"I know of no one I trust more entirely or affectionately," wrote President-elect Woodrow Wilson to Josephus Daniels on February 23, 1913.
"I cannot spare you from my council table."
Ten days later, on March 5, Daniels took the
oath of office as Secretary of the Navy, and began
keeping a diary. His record, presumably intended
for his own reference rather than for future publication, covers the period of his cabinet service
(he was one of only two Wilson cabinet members
to hold their posts throughout both terms), with
the exception of the years 1914 and 1916. The
volumes for these two years are now missing, if
indeed they ever existed. The chronicle of the
other seven years, originally scribbled in Daniels'
own hand and preserved with the Josephus
Daniels Papers at the Library of Congress, has
never previously appeared in print.

Since Daniels seems to have kept this record
largely for his own use rather than with any idea
of eventual publication, some of the entries are
cryptic, some refer to events or persons of little
importance in the grand sweep of history. But,
although he was not a brilliant diarist, Daniels
was a man at the center of things during a com-
plex, crucial, fascinating decade, and his comments over the years provide a host of fresh and
illuminating insights into key personalities and
events. "In these pages," writes E. David Cronon,
"we can feel some of the occasional tension
between Daniels and his supremely confident
assistant, Franklin D. Roosevelt. We can document the decline of Wilsonian cabinet meetings
to mere storytelling and presidential anecdotes.
. . . Daniels adds a new dimension to our understanding of William Jennings Bryan with his
revelation that on December 17, 1919, Bryan
made the extraordinary suggestion that the
United States solve its current difficulties with
Mexico by taking as hostage Lower California
and Magdalena Bay. . . . On another occasion
(January 9, 1920) Bryan confessed that his urging
the ratification of the Treaty of Paris in 1899 had
been 'his great mistake.' "

articles and essays to scholarly publications, he
is the author of Black Moses: The Story of
Marcus Garvey and the Universal Negro Improvement Association (1955) and Josephus
Daniels in Mexico (1960).

The Cabinet Diaries of Josephus Daniels
1913-1921

The Cabinet Diaries

of

Josephus Daniels

1913-1921

Edited by

E. DAVID CRONON

UNIVERSITY OF NEBRASKA PRESS · LINCOLN

Publishers on the Plains

UNP

Preface

WHEN Woodrow Wilson announced his cabinet appointments on March 4, 1913, his choice of Josephus Daniels as Secretary of the Navy occasioned some surprised comment. For like most of the cabinet, Daniels was comparatively unknown outside his native South. Insiders were aware, however, that Wilson had determined from the first to offer him a cabinet post. "I know of no one I trust more entirely or affectionately," the President-elect had written Daniels on February 23. "I cannot spare you from my council table."

Josephus Daniels was not a complete stranger to Washington, though he had never held elective office. In 1893–1894 he had served briefly as chief clerk of the Interior Department under his friend Secretary Hoke Smith in the second Cleveland administration. Daniels had then returned to Raleigh, North Carolina, where he purchased the moribund *News and Observer,* quickly making it an influential force in state affairs and Democratic politics. From 1896 on he was a member of the Democratic National Committee and took an increasingly active role in party politics at the state and national level. A close friend and loyal partisan of William Jennings Bryan during his three bids for the Presidency, Daniels had nevertheless come out for Wilson in 1911 and thereafter had used his newspaper and political influence to advance the cause of the scholarly New Jersey governor. During the campaign of 1912 he had done yeoman service as director of publicity at Democratic national headquarters.

Daniels' background was anything but nautical, however, a point some naval officers were quick to note with mingled feelings of hope and apprehension. True, his father had been a shipwright for the Confederacy and his brother-in-law, Ensign Worth Bagley, had been the only American naval officer killed in the Spanish-American War. But Daniels himself knew little of the Navy or the sea, and his previous experience had been almost entirely in small-town journalism and part-time politics. His appointment to the Navy portfolio struck many observers, as the *New York Times* aptly phrased it on March 6, as "the look of a noble reward for service rendered."

Daniels quickly disappointed those admirals and Navy Leaguers who had hoped that his inexperience would force him to rely largely upon the professionals in running the Navy Department. From the first he took seriously the advice given him by the outgoing Secretary, George von Lengerke Meyer, who tapped the big mahogany desk in the Secretary's office and warmed, "Keep the power to direct the Navy *here*." As Daniels' diary indicates, initially this meant replacing several officers in key posts who Daniels felt were too closely connected to the old Meyer regime to give loyal support to his own policies. For his assistant secretary Daniels chose Franklin Delano Roosevelt, a thirty-one-year-old New York state senator whose enthusiasm for Wilson had been impressive at the Baltimore convention. Like his cousin Theodore, who had earlier also found the Navy post both congenial and politically advantageous, young Franklin accepted with alacrity.

Roosevelt in many respects presented a sharp but complementary contrast to Daniels. Born of the Hudson Valley aristocracy and popular in yachting and high society circles, Roosevelt could move with easy assurance and acceptability among naval officers who merely tolerated the landlubber Daniels with amused disdain. Daniels, slow-moving and deliberate, twenty years Roosevelt's senior, could view the latter's impetuosity and youthful high spirits with the nostalgic tolerance of middle age. But while Roosevelt got on famously with at least some of the admirals, it was Daniels whose tact, persuasion, and conciliation were essential in piloting naval bills through a sometimes suspicious Congress. On the whole Daniels and Roosevelt made a good team, though it was scarcely a case of "love at first sight," as Daniels charitably recalled in his memoirs a quarter century later. Roosevelt sometimes chafed audibly over what he considered ineffective policies of his chief. Daniels, as his diary cautiously suggests, was well aware of his subordinate's occasional disloyalty and at least once even considered the possibility of dismissing him. Fortunately for their respective careers Daniels restrained the impulse and the two men left the Navy Department with a lasting regard for one another.

Daniels was one of only three Wilson cabinet members to hold their posts throughout both terms, a measure both of his devotion to the President and of Wilson's similar high regard. No other Secretary of the Navy save Gideon Welles at the time of the Civil War, moreover, served as long in the post, and few in as important a period of the Navy's history. During Daniels' tenure the Navy adopted important changes in its administrative machinery, underwent an unprecedented expansion in ships and personnel, and devised new weapons and tactics to meet the challenge of modern warfare. Although World War I was largely fought in the mud of northern France, the Navy's contribution in convoying American troopships and containing the threat from German submarines was nevertheless substantial, and despite some postwar recrimination it was accomplished relatively smoothly. Yet probably no Secretary of the Navy was the subject of more controversy or received more personal abuse than Daniels during his term of service. Critics charged that he lacked an elementary comprehension of the role and requirements of a modern navy, that he played favorites in his appointments, that he had no respect for naval custom or discipline. Even the manifest success of the Navy in the war did not still the criticism. During his last year in office Daniels had to endure two hostile Senate investigations sparked by angry strictures from Admiral William S. Sims, who had commanded American naval forces in Europe during the war.

The strength and bitterness of the opposition to Daniels may be explained in part by the nature of the groups he antagonized during his administration of the Navy. He offended much of the Navy's officer corps, for example, by his prompt abolition of the officers' wine mess, a move dictated both by his temperance views as well as by his democratic dislike of the double standard applied to officers and enlisted men with respect to drink. In fact some tradition-minded officers never got over Daniels' revolutionary solicitude for the enlisted men—his compulsory off-duty schools (taught by officers) for the illiterates and poorly educated, his shocking decision to open Annapolis to qualified seamen, and his unconcerned inclusion of no doubt discomfited enlisted and officer personnel at the same social functions. Such actions made Daniels highly popular with the enlisted men, but at corresponding cost of favor with many officers. Similarly, Daniels' effective opposition to the move to create a powerful naval general staff incurred the enmity of some senior officers and their influential supporters in Congress and the Navy League. Daniels believed that a general staff would weaken civilian control of the Navy and reduce the Secretary to a figurehead. Instead he supported the creation of the office of Chief of Naval Operations in 1915 to provide more unified direction of the Navy under the overall authority of the civilian Secretary. This, the critics rejoined, was at best only a partial reform which left the Navy still too subject to the misguided direction of incompetent secretaries like Daniels. On another front Daniels earned the hostility of a significant element of the business community by his blunt accusations that the Navy was being overcharged by its private suppliers. His efforts to use the repair and construction facilities of the Navy's own yards to full capacity, and even more his successful campaign for a Navy-owned steel plant to produce armor plate raised the unpleasant specter of a government price yardstick held over the knuckles of private contractors. Consequently their eagerness to join the ranks of Daniels' critics is understandable. Likewise Daniels' vigilance in preserving the Navy's oil reserves in the West brought him into collision with prominent California oil men and their champion, Secretary of the Interior Franklin K. Lane.

Just how much attention should be paid to the frequent contemporary complaints of Daniels' incapacity and favoritism in running the Navy depends partly on one's conception of the proper relationship between the Secretary of the Navy and his professional subordinates. Certain it is that Daniels tried to staff the bureaus with officers who were personally loyal and who shared his views, especially on such issues as the general staff or his insistence upon adequate sea service as a qualification for high promotion. Such loyalty he rewarded, as when he furthered the careers of Admirals Victor Blue and William S. Benson. But this is hardly a novel or surprising approach for any administrator to take. Some of Daniels' appointments—Admiral David W. Taylor of the Bureau of Construction and Repair, for example—were men of rare talent. There seems to be more merit to the charge that Daniels on occasion was hesitant and indecisive, and that under his direction the Navy, like the nation, was imperfectly prepared for war in 1917. Daniels was profoundly a man of peace who even longer than some of his cabinet colleagues shared the hope of the great majority of Americans that war might be averted. Against this must be set Daniels' novel effort to draw upon American scientific resources as early as 1915 through his Navy Consulting Board headed by Thomas A. Edison, and indeed the creditable record of the Navy when war came.

Daniels began keeping a diary on March 5, 1913, the day he took the oath of office as Secretary of the Navy. His record, presumably intended for his own reference rather than for future publication, covers the period of his cabinet service with the exception of the years 1914 and 1916. The volumes for these two years are now missing, if in fact they ever existed. Located with the Josephus Daniels Papers at the Library of Congress, the diary is in Daniels' own hand, hastily scribbled in pencil onto the pages of seven small leather-bound commercial diaries. Over the years some of the pages have become badly smudged, adding to the often difficult task of deciphering a sometimes illegible scrawl. During his first three months of office Daniels kept an additional and fuller record, evidently dictated to and transcribed by a secretary, which was largely devoted to a recital of events at cabinet meetings. In preparing this published edition I have incorporated this second typewritten diary in its proper chronological place in the handwritten diary.

Like many diarists, Daniels' entries were often irregular and occasionally belated, though he was much more faithful in keeping a record during the second Wilson administration when important war and postwar problems loomed large in his thinking. Unfortunately, many of his observations are trivial and some are so abbreviated as to be cryptic. The historian can only add a fervent "amen" to Daniels' comment on February 19, 1921: "Went over my diary & was sorry I had not kept fuller notes." In spite of its limitations, however, the diary provides an interesting and useful commentary on the Wilson years. In these pages we can feel some of the occasional tension between Daniels and his supremely confident assistant, Franklin D. Roosevelt. We can document the decline of Wilsonian cabinet meetings to mere storytelling and presidential anecdotes. In fact Daniels catches much of Wilson's quick humor, as, for example, when Newton Baker urged him not to ride with President-elect Harding to the inaugural ceremonies if the day were cold and sleety, and Wilson responded wryly: "O that will not matter. I will wear a gas mask anyhow." (January 18, 1921) Daniels adds a new dimension to our understanding of William Jennings Bryan with his revelation that on December 17, 1919, Bryan made the extraordinary suggestion that the United States solve its current difficulties with Mexico by taking as hostage Lower California and Magdalena Bay, which the Great Commoner solemnly noted was "fine country for winter homes." On another occasion (January 9, 1920) Bryan confessed that his urging the ratification of the Treaty of Paris in 1899 had been "his great mistake." In these and many other instances Daniels provides fresh insights into the personalities and events of the period.

In editing the diary I have sought to reproduce the original text faithfully and in its entirety, including errors of spelling and punctuation, obvious trivia, and incomprehensible notations. Since Daniels used periods and dashes interchangeably, sometimes with little or no differentiation, I have tried to use these symbols in the way he presumably intended. If I have occasionally guessed wrong as to whether a particular mark was meant to be a dash or a period, I am confident that this will not affect the meaning of the text. The abbreviated nature of many of Daniels' entries poses vexatious problems for an editor. A really comprehensive set of notes to explain all of Daniels' comments would bulk much larger than the diary itself, thereby ruling out any realistic hope of publication. Besides, such detailed notes would merely intimidate the general reader and probably not really serve the scholar. I have accordingly set some limits to my annotation. As a general rule I have provided an explanatory note only the first time Daniels mentions a person, group, or event, and not thereafter unless changing circumstances require further elaboration. The reader seeking one of these initial explanatory notes may refer to the Index, which I have made as full as possible, recognizing its importance to the serious student of the diary. To keep the notes brief I have not attempted to recount individual careers in detail nor subsequent to the period covered by the diary, believing in any event that this will avoid the danger of distortion by making an individual seem more important than he actually was in Daniels' eyes.

Where Daniels habitually refers to a person by initials, I have provided identification the first few times, but thereafter have assumed that the reader will recognize the pattern. I have tried to avoid superfluous annotation of well-known individuals or developments; conversely in a few instances Daniels mentions persons so obscure as to defy identification.

Like all scholars I must acknowledge my heavy debt to those who have helped make this book a reality. More than most projects, this was a truly inter-university venture. The Henry L. Stimson Fund of Yale University and the Research Council of the University of Nebraska allocated funds for photo-duplicating and transcribing the diary. Between them the University of Nebraska and the University of Wisconsin provided me with a leave of absence during which the bulk of the editing was completed. The Library of Congress on two occasions furnished me with a study room and its unmatched reference collections, without which the task of annotation would have been vastly more difficult. I am deeply grateful to Mr. Jonathan Daniels for his permission to publish the diary and his help in unraveling some of its mysteries. Mr. Howard B. Gotlieb of the Sterling Memorial Library of Yale University facilitated my research and graciously authorized me to quote from the Colonel Edward M. House Diary. My research assistant at the University of Wisconsin, Mr. Roger T. Johnson, helped with the final proofreading and did much of the work in compiling the Index. Lastly, my wife, Jean Hotmar Cronon, merits much more than the customary line of appreciation. Her uncomplaining assistance in deciphering, transcribing, and painstaking proofreading went far beyond anything contemplated in the marriage bond.

E. DAVID CRONON

Madison, Wisconsin
October 7, 1962

Contents

(*Diaries for 1914 and 1916 are lacking.*)

1913

The Cabinet Diaries of Josephus Daniels, 1913

Wednesday, March 5, 1913

The Senate confirmed the nomination of the Cabinet and at 5 o'clock I took the oath of office at the Navy Department. The spacious room was crowded. My wife, three of my sons—Josephus Jr[,] Worth Bagley and Frank A. Daniels Jr—were present, but Jonathan could not be present as he was sick.[1] Mrs. Bagley, Ethel, Belle,[2] and a score of North Carolinians were present, as were Senators Simmons [3] and Overman,[4] Congressman John H. Small [5] and wife, and the National Democratic Committee in a body headed by Chairman McCombs.[6] It was a happiness to me that this Committee on which I had served for more than sixteen years should do me this honor. All the members of the committee have been most cordial and kind to me.

At ten o'clock in the morning an informal gathering of the men chosen to go in the Cabinet met with the President and informally talked over plans.

At eleven o'clock, Mr. Meyers,[7] the retiring secretary, introduced me to all the chiefs of bureaus in the Navy Department and courteously explained many matters about the workings of the Department.

In the evening, my wife and I dined with a charming company, at a dinner at the Shoreham, given by Mr & Mrs. De Saules in honor of Chmn McCombs. She is a beautiful Christian woman [8]

We dined at the Shoreham with Mr & Mrs. De Saules. He took active part in the campaign. His wife is a beautiful Christian.

[1] Daniels' immediate family consisted of his wife, Addie Worth Bagley Daniels (1869–1943), and his four sons, Josephus, Jr. (1894 ——), Worth Bagley (1899 ——), Jonathan Worth (1902 ——), and Frank A. (1904 ——), the latter named after Daniels' elder brother.

[2] Mrs. Daniels' mother, Mrs. Adelaide Worth Bagley, and two unmarried sisters, Ethel and Belle Bagley, residents of Washington.

[3] Furnifold M. Simmons, Democrat, senior U.S. Senator from North Carolina.

[4] Lee S. Overman, Democrat, junior U.S. Senator from North Carolina.

[5] Democrat, U.S. Representative from North Carolina, and a resident of Daniels' birthplace, Washington, North Carolina.

[6] William F. McCombs, early Wilson supporter and chairman of the Democratic National Committee since the campaign of 1912.

[7] George von L. Meyer, Secretary of the Navy, 1909–1913.

[8] John L. De Saulles, wealthy young Wilson supporter and patronage hopeful, subsequently killed by his estranged wife. The following sentences, written in the margin, are evidently an unconscious repetition by Daniels.

Thursday, March 6, 1913

As soon as I received the letter from the President tendering the appointment as Secretary of the Navy, I immediately thought of Franklin D. Roosevelt, of New York, as Assistant Secretary. He had supported Wilson for the nomination, and taken an active part in the campaign, and I found him a singularly attractive and honorable courageous young Democratic leader. I believed in him and was desirous of being associated with him in the Navy Department. And so this morning I went to the White House and told the President that I had decided upon Mr. Roosevelt. He said "capital" and heartily approved. This was gratifying to me.

That afternoon, I consulted Senator O'Gorman,[9] of New York, and asked his opinion. He spoke in high terms of Mr. R. and said his appointment would be acceptable. He had not been gone long before a New York gentleman [10] came and warned me against naming R as Assistant Secretary, saying that every person named Roosevelt wished to run everything and would try to be the Secretary. I listened and replied that any man who was afraid his assistant would supplant him thereby confessed that he did not think he was big enough for the job. I related that conversation to the President who expressed about the same opinion I had entertained.

Dined with Governor Francis [11] at the Metropolitan club. Nearly all members of the cabinet were present.

Friday, March 7, 1913

The first regular meeting of the cabinet was held. One of the topics for discussion was whether the order of President Taft putting fourth class postmasters under civil service should be revoked or modified. A few days before President Taft was defeated, he issued an order that if it stands keeps Republicans in office who were appointed because of their service to that party. The opinion prevailed that the merit system was not advanced by such use of the civil service regulation. But the virtual decision was that Post Master General Burlison [12] should draw up a paper to be presented to the cabinet embodying his views.

[9] James A. O'Gorman, Democrat, U.S. Senator from New York.

[10] In his autobiography Daniels identifies this source as Elihu Root, the Republican senior U.S. Senator from New York. Daniels recalls that when he informed Root he intended to name Roosevelt as his assistant, "a queer look came on his face. 'You know the Roosevelts, don't you?' he asked. 'Whenever a Roosevelt rides, he wishes to ride in front.'" Daniels, *The Wilson Era: Years of Peace, 1910–1917* (Chapel Hill: University of North Carolina Press, 1944), p. 127.

[11] David R. Francis, Democrat, former governor of Missouri, 1889–1893, and Secretary of the Interior, 1896–1897; subsequently Ambassador to Russia, 1916–1919.

[12] Albert S. Burleson, a seven-term Democratic congressman from Texas who as Post-

I presented the request of the Naval board that the ships sent to Mexico should be returned so as to enable them to take part in target practice off Hampton Roads about the 22nd. of March. It was the opinion of the President that, inasmuch as the ships were sent because of troubles, if withdrawn now, it would be construed as proof that the Government was satisfied because of present conditions. It is not satisfied and it was therefore determined that no order for their return be made.

Took dinner with Mr. and Mrs. Homer Cummings [13] at Stoneleigh Court.

Saturday, March 8, 1913

Admiral Knight,[14] who had been ordered to Turkey upon the outbreak of the Balkan war, called at the Navy Department to suggest that two vessels in those waters were no longer needed. He thought one of them ought to be ordered home, cruising slowly along the Mediterranean for a month. He gave an interesting account of his observations. I told him that inasmuch as the ships had been sent at the outbreak of hostilities, it seemed unwise to withdraw them until the troubles were ended. He insisted that one was sufficient to remain near Constantinople, but upon bringing the matter to the attention of the President, I found he thought it best to make no order recalling either ship at this time. One ship is now at Smyrna and the other is cruising off the coast of Asia Minor. The Balkan war is not settled. Adrianople is sure to fall, and how long will it be before Turkey is dismembered?

We dined with Mr. Lane,[15] Secretary of the Interior, and a charming company.

Sunday, March 9, 1913

I had hardly seen our boys since we arrived. They were staying with their grandmother, Mrs. Bagley, at the Dupont, and me at Dr. Sterling Ruffins [16] at 1335 Connecticut Avenue. All the morning was spent with the boys while my wife went to church. We had a fine time. The boys think it fine that their father is in the Cabinet. Worth Bagley thinks I will be president yet! Nothing like being a hero to your own boy!!

Sunday afternoon had long talk with Franklin Roosevelt who accepted as

---

master General throughout both Wilson administrations was actively concerned with patronage and other party matters.

[13] Homer S. Cummings, member, vice-chairman (1913–1919), and chairman (1919–1920) of the Democratic National Committee from Connecticut.

[14] Rear Admiral Austin M. Knight.

[15] Franklin K. Lane, California Democrat and former member of the Interstate Commerce Commission.

[16] Dr. Sterling Ruffin, North Carolina–born friend, chief physician and professor of medicine at George Washington University Hospital and Medical School.

Assistant Secretary of the Navy. He will be a fine co-worker. I look forward with pleasure to the great work we planned to accomplish for the public good. Together we went to the New National Theatre to hear Editor McDonald,[17] of Toronto, to the Y.M.C.A. He is a big Scotchman and made a fine speech. He was introduced by Mr. Bryan,[18] Secretary of State, who gave voice to the friendly feeling existing between that country and Canada. Bryan's speech was his first utterance since his appointment.

Dined with Mrs. Bagley and the boys.

Monday, March 10, 1913

The four officers, constituting the aids to the Secretary,[19] insisted that the ships off Mexico should be returned for target practise, but the troubles in Mexico are not over and we feel that it is better to defer target practise than withdraw them.

Conferred with Naval Board about the necessity of publicity—about the ways to secure accurate news to the people about the doings in the Navy. Too little is published and I planned to see that the public is acquainted with all that happens of interest.

At night we dined with Victor Blue[20] and wife. He is a North Carolinian who won high honor in the Spanish American war.

Tuesday, March 11, 1913

The cabinet devoted the day to consideration of a letter or statement presented by the President outlining the policy of the administration with reference to Central and South American states. During the campaign, there grew up a feeling in some of those countries that a Democratic victory would

[17] James A. MacDonald, managing editor of the Toronto *Globe* and former Presbyterian minister.

[18] William Jennings Bryan, a close political associate and friend of Daniels' since Bryan's first campaign for the Presidency in 1896.

[19] When Daniels took over the Navy Department he inherited an organizational structure headed by a Council of Aids recently established by his predecessor, Secretary Meyer. The current aids were Rear Admiral Bradley A. Fiske, Aid for Operations; Captain Templin M. Potts, Aid for Personnel; Captain Albert G. Winterhalter, Aid for Matériel; Captain William F. Fullam, Aid for Inspections. Partly because he came to dislike Admiral Fiske and partly because he preferred to deal directly with the various bureau chiefs, Daniels gradually abandoned the Council of Aids until it was replaced by the statutory post of Chief of Naval Operations in 1915.

[20] Commander Victor Blue, a North Carolinian, was one of the few naval officers Daniels had known before his appointment as Secretary of the Navy. Daniels liked and trusted Blue and thereafter saw that his career was suitably advanced, as when he shortly appointed him Chief of the Bureau of Navigation (in charge of personnel assignments) with the temporary rank of rear admiral.

be hailed by those seeking to foment revolution as an encouragement. The President and Secretary of State thought it necessary to make a statement. All were agreed. The point of difference was to whether the statement should be delivered to the official representatives of those countries or whether it should be given to the press. It was suggested that it would not be appreciated by those countries having stable governments, and if sent to those only where revolutions were imminent or where there were troubles, those countries would be offended by being singled out. The importance of making known this country's attitude known as encouraging stable government where it is based on the consent of the governed was stressed by the President, whose original idea was to send the declaration to official representatives. After a discussion of nearly two hours it was unanimously agreed that the President should give it out to the press in a way to make it authoritative and impressive. It is a singularly clear and impressive declaration and it is as follows: (Insert here) [21]

This statement will do much good and ought to stop those who foment troubles for personal aggrandizement in the hope of America winking at revolution and holding hands off.

Commander Victor Blue and wife gave dinner to Secretary of Navy and wife and had charming party. He has a lovely wife.[22]

Wednesday, March 12, 1913

The cabinet held its longest session today. It was called at the request of the Secretary of State to discuss the question of the Chinese loan.[23] The Euro-

[21] Daniels occasionally left a blank space in a diary entry, evidently intending to supply later a missing name or the text of a document under discussion. In this case the salient portions of the President's statement to the press were: "We can have no sympathy with those who seek to seize the power of government to advance their own personal interests or ambition. . . . As friends, therefore, we shall prefer those who act in the interest of peace and honor, who protect private rights and respect the restraints of constitutional provision. Mutual respect seems to us the indispensable foundation of friendship between States as between individuals. The United States has nothing to seek in Central and South America except the lasting interests of the people of the two continents, the security of governments, intended for the people, and for no special group or interest, and the development of personal and trade relationships between the two continents, which shall redound to the profit and advantage of both and interfere with the rights and liberties of neither." *New York Times*, March 12, 1913.

[22] This evident repetition of an entry for the previous day suggests that Daniels had already found it difficult to maintain a regular day-to-day schedule of writing in his diary.

[23] In 1909 a group of British, French, and German bankers signed an agreement with the Chinese government to stabilize Chinese finances and construct a railway network. The Taft administration urged that American capital participate in the loan, and in 1911 a new six-power consortium was organized, including Russian and Japanese bankers, along with an American syndicate headed by J. P. Morgan & Company. After Wilson's inauguration,

pean powers had agreed to furnish the new Republic of China [24] money to pay its army and indebtedness upon condition that the money should be disbursed by or under the direction of the foreign governments. A group of American bankers, including what is known as the bankers trust, had stated to the Secretary of State that if requested by the administration they might take that portion of the loan allotted to their country. One of the stipulations made by those offering to make the loan was that if China wished to borrow more money it could be borrowed only from those making this loan. The Taft administration had approved the plan. The matter was discussed two hours, and was opened by Mr. Bryan who luminously stated the objections to the plan. The Secretary of the Treasury [25] thought we could not agree to request the bankers trust to subscribe to the loan. Secretary Lane, who had made a long study of Chinese affairs, thought it would be a mistake to approve this old time favoritism method after China had declared for new ways, and that this country should not be a party to helping China upon condition that it should be beholden to a group of financiers in the biggest nations. Secy Redfield [26] feared if we failed to help in some proper way, the loan would be made by the other nations, and America would lose the chance for building up a large trade. My idea was that we ought to find some way for the Government to help China coupled with the recognition of the Republic of China. The President was clear in his conviction that we could not request the trust group of bankers to effect the loan, and that we ought to help China in some better way. It was decided that the President should draw up a statement to be presented at the next meeting of the cabinet.

Spent a quiet evening at Mrs. Bagley's with her daughters and our boys.

Thursday, March 13, 1913

I attended the meeting of the General Board presided over by Admiral Dewey.[27] He had been a favorite hero of mine since Manilla [*sic*] and it was a pleasure to be received by him. When we went into the room where the

the American bankers were eager to learn whether the new administration would continue the Taft policy of strong support for American participation in the Chinese consortium.

[24] In 1911, Sun Yat-sen led a successful rebellion against the Manchu dynasty in China, forcing the emperor to abdicate the following year, and establishing a provisional Republic of China. The Taft administration had delayed granting diplomatic recognition to the new Chinese government, however, in an effort to coordinate this action with that of the other major powers.

[25] William G. McAdoo, Georgia-born former New York attorney and promoter.

[26] William C. Redfield, Secretary of Commerce, former New York manufacturer.

[27] Admiral of the Navy George Dewey, highest ranking naval officer and hero of the Battle of Manila Bay in 1898.

Board meets, he motioned to me to take the seat at the head of the table indicating that it should be occupied by the Secretary of the Navy. I declined, telling him that as I expected to learn of him I would take a seat at his right. This seemed to please him. The discussion of Navy policies which followed was most interesting. Dewey had been appointed to the Naval Academy by James C. Dobbin,[28] a North Carolina Secretary of the Navy, and he said to me: "Dobbin was an eloquent man, a great Democrat, and I reckon the reason I am such a good Democrat is because I was appointed to the Naval Academy by Dobbin." He had the highest opinion of Dobbin, and at my request wrote the following note: [29] [blank]

My wife and I were entertained at a dinner given in our honor by Captain Wm. Fectkler,[30] of the Navy. He has always been a Bryan Democrat and she is a daughter of Mr. Morrow,[31] long Congressman from California. It was a pleasant evening with a pleasant party.

Friday, March 14, 1913

Yesterday the Mayor of Baltimore[32] called to invite the President and the Secretary of the Navy to go to Baltimore to attend the banquet to be given for the widows and orphans caused by the accident, by which a collier being built for our Government was injured because 300 tons of dynamite exploded in a British vessel.[33] The collier was a mile and a half from the explosion. It was a calamity greater than had been known before. The families of the men killed are destitute and the generous hearted people of Baltimore asked the gifted actors and actresses to give a benefit performance. The President desired me to go to Baltimore to voice appreciation of the Government to Baltimore people and to express the sympathy of the Govt to the people. I was met at the depot in Baltimore by Governor Goldsborough,[34] Mayor Preston, and given a luncheon at the Maryland Club. Afterwards to a crowd that packed the theatre, I made a brief speech. It was in these words: [blank]

The Ambassador of Brazil[35] and his wife gave a dinner in our honor at night at the Brazillian [*sic*] Embassy. She is a Texas woman, a bride of three

[28] Secretary of the Navy under Franklin Pierce, 1853–1857.

[29] In this tribute to Daniels' predecessor and fellow North Carolinian, Dewey declared: "In my opinion, Mr. Dobbin was one of the ablest Secretaries of the Navy the country ever had." Daniels, *Wilson Era: Years of Peace,* p. 511.

[30] Captain Augustus F. Fechteler, president of the Board of Inspection and Survey for Ships.

[31] William W. Morrow, Republican, Representative from California, 1885–1891.

[32] James H. Preston, Democrat, mayor of Baltimore since 1911.

[33] A British freighter, the S.S. *Alum Chine,* had exploded on March 7, killing forty persons and damaging a new Navy collier, the *Jason.*

[34] Phillips L. Goldsborough, Republican, governor of Maryland, 1912–1916.

[35] Domicio da Gama, Brazilian Ambassador since 1911.

weeks and a grandmother. She looks 35 and is a charming woman. He seems a frank man, genuine and outspoken.

Saturday, March 15, 1913

Mr. Frederick [sic] D. Roosevelt, who had been appointed Assistant Secretary of the Navy, arrived to-day, expecting to enter upon his duties, but the Senate, not having acted, he returned to New York. On the very day I received the letter from Mr. Wilson I immediately determined upon having Mr. R. as assistant if it was agreeable to the President. It is singular that I never thought of any other man in that connection. Mr. R told me on the night before the inauguration that if he served in any place in the administration, he preferred to be in the Navy Department. His distinguished cousin TR went from that place to the presidency. May history repeat itself?

The aids to the Secretary brought in a report, signed by Secretary Meyer just before he left Washington, declaring Mare Island a second class navy yard and ending the dredging for which Congress appropriated a million dollars. I declined to transmit the emergency orders until conference could be had with the California Senators.[36] They had secured the appropriation and it seemed to me a grave thing to stop the expenditure of money specifically appropriated by Congress unless it was absolutely a waste. Matter was held up. The action of Congress is not to be disregarded unless the reasons are more than conclusive.

Spent the evening with the boys and Mrs. Bagley.

Sunday, March 16, 1913

Went to church at Mt. Vernon place Methodist (Southern) church [37] with the youngest boys. Senator Overman went with us. The welcome we received was the sort to which I am accustomed at home. The church is a very plain one, out of the mart of fashionable folk, and the people are of the Methodistic type. How courteous and cordial they were! When the service ended, they came up and shook hands and gave words of cordial welcome. On the night before Garfield's inauguration I attended a service at that church with my friend, James Lipscombe,[38] of Wilson

Monday, March 17, 1913

Rose early and went at once to the Executive office. I had heard that John Redmond [39] had sent to the President some real shamrock from Ireland, and

[36] George C. Perkins and John D. Works, both Republicans.

[37] Daniels, a devout Methodist, frequently attended this church while he lived in Washington.

[38] A close boyhood friend in Daniels' home town of Wilson, North Carolina.

[39] Probably John E. Redmond, chairman of the Irish Parliamentary party.

I asked Joseph Patrick Tumulty,[40] Private Secretary[,] for my share of the shamrock on the ground, that though not an Irishman myself, my wife's grandmother came from Ireland and was named Clary—a good old Irish name. My claim was recognized as legal and proper, and wearing the shamrock, sent by the Irish patriot I hastened to the Navy Department and my picture was taken wearing the shamrock. The [blank]

Dinner with Mr & Mrs James Ellison.[41] The other guests were Dr. Sterling Ruffin, Senator & Mrs. Swanson.[42]

Tuesday, March 18, 1913

Nothing of great importance came up in the cabinet meeting to-day. The President, speaking of the fact that a dozen new Federal judges were to be appointed, outlined his idea of the sort of men who should be appointed to the bench. It was illuminating. He said a very different sort of men were needed from those who had too often been appointed. He is in favor [of] finding able lawyers who have no strings tied to them and who are not so in sympathy with the large corporations or trusts as to bias them in favor of the Big interests rather than the superior rights of all the public. He expressed his difficulty in knowing exactly how to find the best man in every State, but urged all the cabinet to assist the Attorney General in finding lawyers of the highest type who would hold the scales of justice equally.

My wife and I left for Raleigh—I to attend to some News & Observer [43] business and my wife to pack up silver, china and other things to go to house keeping in a country home we have rented.

Wednesday, March 19, 1913

Reached Raleigh at 6 a.m. Went home and slept until after nine o'clock.

At night was given a banquet by the Pressman's Union, at Giersch's [Hotel] and greatly enjoyed it. The men who man the presses present were mostly young men and a fine body of men. What pleased me most was the feeling of confidence expressed in the statement made by several, that there would be no trouble between employer and employee if all employers were like their guest. In my speech, I said in part: [blank]

Thursday, March 20, 1913

Attended meetings of the executive committee of the Y.M.C.A.

[40] President Wilson's private secretary, 1910–1921.
[41] James Ellerson.
[42] Claude A. Swanson, Democrat, of Virginia, a key member of the Senate Naval Affairs Committee.
[43] Daniels' newspaper, the Raleigh *News and Observer*.

Friday, March 21, 1913

All the members of the cabinet were present at to-day's meeting except the Secretary of State. The fiasco of Huntington Wilson's [44] resignation as Asst. Secy. of State, because the President had repudiated the Taft program of requesting the banking trust to share with the bankers of other countries the control of the fiscal affairs of the new Republic of China, created only amusement. He took himself very seriously, but nobody else did. Before he left for Nebraska, Mr. Bryan requested Mr. Wilson to remain to look after details. I suggested to Mr. B that it was of doubtful wisdom for him to leave Wilson in charge of his department because he was not in accord with anything in our policy and might take some action that would not be approved. The general opinion is that Huntington Wilson is a great egotist and that his letter of resignation, under the circumstances, was a piece of pertinence and impertinence. The men generally said that for an under secretary, already notified that he was to stay only a few weeks, to seize the opportunity to try to rebuke a new President was unheard of and most out of place. In this city he is generally regarded as having made an exhibition of himself.

Saturday, March 22, 1913

In the evening went with my boys and a company to the Naval Observatory

Sunday, March 23, 1913

Went to Mt. Vernon place Methodist church with the three youngest boys. After church the pastor (Dr. Reggister) [Rev. E. V. Regester] and many of the congregation, were courteous, shook hands and otherwise gave us cordial greeting.

In the afternoon, Mr. A.[lexander] C. Shaw, of Oregon, an old school friend in N.C., called. He was disbarred from practice before the Interior Department by Taft and dismissed from his office in the Land Office because he stood with Pinchot against the land frauds and the hostility to conservation. I have urged Secy Lane to reinstate him.

Mr. Ernest Hamlin Abbott,[45] one of the editors of the Outlook (the Roosevelt publication of which he is one of the editors) discussed with me all the afternoon at the Army and Navy club the attitude of the administration on the Chinese loan and other policies of the administration. He spoke most

[44] Assistant Secretary of State Francis M. Huntington Wilson, a holdover official of the previous Taft administration, resigned on March 19 in protest against President Wilson's public announcement the previous day repudiating American participation in the Chinese banking consortium. The letter of resignation was published on March 21.

[45] Former Congregational minister, an editor of *The Outlook* since 1902.

warmly in praise of the Wilson speech of inaugural, of his cabinet, and of what [has?] been done already and said the country cordially approved the policy of the administration.

Monday, March 24, 1913

Had a talk with the President on the policy of the Navy Department. I presented my view, to wit: that no officer should be promoted unless he had sufficient sea service to make it certain that he would be able to command ships. There have been too many officers promoted who had had soft berths —that is too much shore duty and not enough sea service. The President heartily approved of an order covering this policy which I sent later to the Examining Board. I asked him for authority to request Admiral Andrews [46] (who had never commanded a ship) to tender his resignation and to approve the appointment of Victor Blue, who had won his spurs in the Spanish-American war, in his place. He heartily approved my determination to make sea service essential to promotion and stop easy places for favorities [*sic*], and told me that he took a deep interest in my department. He added "When I was a boy I had ambition to go to the Naval Academy and become a Naval officer, but my father gave me no encouragement." I brought to his attention the fact that it cost $250,000 a year to maintain the Mayflower and the Sylph (the President's boats) and the Dolphin, the boat of the Secy of the Navy, and rather recommended they be put into regular service than kept for our use. I left with him the figures at his request.

Tuesday, March 25, 1913

Cabinet had no grave public question before it. The President said he had nothing to bring before it. The Post Master General said he had formulated

[46] When Daniels became Secretary of the Navy, Commander Philip Andrews was serving as Chief of the Bureau of Navigation, a post which entitled him to the temporary rank of rear admiral and a major role in the assignment of Navy personnel. Daniels evidently was persuaded by Commander Victor Blue (see above, diary entry of March 10) that Andrews and the Aid for Personnel, Captain Templin M. Potts, had played favorites in making assignments to choice shore duty. Daniels accordingly decided to force Andrews' resignation as Chief of the Bureau of Navigation and to appoint Blue in his place. He also laid down the policy—dubbed by some officers the "Single Oak Policy" after the name of Daniels' first Washington home—that promotion to the higher ranks would henceforth be dependent upon a satisfactory record of sea service. Both Andrews and Potts had served for a number of years in Washington and became immediate victims of the Single Oak Policy. Potts attempted unsuccessfully to appeal over Daniels' head to President Wilson. (See entry of April 15, 1913.) Commander Andrews accepted his fall more gracefully, however, and ultimately won both Daniels' respect and promotion to rear admiral after capable service at sea. The Potts controversy lingered many months, for he was retired involuntarily by the dreaded Plucking Board on July 1, 1913, and his champions charged that this was an unfair application of the new rule on sea service.

a plan with reference to fourth class P.M's, put under civil service just before Taft was defeated, which was being considered by the Civil Service Commission. There was long and interesting general discussion over the Page [47] and the Lever [48] bills. The first passed the Senate at the last session, the second passed the House. Both carried large appropriations to aid education. The Lever bill gave aid only to agricultural education, the place where the need is the greatest. The Page bill gave aid to vocational education and to higher education. Secy Wilson,[49] of Labor Department, had earnestly favored the educational plan and presented his views. Nothing was before the cabinet, but the discussion is alluded to here to show that the questions most vital were discussed in the cabinet even if nothing was pending with reference to them.

Wednesday, March 26, 1913

Most important day since I became Secretary of the Navy. Soon after I took the oath I became convinced that it was necessary for me to have as head of the Bureau of Navigation a man who was close to me and to whom I could talk confidentially. I soon decided upon Victor Blue, who was born in North Carolina, and who made reputation in the Spanish-American war. Admiral Philip Andrews, who had been a favorite of the last administration and a favorite who had been advanced by favoritism and who, during his term as captain, had never commanded a ship, held that place. I did not feel safe because all assignments were made by him and the Aid Captain Potts, who did not seem to me to be in accord with my views. I asked Capt. Palmer [50] (my aid) to examine the record of both men, and it showed that neither Potts nor Andrews had been at sea as much as the good of the service required. He dictated for me the accompany[ing] statement which I read to the President.

At 4 p.m. I sent for Admiral Andrews and told him I had been directed by the President to ask for his resignation. He evidently was desirous of remaining, but I added "I have an engagement with the President at 6 p.m. and wish to take the resignation with me." Later he asked a private interview and asked what statement I would make to the public. I told him I would not reflect upon him, but would say I desired an officer in that place who had made reputation in war and who was in close sympathy and touch with me. The change created much comment.

[47] Carroll S. Page, Republican, U.S. Senator from Vermont.

[48] Asbury F. Lever, Democrat, U.S. Representative from South Carolina.

[49] William B. Wilson, Secretary of Labor, former coal miner and union official, U.S. Representative from Pennsylvania, 1907–1913.

[50] Lieutenant Commander Leigh C. Palmer, Daniels' personal aide.

Thursday, March 27, 1913

Spent all the morning visiting the Navy Yard at Washington. Admiral Twining [51] and Leigh Palmer, Naval Aid, called for me at Single Oak [52] in an automobile, and we arrived shortly after ten o'clock. I had requested that there be no ceremonies, but was given the salute by a company of [blank]

For three hours I went from ship to ship and from place to place, saw a torpedo fired from a torpedo boat, and witnessed the making of everything that goes into a battle ship. It was my first visit to a navy yard, and it was a revelation. Capt. Jones, [53] the Commandant, and the master machinist and others explained the various operations. My knowledge of machinery and battle-ships is so slight that I understood very little of the operations or the explanations. Impressed by splendid body of mechanics and crowded conditions showing need for more buildings.

In afternoon had long talk with ex Senator Foster, [54] Senator Ransdell [55] and Editor Ewing [56] of Louisiana. They are greatly worked up over the proposition to reduce tariff on sugar or put it on free list. The last House abolished all the tariff on sugar. They say if the present tariff is reduced 50%, the industry will be destroyed, and it would be better to have free sugar than to have tariff cut so low. They think President Wilson and Underwood, [57] Chairman of Ways and Means Committee favor free sugar, and believe it would destroy the sugar industry and $137,000,000 invested in sugar.

Friday, March 28, 1913

Cabinet

Friday, March 28, 1913

The President read his message to be presented to the Congress when it convenes on April 7th. It is brief, comprehensive, and illuminating. The opening sentence gave the reason why he had called the Congress in extraordinary session and the chief reason given was that the business interests of

[51] Real Admiral Nathan C. Twining, Chief of the Bureau of Ordnance.

[52] Daniels' home on Woodley Lane, rented from Mrs. Edythe Newlands Johnston, daughter of Senator Francis G. Newlands, Democrat of Nevada, who lived next door. In 1915, Daniels moved to 1851 Wyoming Avenue, N.W.

[53] Captain Hilary P. Jones, commandant of the Washington Navy Yard, chiefly devoted to ordnance work and gun manufacture.

[54] Murphy J. Foster, Democrat, U.S. Senator from Louisiana, 1901–1913.

[55] Joseph E. Ransdell, Democrat, U.S. Senator from Louisiana.

[56] Robert Ewing, publisher of the New Orleans *Daily States* and the *Shreveport Times*.

[57] Oscar W. Underwood, U.S. Representative from Alabama, and one of the most powerful Democrats in the House, chairman of the Ways and Means Committee.

the country might know what changes would be made in the tariff so they might adjust themselves to it.

Secretary Bryan suggested that it might be well to add to the other reason given "and that the consumers ought to receive the benefit to be derived from the (reduced) tariff reduction at as early a date as practicable." The President said that he thought that that would be generally understood without being specifically stated and would be glad to incorporate Mr. Bryan's suggestion in the completed draft when it was finished. I suggested that the allusion to possible currency legislation to follow tariff legislation might not be the wisest. I had talked to some of the leaders of the House who felt that it was exceedingly important that after the House had passed the tariff bill or bills that the whole country's attention would be focused on the Senate so that the Senate would have no matter before them except the passage of tariff bills. These leaders of Congress felt that the suggestion in the message of currency legislation would divide the attention of the country and make it easier for the Senate to follow the past precedents and cut the heart out of tariff bills because the public attention would be centered upon currency legislation rather than tariff legislation. President Wilson stated that he had given consideration to this thought and discussed it with members of Congress but in his opinion the currency legislation ought to be enacted at this session of Congress if there could be an agreement and it would be a help to the tariff situation if the suggestion was made in the message that currency legislation badly needed would follow. "In the past," said the President, "when tariff reduction bills were enacted, the question was, if trade expansion follows, where is the money with which to do the increased business of the country? By holding out the expectation of salutary currency legislation, this question would not be asked and the promise of it now would be probably taken up as the tariff bills are enacted would be helpful.["] There was a general discussion on the tariff situation. Secretary McAdoo thought that the President ought to add the word "labor" to the word "industry" in his message, in view of the fact that in the last year. Secretary McAdoo called attention to the fact that the democrats would not give the same care to labor that the republicans had done. Secretary Wilson expressed the opinion that the word "industry" included "labor" and it ought not to be added separately. Secretary Redfield gave statistics of the exports of manufactured goods showing an increase of 20% in the last campaign the republicans made much of the suggestion that the President used the term "competitive tariff" several times and seemed to indicate that the democratic tariff would open the door to competition and asked whether this would be wise. The President said that his message was exactly along the line of his pledges before the election and any suggestion that he should not demand now what he promised then recalled a cartoon recently appearing in a Chicago paper after he made his speech in Chicago on his return from Bermuda. Underneath the cartoon were the words "This fellow actually talks after the election just as he talked before," as if that were a reprehensible thing. "I propose," said the President, "to urge the tariff along the lines of my pre-election promises." Secretary Bryan read a letter which was to be sent to the representative of the bankers that had been requested to take part in the Chinese loan. It suggested to the bankers that they ought to give China further time to pay the obligations already incurred. There was some question as to whether this was wise in view of the Cabinet's refusal to request American bankers to lend China money on the terms proposed by the banking syndicate. President Wilson said, "I feel so keenly the desire to help China that I prefer to err in the line of helping that country than otherwise. If we had entered into the loan with other powers we would have got nothing but mere influence in China and lost the proud position which America secured when Secretary Hay [58] stood for the open door in China after the Boxer Uprising.["] He declared he believed that our position would be stronger not to be in partnership with other countries but to stand ready to aid China and to be able to say to Russia "what are your designs on Manchuria," and to Japan, "What are your wishes on this part of China," and to England, Germany, or any other country, "What are your designs," and being free, this country could help China and restore the relationship which this country occupied toward that country and the world when Mr. Hay was Secretary of State. The President said in connection with the refusal of the Cabinet to request the American bankers to lend China money under terms which would give the lending powers control of Chinese affairs that after his publication the Japanese Minister [59] called at the State Department and asked to be informed of the mind of the United States and it developed then that the United States had asked Japan to take part of the proposed loan to China and Japan had acceded to this in the Taft administration. "It seems," said the President, "in speaking of this matter, that the United States had invited Japan to dinner and than [then] absented itself when dinner was served and Japan did not understand it." Of course he laughed. Mr. Bryan and I both feel this a mistake we made and we ought to have informed the other governments of our actions, but he did not believe any serious result would follow.

Secretary McAdoo brought up the matter of the deposits of American money by the Navy Department in London, the money heretofore being deposited

[58] John Hay, Secretary of State, 1898–1905, author of the Open Door Policy in China.
[59] Viscount Sutemi Chinda.

with bankers who were strong republicans and he had an application from Speyer & Co. who had supported Wilson for President to change the depository in London from the republican bankers to Speyer & Co. Mr. McAdoo thought that inasmuch as Speyer & Co. were in hearty accord with the Administration and help put in power, and thought it a reasonable request. Postmaster General Burleson thought so too and suggested the change at once. In this opinion Secretary of the Navy Daniels concurred and said he would see Secretary Bryan, who was away from the Cabinet and believed that the Cabinet would agree on the change as suggested by the Secretary of the Treasury. The President said he had a talk with Mr. Rea [60] who had a power of attorney from Sun Yat Sen, whose imperial company had the right to build 10,000 miles of rail-road in China and was here to get money to finance this construction. It seems Mr. Rea, who has long been Sun Yat Sen's financial manager, wished to assure the President that the loan as proposed by certain syndicates would not go through and [if] the loans were not made to China on those hard terms the railroad company could get American capital to build the railroads in China, because they had good security. The President said he told Mr. Rea that his public statement was sufficient evidence of what this government stood for in the way of loans and he thought nothing more was needed and he said Mr. Rea seemed to assent to this. Secretary Redfield said he had just seen a letter from a great manufacturing concern in America saying they sent six modern engines to China and this is very good evidence that America leads in the Chinese situation.

Just as the Cabinet meeting closed, Attorney General McReynolds [61] an-nounced that the republican marshall in Texas had resigned thus opening the way of appointing Captain Bill McDonald marshall in Texas. Captain McDon-ald was the body-guard of the President in the campaign and won his spurs as a ranger, as a scout and confederate soldier. The whole Cabinet rejoiced that the way was open and the President advised to send it in as a recess appointment without waiting for Congress. Speaking of the fact that Captain Bill carried in his body many bullets and had been wounded in war and other conflicts, President Wilson said, "you may recall when my scalp was injured in an automobile accident last fall, Captain Bill was with me, and he suffered a severe wrench in his back, and when the automobile was righted and on the way to the doctor, Captain Bill said 'I certainly hate to be hurt—

[60] George Bronson Rea, an American serving as Sun Yat-sen's technical adviser and deputy for negotiation with foreign bankers.

[61] James C. McReynolds, former assistant attorney general, 1903–1907, subsequently appointed an Associate Justice of the Supreme Court in August, 1914.

in an accident. I don't mind it when I have a fair chance and some fellow shooting at me, but being hurt running into a stump is a kind of injury

Saturday, March 29, 1913
Joe Davies.[62] Lunch to French [63]
Mare Island Mayor

Sunday, March 30, 1913
Dr Tudor—The Third in Ohio [?]
Mr. Bryan at dinner   Jonathan & Mr. Bryan   Christian Science
Our first Sunday

Monday, March 31, 1913
B'Nai B'rith banquet

Tuesday, April 1, 1913
Left at 1:30 on the Dolphin for the target practice near Norfolk

Tuesday, April 1, 1913
The meeting of the Cabinet today will be historic. Secretary Bryan read a letter written by the syndicate of American Bankers who had agreed to loan money to China, if the administration should request it, stating that they were unable to give China the six months she had requested on the loans already advanced. This decision was reached after consultation with the bankers of the other five great powers.[1] They stated that they had written to these powers and had asked them to cooperate in giving China the time requested. This letter was in reply to one from Secretary Bryan expressing the hope that those who had advanced money to China would give her six months to pay the loan. Secretary Bryan remarked that this letter was another proof of the wisdom of President Wilson in refusing to sanction the loan to China in that it showed that if we had gone into the agreement with the

[62] Joseph E. Davies, Wisconsin attorney and member of the Democratic National Committee, subsequently appointed U.S. Commissioner of Corporations on May 23, 1913.
[63] Daniels was host to a group of French officers in Washington to confer on radio-longitude determination.

---

[1] Great Britain, France, Germany, Russia, and Japan.

other powers the United States would have been bound to stay with the powers in all of China's matters and this might have put this country in a position where it would be obliged to do things that it ought not to do.

This letter and comment, however, were only preliminary to the greater problems involved with reference to China. President Wilson made the statement that he had been thinking about the Chinese situation and had reached the conclusion that this country ought to recognize China as a Republic and suggested that this should be done next Tuesday when the constitutional representatives elected by the voters of China would meet to fully organize that Republic.

A discussion ensued as to the best method of doing this. Mr. Bryan was inclined to the opinion that the Secretary of State should state to the Ambassadors of the great powers that America would recognize China next Tuesday and would ask the powers to do likewise. Mr. Bryan's idea was that it would be well to inform the public that this had been done after he had talked with the Ambassadors and Ministers. There was dissent among several members of the Cabinet to the suggestion that it should be made public until the Ambassadors and Ministers had been given an opportunity to communicate with their governments.

The Russian Ambassador [2] had suggested that Russia had intended to recognize Mexico in accordance with the action of this government; it might be well for us to follow Russia and recognize the Chinese Republic.

The President thought the conditions were not at all similar in this country and that we should not wait for the other countries to recognize the Republic before this country should do so.

Attorney General McReynolds thought it would be best to ask the powers it [if] they would cooperate with this Republic in recognizing China. The President was not agreeable to this. He thought it was best to announce confidentially to the Ambassadors that they could communicate with their government[s] and say to them that it was his purpose to recognize the Republic of China and he hoped that their countries would take like action. He was not willing to make it a conference in which the powers should have equal voice or by which America would be bound by the action of others. He wished it to be understood that this country was going to recognize China on the great day in its history when the Parliament or Congress of the new Republic will meet, and ask other countries to do likewise and that he did not wish this country's action to be at all dependent upon them. It was finally determined that Mr. Bryan should see the Ambassadors of the powers who have been conferring together about the loan of the money to China and

[2] George Bakhméteff.

let them cable to their governments in the hope that they would take action in recognizing the Republic of China at the time America does and that after the great powers had agreed that the representatives of the smaller powers should be notified.

It was like a breath of fresh air to see the spirit of the President and the Secretary of State in these great matters of international policy, because they were both animated as to this purpose of the Cabinet by devotion to a policy according equal rights. The refusal of this of this [sic] government to join the other powers in loaning money to China on terms that are humiliating to her presaged the recognition of the Republic of China. For months I have been earnestly hoping to see the Chinese Republic recognized and was happy that I found the President and Secretary of State held similar views and that the day was near at hand when this Republic should extend the right hand of fellowship to the great Republic in the Orient.

After the meeting of the Cabinet I hastened with my wife and boys and a number of friends to the Dolphin and began the trip to the Chesapeake Capes to attend the target practice which is now taking place. It was my first trip on the Dolphin since becoming Secretary of the Navy.

Thursday, April 3, 1913

This was another great day. I arose early on the Wyoming, and after breakfast with Admiral Badger,[3] went on the [blank] to the Norfolk Navy Yard with my aid, Capt Leigh Palmer. We were received with every honor and I spent the day inspecting the Yard and the great naval plants in and around Norfolk. There was a sub-marine at the dock and I went down twenty feet under water—my first experience in a sub-marine. It was not at all uncomfortable and I rather liked it. The drilling in the afternoon at the Training School was fine and they had there the largest and best band in the service. Admiral Doyle [4] gave a splendid lunch and we greatly enjoyed it.

At six o'clock, after having walked at least ten miles, we left on the Washington steamer for Washington

Friday, April 4, 1913

The two matters of importance discussed in the Cabinet Meeting today were, first—The tariff question. At the last session of the Cabinet the President had read the first draft of his message to Congress. Today the matter came up as to the sugar schedule and the President stated that, after a conference

---

[3] Rear Admiral Charles J. Badger, commander-in-chief of the Atlantic Fleet.
[4] Rear Admiral Robert M. Doyle, commandant of the Norfolk Navy Yard and Fifth Naval District.

with the members of the Ways & Means Committee and the Finance Committee, he had a talk with the representatives from Louisiana who are chiefly interested in the sugar schedule. He felt that it was a great industry and that it would be proper and wise to give them some time to adjust themselves to free sugar and, therefore, he had told them that if the Louisiana delegation would support the democratic tariff bill, he would favor a tariff of one cent a pound on sugar for three years after which sugar should be free. He insisted on three years because he wished the free sugar to go into effect during his term and he had no authority to make an arrangement that would not be completed while he was President. The matter of the sugar schedule and its effect upon the industry and the maze of schedule which had protected the sugar schedule so long was gone into fully by members of the Cabinet. They all concurred in the President's view that if the Louisiana people would accept the terms offered, it would be the best conclusion of the sugar schedule. The President intimated that he might deliver his tariff message in person in Congress but left it an open question to be decided whether he would do so.

The second important question was with reference to the Chinese situation. Secretary of State Bryan had notified the Ambassadors and Ministers on the 8th of April or on the date when the Constitutional Convention should meet in China, it was the purpose of this Government to recognize the Chinese Republic and it was the purpose of their Governments to recognize it at the same time. The Secretary of State reported that there was a suggestion from the Russian Ambassador to the effect that his Government would take whatever action we took with reference to Mexico and intimated that as his Government must do this about a country within the spher[e] of influence of the United States that the American government ought to follow Russia's example in China. This suggestion that America should be governed by Russia in the Chinese matter did not receive favor with the President or any Member of the Cabinet because of conditions in China and Mexico were in no way similar. The Secretary of State reported that he had heard from none of the other powers and could not state what would be the attitude of the other countries—whether they would join us in recognizing China upon the day when both houses of parliament or congress should convene. The question was discussed as to whether China now really had a Government. The President had had [sic] assumed the range of power without an election by popular vote and there was a suggestion that he was a dictator and not a president, but the discussion brought out the fact that China had elected without any difficulty or any serious division of members of both houses of congress, and that this showed perfect acquiescence in the republic by all those people in China who wished to have a voice. In southern China the people seem to be alive and alert and greatly interested in the republic. The bulk of the people in northern China seem to have no interest whatever in governmental affairs and, therefore, had taken no part and a Chinese doctor, a woman, who had seen the President and Secretary of State, conveyed the impression that the Chinese people were not behind the republic. But she is from Northern China where the people are not yet awake and was not familiar with the enthusiasm and spirit of liberty that permeates the people of South China, particularly Canton and the southern country and, therefore, her suggestion did not seem to carry much weight. Secretary of State Bryan brought to the attention of the Cabinet the information that there had been an assassination of a prominent Chinaman [5] and there was a charge that the assassination would be cured [was secured?] by the new President and this caused comment. Though this assassination had taken place on the 19th of March, no news of it came to America or [was] published in the newspapers. Investigation showed it to be true but the President of China [6] denied he had anything to do with it. The suggestion, however, was that this might change the status of affairs and might delay confirmation by the legislative bodies. Immediately upon this, Cabinet adjourned.

Saturday, April 5, 1913

The Mare Island Navy Yard matter was settled to-day when I gave orders to reverse the order of Secretary Myers [Meyer] made a few days before he went out of office. He had signed an order which stopped the expenditure of the money appropriated by Congress to dredge Mare Island straits, thus fixing the status of Mare Island as a "second class Navy Yard." As soon as I read the order I wrote the California delegation in Congress and asked if they wished to be heard. Both Senators and Congressmen and a delegation headed by ex-Congressman Bell [7] came for the hearing. I was convinced that the Navy Department would be doing an injustice to assume to over-ride the act of Congress. The people of Vallejo felt that the end in view was securing a Navy Yard at Frisco and this was the first step toward the ultimate ending of Mare Island as a "first class Navy Yard." When Congress appropriated money for a specific purpose it is doubtful if a cabinet officer has the right to reverse the action of Congress by virtually annulling its action.

At night we dined with Hannis Taylor [8] and wife. He was born in New Bern, North Carolina and was minister to Spain under Cleveland. Among

[5] Sung Chiao-jen, prominent Kuomintang leader.

[6] Yüan Shih-k'ai, former commander-in-chief of the Imperial Chinese Army and Sun Yat-sen's successor as provisional president of the new Chinese Republic.

[7] Theodore A. Bell, Democrat, U.S. Representative from California, 1903–1905.

[8] Washington attorney, former U.S. Minister to Spain, 1893–1897.

the other guests were Wm E. Chandler,[9] who was Secretary of the Navy under Arthur. He had many anecdotes and incidents.

Sunday, April 6, 1913

Went to Mt. Vernon Place Methodist Church with my three youngest boys, and heard a sermon by Dr. Register on "These were first called Christians at Antioch" and afterward there was communion services.

In the afternoon, we had a flood of company, including Secretary of State and Mrs. Bryan, Admiral Blue and others, including North Carolina friends. Josiah William Bailey [10] took dinner with us. After supper, I had a long talk with Admiral Blue, head of Navigation. He has sense, judgment and poise. We talked over the assignment of officers and the change of personnel. Two naval officers, who had had very little sea service, had been recommended for promotion as rear admirals. They had had very little sea service in their grade, and as I had made an order that no officer could be promoted who had not had adequate sea service I could not advise their promotion. It was a trial in case of these two officers who had been favorites of Secy Myers [Meyer]. He wished them promoted. If I did so, my new rule requiring sea service would have been a failure from the start.

Monday, April 7, 1913

I had a long talk with the Vice President of the Southern Pacific rail-road. That road has many miles in Mexico & he had just returned. He says conditions in Northern Mexico are worse than ever and that the railroad is now being run by the Huerta government [11] and that he could not ride on his own railroad without paying money to the government. He thinks there can be no peace there soon and feels that it is necessary for the American ships now in the important ports to remain there.

Had quite a long conference over the best plan to build a radio station at Colon. The Marconi people declare the specifications are so drawn as to make it possible only for the [blank] company to bid, and they ought to be

[9] William E. Chandler, Secretary of the Navy, 1881–1885. Chandler took a keen interest in Daniels' administration of the Navy, and although a Republican occasionally gave him public support.

[10] North Carolina attorney and Democratic political leader, shortly to be appointed U.S. Collector of Internal Revenue in North Carolina for the period of the Wilson administration.

[11] On February 18, 1913, General Victoriano Huerta had overthrown the government of Francisco I. Madero, who two years earlier had launched one of the significant revolutions of the twentieth century by deposing the aged dictator, Porfirio Díaz. Huerta's connivance in the murder of Madero and his inability to control northern Mexico, where a Constitutionalist force under Venustiano Carranza opposed him, led Wilson to delay diplomatic recognition of the Huerta regime.

allowed to compete. The experts had tried the other system and I stood by them though believing that in all possible ways awards should be given to the lowest bidders.

Tuesday, April 8, 1913
New Willard banquet

Tuesday, April 8, 1913
At Cabinet Meeting today the President came in dressed up for the first time in his Prince Albert, looking spick and span—dressed up properly to break the precedent by reading his message to Congress. Some of us suggested that he had not deemed the members of his Cabinet important enough for him to dress up for them, but seemed to think he thought more of Congress than he did members of the Cabinet. He said he thought he ought to be allowed to dress up occasionally, and that this was the first time he had done so. The President stated that it was expected that the Chinese Government would be formed today and that the Secretary of the American Legation [12]—We have no minister or Ambassador there now—had been instructed as soon as the Government was organized to recognize it. It seems since the murder of a prominent citizen of China last week, there is a widespread suspicion that the new President of China was responsible for the crime or connived at it and this suspicion may make his election impossible. Secretary Bryan stated that the Chinese Ambassador [13] told him yesterday that he thought that the President would have the Senate and that he probably would have the House, but that it was possible for two of the four political parties to unite and defeat him. He has already moved into the imperial palace and whether he feels so comfortable that he will be elected by the Congress today or whether he is preparing himself to stay in power even though he should not be elected are questions upon which the people in China differ. Secretary Bryan said he had a fatherly talk with the Chinese Minister and told him to impress upon the President and his people [not] to have unseemingly [*sic*] spectacle on the occasion of the session of Congress or to do anything that would militate against causing the other nations in following America and recognizing Chinese Independence. So far only the United States, Brazil and Mexico have decided to recognize the Independence of China. Inasmuch as Mexico is in revolution and its President holds tenure by force of arms and not by election, it is doubtful if he has any right to extend any recognition to another country. The big powers are waiting and inclined to join us in recognition of the Inde-

[12] Edward T. Williams, first secretary of the U.S. Legation in Peking.
[13] Chang Yin Tang, Chinese Minister to the United States.

pendence of China. The President and the whole Cabinet devoutly hope that everything will go well in China today and the people will so demean themselves as to justify their recognition by the whole world and give the Chinese Republic an opportunity to take its place among the Republics of the earth.

The Administration is sincerely desirous of promoting the peace of the world and to that end they are prepared to lead or inaugurate movements that will result in hastening the day when war shall be ended. The President stated that he had been talking with Mr. Bryan about the proposition which seemed to him to be a strong step in that direction and he gave a memorandum of the plan which the Secretary of State had suggested and gave a copy to each member of the Cabinet to be considered so that it might be discussed at some later meeting of the Cabinet. The following is a copy of the memorandum:

"Memorandum by Mr. Bryan.

"The parties hereto agree that all questions of every character and nature whatever, in dispute between them, shall, when diplomatic efforts fair [fail], be submitted for investigation and report to an international commission composed of five persons, one member from each nation, two other members, one chosen by each nation, and a fifth member chosen by the four; and the contracting parties agree not to declare war or begin hostilities until such investigation is made and report submitted.

The investigation shall be conducted as a matter of course, without the formality of a request from either party; the report shall be submitted within six months (or one year) from the date of the submission of the dispute, and neither party shall utilize the period of investigation to improve its military or naval status, but the parties hereto reserve the right to act independently on the subject matter in dispute after the report is submitted." [14]

The President said the suggestion of Mr. Bryan reminded him of a rule once made by a great teacher of a military school which was attended by his brother. The boys had a habit of fighting a good deal and he called them all in and said "boys, any boy in this school may fight another boy if he feels he has a grievance, but before doing so he must come to me and state his grievance and the fight must take place under my supervision or somebody representing me and carried on by the Queensbury Rules." The result was that there was no fighting in that school from that time forward. It was suggested

[14] Bryan signed the first such conciliation treaty with El Salvador on August 7, 1913, and subsequently negotiated similar treaties with twenty-nine other nations, including Great Britain, France, and Italy.

that perhaps the other countries would not be able to agree to this. Upon that, the President said "let them say so, it will put them to their trumps to give a reason for not talking over the matter." The suggestion was made by Postmaster General Burleson that the United States ought to offer a conference of all the Powers looking to the purpose of securing uniform action that would be an end to the building of costly battleships and preparations for war. In other words, a conference to bring about disarmament. He thought this country should take the lead and now was the happy time. I agreed heartily to this, but suggested that the first step should be along the line of Mr. Bryan's memorandum. If we could get the nations to agree never to fight until they have talked over the matters in dispute, the day would not be far distant when we would be able to secure disarmament.

Upon the adjournment of the Cabinet, the President left the White House to deliver his message to Congress, thus breaking a precedent. Since John Adams' day, no President had read his message to Congress. Secretary Garrison [15] asked the President whether he desired the Cabinet to accompany him. His answer was that some of the Senators declared in their speeches the day before that the President was reviving an old custom in the nature of an "address from the throne" and was restoring federalism in America. The President laughingly said "the whole idea of a message from the President was an evolution of the address from the throne, but the only thing federalistic about it was delivering the message in person." But he thought it would be better for him to do it in as simple a way as possible without being attended by the Cabinet Ministers, leaving it for each Cabinet Minister either to pursue his duties at his office or go without going in a body. Secretary Bryan stated that he would not go and that his wife had decided not to go. In view of the friction and the more [or] less feeling of Speaker Clark [16] against the Secretary and inasmuch as the Speaker would be the officer to welcome the President to the Capitol, he thought it better on all lines for him not to be present. The President, in a very tactful way, voiced the hope that the feeling the Speaker seemed to have against the Secretary of State would pass away and that friendly relations would be resumed. Mr. Bryan's spirit about the matter all along has been most excellent and he has gone on his way ever since the Baltimore Convention without any criticism or even feeling any criticism against the Speaker who seems to be harboring resentment towards Mr. Bryan and holding him responsible for his defeat for the nomination at Baltimore. This is

---

[15] Secretary of War Lindley M. Garrison, former vice chancellor of New Jersey.

[16] Champ Clark, the Democratic Speaker of the House of Representatives, had not forgiven Bryan for throwing his support to Wilson for the presidential nomination at the 1912 Baltimore convention.

the only cloud that is as big as a man's hand on the political horizon in the Democratic Administration, but it will pass away. Secretary Redfield stated he had some engagements which make it impracticable for him to be at the Capitol. All the other Members of the Cabinet stated arrangements had been made to go, so when the President entered, in a dignified way, to read his message, Members of the Cabinet were in the House Chamber scattered, some in the galleries, others on the floor, as citizens. It was an historical occasion with all the setting suited for the memorable message which the President was about to read. He was in fine form, and there was one spontaneous applause in his few opening sentences, and he read the message with a clearness and distinctness to all parts of the chamber. When he finished, he quietly withdrew amid applause. The precedent of a century had been shattered. Nobody was hurt and Congress heard the message that sounds the key-note of the government's fiscal policy—a key-note not burdened with a detail, but clear, ringing and direct. It was not only heard by members of Congress, but the diplomatic gallery was crowded and an audience representative of men political and governmental with such dignity as had never assembled in the House of Representatives. It was the first time the House had used the new method of seating the members. Up to this session each member had had a desk on which he could write his letters and in which he could keep his mail while Congress was in session. In order to accommodate the increased membership of the House, the desks had to be removed and the members are now seated on benches as in the English Parliament.

Wednesday, April 9, 1913
Potts. Andrews.
First day at home.

Thursday, April 10, 1913
Mr & Mrs Nelson Page [17]
Hopkins Smith.[18]
Ambassador Brice [19]

Friday, April 11, 1913
Armor Plate
Radio

[17] Thomas Nelson Page, Virginia author, subsequently U.S. Ambassador to Italy, 1913–1919.
[18] Probably Newton H. Smith, an office caller from Fayetteville, North Carolina.
[19] James Bryce, British Ambassador to the United States since 1907.

Dewey letter [20]
Navy League dinner

Friday, April 11, 1913

At the Cabinet meeting today the Secretary of War brought up for consideration the matter of whether any aid, except to meet the emergencies, should be rendered by the Federal Government to the flood sufferers in Ohio and Indiana. He said he had received a telegram from the Mayor of Zanesville, Ohio, asking that $1,000,000.00 be sent at once for the flood sufferers, and the idea entertained in the flood district that the Federal Government would reimburse a flood sufferer—for instance, if a man lost a piece of property say of $4,000 valuation, the Government would reimburse him or rebuild his house, and various bills are being introduced into Congress for the relief of the flood sufferers. He thought the matter ought to be adjusted so that the Federal Government should reimburse the Navy and War and other departments for funds already expended and relieve them from further responsibility. Postmaster General Burleson, who had been a member of Congress many years, said there was no danger of Congress assuming any responsibility. The Secretary of the Treasury said that he had offered to send money into the flooded districts to the banks upon security, but as soon as the banks found the Treasury would not deposit money without being secured they did not wish the money. Secretary Garrison suggested that a board of Engineers be appointed to make a careful study of all that section and report whether floods could be prevented in the future and he recommended this be done. He said even if they found no adequate precautionary measures could be introduced, it was of the highest importance that the people in that country should feel, for their own relief, that the Government had investigated the matter and had sought to do everything possible to avert these disasters in the future. In these views the President and all Members of the Cabinet concurred.

The Secretary of War also brought up the serious question of the killing of Americans in the towns on the Mexican and Texas border. It seems that there are fifteen town[s] in which a street or river only divides the Mexican and American people, and that when there is fighting between the Mexican troops representing the Huerta Government and those who deny that he is the actual President the bullets fly over to American soil and injure, and in

[20] Admiral Dewey had written the President protesting Daniels' action in withholding promotions from Potts and Andrews. Daniels sought to mollify Dewey personally (see entry of April 14), and Wilson wrote the Admiral backing Daniels' new sea service rule. Wilson to Dewey, April 16, 1913, Woodrow Wilson MSS., Library of Congress.

some instances, kill American citizens. Only yesterday an American officer, sitting in his tent, on American soil, had the leg of his chair shot out from under him. The Secretary of War thought that something ought to be done, and his idea was that a neutral zone ought to be established, say several miles wide, and that no fighting should be permitted in that zone. It was suggested that the real contention was for the possession of the custom houses on the border. Some of these are held by the Huerta forces and some by those states which have not accept[ed] the Huerta government and are fighting it, and that as intervention by the United States is desired by some, if the United States were to recognize Huerta or recognize the others, or try to recognize both, it might be in a position where it would have to intervene, and as intervention would be acceptable by either or both, it might be difficult for the United States to secure this neutral zone. The Postmaster General, who lives in Texas, said this same condition had been going on on the frontier 2-½ hears [years] and that any action now might jeopardize Americans who are living in Mexico. It was suggested that America might take over the custom houses. There was a long discussion which threatened to last all day and go no where. The Postmaster General said it had been reported to him that one officer of the Army had said that no matter what the orders were, if the Mexicans fired on him he would return it. But somebody said he should be court-martialed and removed from the service. However, this had been investigated and it was not believed the statement was made. He recognized that danger would be great if the Mexicans' fire should kill an American soldier and that without time for reflection the soldiers would return the fire. The Secretary of Agriculture [21] thought that a good many of the people in these towns were Mexicans anyhow and a good many of these people didn't belong to either country, who were mere bummers and that the country would suffer no loss if they were killed. There was a general feeling that no steps ought to be taken looking toward intervention and nothing done which might cause the Americans at this juncture to make it necessary to interfere.

For some days the Navy Department has been anxious to secure the return of the battleships and cruisers sent to Nicaragua and Mexico during the trouble in those countries. At the meeting of the Cabinet two weeks ago it was decided to let one of the ships in Mexico come home and at the last meeting it was decided to make a change in the others. I brought up the matter a few days ago with Secretary Bryan as to whether the ships sent to Bluefields [22] could not be returned, and Mr. Bryan sent a telegram to the Minister in Nicaragua [23]

[21] David F. Houston, former chancellor of Washington University, St. Louis.
[22] A port on Nicaragua's Atlantic Coast.
[23] George T. Weitzel.

that there was no necessity for the ships to remain longer and they ought to come home but should make occasional visits to Nicaragua. Mr. Bryan said the Secretary of the Navy has been very anxious to get the battleships home, and so anxious that he wants to put them in his back yard for use in case of an emergency, and upon receipt of this telegram the Minister said the Secretary of the Navy can have his old ships.

The Postmaster General, among other things, brought up an act of the General Assembly of North Dakota prohibiting the sale of cigarettes and snuff, and also asking the Federal Government to forbid the shipping of cigarettes and snuff by parcel post. The former Postmaster General ruled that whiskey could not be, and that now it was cigarettes and snuff that should be barred from the mails. It was left for this matter to be taken up by the Attorney General and the Postmaster General to see what can be done legally and act upon the matter. It may be it cannot be done now but the day will come when cigarettes will not only be debarred from the mails but outlawed. This prophesy is written here for what it is worth.

At a meeting of the Cabinet some weeks ago the Secretary of Agriculture suggested that the head of the Weather Bureau, Mr. Willis Moore, who had been there many years, be requested to resign. Later I saw Mr. Moore and talked with him. So did the Postmaster General. Mr. Moore was very anxious to be allowed to remain a few months longer, and the Secretary of Agriculture agreed to accept his resignation to take effect July 31st. Since then it developed at the Weather Bureau that in the campaign in endeavoring to secure endorsements to be appointed Secretary of Agriculture in President Wilson's Cabinet, he had spent the public money and had detailed men, who ought to have been engaged in the public service, going about the country trying to get recommendations for himself—all contrary to law, and it had been ascertained this difficulty culminated in a list he had made of promotions that he would make if made Secretary of Agriculture. The Secretary of Agriculture was inclined to believe that Mr. Moore had violated the criminal law and was subject to prosecution. He did not wish any action taken by the Cabinet but he thought that the Weather Bureau Chief should be removed and the matter of prosecution looked into most carefully and he wished to consult with the Attorney General. When the matter first came up the President expressed his severe condemnation of a public officer who would seek to force men in his employ to be active in getting endorsements for him for a Cabinet position and thought it most reprehensible.

The Secretary of Agriculture then brought up a matter which should have most important bearings. For a long time the land grant colleges of the country have been making demand after demand upon the Federal Government to appropriate money to help carry on those colleges. Secretary Houston was once a President of a land grant college and the first time he attended a meeting, the proposition was made to ask Congress to appropriate money to establish a Department of Mines in every land grant college and that there were movements started in all these states to have Congress appropriate money, not to be spent by the Department of Agriculture, but to go direct to these colleges and schools, and the propositions were multiplying and that they had an Executive Committee in Washington wishing to talk with him and he wished to know the policy of the Administration. He thought this a very vicious policy and that the states ought to look after their own institutions and whatever money was appropriated for agricultural development should be spent through the Department of Agriculture and should work in cooperating with state Departments of Agriculture and not land grant colleges; but that money from the Federal Treasury should not go to colleges but should be expended through the National Department of Agriculture. He pressed this matter earnestly and showed he had given it long study and unless such applications to the Government were stopped for drain upon the Treasury, nobody knew where it would end. The President was in hearty accord with the Secretary of Agriculture and said "Oh, how many crimes are committed in the name of education." He also said that a new administration could not succeed upon an important line like this without a program,—we must have a program. He says any man can beat another with a program and without a program everything was at sea. He said "I can take a program and I can defeat most any proposition and without a program nothing can be accomplished." He thought that the purpose of this administration ought not merely to be to meet the measures in Congress it opposed by mere negation but they ought to substitute for propositions it did not approve constructive programs and this is particularly true in matters of development of agriculture and matters of agricultural education.

The Postmaster General brought up a matter that is always the hardest matter to deal with—to wit: policies that are affected by race conditions. In the railway mail service there are a great many negroes who are employed and it often happens that there are four railway mail clerks in one car and when this happens, the white men might often have to do all the work. It is very unpleasant for them to work in a car with negroes where it is almost impossible to have different drinking vessels and different towels, or places to wash and he was anxious to segregate white and negro employees in all Departments of the Government, and he had talked with Bishop Walters [24] and other prominent

---

[24] Alexander Walters, bishop of the African Methodist Episcopal Zion Church and head of the National Colored Democratic League.

negroes and most of them thought it would be a great thing to do. Mr. Burleson thought the segregation would be a great thing as he had the highest regard for the negro and wished to help him in every way possible, but that he believed segregation was best for the negro and best for the Service. The matter then came up generally about negro appointments and how to use them. The President said he made no promises in particular to negroes, except to do them justice, and he did not wish to see them have less positions than they now have; but he wished the matter adjusted in a way to make the least friction. A negro is now Registrar of the Treasury, and Mr. Burleson, the Attorney [Postmaster] General, thought it was wrong to have white clerks, men or women, under him, or any other negro. Secretary of the Treasury McAdoo doubted whether the Senate would confirm a negro even if the President appointed one for this place, and believed it would be very doubtful. As to the segregation of negro clerks in the Treasury Department under the Registrar, Mr. McAdoo feared it would not work. The difference in salaries, etc., would operate against it. The up-shot of it all was that no action was taken, but Mr. Burleson said he would work out the matter in the Railway Mail Service in an easy way that would not go into effect at once and negroes would be employed on railway mail cars in sections where the appointment of negroes would not be objectionable.

The Secretary of Labor brought up the matter and the need of something being done in West Virginia. There is a strike out there between the mine workers and the mine owners which is very aggravated, he said, by the fact that the owners of the mines employ Baldwin Guards, who go to every train and if a new man came to town, they kept him under surveillance, and asking him what his business was, etc., with a view to injuring the strikers. He said this condition had been aggravated so much and said if a striker was arrested and tried, he was tried by a military court and that the state court prohibited him from getting a habeas corpus proceeding, or having his trial by a civil tribunal, and that he was trying, through arbitration, to settle the matter and hoped to be able to secure it but has not yet been able to do so. The President said he thought that it was unthinkable a man should be tried this way, but the beginning of all this was having a town controlled by a mine owner and the keeping out of people not desired by him. It was the root of the trouble. Secretary of Labor Wilson also thought the trouble was aggravated because the mine owners compelled the men to buy at the mine owner's stores and compelled to pay exorbitant prices. The President was very vigorously against the policy of excluding people from a town that did not give all people freedom to come a[nd] go. Secretary of War Garrison thought that the men who were tried by military courts without a jury could appeal to the Federal courts and that something might be done along that line. But, inasmuch as the state courts had held otherwise, there was not much chance. At this juncture, the President arose and said he must be excused to dine with Mr. Bryce of England, not Ambassador Bryce, but his old friend who was shortly going back to England. The members of the Cabinet remained and Mr. Bryan read the address issued by the Chinese Assembly which had been received by the State Department. It was beautiful and had the American spirit. If the prayers of that address can be answered, China will have a republic that will by [be] an example to the Nations.

Saturday, April 12, 1913
  Dolphin.
  Gridiron

Sunday, April 13, 1913
  Jonathans paper
  Dr Ruffin
  Admiral Fiske

Monday, April 14, 1913
  Called to see Dewey. Convention
  Gen Biddle [25]

Tuesday, April 15, 1913
  Col. Thompson [26] din[ner]

Tuesday, April 15, 1913
  When Cabinet met Secretary Bryan said he had a very important diplomatic matter to bring before the Cabinet, a matter in which he himself was more or less involved, speaking in a tone as if the matter was one that would give the Government great concern and might involve it in trouble and yet, from which he hoped there might be a happy issuing. He said he had received a cablegram this morning from England announcing the arrival of a party there whose appearance had not been heralded and arriving on a scene of that kind might involve him in a situation which might not be diplomatic, and after all this preliminary, looking dubious and solemn, he announced that his

[25] Major General William P. Biddle, the Major General Commandant of the Marine Corps, Daniels' host at a dinner at the Marine Barracks.
[26] "Colonel" Robert M. Thompson, Annapolis graduate and ardent Navy supporter, a prominent leader of the Navy League of the United States, a private organization to promote the interests of the Navy.

daughter,[27] who had married Lieutenant Reginald A. Owen of the English Army and who lives at 3 Park Gardens, Eltham, Kent, England, had given birth to a son, to wit, Reginald Bryan Owen.

Mr. Bryan brought up the matter about which he had given a memorandum at a former meeting of the Cabinet looking toward securing a treaty with every country in the world possible that before war should be entered upon, the countries having a dispute should submit the matter to a board of investigation and that pending the investigation by this board of the differences that neither country could enterprise or carry out new policies increasing its naval or military strength beyond the ordinary. Mr. Bryan thought, and so did the President, that a treaty of of [sic] this kind would be free from the objections that have always prevailed against arbitration treaties. Countries have refused to go into arbitration treaties because they said they could not arbitrate a matter of honor and this objection has defeated every treaty yet proposed that would guarantee arbitration. Mr. Bryan's plan is that this investigation shall go on for, say six months, or preferably a year, and then after the boards have made their reports to their respective governments, those governments will not be bound at all by the matter. If they choose after the investigation and its publication to go to war, no finding of the board will prevent them. It is a fact to appeal to public opinion rather than a hasty resort to arms. The Secretary of War thought that it would be as easy to get the countries to adopt a treaty to reduce their armament as it would this, and other members of the Cabinet did not agree with him, and they thought this suggestion of Mr. Bryan to secure investigation and publicity would be much easier to get the approval and adoption by the countries, and it was the opinion of all that if this could be secured, that afterwards it would be possible to secure a conference to discuss the necessity of putting an end to the great use of money for the maintenance of large navies and increased armies. This was deemed to be the entering wedge toward the other decideratum [sic]. It was the unanimous opinion of the Cabinet that this plan proposed by the Secretary of State, and approved by the President was most patriotic and desirable, and upon his suggestion the Secretary of State was requested to take the matter up informally with the Senate Foreign Affairs Committee and if they approved it, ask them to sound the Senators so that the sentiment of the Senate [sic] and if a majority of the Senate favored it, to get the matter out for publication that the whole world might be thinking of it.

The matter that took up the most time in the Cabinet today, and it was of most serious importance at present, was with reference to what attitude the Admin[i]stration should take with reference to Canal tolls on the Panama

[27] Ruth Bryan Owen.

Canal. England claims under the treaty [28] that the law enacted by the last Congress permitted coast-wise American vessels to enter the Panama Canal without paying the same tolls exacted of ships carrying freight of other nations is a violation of the treaty. The President said he had it from pretty good inside information that when the American representatives offered in the treaty before the construction of the Panama Canal to give the same rights to people of all countries through the Canal, Pauncefote [29] was surprised at the gift America was giving him. England did not ask for it and did not expect it, but was offered by America and they eagerly accepted it. Having obtained it, England now, of course, feels that the law is a violation of the treaty. Mr. Bryan stated that if the matter was to be taken up and discussed and a conclusion reached as to whether tolls should be laid or not and the whole question gone into on its merits, he would like to have time for consideration because he needed light on the subject. That the transportation companies had defeated the proposition to build the Nicaraguan Canal, thereby making the trip from New York to the Canal 1200 miles further by the Panama Canal than it would have been by the Nicaraguan route, and he believed that the Canadian Transcontinental railroads and the transcontinental railroads of this country had a working agreement and that it was largely due to this working agreement that the railroads had brought pressure on the Foreign Office in London. The President said it was not his purpose to open it up in its general aspect, but only what was best to do at this time. The arbitration treaty with England expires in June and it was the general opinion that England would be slow to renew that treaty until there was some adjustment of the toll matter. I suggested that the Secretary of State should sound Mr. Bryce; explain to him the dificulties [sic] and the desire of the Administration to postpone the settlement of the tolls question until the next session of Congress and to try to secure an extension of the treaty for one year so that it might be then taken up again after the Congress had a chance to pass upon the toll question. The general sentiment, however, was that England would not consent to renew the treaty for one year with the Panama toll matter unsettled. The President was inclined to think that under the treaty we had no right to charge

[28] The second Hay-Pauncefote Treaty, signed November 18, 1901, provided for the neutralization of a future isthmian canal built by the United States. The treaty stipulated that the canal would be open on "terms of entire equality" to the vessels of all nations. In 1912, Congress exempted American coastwise shipping from payment of tolls and authorized the President to charge lower tolls for American than for foreign-owned ships in the foreign trade. The British quickly protested that this discrimination was an obvious violation of the Hay-Pauncefote Treaty and offered to submit the issue to international arbitration.

[29] Sir Julian Pauncefote, British Ambassador to the United States, 1889–1902.

tolls on English or other vessels more than our own coast-wise trade, and that it was a better economic idea also to take that position. Mr. Burleston [*sic*] thought the bill passed Congress by a very narrow margin and Mr. Redfield said he voted for it under a misapprehension and there was a long debate whether it was best to try to secure the repeal of the law passed by last Congress on Panama Canal tolls as a matter of sound economic policy and try to secure that by this session of Congress, or to accept the construction that the treaty gave England the same right for its ships through Panama Canal that we had for ours. It is a knotty question, and the knottiest that has come before the Cabinet or government in recent years. Why our government should have offered the provision under which England claims equal rights with us is a marvel, and it has involved us in an international complication that is going to be difficult to settle satisfactorily. It is believed that the Senate is strongly in favor of maintaining the present law and Senator O'Gorman has the strong conviction that as America paid money to build the Canal, the treaty does not give England any right except against discrimination, but as America put up money to build the Canal, it does not give England any better tolls than to France, or Germany, or any other country, and that is all the treaty means. England is willing to arbitrate. Mr. Burleson did not believe in arbitration. Mr. Bryan said he would arbitrate anything. Secretary Lane took the ground that it would not be wise to grant England's construction of the treaty but that the proper policy would be to repeal the bill as a matter of national policy. The Secretary of Agriculture thought that the bill passed by the last Congress savored of subsidies of American ships in which view the Secretary of the Treasury concurred and agreed with the President heartily that we ought not to exempt coast-wise trade from freedom of tolls; if we do exempt them, then, of course, foreign vessels will ship all the goods they wish to sell in this country or in the east to New York, put them on coast-wise vessels and escape the Panama Canal tolls. No decision was reached.

The Secretary of War brought up a law passed by Congress which, under certain conditions, permitted the Panama Canal Commission to buy abroad. Its conditions were that whenever American manufacturers charged exorbitant or extravagent [*sic*] prices for anything they desired to sell for use on the Canal, then the President might order such supplies to be purchased abroad. Mr. Roosevelt ruled that in considering whether prices were exorbitant or extravagent that the English price and the price charged by a foreign company should not be considered at the figure offered by him but that to his net price should be added the duty and that the American manufacturers, therefore, should have the advantage which the duty gave him if he were selling to private parties. Colonel Goethals [30] in a letter to Secretary of War Garrison said he had advertised for certain cranes. The American manufacturer, the only bidder, offered to put them in for $1,400,000, in round figures. The lowest bidder, from Germany, offered to put them in for a price so low that after adding the tariff duties he could sell them for $1,200,000, and if Colonel Goethals should buy these cranes from the lowest bidder independent of the tariff he would save over $400,000 upon the purchase. The question was what to do. Colonel Goethals recommended that the contract be given to the lowest bidder and the $400,000 be saved. In his letter he said to pay $400,000 more for these cranes in order to buy from an American manufacturer would go beyond the appropriation and he would not advise it. Mr. Redfield said the American manufacturer had never made cranes of this kind before and was charging the government for all this experimentation as well as profit. The President threw up his hands and said "No need for further argument. Give this contract to the lowest bidder."

I brought up before the President the appeal of Captain Templin M. Potts, U.S.N. Shortly after I became Secretary of the Navy I issued the following order:

"March 24, 1913.

From: The Secretary of the Navy.
To: President, Examining Board for the promotion of Commissioned Officers.
SUBJECT:—Sea service qualification for promotion.

In accordance with Secs. 1493–1510 R.S. (See Navy Regulations, 1913, Chap. 31, Art. 3331), the Secretary of the Navy, from time to time, prescribes the examination for promotion of officers.

The Secretary wishes to inform the members of the Examining Board that he requires that officers coming up for promotion shall have had sufficient sea service in the grades from which they are to be promoted to insure beyond doubt that they are fully qualified and experienced at sea to perform the sea duties of the next higher grade.

(Signed) JOSEPHUS DANIELS."

I looked into the record and found that Captain Templin Morris Potts, U.S. Navy, had been to sea only ten months during his grade as captain, and Commander Philip Andrews, U.S. Navy, had been to sea only two months during his grade as commander. That is, since 1900, Captain Potts had been to sea only 22-½ months, and I was strongly of the opinion that while I hated to withhold the promotions, it was my duty to do so until both of these officers had sufficient sea service. Of course, they claim that the reason they

---

[30] Colonel George W. Goethals, chief engineer in charge of construction of the Panama Canal.

had no sea service was they had been kept away by the Secretary and that it was through no fault of theirs. I became convinced of two things—first, that they did not want to go to sea, and that if I had broken the rule of requiring adequate sea service in the case of these two officers because of their high position, the rule would have fallen down before it came into operation. When I had made the statement of my posititon and presented the petition of Captain Potts at the Cabinet Meeting the President said "The petition is overruled," and then turning in his chair with that delightful smile which radiates his face when he recalls an amusing incident, the President told the following story: "The name of the gentleman who appeals to me to overrule the action of the Secretary of the Navy recalls an incident that happened in a church convention some years ago. I have forgotten the facts, but they are not important. The debate ranged all the morning in the session over a man by the name of 'Potts' and the discussion grew so long that it became wearisome and while the preachers and pious men were discussing what should be done about Potts, or whether Potts was right or Potts was wrong, a layman, not so pious as the rest, had become so utterly disgusted with it said to a neighbor in a tone which he thought would not be heard except by the person to whom he he was talking 'O, damn Potts!' It seemed just as he had uttered that expression, there became a lull in the church so that his remark rang out over the entire church to the astonishment of the Bishop and brethren, but the session terminated, and in the afternoon when the Bishop called the meeting to order again, he turned to the clerk and asked at what point we had arrived before the morning session was adjourned, and the clerk without the suggestion of a smile replied, 'At Potsdam.' "

Wednesday, April 16, 1913
  White House dinner
  ~~Col. Thompson~~ dinner [*sic*]
  Cleveland Dodge [31]   YMCA

Thursday, April 17, 1913
  President Alderman [32]
  Pm
  Cleveland Dodge
  Dinner at Chief Justice White [33]

[31] Cleveland H. Dodge, financier and philanthropist, friend and classmate of President Wilson.
[32] Edwin A. Alderman, North Carolina–born friend and educator, president of the University of Virginia since 1904.
[33] Edward D. White, Chief Justice of the United States.

Hoke Smith [34]
Addie's decision

Friday, April 18, 1913
Tillman [35]
Lodge & Dem
Tom Pence [36] & Press work

Friday, April 18, 1913

As soon as the Cabinet met, Secretary Bryan said he wished to read what he regarded as the most remarkable official document that had been issued in a generation. He read from the Washington Post the following clipping:

"CHINA ASKS FOR PRAYERS—Government makes a Formal Appeal to All Christian Churches.

"Peking, China, April 17—An official appeal was made today by the Chinese government to all the Christian churches in China to set aside April 27 as a day for prayer that China may be guided to a wise solution of the critical problems besetting her. This act of the government is regarded here as striking evidence of the extraordinary changes which have taken place in the nation since the revolution.

"The appeal was distributed broadcast by telegraph today to the governors and high officials within whose jurisdiction Christian communities are to be found. It was also sent to the leaders of the various missions. Prayer was requested for the national assembly, for the new government, for the president of the republic, who is yet to be elected; for the constitution of the republic, for the recognition of the

[34] Democrat, North Carolina–born U.S. Senator from Georgia. As Secretary of the Interior in the second Cleveland administration, Smith had appointed Daniels as his chief clerk, 1893–1894, until Daniels resigned to purchase the *News and Observer*.

[35] Benjamin R. Tillman, Democrat, U.S. Senator from South Carolina, and chairman of the Senate Naval Affairs Committee until his death on July 3, 1918. On this occasion Tillman warned Daniels that Senator Henry Cabot Lodge, Republican of Massachusetts and a strong Navy supporter on the Naval Affairs Committee, was much concerned over a report that Daniels planned to transfer Lieutenant Colonel Charles L. McCawley of the Marine Corps Quartermaster Department to San Francisco. In line with his Single Oak Policy of transferring officers with long service in Washington, Daniels believed that McCawley, who had been a prominent Washington socialite since 1902, should have a term of duty away from the capital. McCawley used every influence, including a personal appeal to Daniels from Senator Lodge, to remain in Washington. Much as Daniels hated to offend Lodge, he believed his policy was right and that the transfer must stand. Daniels was foiled, however, by the timely and probably arranged retirement of Colonel Frank L. Denny, the Marine Corps Quartermaster, in June. McCawley as the next ranking officer succeeded to the post and remained securely in Washington until his retirement in 1929.

[36] Thomas J. Pence, former Washington correspondent of the *News and Observer* and Daniels' assistant in publicity during the 1912 presidential campaign, currently directing the permanent headquarters of the Democratic National Committee in Washington.

republic by the powers for the maintenance of peace, and for election of strong and virtuous men to office.

"The representatives of the provincial authorities are instructed to attend the services.

As soon as he finished reading it, he remarked upon the significant fact that official China was asking Christian churches of that country to pray for the success of the republic. Only a generation ago Christian missionaries could hardly find access to China and that in this generation they have been put to death. The revolution which changes all that and invokes the blessings of the Christians' God for the new republic shows what a tremendous revolution has been wrought in the feeling of the Celestial Empire. The President said that he did not know when he had been so stirred and cheered as when he read that message in the paper this morning and he had in mind to request it though, of course, said he, "I had no right to issue the proclamation that all churches in America on that date will join the churches in China in the prayer for the success of a republic that feels the need of the prayers of Christians." Secretary Redfield thought that the Chinese minds were so different from the minds of Europe and America that it might be well to consider whether the declaration was from the heart or whether it was not rather a play to secure the support of Christian nations and did not represent the real faith of the people. He also raised the question as to whether, in view of the fact that a majority of the people of China are not Christians, it might not hurt the republic if it became understood that the new Government was relying upon the Christian forces of the world for support. That the non-Christians in China, who outnumber the Christians by many thousands, would probably take advantage of this deep interest of the Christians of America and say beware of the republic. These foreign "devils," as they call Americans, are trying to get control of our country, and instead of helping, it might hurt. This did not appeal to the President, who thought that while there might be something in that, we ought to accept the official appeal of wishing the prayers of the Christians as honest and earnest and join with the Christian people in China in praying for the peaceful organization of the republic and its success in administering the government for the people of China. Secretary Garrison raised the question as to what we were going to do with reference to recognizing the republic of China. Mr. Bryan explained that he had sent a letter to our Secretary of Legation of China authorizing him to recognize China as soon as the Congress assembled and organized the government. It was expected then that a President would be elected on Tuesday of last week when the Assembly was scheduled to meet. That expectation had not been realized.

Shortly before the Assembly met a prominent man in China had been assassinated and an attempt had been made to connect President Yuan Shi Kai [Yüan Shih-k'ai] with the assassination and make him responsible for it, and that this had probably prevented the election of a President, but for that assassination and the attempt to connect the President with it undoubtedly Yuan Shi Kai would have been elected. There was opposition made to him as there is a contest between the Vice President and the President and the Assembly has been adjourning from day to day for conferences and there comes no news from China indicating any trouble. There is no suggestion of any turmoil or conflict and it is hoped that the President will be elected and as soon as he is, we will recognize the republic. The President said there had come into his mind a suggestion which might seem irreverent but which was not at all irreverent, i.e., that people would say if we pray that China may become a peaceful and progressive republic, why does not this country help answer its own prayers by immediately recognizing China? Secretary Garrison thought the country would say that you better recognize China first and pray afterwards. My suggestion was that faith without works is dead, that we ought to pray and also recognize China just as soon as we had enought [sic] facts to justify it. Secretary Bryan was requested to wire China and get all the facts. He has been hearing very little from China and we have no information of what is going on and the opinion was expressed by the President and others, particularly Mr. Bryan, in favor of recognizing China and that by Tuesday we would get enough information to recognize China by April 27th, on which date the churches would all offer prayers for the republic of that country.

The Mexican situation next came up for consideration. Some weeks ago when Secretary Bryan informed the the [sic] Ambassadors and Ministers from other countries that it was the purpose of the United States to recognize the republic of China as soon as the Assembly met and elected a President. He instructed his Secretary to notify all the Ambassadors and Ministers to come to see him and he made known his request. The American [Mexican] Ambassador [37] was included in that request and Secretary Bryan read a letter from our Minister at Mexico [38] stating that it was contended by the Huerta Government that this was equivalent to recognition of that government although no act of recognition has never [sic] been given. The President suggested that Mr. Bryan say to the Mexican people that his summoning the Mexican Minister was a courtesy and not recognition. What to do with Mexico is the great

[37] Presumably Arturo de la Cueva, first secretary and chargé d'affaires of the Mexican Embassy.
[38] Henry Lane Wilson, U.S. Ambassador to Mexico, 1909–1913.

problem and was discussed at length. Secretary Garrison had information which made him believe that conditions were worse than they had been and that it was doubtful whether the Mexicans could ever organize a government and that in this country it might be well to consider whether it would be well to recognize a brute like Huerta so as to have some form of government which could be recognized and dealt with. It was a general point of doubt that if we communicated with Huerta, he could not communicate with the northern states which are in revolution against him. The general opinion in the Cabinet was that the chief cause of this whole situation in Mexico was a contest between English and American Oil Companies to see which would control; that these people were ready to foment trouble and it was largely due to the English Company that England was willing to recognize Mexico before we did. What to do as to property that had been destroyed in Mexico was earnestly discussed. American property is being destroyed. The President of the Harriman railroad had been to see the Cabinet officers and it was said that 300 men in their employ were retained at a place where their shops were located in Mexico (Guaymas, I think) and that property and life were in jeopardy. Mr. Bryan offered to give them a convoy or make it certain that they could be taken our [out] of the country and their lives be saved, but the President of the railroad did not wish that but wanted them to stay and protect the property. But, if they chose to stay and protect the property, Mr. Bryan could not see that this government could do anything. It was certain that this government could not send an army to make safe conduct and who wished to stay in order to protect their property. The news from Mexico and our Minister and Consul General [39] is not as definite as is desirable and the question was whether a special man should be sent, a confidential man, to study the situation and get at the exact facts as they exist, but nothing went beyond discussion. This is Mexico's last chance at the President. Huerta and Diaz [40] now have the opportunity to see if they can maintain a constitutional government. An election has been ordered to be held in a month or two and unless they can elect a constitutional government, there is no hope for it and when they throw their hands up, both parties will call upon America to interfere. If it should intervene without being called upon, it would have to go in and conquer Mexico which is unthinkable and it is greatly to be hoped that a constitutional government can be organized in Mexico so that America will not have to intervene. Secretary Garrison thought that many Americans and Mexicans want intervention. Secretary Lane said he did not think there were 500

---

[39] Arnold Shanklin, U.S. Consul General in Mexico City since 1909.

[40] Félix Díaz, nephew of the deposed Mexican dictator Porfirio Díaz, had collaborated with Huerta in the overthrow and murder of Madero.

Mexicans who wished intervention. Postmaster General Burleson said the people in Northern Mexico, who are in opposition to Huerta, would like intervention provided they though[t] the Huerta government was going to succeed because they did not wish to be under his rule believing him to be a brute. But he was strongly against any intervention and thought the policy being pursued now was the only correct one and that this government should never intervene until Mexico saw there was no hope. Mr. Burleson lives in Texas just across the line from Mexico; he knows a great many people in that country and knows the situation from a neighborly attitude. He told a horrible story of a young man whom he knew well, employed by an American railroad in Mexico, who sometime last fall was out surveying for a new line for the railroad and was taken by the Insurrectos who cut his head off and the body was shipped to Cincinnati. This recital of this horrible and murderous thing shocked the Cabinet. The suggestion was made as to what was the best way to reach and punish the criminals. The President pointed out that this was done by men who were in insurrection against the government and nobody knew who did it, and unless there was some way of reaching the responsible parties, we could do nothing except to send an army down to fight the whole insurrection in a body in order to reach the culprit and this seemed impossible.

The third big matter before the Cabinet, and this was a day for the discussion of real problems of world wide interest, was the statement of the conversation between Secretary Bryan and Ambassador Bryce. They had talked over an hour over the matter of tolls on the Panama Canal. Ambassador Bryce, whose term soon expires, urged upon the Secretary of State that the President should announce that unless Congress repealed the bill under which coast-wise vessels had an advantage through the Panama Canal over English vessels he would submit the controversy between England and America to arbitration. Mr. Bryce was very earnest about this matter and Mr. Bryan detailed the conversation and argument between them and he told the English Ambassador that after 20 years of struggle the democrats were now in power and were in the midst of a fight to secure a reduction in the tariff law and that in his opinion the President would not be justified in taking up any important matter that would divide his party in the midst of this great tariff struggle. He pointed out to Mr. Bryce that there was no hurry about this Canal matter as it would not be open to vessels for about a year, possibly longer, and this matter might well be postponed until the President had the opportunity to put the tariff fight behind him and that England ought not to urge that this matter be taken up and some statement made until the tariff matter was settled. Mr. Bryan detailed his argument to Mr. Bryce along this line which was so convincing to the Cabinet as to lead me me [sic] to ask what answer Mr. Bryan could make to his argument on arbitration and Mr. Bryan answered that Mr. Bryce did not seem to be satisfied and did not understand why any man in America could oppose arbitration to which Mr. Bryan replied that it might be hard to understand but the fact existed and nevertheless it had to be dealt with. Although he could not speak for the President, he certainly would advise him that the only course would be not to permit this matter to be taken up now and make it an Administration policy until after the tariff measure had become a law. Mr. Bryce said in that event it might be that England would refuse to continue the arbitration treaty between that country and the United States which would expire in June. Mr. Bryan expressed surprise at this and quoted Mr. Bryce as saying that English leaders understood thoroughly the American favorable attitude toward arbitration and then asked Mr. Bryce if they understand it, why do you wish to press us to take it up now when the tariff matter is pressing? Mr. Bryce replied that while he and the leaders understood it, the people did not understand, and he was urging their government for action. The President said, "I have talked all this matter over with Mr. Bryce, not as Ambassador of Great Britain but as my old friend, and I am determined that I shall not make any statement about the matter or permit it to interfere with the policy of the Administration until the tariff bill is out of the way.["]

The Postmaster General brought up the fact that South Dakota had passed a law regulating the selection of postmasters. The law was passed by a republican legislature, after Mr. Wilson was elected President, providing that nobody but members of the party in power shall be voted for but all qualified electors shall vote in the appointment of postmasters. Mr. Burleson pointed out that the law was defective in many ways in that no man could vote for postmaster unless he lived in the corporate limits of the town in which the post office was situated and Mr. Burleson pointed out further that patrons of the office lived in the country and should have a voice if the postmaster is named by a primary election. He further said that if republicans can vote on the matter, that they will always take the weakest sort of a democrat and vote for him and never permit the democrat who was desired by the militant democracy to secure a majority of the votes and that he had notified the South Dakota Committee, who waited on him, that he would consider the vote in the primary just like any other petition, but that it would not be binding on him in naming the postmasters. The President said that those who had come to him seemed to have some opposition to the democratic organization in South Dakota and wished to defeat the man they recommended and that this had made him suspicious of the whole affair. The democratic leader in South Dakota whom they were criticising was Mr. E. S. Johnson,[41] long member of the National Committee and candidate for governor last year. It was the opin-

[41] Edwin S. Johnson, subsequently U.S. Senator from South Dakota, 1915–1921.

ion of all members of the Cabinet who took part in the last campaign that no policy looking to the unhorsing of Johnson should receive the least countenance. Mr. Bryan stated that as a principle it would be well to have the people in the community elect their own officers, and in this there was acquiescence, but did not believe this should be done where a law had been passed by a republican legislature to deny responsible democrats the power to recommend the officers they desire. It is my opinion that the day is not far distant when the postmasters and other federal officers will be elected by the vote of the people and this should be the method. It is the only proper way of ending the patronage troubles and of giving the people full control but it should be done under a national law and made uniform.

Secretary Redfield stated that he had investigated the question of meat supply of America and that he found that as the population increased and more need for meat, the amount of cattle produced in the country had steadily decreased and that now America was the fifth country in the raising of cattle and if it decreased the next few years as it did in the last few years the United States would be importing meat instead of exporting it. "What effect will this have on the tariff legislation," asked the President? Secretary Redfield said he did not know but thought the matter ought to be given out while it is being considered. Secretary McAdoo thought that meat was so high and this country was exporting so little that meat ought to be put on the free list and that it would help tariff legislation.

Saturday, April 19, 1913
  Badger
  Page [42]
  Fiske

Saturday, April 19, 1913
  Admiral Southerland [43] called this morning. He was in charge of our vessels on the Pacific Coast during the time when they were stationed at Mexican ports while the recent troubles were going on in that country. Admiral Southerland stated that in the northwestern province of Mexico the rebels appeared

[42] Walter Hines Page, North Carolina–born journalist, and newly designated U.S. Ambassador to Great Britain. Daniels and Page had at one time been close friends. When Daniels took over the Raleigh *State Chronicle* in 1885, a weekly originally edited by Page, the latter offered to write a regular column from New York. Gradually the two men drew apart politically, however, until in 1896 they split on the question of party regularity, with Daniels an enthusiastic supporter of Bryan and Page preferring McKinley. By 1912, Page's antipathy for Daniels was sufficiently deep for him to try to block Daniels' appointment to the cabinet, though Daniels was not aware of this.

[43] Rear Admiral William H. H. Southerland, commander of the Pacific Fleet.

to be gaining ground very rapidly; that the federal troups were not numerous; that near Guaymas we had an American city with about 200 women and children in addition to the men. He reported that the people did not like Huerta, but that they were willing to get together for the sake of peace. About the time they were supposed to be arriving at an amicable agreement, one of the government officers landed and took possession of the provisional governor and his staff near one of the coastal towns and carried them away to the City of Mexico where they were imprisoned. This incident carried out on the responsibility of this officer alone, effectually stopped any further attempts at an amicable agreement. Admiral Southerland states it is the general opinion in Mexico that one Federale is equal to five Insurrectos but that the people in this province and in adjacent provinces have, during the Madero Administration, tasted the pleasure of a little liberty where before they had always been ruled by an iron hand, and that having once enjoyed this privilege they will never again be willing to put up with anything less than a free representative government. Admiral Southerland further states that he believes we are likely to have a war with Mexico at twenty-four hours notice in case the troups should enter the American town near Guaymas and massacre some of the women and children. He believes that our vessels should remain on that coast or that others should relieve them so that every port could be occupied. He thinks that the display of force will over-awe them and that in case of trouble the United States forces, represented only by the Navy on the West Coast, would be able to cut communications, divide the country in two parts, and get control by sending sailors and marines up the local railroads from each port to the main line. He believes that we should send the larger ships back to San Francisco and Puget Sound for thorough repairs, taking their officers and men and commissioning all the smaller vessels to return to the Mexican ports. He further states that if trouble came, he is confident that the Navy on the West Coast could end the war in three months.

In the course of his conversation, Admiral Southerland called attention to the fact that two of the armored cruisers left the Mare Island Navy Yard in poor condition on account of the fact that they were resting on the bottom, due to lack of depth at that place and that the plain necessity for the Navy on the West Coast was to have not another navy yard, but a suitable place for docking vessels in San Francisco Bay and away from Mare Island.

Sunday, April 20, 1913
Bishop Wilson [44] Eph 10 Ch 11:12 verse

[44] Probably Alpheus W. Wilson, Baltimore bishop of the Methodist Episcopal Church, South.

Dr. Geo Thomish [?]: "I am doing nothing & paid for doing it"
Henry Bagley.[45]
Lady. Marshall's [46] speech.
Dr J A Holmes [47]   Alaska Coal

Monday, April 21, 1913
Badger—The President.
War is an attitude
Meeting of chiefs. A ship a school-room.[48]
Senator Lodge. McCauley.

Tuesday, April 22, 1913
As soon as the Cabinet met this morning, the President said he would like
to ask the views of the members of the Cabinet as to whether it would not
be wise for him to request the Secretary of State to go to California and confer with the Governor and Members of the Legislature with reference to the
pending bill relating to alien ownership of land.[49] Since the last meeting of
Cabinet, there has been a distinct change in California. It looked a week ago
that the legislature in response to the suggestion of the President and the
Secretary of State that the legislature would pass an act that would apply to all
aliens and not only to the Japanese. But yesterday the Governor of the State,[50]
a Roosevelt Republican, gave out a statement in favor of the bill as originally
introduced which excludes ownership of land by the Japanese and Chinese, but
no other aliens. This is very offensive to the Japanese who are very sensitive and
and [*sic*] feel that it is a reflection upon their race. The President thought
Mr. Bryan, who is very popular in California, particularly with the labor
people and others who mostly give their expression to the hostility against

[45] W. Henry Bagley, Mrs. Daniels' brother, currently business manager of the *News and Observer*.

[46] Vice-President Thomas R. Marshall, former governor of Indiana, 1909–1913.

[47] Joseph A. Holmes, director of the Bureau of Mines since its creation in 1910. Daniels was much interested in the idea of developing the Alaskan coal fields as a supply source for the Pacific Fleet.

[48] Daniels was shocked at the meager education of many Navy enlisted men. One of his more controversial reforms (General Order 53, October 1, 1913) required the establishment of off-duty schools on every ship and naval station for compulsory training in various elementary subjects, using officers as instructors. The program was generally unpopular and functioned with varying success until wartime conditions made it impractical.

[49] Anti-Japanese sentiment in California, strong for more than a decade, had been whipped to a new high by demogogic oratory in the 1912 political campaign. When the California legislature met in March, 1913, it immediately began to consider legislation to prohibit the ownership of land by Japanese residing in the state.

[50] Hiram W. Johnson, Republican-Progressive, governor of California since 1911, subse-quently U.S. Senator after 1917.

the Japanese, could tell them the legislation desired by the passage of the bill forbidding alien ownership without making the bill apply only to the Japs, and that he could do this by his presence better than by writing. Secretary Garrison raised the question that it might make a precedent that would come up to give trouble in the future as well as now. It was a very serious question for the Secretary of State to go into any state to confer about pending legislation and that there would be resentment against it. It would be contrary to the old democratic doctrine of "States Rights," and that it might inflame the people and do more harm than good. The President did not think that this would raise such a precedent because it was not supposed to take any action or do anything limiting the states in their rights, but only to point out to legislators and the Executive that the state ought not to do anything that might be contrary to the treaties which the federal government had made with any foreign power. He said that it had never been determined by the courts whether a state was bound by any treaty stipulations and this was a matter still to be decided. Secretary Lane, of California, believed that the people of California wished the most drastic law against the Japanese that could be enacted and that they were not in a mood to have anything but drastic laws but as Mr. Bryan is very popular in California, and if anybody could persuade them that the Kaminetti [51] Bill which forbade all alien ownership should become a law, Mr. Bryan is the man that could do it. According to Mr. Lane, the most unpopular people in California, led by Harrison Gray Otis,[52] who is despised by the labor organizations had advocated a conservative course and Governor Johnson, a politician, had seized upon the advocacy of a conservative measure by the unpopular force to advocate a more stringent measure and doing this to strengthen himself politically and to strengthen the progressive party. Secretary Wilson thought that if Mr. Bryan went out to California, not to carry any word from the Administration, demanding something to be done, but in the spirit of cooperating with the people to secure what they desire in a way that would be the least objectionable, it would be very well, but if he went in any other way it would be with bad effect. Mr. Bryan discussed at some length the matter, prefacing by saying it was not a job he would solicit and that he had but one spirit in coming into the Cabinet and that was to help and [be] ready to do anything that the members of the Cabinet and the President thought he ought to undertake. His idea was that nobody should go from the Administration to California unless invited to do so by the California people. He suggested that inasmuch as the California people had put

[51] Anthony Caminetti, Democrat, former U.S. Representative from California, 1891–1895, California state senator, 1907–1913, U.S. Commissioner of Immigration, 1913–1921.

[52] Editor and general manager of the *Los Angeles Times*.

in their constitution the referendum, it might be well to advocate the submitting to the people the choice between the two acts—the one forbidding all alien ownership and the one forbidding ownership by the Japanese and then whatever action they took the Administration could say to the Japanese that the Administration is up against a fact and it could not fly in the face of a registered will of the people of a whole state. Secretary Lane raised this question: What would you advise the democrats in California to do? Would you advise them to vote for the conservative bill forbidding all alien ownership or for the bill advocating the forbidding only Japanese ownership? The President brought out the fact that four years ago when the Californians were passing acts forbidding the Japanese from coming to public schools and Mr. Roosevelt were [sic] asking them to hold it up, the democrats made political capital out of this; and if this Administration urge the more modern measure, the progressive party would make capital out of it and put the democrats in the hole because that was theirs when Roosevelt was trying to control the matter. Mr. Bryan's suggestion of a referendum to the people of California would not meet with favorable consideration as the general opinion being that the people of California would vote for the most stringent legislation against the Japanese and instead of helping the diplomatic situation with Japan, would complicate it. Moreover, it would be embarrassing to the democrats and if they stood by the Administration, they would have to change their position of four years ago and it would be embarrassing for them to join against the measure. The President stated that he had that morning sent a telegram, which he had given to the Press, to the members of the Assembly of California to do nothing to abridge treaty rights. But the general opinion was that the Governor of Cal[i]fornia was playing politics and nothing was to be expected from him that would help the Administration but on the contrary he would take the opposite view. While Mr. Bryan was stating his views, the President wrote a message which he stated he thought of sending to the legislators in California suggesting that Mr. Bryan will come out to confer with them if they desired it. Secretary McAdoo agreed with me that it would probably be best to wait until the President heard from his telegram he had given out this morning before any further message should pass and that was the course pursued. Mr. Bryan said he had had a very hard time. He was trying to find a position paying about $4,000 a year for the brother of the Senator who was Chairman on the National Democratic Committee and that he was not particularly qualified to go in the Consular Service, but that he was particularly anxious to get him a position and he said to the Members of the Cabinet that he would make a trade—"I will give a man a position at $4,000 if you will give me a $4,000 job in another Department." The Attorney General,

Mr. McReynolds, said, "All right, I will give him a place if you will let me name the Minister to Persia." Mr. Bryan accepted it speedily and said "Send over your man." [53]

Thursday, April 24, 1913
  N.Y. Asso Press
  Paper burned [54]

Friday, April 25, 1913
  Went to Raleigh

Wednesday, April 30, 1913
  Left for Wilson

Thursday, May 1, 1913
  Wilson [1]

Friday, May 2, 1913
  Raleigh [2]

Saturday, May 3, 1913
  Left for N[ew] O[rleans] [3]

Sunday, May 4, 1913
  Tallahassee

Monday, May 5, 1913
  New Orleans

[53] McReynolds may have used this patronage swap to protect the position of the incumbent minister to Persia, Charles W. Russell, whose previous service as an assistant attorney general from 1902 to 1910 had overlapped that of McReynolds. In any event Russell remained at his post until 1914.
[54] Just minutes before he was to address the Associated Press banquet in New York, Daniels received word that the plant of his newspaper had been destroyed by fire, with estimated damage of $75,000 covered by only $40,000 insurance.

----

[1] The citizens of Wilson, North Carolina, where Daniels had lived as a boy, were giving a banquet in honor of his appointment as Secretary of the Navy.
[2] This was the Daniels' twenty-fifth wedding anniversary, and their Raleigh friends were celebrating the occasion.
[3] For the next ten days Daniels inspected various Navy facilities in the South.

Tuesday, May 6, 1913
Pensacola

Wednesday, May 7, 1913
Jacksonville

Thursday, May 8, 1913
Key West

Friday, May 9, 1913
En Route to Charleston

Saturday, May 10, 1913
Charleston

Sunday, May 11, 1913
Port Royal
Savannah

Monday, May 12, 1913
Raleigh

Tuesday, May 13, 1913
Cabinet

Tuesday, May 13, 1913
I reached Washington at 8:30 this morning from Raleigh after a long trip in the South to find a great accumulation of mail and other matters requiring my attention. During my absence, the matter of the land legislation in California had reached an acute stage. Secretary Bryan had returned from California where he had been unable to induce the Legislature to change the law relating to the holding of land by aliens. He had suggested that the law should be changed so that it would apply to all aliens alike and that the words "eligible to citizenship" offensive to the Japanese could not occur in the bill, but inasmuch as German and French capitalists have much money invested in California, they were not willing to do this so that the only thing directly accomplished was that the bill was changed so as to contain the terms of the treaty with Japan and to guarantee that all treaty rights should be protected in California, or rather the bill was drawn in accordance with the treaty.

Upon Mr. Bryan's return from California, the President presented to the Governor of California the objections raised by Japan to his signing the bill. Mr. Bryan had suggested to the Legislature of California the wisdom of appointing a commission to consider the matters treated in the alien land bill to be reported at the next session of the General Assembly. That suggestion would not have caused California to lose any of its rights, but simply deferred action until a more convenient season. If Japan feels so hostile to the Legislation that it would be disposed to consider California's action as casus belli, the delay would have prevented the passage of the act until after the Panama Canal is opened and our battleships can go through to the Pacific quickly and easily. That suggestion was one that appealed strongly to the people of the country, but Governor Hiram Johnson and his followers in California seemed to think there was a great party advantage in passing the bill now and they seemed to have an idea that it would put the Democratic Administration in a hole should they pass the bill at this time. They seemed wholly indifferent to the fact that it might involve this country in serious trouble, whereas delay and consideration and consultation might prevent any trouble. Governor Johnson seems to put politics and partisan advantage above everything else, and in this crisis, he and his friends in California have not risen to the height of patriotism but seem to play local politics even in so doing they are playing with fire. From the moment the President suggested that Mr. Bryan go to California, Secretary Lane, a Californian who knows the temper of the people, felt that Governor Johnson would do nothing at all that the Wilson Administration might desire, but would seize upon any request of the Administration as a means of making capital for himself, and this was brought to the President's attention. However, the President's attitude was that if this was Johnson's position, it was the Administration's duty to put the patriotic matter before him and give him the benefit of every bit of information and every view from the Administration's standpoint, and if Johnson then preferred political stunts to statesmanship, he must take the responsibility. It was the hopw [hope] of the President that the California Legislature and the Governor would not be precipitate, but the other members of the Cabinet have little faith in the ability of Mr. Bryan or anybody else deflecting Johnson and the party from the course they had marked out for themselves. The discussion over the California situation occupied much of the time of the Cabinet and was generally participated in. The President read Baron Chinda's protest against the legislation in California. The words of the protest were very strong—stronger than the circumstances seemed to warrant. The language, while diplomatic, was such as to cause Secretary Redfield to feel that it might imply that in the event this government was unable to meet the demands and wishes of Japan, the worst results might follow. All the members of the Cabinet seemed to think the language was stronger than ought to have been employed and should give them pause, but did not think it implied anything except a very earnest desire to secure the same rights for the Japanese in California that are given to other aliens. This protest, of course, will be made public when the President and the Secretary of State, Mr. Bryan, reply to it and it will take the subsequent results of history to determine whether the language really had in it the implication of possible force that the Japanese might employ. Secretary Redfield thought that what ought to be read into it was all which it implied by considering it in the light of diplomatic utterances.

Secretary Bryan spoke of his trip to California and of the feeling in California that some legislation ought to be enacted but he had to leave the Cabinet Meeting early to go to Harrisbury [Harrisburg] to address the General Assembly of that State. He said if the President sent him on many other missions—the President had requested him to go—he said, laughingly, that he would not have time to attend to the duties of his office. The California mission had consumed considerable time and he had been requested now by the President to go to Pennsylvania and the President expressed his great appreciation of Mr. Bryan's making the trip to Harrisburg at the request of the Pennsylvanians.

I brought up the question before the Cabinet as to whether the three ships, the SARATOGA, the MONTEREY, and the MONADNOCK, which are in the Chinese rivers, ought to be ordered to the Philippines in accord with the suggestion of the Aid for Operations of the Fleet, Admiral Fiske. I had read a statement on the possibility of war with Japan from the Aid for Operations to the Cabinet, which is appended hereto.

IN REPLY ADDRESS
THE SECRETARY OF THE NAVY
AND REFER TO NO.

Op–BAF–JVD

NAVY DEPARTMENT
WASHINGTON
May 13, 1913.

From: The Aid for Operations.
To: The Secretary of the Navy.

   Subject: Possibility of War with Japan.

   1. While I do not believe that our present

tension with Japan will result in war, while I

realize the reasonableness of the belief of many
people that Japan does not desire war, and while I
earnestly hope that war will not result, yet I beg
leave to present the following statement of facts:—

(I)   The Islands of Japan are not at all
fertile; the climate is very trying; the people
have a hard time to subsist on the Islands.

(II)   The Philippine Islands, which lie to
the southwest of Japan, are extremely fertile, are
very sparsely inhabited, and would be an
extremely desirable possession for Japan as an
outlet for their surplus population.

(III)   From their geographical position with
reference to Japan and to the east coast of Asia,
the Philippines would be an extremely desirable
possession for Japan as a strategic position from
which to command the coast of China.

(IV)   The Hawaiian Islands also are very
fertile, and would be an extremely desirable
possession for Japan.   Japanese people are already
on the Islands in great numbers; and it has
frequently been stated that Japan declared, just
previous to the Spanish War that she did not desire
the United States to take possession of the
Hawaiian Islands.

2. It is not impossible that Japan, in spite of her poverty, may decide that it is worth her while to go to war with the United States in order to secure possession of the Philippine Islands and the Hawaiian Islands.

3. Should she decide to go to war, she could at once occupy the Philippine Islands and the Hawaiian Islands, and hoist the flag of Japan on those Islands.

4. After doing this, after placing in the Hawaiian Islands, say, 60,000 men, and in the Philippine Islands 150,000 men, she could withdraw her fleet to Japan, and, to use a slang expression, "standpat"; that is, she would withdraw her fleet to a place in the Inland Sea, and not do any fighting whatever.

5. All the United States could do would be to send her Fleet to Japan; we could cut off most of the trade of Japan with the rest of the world by means of our Fleet, but not all of it. We could cut off her trade to the westward, and south'ard [sic], and eastward, but probably we could not cut it off to the northwestward. Probably Japan would be able by means of mines and

destroyers, even without the use of her battleship
fleet, to keep the Sea of Japan sufficiently open
for her vessels to communicate with Korea, and from
there to make land communication with the rest of
the world.

6.   This would undoubtedly place Japan in a
very distressing position; but her people are very
frugal, and if they have to do so, can live in a
very simple and inexpensive way. They have
tremendous national feeling, a great deal of
endurance and determination, and probably could
stand this condition for, say, two years, or even
more.

7.   During these two years our entire fleet,
practically speaking, would have to be maintained
off the southern coast of Japan. To do this would
be enormously expensive; and even if no actual
battleship battle were fought, it is probable that
many of our ships would be lost through the agency
of submarines, mines, and torpedoes.

8.   What the issue would be would depend upon
the relative state of mind of the people of the
United States and the people of Japan.

9.   It is possible that Japan may believe that

there is so large a number of people in the United
States who would be glad to get rid of the
Philippine Islands, that they would easily come to
terms with Japan after an inglorious and expensive
war that lasted, say, two years.

   10.   In other words, it is conceivable that
Japan may conclude,—may have already concluded,——
that, if she should go to war with the United
States, she could, by enduring a period of privation
and distress lasting about two years, acquire
possession of both the Philippine Islands and the
Hawaiian Islands.   Her war against China supplies
a precedent for such a procedure.

                                 Bradley A. Fiske,

There was considerable discussion of the matter. I recommended that no
movement be made at this time. The "yellow press" in America are so aggra-
vating and the Japanese are in such an inflammatory mood, I thought that
any movement might give them an opportunity to inflame the people of Japan,
who do not fully understand our attitude in regard to the movement of ships
in the Yellow Sea, as evidence of our unfriendliness and our expectation of
war. I have observed that if a man puts a gun on his shoulder and walks down
the street, particularly down a street in which he knows there is a man with
whom he has some misunderstanding, it is pretty likely to cause the other man
to get a gun himself and that death or something else serious results, whereas
if the man had not started out with the gun on his shoulder the difficulty
would have ended peaceably.

Wednesday, May 14, 1913
Garrison
Goethals
H A London [4]

Thursday, May 15, 1913
Garrison
Bassett Moore [5]
Spain blew up Maine
Inevitable
Tom Reed's [6] joke
   Lion in tree   Man shot. Couldn't convince lion that dog under tree shot
   gun.
Go to Balti Sat—
Enlisted men for pay corps [7]

Thursday, May 15, 1913
Yesterday the Joint Board of the Army and Navy held a meeting and unanimously reported the conclusion that the three ships in the Yang-tze River,
which were sent there about the time the Chinese began to change their form
of government, should at once be sent to Manila. The War Department earnestly urged this on the ground that these ships could protect Corregidor Fort
and that if these ships were there they could prevent the entrance of the
Japanese Fleet which might come and it would be very difficult for the Japanese to take Manila if these ships were in Manila Bay or near by able to cover
the approach to the Fort.
   Admiral Fiske, Aid for Operations, who earnestly pressed this action of
withdrawing these ships from China, gave me a memorandum giving his
reason and his argument on the possibility of war with Japan. This memorandum is appended hereto.
   ~~I had a talk with John Bassett Moore with reference to the right of a country~~
~~to take out its ships after war had been begun.~~ [*sic*]

[4] Major Henry A. London, a pre-Baltimore Wilson leader in North Carolina, whom
Daniels took to the White House on this date.
[5] John Bassett Moore, experienced diplomat and expert on international law, serving at
this time as Counselor of the Department of State.
[6] Presumably Thomas B. Reed, Republican, U.S. Representative from Maine, 1877–1899,
three times Speaker of the House.
[7] As part of his campaign to increase opportunities for the enlisted men of the Navy,
Daniels ordered that the ten vacant commissions in the Pay Corps be reserved for enlisted
men, a policy regarded by some Navy officers as revolutionary.

JH   Op-

May 14, 1913.

From: Aid for Operations;
To: The Secretary of the Navy.

SUBJECT: Possibility of war with Japan.

1. While hoping that no war will result from
the present tension between this country and Japan,
I believe from a mature and careful consideration
of the situation, and a careful study of the
historical precedents and actions of the Japanese
government and people, that such a war is possible,
and even probable, and deem it my duty to submit
for your consideration the following statements:—

(1) The Japanese are a highly-strung,
proud, sensitive race, extremely jealous of
their national rights and claims to equality
with all races and nations; and are possessed
of a patriotism of the intensity of a religion.
These qualities are not fully understood either
in this country or in Europe, except by the
few who have been brought in contact with
them, and made a study of their race.

(2) The Japanese are a vigorous, growing,
expanding race with whom expansion is a
necessity for national life, since Japan
itself is not capable of supporting the
increasing population. It was this necessity
that lead to the Japan-China war in 1894-5,
and the acquisition of Formosa; the European
powers, lead by Russia, depriving her at that
time of further intended expansion in Corea.
It was the same necessity, coupled with
natural enmity against Russia for the latter's
action in 1895, and her arrogant attitude in
the Corean negotiations, that lead to the
Japan-Russian war in 1904-5, with the acquisition of Corea, lower Sakghalien and dominant
influence in Manchuria.

(3)   Japan has not been particularly
successful in colonizing either Corea or
Sakghalien, nor are her own northern islands
well populated. The climate in all these is
rigorous and inhospitable, and the race does
not thrive there. They do thrive vigorously
in warmer climates as in the Hawaiian Islands,
which are largely populated by them, and in
Formosa, which is receiving considerable
development.

(4)   The natural outlet for the increasing
surplus of the race is to the southward, and
the fertile Hawaiian and Philippine Islands
form ideal places of Japanese colonization.
These are both in the possession of the United
States which blocks their expansion in this
direction and are very loosely held while the
battle fleet is in the Atlantic. They could
both be seized and occupied in force and then
held without the support of their fleet, before
our fleet could enter the Pacific at any time
previous to the completion of the Panama Canal.

(5)   Japanese commerce and trade is increasing enormously and she aspires to commercial supremacy in the Pacific, especially
on the Asiatic continent. Her chief rival in
this is the United States, which from its own
position in the Eastern Pacific, and its
position of advantage in the Philippines in
the Western Pacfic, hems in and cuts off Japan
commercially as well as in racial expansion.

(6)   The United States thus, by refusing
citizenship to Japanese, and by such state
laws as are now pending on the west coast,
hit the Japanese in their tenderest spots—
their sense of honor; their pride of race and
their patriotism; by the occupation of the
Hawaiian Islands and the Philippines, cut off
their natural lines of expansion necessary to
their physical life and national growth; and
by superior wealth and position hamper their
commercial growth. With the fearlessness of
their race, their contempt of death, any of
those causes make war possible, and, all

combined, probable; and my study of the race and its history leads me to the conviction that it is only a question of whether they themselves believe their preparations are sufficiently advanced to seize and hold the Philippines, Guam and Hawaiian Islands and inflict an enormous damage on us before we can bring any adequate force in the Pacific that will decide whether they will go to war or not. If they decide they can accomplish these things war will come; and when we appear finally in the Pacific in superior force, they will retire their fleet to Japan, hold the Hawaiian Islands, Guam and the Philippines, prolong the war with torpedo and mining tactics, and trust to the enormous cost of the war to us and the influence of the great numbers of our people who love peace at any price and would be glad to give up the Philippines, to bring the war to a successful conclusion for them.

(7)   Japan has proved in both her wars with China and with Russia that she can and does make war effectively without previous warning when she considers that her interests demand it and justify it, and that her state of preparedness justifies the risk and is equal to the accomplishment of her desires.   In 1894, Japan began war with China by the "NANIWA" capturing the "KOWSHING" on July the 25th without warning.   China acknowledged a state of war on July 31st, and Japan only on August 1st.   In 1904 the first intimation the Russians had that war existed was the attack on the Russian Fleet at Port Arthur and the Division at Chemulpo.

(8)   The people of the United States believe almost universally that war is impossible.   The Russians had the same belief— shared universally by continental Europe—in 1904.   The disparity between Russia and Japan then was greater than between the United States and Japan now, and the stake no greater. Russia and all Europe believed then that Japan would not dare, that she had not the means,

to make war, yet she did, and successfully.
The people of the United States believe the
same now; and have not learned that the
Japanese with their superb courage, intense
patriotism, frugality and perfect probity in
governmental expenditures can make war on a
small fraction of what it costs us.

(9) The treaty of alliance with England
made by Japan in 1902, which enabled her to
prosecute her war with Russia without fear of
outside interference was renewed in 1905, and
again in 1911 for ten years and gives her the
same assurance of freedom of action now.

(10) This condition of affairs, relative
to what Japan could or could not do in the
Pacific, will last only as long as the Panama
Canal is not finished, with our fleet in the
Atlantic; or until we put a superior fleet in
the Pacific. This is a fact well-known to
Japanese statesmen; and will, I believe, have
great influence in governing their decision
for prompt action, should their inclination be
for war; for they know the opportunity lost
now is lost forever.

(11) In diplomatic justification of war no
nation has ever shown greater astuteness than
the Japanese. Their correspondence with
Russia leading up to the war was a masterpiece
of diplomacy. A parallel correspondence was
begun with this country at the time of the
school incidents and San Francisco riots in
1906. This situation was relieved by the
temporary transfer of the fleet to the Pacific,
assisted by similar riots occurring opportunely
in Vancouver, a port of Japan's ally. The
present attitude of California, with which all
Pacific states sympathize, gives better
grounds for justification than the school
incidents and riots of 1906.

(12) It is believed here that war is impossible because we have no "reason" for war.
War is rarely made for "reason", and we have
no reason. But the question depends not on

us but on the Japanese, who, I believe, can
show reason to the world, and add to it
passion, interest and race antagonisms, which
are the true causes of war.

2. Considering these facts, I believe, as
stated above, that war is not only possible, but
even probable, and that my duty demands that they
should be brought earnestly to your attention, in
order that, should our hopes of continued peace be
disappointed, the country may not be found in the
same state of unpreparedness that overtook China
and Russia in 1894 and 1904.

                              Bradley A. Fiske
                              Rear Admiral, U.S.N.

Friday, May 16, 1913
  Cabinet
  Garden Party

Friday, May 16, 1913
  When the Cabinet met, the President presented a draft of his reply about
Baron Chinda's protest over the California-Japanese legislation. It and the
matters surrounding it were discussed for nearly two hours and all the col-
lateral matters were gone into, particularly as to touching whether the Federal
Government had any powers it could assert to meet the feelings of the Japanese
Ambassador. Many suggestions as to changing the verbiage were made and
noted by the President, all looking toward trying to guard against any expression that might be taken up by jingoists in this country or Japan to make
friction between the two nations. On the day prior to the meeting of the
Cabinet, the Joint Board of the Army and Navy held a meeting and had
urgently recommended that the three largest ships in the Chinese rivers be
sent at once to the Philippine Islands. Secretary Garrison approved the finding
of the Joint Board. Secretary Garrison asked me to come over to his office
to discuss this action of the Joint Board. He was very strongly in favor of
its being carried out and having the ships moved at once and thought we
ought to unite in a recommendation to that effect to the President, and I told
him I could not do so chiefly for the reason that there was a very excited
condition in Tokyo among those who are against the Government and hostile

to the United States and the movement of any American ships now in the Yellow Sea would be taken up by the jingoists to inflame the popular mind there though these ships were not dreadnoughts and only one of them powerful. All Japan would be made to believe that we had mobilized our Navy in the Yellow Sea and it might so inflame the people of the Islands as to make possible a feeling that might provoke war. I told him that my feeling was that if the ships were moved out of Chinese waters to Manila there were not enough of them of powerful type as to be able to meet the Japanese fleet, that they could do very little good even if they got to Manila and that their movement would be heralded all over the world as indicative of the fact that we expected war with Japan and were getting ready to meet them in the Philippines. Even if we were expecting it, I went on to say, we could not prevent the Japanese Navy from taking the Philippines if they decided to concentrate their forces on those possessions. I told him that if I had known as much as I do now when I first became Secretary of the Navy, I would have taken steps to send our Fleet in the Pacific Ocean. Since I have been here, I learned that we came near having war with Japan in the Roosevelt Administration and was only averted by the most careful measures which caused Japan to think in a sense that America was afraid of it and that the action then opened the way for the Japanese jingoists to stir the people up now to the hatred of America. The last Administration should have had the Fleet in the Pacific and, of course, if we had foreseen the California legislation, they would have been despatched off the coast of California, Hawaii, or the Philippines, but until the Panama Canal is opened, the journey to the Pacific is such a long one that we could not now send the Fleet to the Pacific in time to save the Philippines if the Japanese Navy has any desire to strike a blow there. Secretary Garrison took the ground that we had a perfect right to move our ships when and where we pleased and moving them from the Chinese waters to the Philippines was nobody's business and could not create any trouble and they could help protect the Philippines and back up the Army at Fort Corregidor in case of trouble and it would be a great mistake for us, who knew so little about military warfare, not to take the advice of the Joint Board. He put his argument along that line very ably and strongly but it seemed to me the weight of the argument was the other way and could not sign the recommendations, but we agreed to go see the President and we did. The Secretary of War urged upon the President that it was wisest and necessary to send the ships to the Philippines and to make every preparation for the protection of the Islands possible, and I advanced to the President the views I had put forth to Secretary Garrison, adding that I did not regard the Chinese situation in such shape as to make it wise to take the ships out of the rivers in China except in an emergency. After discussing the matter at some length, the President said that it was a matter of such importance that it would have to come up in Cabinet the next day but until then he would not consent to have any ship moved in the Pacific Ocean. In the Cabinet Meeting Friday, this matter came up and was threshed out after lengthy discussion. Secretary Garrison presented his view with ability of the action of the Joint Board. I presented, briefly, the reasons why I could not agree with the Joint Board and while [why] I believed at this time any such action which might inflame the passions of the people of Japan and lead to a war which we would all regret. Secretary Redfield was strongly supporting Secretary Garrison as did Secretary McAdoo. The Secretary of State and the Secretary of Labor took strong grounds against moving any ships in the Pacific and helped me hold up my end of the argument. Secretary Lane also indicated that it might be unwise to move the ships at this time. Attorney General McReynolds was inclined to agree with the Secretary of War. The Secretary of Agriculture took my side. I do not recall that the Postmaster General had any statement to make but I gathered that he was with me. On Mr. Bryan's earnest advocacy of peace, he could not approve any movement now that might make war. Most of the time of the discussion was taken up with the arguments of those who wished to withdraw the ships. When all was said and done the President said, "The Joint Board, of course, has presented the military aspect of the situation as it sees it and it may be right, but we are considering this matter with another light, on the diplomatic side, and must determine the policy. I do not think any movement should be made at this time in the Pacific Ocean and I will, therefore, take the responsibility of holding the ships where they are at present." He spoke at more length and made me very happy to find that he was in accord and agreement with the views I had made in supporting me in his clear and logical power.

In the afternoon the President and his wife held a garden party in the White House grounds, and I was made very happy by his taking me aside and saying, "I think we did right today. At one time I think we had a majority of the Cabinet against us, but when I looked down the table and saw you upholding what you thought was the right course, it cheered my heart. We must not have war except in an honorable way and I fear the Joint Board made a mistake."

Saturday, May 17, 1913
  Adml Fiske
  Joint Board's Action.
  Fiske—

Jos K. Ohl.[8]
President

Saturday, May 17, 1913

After the Cabinet Meeting yesterday, I called in Admiral Fiske and told him that the President determined no ship should be moved in the Pacific for the present and that he was entirely in accord with the view I had expressed in this respect. The Admiral was greatly disappointed because he felt keenly that the wise course was to take the ships out of the rivers in China and send them to the Philippines. Nearly all the naval officers, including the Admiral, ever since the California matter came up, believed that no power would prevent the Japanese from taking the Philippines. Therefore I was surprised when the Joint Board unanimously demanded that these ships be moved and the movement of these ships might avert that disaster. This morning Admiral Fiske came to me with a resolution which he said had been passed by the Joint Board which bore date of May 16th and he was very emphatic and earnest that whatever happened, the Joint Board wished it presented to the President so that the President might have before him their view upon what he thought was a very serious situation. He said that the Joint Board thought the President and the Secretary had made a great mistake in not having these ships brought out from the Chinese waters and now they presented a formal recommendation that at once all the torpedo boat destroyers and torpedo boats and a number of our other small craft on the California Coast be sent at once to Hawaii. I told him that I thought the President's determination not to move anything in the Pacific Ocean had settled this matter for the present and thought it not worth while to re-open it, but the Joint Board seemed insistent, and he pressed it upon me to take it to the President so that he could have their point of view. Naturally in a matter of this importance I felt some little hesitation by standing on my own view when it was opposed to that held by the distinguished Army and Navy officers on the Joint Board, and action gave me pause and did not convince me at all, but later in the day the Admiral came to me with a map of the Philippine Islands and urged also that the two gunboats at Manila be taken away and sent to the Corregidor Fort so that they could mine the channel or entrance to Manila Bay and be ready for any emergency. Shortly after these statements were brought to me the map and later the recommendations of the Joint Board. [*sic*] The correspondent of a big newspaper came in to see me and

---

[8] Joseph K. Ohl, just returned from a six-year tour as the *New York Herald*'s Far Eastern correspondent. Daniels lunched with Ohl on this date, and he probably was the correspondent referred to subsequently who knew of the Joint Board's disagreement with the administration.

asked if I had approved the action of the Joint Board of taking all ships on the Pacific Coast and sending them to Hawaii or Manila. The question came to me like a clap of thunder from a blue sky. Evidently there had been a leak. Evidently the newspaperman knew what he was talking about and I was at a loss how to parry his inquiry and put it off by saying now [no] action whatever had been taken to move any ship in the Pacific and none was contemplated. He pressed at the matter a little but went off. I then sent for Admiral Fiske and told him about the interview and told him there was a leak in the matter somewhere. Of course, I knew that no employee of the Navy Department would consciously give out such important and confidential matter, but that it was a very serious matter. Of course, the Admiral was as much distressed as I was that anything had leaked but thought the newspaperman was talking about something else. Late in the afternoon I went to the White House to see the President with the map and recommendation of the Joint Board urging the immediate removal of the Fleet on the Pacific Coast and told him about the leak. He was greatly put out, not only about the leak, but chiefly because after he had announced his policy on the Pacific Coast the Joint Board had a meeting and taken action relative to moving ships on the Pacific. He felt that this was a breach of military discipline and spoke his mind freely: He said in substance: "After we talked this matter over in Cabinet Friday and you and Secretary of War informed these Navy and Army gentlement [sic] that there was to be no movement now, they had no right to hold a meeting at all and discuss these matters. When a policy has been settled by the Administration and when it is communicated to the Joint Board, they have no right to be trying to force a different course and I wish you would say to them that if this should occur again, there will be no General or Joint Boards. They will be abolished." We talked the matter over considerably and it was a glorious thing to see the President's determination that the policy of the Administration should be carried out and no officer in the Army or Navy should be permitted to make war plans along certain lines after they had been notified when such policy was contrary to the spirit of the Administration. That night I called Admiral Fiske to state to him the President's spirit and purpose and to notify him that I wished no more meetings held until I returned to the city and could have a talk with him, but he had gone to the theatre, and I talked it over with my wife and as I was preparing to leave on the train, I communicated with my Naval Aide, Captain Palmer, and asked him to communicate this information to Admiral Fiske.

Sunday, May 18, 1913
    Reached Ral[eigh] 1 a.m. Did not go to bed, but finished writing my speech for Washington N.C. Taught my A&M College Sunday School class for the

last time. Talked of Joseph and his dreams. Went on ACL [9] to Washington NC Met at depot by committee and went to Wiley Rodman's house on the very site on which I was born 51 yrs ago.[10] Saw my Mother at Mr Geo Hackney's [11]

Dinner—Grimes [12] & wife. Small [13] & wife

Monday, May 19, 1913

Shortly after 10 a.m. Naval Reserves & band escorted to School Auditorium where I spoke. See speech.

Introduced by E. A. Daniel. Rev N. Harding John H. Small introduced mother.

Luncheon at Elks Hall—matrons of town prepared dinner. It was served by beautiful maidens of the town. Henry & Adele [?]

Left at 3⁰⁰ p.m. for Raleigh.

Spent evening in Raleigh looking over plans for new building. Went to Moving Picture show & saw myself walking out of N&O burned building. Saw Gov. Craig [14] Freight [?] rates. Returned to Washington

Tuesday, May 20, 1913
Cabinet

Tuesday, May 20, 1913

At the Cabinet Meeting this morning the Secretary of State announced that immediately upon the signing of the California Alien Land Act he had delivered to Baron Chinda, the Japanese Ambassador[,] the note in reply to the protest of Baron Chinda against the California legislation. This note was submitted to the Cabinet at its last meeting and gone over by them carefully after which the President rewrote it after conference with the Secretary of State. It ought to be satisfactory to the reasonable people of Japan and clearly shows that the spirit of the Administration is one of the utmost friendliness and that the good offices of the Administration have been employed to induce every American state to legislate in a way as to make as little friction as possible with any foreign country. Of course, the answer cannot give to

[9] The Atlantic Coast Line Railroad.

[10] Daniels was born on May 18, 1862, in Washington, North Carolina. On this occasion he had returned for a birthday celebration tendered by the town in honor of his appointment as Secretary of the Navy. Appropriately, he and Mrs. Daniels stayed at the home of Captain Wiley Rodman, located on the site of the old house in which Daniels had been born fifty-one years before.

[11] A boyhood friend, and host of Daniels' mother, Mrs. Mary Cleaves Seabrook Daniels.

[12] J. Bryan Grimes, the North Carolina secretary of state.

[13] Representative John H. Small, also born in Washington, N.C.

[14] Locke Craig, Democrat, governor of North Carolina, 1913–1917.

Japan all that it desires, and under our Constitution the Federal Government has no power over land laws and each state may make laws to suit itself being bound thereto only by stipulations in treaties and in the Constitution. Japan cannot treat with California and, therefore, it must make its protest to the United States. Mr. Bryan was asked how the Japanese Ambassador seemed to accept the answer to the protest of his government. He replied that he read it in the office of the Secretary of State, and from his manner one would not suppose that it caused him any great agitation. At a former meeting of the Cabinet when Mr. Bryan was absent and John Bassett Moore was present, Mr. Moore stated that the Japanese Ambassador seemed much agitated and so much so that when he left the room he seemed almost to stagger under some influence that oppressed him and, of course, the inference was that the outcome of this diplomatic controversy might be such as to greatly depress the Ambassador. No such feeling was shown by him or no such attitude at this meeting and Mr. Bryan felt from his attitude and bearing that there was cause for congratulation and encouragement though, of course, the Baron gave no such statement. In addition to the formal answer to the protest, Mr. Bryan stated, after consul[t]ation with the President, that he had told the Japanese Ambassador that the Federal Government, of course, would recognize that if the California Alien Land law brought any loss to any Japanese citizen, the President would recommend to Congress that money be appropriated to compensate for such loss. There are several precedents for this and Mr. Bryan said that he had told the Ambassador that the Administration would use all its influence to prevent any financial loss by the Japanese. Another addition was made to the formal note verbally to the Ambassador that was that this government would use its good offices to insure and advance its hearings in the courts of any case that any citizen of Japan might bring who felt himself aggrieved. Mr. Bryan said he had suggested to the Ambassador that these verbal statements be not sent to the Government at once but wait until that Government had received and considered the formal answer to Japan's protest. He thought it wisest to let them consider that and determine their policy before adding anything. These might be added later. Of course, he did not say so but, of course, Mr. Bryan meant that if the Japanese Government is embarrassed by jingoists, he thinks more ought to be offered by this country. The Ambassador could then add these two expressions and offers of speedy trials and indemnity as reasonable assurance why Japan ought to understand the friendliness of this country and its sense of justice.

Secretary Garrison asked if it were true that Mexico had protested against the Arizona Alien Land Act. Mr. Bryan said that no such protest had been received but that Baron Chinda, having in mind the statement of Governor Johnson of California, that if Arizona passed a law similar to that of California, had called and entered Japan's protest against Arizona's action, stated that the Japanese Government had not known of the passage at the time, but were as much opposed to the act passed by that State as that by California. The Secretary of War asked if the report was true that there had been a secret treaty between Mexico and Japan by which Mexico ceded Magdalena Bay [15] to Japan. Secretary Wilson in a hearing before Congress had been informed that there was such a treaty but had no further information. Secretaries Burleson and Lane, who live nearest to Mexico, said that they had been assured no such treaty had been ratified or considered. Secretary Lane thought it grew out of the fact that there is a large body of land 300 miles long and 50 miles wide on Magdalena Bay owned by a syndicate and the syndicate offered to sell it to Japan for purposes of colonization but the proposed deal had not gone through and thought this whole talk that Japan was to have Magdalena Bay grew out of this. Mr. Bryan stated that he had read in the morning papers that at a meeting in Japan, Count Okuma [16] had said fifty years ago that Japan was so ignorant of foreign nations that it despised them all and had a narrow provincial spirit, but that it had learned more about foreigners and made so much progress itself that it was now in a position to look at California's unwise action in a proper light. "We were as ignorant virtually," he said, "fifty years ago of foreigners as California is now," and he wished the Japanese to look upon California's unreasonable action as sure to be outlived as was Japan's hostility to foreigners when California should become as progressive and as wise as Japan. This statement by Count Okuma, Mr. Bryan said, gave him great encouragement and that Japan might take this view of the situation and might let time adjust the differences more surely than they could be adjusted by resort to arms. Secretary Garrison, reverting to the Mexican situation, said he believed that recognition of the Huerta Government was the only alternative to intervention and that he would like to read to the Cabinet an editorial by Paul Hudson,[17] editor of the Mexican Herald, which gave strong reasons for the recognition of the Huerta Government by this country. He said he entirely agreed with the editorial. The President said, "That reminds me of a statement made by Carlyle, who said that 'every man regarded an editorial in a newspaper as very wise and able if it voiced

[15] A strategic site in Lower California. During 1912, Senator Lodge and other American leaders had expressed concern over rumors that Japan was seeking to acquire a lease over Magdalena Bay, a potential naval base that would threaten American communications with the nearly completed Panama Canal.

[16] Shigenobu Okuma, prominent Japanese statesman, subsequently premier, 1914–1916.

[17] Resident of Mexico City since 1896, editor and publisher of the English-language *Mexican Herald,* ex-president of the American School in Mexico City.

the opinion which he himself held," the intimation being that Secretary Garrison was applauding the editorial of the Herald because it was expressing the views he entertained. Secretary Lane said "You ought to know who owns Paul Hudson before you give much weight to what he writes." "I would not care who said it," replied Secretary Garrison, "if it came out of a phonograph; if it is sensible, I will take it just as quick." Then he proceeded to read the editorial, and in two or three places the President interjected remarks showing that some statements in the editorial were not true, and when he finished someone remarked that this was the first newspaper editorial that had been read at a Cabinet Meeting—(and I don't think it will be the last.) I asked Mr. Lane what he meant by saying, "Do you know who owns Editor Hudson," and he replied that it was well-known that Hudson and his paper had been long subsidized by people and parties and interests wishing special privileges in Mexico, and what he said should be taken with many grains of allowance. Mr. Lane thought that recognition of the Huerta Government would cause the northern states of Mexico, which are hostile to Huerta, would be so incensed with America that they would destroy the property of Americans in that country. Mr. Garrison thought that they could not destroy it any more than they were now.

Secretary Bryan brought up the question of sending an Ambassador instead of a Minister to the Argentine Republic and said that this great South American Republic wished this recognition. He said he had taken the matter up with the Chairman of the Senate Committee on Foreign Relations and Senator Bacon [18] thought it would be a fine thing if we would send an Ambassador to Spain. This suggestion met with the approval of the whole Cabinet, voiced by the President, and after discussion, it seemed to be the sense of the Cabinet that our diplomatic relations with both Spain and Argentine should be carried on through an embassy and not by a minister. Mr. Bryan said then "I take it that it is the sense of the meeting that I shall speak to the Foreign Affairs Committee in favor of having ambassadors for these countries and will do so."

Secretary McAdoo brought up the question of California appointments. The political situation in that State during the last campaign, so far as the democrats are concerned, gave more trouble to the National Committee than any other state. They went by factions. The organization, backed by the Hearst papers, carried the state primaries, and after the Baltimore Convention, the factional fight continued so the National Committee gave many troubled hours trying to straighten out the California situation. It is, of course,

[18] Augustus O. Bacon, Democrat, U.S. Senator from Georgia and chairman of the Senate Foreign Relations Committee.

now very acute in the matter of appointments to office and there was much discussion of the California situation. Mr. Lane asked if the President had in mind appointing Mr. Phelan [19] of California to the Diplomatic Service. The President said he had him in mind for a mission. He said it has been always customary to appoint a catholic to Vienna and had Mr. Phelan in mind for it, but had information that while Mr. Phelan was a member of the catholic church, his appointment would not be satisfactory and thought this came from a pretty direct source. Of course, if a catholic is to be sent to that country, he should be one that would be recognized by the catholics. Somebody suggested Mr. Phelan for Italy, but it has not been the policy of this country to send a catholic to that country, and Secretary Lane laughingly said, "It seems Mr. Phelan cannot go to Italy because he is a catholic and he cannot go to Vienna because he is a catholic."

Secretary Lane brought up the matter of his first assistant Secretary of the Interior and the Commissionership of Indian Affairs. He recommended Mr. Jones,[20] member of the National Democratic Committee from New Mexico for first assistant, and asked if he was known to the Cabinet, and suggested for Commissioner of Indian Affairs Mr. Cato Sells,[21] from Texas, member of the National Democratic Committee from that state. I remarked that I thought Mr. Sells was a man of the highest character and ability and I hoped that he would be named and the only objection to him was that he was a little vain. The President said "a little vain!" I said, "add your little vain to my little vain and I think it is very vain, but it is a vanity that has about it nothing that could injure the public service and at least when a man has anything about him no worse than vanity when that vanity injures nobody, it is a very little draw-back though sometimes it annoys one's friends." Mr. Bryan said "I think Mr. Sells is the man for the place; he has ability and capacity, and is of the right character. He does love to talk about himself a good deal, but I think he always feels when he is telling anyone about himself that he exercises a great deal of self-repression," and the President said, "Yes, when he talked to me about himself, and unduly, I recognized all th[r]ough it that he was a man wholly devoted to the public service." Mr. Burleson, of Texas, in whose state Sells lived, urged that he be called to the high station and said he had been a leader for the progressive cause though not living there long, and that the papers opposing him were rather taunting Sells

[19] James D. Phelan, prominent California Democrat and former mayor of San Francisco, U.S. Senator from California, 1915–1921.

[20] Andrieus A. Jones, prominent New Mexico Democrat and attorney, U.S. Senator from New Mexico, 1917–1927.

[21] Iowa-born Texas banker and Democratic leader. Both Jones and Sells were appointed as Lane recommended.

because he had done so much for the progressive cause and could get no recognition.

Wednesday, May 21, 1913
   Annapolis
   Hydroplane [22]

Friday, May 23, 1913
   Banquet. Milburn [23]
   Webb,[24] Small, Pou [25]
   Bryan. Redfield

Saturday, May 24, 1913
   Went to Balti—S.S.   May Walk [26]

Sunday, May 25, 1913
   Spoke at Temp. meeting.
   Mt Vernon & Northern Meth Ch[urches]
   Temperance

Wednesday, May 28, 1913
   Went to NY

Thursday, May 29, 1913
   Inspect Navy Yard
   Hearst [27] dinner

Friday, May 30, 1913
   Spoke at Maine Memorial.
   Lunch.
   Taft. Cuba repre [28]

[22] While visiting Annapolis, Daniels took his first airplane ride, an eight-minute flight.
[23] Frank P. Milburn, prominent Washington architect, who gave a large banquet in Daniels' honor on this date.
[24] Edwin Yates Webb, Democrat, U.S. Representative from North Carolina.
[25] Edward W. Pou, Democrat, U.S. Representative from Daniels' district in North Carolina.
[26] Daniels took part in the annual Sunday school convention and parade in Baltimore.
[27] William Randolph Hearst, prominent newspaper publisher, gave an elaborate dinner for Daniels and the officers of the Atlantic Fleet.
[28] Among those taking part in the dedication of the victims of the sunken battleship *Maine* were ex-President William Howard Taft and the officers and men of a Cuban gunboat, the *Cuba*.

Geo. Gordon Battle [29]
Dolphin to West Point

Saturday, May 31, 1913
Reached West Point at 11 a.m.
Salute. Reviewed drill
Lunch with Commandant—
Organ "The Son of God goes forth to war."
Score 2 to 1.[30]
Reached NY 10 p.m. Left for Newport

Sunday, June 1, 1913
B. Graff—USS Constellation
Reached Newport, via Providence, at 9 a.m. Went with Capt Rogers [1] to
War College. Spent pleasant morning with R & sisters—Miss Helen &
Mrs ———. Flight [?] John Rogers, aviator. Auto with Mr. Weatherly, navy
man who is ow[ner?] of airship.
Spoke at Y.M.C.A. in Army & Navy Bldg. Mrs. T. J. Emery, who gave
building was present.
Dinner at Capt Rog[ers]
Services: War Tng [?] needed

Monday, June 2, 1913
Monday.
Spoke at War College
Adl Caperton [2] & wife
Went on board Constellation
Inspection.
Inspected Melville. 600 foot longer dock   Rohange [3] Chf Boatswain

[29] North Carolina–born New York attorney.
[30] Daniels neglected to record that Army won the annual baseball game.

---

[1] Captain William L. Rodgers, president of the Naval War College.
[2] Rear Admiral William B. Caperton, commandant of the Newport Naval Station and Second Naval District.
[3] Chief Boatswain Robert Rohange, assigned to the coal depot at Melville Station, where Daniels caught the train to Providence.

The Morris.[4] Capt. William S C Oliver, Charlotte

Saturday, July 12, 1913

Left at 6:45 for trip to the Pacific. My wife, Capt. Leigh C. Palmer & self going to inspect Navy stations and attend several celebrations.

Jonathan and Frank went to train with us

Dr. Stokes,[1] Surgeon General of the Navy, also accompanied us.

Sunday, July 13, 1913

Reach Chicago at 2 o'clock. Hot as blazes. At 4 went to Lake Forest. With Capt. Palmer visited Naval Training School. After the heat in the city, the stay there on the lake was delightful. Capt. & Mrs. Clark[2] had invited all officers and their wives to meet us. Among them Dr. Taylor,[3] nephew of Dr. Chas. E. Taylor[4] Pres of Wake Forest College. Inspected the dining halls & saw food prepared for enlisted men. This is the best station in the Navy.

Later went to dinner at Forest Park with Mr. and Mrs. Jonathan Worth Jackson[5] and had delightful evening, leaving for Chicago in time to take 10 o'clock train for the West.

Monday, July 14, 1913

Reached St. Paul

Walked out in station. Palmer had my ticket. I forgot time train left, and asked the Bureau of Information what time train left. He said "Let me see your ticket." I said "a friend has my tickets," and he looked as if he thought I was faking.

Tuesday, July 15, 1913

Traveled on Great Northern. Passed beautiful Glacier Park.

[4] A Navy torpedo boat, assigned to the Reserve Torpedo Division at Newport, which took Daniels to Bradford.

---

[1] Rear Admiral Charles F. Stokes, Surgeon General of the Navy and chief of the Bureau of Medicine and Surgery.

[2] Captain George R. Clark, commandant of the Great Lakes Naval Training Station.

[3] Lieutenant Commander James S. Taylor, a Navy surgeon.

[4] An old friend of Daniels' despite their involvement on opposite sides of a Baptist-led fight in 1894 to cut the appropriations for the University of North Carolina. Throughout his life Daniels was an ardent champion of education and particularly the University of North Carolina, serving for many years on its board of trustees.

[5] A cousin of Mrs. Daniels'.

Had much fun with Dr. Stokes because he was in conversation with a handsome woman who left the train at Glacier Park.

Wednesday, July 16, 1913

Reached Seattle at 6:30. Met at train by Mayor,[6] Chairman Foster [7] of Potlatch celebrations, Editor Blethen [8] and others, and taken to the Washington hotel and given the President's suite, which had been occupied by President Taft when he visited Seattle.

I attended banquet of Democratic Club and reviewed the Potlatch parade and celebration.

After the Potlatch exercises were over, went to supper with Chairman Foster. Editor Blethun [sic] refused to come because Mayor Cortterell [sic] and wife were there. A long standing feud pends between them.

Thursday, May 17, 1913

Went early in morning with Mayor, Mr. Foster in automobile ride over city to view its splendid park systems and the plan for a great inland fresh water lake. Spoke at lunch given by Commercial Club. Spoke on the new era where partisanship is made secondary to patriotism. Was initiated into the order of Tilikims [9] with imposing ceremonies. After lunch, reviewed the beautiful procession that is the event of Potlatch and was presented with a canoe by Tyhee Cobb.[10] Then by appointment met the Democratic Committee. At night, attended banquet given me at Rainer Club—a beautifully served one—presided over by Judge Albertson,[11] a former N.C. man. T. M. Vance [12] one of speakers. Spoke on the flag.

My wife had dinner at Mrs. Fosters & lunch with Mrs. Trimble.[13]

Friday, July 18, 1913

Left early for Bremerton Navy Yard. Met by Capt Cottman.[14] We went first to inspect proposed site for torpedo range. Glorious day & beautiful trip. Received with all honor at Navy Yard and after inspection, visited

[6] George F. Cotterill, Democrat, mayor of Seattle, 1912–1914.

[7] Walter F. Foster, chairman of the Seattle Carnival Association which sponsored the annual Potlatch celebration commemorating the arrival of the first Klondike gold ship.

[8] Alden J. Blethen, editor and publisher of the *Seattle Times*, which was currently attacking Mayor Cotterill for failing to deal more sternly with the Industrial Workers of the World.

[9] The Tillicums, a Seattle civic group, named after the Indian word for "friends."

[10] Presumably "Tyee" Roland P. Rice, branch manager of the Ford Motor Company, serving as the honorary Indian chief at the head of Potlatch.

[11] Judge Robert B. Albertson of the Superior Court of King County.

[12] Thomas M. Vance, former attorney general of Washington state.

[13] Cannie Ford Trimble, wife of a prominent Seattle attorney, William P. Trimble.

[14] Rear Admiral Vincendon L. Cottman, commandant of the Puget Sound Navy Yard and Thirteenth Naval District.

Y.M.C.A. & afterwards arrived Commercial Club. Met Mrs. Dr. Shepard [15] who said her father who lived in Ohio was named Josephus Daniels. I claimed kin for she is good looking, and I claim kin with every Daniels who is good-looking. After visiting Disciplinary Barracks and docks [?] & reception, returned to Seattle. Went on board West Virginia & dined with Admiral Reynolds [16] & party. Then went to Potlatch ball and shook hands with thousands.

Saturday, July 19, 1913

At 7 a.m. left for Tacoma. Met by Maj. Grist, Mrs. Martin & Mr. Scofield & after a few minutes at the Commercial Club, went by automobile to Country Club where were joined by Mrs. Wagner, sister of Col. Grist, and went to Mount Tacoma, officially called Mt. Ranier. Stopped at Ranier Park lodge and met Ethen Allen [?] and foresters. Arrived at the Inn for lunch, and then went on up the mountain. Visited the glaciers and waterfalls and had a glorious day. Cut a piece of ice out of glacier. Mr. Allen had road closed to vehicles so our two autos could have right of way. Engaged in snow balling. Met Col. De Thrope [?], the first white man who went to top of Mt. Ranier. Returned & spent night at Inn. Mr. Allen presented me with a wild mountain goat. Rode 95 miles in auto.

Sunday, July 20, 1913

Rose early and left at six o'clock on trip down the mountains, taking a last regretful look on the snow topped mountain. It was cool and delightful trip. We stopped at the Tacoma Power house where power is generated to run factories in Tacoma. Reached Country Club at ten o'clock, & were given an elegant breakfast at 10:30—I spoke on "The Conservation of the Almighty." Rode to Tacoma and took train at 12:30 for San Diego. At Portland, a delegation met us and asked to return for a banquet to be given by Chamber of Commerce. Twice in night reporters woke me asking about the Seattle I.W.W. troubles.[17]

[15] Frankie G. Daniels Shepard, wife of Lieutenant George W. Shepard, a passed assistant surgeon stationed at the Puget Sound Naval Hospital.

[16] Rear Admiral Alfred Reynolds, commanding the Pacific Reserve Fleet.

[17] By speaking "on the flag" at the Ranier Club dinner on July 17, Daniels inadvertently added fuel to the political feud between Mayor Cotterill and the *Seattle Times*. Using material from an old speech, Daniels had innocently elaborated on the ancient theme that Old Glory was the only flag for Americans. Daniels' remarks were supposed to be off the record, but the *Times* headlined them as a public rebuke of Cotterill for his alleged sympathy for the "Red Flag" Industrial Workers of the World. The following night a group of sailors attacked and burned the I.W.W. headquarters in Seattle, which led I.W.W. and socialist spokesmen to charge that Daniels had incited the riot. Mayor Cotterill also closed down the *Times* temporarily until frustrated by a court order.

Monday, July 21, 1913

Passed Shasta at 10:30 and drank of that famous spring and travelled in view of the snow-clad mountains. This was the first hot day since we left Chicago.

Reached San Francisco about 9 o'clock. Were met by Capt. Pond,[18] USN & Mr. Lathrop of the Southern Pacific, and escorted over on the ferry to our train which left at ten o'clock for San Diego, going by the shore drive of the So. Pacific.

Tuesday, July 22, 1913

Traveled through beautiful country with the view of the Pacific for a long part of the journey. Met at Los Angeles by Mr. Kinney,[19] Pres. Chamber of Commerce & Secy Wiggins [20] & others who had automobiles to transfer us across city to connect with our train for San Diego. There we were joined by Mr. Lee,[21] Ch. Admiral Manney,[22] H. M. Holleman, formerly of Apex, N.C. and others who went with us to their city of San Diego. Col. M. F. Tarpie [Tarpey] former National Committeeman for California joined us here and this added to the pleasure of the trip. Also Mr. Collier,[23] Pres. of Exposition at San Diego, and as soon as we reached San Diego we rode out to the Expo. grounds. Had elegant apartment at Hotel Coronado. Beautiful bouquet like deck of ship was given.

Wednesday, July 23, 1913

Left at 9 a.m. on John D. Spreckels [24] yacht with party to inspect San Diego harbor and Pacific shore from San Diego to Los Angeles. My wife & ladies left at 11 on the South Dakota for Los Angeles. Had a very pleasant day on the ocean. At a little after 4 we went aboard the South Dakota where all the men were in formation. After the naval honor and salute, I made a brief address to the officers and men. Then, received by a large committee of Los Angeles citizens, we went from the harbor to the Alexander Hotel. After a hasty dinner, went to auditorium where I spoke to an audience of 3,000 under auspices of Chamber of Commerce. Never saw a more magnificent body of men together. Leaving auditorium, went to banquet given by the

[18] Captain Charles F. Pond, commandant of the Thirteenth Naval District.
[19] Arthur W. Kinney, president of the Los Angeles Chamber of Commerce.
[20] Frank Wiggins, secretary of the Los Angeles Chamber of Commerce.
[21] Fred J. Lea, president of the San Diego Chamber of Commerce.
[22] Rear Admiral (Ret.) Henry N. Manney, San Diego police superintendent.
[23] David C. Collier, president of the Panama-California Exposition of 1915.
[24] Prominent California capitalist, whose yacht, the *Venetia,* was used to tour the San Diego harbor facilities.

Press Club—a very novel and beautiful one. Presented by the President with a gold card showing my election as member of Press Club.

Thursday, July 24, 1913

Left hotel early with large committee headed by Mayor Rose [25] and Chairman Kinney to inspect work on harbor of Los Angeles. Much work has been done here, large craft were in the harbor, and the faith and enterprise of Los Angeles. Also visited army station and range overlooking ocean. Were taken to Long Beach to dine at Virginia Hotel. Scores of members of Los Angeles Chamber of Commerce, together with our party, were entertained. I spoke and was presented with a gold card [blank] and a great laugh was created when Mr. [blank] also presented me with the Pacific Ocean and a miniature bathing suit. Leaving Long Beach regretfully, for it is a lovely & cool place, I was driven in auto through beautiful Pasadena, and back to Los Angeles in time for a dinner given by the North Carolina Society. Dr. [J. E.] Cowles was President. Mr. Newby [26] toast master.

Left at 8 p.m.

Friday, July 25, 1913

Reached San Francisco at 9:45 & went at once to launch & visited Training Station at Goat Island. Fine place and splendid body of men. Then called on President Moore [27] of Panama Expo Com. & went with him to lunch at the Fairmont hotel given by the Exposition. It was a pleasant occasion. Then we visited Expo. buildings and grounds, and at 3:30 I talked on [blank]

Sunday, August 3, 1913

Did not wake till 11 a.m. & read N&O so long did not get up until train was pulling in station at Emporia for Lunch. Day was very hot. Lack of rain has almost destroyed crops in Western Kansas and all day it was oppressive on train. As I was sitting in smoking room, one man told another "We have a big man travelling [with] us today—Mr D—— Secy of State." See how I was advanced Reached Kansas City at 5. Hot and uncomfortable. Have fine dinner leaving Kansas City and went to bed at 8 o'clock

[25] Henry H. Rose, Republican, mayor of Los Angeles since June, 1913.

[26] Nathan Newby, North Carolina–born Los Angeles attorney.

[27] Thomas M. Moore, commissioner general of the Panama-Pacific Exposition at San Francisco, 1915.

Monday, August 4, 1913
Reached Chicago 7.28 am on Santa Fe. Left on Pa 10:30. Mr. Chapman [?]
of the International Press Bureau.

Saturday, August 23, 1913
M E Stone [1] to make eng[agement?] with Pres

Tuesday, August 26, 1913
Stone   DeLa Barre [2]

Wednesday, August 27, 1913
—Pres. read message [3]
Armor bids [4]
Stones telephone mess[age?]

Thursday, August 28, 1913
Dr Couglan [5]—Patrick
Stone

Friday, August 29, 1913
Bassett Moore
1 2   Stone. President Mexi[co]
DeKay $1,000 a day.
DeLa Barre.
Let Huerta resign & take field
Could not let help Huerta fight the Constitu[tiona]ls

---

[1] Melville E. Stone, general manager of the Associated Press since 1893.

[2] Francisco de la Barra, Mexican foreign minister in the de facto Huerta government until his resignation on July 8, had recently visited the United States to try to bolster the Huerta regime.

[3] Wilson's report to a joint session of Congress explaining his Mexican policy, and calling for "watchful waiting" while the two sides fought it out in civil war.

[4] Upon opening the bids for armor plate for Battleship No. 39, Daniels discovered that the three American firms supplying armor plate to the Navy—Bethlehem, Midvale, and Carnegie—had offered identical bids down to the penny. They denied any collusion, but Daniels rejected the bids and issued a scathing public denunciation. He now began a campaign, ultimately authorized by Congress, to construct a Navy-owned armor plate factory as a yardstick of private manufacturing costs. He also sought to stimulate competition among American and foreign suppliers for the Navy with considerable success in reducing costs.

[5] Dr. John W. Coughlin, former mayor of Fall River, and currently a member of the Democratic National Committee from Massachusetts, an office caller.

Tuesday, October 21, 1913
   Colorado mines. Ammon [1]
   Civil Service

Wednesday, October 22, 1913
   Kansas City.

Thursday, October 23, 1913
   Armor plate   65 £ Argentine—100 £ here

———

Friday, November 7, 1913
   Mexico—

Sunday, November 9, 1913
   Spoke at Newport News

Monday, November 10, 1913
   Baptists—Annapolis
   Fiske discussed paying inventors in Navy.[1]
   90% stay for retired list.
   E. O. Wood [2] & Mich delegation.
   Pindell [3]—Russian Ambassador
   Gov. Walsh [4]   Mass
   Read letter to chickens—the President [5]

[1] Elias M. Ammons, Democrat, governor of Colorado.

———

[1] Rear Admiral Bradley A. Fiske, the Aid for Operations, was a naval inventor of some ingenuity, an early advocate of fire control and the torpedo plane. Understandably, Fiske was eager to establish the principle of royalty payments for inventions developed by Navy personnel.

[2] Edwin O. Wood, Michigan editor and member of the Democratic National Committee since 1908.

[3] Henry M. Pindell, Peoria editor whose appointment as U.S. Ambassador to Russia had caused a controversy and his ultimate withdrawal.

[4] David I. Walsh, Democrat, currently lieutenant governor of Massachusetts, governor, 1914–1915, U.S. Senator after 1919.

[5] This is evidently a reference to one of President Wilson's many jokes, about the man who wrote an angry letter to his neighbor protesting that his garden was being ravaged by the latter's chickens. The next day the chickens were back in the garden as usual, and the aggrieved neighbor demanded an explanation. "Why, I just don't understand it," was

Tuesday, November 11, 1913
Cabinet.
Mexico. 1. To grant arms—
           2. Withdraw diplomats
Garrison preferred giving 24 hours notice and then putting Huerta out
McAdoo suggested recognition of belligerency
McReynolds: Pres. has right to permit Constitutionalis[ts] to bear arms
England's attitude.
President rather weary
Bryan—concessions give foreign control
Wilsons Mobile speech [6]
Church at Annapolis—Presbyt[erian?]
Karnody—divorced

---

the innocent reply; "I read them your letter." President Wilson enlivened many a cabinet meeting with similar stories, and Daniels, as subsequent diary entries will indicate, sought faithfully to record them, good and bad alike.

[6] Wilson was at this time much exercised over the failure of his diplomatic campaign against the Huerta regime in Mexico. On October 10, Huerta had arrested 110 opposition deputies and assumed dictatorial powers. The very next day a new British Minister, Sir Lionel Carden, arrived in Mexico and ostentatiously presented his credentials to Huerta, announcing to reporters that Great Britain had no intention of withdrawing recognition of the Mexican strong man. Wilson was furious, convinced that British oil and other interests had persuaded London to strengthen Huerta just as he was about to collapse. When he addressed the Southern Commercial Congress at Mobile on October 27, therefore, Wilson publicly denounced foreign concessionaires in Latin America and promised United States support in freeing the region from their alleged domination. Daniels had helped arrange the invitation to address the Southern Commercial Congress and accompanied the President to Mobile.

Daniels aboard ship.

A Loving cup presented to JDR upon his departure prior to his retirement as Asst. Sec. on Monday when he accepts the presidential nomination — I was requested by Mr. Morning Star, Chief Electrician of the Washington Navy Yard, to make the presentation for the men in the service — [illegible] of only the compensations for men in public office — consciousness of [illegible] both to the public weal & appreciation & friendship of co-workers — JDR had both. He left in afternoon, but before leaving wrote me a letter most friendly & almost [illegible] made me glad I had never acted upon my impulse when he seemed to take sides with my critics.

Sun McGowan wants to retire in December — JDR appoints no Asst. Sec. [illegible] appointed now. He [illegible] him for a short term [illegible] him who had [illegible] offer of $20,000. He believes it but [illegible] a great [illegible] but cannot [illegible] that [illegible] to the shipbuilders that they must make more progress on [illegible] they are building —

George Creel here the letter to get Pres W to [illegible] and let him publish & sell to all countries. He said he could make Wilson a [illegible] man —

One of the more legible pages of the Daniels Diary.

Daniels as Secretary of the Navy.

Woodrow Wilson and his private secretary, Joseph P. Tumulty.

President Wilson and his first cabinet, 1913. Left to right: Secretary of the Treasury William G. McAdoo, Attorney General James C. McReynolds, Daniels, Secretary of State William J. Bryan, Secretary of Agriculture David F. Houston, Secretary of Labor William B. Wilson, Secretary of War Lindley M. Garrison, Secretary of Commerce William C. Redfield, Postmaster General Albert S. Burleson, and Secretary of the Interior Franklin K. Lane.

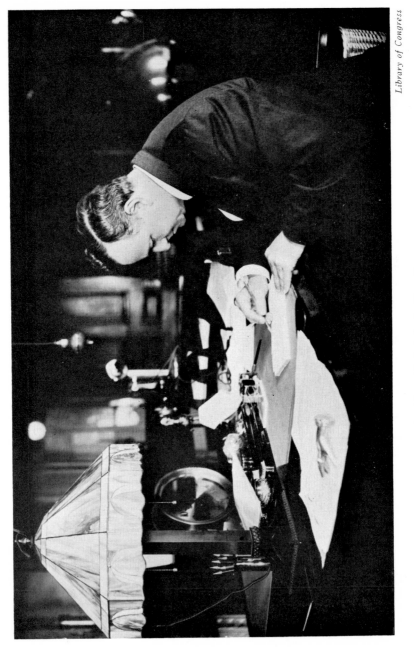

Daniels at his desk in the Navy Department.

Daniels and his first Council of Aids, 1913. Left to right: Chief, Bureau of Navigation, Admiral Victor Blue, Commandant of Marine Corps General George Barnett, Aid for Inspection Captain Augustus F. Fechteler, Aid for Matériel Captain Albert G. Winterhalter, and Aid for Operations Admiral Bradley A. Fiske.

Daniels family group, at target practice, April 1–3, 1913. Left to right: Worth B., Daniels, Jonathan W., Mrs. Daniels, Frank A.

Daniels looking through gunsight aboard U.S.S. *Wyoming*, probably 1913.

At target practice, April 1–3, 1913. Left to right: F.D.R., Admiral Charles J. Badger, unidentified officer, Daniels, Secretary of Commerce William C. Redfield, Secretary of War Lindley M. Garrison.

At Daniels' first visit to Atlantic Fleet, April 1–3, 1913. Daniels, Secretary of War Garrison, and Secretary of Commerce Redfield, with unidentified officers.

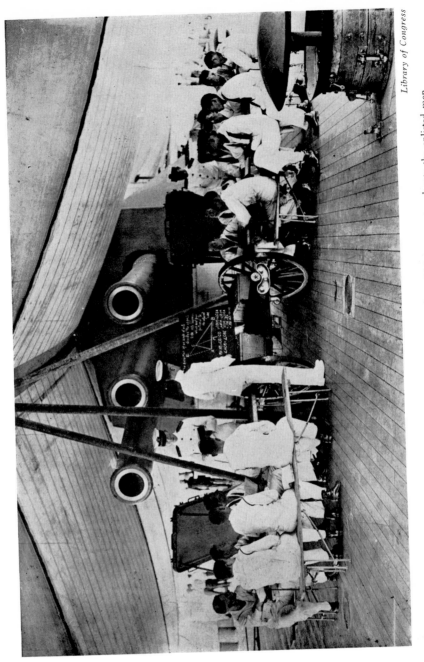

Mathematics class aboard U.S.S. *Oklahoma*—illustration of Daniels' program to educate the enlisted men.

"Single Oak," Daniels' first Washington home, 1913–1915.

The Council of National Defense and Advisory Commission; photograph taken 1916. Left to right: Julius Rosenwald, Bernard M. Baruch, Hollis Godfrey, Daniel Willard, Secretary Wilson, Houston, Howard E. Coffin, Daniels, Franklin H. Martin, Baker, Redfield, Samuel Gompers.

Daniels giving the first Navy wireless order, May 16, 1916.

The Wilson cabinet in 1917. Left to right: first row—Redfield, Secretary of State Robert Lansing, Houston, President Wilson, McAdoo, Burleson; second row—Daniels, Secretary Wilson, Secretary of War Newton D. Baker, Attorney General Thomas W. Gregory, Lane.

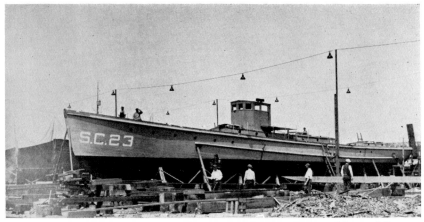

A small wooden subchaser of the class F.D.R. favored early in the war and which Daniels and others questioned. See entries of March 21, 25, 26, 29, and April 4, 1917.

Daniels, F.D.R., and the wartime Navy Department bureau chiefs. Left to right: General George Barnett; Captain William C. Watts; F.D.R.; Admirals Samuel McGowan, Robert S. Griffin, David W. Taylor, William S. Benson, Ralph Earle; Commander Sparrow; Admirals Charles W. Parks, Leigh C. Palmer, and William C. Braisted. Seated: Daniels.

Wartime destroyer construction.

Daniels and a group of Navy enlisted men. Daniels was more popular with enlisted men than with many officers because of his devotion to democracy and willingness to modify ancient traditions.

The U.S.S. *Dolphin*, Daniels' Navy yacht.

At the christening of the U.S.S. *Bagley* (named for Mrs. Daniels' brother, killed in the Spanish American War), October 19, 1918. Left to right: Mrs. Daniels, her mother Mrs. Adelaide W. Bagley, Daniels, Belle Bagley and Ethel Bagley (Mrs. Daniels' sisters).

U.S. Navy 14-inch gun at Thierville, France, firing on the German-held town of Longuyon, France, 1918.

Daniels and wartime Naval Consulting Board.

Daniels and a potential Navy recruit, identified only as "the Edwards boy."

Mrs. Mildred McLean Dewey, widow of Admiral George Dewey and a close friend of the Daniels family.

The Daniels family in 1919. Left to right: Worth, Jonathan, Josephus, Jr., Mrs. Daniels, Daniels, Frank.

Daniels and General John A. Lejeune at Vallendar, Germany, during European tour, 1919. See entry of April 18, 1919.

Daniels trying his hand at stoking coal aboard ship. European trip, 1919. See entry of May 14, 1919.

Daniels in cockpit of Navy plane NC-4, first to fly the Atlantic, 1919, with Lieutenant Commander Albert C. Read, the NC-4 commander. See entry of October 16, 1919.

U.S.S. *New York* at Honolulu, Daniels' ship for his Hawaiian tour, 1919. See entries of August 12–30, 1919.

Reviewing parade at San Francisco during fleet review. Left to right: Governor William D. Stephens and granddaughter, Mrs. Daniels, Daniels, Mayor James Rolph, Jr., and Admiral Hugh Rodman. See entry of September 2, 1919.

A Marine detachment aboard U.S.S. *New Mexico* at the San Francisco fleet review, September, 1919.

F.D.R., Daniels, the Prince of Wales, Admiral Archibald H. Scales (Superintendent of the Naval Academy) during the Prince of Wales's visit to Annapolis, 1919. See entry of November 14, 1919.

Daniels family Christmas, 1919. Left to right: seated—Jonathan, Daniels, Mrs. Daniels, Josephus, Jr.; standing—Worth, Frank.

Members of the last Wilson cabinet, 1920. Left to right: Attorney General A. Mitchell Palmer, Secretary of State Bainbridge Colby, Burleson, Secretary of the Interior John Barton Payne, Daniels, and Baker.

Photograph by Edmund D. Cronon, Sr., 1962

Daniels' second Washington home while Secretary of the Navy, 1915–1921.

Pro-Daniels cartoon, during Sims investigation, 1920.

Daniels, Senator Key Pittman, and naval officers leaving congressional hearing over Admiral Sims's charges against Daniels, 1920.

Daniels during the congressional investigation over Sims's charges against Daniels' administration of the Navy, 1920.

Daniels and key Navy advisers, about 1920, taken evidently in Daniels' study at his home. Left to right: Admirals Henry B. Wilson, Robert E. Coontz, and Hugh Rodman.

Daniels and his Navy Council, including F.D.R., probably taken shortly before F.D.R.'s resignation in the summer of 1920. See entry of August 5, 1920.

Daniels presenting loving cup to F.D.R. upon F.D.R.'s resignation, August 6, 1920. See entry of that date.

Daniels and Gordon Woodbury, F.D.R.'s successor as Assistant Secretary of the Navy, late 1920.

One of Daniels' characteristic social obligations—transporting visiting dignitaries to Mount Vernon on the presidential yacht *Mayflower*, October 2, 1920, celebrating the *Mayflower* tercentenary, 1620–1920. (Mrs. Daniels is second from the right, Daniels is fifth from the right.)

Daniels and Navy bureau chiefs, December 27, 1920.

Daniels, Admiral Newton A. McCully, and Russian orphans. See entry of January 5, 1921.

Daniels with his successor, Edwin Denby, 1921

Daniels at the swearing in of his successor, March 5, 1921. Left to right: Secretary of the Navy Edwin Denby, Daniels, retiring Assistant Secretary Gordon Woodbury, and incoming Assistant Secretary Theodore Roosevelt, Jr.

1915

The Cabinet Diaries of Josephus Daniels, 1915

Friday, January 1, 1915

Goldsboro—reached there 6. am. Brother Frank[1] at depot. C. C. D[2] &
G—— letters.

Went to Raleigh 4 p.m.

Attended New Year's reception at Y.M.C.A. & made brief speech "I stay
in Washington but I live in Raleigh["]

Saturday, January 2, 1915

Raleigh—Went to Durham to attend funeral of Rev. J. N. Cole.[3] Stuck in
the mud, nearly. Pulled H. A. Page[4] out. Judge Biggs,[5] Rev. M. Bradshaw &
C. B. Edwards.[6]

Sunday, January 3, 1915

Returned from Raleigh.

Josephus left that night for R—— to begin work as cub reporter on N&O.
For months he had been anxious to quit school & go on the paper, & we
consented. I went to the train with him. He was happy to be going home
and to work. In addition to his travel, I gave him a $20 bill, and told him
that over 25 years [a]go I had gone to Raleigh to make my way in journalism
I had $20 and I wished him to begin with the same amount of money.

Tuesday, January 5, 1915

Cabinet.

At night attended conference at home of Secretary Garrison to discuss policy

[1] Franklin A. Daniels, Daniels' elder brother, a superior court judge of Goldsboro, N.C.

[2] Charles C. Daniels, Daniels' younger brother, an attorney.

[3] John N. Cole, much beloved superintendent of the Methodist Orphanage in Raleigh and former pastor of Daniels' Raleigh church, the Edenton Street Methodist Church.

[4] Henry A. Page, president of the Asheboro and Aberdeen Railroad, and brother of Walter Hines Page.

[5] J. Crawford Biggs, former superior court judge, subsequently special assistant to Attorney General Gregory, 1917–1918, in charge of Navy oil litigation against the Southern Pacific Railroad in California.

[6] Cornelius B. Edwards, prominent North Carolina printer and part-owner of the *Biblical Recorder*.

to be pursued by Democrats as to military preparedness, appropriations &c. Garrison had advocated very big increase of the army—I same naval program as last year.

Tillman and Padgett [7] represented Navy Cong. Com. Chamberlain,[8] Hay [9] & Sherley [10] Army Cong. Com. Also Oscar Underwood present.

Discussed probable revenues. Underwood, Hay, Padgett & I advocated the regular program. Tillman some change. Garrison larger increase. Sherley some step of real progress.

Left for N.Y. with wife at midnight.

Wednesday, January 6, 1915

Reached N.Y. 7 a.m. & went to Admiral Usher's [11] where we were entertained. Lt. Wurtzbaugh [12] went as my aid.

In afternoon on the Florida presented medals to [blank] sailors who were awarded them for conspicuous bravery at Vera Cruz—All the men on ship drawn up in line.

Dined that evening on the New York with Admiral Fletcher.[13] My wife the only lady present. The others were Admirals Fletcher, Usher, Boush,[14] Captains Rogers (TS) [15] Albert Gleaves,[16] W. R. Rush,[17] Hillary Jones,[18] H P Huse,[19] W R Shoemaker,[20] A. W. Grant,[21] Yates Sterling,[22] C C Richards,[23] Frank Jack Fletcher,[24] Arthur Crenshaw,[25] John Halligan,[26] Thos A Kearney,[27] & Howard A. Banks.[28]

[7] Lemuel P. Padgett, Democrat, U.S. Representative from Tennessee, chairman of the House Naval Affairs Committee until the Democrats lost control of the House in 1919.

[8] George E. Chamberlain, Democrat, U.S. Senator from Oregon, a member of both the Appropriations and Military Affairs Committees of the Senate.

[9] James Hay, Democrat, U.S. Representative from Virginia, chairman of the House Military Affairs Committee.

[10] J. Swagar Sherley, Democrat, U.S. Representative from Kentucky and an influential member of the House Appropriations Committee.

[11] Rear Admiral Nathaniel R. Usher, commandant of the New York Navy Yard.

[12] Commander Daniel W. Wurtsbaugh, subsequently Daniels' private aide.

[13] Rear Admiral Frank F. Fletcher, commander-in-chief of the Atlantic Fleet.

[14] Rear Admiral Clifford J. Boush, commanding the second division of the Atlantic Fleet.

[15] Captain Thomas S. Rodgers, commanding the U.S.S. *New York*.

[16] Captain Albert Gleaves, commanding the U.S.S. *Utah*.

[17] Captain William R. Rush, commandant of the Boston Navy Yard.

[18] Captain Hilary P. Jones, commanding the U.S.S. *Florida*.

[19] Captain Harry McL. P. Huse, chief of staff of the Atlantic Fleet.

[20] Captain William R. Shoemaker, commanding the U.S.S. *Arkansas*.

[21] Captain Albert W. Grant, commanding the U.S.S. *Texas*.

[22] Commander Yates Stirling, Jr., commanding the submarine flotilla of the Atlantic Fleet.

[23] Lieutenant Clarence A. Richards of the *Utah*.

[24] Lieutenant Frank Jack Fletcher of the *New York*.

That night went to Seventh Regiment Armory, with all Admirals &
Captains & reviewed the regiment. Afterwards banquet & dance
Col Appleton [29]—Night at Vanderbilt

Thursday, January 7, 1915
At Vanderbilt, New York
Had call from Judge Hudspeth [30] & Mr. Spears, representing Electric Boat
Company to talk submarines.
Talked over phone with Herman Ridder [31] who was too sick to be seen.
German America & the war was subject I wished to talk with him about
Bought record "Looking This Way," the favorite of Admiral Dewey. He
had told me on his birthday that it was his favorite—had told me while
tears were in his eyes as it was played in his home.
Went to Winter Garden—heard Al Jolson [32]—"My soul belongs to O'Sul-
livan"
In afternoon went to Waldorff [*sic*] to hear Irvin Cobb [33] who had just
returned from war in Europe. He had personal pass from the Emperor.
Stench from trains (slow) carrying the wounded.
Dined at Waldorf with Col. John Wilson & wife & their friends from Erie
Went to Hippodrome with Evelyn Hope [34]
I left at midnight for Washington, my wife remaining in Washington

Friday, January 8, 1915
No cabinet meeting. President spoke on Jackson Day at Indianapolis

Sunday, January 10, 1915
Went to mass 11 am at St. Patricks & afterwards to luncheon with Mon-

---

[25] Lieutenant Commander Arthur Crenshaw, commanding the 6th division of the torpedo
flotilla, Atlantic Fleet.
[26] Lieutenant Commander John Halligan, Jr., fleet engineer.
[27] Lieutenant Commander Thomas A. Kearney, fleet gunnery officer.
[28] Daniels' private secretary, a former North Carolina journalist.
[29] Daniel Appleton, New York publisher and colonel of the Seventh Regiment.
[30] Robert S. Hudspeth, New Jersey attorney and former judge of the Court of Common
Pleas, member of the Democratic National Committee. Hudspeth's client, the Electric Boat
Company, was the major U.S. firm constructing submarines for the Navy and was seeking
to monopolize submarine construction.
[31] Prominent German-American and Democrat, publisher of the New York *Staats Zeitung.*
[32] Actor and singer, then nearing the peak of his career.
[33] Irvin S. Cobb, journalist and author, just returned from service in Europe as a war
correspondent for the *Saturday Evening Post.*
[34] Daniels' niece, Evelyn Hope Daniels, daughter of his younger brother, Charles C. Daniels.

signor Russell [35] to meet Cardinal Gibbons.[36] Made brief speech telling of the Cardinal's stay & influence in North Carolina

"May you live as long as possible"

Mon Russell sent roses to my wife

Many callers—among them Secy & Mrs. Lane   Lane talked of Mrs. Belmont [37] and expressed abhorrence &c.

Tuesday, January 12, 1915

Cabinet.

Mexican situation.

Wednesday, January 13, 1915

Dined at 8 pm with Dr & Mrs. [John C.] Boyd

Friday, January 15, 1915

Cabinet meeting at night in White House.

Discussed trip to Panama [38] and itinerary of President, places where he should speak returning.

Addie went to Raleigh to attend reception given by the Governor to the General Assembly.

Saturday, January 16, 1915

Left Saturday night for Raleigh

Sunday, January 17, 1915

Raleigh. Taught my old A&M College class at Edenton Street Sunday School. Had liberty

At 11 am, with mother & wife heard Bishop Kilgo.[39] Greet congregation "You can be brutal. You can be worse. You can be Germanic."

---

[35] William T. Russell, rector of St. Patrick's Roman Catholic Church in Washington since 1908, and formerly private secretary to Cardinal Gibbons.

[36] James Gibbons, Roman Catholic cardinal and archbishop of Baltimore since 1877, formerly bishop of North Carolina, 1868–1877.

[37] Presumably Alva E. Smith Belmont, widow of Oliver H. P. Belmont, social justice crusader and woman suffrage leader, currently operating a soup kitchen in New York for unemployed women.

[38] Wilson was at this time contemplating a visit to Panama to take part in the ceremonies opening the Panama Canal.

[39] John C. Kilgo, Methodist bishop and former president of Trinity College in North Carolina, with whom Daniels and his newspaper had formerly clashed over Kilgo's hostility to the University of North Carolina and other state schools.

Monday, January 18, 1915
  Visited Legislature. The Governor
  Talked to Dr Anderson.[40]
  Went to Wilson to see Hon F. A. Woodard.[41] So did Addie
  New Federal Building at Raleigh opened; Speeches by Judge Connor,[42]
F. S. Spruill [43] & others.
  Returned on night train for Wash

Tuesday, January 19, 1915
  Left R at 2 a.m. & got to Wash. 12.30, just in time to attend closing minutes
of cabinet meeting. *Cath[olic] & Protest[ant]*
  Pres. "We will set up a standard here to which the prudent will resort[."]
(See Wash)
  The Menace
  Hon. E. W. Pou—on P.M. at Raleigh. Mrs. Aycock [44]

Thursday, January 21, 1915
  Bailey & P.M at Raleigh. Bailey came out to dinner

Friday, January 22, 1915
  Cabinet meeting at White House—All present but R[edfield] & H[ouston?].
Pres. had talked with U & F [45] who felt it absolutely necessary to reduce budget
60 mil dollars. Discussion as to how & where. Pres. seemed to think could
reduce to one battleship & save 5 mil, War could reduce 5 mil. No others.
Sentiment seemed to favor making cut in army & navy, & then to urge Congress to continue war tax till war in Europe ends.
  Pres. in fine spirits. "I am no hero. I just swam out, turned the man over,
saw he was not Lloyd George [46] & brought him out" Pres. read extracts from

[40] Albert Anderson, superintendent of the North Carolina State Hospital at Raleigh.
[41] Frederick A. Woodard, Wilson attorney, trustee of the University of North Carolina, former Democratic U.S. Representative from North Carolina, 1893–1897.
[42] Henry G. Connor, former North Carolina supreme court justice, now U.S. district judge for eastern North Carolina.
[43] Frank S. Spruill, prominent North Carolina Democrat and attorney.
[44] Mrs. Cora Woodard Aycock, widow of former Governor Charles B. Aycock, whom Daniels had strongly supported in his term, 1901–1905.
[45] Probably Oscar W. Underwood, powerful chairman of the House Ways and Means Committee, and John J. Fitzgerald, Democrat of New York, chairman of the House Appropriations Committee.
[46] David Lloyd George, British statesman, currently Chancellor of the Exchequer since 1908, subsequently Minister of Munitions, 1915–1916, Secretary of State for War, 1916, and Prime Minister, 1916–1922.

[blank] book by author of Rulers, Rustics &c [?]—upon certain English leaders. "I have the honor never to have known Lord Northcliff." [47] Told good stories of summers spent in England. Severe on Chamberlain.[48] Houston told of spending days in Parliament hearing debates. Bryan said C—— was the most popular & convincing speaker he heard in E & he heard a number of them.

Saturday, January 23, 1915

Spoke at banquet of Navy Yard and Arsenal Machinists at Hotel Walton, Phila. Subject: "Put Yourself in His Place." Carroll, former employe, Wash. Navy Yard, toast-master, told how he had visited Raleigh to investigate me when I was made Secy of Navy. Had lived in R fifteen years ago. Found saloons, gambling & brothels driven out & their keeps all enemies of D——

Chief Machinist S.A.L.[49] was member Legislature. Praised D——   I called him Sherlock Holmes & told Mark Twain's story of "they will lie for you as I would for them under like circumstances."

Had meeting, as per arrangement at cabinet meeting, at Sec. of T's office, to discuss reduction of estimate. House leaders wanted $60,000,000 reduction. Nobody could scale—or said they could not, except G, W & I.[50] We said we ought not, but W—— said he could $900,000. G & I said if President felt it essential we could scale $5 mil each.

Sunday, January 24, 1915

Dr. Wood: [51] Mangoes. Singapore "Morsel of deliciousness. Shell, hard & ugly. But Duty may be hard, & the reward is sweet.

Dr. McCullers:

Fiske & Knapp: [52] Want German staff [53]

---

[47] Alfred C. W. Harmsworth, 1st Baron Northcliffe, influential British newspaper publisher, subsequently chairman of the British War Mission to the United States, June–November, 1917.

[48] Presumably Joseph Chamberlain (1836–1914), British statesman and leader of the Liberal Unionists.

[49] The Seaboard Airline Railroad.

[50] Presumably Secretary of War Garrison, Secretary of Labor Wilson, and Daniels.

[51] Charles Wood, Presbyterian minister of the Church of the Covenant in Washington since 1908. Although Daniels was a staunch Methodist, his wife had remained an equally dedicated Presbyterian, and they compromised by attending both churches, sometimes separately, sometimes together.

[52] Captain Harry S. Knapp, a member of the General and Joint Boards of the Navy.

[53] Since the turn of the century there had been agitation for an administrative reorganization of the Navy Department. Some Navy officers had long advocated the creation of a Navy General Staff to secure professional direction of the day-to-day operations and long-range planning of the Navy. Daniels' predecessor, Secretary Meyer, had established his

Monday, January 25, 1915

Talked personnel legislation with special committee which ended Plucking Board & promote by selection after examination.[54]

Banks left for San Francisco. Cyclorama [55]

Tuesday, January 26, 1915

"I desire you, Mr. Secretary, to convey to the Admiral who discussed administration policies in New York last night, that he should confine his remarks to questions asked him by committees of Congress." These were the words used by the President to me when the Cabinet met to-day. He was aroused and indignant. In the afternoon I conveyed the message to Admiral Knight [56] who was much perturbed. He is obsessed by the belief that the Navy Department should be organized on the German system and in order to bring about that plan is guilty of doing injustice to the service and criticizing the administration's policy. He averred that he was loyal to the administration & never dreamed that what he said would be construed into a criticism of the Secretary's or President's policy.

I told him if he was right in saying the Department was not organized for readiness for war, he, the War College, the General Board, the Aids and the Secretary were incompetent and should be removed.

Council of Aids as a step in this direction. The campaign for a Navy General Staff was led by Admiral Fiske, supported by several younger officers, including Captain Harry S. Knapp. Without Daniels' knowledge, Fiske drafted a bill, which was introduced in Congress early in 1915 by Representative Richmond P. Hobson, a former naval officer, to establish a powerful Chief of Naval Operations who with his fifteen assistants would constitute a General Staff responsible for the general direction of the Navy. Daniels saw this proposal as a threat to civilian control. While he favored some reorganization, he was instrumental in watering down the measure to insure that the Chief of Naval Operations would operate under the direction of the Secretary of the Navy, rather than as head of a largely autonomous general staff.

[54] By long-standing tradition, promotion in the Navy was based on seniority. The system had many defects, not least of which was its tendency to reward mediocrity and its inability to recognize efficiency. As a partial reform the Personnel Act of 1899 had authorized a board of officers—the dreaded Plucking Board—to select a certain number of officers for involuntary retirement each year. The Plucking Board could thus remove the least capable, but there was no provision for rapid advancement of the ablest younger officers. Daniels believed that promotion should be chiefly by merit rather than seniority and in 1916 he secured a sweeping revision of the system of promotion to achieve this end.

[55] The Navy exhibit at the San Francisco Panama-Pacific Exposition.

[56] Rear Admiral Austin M. Knight, president of the Naval War College and commandant of the Newport Naval Station, and a senior member of the General Board. In an address before the Efficiency Society the previous evening, Admiral Knight had called for the establishment of a Council of National Defense as well as a Division of Strategy and Operations in the Navy Department—the general staff proposal which Daniels opposed.

In the Cabinet, the President expressed faith that the ship bill [57] would pass, decided to change Friday night cabinet meetings to day meetings, combatted the suggestion that we might declare it was not the purpose to buy the German merchant ships interned, but that we should insist upon our right even though we should not exercise it. "England is trying the old game of bluff" was Burleson's opinion. Bryan was rejoiced to get news that gave the lie to the oft repeated story that nuns had been violated in Mexico. Some Republican Catholics had been using that canard against the administration. Goethals had told President he could not be certain the canal would be ready in March. Decided to postpone celebration till July. When will Senate filibuster end. "Reps are not open to reason" said W.

Bryan, Houston, Wilson, Lane, Daniels lunched at Shoreham   Talked about early struggles. Bryan $50. Lane 75   Wilson $600 a year   H—— no help from home.

Young Wise & San Domingo place. Had his nerve.

Maj. Bass [58] & turkeys.

Roosevelt & Branch's letter on grog to midshipmen

Wednesday, January 27, 1915
Dined with Peter Ten Eyck [59]
Hamlin,[60] Lansing [61] & others.

B[ryan]. Pig—one tail curled in a W, one into J., & one into a B—& the owner of pig voted for Bryan. Only vote I ever got that was not because voter was casting his real sentiment

Bryan & the buttons $15 for McKinley, $8 for Bryan   boys do not care what they buy

Thursday, January 28, 1915
Guilford Battle Ground.
Arlington Memorial meeting

[57] Since August, 1914, the administration had been seeking enactment of a Ship Purchase bill creating a government corporation to purchase foreign merchant ships, presumably mostly German, to relieve the badly congested American export trade. In a bitter legislative battle at this time congressional Republicans, aided by some rebellious Democrats, defeated the measure, charging that it was both undesirable state socialism and would very likely involve the United States in serious diplomatic difficulties with the British and French.

[58] Joseph P. Bass, elderly publisher and former mayor of Bangor, Maine.

[59] Peter G. Ten Eyck, engineer and inventor, Democrat, U.S. Representative from New York, 1913–1915.

[60] Charles S. Hamlin, former Assistant Secretary of the Treasury, 1893–1897 and 1913–1914, Governor of the Federal Reserve Board, 1914–1916, reappointed as member of the board for a ten-year term in 1916.

[61] Robert Lansing, counselor of the Department of State since 1914, subsequently Secretary of State from June 23, 1915, to February 13, 1920.

Y.M.C.A. speech.

Press Club banquet

Dr. Lownes [62] at dinner   Undertaker told Dr. Lownes he was glad to see him back in Washington

Friday, January 29, 1915

Cabinet in White House—first time we met in the White House. Rather informal   Revenues again

Cabinet. Garrison. Cosmos club

Went to New Willard and heard the President make speech. At first his audience (Am. Elec. Ry. Asso.) seemed cool, but he got them in a weaving way by his best speech.

Reception by N.C. Society. I did not attend, but heard instead debate in House on Naval bill

Saturday, January 30, 1915

Naval Bill in the House.

Pou & Anderson—Raleigh post office

Mrs Marshall & Mayflower din [?]

Sunday, January 31, 1915

Went to Mt. Vernon church, with the boys

Monday, February 1, 1915

Jonathan went up to the 8th Grade & Frank into Class B Fourth Grade.

C C D [1] here—O'Bryan & C

Addie had big luncheon, given in honor of Mrs. Walter H. Page, wife of Ambassador to England

Dinner with the Hamlins. The V.P. [2] told of the 7 Dem Senators who deserted on the Shipping bill. Stone's [3] plain words.

Stood in line at Southern Relief Ball at New Willard

[62] Commander Charles H. T. Lowndes, a Navy medical inspector assigned to the Marine Barracks at Washington.

---

[1] Charles C. Daniels.

[2] Vice-President Thomas R. Marshall.

[3] Senator William J. Stone, Democrat of Missouri, the administration's floor leader for the Ship Purchase bill.

Tuesday, February 2, 1915

No Cabinet meeting. The President in conference with Senators about Ship Purchase bill—

Saw Gathman [4] & Pence about armor plate & factory

Dined with Mr & Mrs. Carl S. Vrooman [5]—Gen. Hugh Scott [6]—& Mrs. Matthew Scott [7] among others. Later, Poet Lindsey,[8] & Poet Steel Maceye [?] read from their own poems.

Secy. Bryan read Theodosia Garrison's [9] poem on Peace, & Lindsey read "When Bryan Speaks" while Secy B—— was called to telephone.

Wednesday, February 3, 1915

Secretary Herbert [10]—Talked on Roosevelt's "Hell or Utopia" Questions of honor should be left to arbitration. Even duels were left to arbitration.

Isham: [11] "This Dept is controlled by the Armor Plate Trust["]

Dinner with Mr. & Mrs. John H. Small

Thursday, February 4, 1915

Lunched at Cosmos Club with Gov Folk.[12] He had Harry Hawes,[13] Bates of St. Louis & J J Dickinson. Dickinson told of European war. Said he cried all the time he was in France. Says you would hardly know there was any war going on in England. London lively. Decidedly anti-English.

Attended meeting of Arlington Memorial Commission. Decided upon Danby granite after Woods [14] & I had stood out for justice to Southern granite.

[4] Louis Gathmann, inventor of the Gathmann high explosive shell and the triple hull for warships, who charged that high Army and Navy officers were in league with the Armor Plate Trust.

[5] Assistant Secretary of Agriculture.

[6] Brigadier General Hugh L. Scott, Army chief of staff.

[7] Julia Green Scott, widow of Matthew T. Scott, and former president-general of the Daughters of the American Revolution.

[8] Nicholas Vachel Lindsay, gifted Illinois poet and writer.

[9] Theodosia P. Garrison, poet and author.

[10] Hilary A. Herbert, former Secretary of the Navy, 1893–1897. Herbert, the last Democratic Navy Secretary, took a lively interest in the affairs of the department under Daniels, and occasionally voiced public support of Daniels' policies.

[11] Willard S. Isham, inventor of a naval shell designed to strike below the waterline on the lightly armored part of the ship. Ordnance experts were skeptical of the feasibility of the Isham shell, but Daniels ordered it tested subsequently.

[12] Joseph W. Folk, Democrat, former Governor of Missouri, now chief counsel of the Interstate Commerce Commission.

[13] Harry B. Hawes, prominent St. Louis attorney and Democrat.

[14] Elliott Woods, superintendent of the Capitol, like Daniels a member of the Arlington Memorial Amphitheater Commission.

Dined at Army & Navy Club with Assistant Attorney General Graham.[15]
In afternoon, party to Mary Cleaves [16] & Evelyn Jackson [17]
Worth made average of over 91 in every study. Had examination

Friday, February 5, 1915

Cabinet in the White House. Discussed German Admiralty statement [18] of war zone in North sea & danger to Am. Shipping. Lansing to ask German Emperor.

What to do as to Van Horn,[19] who tried to blow up bridge between Maine & New Brunswick. Better keep him in Maine & avoid international trouble, said Atty Genl. Shall we make a Declaration?

Pres. tried last summer to get England to agree to Declaration of London,[20] but it then declined what it is now insisting upon.

Pres. said he hoped Page's letters would be printed. Said they were the best he had ever read & the most illuminating. They gave you the atmosphere

Armstrong & Maxim [21]—wanted to go to Indian Head [22] to learn how to make smokeless powder. Stand so firm we lean backward.

Turkeys from Col. J. P. Bass, for Cabinet dinner   Pecans from Col. Wm. Bailey Lawson [?] for Cabinet dinner

Naval bill passed House. Underwood

Ambassador Naon [23] with Argentine Capt. $3 mil dollars demanded by N.Y. Ship Bld Co in excess. Holding ship. Sailors present

Lunched at Shoreham with Cabinet & McReynolds

---

[15] Samuel J. Graham.

[16] Daniels' niece, daughter of his elder brother, Judge Frank A. Daniels.

[17] Daughter of Mrs. Daniels' cousin, Herbert W. Jackson, a Richmond banker.

[18] The day before, on February 4, the German government had announced a submarine blockade of the British Isles, warning that neutral shipping would enter this war zone at its peril because of the difficulty of clear identification.

[19] Werner Van Horn, an admitted German reservist arrested in Maine on February 2 after attempting to destroy a Canadian Pacific Railroad bridge. Canada was asking his extradition.

[20] The London Naval Conference of 1909 had drawn up the so-called Declaration of London in an attempt to codify rules for maritime warfare. The declaration protected a large degree of neutral trade in wartime, and for this reason Great Britain had not accepted it. This in turn had led the United States and other nations to withhold their final ratifications, so that when war began in 1914 the declaration was no more than a pious hope.

[21] Hudson Maxim, inventor of explosives and smokeless powder, subsequently a member of the Naval Consulting Board.

[22] A Navy proving ground on the Potomac south of Washington.

[23] Rómulo S. Naón, the Argentine Ambassador, who was seeking Daniels' intercession to obtain the release of the new Argentine battleship *Moreno*, whose builder, the New York Shipbuilding Company, was demanding additional money.

Saturday, February 6, 1915

Japanese cruiser [24] aground near Lower California. Sent radio to Admiral Howard [25] to go and render assistance in name of humanity, but to inform Japanese captain that if ship were saved we must bring it into port to be interned. Awful to think of what this war compels—cannot save a belligerent ship without imposing such conditions. Lansing & Fiske advised saying *"Do not* save unless" &c

Lunched with C C D at Press Club. Talked Minnesota land cases

Talked about coming of Japanese Admiral & plans for entertainment.

Attended dinner at New Willard Presidential suite given by Justice Mc-Reynolds [26] to Chief Justice—Cabinet, Supreme Court, wives, 60 in all. Same place in which Cabinet gave dinner on first anniversary of administration. I went in with Mrs. Bryan—my wife with Houston. Talked with Judge Lamar [27] about his dissent in white slave case. Out of 60, five North Carolinians—Houston, J D & wife & Yates Webb and wife.

Sunday, February 7, 1915

Admiral Howard reported that Jap cruiser had help—colliers & another cruiser. He had offered neutral assistance which was not desired. He was given power to exercise discretion

Went to Church of the Covenant. Sermon by Dr. Wood—Choose your path &c. Robber reversed engine, which was full & gloried in it. Turning a curve it was smashed. Young man free from order goes to ruin. Prodigal. When "I ought" takes the place of "I must"

In afternoon went with wife to Alexandria to speak to young men in Presbyterian Westminster hall. It was crowded. Talked of making a life, not merely a living. The President boos—ridden [?]. All crowned heads try to prove alibi for bringing on the war. Later tea at Editor Barrett,[28] of Alexandria Gazette. It is 105 years old. Every person in his family ex. 3 year old got a bread-winner—Daughters as well as sons. South poor partly because

---

[24] The Japanese armored cruiser *Asama*, grounded and wrecked at San Bartolomé, or Turtle Bay, on Lower California on February 4. The incident sparked some American concern that the Japanese might be attempting to establish a naval base in Mexico, since there seemed little reason for a Japanese force to be in Mexican waters.

[25] Rear Admiral Thomas B. Howard, commander-in-chief of the Pacific Fleet.

[26] In August, 1914, Wilson had appointed Attorney General McReynolds an Associate Justice of the Supreme Court.

[27] Associate Justice Joseph R. Lamar, who had dissented from the Court's February 1 decision that women might be charged with conspiracy under the Mann White Slave Act.

[28] Robert S. Barrett, editor and publisher of the *Alexandria Gazette*.

there is generally only one bread winner in the family & people without property.

Auto broke down but no harm done.

Tuesday, February 9, 1915
Cabinet

Dinner on Mayflower—Members of Cabinet & their wives to meet Atty Genl & Mrs. Gregory [29]

Went to Capitol to see the Senate in session where Republicans were filibustering

Wednesday, February 10, 1915
Admiral Dewa,[30] Japanese Admiral & staff, called & met all aids & bureau chiefs. Later I called on him at the Shoreham. Had our pictures taken

Dinner of Mayflower to Admiral that night. American & Japanese National air.

Speeches by Bryan, Japanese Admiral & Ambassador, Padgett.

Thursday, February 11, 1915
Lunched with Bryan to meet Japanese Admiral.

Bryan: Mediterranean did not separate Roman Empire, but united it.

Dined with the Padgetts

Friday, February 12, 1915
Dined with Col & Mrs McCauley

Italian Ambassador [31] stayed late—I rose to leave before Ambassador & my wife gave me seat [32]

Saturday, February 13, 1915
Gridiron Dinner

Sunday, February 14, 1915
Mt Vernon Place Methodist church   wife, Jonathan and Frank

[29] Thomas W. Gregory, Attorney General of the United States, 1914–1920.

[30] Admiral Baron Shigeto Dewa, Japanese representative to attend the opening festivities of the Panama-Pacific Exposition at San Francisco.

[31] Count Vincenzo Macchi di Cellere.

[32] Daniels had evidently forgotten the protocol requirement that guests at a social function should remain until after the ranking or guest of honor has departed.

Visited Lanes & Redfields.

D. F—man on train & McAdoo

Tuesday, June 8, 1915

Franks birthday all kinds of presents [1]

Saturday, June 26, 1915

Reached Newport 8. a.m.

Admiral Fletcher & Capt. Huse called 9 am

9.20 went to Training Station, reviewed the 1200 boys at station & inspected the station & spoke to the boys who made very fine appearance.

At 11 a.m. delivered address at War College. The Gov. of Mass & R.I.[2] were both there & also officers of the fleet.

1. pm. Luncheon at Adml Knight

3 p.m. Visited Torpedo station, guests of Capt. Robinson,[3] & saw the wonderful work going on. Addition to plant nearly completed. It will enable us to double the supply of torpedoes made there. Reception.

David [4] came to dinner on Dolphin. Afterwards Governor Walsh, Mrs. Slater,[5] & Mrs. B [blank] called on Dolphin.

Mrs. S—— with 30 mil. Will she marry the Gov of Mass. Only gossip he said

Sunday, June 27, 1915

Left Newport 6. am.

Monday, June 28, 1915

Reached Wash. from Newport 7 am

Conference with Neutrality Board and they went over telegrams sent from Sayville to see if they were contrary to laws of Neutrality.[6] Saw Lansing who

---

[1] This entry, written in a boyish scrawl, was obviously intended as a reminder from Daniels' youngest son, Frank.

[2] Governor David I. Walsh of Massachusetts, and R. Livingston Beeckman, Republican, governor of Rhode Island, 1915–1921.

[3] Commander John K. Robison, in charge of the Newport Naval Torpedo Station.

[4] Lieutenant David Worth Bagley, Daniels' brother-in-law, a career naval officer with the Atlantic Fleet at this time.

[5] Mabel Hunt Slater, wealthy widow of Horatio N. Slater, a Massachusetts manufacturer.

[6] Shortly before the war a German company had established a radio transmitting station at Sayville, Long Island. The military potential of such a station was obvious, and on

agreed to send brief to the President in re taking over S[ayville] station. He and Redfield & Roosevelt all favored it.

Telegram from Windsor, Vt. from the President.[7] He had seen telegram from Admiral Howard suggesting a permanent settlement of Marines in Yaki Valley,[8] with radio. The President said "Don't you think we had better not depart from our original plan not to send marines in only to bring out Americans." I wired that original plan without change would be carried out & wired Howard not to send in marines.

Mr. Cadwallader[9] called. He claims he can make heat, light & power from the attraction of the earth. Will see him again tomorrow

Delegation from Washington Navy Yard about wages—Division of $240[,]-000 bet. Wash & Indian Head cuts down Wash wages.

Spent hour in National Library

Fiskes Isham Shell Board report.

Tuesday, June 29, 1915

Shall Federal Company be given right to erect radio in Philippines. General Board says "No." Garrison seems to favor. Bullard[10] thinks it good opportunity to try government ownership. I asked officers to submit plan to sell to Gov—— at stipulated time & price, without water. Will submit next week.

Benson.[11] How to fortify Guam? Submarines may be better   Shall the Joint Board meet to consider? Benson thinks if war with Yellow,[12] we should make Puget Sound our base & not Guam as General Board has approved. It is not

August 5, 1914, Wilson had prohibited the transmission of unneutral messages from American radio stations, directing the Navy to supervise both the Sayville station and a similar German-owned station at Tuckerton, New Jersey. On July 8, 1915, the Navy took over direct operation of the Sayville station to insure that it would not be used for belligerent purposes.

[7] Wilson was vacationing at the Cornish, New Hampshire, estate of novelist Winston Churchill.

[8] The administration was concerned over the safety of American farmers living in the Yaqui Valley of northwestern Mexico, who were threatened by the unsettled conditions resulting from the Mexican Revolution.

[9] Bassett Cadawallader, of New York, according to Daniels' office register.

[10] Captain William H. G. Bullard, superintendent of the Naval Radio Service.

[11] Rear Admiral William S. Benson, whom Daniels had appointed on May 11 to be Chief of Naval Operations, the new post recently established by Congress to meet the demands for more centralized direction of the Navy. By selecting Benson, then commandant of the Philadelphia Navy Yard and only a captain, Daniels had shown his determination that this important post should be filled by an officer who would be personally loyal and, like his chief, dedicated to the concept of ultimate civilian control. Benson's appointment antagonized Admiral Fiske and other proponents of a Navy general staff, and was one of the reasons for Fiske's retirement at this time.

[12] Code name for Japan.

much further. He thinks ships might go from Panama & coal under lee of coral islands or reefs.

Move big dry docks? Stanford [13] favors & Benson doubts whether we will go on building dreadnaughts, & smaller craft may take their place.

N.Y. Ev. Post man—Roy Vernon [14] talked on dif. between Myers plan and mine.

Straus,[15] Fiske, Isham—

Wednesday, June 30, 1915

Admiral Fullam—reported 5 arrested for hazing.[16] He thinks original 7 guilty of gouging [17] & none others. Says he is on trial, showed me editorial in Balto Sun severely criticizing system at Annapolis. He thinks it perfect.

He feels if he is not retained at Academy he is put in bad light. "Fullam never looks beneath surface" writes a frank & discriminating midshipman

Labor Com. called about $240,000 division of wages between Washington and Indian Head, worked up because Wash. must give part to Indian Head. Rather difficult matter. My statement in today's Star greatly pleased Tumulty

Knight & War College

Redfield. Bureau of Standards & soap.

Benson & Redf[iel]d. talked of making surveys in Pacific with Commerce boats to see if there were not place where fleet could be protected & coal & get supplies.

Howe [18] & Edison [19]—letters.

[13] Rear Admiral Homer R. Stanford, chief of the Bureau of Yards and Docks.

[14] Probably Leroy T. Vernon, Washington correspondent of the *Chicago Daily News* since 1903.

[15] Rear Admiral Joseph Strauss, chief of the Bureau of Ordnance, 1913–1916.

[16] Daniels was determined to stamp out the degrading and sometimes sadistic practice of hazing first-year midshipmen by the upperclassmen at the Naval Academy at Annapolis. Not all officers, including the current superintendent, William F. Fullam, considered hazing such a serious matter. Despite pressures from parents and interested congressmen, however, President Wilson upheld Daniels' policy of instant dismissal for any midshipman convicted of hazing.

[17] Cheating on examinations.

[18] Louis McH. Howe, former New York journalist now serving as Assistant Secretary Roosevelt's private secretary.

[19] Thomas A. Edison, the famous inventor. Howe was evidently helping to draft Daniels' letter to Edison of July 7, in which he asked the Wizard of Menlo Park to help organize and head a naval consulting board to advise on naval experimentation and invention.

1917

The Cabinet Diaries of Josephus Daniels, 1917

Sunday, January 7, 1917
Went to hear Billy Sunday's [1] opening sermon.
Lunch with Dr. & Mrs. Wood at Service Club to meet men of the Navy

---

Friday, February 9, 1917
See Lane's book—Page 233 [1]

Friday, February 16, 1917
Lane—Page 235–37

Tuesday, February 20, 1917
Lane   Page 238

Friday, February 23, 1917
Lane   Page 239–240
Red—Shall I give a tip to Gardner [2]   "The only tip I would like to give him is to go to hell[."]

Sunday, February 25, 1917
Last Cab. meet— W W: Why don't B[ritish] convoy ships?
B[ritish] A[dmiralty] do not believe in it—think dispersion better & some Am. Adls agree.

[1] William A. Sunday, prominent Presbyterian evangelist.

---

[1] In this and subsequent entries Daniels refers to the published letters of his cabinet colleague, Franklin K. Lane. (*The Letters of Franklin K. Lane, Personal and Political,* Anne W. Lane and Louise H. Wall, eds. [Boston: Houghton Mifflin, 1922].) Daniels' references, obviously added years later, are to various Lane letters written on the dates in question.
[2] Augustus P. Gardner, Republican, U.S. Representative from Massachusetts, a strong critic of the administration's preparedness policies.

W W: ought to convoy [3]

Tuesday, February 27, 1917

The Cabinet today decided to send a division to Santiago, Cuba, to make demonstration to help Government against revolutionists. W said I am very free from G[erman] suspicions but so many things are happening we cannot afford to let Cuba be involved by G plots.[4]

Benson did not think it necessary but—

I said to Lansing "You are never happy except when you are breaking up naval operations—" Manouevering [*sic*]

W: Gerard's [5] remark to Von Jagow [6] who said to G "If there is war bet. G[ermany] & US, you will find there are 500,000 German reservists ready to take up arms for mother country & you will have civil war." G replied "I do not know whether there are 500,000 or not. But we have 500,001 lamp posts & every man who takes up arms against his country will swing from lamppost.["]

[3] Significantly, Daniels' account of this cabinet meeting is both shorter and different from that of Lane, one of the war hawks in the cabinet. Moreover, it is perhaps also significant that Daniels' entry is on Sunday, February 25, although the meeting was held the previous Friday. That Daniels may have added his entry after reading Lane's version is suggested by the date of Lane's letter to his brother, February 25, which corresponds to the date of Daniels' entry. Lane says in part:

"On Friday we had one of the most animated sessions of the Cabinet that I suppose has ever been held under this or any other President. . . . This led to a discussion of the great problem which we all had been afraid to raise—Why shouldn't we send our ships out with guns or convoys? Daniels said we must not convoy—that would be dangerous. (Think of a Secretary of the Navy talking of danger!) The President said that the country was not willing that we should take any risks of war. I said that I got no such sentiment out of the country, but if the country knew that our Consuls' wives had been treated so outrageously that there would be no question as to the sentiment. This, the President took as a suggestion that we should work up a propaganda of hatred against Germany. Of course, I said I had no such idea, but that I felt that in a Democracy the people were entitled to know the facts. McAdoo, Houston, and Redfield joined me. The President turned on them bitterly, especially on McAdoo, and reproached all of us with appealing to the spirit of the *Code Duello*. We couldn't get the idea out of his head that we were bent on pushing the country into war. Houston talked of resigning after the meeting. McAdoo will—within a year, I believe. I tried to smooth them down by recalling our past experiences with the President. We have had to push, and push, and push, to get him to take any forward step—the Trade Commission, the Tariff Commission. He comes out right but he is slower than a glacier—and things are mighty disagreeable, whenever anything has to be done. . . ." *Letters of Franklin K. Lane*, pp. 239–240.

[4] A revolt had broken out in Cuba in a dispute over the recent presidential election. United States support of President Mario G. Menocal was ultimately decisive, though American intervention was limited to minor patrol duty by Marines from Guantanamo.

[5] James W. Gerard, U.S. Ambassador to Germany, 1913–1917.

[6] Gottlieb von Jagow, the German foreign secretary.

L repeated there was rumor that 500 German Reservists had gone to Mexico to make trouble. Also McAdoo—200 Japs to make munitions. Wilson, W B "Strange that G & Japs both going to Mex seeing they are at war.["]

Discussed resolution for arming ships.

Lunched with French delegate to Economic Conf. in Paris. It was said the Entente powers had decided to control the trade of the world. Frenchmen desired it & said it was not even discussed. If G—— should by unfair & monopolistic methods try to control trade, they would be forced in self defense to stand together. But not against America. Against the Germans &c &c

Hudson Maxim & 12,000.

Gompers [7] & enlisting personnel.

Thursday, March 1, 1917

McAdoo, Burleson & I talked with Swanson, Kitchin,[1] Fitz,[2] Sherley about bond issue.

McAdoo & Fitzgerald—cussing—Kitchin said: "When you members of the cabinet get through cussing, I will take up the question.["]

I said: "Don't confuse members of Cabinet. Say instead "When you two New Yorkers get through cussing. It is confined to the Empire State folks.["]

Friday, March 2, 1917

Dined with Burleson & we went to Senate to try to get an agreement to vote. P.O. bill. Bone dry & tubes. B wanted veto, but consented.[3]

Japanese attache: Who is this Mr. Bone who makes Washington dry? Must be a very influential man.

[7] Samuel Gompers, president of the American Federation of Labor and a member of the Advisory Commission of the Council of National Defense. Both the Council and its Advisory Commission were established in 1916 to coordinate the national preparedness effort. The Council was composed of the Secretaries of War, Navy, Interior, Agriculture, Commerce and Labor. In addition to Gompers, the Advisory Commission included Daniel Willard, Bernard M. Baruch, Howard E. Coffin, Julius Rosenwald, Dr. Hollis Godfrey, and Dr. Franklin H. Martin.

---

[1] Claude Kitchin, U.S. Representative from North Carolina, Democratic majority leader.
[2] John J. Fitzgerald, Democrat, U.S. Representative from New York, chairman of the House Appropriations Committee.
[3] The Post Office appropriations bill had been held up in a congressional wrangle over amendments which would end pneumatic tube service and forbid the mailing of liquor or liquor advertising into states where prohibited. Burleson finally consented to the "bone dry" amendment in order to get the bill.

Saturday, March 3, 1917

Hudson Maxim $1,000 a month

Japan Naval Attache asked who is Mr. Bone who secured passage of dry bill.

Naval bill passed at 2 a.m. Tillman & Conference took 5 hours for agreement. Charleston Dry Dock—Pacific Navy Yard—Wages at Navy Yards. Swanson said to Tillman: "I will not sign unless you do, but if we in this emergency kill this bill, what will the country say?"

"O, Claude, I will not hold you to the promise & I will sign. I put the country ahead of any local interest."

Sunday, March 4, 1917

Went to capital to see close of Congress—Adjourned without action. Lane, Bn [Burleson?], Baker [4] & I suggested to President that he go before Congress & ask for passage of bill.[5] B & B & L were enthusiastic. The dramatic setting appealed to them. Pres. said "if I ought to have gone, should have gone sooner.["] Said he thought he ought to speak only when he could accomplish something & he thought it could not change the determination not to act. He convinced all he should not go.

Got pen with which President signed Naval bill.

Left capitol & went to Mt. Vernon church in time for communion.

Monday, March 5, 1917

Inauguration. McAdoo & President's daughters [6]

Bob & the sunshine.

Vardeman [7] & John Sharp [8]

Marshal[l] said "so help me God in whom I believe."

Homer Cumings [*sic*]: Electric Boat Company. Conflict between owners. Voting trust controls. Wanted me to take over plant.

Cold out on reviewing stand. I went in & asked her [9] to invite the ladies in.

[4] Newton D. Baker, former mayor of Cleveland, succeeded Lindley M. Garrison as Secretary of War in March, 1916, and served throughout the second Wilson administration. Daniels was much closer to Baker than he had been to the more aloof Garrison.

[5] The administration's request for congressional authority to arm American merchant ships against possible attack by German submarines. Germany had begun unrestricted submarine warfare against vessels in the war zone around the British Isles on February 1. The bill to arm American ships was defeated by a Senate filibuster, but after Congress adjourned Wilson ordered the ships armed under executive authority.

[6] In 1914, Secretary of the Treasury William G. McAdoo married the President's daughter, Eleanor, thereby gaining a particularly close relationship with the Wilson family.

[7] James K. Vardaman, Democrat, U.S. Senator from Mississippi.

[8] John Sharp Williams, Democrat, U.S. Senator from Mississippi.

[9] Presumably Mrs. Wilson.

Tuesday, March 6, 1917

Conference with ship builders. Read them the new law [10] on speeding up & tried to ascertain how many ships each could [?] build & when & cost.

Talked with Wilson & Gompers about labor

Phelan called about Navy Yard at San Francisco.

Walsh [11]—Said Southern control hurt Dem party as seen in election of Martin [12] as leader.

President called at Navy Dept to talk over arming ships & danger of submarines in American waters & about bringing the fleet North. He thought in addition to arming, we ought to have 3 motor boats on each ship to be lowered in smooth seas & hunt submarines. When in England he saw the annual occasion where a shepherd would stand in a circle & by calls & whistles herd three sheep distant from him in a pen. It wasn't hard to manage 2, but very difficult with 3. They would expect a boat on each side of ship but the third boat would confuse them.[13]

Wednesday, March 7, 1917

Conference with ship builders. Big program—10% profit.

Gotting: Lived in Germany for years. They are educated barbarians, more like Tom Cats than men. In 1913 he saw 13 million rifles in Germany & it was prepared & armed to the teeth.

If G wins America must fight for existence.

George Creel [14] to dinner. Paper [?] fight.

Went to train with Britton.[15]

Thursday, March 8, 1917

At night had message from Hoover [16] at White House saying Mrs. Wilson wished me to call. Upon arrival she said she was a blind—that Pres. was

[10] The Naval Appropriations Act of March 4 had authorized cost-plus contracts to speed ship construction.

[11] Probably Thomas J. Walsh, Democrat, U.S. Senator from Montana, a member of the Senate Naval Affairs Committee.

[12] Senator Thomas S. Martin of Virginia, new majority floor leader.

[13] Wilson's analogy between sheepherding and submarine hunting did not impress the admirals. See entry of March 9.

[14] Midwestern editor and writer, shortly to be appointed (April 14, 1917) chairman of the Committee on Public Information, the official war propaganda agency.

[15] Edward E. Britton, longtime reporter for Daniels' newspaper and its editor since 1913 while Daniels was in Washington. In September, 1917, Britton left the *News and Observer* to serve as Daniels' private secretary in the Navy Department.

[16] Irwin H. (Ike) Hoover, White House usher.

declining to see anybody & that was why she called. He was suffering from cold.

We discussed arming ships—wished it all kept secret. Decided to arm ships. We had prepared regulations in event we armed & I had sent to him that afternoon. He suggested changes and particularly to omit "No ship shall go to rescue of ship attacked." England had adopted that rule after three ships were sunk that went to rescue of ship attacked. It seemed inhuman said President. Upon returning I called up Benson & Palmer,[17] & Benson went that night to NY to see P S B Franklin [18] of American lines & arrange to have guns & armed guard put on all ships. He saw F—— who thought visit & search should be permitted outside of zone. F called me up by telephone & wanted to know if he should arm Manchuria ready to sail.

Lunch Barney Baruch [19]—Profits in munitions.

Josephus went to Raleigh.

Friday, March 9, 1917

President sick—no cabinet.

Called to White House again to see President about armed guard on ships. He had sent Lansing my memorandum of instructions. Should naval officer control or master? Or should they agree? I thought if both must agree, it might be debating society, & ship might be sunk waiting for decision.

Shall visit be permitted outside zone? That is required but safety of passengers is also required. If they conflict what? The President say [said] it was not to be permitted that they should be put to sea in small boats 300 mi. from shore & German sub-marines would not dare to tow them near to land. Therefore preservation of life demanded leaving no chance by inaction outside of zone.

Was to see Lansing & request him to see Spring Rice [20] & request protection of our ships near Great Britain as they protected their ships.

Danish West Indies [21]

Taylor's [22] statement about small boats seemed to convince the President his idea was not practical

[17] Rear Admiral Leigh C. Palmer, Daniels' personal aide when he became Secretary of the Navy; since August, 1916, serving as chief of the Bureau of Navigation.

[18] Philip A. S. Franklin, vice-president of the International Mercantile Marine Company.

[19] Bernard M. Baruch, member of the Advisory Commission of the Council of National Defense, and chairman of its Committee on Raw Materials, Minerals, and Metals.

[20] Sir Cecil A. Spring Rice, the British Ambassador.

[21] The administration was at this time completing arrangements for the purchase of the Danish West Indies (Virgin Islands) and Daniels was necessarily concerned about their defense in the event of war with Germany.

[22] Rear Admiral David W. Taylor, chief constructor of the Navy and chief of the Bureau of Construction and Repair.

Saturday, March 10, 1917

Lansing & Polk: [23] Man arrested in Phila. who had obtained chronomators &c from Frederick Eitel interned.[24] They implicated captain & next officer, & Dept. of Justice wanted to arrest German officers for smuggling, & wished it done so as to get statement of each before they could manufacture a story. Benson strongly opposed arresting them, favoring investigation by Commandant & I asked Dept. of Justice not to proceed, but leave to Navy. In ordinary times, such charges would be taken up with Embassy & we ought not to subject German officers to the indignity. Polk said they could not be relied upon to tell the truth & we could not trust them. If we arrested them, would the sailors in Germany be allowed to leave. I said "If Germans lie & do wrong, we should conduct our affairs to make marked contrast.["]

McAdoo called to urge right in arming ships, said war was inevitable, & would unite people & bring blessings in its wake.

E. A. Filene,[25] of Boston: If we have war its expenses should be borne by the people who have big incomes. If rich men could emerge from the war with what they have & should be satisfied to pay at least 50% of their income tax. Some might pay 100%. All should pay tax who get over $1,000, but it should [be] very low rate.

McAdoo agreed that reliance to pay costs of war should be on taxes not bonds. If bonds are issued it should be provided that if subsequent bonds are issued, all subsequent issues should bear the same rate of interest. This would induce men to buy bonds. Would it not also tend to make men favor bond issues instead of taxes.

Sunday, March 11, 1917

Had telephone from F. D. R. in New York and asked him to see newspapermen about publishing news of sailings—to get their advice. Also to see Usher [26] about fixing merchant ships with guns.

Saw Lansing after church. Gave him copy of tentative instructions to officers going on merchant ships & asked him to suggest any changes necessary. He showed me letter from Mexico (furnished by Spring Rice) quoting Minister from Argentina saying that Mex. Min of Foreign Affairs [27] predicted that if Germany and U.S. became engaged in war, war would follow between U.S. & Mexico. Carranza is supposed to be author of this

[23] Frank L. Polk, Counselor of the Department of State.
[24] The *Prinz Eitel Friedrich,* an interned German auxiliary cruiser, named after one of the sons of Kaiser Wilhelm II.
[25] Edward A. Filene, prominent Boston merchant active in the League to Enforce Peace.
[26] Rear Admiral Nathaniel R. Usher, commandant of the New York Navy Yard.
[27] General Cándido Aguilar.

Capt. Hood,[28] of Reserve fleet, called to protest against any men in reserve fleet, being put on merchant ships. He had a grouch because he didn't have everything exactly as he wanted it and wished to advise me about regulations & what arming ships meant as if they had not been considered. I told him the first lesson was to learn to carry a message to Garcia.

Benson & Palmer called at night. Palmer directed to get best men from active fleet as crew to man guns on merchant ships. Benson to see Gen Scott about protecting oil wells at Tampico & care of men on German interned ships at Phila. Also ordered to send armored cruiser in Pacific & destroyers to Panama canal as precautionary measure.

Boys on victrola & happy evening.

Monday, March 12, 1917

Conference with Westinghouse & General Electric Co, Carnegie Company, Baldwin Locomotive Works & others with reference to speeding up in work of furnishing material to build ships. Also conference with a score of men about building 110 foot motor boats for patrol duty. We hope to build 200.

Senator Jones,[29] of New Mexico, telephoned about who should christen the New Mexico. Gov. McDonald [30] who went out of office in January, had recommended the daughter of Governor deBaca,[31] his successor, to christen the ship. DeBaca (Dem) died a short time ago and was succeeded by the Lt. Gov. (a Republican).[32] Mr. J. said the new Governor proposed to displace Miss [Margaret C.] DeBaca & name his own daughter. I nipped that one in the bud by naming Miss DeBaca before new Governor could make recommendation. I am her deBacka [?].

Sent to the President draft of orders sent to men on armed ships this afternoon, embodying suggestions from Lansing which would omit statement of policy. At ten o'clock received instructions from President approved as amended, with a note in which he wished me to give orders that nothing should be given out & he would wish any officer court-martialed who gave out any hint of instructions.

Swanson urged graduating midshipmen who had three years.

Tuesday, March 13, 1917

At 6:30 signed instructions to Naval officers who command Armed Guard on merchant ships. Before doing so, submitted them to Attorney General &

[28] Captain John Hood, commander of the reserve force, Atlantic Fleet.
[29] Andrieus A. Jones, Democrat, First Assistant Secretary of the Interior, 1913–1916, newly elected U.S. Senator from New Mexico.
[30] William C. McDonald, Democrat, governor of New Mexico, 1913–1917.
[31] E. C. De Baca, Democrat, governor of New Mexico briefly in 1917.
[32] William E. Lindsey, Republican, De Baca's successor, 1917–1919.

talked with the President & Secy. Lansing over telephone[.] I signed ten copies which Palmer sent over to New York by officer. Benson, Roosevelt & I went over the instructions first. It was a rather solemn time, for I felt I might be signing what would prove the death warrant of young Americans and the arming of ships may bring us into war. To-night officers, armed with these instructions, started leaving admonished not to mention a word of their instructions.

No cabinet. President sick, but talked with him on phone

Adams,[33] of the Portsmouth Navy Yard, could build 10 sub-marines. He thought Dems. could elect successor of Cy Sulloway.[34] Talked to Hollis.[35]

Plans for organizing motor boat flotilla.

Dined with Senator and Mrs. Newlands.[36] Frank B. Noyes[37] discussed censorship and how stupid it generally was. He thought Stone[38] ought not to have been re-elected Chmn. of Foreign Affairs [sic] while Newlands argued the other way. I said little.

War news & ships [?] & tariff

Wednesday, March 14, 1917

Opened bids to build Scout-cruisers and had long conference with ship builders. "I almost wish the old man had not died."

Roosevelt, Benson & the ships for patrol service—

Miss Boyle O Reilly,[39] just from Russia. Here to write preparedness articles for Scripps McRae league of papers. She could not conceal her deep feelings, as she said, that this country was being made the pawn of England in this war. "But this is not the great war   Oh no the great war will come later when Russia, Germany, Japan & Turkey will unite against England, France & the U.S. Already a great Russian had informed her that the big gun was in the making in Japan for "this great war."

Dined with Russian Ambassador, Nona [?] McAdoo[40] and her Russian betrothed. Had quite a talk with Mr. [blank] who had lived years in Russia. He said: ["]Russia like America is democratic. The autocracy is a myth." He quoted President of great Russian University as saying to him the two coun-

[33] Commander Laurence S. Adams, industrial manager, Portsmouth Navy Yard.

[34] Cyrus A. Sulloway, Republican, U.S. Representative from New Hampshire, who had died on March 11.

[35] Henry F. Hollis, Democrat, U.S. Senator from New Hampshire.

[36] Francis G. Newlands, Democrat, U.S. Senator from Nevada.

[37] President of the Washington *Evening Star*.

[38] William J. Stone, Democrat, U.S. Senator from Missouri, chairman of the Senate Committee on Foreign Relations.

[39] Mary Boyle O'Reilly, social worker and foreign correspondent in Europe, 1913–1917.

[40] Nona H. McAdoo, daughter of the Treasury Secretary, was engaged to Ferdinand de Mohrenschildt, second secretary of the Russian Embassy.

tries had more in common than any other two. I was doubtful. Just while we were talking, the Russian Revolution was going on and the Duma was deposing the Tzar, who was supposed to be under German influence.

Thursday, March 15, 1917

Had conference with ship-builders. Agreed to build battle cruisers on 10% profit with overhead charges and rental for ships & shops to be fixed by a Board of Naval officers. I hated to do this, knowing the danger of overhead and rental being fixed at too high figure but in the emergency nothing else to do.

Went to luncheon with Gen Gorgas [41] at Cosmos club to meet Dr F [blank] who had just returned from Germany (came with Gerard) where he had been since the war began. Has seen much of prison life in Germany & helped to ameliorate conditions. He said the treatment of prisoners depended upon the temperament of the officer—if he was kind, it was tolerable, if a martinet it was hard. Instanced that prisoners were allowed to buy whiskey in German canteen. If they became drunk, they were put in prison three months. He told them they had no right to such rigorous punishment if they allowed men to get liquor. They were so miserable some would drink to drown their sorrows.

Conference with Lansing, Gregory, Baker & Polk on German ships at Phila. "I would not believe any German of [blank]— The easiest man in the world to fool is a German officer" said L.

Night at home. Gilson Gardner [42] & ———— representative of Scripps McRae league of papers called. He wanted to enlist for 3 weeks & write the story of life in the Navy.

Friday, March 16, 1917

Swanson called. Grayson—a good navigator— [43]

[41] Major General William C. Gorgas, Surgeon General, U.S. Army.

[42] Washington correspondent of the Newspaper Enterprise Association.

[43] When Wilson entered the White House he selected as his personal physician a Navy surgeon, Lt. Cary T. Grayson. Grayson proved to be both a capable physician and a devoted friend. In 1915, Wilson asked Daniels if there was anything he could "properly and legitimately do to set forward" Grayson's chances of promotion. (Wilson to Daniels, July 2, 1915, Daniels MSS.) When Congress authorized the rank of rear admiral for two members of the Navy Medical Corps, Daniels recommended the appointment of Grayson and William C. Braisted, already an acting rear admiral by virtue of his position as Surgeon General. In Grayson's case the promotion meant a considerable jump in rank over the heads of 127 older, senior officers. The appointment of Grayson to be a rear admiral in August, 1916, brought angry Republican charges of favoritism by Wilson and an attempt by Senator Henry Cabot Lodge and others to block Senate confirmation of the appointment. Wilson was adamant, however, and with skillful support from Senator Claude A. Swanson of the Naval Affairs Committee, Grayson finally was confirmed.

Barney Baruch—copper. Saw Baker. Thinks plunderbund [?] will reduce price one half for Army & Navy.[44]

Council of National Defense. Lane wished telegram sent to Daniel Willard [45] (Pres of B&O) to confer with Brotherhood to try to end strike.[46] This would have been equivalent to taking side of RR owners against the employees. Amended to send Lane & Wilson of National Council & Willard & Gompers of Advisory Commission to New York to confer with both sides. At cabinet the President, not yet well, talked of the threatened strike & the difficulty of doing anything. He said R.R. owners declined proposition last fall when employees accepted. They had carried Adamson law to Supreme Court, & might have averted the trouble. He said he had no influence with them & most [of] them would not be open to reason. But he added that was no justification for the brotherhood at this time to engage in a strike & tie up business, particularly since the country was in critical position. Said also the strike leaders had told him last fall they must strike then or not at all, since the vote to strike would not late[r] give them power. Now they contend they can act on old strike vote.

Eberle—Civilian head of Department of English.[47]

Dr. Grayson came over after commission which President had signed.

Houston: I want a leader [?]

Saturday, March 17, 1917

Had conference with Press Asso. men about censorship. Baker present. Noyes & others wished to save us from the stupidity that was practised in English censorship. They wished a civilian at head of censorship, & protested against military censorship.

In England, censor cut out "The Captains and the Kings depart." In

[44] Both the Army and the Navy were seeking to obtain large stocks of copper at this time, and Baker and Daniels were disturbed over the prospect of having to pay greatly inflated prices. Spot copper, for example, was selling for as much as thirty-seven cents a pound. Working through Baruch, who appealed to the patriotism of the copper suppliers, the two services were able to get copper at sixteen and two-thirds cents a pound, a figure based on the average price of the ten years preceding the war.

[45] President of the Baltimore and Ohio Railroad and a member of the Advisory Commission of the Council of National Defense.

[46] The Railroad Brotherhoods were threatening to strike on March 17 over the failure to implement the Adamson Eight Hour Act of 1916.

[47] Captain Edward W. Eberle, superintendent of the Naval Academy, was opposed to Daniels' proposal to appoint a civilian professor as head of the English department at Annapolis. In an attempt to strengthen instruction in the humanities at the academy, however, Daniels overrode objections by Eberle and other officers and brought in Dr. C. Alphonso Smith to head the English department. Smith, a distinguished scholar and former graduate dean at the University of North Carolina, did a good deal to raise academic standards at the Naval Academy after his appointment in 1917.

Spanish-American war, American censors made men say the opposite of what they did say, & Noyes protested to McKinley. Willing to [accept?] a voluntary censorship same as of law.

Oswald Garrison Villard [48] called to talk about censorship & then about pending bill. Said if bill passed he might go to jail. I replied: "In some circles, your being put in jail would be a very popular act."

Thomas Mott Osborne [49] came down at my request to further discuss prison reform in Naval Prisons. With Judge Advocate Watts,[50] we went over his recommendations. I had already upon his first report given orders not to put numbers on prisoners clothes, not to clip their heads, and one or two other reforms. We plan now to restore to the service those who show good qualities & discharge most of those who are not suited or demoralize good men. Watts had evolution. At first he felt whatever is is right, then came around & we will find him, I trust, an ally in the program to make navy prisons model prisons and have the best system of discipline and punishment in the Navy to be found anywhere.

Mr. Osborne came home with me.

Sunday, March 18, 1917

Went with boys to Mt. Vernon place Meth chr. Dirt for new building to be dug next week. All went to Granny's to dinner.

Letter from Miller [51] of N.Y. Times wishing information about condition of Navy. Are we ready? Gave answer. See my files.

Letter from Melville Stone protesting against censorship at Sayville.

Ships went out yesterday under armed guard, saluted by every ship in the harbor including German interned ships. Examined New York papers and not a reference to it though it was the best news story of the week. All by voluntary acquiescense in censorship.

Awful night. Three American ships reported to be torpedoed by German submarines.

Secretary Baker promised to go to University of North Carolina to deliver commencement address.

Monday, March 19, 1917

President called at Navy Department. I had asked to see him. He called on me. Wished everything possible done in addition to Armed Guards to

[48] President of the *New York Evening Post*, known for his progressive political views and interest in civil liberties.

[49] Prison reformer and former warden of Sing Sing Prison whom Daniels subsequently commissioned a lieutenant commander and put in charge of the naval prison at Portsmouth, New Hampshire.

[50] Captain William C. Watts, Judge Advocate General of the Navy.

[51] Charles R. Miller, editor-in-chief of the *New York Times*.

protect American shipping, hoping this would meet the ends we have in view. He had been urged to call Congress to declare war. He still hoped to avoid it and wished no cost & no effort spared to protect shipping, putting efficiency above prudence in the usual meaning of prudence. I asked Capt. Oliver [52] to learn what English were doing to stop or lessen sub-marine warfare. I told the President I would call General Board to consider every method to protect our shipping, it being paramount, and send him their report. He was gratified that the strike had ended as it had—eight hour law being upheld. Approved working over eight hours in emergency, his approval being necessary. Strongly approved my plans of putting educators rather than officers at head of non-military studies at Annapolis.

Speaking of Arias [?], knew an old woman in Conn who was a nuisance. Is she ill? "Yes." Are you her Doctor? Yes! Well, if your physic fails to cure her there will be no criticism or complaint.

Lincoln Steffens: [53] Opposed our going into Haiti & Santo Domingo. After visit there, said we could not withdraw and our presence now was necessary. Praised Admiral Knapp [54] who understood the dif. bet. intervention and keeping order so that natives may come into their own when able. Said at present each faction preferred America to the other faction.

Osborne—Board of Rehabilitation—Indeterminate sentence—

Josephus [?] went with Osborne to dinner & theatre.

Roosevelt: Should consult French & English.

Tuesday, March 20, 1917

Cabinet discussed: Shall Congress be called earlier than April? And what message shall be given? That was what was propounded by the President, who was grave. He pointed out that he had told Congress he did not believe Germany would do what it threatened; if so he would ask for power. G—— had. He had the power to put Armed Guard on ships & to use the Navy to protect. He needed no other power, unless we should go the final step and declare that Germany was waging war against us. He opposed G—— militarism on land and E's militarism on sea. Both were abhorrent. He was disinclined to the final break. Spoke of the glorious act of Russians, which, in a way, had changed conditions, but he could not give that as reason for war. Asked cabinet's view. All declared for war except B & I, & the President said: "Burleson, you & Daniels have not spoken." B—— said he thought we were already at war, & that unless President called Congress the people would force

[52] Rear Admiral James H. Oliver, director of Naval Intelligence.

[53] Joseph Lincoln Steffens, former muckraking journalist, now a free-lance writer and lecturer.

[54] Rear Admiral Harry S. Knapp, military governor of Santo Domingo, 1917–1918.

action. The Pres said "I do not care for popular demand. I want to do right, whether popular or not." It was a supreme moment in my life. I had hoped & prayed this cup would pass. But there was no other course opened, & I said our present attempt by Armed Guard could not be wholly effective & if it succeeded we must co-operate with English & let them convoy our ships while we patrolled this coast. Having tried patience, there was no course open to us except to protect our rights on the seas. If Germany wins, we must be a military nation.

President was solemn, very sad!!

Decided after talk with Baker & myself to put D[anish West Indies] islands under Navy.

Attended meeting of General Board & discussed how we could protect Am. lives & ships. Badger.

Baruch & copper. Gifford [55] & publicity.

Gov. Manning: [56] Time has come to go to war with Germany.

Wednesday, March 21, 1917

Frederick Palmer,[57] lectured on "Battle of the Somme," called. Hot for war and universal service.

Cal O'Lauchlin,[58] who was in Russia in Japanese war, predicted another Russian revolution. Did not think the Pro-German ministry dismissed would submit. They have big influence and will attempt to regain power. He thinks Germany will next make drive on Italy.

Admiral Oliver to go to new Danish islands—the President wanted a naval officer who had some statesmanship. Talked to Oliver whose views accord. Hope for civil government.

Polk showed me telegram (stopped from G) ordering the Geier (at Hawaii) to be put out of commission. Shall we withdraw Des Moines and Caesar from Alexandria? Sent there to bring Americans from Turkey, but permission could not be given. Navy says yes, but it might save Americans & to withdraw now might cause it to be torpedoed.

Roosevelt urged more motor boats to be used for patrol. Will order many, but are they valuable? How much of that sort of junk shall we buy? [59]

---

[55] Walter S. Gifford, former chief statistician of the American Telephone and Telegraph Company, now director of the Council of National Defense and Advisory Commission.

[56] Richard I. Manning, governor of South Carolina, 1915–1919.

[57] Author and journalist, recently returned from two years' service as a war correspondent with the British Army and Navy.

[58] John Callan O'Laughlin, Washington correspondent of the *Chicago Herald*.

[59] Assistant Secretary Roosevelt did not always see eye to eye with his chief, whom he considered too deliberate and inexperienced in nautical matters. With American entry into the war likely, Roosevelt was convinced that the Navy was not adequately prepared for anti-

Swanson urged calling for the 87,000 men now and the President asking for one million men, but no compulsory service.

Delay in Mississippi.[60] No!

Women to be enlisted in reserves for certain duties. First time in history of woman enlisted in the Navy.[61]

Thursday, March 22, 1917

President: The present Russian Ambassador Bakhmeteff tried to have Prof Milukov [62] removed as Professor. What will Milukov do to B? He must be uneasy.

When Benedict Arnold was given a roving commission to destroy he went South, met a N.C. man who was denouncing Arnold. "What" asked Arnold "would the people of N.C. do to Arnold if they captured him?" The unsuspecting N.C. said: "They would cut off the leg injured when he bravely followed Washington & give it an honorable burial. Then we would hang the balance of the d—— rascal." This apropos of seeing John Paul Jones' sword given by Willie Jones of N.C.

Mrs. W hangs on the President's stories & comments with enthusiasm. "Sweetheart"

McGowan: [63] Boy grad at Annapolis had impediment in his speech & McG urged he graduate and go in the pay corps. I demurred because of his infirmity of speech. McG "It would be better for the service if every paymaster was dumb.["]

"Including the Paymaster General" I replied & all laughed & McG said "You have one on me"

Friday, March 23, 1917

When cabinet met, the President, grave within, told several stories before proceeding to business. Hope was expressed that Russian revolution would be permanent. "It ought to be good" said W W with a smile, "because it has a professor at the head." He seemed—in fact—stated his pleasure—that America

---

submarine patrol duty. He accordingly conceived the idea of building hastily a number of small 50-foot motor patrol boats rather than the more elaborate 110-foot boats favored by the department. As this and subsequent entries indicate, Daniels and some of the senior officers of the department were highly skeptical of Roosevelt's small-boat plan.

[60] A dreadnaught-type battleship under construction by the Newport News Ship Building Company.

[61] To cope with mounting clerical work and free enlisted men for other duty, the Navy in 1917 broke precedent and accepted the enlistment of women as Yeomen (F) in the Naval Reserve. Ultimately some 11,000 women wore the uniform of the Yeomen (F) during the war.

[62] Paul N. Miliukov, new foreign minister in the Russian provisional government.

[63] Rear Admiral Samuel McGowan, Paymaster General of the Navy.

was the first nation to recognize the new Russian government. Crane [64] knew well the leading spirits & said they were men of ability and had the confidence of Russia.

Redfield, ought not to permit transfers from one Department to another. Small matter in time of great moment.

Burleson said it made him hot to read Gen. Wood's [65] fulminations. President spoke strongly of lack of loyalty by some Army & Navy officers. Said he came here without any prej[udice] vs Wood, but his conduct had been most reprehensible. Early in administration, W said [?] the Dems criticized R & the Reps criticized administration. Some members of cabinet asked Baker if Wood did anything but fulminate. "The most prodigiously busy man you ever saw" he replied. Asked if he had called his attention to impropriety. "Yes" he said with a smile, "and he always acknowledges receipt of my letter." All laughed, Baker leading

President said call for 87,000 men to fill up the Navy

Also use money for communications.

Talk with Vance McCormick [66] & F D R about spectacle of Gen Wood & Goethels saying America could be taken, had no army and no navy to defend itself. R defended Wood's propaganda. He ought to retire from the army and take the stump or observe military orders.

Lunched with Baruch & McCormick & talked about uniform prices & supplies by steel manufacturers.

Talked to Benson & Taylor about standardizing construction of destroyers. Gunner "creditable record." Should have a hearing—

Saturday, March 24, 1917

Council of National Defence met at 10 am. Advisory Commission urged compulsory military service of boys between 19 & 24. Nearly all favored it. Baker, Wilson & I had objection. I said it should be resorted to only as the last resource to protect American liberty—it was unAmerican. Not right to limit to boys & very young men, but to all who volunteer. Why should not men of 30 fight as well as boys of 21? It would inject a new question when Congress meets whereas the simple question should be a declaration that war exists & the President should be authorized to enlist 1,000,000 men in army if necessary and as many as needed in Navy. Would be unwise to inject compulsory service. Why introduce Prussianism to fight Prussianism?

[64] Charles R. Crane, Chicago manufacturer long interested in Russian affairs.

[65] Major General Leonard Wood, outspoken critic of the Wilson administration's inadequate preparedness program.

[66] Vance C. McCormick, newspaper publisher and chairman of the Democratic National Committee since 1916.

Conference with ship-builders to construct destroyers. 24 ordered on 10% basis. Did so only because of emergency.

Late in afternoon President and Mrs. Wilson called at Department—the first time she had been there. "Most beautiful office in W." She admired John Paul Jones' sword. President told of new head of affairs in Russia, Prof Milukov. Invited to lecture by Crane at Univ of Chicago. Could not speak English but promised to learn in a year. Attended meeting to plan reforms, put in jail for 1 yr, began to study English, & wrote his lectures in English, painfully, & then reflected that though he wrote English he could not speak it. Resolved to learn & asked & obtained 3 months from jail to go to England. Strange to say granted & in that time learned to speak English well. Returned, went into prison, had to break in. Obtained interview with Prime Minister, who after long talk, was so pleased with him, he offered him Minister of Education. Declined because he was not in sympathy with spirit of Government. And now he is the head of the Russian Gov.[67]

Sunday, March 25, 1917

Frank not well. Remained from church with him.

Admiral Palmer came at my request. President had last night signed an order increasing naval enlistment to 57,000 men. I decided to send telegram to every editor in America asking him to emphasize the need of this number of men and told Palmer to telegraph every recruiting station to increase their force and engage doctors to examine applicants so there would be no delay.

Fleet had been ordered North—D W B [68] here & he thought it was safer near Guantonimo [*sic*] than in C[hesapeake] bay. That was my personal idea & Benson agreed. But Gen. Bd. insisted it should come to our shores & public men & other officers had the same view. But I hate to see it come up—harder to protect than in Southern waters.

Pres. consulted about whether we should send Naval officers of high rank to England to study & co-operate to protect our merchant ships or ask them to send officers here. Decided to send H. B. W.[69] who becomes an Admiral in a few days. Must work with Navies of Nations to which our shipping goes.

F D R & 50 foot boats—his hobby. Good in smooth water. I fear buying a lot of junk.

Had long talk with Edwin LeFevre.[70]

[67] Daniels is confused here. Miliukov was the foreign minister, not the prime minister of the new Russian provisional government.

[68] Lieutenant Commander David W. Bagley, Daniels' brother-in-law.

[69] Captain Henry B. Wilson.

[70] Author and journalist.

Monday, March 26, 1917

Telegram to Mayo [71] to come to Washington. Also Sims [72] who will go to England.

Must take over Danish islands by Saturday. That country insists upon it before possible war with Germany.

Rodman [73]—angry. R[oosevelt] had urged 50 foot boats & Rodman had opposed & obtained information that 110[-foot] boats could be had.

4:30 p.m.   President came when I was being interviewed by the press. Took a seat & did not know he was present. Said we must keep in close touch. Had letter from McAdoo opposing taking German ships & anchoring them in midstream. Thought, inasmuch as Germans had tried to destroy ships, they were now derelicts & ought to be taken in charge by Marines to prevent sinking and injury.

Good to marry in the Navy—must be happy at least half of the time—for husband is away from home half of the time.

5 P.M.   The President showed me letter from E. M. H.[74] saying friend had informed him that Austrian had arrived on sub-marine—called upon Austrian consul who sent for Austrian Ambassador and gave him papers brought from Europe on sub-marine. He understood that two sub-marines had come over from Germany. I told Benson to send out All-Nav wireless to be on the outlook.

10 P.M.   Benson called up & said he had message from Usher two sub-marines had been sighted off Montauk Point. Inquiry found that no American submarines were in that vicinity. Army was informed & destroyers & motor boats sent out to locate and run down.

German sailors had oil & inflammable material in close proximity to cans of kerosene—50 automatic revolvers found in a barrel.

Tuesday, March 27, 1917

Cabinet. McAdoo wished German men on interned merchant ships taken off, believing when declaration of state of war was made they would blow them up & might injure docks & do great injury. Thought their action in Charleston & elsewhere justified taking this action. Lansing doubted the authority. Gregory thought the danger was magnified & thought no legal right now

---

[71] Rear Admiral Henry T. Mayo, commander-in-chief of the Atlantic Fleet.

[72] Rear Admiral William S. Sims, shortly to be appointed (April 28) commander of American naval operations in European waters, with headquarters in London.

[73] Captain Hugh Rodman, currently a member of the General Board.

[74] Edward M. House.

to take ships belonging to private citizens. McAdoo thought they were controlled by government of G. Gregory laughingly said "McAdoo wants those ships." I said we criticized Roosevelt for saying we ought to seize those ships. McAdoo said conditions had changed. The President firmly declared we would run any risk—we must be good sports & take our chances, & do nothing questionable & nothing that looking [*sic*] like profit for ourselves.

I brought up proposition for Navy to buy all wireless stations & make wireless a government monopoly.

Burleson: I serve notice that when peace comes it must be under PO Department.

President: Is that a threat or a prophecy

Daniels: It is a bluff or a boast.

Resolved to ask Congress for that authority

Redfield: "I think of getting off Council of Nato Defense—Talk & talk & do nothing[."]

Baker to Lansing: The talk of Germans going to Mexico is exaggerated

Germans left ships in Philadelphia & the 6 left behind had explosives, so they could have blown up ships and Navy Yard. Took them all off.

Wednesday, March 28, 1917

Telegram from Page in London enclosing recommendation from McDougall [75] advising converting ship with armed guard into naval auxiliary—it would then become a naval vessel & its officers & crews if captured would have the honors of war. Otherwise if taken, might be killed—treated as pirates by G—— Sent over by Lansing. I went over to see the President who said we had a right to put armed guards on ships & the piracy talk was absurd & if such spirit prevailed the change in character in ship would not avert it. Such change would prevent merchant ships carrying trade & prohibit contraband. Lansing said suggestion was absurd. Pres said "Page meddles in things outside his domain. I do not mind this if he gave us his own opinions but he is giving him [*sic*] English opinion. ["]

Conf. with Lansing & Baker. President wished us to confer as to protection if Cuba & Panama followed our lead as to Germany. Baker in Panama—Navy in Cuba—could send marines to Cuba. Baker would furnish transport & have soldiers at Galveston to send to Tampico if necessary

6 p.m. Went to Annapolis to present Diplomas to graduates. Asked the President to go. Said he wished to do so but did not like to go without saying something, and this was not a time to speak. "I would like to talk to the youngsters and incite them to splendid service, but now anything I might say

[75] Captain William D. MacDougall, naval attaché at the U.S. Embassy in London.

would be subject to being interpreted in a wrong way & I wish to say nothing until I give my message to Congress."

He could not speak unless he said something; therefore I could go as I could speak without saying anything.

Thursday, March 29, 1917

Annapolis

Slept late & had breakfast in bed. Had bad night. Had written speech but not satisfied with it and that made me restless. Made some notes & decided not to read speech even if I failed. Sun came out & Day was beautiful. Got along well for me & presented 180 diplomas. Spoke on "Get you a hero— Dewey." After exercises, visited site of proposed addition to Bancroft Hall & Ishewood Hall. Will enable us to accommodate 1,500 midshipmen.

Talked with Eberle about building a bridge across the river at Annapolis so as to utilize our land across the Severn. Crowded on this side—why not expand by tunnel or bridge in the only way Academy can expand. This worth looking into.

Benson received telephone that the submarines supposed to be on Montauk Point had turned out to be motor boats & that relieved us.

Talked to Roosevelt about not working on battle cruisers & putting all force on destroyers & small craft.

Sun Ship Yard Co (Mr. Pugh) [76] wished to continue building Merchant ships & do no navy building though it is needed. Will see him Monday.

Palmer & Ward: [77] To what ship do you go?

"I am forbidden to state."

Wertzbaugh [sic] —Record of Texas & his desire for cruiser.[78]

Friday, March 30, 1917

Telegram from McDougall about defective shells on St. Louis & injury to gun lining from explosion. Shells made in 1904 & were tested, & records show they were very good. Talked to Earle [79] who will at once test all shells and all guns. Never so depressed & troubled since in Washington.

[76] Probably Joseph N. Pew, Jr., an official of the Pew family firm, the Sun Shipbuilding and Drydock Company.

[77] Probably Ensign Hervey A. Ward.

[78] Commander Daniel W. Wurtsbaugh, at one time Daniels' personal aide (see entry of January 6, 1915), was currently second-in-command of the battleship *Texas* and evidently anxious to get his own command of a cruiser.

[79] Rear Admiral Ralph Earle, chief of the Bureau of Ordnance. The Navy gun crew aboard the S.S. *St. Louis* had damaged a gun with defective ammunition in practice firing.

Victor Blue [80] here—the truest of the true—Texas is E of ships. Says spirit of fleet is fine. Good treatment of men shows good results.

Swanson & Richmond delegation for projectile factory

Cabinet Meeting. President, grave, told an anecdote or two, and then spoke of the message to Congress he was writing. He stood up at his end of table & practiced calisthenics, saying he had been sitting at his desk writing all the morning and was stiff. Lane read several telegrams from Cal.[ifornia] saying sentiment was nearly all for war. President discussed the method of his presentation & the changed conditions since he addressed Congress. He wished to know if, in presenting the miasma of German enemies here he could safely trace them to the Embassy—not necessarily to Bernstoff,[81] but to others in Embassy. Von Papen,[82] Boy Ed [83] & others said L & G, & G added that men had been convicted in N.Y. for carrying out crimes against this country & paid for it by G—— Consuls.

He wished no argument and no feeling in his message, but wishes to present facts, convincing from evidence, justifying position. McAdoo thought all crimes of G's should be set forth to arouse & stir the people. Redfield told of how 6 chauffe[u]rs had sought places with a woman who talked German & every one said: "And are you, too, true to the Fatherland?" The President recounted some of the absurd stories told of what G's were doing. "There's a German in the cellar" said White House house-keeper referring to inoffensive German employed in White House to tend the fires. "I'd rather the blamed place should be blown up than to persecute inoffensive people.["]

Would hold places for Gov employees.

Baker & I: Have efficiency keen in war. [?] Be cold blooded.

Saturday, March 31, 1917

Council of National Defense. Mr [blank], correspondent in Russia of London Times, urged that Americans offer to take over Siberian Ry as the greatest help to enemies [?] of Germany. He fears German submarines will prevent shipment of arms through Baltic & road from Archangel may be closed & Russia's only chance of help will come from Americans over Siberian Ry, 5,800 mi. long. It is in bad condition & poorly managed. Russians were armed

[80] Captain Victor Blue, Daniels' first appointment as chief of the Bureau of Navigation (see entry of March 24, 1913), currently commander of the battleship *Texas*.

[81] Count Johann H. von Bernstorff, the German Ambassador.

[82] Captain Franz von Papen, former German military attaché.

[83] Captain Karl Boy-Ed, former German naval attaché. In December, 1915, the United States had demanded the recall of von Papen and Boy-Ed for their flagrant espionage and other hostile activities in the United States.

with different kinds of guns and there is opinion this & Ry was due as much to treachery as to incompetence. Why hasn't [sic] England and France helped? They had their handfuls [sic] and pro-Germans appealed to ingrained prejudice of England. Hard to overcome. People do not read papers & England is sending films showing what England is doing in war. Russia would welcome us. [?] Fears a German drive might enable them to take Petrograd and with Russia disabled, the only hope of victory would be by American troops to take place of Russians.

Com. named to look after nitrates in Chili.

Plan to have Board to look into purchases and get uniform prices and speed for Army and Navy & to standardize.

Present when $25,000,000 paid to Minister from Denmark for islands.

Advisory Council met & discussed estimates. Hope Congress will vote a lump sum so can be used for the pressing needs.

Baruch & Coffin [84] & I talked steel. Gary [85] had written 3.50 for plates we paid 2.90 for. I wrote too high.

Dined with Japanese Ambassador.[86] Col. Thompson said Red Cross objected to Navy League raising money to help families of sailors who enlisted.

Sunday, April 1, 1917

Had talk with Admiral Fletcher about Armor plate plant.[1] He will go to Richmond at Senator Swanson's request.

Heard Bishop Cranston.[2] All sins require blood atonement. Abraham offer-

---

[84] Howard E. Coffin, vice-president of the Hudson Motor Company, and a member of the Advisory Commission of the Council of National Defense and the Naval Consulting Board.
[85] Elbert H. Gary, chairman and chief executive officer of the United States Steel Corporation.
[86] Aimaro Sato.

---

[1] After a long battle Daniels had secured congressional authorization for the Navy to construct its own plant for the manufacture of armor plate. Both Daniels and Senator Tillman were convinced that the Navy had long paid too high a price for its armor plate, and that a Navy plant would be a useful yardstick in dealing with the three private suppliers. This entry refers to Daniels' appointment of Rear Admiral Frank F. Fletcher, a member of the General Board, as head of a committee to find a suitable site for the plant. Ultimately the committee selected Charleston, West Virginia, and construction of the plant began in August, 1917. Because of the relatively low priority given to the construction of heavy capital ships during the war, however, the armor plate facilities were never fully completed, though the Charleston plant did manufacture some steel and shells. Under the Harding administration the Navy abandoned further development of the plant, much to Daniels' unhappiness.
[2] Dr. Earl Cranston, retired Methodist bishop in Washington.

ing Isaac, the Passover in Egypt, the Crucifixion—is America to make sacrifice for good of the world.

Call at Department of Justice to talk about espionage bill and penalties for printing incorrect news & for wilful mis-statements. Suggested conference between him and committee of N.E.A.[3] who wished act drawn so as to catch men guilty but not to get in the net men who were not guilty. Will see him Monday morning. He showed me telegram from Dist Atty in New York saying three disabled Germans at Tottenville (Staten Island) could be sunk to impede channel. Admiral Usher suggested they should be moved to 133rd Street. Later I talked with McAdoo who urged it. Baker has authority to fix places for ships in navigable streams.

Took long ride with David & Mrs. B——[agley]

Requested by Edgar Harris[4] to speak in Petersburg for enlistment. Could not go.

Lane   Page 243

Monday, April 2, 1917

Went with committee of editors to see Attorney General about press censorship bill. They feared it was too drastic. Later in the day, with Baker and Polk, had talk with editors about censorship. We wish to censor as little as possible.

Baker called with Mr. Scott,[5] head of Board to secure munitions and supplies more rapidly & with right priority. I named a committee to act with others. It looks to a Commission of Munitions & Supplies

President called during meeting of Council—he had heard Navy intended to take over German merchant ships and search them. Message had come to Collector Malone[6] that naval officer said Navy would do this. Members of Cabinet & others had urged this but President had taken the ground that ships belonged to German private citizens & we must save them. Report was error, but I telegraphed to all places where German ships were and instructed not to board them.

8:30 went up to hear the President's speech on Germany making war on us. Distinguished body, diplomats on the floor, Supreme Court, & galleries filled. Addie up there. Jonathan got in through kindness of Kitchin. President grave and serious but dominated by feelings he was standing for human

[3] Newspaper Enterprise Association, a wire service to over one hundred daily newspapers.

[4] Possibly Walter Edward Harris, publisher of the Petersburg *Index-Appeal*.

[5] Frank A. Scott, Cleveland industrialist, chairman of the new Purchasing Board of the Council of National Defense, subsequently chairman of the successor General Munitions Board and the War Industries Board.

[6] Dudley Field Malone, Collector of the Port of New York.

rights. Said he did not want Capitol guarded by soldiers but it was done.

Went to Department and heard about sinking of Astec [7]—Lt Gresham [8] & boys on Dolphin [9] safe.

Tuesday, April 3, 1917

Council of National Defense. Advisory Council suggested a Board of Censors —No—Baker suggested motion not to let labor lose what it had gained. Speeding up could not last if labor had too long hours.

Talked with Oulahan [10] and others about a law to give us censorship.

Lunch at Shoreham—Alderman [11] with us, Univ of Va aflame with patriotism. Talked with Lane about getting new Interior Department. He said "No," but would let us use the land office.

Cabinet. Discussed what to do with German ships in American ports— McAdoo wished to take them. 700,000 tons of shipping would help make up for what G—— had sunk. Hard to tell which Department had authority & responsibility. Finally decided G—— sailors (Reservists) should be removed by Secy. Wilson to Ellis island. President said it offended him to see people covet these ships—America must set an example of splendid conduct of war. He said it was remarkable what stories people would believe, instancing that many people in Canada do not believe Kitchener [12] was drowned, but that he was taken away because he was a failure.

President said munition makers must give reasonable rates or we would take them over. Give orders at fair prices & invoke the law.

Told me the applause in capitol grated on him because he felt the gravity & seriousness of the situation & the necessity make applause far from his feeling. George Creel.

Wednesday, April 4, 1917

Ordered Bliss Torpedo Company [13] to make torpedoes at $7700 instead of $9,500 under new act.

[7] An American merchant ship sunk by German submarine the day before with a loss of twenty-eight lives.

[8] Lt. William F. Gresham, commander of the Navy armed guard on the *Aztec*, commended for his heroism in the action.

[9] U.S.S. *Dolphin*, a small gunboat, formerly Daniels' yacht now assigned to the Atlantic Fleet.

[10] Richard V. Oulahan, Washington correspondent of the *New York Times*.

[11] Edwin A. Alderman, president of the University of Virginia and chairman of the Board of Visitors to the Naval Academy; an old friend of Daniels'.

[12] Horatio H. Kitchener, First Earl Kitchener of Khartoum and Broome, Secretary of State for War until lost at sea June 5, 1916, in the sinking of the cruiser *Hampton*.

[13] The E. W. Bliss Company, the major private supplier of torpedoes for the Navy.

Telegraphed Judge Gary requesting him to come to W to consult about steel prices.

R—— wrote letter about 110 foot boats roasting Griffin [14] and Taylor. He wants 50 foot boats. I saw Capt. Henry Wilson and he said he would not waste public money building 50 foot boats. Interview with R, G & T not very agreeable. Left a bad taste in the mouth.

Braisted—crowded at Great Lakes Training Station

Jared Y. Sanders,[15] of La, called & we recalled when I went to Louisiana to study their constitutional convention.[16] Gen Estoppinol [17] & New Orleans Navy Yard. Senator Broussard [18] trying to get credit—

Thursday, April 5, 1917

Senator Tillman: What are you going to do for Charleston out of the 18 million.

"You are stubborn as a mule" he said [19]

Lane [20] & Rogers, of Bliss & Co. torpedo works, accepted order at $2¼ mil less than they had bid after I let them know they must make at decreased prices or I would take them over

12:30   By his request went to see Vice President who is deeply interested in Armor plant at Evansville. We were hurt in campaign by charge that too much had been done for the South & it would be good for the party and the country to locate plant at Evansville.

Redfield: Coast Survey to come into the Navy

6:30   Talked to Baruch about steel. He is fine & thought it ought to be settled at once & while thinking 3:30 a good price & fair felt the importance of securing 2.90 if possible.[21]

Roosevelt & Howe (Board on Compensation) [22]

[14] Rear Admiral Robert S. Griffin, chief of the Bureau of Steam Engineering.

[15] Democrat, U.S. Representative from Louisiana.

[16] Sanders was a prominent member of the Louisiana constitutional convention of 1898 which effectively disfranchised the Negro. Daniels, who was active in a similar fight in North Carolina at that time, had followed the Louisiana developments with interest.

[17] General Albert Estopinal, Democrat, U.S. Representative from Louisiana and member of the House Naval Affairs Committee, with a pork barrel interest in the New Orleans Navy Yard.

[18] Robert F. Broussard, Democrat, U.S. Senator from Louisiana.

[19] Senator Tillman's paternal concern for the development of the Charleston, S.C., Navy Yard was notorious.

[20] James W. Lane, president of the E. W. Bliss Company.

[21] Daniels was determined to prevent profiteering at Navy expense during the war. In this instance he held out for a preferred price of 2.9 cents a pound for steel plates.

[22] To make advancements to shipbuilders and otherwise supervise payments for the vast naval construction program during the war, Daniels created a Compensation Board headed by Rear Admiral Washington I. Capps, an experienced naval constructor.

Friday, April 6, 1917

Mr. Farrell,[23] president Steel corporation, called by appointment. Had long talk. He finally agreed to reduce from 3.30 to 3 if we could settle to-day and he would guarantee all our needs for a year. Other concerns unwilling to come in but his committee could secure help of others or furnish all plates &c. from their own plants. Talked it over in Cabinet. McAdoo, Redfield, Lane & others thought 3¢ very good and we ought not to press for lower price. The President felt that we should stand for .0290. After cabinet I saw Farrell again & told him it was .0290 & he agreed & I figured it would save $18 mil from current prices.

Burleson proposed excluding papers from the mail, papers that criticized. Lansing thought no papers should be printed in German. B—— opposed. I said you have made a net that will catch the innocent & most Germans will be loyal. President spoke strongly against action that was more than moderate. Baker & I agreed that there should be no censorship of opinion or comment, only to exclude publication of military news that would aid the enemy.

Wilson reported Germans had been taken off ships & put in Ellis island.

Saw Col. Thompson about Navy League & Red Cross

Spoke with Baker at Red Cross meeting

McCandless [24] signal "War" & message sent out

Saturday, April 7, 1917

Arrangements made to see English and French Admirals to discuss best plan of co-operation.[25]

R—— brought in request from Norfolk to work 12 hours. Declined to approve it.

Council of National Defense. Resolution adopted not to disturb labor conditions but to continue 8 hours except when emergency demands otherwise (see proceedings). Resolution passed to request Hoover [26] to head committee on Food problems.

F D R wanted me to sign order for Winslow [27] to come here to assist him.

[23] James A. Farrell, president of the United States Steel Corporation.

[24] Lt. Byron McCandless, Daniels' personal aide at this time, who semaphored the news across the street to the department as soon as President Wilson signed the war resolution.

[25] A reference to the forthcoming visit of the British and French missions to discuss American participation in the war.

[26] Herbert C. Hoover, prominent engineer and Commissioner for Relief in Belgium; chairman of the food committee of the Council of National Defense, April–August, 1917; thereafter U.S. Food Administrator until June, 1919.

[27] Rear Admiral (Ret.) Cameron M. Winslow, former commander-in-chief of the Pacific Fleet.

Declined[.] should [?] not have a retired Rear Admiral for such service. Had long talk with B[enson] at night. He thought it was aimed at him & R wanted W——— to advise as to operations. No division of power as to operations.

Decided to ask all ships to aid & to hurry up work

Sunday, April 8, 1917

Went to church. Dr. Wood preached. Dr. Johnson asked if sermon did not convince him of truth of resurrection. "Yes, but I would like more evidence." Can we receive messages from the dead? Sir Oliver Lodge [28] lost his son, Raymond at Ypres. Brilliant man & father idolized him. His father received message "pledge [?] my head and heart thrice. There is a Christ. Cannot describe his raiment &c.["] (See Lodges book "Raymond")

Went down to Department, read telegrams, went over to Interior Department buildings & examined room in one building. Cramped quarters.

Saw Admiral McGowan about commissions in Pay Department—not all from D.C., but must be divided between States.

Saw Admiral Taylor about rushing 110 foot boats & about plan for hastening work on ships being built on profit plus.

Saw Homer Cummings about Sharp property at New London. Thinks Navy will need it or should buy it. Talked about story of Electric Boat Company

Worth's Birthday

Monday, April 9, 1917

Lansing & Baker—more room.

5 p.m. Saw the President. Decided to approve the site of armor plate factory recommended by the Board—Charleston, W Va.

Named the 5 battle cruisers after famous ships of early era.

Talked about censorship. He will appoint George Creel as head.

Talked about Com. of Munitions. Would Baruch do? Yes, I said. He is somewhat vain. President: Did you ever see a Jew who was not? Told story about North Carolinian—how he would bury Benedict Arnold.

Benson went down on steamer to meet English & French Admirals at Old Point with Mayo & Wilson, to discuss best method of co-operation. R wished to go down to meet them as honor. I said no. He did not like it but—

Knauss,[29] first of the armed guard, to get back from England. He went

---

[28] Sir Oliver J. Lodge, principal of the University of Birmingham and author of a number of books on psychical phenomena, including *Raymond, or Life and Death* (London and New York, 1916).

[29] Lieutenant Harrison E. Knauss.

over and came back on St. Louis. One submarine sunk 40 mi S & one 120 mi N. Germans determined to get his boat. Defective shells discovered & injured gun. Might have lost ship by reason. Jellico [30] said, "If a sub-marine had found you, you would not have known what hit you[."]

Tuesday, April 10, 1917

Representatives of W.R. Grace & Co. called and wished to sell us 2 dreadnaughts belonging to Argentina which is hard up for money. Would also sell destroyers if Chile & Brazil would sell part of theirs so as not to disturb the balance of strength. Took matter up in cabinet & President thought we ought not to buy.

Call from Capt. I. Mishtowt,[31] Russian Naval Attache, who asked us to send destroyers, trawlers &c over to help Russia. Said transportation was bad & whereas 100 cars a day were handled a year ago now they could handle only 30.

Should Germans, not citizens be naturalized now. W. B. Wilson read a letter from a German, who wrote he had not taken out papers because he had a father & brother & Sister in Germany & he was a reservist in G—— & would be regarded as traitor if he became citizen & therefore could not visit then. Now he was for the U.S. & wished to be naturalized.

Named the new 5 battle-cruisers

Knauss & wife took dinner with us.

Armor plate plant. V.P. was very much upset as he had his heart set upon Evansville, Indiana. Said Indiana had no chance &c &c.

Wednesday, April 11, 1917

Conference with Lansing and Lane about taking over coast wise ships to carry goods to Europe. Lane favored, thinking railroads would carry freight at reasonable rates. New Orleans people say they cannot secure cars now.

Ambassador Spring Rice called with Vice Admiral Browning [32] & Admiral Grasset,[33] who had come to talk over our co-operation with the Navies of their countries. In the afternoon at General Board headquarters we had long conference. Admiral B—— presented the requests of the Admiralty—to patrol the Atlantic Coast, send destroyers off the Irish coast, & otherwise work together. Admiral G—— wished the same, but thought the destroyers should be sent to France & earnestly desired other small craft which F greatly needs.

---

[30] Admiral Sir John R. Jellicoe, First Sea Lord and subsequently chief of naval staff of the British Admiralty.

[31] Captain I. V. Mishtowt.

[33] Vice Admiral Sir Montague E. Browning, a member of the visiting British mission.

[33] Rear Admiral R. A. Grasset of the visiting French mission.

O for more destroyers! I wish we could trade the money in dreadnaughts for destroyers already built.

Told Grace & Co we would consider buying destroyers but not dreadnaughts.

Creel came over & helped me & Baker & I will try to get Department of Information going.

McGowan & Geo. Daniels [34] for pay corps.

Armor plate plant located at Charleston W Va

Page 244 Lane

Thursday, April 12, 1917

Council of National Defense. Shall we take ships off coast wise trade to send them on trips to carry cargoes to Europe? Aeroplane 2 yr program

I had tentatively agreed to send colliers to carry rails to France where they are greatly needed. The President thinks better that we send to Chile for nitrates so that farmers may have fertilizer. Shall we send destroyers to England & France.

Baker & I sent letter to W. W. as to Committee of Publicity, & suggested appointment of George Creel. He approved his appointment but waits for the method & the pay.

Dinner at Mr. Hewsons [35]   (He married Mrs. Schofield)

Gen Kuhn,[36] who spent 2 years in Germany, expected Germany to fall by Apr. 1. Thinks it cannot hold out very much longer because people lack food. The stomach is the test.

Lane Pg 246

Friday, April 13, 1917

Cabinet. Lane had letter from Ala. quoting statute that any person who furnished intoxicants to an Indian was guilty of a crime & that Mr Wilson was an Indian & the President violated the law when he served wine at White House dinner.

Pres. agreed that I at once order work on German war ships. They are damaged and cannot easily be put in commission. The officers evidently intended to make it impossible to use them.

Knight [37] telegraphed from China he would intern ships. We ordered him (Lansing & I) not to intern without specific orders. We have prevented revolu-

[34] Daniels' nephew, George S. Daniels, who desired a commission in the Navy Pay Corps. See entry of May 18, 1917.
[35] John H. Hewson.
[36] Brigadier General Joseph E. Kuhn.
[37] Admiral Austin M. Knight, commander-in-chief of the Asiatic Fleet.

tion in China & protected people, & hope still to do so. Japs may demand to go in if we stay. Delicate question.

President appointed George Creel as chief of Information & Lansing, Baker & I to control. Creel went to L to sign letter whereupon, L wanted it written on State Dept. paper & he sign first. Precedence!

Talked to Portuguese Minister [38] who said shipping was dangerous on his coast by means of sub-marine warfare.

We allowed Italy & Russia to take out fast boats we had need of.

Littman & School of Journalism

Saturday, April 14, 1917

Baker about rooms. Lane willing to fix up the War Dept but not willing to let War Department have room to conduct war.

Oulahan called to ask about report of shells and guns on the St. Louis. His managing editor had the story & felt like printing it. At night I called up Oulahan and urged it be not printed because of bad effect on the other side.

Sims sent telegram from Great Britain—so confidential he sent it in the State Department secret code. Feared it might help the enemy's moral[e] if known. It will be delivered to-morrow.

Shall we send the Caesar [39] home from Alexandria?

Letter from Capt of Scorpion [40] complaining that the Ambassador wished him to stay when he would do no good

Talked to co-editor of Parisian—able man   Happy over to-day's legislation.[41] Shows this country has ideals & a soul. His name is Georges Lechartier, of the staff of the Petit Parisien et au Journal Des Debats. Owner was bailiff who married widow who owned the paper.

Dinner at French Embassy to meet Vice Admiral Grasset & others. Mrs. J——[42] talked about E's slow going into war. President of France asked King of England to say they were going in but would not say anything.

The Ambassador toasted the Navy & I replied.

J—— showed copy of order issued by German commander at Liege & threatening to shoot any who did not do the will of German officers. Horrible. It boasted of the killing of 110 in village they had taken.

[38] Viscount de Alte.
[39] A small fuel supply ship.
[40] A small converted yacht regularly stationed at Constantinople for the use of the American Ambassador, at this time Abram I. Elkus.
[41] The House of Representatives had approved the $5,000,000,000 war revenue bond bill, with suitable expressions of solidarity with the Allies.
[42] Elise R. Jusserand, the wife of the French Ambassador, Jules J. Jusserand.

Sunday, April 15, 1917

Mr. Bryan took dinner with us. He opposed war but when his country spoke, he telegraphed his readiness to serve. He refuses to discuss any of the President's policies—"If I discuss those I approve" he said "I must discuss the others. And at this time I wish not to say anything except to serve in the way I can do so best." He begins a lecture tour in California soon and will urge all the people to plant big crops, economize, and serve the country. He hopes democracy will come in Germany and hasten close of war. Twelve years ago after visit to Russia, he predicted it would be the first country in Europe to become a Republic.

Talked to Lansing about China & interning our ships. He hopes China will enter the war so our ships & Englands will have free access. In the meantime, manana—playing for time. He saw no reason for keeping Des Moines and Caesar at Alexandria, & orders were sent for them to come home

Benson learned that German sub-marines were on our coast & we wired all ships secretly to be on their guard, & directed that no merchant ship leave any port until after dark and sail without any lights. His information convinces him of danger.

Took Worth to train

Monday, April 16, 1917

George Creel came down to take chg. The press generally cheered [?], but some plutocratic papers snarled.

Mr. Willard called about ships to France and whether we could place guns on them. Ships from coast wise trade must be withdrawn & taken into ocean traffic.

A delegation of sailors from the French ship at Annapolis called at the White House & telephoned to see if they could come to the Navy Department. Yes. They came over with a French woman who lives here. Fine fellows, some young and some middle aged[.] Pleased to see John Paul Jones's sword & remembered he lived in France. Later Vice Admiral Grasset & staff called to thank & to ask for ships to patrol at Brest and Bordeaux. He was astonished when he learned that the sailors had been received by the Minister of Marine in his office! I told him France & America not only preached Democracy but practised it also.

Capt. Gerardi [43] (naval attache to Germany) told me remarkable story.

[43] Commander Walter R. Gherardi.

Admiral von Holtzendorf,[44] Chief of Admiralty staff, wrote letter in Jan. saying if given full rein with submarines he could make England sue for peace by August. Hindenberg [45] sent his chief of staff to the front & reported it was impossible for his troops to advance. Then & then only Hindenberg approved & the Emperor wrote "Approved" on von Holtzendorf's letter & the submarine warfare began. Von H had kept submarines on bottom of sea and had reported how many ships they could have sunk. If they cannot starve England by August, what will G—— do? They will fight to the last, said G——

Tuesday, April 17, 1917

10 a.m. Meeting with Lansing and Baker and Creel & Polk in L's office to talk about censorship. "We know nothing about it" said L & P "Let us ask England to send an experienced man. Page says they are willing to do so." All mail to South America should be censored, said L. "The Germans have subsidized S. American papers. We should do the same." Idea of L & P was for following E's plan to create a great censorship, touching all countries to the South of us and Europe—to cost millions of Dollars. Not so B & I, & later we talked to the President who said he wished nobody brought over from E—— & did not wish C'sorship to be big

Presided at National Council. Doctors (eminent ones) presented resolutions for continence and for prohibition around military and naval camps. They had previously declared for national prohibition. Mr. Fisher [46] gave statement. Council of National Defense.

W. W. How the English mind works—In Oxford wished to buy single ticket to hear one lecture & not whole course. Could not let him have one. He walked in with speaker & sat on stage.

Padgett & Swanson. Not so many promotions as Navigation recommends. Ran wild & would make bad impression

Presided at Woman's Miss. Conf. Jubilee Met Meth Ch. [?]

Lord Balfour [47] coming. "I believe in a personal God to which I can pray & who answers prayers.["]

A practical statesman with touch of mysticism

Pres said: "Let Destroyers go to other side[."]

---

[44] Admiral Baron Holzendorf, German submarine expert.

[45] Field Marshal Paul von Hindenburg, German army chief of staff.

[46] Probably Irving Fisher, professor of political economy at Yale and prominent prohibitionist, chairman of the subcommittee on alcohol of the Council of National Defense, 1917–1918.

[47] Arthur J. Balfour, British foreign secretary and former prime minister, head of a British commission en route to the United States to discuss American participation in the war.

Wednesday, April 18, 1917

C. Alphonzo Smith: Eberle had written him that Raby [48] was doing very well and &c. Preferred he should not come. S—— disturbed. I told him to wait till Board of Visitors made their report & teachers of experience wd be named.

Council of National Defense. Shall we have a body of women? How to select them & shape their work. W said unless what they did was mapped out there wd be trouble. Ships? Shall we build battle cruisers or postpone them & build only destroyers and merchant ships? Will wait to see Shipping Board [49] &c

B. M. Baruch—Some conflict. Munitions Board should [?] be named to fix prices. Unless he has authority, how can prices be fixed & people know he had the right specialty [?].

McGowan & Paymasters—

Watt, Palmer & promotions—Padgett & Swanson

Burleson: Wireless should be made government monopoly—He wants it to go to PO Dept

Benson: What course shall we (the Navy) take in the war. He thought some policy should be pursued by which subs were retained in German waters. Discussed the use of German war ships at Phila——

R[oosevelt] & steel ships to be made by concern making structural steel, & keels as with wooden ships—

Edison [50] thinks he can put bouys [*sic*] (containing 2 or 3 men) to detect submarines &c

Thursday, April 19, 1917

Council of National Defense. Resolution of doctors for continence and temperance, for zones where bad women & liquor will not be allowed, came up. I moved its adoption & Redfield seconded. Lane wanted to postpone. Baker had found publicity in such matters not desirable & wanted a statement prepared before voting. Wilson doubted attitude [?], I think, of Labor. Houston favored   Postponed till Saturday.

Long talk with Scripps-McRae league editors who wanted to send an army to France or something done to stir up our people.

[48] Commander James J. Raby, current head of the English department at the Naval Academy. See entry of March 16, 1917.

[49] The U.S. Shipping Board, created by the Shipping Act of August, 1916, to purchase, construct, and operate ships so as to increase the size and effectiveness of the American merchant marine.

[50] Thomas A. Edison, president of the Naval Consulting Board, created by Daniels in 1915 to advise the Navy on anti-submarine research and other naval problems. See entry of June 30, 1915.

Saunders[51] of Naval Civilian Consultive Board, talked about Board—whether I approved what it was doing &c &c. I did not want it a gov-board. One reason: Some of its ablest members sell to the government. Should have no responsibility.

Prohibition—up to the President.[52]

C Alphon[so] Smith—& Eberle.

Cablegram from Sims who seemed to feel Great Britain had done all possible against submarines

Friday, April 20, 1917

Overman's son-in-law and Chilton bought ship which German captain took to Pernambuco [Brazil]. Interned, because Gt Brit suspected it was serving coal to G raiders. The captain sold it to Danish people. The day Eng. got to Pernambuco, L Miller,[53] Foreign Minister, gave it right to sail, & now Eng & Co may lose all. Wish us to overhaul it & bring it into American port so they will prove title. Story a remarkable one. (See Overman letter).

Cabinet. German ships to be repaired by Navy in N[ew] O[rleans] Charleston & Norfolk. McAdoo discussed reserve bill. 3¢ postage stamps. (B—— said to L—— aside that President [will?] not adopt prohibition). I spoke to him about seeing Fisher & others on Prohibi[tion]. He said F wished to take the wrong [?] time & he would not see them. Does not seem interested. Fear can do nothing.

Reuterdahl[54] wants commission in Naval Reserve. The gall & the cheek. Will welcome his service but no commission.

Col. Robt. Thompson and pensions for enlisted men. I talked to President who fully agreed not to do it.

Approved asking a building for Navy Department.

Saunders—Naval Consulting Committee wishes quarters in Washington as Board of Inventions.

Saturday, April 21, 1917

Council decided to appoint Woman's Defense Committee to aid in prosecution of war with Mrs. Anna Shaw[55] chairman.

Vance McCormick came with indictment from Penn Com on Safety—not enough ships and no protection. Slow in obtaining ships. Regular jeremiad

---

[51] William L. Saunders, chairman of the Naval Consulting Board.

[52] Like other prohibitionists, Daniels hoped to use the wartime emergency to further the temperance cause.

[53] Dr. Lauro Muller, Brazilian foreign minister.

[54] Henry Reuterdahl, naval artist and sharp Daniels critic in the Navy League. Daniels evidently relented, for Reuterdahl was given a commission as a lieutenant in the Naval Reserve on May 25, 1917.

[55] Anna Howard Shaw, prominent woman suffragist.

with charge of incompetency and drunkenness against Capt Russell [56] & Comd. Nelson.[57] Partly honest, mostly political & vicious. But must get their help to secure more ships. Prices there extortionate.

R—— proposed we would send destroyers to England & tell her we would expect her to furnish in return some of her best dreadnaughts. "We are in this war for—what? To crush autocracy & ruthless murder or nothing. Could we suggest some return in ships. L—— had made same suggestion to Cabinet & President had not approved.

Ride with Mrs. Helen Ring Robinson [58] of Colorado—State Senator who wrote the best article on Wilson during the campaign in the Independent.

Lansing telephoned he had telegram—So confidential could not talk over phone—Tel from S[ims]—13 ships (44,000 tons) lost in 24 hours, not counting 4 mine sweepers, mostly S.W. of Ireland. In 18 days 408,000 tons sunk. Appeal for destroyers. Critically serious & growing worse. Maximum assistance urgent. Secret. Telephoned to Benson

Sunday, April 22, 1917

Josephus came today. Train late and I did not go to church. He told me about vicious article in the Greensboro News, saying none of my boys had enlisted—a vicious, dirty article that wounded him. We had a heart to heart talk and a cry. The dear boy's health did not permit him to study and he is not prepared for leadership in any military training & both of us are at sea as to what we ought to do. Marine Corps may be best. He goes to NY to-night to Publishers meeting.

Admiral Fletcher called to report about his trip to meet Balfour, Admiral de Chair [59] and others of the British Commission. He said they felt the [?] allies would win but regarded the German submarine warfare as very serious and were not unmindful of the terrible struggle before victory. He had known the Admiral before & had a pleasant & interesting experience.

Three flags—American British French—flag raised on our home to-day. They reached Washington at 3 p.m. & thousands were out to greet them.

Monday, April 23, 1917

Board of Visitors [60] to Annapolis called at Navy Department. Discussed plan of having civilian heads of history, languages & English. Had picture taken &

---

[56] Captain Robert L. Russell, commandant of the Philadelphia Navy Yard.

[57] Lieutenant Commander Charles P. Nelson, stationed at the Philadelphia Navy Yard.

[58] Journalist and member of Colorado State Senate, 1913–1917; subsequently appointed by Daniels as a member of the Navy Department's Commission on Training Camp Activities.

[59] Rear Admiral Sir Dudley R. S. De Chair, former British naval attaché in Washington, 1902–1905.

[60] A board of civilians charged with visiting the Naval Academy annually and reporting on

called to see the President who said upon being asked what he thought of faculty meetings said he thought they were a means of grace. Board went to A.

Admiral de Chair called & we discussed naval part of war.

Conference with L & B & C on Publicity—whether to have censorship of cables &c. Afterwards called up Cable Co. President to see about it on Wednesday a.m.

Admiral Howard [61] will go to Phila to look into charges against Russell & Nelson.

Schwab [62]—felt he could build ships.

Called on Admiral de Chair—Benson ran the auto. Wasn't that true American democracy—a full Admiral driving the car? He told of capturing submarines.

Shall we print the news just reced. from the Mongolia? [63] England never claimed to have sunk a sub-marine unless it captured it and its men. Sometimes when gunmen thought they had brought down sub-marine they were mistaken.

Dinner at the White House to British Commission. Sat between Balfour and De Chair. Discussed sub-marine warfare &c. Maj. L. W. B. Rees [64] of Royal Flying Corps, who single-handed fought 10 German planes, bringing down seven.

Champ Clark wanted to go home. Said to the President: "Mother, let's go to bed so the company can go home." Then worked at Department until one o'clock

Tuesday, April 24, 1917

Short session of Cabinet. I brought up purchases of destroyers from Argentina. Lansing was to "sound" the Government

Six destroyers sailed for England to aid in the war—the perilous step—but Sims says destroyers are needed more than everything else and few have been sunk. Subs are afraid of them.

---

its operation. Concerned about academic standards at the academy, Daniels had abandoned the traditional practice of naming politicians and Annapolis graduates to the board, and had instead appointed educators. The board was currently headed by Edwin A. Alderman, president of the University of Virginia.

[61] Rear Admiral (Ret.) Thomas B. Howard, ordered to active duty as superintendent of the Naval Observatory, April, 1917–1919.

[62] Charles M. Schwab, chairman of the board of Bethlehem Steel Corporation; subsequently named director general of shipbuilding of the Emergency Fleet Corporation in April, 1918.

[63] The Navy armed guard aboard the S.S. *Mongolia* was reported to have sunk a German submarine in a recent encounter, a report later deemed untrue.

[64] Major Lionel W. B. Rees, British war ace.

Commander Kempff,[65] of Jupiter, called "I hear you wish a French hat." Getting ready to carry freight to France. He was brave but fearful. Asked me to drop a line to his wife. The tragedy of it

Breckinridge Long[66] sent quantities of drinkables to Mayflower for the French Commissioners. Berry[67] would not allow him to land it. He came to see me & spoke of the French habit of wine at meals. "Is it final?" *Final.*

Gave dinner at home to English Admiral with nobody but Admirals & officers present, except Chairman Padgett. Admiral was very fond of the N.C. ham. My wife gave him the British Admiral's flag with which she decorated the table. He took the place cards. Then we went to Pan American reception.

Wednesday, April 25, 1917

Met heads of all cables & telegraph companies with Creel and Todd[68] to discuss censorship. All willing to abide if an executive order was issued. Atty General has drawn up ex. order, but not yet signed.

Council of National Defense met. Discussed shipping & multiplication of boards. We had appointed a Shipping Board[69] which had crossed wires with Shipping Board. Houston said President would co-operate only with Shipping Board. Other must be advisory. Lane said the Com. with Willard chairman, would not work with Shipping board & there was division. Decided Shipping board must be "it."

French Com. arrived—None speak English—French Ambassador & the lemon [?] on the Mayflower.

Wrote President about composition of the Russian Commission.[70]

Reported American sailors had sunk submarine on the Mongolia. Officer thought so, but would not claim it.

Talked to Phillips about dinner to the French visitors.

Thursday, April 26, 1917

Admiral Howard made report of his visit to Phila about Russell & Nelson. R—— "made fool of himself" but Pepper[71] & others did not wish any action.

---

[65] Commander Charles S. Kempff, commander of the U.S.S. *Jupiter,* a large and relatively slow Navy fuel ship.

[66] Third Assistant Secretary of State, and as the entry indicates, not a subscriber to Daniels' temperance views.

[67] Lieutenant Commander Robert L. Berry, commander of the *Mayflower,* the presidential yacht.

[68] Commander David W. Todd, director of Naval Communications.

[69] A reference to the Advisory Commission's sub-committee on transportation and communication headed by Daniel Willard.

[70] The U.S. mission, headed by Elihu Root, to visit the new revolutionary government in Russia.

[71] George Wharton Pepper, chairman of the Pennsylvania Council of Defense.

N—— drank too much. He is a kindly soul and recommends nothing further.

Council of National Defense—Lane & Willard vs. Denman [72] and shipping board. Houston wanted the lawful body to control & Willard's Com to be advisory. Houston tired of trying to make side shows the real circus & wanted Govt. agencies to control.

Nitrates for fertilizer. Can we take part from navy & army & help the farmers, and later replace it?

Admiral Chocheprat [73] & his staff called to pay respects & talked over the naval needs. Ships and ships and then more ships.

Signed contract for the Lexington.

Dined at White House to meet Joffre [74] & other French in the mission to this country. J—— fine old fellow. French officer said 5 in his family killed.

Soldier greeted an officer familiarly "How are you my father?" Officer looked at him sternly. The soldier said: "I beg your pardon—I thought I was speaking to Gen Joffre.["]

Friday, April 27, 1917

Lansing Baker & I & George Creel went over the executive order to censor cables. Todd wanted to give commissions to all who censor.

Council of National Defense discussed ships again. Willard made long statement of how he had, at request of French Ambassador sought to obtain ships.

Schwab said Jellico had cabled to ask him to construct 100 steel ships at $1 million dollars each, or would advance $25 mil. to construct new plant. Would not quit work on navy ships. He was asked to see Denman and see Ship Board again.

Ship to be made ready to take Russian Commission.

Orders for six more destroyers to be made ready to go to Europe. Must also send small craft. French Admiral gave statement of what he wished us to do—destroyers & small craft imperatively needed.

Dined at French Embassy with French Mission. Viviani [75] & Marshall spoke, the first in French. Marshall made nice speech. Am [?] of Austria told the Cardinal "God does not pay weekly but he pays & you will find it out." That is what Germany will learn because it took Alsace & Lorrain. All countries represented. Addie and ladies came in after dinner.

---

[72] William Denman, chairman of the U.S. Shipping Board, December, 1916—July, 1917.

[73] Vice Admiral P. L. A. Chocheprat, naval adviser on the visiting French mission.

[74] Marshal Joseph J. C. Joffre, former commander-in-chief of the French armies, a member of the visiting French mission.

[75] René Viviani, head of the visiting French mission, former vice-premier and Minister of Justice in the recent Briand cabinet.

Saturday, April 28, 1917

Josephus came from New York & we talked over what he should do. Saw Lejeune [76] too. His heart is in the paper and he has a hard time to decide.

Went to Naval Consulting Board and spoke before that body, outlining its work, &c.

Came back—went to church with Josephus who was silent and thoughtful. He had enlisted as a private in the Marine Corps.

Conferred with ship builders about more destroyers. Had telegram from Sims. Conditions critical because of submarine warfare. Put him in charge of our destroyers going to Europe.

Dinner to Vice Admiral C[h]ocheprat & then with French and English members of mission[.] Baker & I received at Army and Navy Club.

Sunday, April 29, 1917

McAdoo called me about new Navy building in response to suggestion that a special commission instead of Supervising Architect erect new Navy building.

Left home at 12:30 for trip on Mayflower to carry the English and French to Mt. Vernon. Beautiful afternoon and delightful crowd. Met at Mt. Vernon by Regents—Miss Commages [Comegys]. She made brief address. Viviani, Joffre, Balfour & Governor Stewart. [77]

My three boys were introduced to Joffre, whose eyes brightened, & he said "You are a very rich man (I had told him I had four sons) and your wealth is in what is more valuable than anything else in the world—fine boys— 1,2,3, he counted the boys—where is the fourth?["] "At the University" I told him, ["]where we are drilling every day.["]

Went to train with Josephus

Monday, April 30, 1917

Admiral Gleaves [78] complained that destroyers were taken from him & given to Sims. Then Mayo plead[ed] for him & wished him made a Vice Admiral. Never.

Council of National Defense. Houston's resolution to give President power to fix prices and make prohibition. Lane wanted us to approve sending Hoke Smith's resolution [79] to committee to burial. That is what RR's wanted.

[76] Brigadier General John A. Lejeune, of the headquarters staff of the Marine Corps.

[77] Henry C. Stuart, Democrat, governor of Virginia.

[78] Rear Admiral Albert Gleaves, commanding the destroyer force of the Atlantic Fleet.

[79] The Smith resolution directed the Interstate Commerce Commission to be vigilant in approving railroad rate increases and to hold hearings at which shippers could testify against rate increases.

I objected & said this was a time to make sacrifice & RR's wanted increase of rates. Denman wished U.S. to build ships instead of England so after the war we would have them. Opposed Schwab's plan of building for England.

12.40: Went to see President. Talked about sending our ships to England & France & decided to send 36 & try to secure other small craft. Must act now. He did not like Com. named by L & W—all of them had fought shipping bill.

Lunched with the President and Mrs. Wilson & he had good stories. Discussed "Damn"—He told of a Judge, a Federalist, the Democrats wished to impeach—Chase [80] I think. It was charged he used profanity on the bench—said damn. His lawyer argued that Damn was not profane—just emphatic. Acquitted. Pres. said he saw Jefferson Davis being taken to prison. Waffles [?] —Don't stop to print em. Dr. McCosh [81] showed Garrett plans of a new building—Got $10,000 & it was reported he asked him while a guest in his house. Mrs. McC resented it & said "My husband merely showed him the plans["] & added "I have all the money needed except $10,000. What do you say"—Say Mr. Yankee!

Reception at Pan American to French Mission.

Tuesday, May 1, 1917

Received Cuban mission, who came to discuss ways of help in war & to receive aid. They promptly followed our lead and declared war upon G—— Wanted us to repair & furnish ships.

French Admiral called to say good-bye, express thanks for courtesies, & bluntly through Naval attache [1] express hope that our good sentiments would be followed by acceding to their claims for practical help.

Battle of Manila Bay [2]—Called on Mrs. Dewey [3] with General Board. Mrs. D received us & showed portrait of Admiral paid for by C. M. Schwab. She felt Gen. Board were her brothers & children, depending upon age.

---

[80] Samuel Chase, intemperate Federalist and Justice of the Supreme Court, acquitted at his impeachment trial in 1804.

[81] James McCosh, Scottish-born president of Princeton, 1868–1888.

---

[1] Commander de Blanpré.

[2] The nineteenth anniversary of Admiral Dewey's victory at the Battle of Manila Bay in the Spanish-American War of 1898.

[3] Mildred McLean Hazen Dewey, the Admiral's widow, a good friend of Secretary and Mrs. Daniels.

Council of National Defense gave out statement to have zones for protection against drink & venereal diseases.

Cabinet—One of the few times that the President asked about assignments. Helm [4] had been ordered to Mare Island, & Pres. thought he was being shelved. I think due to Miss Benham [5]

He wished destroyers not all sent now, but some held to act as convoys when troops are sent to France. Talked to Baker & felt if we were to send troops we should send them *at once.*

Swanson & Navy bill. We could add to it or change it in the Senate as desired. Add Jamestown [6]

Wednesday, May 2, 1917

Wedding Day [7]—David came to say good-bye before leaving on the Jacob Jones [8] for Europe. He is brave and courageous, but felt tender when he said good-bye.

Council of Representatives of all the States on defense met in War Department. Baker, I & Lane spoke. Then called to see the President, had picture taken, and discussed plans of how State & Federal Gov—— could work together. President naming German ships.

Sub-Marine contract with Lake people who promised earlier construction.[9]

Argentina will sell Destroyers to China & that country will sell to us. Are they good? "Made in Germany" and England at that time said they were not well built—structure not strong enough to cross the ocean.

General Board reported that sub-marine warfare critical & action must be taken at *once.* Advised destroyers, trawlers, mines, tugs &c at once

Thought in a few months England would be starved *into submission*

Thursday, May 3, 1917

Russian Naval Attache called and requested ships for White Sea to protect shipping to Archangel as soon as the ice broke up. Russia had no destroyers

[4] Rear Admiral James M. Helm. Evidently the President's interest had some effect, for Admiral Helm remained in Washington at his post of senior member of the Commission on Navy Yards and Naval Stations until January, 1918, when he was named commandant of the Fourth Naval District at Philadelphia.

[5] Edith Benham, Mrs. Wilson's private secretary, who subsequently married Admiral Helm.

[6] The Navy was interested in using the site of the Jamestown Exposition as a training facility.

[7] Daniels' twenty-ninth wedding anniversary.

[8] One of the newest destroyers of the Atlantic Fleet, commanded by Daniels' brother-in-law, Lieutenant Commander David W. Bagley.

[9] The Lake Torpedo Boat Company of Bridgeport, Connecticut, a financially weak firm which Daniels wished to survive to provide competition with the dominant Electric Boat Company in Navy submarine construction.

except those in repair and greatly needed small craft. R.R. through Siberia needed rails, cars, & engines—

Attended session of Appropriations Committee of Senate to discuss appropriations pending for Navy & urged particularly site at Hampton Road—Sewall Point and the Jamestown Exposition site & temporary barracks elsewhere.

Saw Padgett. Naval Affairs Com. wanted to hear the French and English Admirals & Benson is to see if it can be arranged.

Mr. Bok [10] came about his son who enlisted as reserve and was ordered to report—Where am I to go? "What in the hell do you ask me for?["] Warrant Officer advised young men to be immoral & told them he could prevent disease. Officer swore at young men and he was outraged because of the roughness profanity & the like. I telegraphed Tappan [11] to come to W and I will investigate.

Council of National Defense met with delegates from Govns of all the States.

Lake [12] said he had an invention that could prevent the destruction caused by the sub-marines.

Everybody wants to be an officer & get a Bomb-proof-position.

Lane Page 250

Friday, May 4, 1917

Representative of Flint & Co.[13] called about buying destroyers from Argentina. I told them they must guarantee they are in good condition. They cabled to Argentina.

Spear [14] came to see about submarines & wished to build on their plans rather than Gov. plan. Taylor rather recommended & Benson assented. Hard question to decide.

Meeting of cabinet. President talked about the sub-marine task. He returns to his original idea that merchant ships should be convoyed by naval ships, but expressed his view, as he said, without confidence as he is no expert. He also outlined his views as to changing course & ports on trips to England of our ships. Discussed sub-marines. Redfield thought a net could be stretched across the North Sea—250 miles—a net 5 mi. long had been used in Alaska and will talk to Admiral De Chair about it.

---

[10] Edward W. Bok, editor-in-chief of the *Ladies' Home Journal.*

[11] Rear Admiral (Ret.) Benjamin Tappan, currently commandant of the Philadelphia Naval Station.

[12] Simon Lake, naval architect and submarine inventor, president of the Lake Submarine Company and related firms.

[13] A shipping and ship brokerage firm with a specialty of supplying warships to belligerents.

[14] A representative of the Electric Boat Company.

Stop enlisting. Editor Fort Worth (Texas) wrote that his son enlisted, went to Chicago to Training Station, very cold & change in climate made him ill, & he died. Not a harsh word either in letter or paper, but protested against Southern boys being sent to Chicago. He thought they ought to be sent to stations on the Gulf. I directed Palmer to prepare places at Charleston & Pensocola [sic]

Saturday, May 5, 1917

Addie went to Raleigh. Drove with her to the train

The President called up. He did not like the papers discussing methods to be employed to fight submarine warfare. Talked about naming two German war ships. Change Kron Prinz Wilhelm [15] to Von Steuben & Eitel Frederick to the De Kalb—good German names of men who helped us to win our battle for independence.

Balfour & British Commission met Council of National Defense to discuss how co-operation can be secured. He said the need was for American manpower in France. That country he said would not have as many soldiers next year as this, and England's number could increase little if any. He said it was not for his body to pass upon what America could do. He pointed out that differences in guns &c was undesirable & had been found so because England & France had different patterns.

Gov. Lister,[16] of Washington. He had stood for prohibition. Wets formerly were able to "hold up" candidates. He broke with the Ch of Central Com. because he was wet & he would not carry water on both sh——

W. L. Saunders thought the antidote for submarines had been discovered. I had not received report & doubted. Would not say until it was demonstrated

Barnett [17] telegraphed Josephus to report when ordered

Lane 253

Sunday, May 6, 1917

Dr. Braisted called to talk about need for hospital accommodations—New men come in so fast that some have brought measles & other contagious diseases. Only one hospital ship ready.

Went to church (Mt. Vernon Place). Boy wished chance to stand examination. Other requests. Dinner at Mrs. B's [18]

Baruch called up about article in Sun saying there was friction between

---

[15] An interned German auxiliary cruiser used as a commerce raider.
[16] Ernest Lister, Democrat, governor of Washington.
[17] George Barnett, Major General Commandant of the Marine Corps.
[18] Mrs. Adelaide W. Bagley, Daniels' mother-in-law.

Navy Department and Munition Board; they had fixed a price at .0350 as against .0290 I had obtained for steel plates. I have the contract in writing & we will pay no more.

C C D [19] came from New York. Opposition to Root to head Commission to Russia.

Monday, May 7, 1917

Benson & Palmer wanted to send an Admiral to France as well as England. I waited. After cablegram from Sims it was clear that there ought to be only one command abroad.

Named German ships for von Steuben and De Kalb after men who fought for American liberty in the Revolution.

Young enlisted man became an Assistant Pay Master—hurried his nomination to Senate & he was confirmed. One day later would have lost him place, for he would have been over 26.

Winston Churchill,[20] author[,] grad Naval Academy, called. He is going to write book on the Navy. He was at Annapolis with Worth [21] & Breckinridge. The latter a real Kentuckian, with deep love & deep hatred.

Addicks [22] and Naval Consulting Board. Wants more money and pay for those who experiment

At night dined with Secretary Wilson who has as guests the British Labor Commission—Mems—

Told of the crucifixion of English soldiers by Germans & the finding of French girls in trenches who had been compelled by German soldiers

Long talk with Hoover. There must be, he said, a Food Dictator, & no wheat or barley should go into intoxicants. As an ethical question he believed in it, but he advocated it purely as a war plan. He wishes to be Food Dictator. Thinks it should not be under Agriculture. People fear beaurocrocy [*sic*] & would wish dictatorship ended when war closes.

Tuesday, May 8, 1917

Conference with McAdoo and Baker about Commissioner to buy everything. McAdoo wanted Baruch. Baker liked him, but said country regarded him as daring speculator on Wall Street. No conclusion. McAdoo's plan would center everything, including food, in one hand. Baker thought Council of National Defense could do it very well.

Council of National Defense. George Wharton Pepper wished to enroll

---

[19] Daniels' younger brother, Charles C. Daniels.

[20] Winston Churchill, the American author, a graduate of the Naval Academy in 1894.

[21] Ensign Worth Bagley, Daniels' brother-in-law, killed in action during the Spanish-American War.

[22] Lawrence Addicks, metallurgical engineer and member of the Naval Consulting Board.

for Service—Only one more of the plans that sound very well, but get no service. Wait till after selective draft.

Newspaper men all hot at Lansings order that nobody should talk.

Cabinet. President brought up resolution giving him power to fix priority in shipments on RR & by water, & to let RR violate letter of law against preference. If only lawyers would let us alone. They are so technical.

Shall we bring German prisoners from England to this country?

Prof Abbot [23] of Yale wished to know if boys should leave college to enlist in the Navy? No. Should doubtless [?] be getting ready, but best preparation is for young boys to stay at school

Sperry [24] & others of Naval Consulting Board, with us at dinner. After discussed practical plans to meet submarine menace—Aerial torpedo, carrys T.N.T. could be sent 50 miles & create lane. Also Elec [?] mine. When sub marine struck the net, it would turn on a light & a bouy [sic] would whistle 1½ hour & patrol boats could arrive [?].

Lane 254

Wednesday, May 9, 1917

Saw Mr. Tichnor [25] before getting up. Rev McFarland had said I wished no increase in chaplains & Welfare Secretaries to displace chaplains. Corrected that.

Council of National Defense. Houston did not wish Food Controller, but for the Dept of Agriculture to control it. Hoover told us about conditions abroad. Holland sold to Germany, getting its own supply from abroad. Temptation very great. A Dutchman can carry enough lard into Germany on his back & get enough money at present prices to live 6 months. He enlarged upon ideas stated in previous conversation with me.

Saw Saunders and Addicks & arranged funds for larger experiments as to Sub marines.

Mrs. Mary Rinehart Robert [26] going to the fleet.

John H. Small—40 foot at Hell Gate Harbor [?] of N.Y. Letter from the President. Saw Baker & we will do it lest C & W in the Senate claim party advantage *now* though it could wait till next year [27]

---

[23] Wilbur C. Abbott, professor of history, Sheffield Scientific School of Yale University.

[24] Elmer A. Sperry, electrical engineer and member of the Naval Consulting Board.

[25] Probably John S. Tichenor, subsequently a member of the Navy's Commission on Training Camp Activities, referring to Charles S. MacFarland, general secretary of the Federal Council of Churches.

[26] Presumably Daniels meant Mary Roberts Rinehart, the author.

[27] Probably a reference to a dredging operation projected for the New York harbor. Representative John H. Small was chairman of the House Rivers and Harbors Committee; both New York senators were Republicans, William M. Calder and James W. Wadsworth, Jr.

Thursday, May 10, 1917

Small came up & we will try to put through 40 feet at Hell Gate.

Saw Lansing about Naval member of Russian Commission—Scott [28] goes & Navy man should be junior.

Council of National Defense heard Mr. Thomas [29] MP (Labor delegate from Great Britain) who traced the labor legislation & labor's sacrifice in the war. Said 1¼ [million?] women are doing work women never did before. Long hours at first made for sickness & was found to be not wise or economic. Mr. Balfour present & nodded approval to most that Mr. Thomas said. Other labor leaders will be heard Monday

Munitions Board & forgings—Wanted 39¢ & 15¢ per pound extra to build & pay for plant. I sprung a surprise that shocked Grace [30] when I proposed to advance money and pay 10–15% profit. They opposed & Grace actually turned pale, but I was firm and won over part of the Munitions Board that had accepted the statement of Grace with slight investigation

Friday, May 11, 1917

Admiral Winterhalter [31] returned from China. He says Japanese conveyed impression that they wished to get in the war & felt hurt that they had not been invited to send soldiers to the front. Their army leaders are pro German & Navy officers pro-English. Speaking of Vice President of China, he said he asked why V.P. was not a General. Thought all VP should wear uniform.

Cabinet. President was most amusing describing how John Barrett [32] elbowed him at Balfour reception & said not to swear at him proved his Christian character. Wanted to tell him to go to h——. Lansing said B—— was very energetic. President told story of woman who praised the devil by saying "You know he is very energetic." President talked of Russian mission & gave names of men appointed—3 may be said of capitalistic turn of mind & 4 Democratic—one of them a Socialist.[33] They leave next week on Buffalo. Not to tell Russians how to manage their business, but to be ready to co-operate with them

6 destroyers by Newport News—1 yr—

[28] Major General Hugh L. Scott, former Army chief of staff.
[29] James H. Thomas, Privy Councillor and Labor M.P. from Derby.
[30] Eugene G. Grace, president of the Bethlehem Steel Corporation.
[31] Rear Admiral Albert G. Winterhalter, commander-in-chief of the Asiatic Fleet.
[32] Former American diplomat, director general of the Pan American Union since 1907.
[33] In addition to Elihu Root, the members of the mission to Russia were: John R. Mott, Charles R. Crane, Cyrus H. McCormick, Samuel R. Bertron, James Duncan, and Charles Edward Russell, with Major General Hugh L. Scott and Rear Admiral James H. Glennon as military and naval advisers.

Coal contract lower

Sprague [34] believes he has *the* idea & I gave him $5,000 to carry on experiments.

Saturday, May 12, 1917

Mr. Peabody [35] of Coal Committee, $2.85 delivered $2.95 at the mine plus freight & wage increase. Market price $5.00

Red Cross building opened—President, Taft & Baker spoke & women march

Left at 7 p.m. on Mayflower to visit fleet. Baker, Benson, Braisted, Palmer & boys.

Sunday, May 13, 1917

Reached Yorktown 9:30. Mayo called & then we went on Pennsylvania [36] to church. Afterwards all Admirals and Captains called & then luncheon on ship, after we had made a tour of inspection of the ship. The French Admiral had said: "It is a great ship—beautiful, magnificent." All ships there & beautiful with launches & green hills.

After lunch newspaper writers came aboard and then we went ashore and visited monument, the oldest house, house where Cornwallis had his headquarters, & the playground. New recruits looked fine & were looking happy & full of purpose.

Wertsbaugh [Wurtsbaugh] and promotion of warrant officers. Is to write me.

Came back—beautiful, clear night.

Stories Palmer, McCandless—Creel.

Baker: "I did not steal the tube [?]. But Jim, you see, had married my sister. There were the children. He could not afford to do time and I had no family."

Monday, May 14, 1917

Council of National Defense again heard the British Labor delegation. One [blank], who was a part of the Welfare department of government, affected a lackadaisical [?] air & spoke of the slackers in England where double pay was allowed for double time. "We are not all saints" said Thomas M.P.—"and when men work 14 hours a day & longer, they become unnerved[.]" 1911, he said was the hottest year known and there were more strikes and labor

---

[34] Frank J. Sprague, electrical engineer and member of the Naval Consulting Board.

[35] Francis S. Peabody, president of Peabody Coal Company and chairman of the coal production committee of the Council of National Defense.

[36] The battleship U.S.S. *Pennsylvania*, the flagship of the commander-in-chief of the Atlantic Fleet, Admiral Mayo.

troubles than ever known. When people are hot, work over time, they lose their nerves & poise. Moral: Keep men cool

At 1 p.m. lunched with Lansing to meet Russian Commissioners. Root laughingly said he could have nothing to drink on the voyage. Charles Edward Russell: "We thank you for all you are doing for righteousness." [37]

Saw Couchprat [*sic*] (French Admiral) who wished more help for France. Benson wanted united action & more information

Saw Simmons [38] about tax on newspapers. Prefer per cent on advertisements.

Tuesday, May 15, 1917

Saw Rogers [39] about getting estimate of how much revenue 5% tax on advertisements in newspapers would bring the government.

Council of Nat. Defense. Discussed coal contract. 2.85 now at Hampton Roads. Offer $2.95 at mine making $4.45 at least. Shall we pay it. Questions of buying—Shall we get the same price for allies as we get for ourselves? Will see the President about policy.

Talked to Palmer about getting list of best petty & warrant officers and making them Ensigns, so as to reward good service & make incentive to enlistments

McFarland, of Boston American, said was organized purpose to drive B[aker] & D out of cabinet. Was willing to buy space in papers to reply to unjust attacks. I thanked him and said "No—if criticism is unjust it will react. If just, it ought to be made."

Lunch at Shoreham—saw John R Mott [40] & wife. "All mothers bless you for your practical temperance" said Mrs. Mott

Went to McAdoo wedding with Mrs. Pitney.[41]

Wednesday, May 16, 1917

Saw Morgenthau [42] and he agreed to go to Raleigh and speak at A&G

---

[37] A reference to Daniels' ban on intoxicants on naval vessels.

[38] Senator Furnifold M. Simmons of North Carolina was chairman of the Senate Finance Committee.

[39] Probably Samuel L. Rogers, director of the Census Bureau.

[40] General secretary of the International Committee of the Y.M.C.A., and member of the Root mission to Russia.

[41] Florence S. Pitney, wife of Associate Justice Mahlon Pitney of the Supreme Court. McAdoo's daughter, Nona H. McAdoo, was married to Ferdinand de Mohrenschildt, second secretary of the Russian Embassy.

[42] Henry Morgenthau, Sr., prominent Democrat and U.S. Ambassador to Turkey, 1913–1916.

College. Came in with a Hebrew from N.Y. who wanted to render some service. Cotton expert—

Settled Asst. P.M's [Paymasters] with McGowan—confirmed all appointed in rush, but regretfully, and will have exam for 100 more open to all.

Went with Baker to see the President about buying. He approved my plan of 10 to 15 per cent profit for for [*sic*] forgings & advance money when necessary. Watch Schwab & Grace wince. He did not approve increase in price of coal.

Telegram from London saying our destroyers had arrived—Admiralty gave it out. Got out press notice & sent to the President who wrote "Dear Daniels, This is all right, but I hope Creel will remind the newspaper men of their agreement *not* to publish news of movements of our naval vessels." I telegraphed Sims to await advices before giving out news from London.

Con of Nati Defense—Coffin and others appeared and spoke on aviation & the need for enlargement—stations, schools &c. Trouble is we can get only learners craft & very few suitable for war. Stress on Stations & training men, & little on getting fighting craft.

English Admiralty gave out that our destroyers had arrived & well received.

Thursday, May 17, 1917

Call from Italian Ambassador [43] & Naval Attache [44] who urged us to send coal to Italy—only enough to last till June 6—Doubtful for England is supplying them with some

Lunched with British Labor Mission at New Willard—Thomas, M.P. spoke rather despondently—predicted change of ministry & overthrow of Lloyd George. Spoke of Churchill's [45] blunder in seizing ships built in England and paid for by Turkey. This offended young Turks. Said he did it without consultation. Said blunders were not made by Asquith [46] & Gray [47] as alleged but by military leaders. Bowerman,[48] who presided seemed much impressed by fact that Cabinet officers had met them twice & were at lunch with them & praised the President.

Council of National Defense met. Decided to make statement that would show good work done in answer to Congressional criticism

[43] Count Macchi di Cellere.
[44] Captain Lamberto Vannutelli.
[45] Winston L. S. Churchill, First Lord of the Admiralty, 1911–1915; currently Minister of Munitions.
[46] Herbert H. Asquith, leader of the Liberal party and prime minister, 1908–1916.
[47] Edward Grey, First Viscount Grey of Fallodon, foreign secretary, 1908–1916.
[48] Charles W. Bowerman, Labor M.P. and secretary of the Trades Union Congress.

Friday, May 18, 1917

Birthday.[49] 35 roses from Admiral W.[50] Girl—18 roses

McGowan and Assistant Pay Masters. G S D [51]

Cabinet—The delay of action by Congress. Baker said Panama RR, though entirely owned by Government, could bring nitrates from Chili, though a Gov. vessel could not. "Nobody but a lawyer" said the President, "could say that with a straight face." President told of Dr McCosh. Committee called to protest against his action. Chairman tried to give rebuke. Dr. McC quoted appropriate scripture about men receiving [52] rebuke in proper spirit, & turned to the Chmn & said "let us pray Gods [?] lead." It was a hard prayer & the Com left after the prayer without a word. Lecture on Plato (Flaps [?] open)   Checks & balances were carefully adjusted & promptly kicked over. All questions revolve around a dictum or phrase. When Constitution was formed Newton's idea possessed the thought of the world. Centrifugal & centripetal forces marked references to those who discussed the Constitution. Later came Darwin & all the talk was of evolution. The President very interesting & illuminating.

Council of National Defense—10% on cost approved—

Pickets (Woman Suffrage) at White House—Asked what the President thought of it, one said: "O, he likes it, for it brings him into prominence."

Said woman pickets are not paid

Saturday, May 19, 1917

Conference of aids on more room.

Swanson, McGowan and the appointment of Assistant Pay Masters. Examination to be held in all 14 districts.

Dr. Bryant [53] & the dental scandal.

Mother and Addie came.

Sunday, May 20, 1917

Went to church

[49] Daniels' fifty-fifth birthday.

[50] Probably Admiral Winterhalter, recently returned commander-in-chief of the Asiatic Fleet.

[51] Daniels may have been troubled about the propriety of appointing his nephew, George S. Daniels, an assistant paymaster with the rank of ensign. He did so on May 24, however. See entry of April 11, 1917.

[52] Here Daniels has inserted: (Would have served father right if boy [?] had parted [?])

[53] Probably Lieutenant (Junior Grade) Emory A. Bryant, Navy dentist at the Washington Navy Yard.

John Jenkins [54] & Banks here to dinner

Grandfather's death troubled little boy, but it was explained that the body was like an egg shell & he was really in heaven. Later when sympathized with the little boy said: "Rats, grandfather is all right. Nothing the matter except his insides are blown out.["]

Banks told of amendment to tax on newspapers. Making it on adv & not increased rate of postage.

News that shell had burst on the Mongolia, came back, & killed two nurses. Ship will reach New York to-morrow

Auto to Cabin John Bridge [55] & beyond

Cable—that David had arrived safe.

Monday, May 21, 1917

News that 2 nurses killed on Mongolia. They were going to Europe & when in practise shell was fired, the brass put on to keep out the moisture fell from shell it was blown violently back on the ship, & instantly killed. Earle was so depressed & it was distressing. Statement made in newspapers.

Orders for 24 ocean tugs & mine-sweepers.

Council of National Defense. Objection made by Jacksonville ship-builders that Navy paid too much and took employes from private plants.

Filipeno [*sic*] boy came to see & said he had been knocked down and beaten by Lieut. Osterhaus [56] & cursed. He will call to see me to-morrow night.

Tuesday, May 22, 1917

Admiral de Chair called and left a memoranda [*sic*] of what small craft and mine layers Great Britain wished to obtain from this country. Spoke in high terms of the Navy & his reception. In afternoon went to lay wreath on Dewey's grave.

Mr. Bonner [?] (*of Carnegies*) wished to know if we would surrender plates as France was very anxious to obtain some.

Cabinet. Decided to hold united Flag day celebration at foot of monument. President to speak. He was not favorable to the temporary chicken coops Lansing suggested we put up. Burleson opined Congress would not permit.

Baker & I took up copper & lead with President. Baruch said copper co. thought they ought to have 25¢ instead of 19. Baker said, & all agreed, we should get same price for allies. President said we should offer good prices—

[54] John Wilber Jenkins, former *News and Observer* reporter, now handling Navy public relations.

[55] A landmark along the Potomac River in nearby Maryland.

[56] Lieutenant Commander Hugo W. Osterhaus, serving on the battleship U.S.S. *Arkansas*.

10 to 20 per cent—offer that, if they declined, let them do so in writing & he would appeal to the country & demand they sell to all at fair prices. Baker to see Baruch and convey President's idea

After cabinet, I went with Mr. Balfour who had agreed to speak at Cotton Manufacturers Association. Big crowd in Willard. I spoke of the Cotton King & Queen of Oil. Referred to Sims and "blood is thicker than water." [57] Mrs. Balfour made address on America & the war.

Ride with my wife. Josephus & his going.

Earle furnished statement about defective shells.

Wednesday, May 23, 1917

Italian Mission here

Polk said Balfour would like to have one of my pictures & would send one of his to me

Council of National Defense. I proposed that the Gov. fix the price of coal, oil, copper & all such raw material & thereby early take the course that England and France took after the few men owning these necessities had become rich. As to transportation, we must also, I said, virtually control RR's which were demanding increased freight rates when all others were expecting to make sacrifice in time of war

Presidents statement showing good work of Council

Thursday, May 24, 1917

Mission from Italy called—Marconi [58] with them—The Prince [59] & others. Speak English & high class men

More quarters for men in Boston & elsewhere

Sims to be Vice Admiral

Class to graduate at Annapolis in June—

Council of National Defense—Discussions of how to get raw materials at fair rates. Must find a way. Baruch & Baker do not think a per cent basis is feasible.

Specifications for cots (made by certain Mfgr. who afterwards got contract). Fitzgerald roasted War Department. If true Baker said he wished to know it.

[57] Probably a reference to Admiral Sims' famous Guildhall address of 1910. Sims, then a commander, had responded to an address by the Lord Mayor of London welcoming the visiting U.S. fleet by asserting that if the British Empire were ever seriously threatened England could count on every assistance from America. Sims was reprimanded by President Taft for this indiscretion.

[58] Guglielmo Marconi, inventor of wireless telegraphy.

[59] Ferdinand of Savoy, the Prince of Udine, head of the visiting Italian delegation, and a first cousin to King Victor Emmanuel.

Dinner to the Italian Mission at White House

Told Mann [60] I would have kept him in the Caribbean sea if necessary to organize the House—

Friday, May 25, 1917

Cabinet. President asked about defective shell & I gave statement and afterwards sent Admiral Earles state[ment]   Swanson called to say that Freylinghuysen [61] had introduced resolution to appoint 5 Senators to investigate shell. I arranged for Earle to go to see him to-night & give him facts.

Gregory said necessary not to let German aliens continue as officers of ships in New York harbor. Said should be careful that none were in arsenals or navy yards

Sims wired Germans knew of our torpedoes [destroyers] going over & had mined the harbor where they had their base. Necessary to be vigilant to keep movements secret. This shows it to be needed

Secretary Herbert called and talked about Confed. vets. I saw Lansing & Mrs. L—— They will give reception at Pan American & cabinet to receive with them.[62]

Baruch & cement. He was criticized by Clark & others in the House.

Spoke at Editors of Com journals at New Willard A man ought to be ashamed to get rich out of war profits & the man who made more than normal profits was little less than a traitor

Winterhalter told of officers wife who told at a dinner the contents of a coded message.

Saturday, May 26, 1917

Spoke in the e[l]lipse before the Merchants Association in behalf of recruiting of the Marine Corps. Boosters went down the river to try to get recruits & gave up their annual meeting to secure business to boosting marine recruiting.

Went to wedding at Delanos [63]

Dined at Italian Embassy to meet the Prince Udine and the Italian mission. Large company came in after dinner. "What did you call the Prince—His Royal Highness

[60] James R. Mann, Republican, U.S. Representative from Illinois, and House minority leader.

[61] Joseph S. Frelinghuysen, Republican, U.S. Senator from New Jersey.

[62] Daniels was active in planning the forthcoming Confederate reunion, intended partly as a gesture of wartime unity.

[63] The wedding of Laura Delano, daughter of Frederic A. Delano, vice governor of the Federal Reserve Board, to James L. Houghteling, Jr.

Sunday, May 27, 1917

Slept late—Herbert [64] & wife came from Richmond. At 1 o'clock went on Mayflower to Mt Vernon and took the Italian Mission. I introduced the Prince and Marconi who made addresses at the shrine. It was a perfect day—cloud—

Admiral Winterhalter took Marconi in the wireless room, & laughingly told him not to touch that red wire—it would kill you. Marconi, not knowing the Admiral knew his expertness, said: "I have been in a wireless before"

Eberle told H W J the plan of a civilian head of English would not suit at Annapolis and predicted that it would not succeed

Hoke Smith and his son-in-law for the Pay Corps. Had taken an examination & been held up.

Monday, May 28, 1917

Council of National Defense—discussed coal & raw material.

Talked to Swager Sherley about fortifying Fort Henry [65] and said he had opposed it 4 years ago, but since ordnance had made such progress guns could now protect. Talked to him about young man who had taken examination in the Pay Corps & stopped by my order.

At night McAdoo, Baker, Baruch & Hoover & I went to talk with the President about the best method of purchasing for us and for the allies. It was agreed both must get the same price & price must if possible be fixed so that it would not be high & that it could be high enough to keep production. Hoover wanted to control food purchases & felt it necessary to have that power. McAdoo wanted B[aruch] to be the purchaser for all. The President wished to find a way by which citizens should get the same price as the government. Complicated & difficult   Baruch to draw a chart & meet again on Wednesday.

Tuesday, May 29, 1917

Conference with coal people. Told them it would be a crime to make more than normal profits out of war contracts

Cabinet. Question brought up whether the President should make a definite declaration of what we are fighting for as differentiated from aims of France and England & others. Cecil [66] had declared war would not end until G—— gave indemnity and Ribot [67] had declared France would go until

---

[64] Herbert W. Jackson, Mrs. Daniels' cousin, a Richmond banker who often advised Daniels on personal financial matters.

[65] At the entrance to Chesapeake Bay.

[66] Lord Robert Cecil, British Minister of Blockade.

[67] Alexandre F. J. Ribot, briefly French premier at this time.

Alsace and Lorrain are restored. All agreed this most unfortunate, but W——
thought nothing should be said now "We are in an alliance or agreement
and I have not permitted myself to think of plans & policies when war ends. We
trust our allies but make no alliances & this country will be ready to see that
right settlement is made when all sit at the table." Wilson (W B) thought
if we had dif. views from F & E and we wished to withdraw our troops, F & E
might by force seek to prevent it. "We want nothing for ourselves ["] said
W W. Long talk & W W was earnest & confident America would have its way
when it proposed what was right.

H. A. Garfield,[68] President of Williams College, called. During last campaign,
my brother James R.[69] wrote my mother [70] (age 85) "Do not let Harry influence you to be for Wilson. Remember we are Republicans." Harry asked her:
"What did you tell Jim?" Answer: "I told him you could not influence me
and neither could anybody else, & that if I had ten votes I would cast them
all for Wilson."

Wednesday, May 30, 1917

Attended Decoration Day exercises at Arlington. The President spoke and
Col. Sherwood [71] told of the songs which the war evoked.

Capt Bullard [72] came to see and I sent for Filipeno [sic], F. Boron, who
reported that Mr. Osterhaus had abused him and kicked him about and he had
rather go to prison than go to the Arkansas to be abused by Mr. O. All other
Captains, he said, had treated him well. Bullard said he had never heard of it
& was indignant if such things could occur—Will investigate.

Thursday, May 31, 1917

Thos. Mott Osborne talked of prison reform. He expects to have all in-
dictments over before 2 weeks and then he can be eligible to head the Portsmouth prison.

Council of National Defense met. Lane wished it to endorse bill to appropriate 5 mil. dollars to clear and level reclamation land in the West as a
war emergency. No.

Decided to increase wages at New York Yard after advice of Secy. Wilson
had been obtained.

Prince Udine & staff called. He will meet the Gen Board & talk on submarines.

[68] Harry A. Garfield, subsequently U.S. Fuel Administrator, August, 1917—December,
1919.
[69] Secretary of the Interior in the second administration of Theodore Roosevelt.
[70] Lucretia R. Garfield, widow of President James A. Garfield.
[71] Isaac R. Sherwood, Democrat, U.S. Representative from Ohio, a Civil War veteran.
[72] Captain William H. G. Bullard, commander of the U.S.S. Arkansas.

Telegram from Canada indicated that sub-marine had encountered cruiser in mid-Atlantic. Is the sub-marine warfare to be transferred to America?

Dinner with Miss Myers [73]—teaches at St. Albans.

Decided to send Abram Flexner, Dr. Welch & Nathan Straus to go to the Solace and investigate report [74]

Friday, June 1, 1917

Cabinet. Discussed "What after?" "Not a word of what we have been talking about[,"] said the President.

Dr. Welch, Nathan Straus & Dr Abraham Flexner on the way to Norfolk to make investigation on the Solace.

Saturday, June 2, 1917

Wrote Pres. suggesting Tuesday [1] there be sunrise service in all churches for the asking of the guidance of the God of our fathers.

Went with Earle before Senate Naval Affairs Committee investigating killing of nurses on Mongolia. Some Rep[ublican]s disposed to be ugly.

Council of National Defense. Willard & Advisory Council advised not applying 8 hour law to work done for government by concerns not now doing such work

Willard said "Baker can not give such order[."] Lane "And Baker would be impeached[."]

Josephus & Worth came up from R—— in auto—had paid [?] $7 to be pulled out of mud

Dined Asst Scy Longs to meet Italian mission.

Sunday, June 3, 1917

Telegram saying Buffalo [2] had arrived at Vladivostock with Russian Commission. I called up Lansing and the President & the latter said give it out.

[73] Gertrude W. Myer, probably a teacher of one of the Daniels boys.

[74] To investigate reports of poor conditions aboard the Navy hospital ship *Solace*, Daniels appointed a distinguished committee of three civilians: Dr. Abraham Flexner, secretary of the General Education Board, Dr. William H. Welch, director of the School of Public Health at Johns Hopkins University, and Nathan Straus, retired New York merchant and philanthropist. The committee's investigation disclosed undesirable crowding on the *Solace*, but it dismissed the other charges as grossly exaggerated.

---

[1] The date set for the scheduled nationwide registration for the selective service draft.

[2] A Navy transport of the Pacific Fleet which carried the Root mission to Russia.

President said he liked my idea of church service on Tuesday, but feared it might be the occasion for pacifists to say things that might cause trouble.

Council with officials who went to Jamestown to arrange for opening Navy Station

Travel to Arlington to Confed. Memorial. Clark [3] (Fla) spoke & brought in the days of negro rule &c. Rather inappropriate Col Bennett Young [4] spoke of the fact that in the Confed army there was no German & no negro. Bad taste. Otherwise speech excellent

Monday, June 4, 1917
Greatest rush of the year.

Baruch & Peabody on coal. P—— accused B—— of wiring me not to be guided in my prices of coal by what was paid by Italy & others thwarting the proposed prices by the coal dealers.

Council of National Defense. Debated proposition of Munitions Board to suspend the 8 Hour law requiring all factories doing work for the government to work only 8 hours & let new concerns on a 9 hour basis continue the work at 9 hours per day. Created most interesting discussion of the day. Gompers, Wilson & Redfield & I stood for no change in law. Coffin, Willard, Voplane,[5] & others for the change. The English & French had warned us against changing labor conditions.

Josephus saw Gen. Barnett and will go to Phila Friday. He came down & drove me home in his auto.

Did not go to dinner at Army & Navy Club—Stayed home with Josephus.

Saw Eberle about C. Alphonso Smith & he will go June 10th. Eberle died hard

Mrs. F D Roosevelt went to NY to see about the Navy Relief.

Tuesday, June 5, 1917
Spoke at foot of Washington monument at close of Registration Day & then went home to help greet the sponsors at reception. Left at 9:30 with Baker for Chapel Hill

Wednesday, June 6, 1917
Reached Raleigh 6:30 a.m. Breakfast at Capt. Brodhurst [?] & then with Jack London [6] as aid went to Chapel Hill with Secretary Baker. Glorious sum-

[3] Frank Clark, Democrat, U.S. Representative from Florida.

[4] Bennett H. Young, served with Morgan's raiders in the Confederate attack on St. Albans, Vermont, in 1864; commander-in-chief of the United Confederate Veterans, 1912–1916.

[5] Samuel M. Vauclain, vice-president of the Baldwin Locomotive Works, chairman of the Committee on Army and Navy Artillery of the General Munitions Board.

[6] Lieutenant John J. London, a native of North Carolina currently serving as inspector of ordnance at the Raleigh Iron Works.

mer morning & drive through the country was exhilarating. Baker made LLD & fine speech. Graham [7] very cordial in introduction. I spoke of how people loved leaders who held back from war as long as Duty permitted & instanced Washington, Vance [8] and Wilson.

At 4 p.m. spoke in Durham to great crowd of very enthusiastic men & women. Told of Joffre & his chaffeur [sic]. Asked when war would end & told of old Confed. who said he had the biggest gun & had cast it overboard to keep out of hands of Federals. Now wished it brought up—

Reached Raleigh. Meeting of directors.[9] Agreed to pay off bonds $37,000 from receipts from contest.

At night spoke in Raleigh from Governor's Mansion & Baker spoke well.

Returned to Wash—at midnight with Bickett [10] & others

Thursday, June 7, 1917

Reached R—— [Washington] at 9:30 With President watched the Confd vet. march by reviewing stand. Wonderful sight of the brave old men, some tottering, but most of them holding their heads high. Chief Justice White marched with Louisiana veterans. Gregory cried—his father was a soldier & Burleson tearful. Many touching scenes.

In afternoon, Reception to veterans at Pan American by Lansing and all Cabinet. No handshaking by decree of Lansing.

At night gave the Generals a dinner on the Mayflower. Speeches by Herbert, Tanner,[11] Harrison [12] & others.

Friday, June 8, 1917

Cabinet—discussed with the President the Jamestown Exposition matter. He favored it. McKean [13] got back. His wife in distressful condition & afraid her mind was gone—

Council of National Defense—No more committees. Baker told of the officer who wished to resign because his father was born in Germany & his wife was an Austrian No

---

[7] Edward K. Graham, president of the University of North Carolina.

[8] Zebulon B. Vance, U.S. Representative from North Carolina, 1858–1861, and wartime governor, who opposed secession until Lincoln's call for troops.

[9] Of Daniels' newspaper, the News and Observer.

[10] Thomas W. Bickett, governor of North Carolina.

[11] Probably James Tanner, prominent member and former commander-in-chief of the Grand Army of the Republic.

[12] George P. Harrison, commander-in-chief of the Sons of the Confederacy.

[13] Captain Josiah S. McKean, the Assistant for Material in the office of the chief of Naval Operations, Admiral Benson.

Saturday, June 9, 1917

Swanson & Martin—Jamestown.

Swager Sherley thought might buy Jamestown site if could get Naval affairs committee to approve.

Swanson brought letter written by Freylinghuysen who evidently is resolved to try to make trouble & has a letter from fuse makers who are piqued because Ordnance buys the Semple fuse. Also thinks he has something on me because Raleigh company obtained contract to make shells. Wired for Straus [14] & Twining [15] to come before committee—

Saunders (W. L.) thinks he has plan by which he can prevent sinking of ships by sub-marines, putting in wooden boxes and keeping in the air. Lumber floats in a ship even when submarined. Will discuss it with ship builders & then see McAdoo about insurance.

Hearing before Naval Committee ordered for Monday morning

Sunday, June 10, 1917

Slept very late & then went to Navy Department to catch up with correspondence that had piled up & to sign Saturday's mail   First time I had done regular work on Sunday

Spent afternoon riding with Josephus & mother & Addie. He is quiet and loves to be with me & all the time I am yearning to take his place & help him. The saddest thing about being a father is the striving to help a boy grown to age and not be able to do it. He does not like to talk of going and says little about it & prefers to talk about the paper where his heart is.

Talked with Ralph Earl[e] about Freylinghusens letter (anonymous) about fuses. Some one at Indian Head or Washington has been giving out letters & seem[s] to be working for some fuse concern. Also about the Raleigh Iron Works, thinking to injure me. F—— is two faced.

Wrote to Miss H [16] about bonds on N&O which we will pay off

Long talk with Braisted about what we we [*sic*] were doing to preserve health of men in Navy

Monday, June 11, 1917

Before Naval Affairs Committee of Senate on **Freylinghuysen resolution.**[17]
Then went before House committee on Jamestown site.

[14] Captain Joseph Strauss, commander of the battleship U.S.S. *Nevada* and former chief of the Bureau of Ordnance, 1913–1916.

[15] Captain Nathan C. Twining, on the staff of the Naval War College and former chief of the Bureau of Ordnance, 1911–1913.

[16] Mary H. Horton, vice-president and cashier of the *News and Observer* since 1900.

[17] To investigate the accidents on the *Mongolia* and *St. Louis* resulting from defective shells. See entry of May 25, 1917.

Tuesday, June 12, 1917

Asked President to write letter about Jamestown. Wrote a strong letter to Mr. Padgett—

Saw Dr. Alderman about Civilian Instruction at Annapolis

Cabinet. President said he had written his Flag Day speech—so as to avoid J Ham Lewis [18] state[men]t that when he spoke extemporaneously he was apt to say things he did not intend to say. Food control legislation discussed

The General Board wrote letter approving Jamestown & I hurried up to the capitol so as to use it, but Naval Affairs Committee had agreed unanimously.

Wednesday, June 13, 1917

Mr. Fahy,[19] of Boston, said B. Baruch would not do—there should be a board. No Wall Street speculator.

Went home to lunch with Josephus and then went to Star office with the dear boy.

Council of National Defense—How to co-ordinate. Nothing to do until the President decides upon purchasing.

Mr. Gompers made long speech upon the unrest of labor, demanded labor representatives on all committees. He was greatly impressed with serious conditions and said labor could not pay present prices & demanded provision to control price of food stuffs.

Benson & Palmer here to talk about caring for enlisted men. New barracks

Thursday, June 14, 1917

Council of Chiefs. Discussed how to utilize Jamestown for enlisted men.

Senator Lodge called & spoke cordially & I told him of Navy training gun crews & men to man ship. Closed by talking for Dr. Bryant. Swanson said he thought Freylinghuysen would agree to report & was satisfied. Felt that I had impression he was animated by partisan ends.

Flag Day. Rained so that President spoke in rain coat. Looked grave and severe.

Friday, June 15, 1917

Lord Northcliffe called with British Ambassador. We discussed censorship. He said England had been stupid. Every day said "Don't print this—would not let us print about Servia, &c." He thought they ought to give out vessels sunk by submarines & submarines captured.

[18] James Hamilton Lewis, Democrat, U.S. Senator from Illinois.
[19] Probably John H. Fahey, Boston newspaper publisher.

Alfred Pollin,[20] naval expert & writer, called. Thought England should have destroyed Zabrigge [21] before Germany took it and fortified it. But England believed she was mistress of the seas until recently if she could keep her fleet.

Cabinet. Hannis Taylor had written pamphlet alleging it was unconstitutional to send soldiers to fight across the water. Is not that treasonable—certainly discouraging enlistment &c. Pres. thought some examples must be made of men who circulated statements calculated to aid the enemy or discourage &c "I have a mind to go to G—— [22] & say 'I have come to consult with you as I never have any support from your Senators[.']" Burleson thought no— Congress had acted well & better than ever, & it was best not to have any conflict. But they always criticize? [sic] "I don't mind their hitting if I can hit back" said W. W.

McAdoo reported bonds fully subscribed & happy.

Farm conservation more important to push than revenue measure.

Banks & why I issued Wine Mess Order.

Saturday, June 16, 1917

Gave order to steel people for certain steel for $1\frac{1}{2}$ cents less than they quoted. That is the big question to be settled

Luncheon with M. Tarde,[23] French Commissioner, to meet Lord Northcliffe. He was greatly interested about the conditions in the South, and he felt that the Southern attitude toward the negro was the correct one. Knew Ambassador Page well—was the last man he saw before leaving England.

Josephus had 40 hours leave & came home from Philadelphia to spend Sunday. He was in excellent spirits and entering with proper feeling upon the work of a private in the Marine Corps He isn't very strong. I had to waive defect in eyes for him to enter & feared he would not be able to stand it; & that sleeping in room with 30–40 men &c would go hard with him. He takes it all bravely & cheerfully—

Sunday, June 17, 1917

Brother Frank & George [24] came to-day. Spent the morning reading old letters from the Seabrooks [25] & talking.

[20] Arthur J. H. Pollen, British writer on naval affairs and pioneer of naval fire control, attached to the Northcliffe mission.

[21] A reference to the heavily fortified German submarine base at Zeebrugge, Belgium.

[22] Jacob H. Gallinger, U.S. Senator from New Hampshire, Republican minority leader.

[23] André P. G. A. Tardieu, Paris editor and political leader, recently arrived as French high commissioner in the United States.

[24] Daniels' elder brother, Judge Frank A. Daniels, and son.

[25] The family line of Daniels' mother, Mary Cleaves Seabrook Daniels.

In afternoon went to ride. Josephus driving his car. He was in good spirits & we had our picture taken, J protesting. He had on his uniform of private in Marine Corps.

W. G. McAdoo said his boy [26] had been up only 5 minutes & wished training. I sent Towers [27] to see him. Complimented him on the wonderful success of the bond issue. The Navy had taken 3 mil. dollars.

Monday, June 18, 1917

Simmons—army camp for North Carolina

Wood—Baker. You know he is another Fisk.[28]

Council of National Defense. Advisory Commission wanted to turn the oil reserve over to S. Pacific Ry. No. Lane said he had made up his mind to say nothing ab[ou]t it. Redfield hot for it. Will get data.[29]

Dinner at the White House to meet the Belgian Mission. Gen ——— [sic] said when the Germans invaded Belgium, a lady said: "What shall I do? I have 9 children to feed?" The German officer killed four & said ["]You now have only 5."

He had 88 men in his military school   All but 9 killed in the war

Tuesday, June 19, 1917

Melville Stone. We let Hearst man go to Europe on Navy ship because a ship is American soil and we could not let England decide who should go on our ships. The matter of Hearsts being persona non grata to England [30] is not our quarrel. Stone approved.

Received & approved articles written for New York Times about Naval policies. Showed it to Benson who approved.

Cabinet. Baker read figures of registration showing 300,000 more than census figures show we had. N.C. 106 out of expected 100. Wash & Oregon less than 60%   Why? One officer had told Baker it was because these states had voted prohibition & there had been an exodus of business & others. W W said "Baker likes to start something," & looked at me & B—— I said ["]if

[26] Probably Francis H. McAdoo, subsequently commissioned as an ensign on September 15.

[27] Lieutenant John H. Towers, a naval aviator from the office of the chief of Naval Operations.

[28] As Aid for Operations until May, 1915, Rear Admiral Bradley A. Fiske had opposed much of Daniels' program, and after he retired in 1916 he became an open and sharp critic of Daniels' administration of the Navy. Major General Leonard Wood was similarly critical of Secretary Baker's administration of the War Department.

[29] Throughout his term as Navy Secretary, Daniels fought vigorously and successfully to protect the Naval Oil Reserves in California from the encroachment of private claimants.

[30] Because of his sharp editorial criticism, the British and French had denied Hearst the use of their cable and mail facilities late in 1916.

prohibition cuts down registration how about N.C. 106? It is a dry state."

Refer to Belgian & R mission, the Pres. said it meant more conversation. Reminded him of Sampson-Schley controversy [31]—"One year of war & 10 years of conversation"

Gov. of Wash, said truth was Washington's census was padded at last census. Are either liars or slackers. Between the two, prefer to be liars.

Talked to Denman about price of steel.

Gave interview with London editor [?]

Wednesday, June 20, 1917

Industrial Trade Commission [32] called to discuss how to fix price of raw materials. The President has furnished them the money to make investigations.

Mr. [blank] [33] President of Standard Oil Co & Mr. Doheney [34] urged to accept high price proposed. Standard gets unholy profits though Rockefeller may think they are holy.

Thursday, June 21, 1917

Called on McAdoo who was ill. In fine fettle. Why should we not fix the price of money? Must fix price of other things.

Dinner at White House with Russians

Council of National Defense—studied the plan of organization submitted & we are to suggest names to the President

Friday, June 22, 1917

Talked to Baruch who advised me not to pay prices charged for oil and gasoline.

Had call from Ambassador Menshuiteff [?] [35] of Russia, Gen Rope [36] & aid & talked of kindred aims of Russia & America.

Cabinet. President asked if it would not be feasible to produce coal from the

---

[31] A reference to the long and bitter controversy in naval circles as to who should get credit for the Battle of Santiago in 1898, the actual commander, Captain Winfield S. Schley, or his absent superior, Captain William T. Sampson.

[32] Daniels probably meant the Federal Trade Commission.

[33] Alfred C. Bedford.

[34] Edward L. Doheny, oil producer with substantial interests in the United States and Mexico.

[35] Undoubtedly Boris A. Bakhmeteff, newly arrived special ambassador of the Russian provisional government, not to be confused with the old czarist ambassador, George Bakhméteff, who had resigned on April 17.

[36] Lieutenant General Wladimir H. Roop, chief of the Russian military mission to the United States.

public lands of Wyoming & Western States—had long thought it could be done & if done in war it would not end. Would look into it further.

Baker & I talked to him about prices for steel &c. & he took the ground that they [the] price to be paid would be determined after investigation into cost of production—pay them old prices till then

Long talk with Mayo—wants to go to Europe with staff—thinks he might be displaced

Dinner at White House

Saturday, June 23, 1917

4 hours before the Public Lands Com. of the Senate & discussed oil reserve in California. Long grilling.

Garden party at Pan American

Sunday, June 24, 1917

Slept late. Went to Mt Vernon on Mayflower to carry delegation from Russia and Belgium.

Mr. Paul May, minister from Belgium to China, in the party, was talking about his wife & her anxiety, & tears came into his eyes & he apologized. I said "I honor you for it."

Bakhmetiff said the revolution came suddenly even to Russians. No orders were given to confine the Czar. RR men did it after the soldiers had guarded the Duma.

Monday, June 25, 1917

Went before the Military Affairs Com. with Baker on bill to appropriate 600 mil. dollars for aviation. We both opposed a new cabinet place for that. Why not Secretary for Artillery? said Baker.

Council of National Defense to discuss organization and suggest men as Munition Board & get quicker action in purchasing—No action   Difficult to find men to fill bill.

Capt. Volney Chase [37] found dead. Without fear & without reproach

Council—I presided—

Denman and Shipping Board present. Expected an airing of differences but not so. They were in harmony. Denman & Redfield opposed Navy taking over ships to carry troops to Europe. Denman said all British troops were transported by Merchant captains & crews. I doubted if officers & crew, capable, could be found. Silent at meeting: After meeting agreed with me.

[37] Captain Volney O. Chase, the Assistant for Operations under Admiral Benson.

McAdoo about the Purchasing Com. He favored *3*
Mayo wanted to go to England with his staff.

Tuesday, June 26, 1917

Went before Naval Com on bill to authorize Navy to carry commercial radio messages. It was not a war measure & could not take it up. Might prejudice gov. control of radio.[38]

Went to meeting of coal operators. Spoke to them. They should enlist. They owned coal only as trustees for the country. The only business in America is to successfully carry on the war. Coal men should not accept more than normal profits

Cabinet. Reported that leasing bill and trading with enemy act would be tacked on to food control bill. Presd indign[ant] I'll be d——d if I sign it. But, said B—— They have put prohibition on it— But that said W.W. is pertinent, & along similar line. Others are not.

Thought Mayo ought not to go till our policies are more settled.

In asking big appro. we should consult with Secy of the Treasy who is consulted by the men who raise revenue

Wednesday, June 27, 1917

Council of National Defense. Selected three on Board of War Industries Daniels dissenting

Would we send dreadnaughts to Norway? "G[reat] B[ritain] is very careful of her ships" said W W

Funeral for Capt Chase

Thursday, June 28, 1917

Baker—Creel &c [?]

Dined at Ambassador Jusserands.

Friday, June 29, 1917

Coal agreement—Lane & others. President was indignant at the arrangement and wished the Council of National Defense to repudiate it.[39]

Cabinet. Anti-Saloon L[eague] wished President to request them as public duty not to press the beer amendment. Said he did not feel that he should

[38] Daniels consistently advocated making radio broadcasting a government monopoly, hopefully under the Navy which led in its development and which had an obvious interest in radio communications.

[39] Lane had helped to work out a plan whereby coal prices would be fixed by a joint board representing the producers and the government, the producers promising vaguely not to profiteer.

request anybody to let the Senate proceed. I asked if the beer amendment was to be killed. He said he was anxious to omit anything that would delay bill in the Senate & would trust to Conference to write the bill.[40]

Miss Hobson [?]: Only one man can win the war. Told of her dream. The vision

Saturday, June 30, 1917

Council to discuss right to use lump sum money to increase salaries & make new positions. Roosevelt & Benson to see Fitzgerald

Baker's statement on coal &c

Cary Dowd [41] & Cam Morrison [42] came to try [to] get camp for Charlotte. Gen Wood had insulted a delegation from C & said "There are two kind of folks who never learn anything—Democrats & D—— fools." They told him he had promised to come to Charlotte & had broken his word—that an army officer should tell the truth. Then he promised to go

Prof. Irving Fisher[:] had long talk with him about action of Pres—requesting temperance forces not to press wine & beer exclusion provision on pure food bill. He thought W. W. had thereby helped the beer forces. It was they who were endangering the food bill by pledging as Penrose [43] said "to fight till hell freezes over" to prevent passage of House bill. He said the fight had been won till President took a hand & it had strengthened the beer forces though he admitted it would have taken a long time to pass it. Wished the President to pass prohibition in a separate bill & thought he ought to come out and say so. He was much depressed & so are the temperance leaders generally.

Baker (inspired by W W) wrote vigorous letter to Gifford repudiating action in fixing price of coal made by Lane Coal Committee and Trade Commission. The Council of National Defense had no part in it.

Josephus came with Joseph Yaegar [44]

---

[40] The House had approved a "bone dry" amendment to the wartime food control bill (subsequently known as the Lever Act after its adoption on August 10). The bill was delayed in the Senate for nearly two months in a bitter fight over whether to permit production of beer and light wines.

[41] William Carey Dowd, editor of the *Charlotte News* and former speaker of the North Carolina General Assembly.

[42] Cameron Morrison, Charlotte attorney and Democratic politician, subsequently governor of North Carolina, 1921–1925.

[43] Boies Penrose, Republican, U.S. Senator from Pennsylvania, a member of the Senate Naval Affairs Committee and occasional Daniels critic.

[44] Joseph A. Yeager, a friend and fellow Marine occasionally invited home by Josephus, Jr.

Sunday, July 1, 1917
Went to Church of the Covenant
Had talk with Palmer about promoting enlisted men.
Saw Jayne [1] about Pensacola and air craft in the Navy. Our balloons can see
5 mi—& is [*sic*] protection against sub-marines
Ride at night with Worth & Jonathan

Monday, July 2, 1917
Naval officer from Italy called and talked interestingly about aeroplanes.
Said his country had the largest in the world and one would arrive shortly
and he would fly to W from New York.

Lord Northcliffe called & had a special telegram from Lloyd George: "Must
have 200,000 tons of oil   Situation most serious and lack of tonnage required
to bring oil fuel here from U.S. threatens to lead to the immobilization of the
Fleet. In fact mobilization will be stopped unless the 200,000 tons referred to
are not received by the end of August, and even then a further 100,000 tons
will be essential before the end of September. Please do everything possible to
secure this supply, since failure to do so will render our naval supremacy itself
insecure and will create a position of the utmost danger. I presume that what
is needed is strong executive action in the commandeering of American tonnage, which the trading interests concerned appear to be reluctant to divert.
I leave this matter, which is quite apart from the general question of the
control of oil tonnage and the International Oil Board, entirely in your hands
and rely on you to see it through." I promised to take action & put Benson
to work to find tankage.

Went to theatre with boys. Pouring rain.

Tuesday, July 3, 1917
Gordon Smith [Gordon Gordon-Smith], newspaper correspondent from
Servia, an Englishman, called with letter of introduction. He said you saw
khaki everywhere in England, 1½ million soldiers on the island with Haig [2]
calling for more. England was suffering from the fictitious fear of an invasion & leaving the most important front undefended. He maintained that
Salonica was *the* important front and that England could have saved Servia
if it had conceived the importance of helping & cutting off Germany from

[1] Captain Joseph L. Jayne, commandant of the Naval Aeronautic Station at Pensacola,
Florida.
[2] General Sir Douglas Haig, commander-in-chief of the British Expeditionary Force in
France from 1915 to the end of the war.

Turkey. Instead of recognizing its importance, England told Servia not to attack Sofia, & that she desisted & was crushed by Bulgarians & Germans. Now he wishes America to mobilize all the Servs, send them to Canada for training & that will save allies. Turkey would have to quit if the railroad was cut & Germany would starve.

Pres. W. W. sent telegram to be sent to Sims. He wanted offensive in submarine warfare & merchant ships to be convoyed. I wrote that England had decided to convoy.[3]

Worth went to Hospital for operation

News came that last ship carrying troops to France had arrived after being attacked by submarines. One submarine sunk & probably others

Spent evening with Worth

Wednesday, July 4, 1917

Went with Jonathan to front of monument to hear Speaker Clark & Jusserand speak. Told Spring Rice: "Listen to indictment of your country." It sounded exactly like W. W's indictment of Emperor of Germany. J—— referred to America's paying return trip of Rochambeau's visit 145 yrs ago. Russians & Belgians also present

W W sent telegram to Sims

Took lunch & dinner at Army & Navy Club with Jonathan & at night with Charles [?]

Thursday, July 5, 1917

A.P. had story that officers in fleet at Queenstown had denied my statement that ships were torpedoed by sub-marines en route to France. M. E. Stone telephoned me & told him it was not correct. He said he would ask Elliott[4] to see me. But, contrary to my thought, he printed the story. Eliott [*sic*] said he felt a big mistake had been made and he called up the AP & it killed the story. It was correct but had been written in rather a thrilling style with a suggestion of exaggeration. When boys came in they bombar[d]ed me with questions. I said it had been withdrawn & was a closed incident.

Lansing, Baker, Creel and I met to consider more perfect censorship. Creel goes to New York tomorrow to arrange things.

Council of National Defense—discussed men for Industrial Council. Baker

---

[3] The British Admiralty had previously resisted the idea of convoying merchant ships to protect them from submarines, arguing that it was safer to disperse the vessels. Wilson had lost patience with the British reluctance to try new tactics.

[4] Jackson S. Elliott, head of the Washington Bureau and Southern Division of the Associated Press.

had suggested certain names. WW asked their politics 2 R & 1 D. He said that would not do.

George Creel said he elaborated story of attack of sub-marines. Kirby [5] of World said it was made up. Pulitzer [6] wired for text of Gleaves message. I declined to give it

Friday, July 6, 1917

Lord Northcliffe and oil for Great Britain. Also wanted plates shapes to hurry construction of ships.

Ambassador Elkus called at same time. He said Turkey was very tired of the war. Germans control War Department and others hate Germans. Money greatly depreciated and gold cannot be had.

Cabinet. I told what Gen. Wood told Charlotte people: "Two kind of folks learn nothing Dems & D—— fools." President said there were once two professors—one a renegade Southerner who always sneered at the section of his birth and the other a soldier who had served under Grant. The Yankee soldier hated the Southern renegade and would not speak to him. When his father visited W. W. the Southern renegade called & after being introduced asked: Where do you live Dr. Wilson? President's father said "Wilmington, North Carolina.["] "I am thankful to say my foot never touched the soil of that State.["] "If you should visit it, the feeling would be mutual and they would wish you to leave it,["] or words to that effect

How far shall President fix the distance of saloons from camps & cantonments? Baker thought should be left to camps [?]. I said 4 or 5 mi—enough to prevent easy access—

Talk of spies. Greg—— thought hysteria.

President who has always believed in convoying, wanted to know why there should not be a single lane for ships to reach Britain, with plenty of patrol boats & hydroairplanes so as to make sub-marines operations there impossible. I telegraphed to Sims.

Louis Siebold [7] & Creel.

Frank returned from Adirondacks

Saturday, July 7, 1917

Talked to Baruch about price of raw materials & getting steel &c for Great Britain. No conclusion.

[5] Rollin Kirby, political cartoonist of the *New York World.*

[6] Ralph Pulitzer, president of the *New York World,* commissioned as a lieutenant (J.G.) in the Naval Coast Defense Reserve two weeks later on July 23, 1917.

[7] Correspondent for the *New York World.*

Swanson came to talk about the article of encounter with submarines. Showed him the telegrams.

Baker had a talk with the President and will call a meeting of the steel committee on Tuesday to tell them he must know the cost of production before price is fixed. If they cannot give right prices, he will take over mills and run them and fix reasonable prices. Denman is also to be there.

Saw Denman about the ships we need to use as transports. He wanted more conversation—Baker said "D—— is impossible," but he is honest. That's the main thing

Mayo returned to fleet.

Rodman felt sure the submarine had been sighted off Hampton Roads.

Josephus came home, with cold. Gave him calomel

President turned over 12 German ships to Navy to be used to carry troops to France

Sunday, July 8, 1917

Slept late & then went to hospital to spend morning with Worth. He was ready to come home—only 5 days in hospital. Everybody liked him. I phoned for auto & we were at home before [*sic*]

Talked with McAdoo over the telephone. He wanted his son, F. H. to go to Annapolis. Said he thought it tough Roosevelt's boys and others could get into important places, while boys who had gone into the reserve last year had no chance. Said the N.Y. Tribune rented many offices to men who were pro-German & that Secret Service of Army & Navy & Treasury should co-operate to find spies.

Gen. and Mrs. Barnett called. "I am ready to swap a girl for your boy Frank" she said. Frank had been with them 4 weeks in camp in New York. They had been to lunch with T. P. O'Connor [8] who said he thought the war would last ten years.

Surgeon G Braisted called—wanted hospital units to go abroad to be ready. He thought we should not greatly extend camps in temperate climate—too cold in Chicago & New York for men unless buildings were modern.

Letter from Judge Brown [9] who demanded .03 premium for his N&O bonds. Sent the check.

J D Jr. said the worst thing about marine life was the cursing and swearing at men & the vulgar language. Must be ended

[8] Thomas P. O'Connor, Irish nationalist M.P. since 1885.
[9] George H. Brown, Associate Justice of the Supreme Court of North Carolina.

Monday, July 9, 1917

Gov. Beekman of R.I. brought a letter from Mr. Rathom,[10] Editor Providence Journal, who had obtained evidence proving awful conditions in Newport, saying 30 houses had been closed & women driven out, some diseased had returned. Both, especially the Governor, blamed Navy Department more for not having quarters than they blamed evil conditions. Gov. was interested in our buying Codington Point.

Council of Aids—all had tremendous estimates for deficiencies for Navy.[11]

Council of National Defense. I presided. Willard was not satisfied—did not think war preparations moved fast enough. Commission did not feel it could do all that it desired, and felt the need of more co-operation. Baker told graphically of the great things that had been done, how all had helped. He said he worked 16 hours a day & yet each night he felt that he had accomplished nothing because there was so much more to accomplish. All felt better.

Lunched with Wm. Kent [12] to meet Walter Camp [13] who wished to organize class of Cabinet & others to exercise. Told how class of 220 men in Hartford between ages of 46 & 73 had been made strong & healthy by exercise.

Penrose introduced resolution for telegram from Gleaves & roasted Creel & Information for making it news. Creel greatly disturbed

Tuesday, July 10, 1917

Cabinet. W W told [how the] President & Mrs. W. went to Pohick [14] to church. Secret serviceman told he was coming. "President of what?" President of U.S. Dismissed S[unday] S[chool] so children could go home to tell the parents. Preacher told sexton to ring the bell. "Cannot" said sexton. "I must go home & shave." Preacher had to ring bell in rain. Good congregation came out. Service delayed while preacher was trying to find the special prayer to make when the President was present. Couldn't find it. Had to make usual prayer. President enjoyed telling story.

Council of National Defense. Discussed proposed organization. They did

[10] John R. Rathom, editor of the *Providence Journal,* a Daniels critic.

[11] A reference to supplemental or deficiency appropriations.

[12] William Kent, Progressive Republican and Independent, former U.S. Representative from California, currently a member of the U.S. Tariff Commission. Kent was a Yale graduate.

[13] Author and sports writer, active in the direction of the Yale athletic program, subsequently a member of the Navy Commission on Training Camp Activities.

[14] An historic old Anglican church overlooking the Potomac south of Washington where George Washington had once been a vestryman.

not (Advisory Board) seem to approve. I told Lane & Baker I did not think it would work—too many committees now & they did not concentrate. Baruch & Rosenwald opposed, or rather said they could not see that it would help. All Council except J D thought it answered all criticism & would work. I talked to McAdoo after the cabinet, & he wanted three purchasing agents to do the work in connection with our allies who are buying here.

Saw T. P. O'Connor who said it was disheartening to talk to the Irish in America—they hadn't passed 1845 & thought the England of to-day was like it was years ago. Said Asquith held on to Kitchener a year after everybody knew he was a failure. English slowness & lack of understanding of Ireland. He had held no public meeting—felt sure some Irish would disturb the meeting by hostility to England

Dinner at E. B. McLeans [15]

Wednesday, July 11, 1917

Conference with Judge Gary, Chas Schwab about steel.

They wanted us to agree upon a fixed price for what this Government needs. Gagged at making the same price for the allies as for us & at commandeering the whole supply. But after an all day talk adjourned to sleep it off.

Thursday, July 12, 1917

President's statement [16] great.

Met the steel men at 9 a.m. They had evidently read the President's letter. They came in and said they were ready to do whatever the Government desired.

Council of National Defense. Labor Board—Gompers made a great speech urging that union labor be recognized and union wage rates be required everywhere

Redfield, Wilson & Willard

Friday, July 13, 1917

Cabinet. W. W. said Dr. G T W [17] once asked "What do you think of faculty meetings?" "They are a means of grace. If a man can keep his temper during a faculty meeting, he shows he is a Christian"

Baker brought up labor matter and told of Gompers speech. President agreed 8 hour, union labor.

IWW & Socialists, & Peace party

[15] Edward B. McLean, publisher of the *Washington Post,* a Daniels critic.
[16] Wilson had issued a public appeal to businessmen to be unselfish in setting prices in wartime.
[17] Probably George T. Winston, North Carolina–born educator and former university president, a friend of Daniels.

Saturday, July 14, 1917

Thomas Mott Osborne—prison reform. Will put him in charge of Naval Prison at Portsmouth.

Gavin McNab [18] called—Wilson leader in California. Said two great mistakes: McAdoo had failed on his visit to thank the women of California for carrying the State for Wilson but had time to dance at Phelan's with people most of whom supported Hughes. & I had caused them to feel they were wronged by opposing the oil leasing bill. Urged compromise. Said Justice [19] was obsessed with feeling that Californians were thieves

At night

Went to French Ambassadors where they celebrated the falling of the bastile [*sic*]

Sunday, July 15, 1917

Mayo came in—meeting of Board of Selection.[20]

Council of National Defense. Resolution asking Embargo Council to bear in mind that Army and Navy would need most of the iron and steel products of our mills, and to give great consideration to any license to export steel. Japan has been buying & there is report that other country would buy to hold.

Wrote letter to Tillman in re Creels story

Sprague called at night. Pollen had made statement, or would to-morrow, that the way to defeat submarines was to make a lane & to have boats to patrol it & use small torpedoes for 150 foot boats that could send torpedoes under water to hit submarines 2,000 yards off. He believed it was the antidote. He had been looking into & experimenting with Leavitt [21] & Bliss & believed he had found the real way to defeat submarines.

Mr. Bo Sweeney [22] died suddenly.

Wrote letter to Speaker Clark for $45,000,000 for air craft

[18] Prominent California Democrat.

[19] Edwin J. Justice, lawyer and former member of the North Carolina legislature, serving at Daniels' recommendation as special assistant to the Attorney General in charge of litigation over the Naval Oil Reserves in California. Throughout his administration of the Navy Department Daniels waged a vigorous fight to protect the Navy's claim to the oil reserves, withdrawn in 1909 by the Taft administration for the use of the Navy. Subsequently private claimants had challenged this withdrawal.

[20] In 1916, Congress had changed the method of promotion in the Navy, modifying the traditional emphasis upon seniority by introducing the principle of selection for merit. The old Plucking Board was abolished, and in its place a Selection Board of nine rear admirals made all promotions from the grades of lieutenant commander, commander, and captain.

[21] Frank M. Leavitt was the chief engineer of the E. W. Bliss Company, the major private supplier of torpedoes for the Navy. Leavitt had developed the Bliss-Leavitt torpedo used by the Navy.

[22] Bo Sweeney, Assistant Secretary of the Interior.

Monday, July 16, 1917

Cabinet. Grant [23] made Vice Admiral. "I was more foxy than you thought" said the President "in my letter to S—— His friends would say later 'Sims is original. If he had been given his way, he would have started along lines of such vigor as to win success.' Now he has advised only what the English are doing, &c.["]

Report that I.W.W. was so determined to make trouble by burning the wheat & the President had letters wishing protection from I.W.W.'s. It was not deemed an imminent danger.

W. W. had a letter from Mr. Burnett [24] who wanted to deport aliens who did not fight for this country or their own country. Gregory said: Their own countries should be allowed to draft them here. There are many aliens here who ought to serve in the army & who escape military duty.

Complaint of partisan sectionists because many camps have been authorized in the South.

Tuesday, July 17, 1917

Worth went to Yellowstone & Alaska. I secured letters for him.

Council of National Defense. Mr. Bell,[25] of California, came as representative of eight Western Governors who wished the Federal Government to take up question of I.W.W.'s. They are said to be burning wheat fields & provoking labor troubles and preaching against enrollment. He wanted the Fed. Government without trial to intern all IWW who agitated to prevent work—Wilson said Am. citizens could not be interned without a hearing. We could intern aliens but not Americans. Houston & Lane agreed with Bell, but I doubted the wisdom of such an action without proof. Bell wanted to see us with the President. No. He was to write to us a concise statement.

At night spoke with Aviator La Grande [26] at Central High School. Large crowd

Wrote to Governor of South Carolina [27]

Cabinet [28]   Spoke to the coal people   A privilege to make sacrifice

[23] Albert W. Grant, new commander of Battleship Force One of the Atlantic Fleet.

[24] John L. Burnett, Democrat, U.S. Representative from Alabama, chairman of the House Committee on Immigration and Naturalization.

[25] George L. Bell, California attorney and executive officer of the California Commission of Immigration and Housing. Daniels is in error about the date of this meeting, which took place the following day, July 18.

[26] Captain Amaury de la Grange of the French aviation mission. This meeting also took place the following day.

[27] Richard I. Manning, Democrat.

[28] Daniels has drawn a line through the word "Cabinet."

Wednesday, July 18, 1917

Talked to Creel about censorship in NY

Sprague called to see me about building 600 boats 150 foot long with torpedoes weighing 175 pounds which two men could handle. He thinks that with a lane would end submarines.

Spoke at Central High School with Capt La Grande of France Aviation Corps—"Two countries ties[,] ours & France[."]

See Wash. Post.

Worth left.

Thursday, July 19, 1917

W L Saunders—lunched—the unsinkable boat. He had plan which he thinks would let a boat float even if torpedoed. It would reduce cargo carrying space 20–30 per cent

Attended funeral of Bo Sweeney—Cremated. He had been with me in oil fight and he & Lane were not on good terms. He refused to sign certain papers without written instructions

Dined with Winterhalter—Mayo, Usher and others. W—— said he was dined by V.P. of China, & champagne flowed. When W entertained him, he said "it is against navy regulations." The Chinese VP said "that is very interesting to me. I would like to put it in effect in our Navy."

Usher told of Russians in N.Y. Navy Yard. After revolution, enlisted men did not salute officers & they became so lazy Usher said they let their ships get dirty & he had to tell them they must salute while they remained under American control.

Went to see Senator James [29] & talked about the Penrose resolution.[30] He still following [?] his partisanship

Friday, July 20, 1917

Long conference with Tillman & Swanson. Will write letter to Tillman about the statement of attack of the boats given out by me on July 3d

Ordered 20 new destroyers

Cabinet. President W—— spoke of Smoot resolution to send to Congress all about ship contracts.[31] "Why will Democrats pass any old resolution of inquiry a Republican offers?"

[29] Ollie M. James, Democrat, U.S. Senator from Kentucky.

[30] Penrose had demanded an investigation of George Creel's Committee on Public Information for its embellished story about the alleged submarine attack upon the first American troop convoy.

[31] The day before, the Senate had adopted Smoot's resolution asking data on the badly

Discussed Mr. Bell & IWW. His plan was to intern when cases were suspicious, ask the papers to print nothing because it made the IWWs martyrs & try to get better conditions. W. B. W. said mine operators this week refused to meet a committee of mine employes & much of the friction came from unfair treatment. W. W—— was willing to have [sic] & favored secret service men but not taking over a function of the separate States. He will see Bell before he goes back.

Letter from Page & Sims wanting more officers in England.

Saturday, July 21, 1917

Talked to Tumulty about my statement to be made in letter to Tillman and made some changes in it.

Bo Sweeney was asked to resign by L[ane,] & T[umulty] advised not. Only D[aniels] on guard.[32]

Rodman wished change from training ships to newer ones & came to see me. I sent for Benson. He said "Why did you not speak to me first?" R—— was in good spirits & I told B—— it was OK for R to express his preference

Roger Wells [33] brought in recommendation for enrollment for Navy Leaguer who had been busy with the gang. I tore it up.[34]

Capps & Compensation Board—

Strike in NY ship yards compelled taking yachts to Navy Yard to get ready for France

Long ride in the country—J D Jr OK—

Sunday, July 22, 1917

Went to Meth church.[35] District Day of Prayer for National Guard & others. Mr. Harden preached. Quoted Benjamin Franklin when he wished Congress to open with prayer & quoted Washington's religious faith.

Arthur Brisbane [36] called & showed me editorial which was to appear in

---

snarled ship construction program, an inquiry stemming from the current feud between William Denman, chairman of the U.S. Shipping Board, and Major General George W. Goethals, general manager of the Emergency Fleet Corporation.

[32] During the long legal fight over the disposition of the Naval Oil Reserves and again during the war when California faced an oil shortage, Secretary Lane, a Californian, sided with the California claimants against the Navy.

[33] Captain Roger Welles, director of Naval Intelligence since April 16, 1917.

[34] Daniel did not get along well with most of the leaders of the Navy League. Before the United States entered the war and especially during the political campaign of 1916, the league had strongly criticized Daniels' administration of the Navy and had attacked his preparedness program as inadequate.

[35] Probably in Richmond, where Daniels was visiting for the weekend.

[36] Owner and editor of the *Washington Times* as well as editor of the *New York Evening Journal*.

the Times on making the Navy democratic. Also wished Nathan Straus Jr.[37] brought to Washington

Frank Smith [38] came and I sent him to find Dave Lawrence [39] and give him my letter to Senator Tillman.

At night spoke to the men training to be officers at Fort Myers on clean living.

Monday, July 23, 1917

Senator Nelson [40] said a Norwegian ship really belonging to Standard Oil Company, carried oil to certain islands off Norway and supplied Germans. Thought it important to look into

Standard Oil man objected to my fixing prices for carrying oil at $4.25 per ton "tentative price" Commandeered 10 oil ships.

Two young men with German names wished authority to speak & organize for recruits for the Navy. Naval Intelligence had them under suspicion. We have enough men now in the Navy & I sidestep—

Went to Baker's office where talked with the Pres about G & D.[41] It was painful. "I have so many pains—it is like a tooth that hurts—you get pleasure only in pain." Then Council of National Defense. Shipping Com. wished to know what they were to do. Said their position with Denman as chairman was intolerable. He had asked them in writing to suggest prices for carrying freight to Europe. They asked whether all ships would be commandeered or some. He did not answer—too busy. Part of the friction was due to Denman's insistance upon just prices

Tuesday, July 24, 1917

Went to Naval Hospital just before operation on Admiral Earle. He is the salt of the earth.

Talked to Capt. Bryan [42] of Charleston. Negro women had registered to work in clothing factory & no white women could be appointed. Arranged to have segregation & 2 buildings, one for each race. Necessary or could not do work necessary.

[37] Nathan Straus, Jr., the son of the prominent New York merchant and philanthropist, was commissioned an ensign in the Naval Coast Defense Reserve the following day, July 23, 1917.

[38] A civilian employee of the Navy Department.

[39] David Lawrence, Washington correspondent for the *New York Evening Post* and syndicated columnist. Daniels' letter to Tillman dealt with the alleged submarine attack upon the troop convoy.

[40] Knute Nelson, Republican, U.S. Senator from Minnesota.

[41] To settle the embarrassing Denman-Goethals feud, Wilson had asked for the resignation of both.

[42] Captain Benjamin C. Bryan, commandant of the Charleston, S.C., Navy Yard.

Talked to Benson & Mayo about securing co-operation in naval warfare with England and France. Mayo thought he ought to go & I later talked to the President who rather thought it wise. Sims had written to the President who gave me the letter unsealed to read and tell him whether anything new. No propositions from England for conference to determine upon joint program—we are asked to send & send, but not a conference where we have equal voice

Cabinet. Shall we recommend increased salaries? No. Redfield said he had experts (24) who would resign & they could not live on $2,4000 [$2,400]. Wilson said they could live very well, but might not be able to keep up with the Joneses.

Berry—Palmer—Both boats   The President did not like it

Wednesday, July 25, 1917
Baruch talked about new organization of Council of National Defense & wanted to know who and what. Could not tell him.[43]

Secy Wilson and labor troubles.

Telegram of sudden death of Ed. Justice in San Francisco. His great fight in oil litigation.

Went to dinner at Barnetts. Miss P—— wanted to know why we were not doing more in the war. She was violently anti Wilson & pro-war & talked against taxes

Thursday, July 26, 1917
Mr. Bedford [44] protested against requisitioning oil tankers, particularly the one belong[ing] to Stand Oil. Hilton [45] held his ground and we said it was national necessity.

Com. on Training Station activities met & discussed ways to make lives clean and surroundings wholesome. They were at lunch with us.

Secret service man in Newport wrote report quoting a gambler saying everything would be open soon for Gov. Beekman had bought up Secretary Daniels —Roosevelt ha ha'd.

Mr. R. Hutch brought letter purporting to be from Frank. Shrewd rascal had obtained $250 from him, passing off as my son.

At night went down on the river with Mr. & Mrs. Redfield on the Surveyer [?] &

[43] For several weeks the Council of National Defense had been considering replacing the cumbersome twenty-two-member General Munitions Board with a more efficient organization to be known as the War Industries Board.

[44] Alfred C. Bedford, president of the Standard Oil Company (New Jersey).

[45] Lieutenant Commander James C. Hilton of the Logistics and Fuel Division of the Bureau of Supplies and Accounts.

Friday, July 27, 1917

Council of National Defense. Johnson [46] & Phelan wished to discuss oil in California. We had not heard other Senators—should we hear them. Decided to submit to the President. He rather thought not for he had heard all sides.

Discussing Georgia Senators [47] he quoted that a man had said "the difference between Rudyard Kipling & Richard Harding Davis was that Kipling was a genius & no gentleman while Davis was no gentleman.["]

Redfield was hurt. McAdoo had asked to have clearances taken from Commerce & put in Treasury. He had been off[ere]d $40,000 a year but had decided to stick it out, but that if it was open he would take it. He was too old for squabbling and could not submit.

Discussed labor troubles. Bell, of California, last week wanted Fed Gov. to take up IWW trouble. Now Gov. of California [48] had requested not to send troops except upon his request. Bell very anxious to intern suspected IWW. Presid[en]t said "no." He showed he was a very young man hoping to control the press

Had for dinner Commander Wertsbaugh & Private Woodson (Hospital Apprentice from NC) [49]

Long conference with Benson and Mayo

Saturday, July 28, 1917

Council of National Defense moving on the Industrial War Board—planning the best public statement. Then Baker took it over to the President and we met again in the afternoon, improved by the President. ["]I move we approve his suggestions" said Houston and we all laughed.

Had talk with Admiral Gleaves who was indignant that any reflection had been made upon his statement that the transports had been attacked by submarines. I wired Sims for statement from Associated Press reporter & his own statement of why the article denying my statement was allowed to be sent out.

Discussed oil in Council.

Went down the river on Sylph [50] with Frank, Addie, Mrs. B[agley] & the girls [51]—Cool & delightful. Slept ten hours

[46] Hiram W. Johnson, Progressive and Republican, U.S. Senator from California since 1917.
[47] Hoke Smith and Thomas W. Hardwick, both Democrats.
[48] William D. Stephens, Republican.
[49] Daniels often entertained both enlisted men and officers at the same social functions, much to the dismay of some of the tradition-minded admirals.
[50] A small Navy yacht used by Daniels, Roosevelt, and occasionally the White House for entertaining and relaxation.
[51] Mrs. Daniels' two sisters, Ethel and Belle Bagley.

Sunday, July 29, 1917

Spent most of the day reading Paul Kester's "My Own Country" [52] and was so absorbed in his powerful story of race feeling I forgot there was any navy or even war

Q. M. Martin—Grayson saved my child's life. "I was at hospital & when Grayson was named admiral, I approved. The nurse was vicious against it & treated me as rough as she could because I championed Grayson and I left the hospital[."]

Monday, July 30, 1917

Went before Naval Affairs Committee on bill to increase pay of commutation of ration, to make new grades for engine tenders & men with machine knowledge, and pay the cost of what a soldier lost on ships in time of war.

Talked with President. He wished to mobilize the initiative of the Navy & ask every naval officer to send his views of how we ought to fight to win naval victories. He wanted young men, who would be as courageous as Hobson [53] to be called to the front.

Council of National Defense heard Phelan, Kahn,[54] & Raker [55] on opening the California oil fields.

Jonathan—Winston Churchill [56]

Took dinner in the country with Dr & Mrs Grayson. Dr. Rixey [57] & wife there. Fine farmer

Returned on Sylph & met company of Engineer Corps passing White House

Tuesday, July 31, 1917

Strike in New York on ships we must have to send to France. Employers refused even to talk to their employes.

Cabinet. Discussed I.W.W. Haywood [58] had sent telegram to President that

[52] Paul Kester, *His Own Country* (Indianapolis: Bobbs-Merrill, 1917), a melodramatic novel of race relations in Virginia after the Civil War with strong anti-Negro overtones.

[53] A reference to the bravery of Richmond P. Hobson during the Spanish-American War when he and a group of Navy volunteers attempted to block the exit of the Spanish fleet by sinking the collier *Merrimac* in the channel of Santiago harbor.

[54] Julius Kahn, Republican, U.S. Representative from California.

[55] John E. Raker, Democrat, U.S. Representative from California.

[56] Churchill, the American novelist and Naval Academy graduate, interviewed Daniels in the presence of his son Jonathan in connection with a report Churchill was preparing on the Navy.

[57] Surgeon General (Ret.) Presley M. Rixey, former White House physician, 1898–1909, recalled to active duty when the United States entered the war and currently serving in the Bureau of Medicine and Surgery of the Navy.

[58] William D. Haywood, leader of the radical Industrial Workers of the World.

unless IWW were returned to Bixby, Arizona, from which they had been driven out,[59] strikes would occur in West—mines. Then he sent another, that unless this were done, other strikes would take place. Presid[en]t was indignant, but said what Haywood desires is to be a martyr—What shall I do? Referred to Gregory & Wilson.

Saw Gleaves again and read his report & he said he would demand that investigation be made of telegram from Asso Press

---

Wednesday, August 1, 1917

Council of National Defense met with the National Industries Board to discuss their duties. Lord Northcluffe [*sic*] had called to see what could be done about purchases for the allies. The Steel Institute [1] had promised to sell for the same prices but had made an offer for plates for 8c while I am paying .029. The steel people are trying to escape their agreement. It should have been taken down in writing.

Lane said Phelan wanted a Commission (Lane & I) to lease land but Lane said we could not agree & he could not favor it. That oil fight, which I had won, is in peril because of California's need & the national emergency.

Frank Noyes & Creel.

Telegram said Asso. Press correspondent had been fired because of report he had sent out

Thursday, August 2, 1917

Winston Churchill on naval organization. He wrote suggestion which rather looked to ending the General Board and putting power under operations in younger men. I had heard he was going to criticize me rather severely, but I think not. Jonathan who rode with us said I made a good impression.

Vance McCormick came to dinner & discussed our export attitude. Had taken tons of ore off Swedish ship at Norfolk. Captain & others said if they

[59] A reference to the strike of 15,000 miners in the Warren district of Arizona, mostly members of the A.F.L.'s International Union of Mine, Mill, and Smelter Workers but including some members of the I.W.W. Sheriff Harry Wheeler had deputized 2,000 armed men and arrested 1,186 persons, not all of them strikers, in the town of Bisbee, Arizona, and after a three-day train ride in boxcars had unloaded them in the desert near Hermanas, New Mexico.

---

[1] The American Iron and Steel Institute, the trade association of the steel industry, headed by Judge Elbert H. Gary of U.S. Steel.

did not furnish ore to Germany, that country would go to war with them. Small countries obtained supplies here to feed themselves & sold what they raised to Germans. If President approves strict export rules McCormick said war would end in April.

Council of Defense. Owners of coal mine in New Mexico violated agreement made for 2 years with former men. They struck & have been transported by train to some place. Mine workers warn President unless they are returned there will be general strike. Threat to strike by employees of Southern Pacific Ry. Employers which would tie up transportation on Pacific. Wilson authorized to see President & try to get Board of Conciliation.

Friday, August 3, 1917

The President told this: Some years ago he went to a stomach specialist Dr Janaway [2] who said "What I am about to do, you will find very uncomfortable, but not intolerable." Tried to get doctor to talk, but he was very economical in conversation. A Princeton foot-ball player went to see Dr. J. who gave prescription. The coach could read only [one] word & it was "strychnine." He said: "Don't take it. Dr. J—— is a Yale man and he may be trying to poison you." He did unbend then.

Discussed labor troubles. Case of owner of coal mine who sent men to other State. Decided to get Judge Covington [3] to go to Governors of certain Western states & urge them to see law enforced; if not, in war Federal government must find a way.

Addie came back from Philadelphia.

Jordan [4] died today—peacefully.

Decided to build aeroplane factory in Phila.

British Admiralty notified correspondent of Asso. Press he could not remain with the fleet, having sent out story that Admiral Gleaves's report of attack by submarines was incorrect. AP about to send out story that would be a virtual attack upon Creel. I said such a story should not be published. Tables are turned. They were ready to crush me & virtually were behind Penrose resolution. Now they see that I was vindicated

[2] Dr. Theodore C. Janeway, professor of medicine at Columbia University, 1907–1914, and professor of medicine at Johns Hopkins University until his death on December 27, 1917.

[3] Chief Justice James Harry Covington of the Supreme Court of the District of Columbia, Democrat, and former U.S. Representative from Maryland. Covington continued to act as an administration trouble-shooter when he was appointed a member of the Railway Wage Adjustment Board in January, 1918.

[4] Probably Burl L. Jordan, Negro coachman assigned to Daniels by the Navy Department.

Saturday, August 4, 1917

Polk came to see me. Said Balfour would consider letting us have option to take over a number of dreadnaughts & battle cruisers after the war was over in consideration of our deferring such construction in favor of destroyers and small craft during the war. Real reason? J—— "We could then by prior arrangement obtain ships we might need without any complications if G or J should be at war with us.["]

Admiral Browning of the English Navy, telegraphed he wanted conference. I told B to telegraph to him to come to W from Hampton Roads. Then Belknap [5] told me that B—— was not very well and needed rest. So I told B I thought it best to go down to HR—to take the Sylph & stay several days, visit the fleet, the Navy Yard & Jamestown.

Went down the river on the Sylph.

Sunday, August 5, 1917

Beautiful day. Spent most of it reading Irving Bacheller's Book "The Light in the Clearing" [6] after I had finished "In His Own Country."

In the afternoon the Burlesons and Crane [?] came on board the Sylph and we had a nice sail. B—— talked about war & his denying the use of the mail to disloyal papers. He had in mind shutting up big papers—that were disloyal. He said he was going to advise W W to give a garden party, invite members of Congress who had stood by him, & leave out the others like Weeks,[7] LaFollette,[8] & others so the country could see they were not trusted. He was full of that & thought it would pillory them before they could go out to the country & speak against the plan before the second draft was called

Kennesaw Mountain Landis [9]

Monday, August 6, 1917

Called with War Industries Board to see the President and discussed their duties. He said it had been reported to him the steel trust had agreed to sell

[5] Lieutenant Commander Charles Belknap, Jr., serving in the office of the chief of Naval Operations.

[6] Irving Bacheller, *The Light in the Clearing; A Tale of the North Country in the Time of Silas Wright* (Indianapolis: Bobbs-Merrill, 1917), a sentimental novel set in upstate New York in the early nineteenth century.

[7] John W. Weeks, Republican, U.S. Senator from Massachusetts, currently advocating the creation of a committee on the conduct of the war.

[8] Robert M. La Follette, Republican, U.S. Senator from Wisconsin, an opponent of American entry into the war and subsequently a critic of various war measures.

[9] U.S. district judge for the Northern District of Illinois.

to the allies & our country at the same price & that they now were trying to make dif price. In fact America furnished the money for allies who need it just now more than we do & it should be at the same price.

Council of National Defense & Advisory Council

Willard wanted to stop assessing railroads for taxation.

Gompers protested if food law contained anything that interfered with Clayton anti trust act (not applicable to labor unions) it would begin [?] trouble. He & Willard agreed law could not prevent strikes. Gompers had heard that Lane said the food bill was intended to prevent strikes.

Willard said we needed to send RR men to Russia & more engines. I am to see W W & N D B [Baker].

Went to Sylph to see Benson about taking over ships of Commerce Dept & President's visit to fleet.

Tumulty overcome by heat

Tuesday, August 7, 1917

French scientists called to say "good bye." They were depressed about sub-marine sinkings, and hoped the Navy would not depend too much upon scientific discoveries but more on fighting ships & guns. Better build fighting craft than merchant tonnage. Evidently anxious & urged quick action.

Cabinet. Furnishing engines & men to Russia—Depended upon money. Very difficult to get statement of exact & most pressing needs. Rus Am[bassador?] "Please let us have $165,000,000 [?] dollars. If this is not done it will cause misunderstanding"—No particulars. Must have detailed list & secure treasury loan before can determine what can be advanced. English Ambassador wrote to W W gloomily about rr's in Russia, but President did not think he knew much about it.

Gompers strike of carpenters in New York over Navy work. Saw Mr. [blank] [10] head of Carpenters Union who said our contractor would not work with organized labor

At Cabinet—Burleson wanted something done with Tom Watson [11] whose articles against the draft were printed in Socialist papers. "We cannot go after all the DF's [Damned Fools] we know [?]. Tom Watson is a fool. We have better things to do.["]

[10] Probably William L. Hutcheson, president of the United Brotherhood of Carpenters and Joiners since 1915.

[11] Thomas E. Watson, former Populist leader and U.S. Representative from Georgia, sharp critic of conscripting men to fight overseas. Subsequently Burleson closed the mails to *Watson's Jeffersonian Magazine* and the *Jeffersonian Weekly*.

Wednesday, August 8, 1917

Delegation from Norway called. Over 600 of their men had been submarined by Germans. Their crops were short—no rain. Conditions were not good. If Russia had made separate peace with Germany it would have been given port in North Atlantic, making it a menace to England & injury to Norway. That was the plan. One trouble in Russia is that its people for generations have been trained to hate the English. If Czar had not been forced to abdicate a separate peace would have been agreed upon with Germany before now.

Arthur Pollen looks for more vigorous offensive because of change in English Admiralty. He had heard we would send a mission to confer. He said a civilian should head it, & its report should not be separate but as one body. Should visit fleet & be bold to take issue with English Admiralty & try out what it had failed. Should demand to be shown. Our naval officers abler in scientific & practical learning than English. They lack strategy—too material. War depends on policy Secretary of Navy can secure & your responsibility great.

Council of Defense. Labor Troubles. Members of Shipping Board should be on the labor board. Fore River [12]—must it pay Navy Yard wage? Lowlers [?] had to do so. Harris [13] goes to NY to try to settle strike with carpenters.

Winslow—desires to go to England to study conditions.

Thursday, August 9, 1917

Benson had been down to the fleet & saw Admiral Browning. He went on the Sylph & picture was taken of flag of our country, our Admirals flag & flag of the Vice Admiral of England flying—something never seen before.

When ship went band on Penn played "God Save the King."

B & B discussed naval policies & co-operation between the two countries. Nothing particularly new. Seemed surprised we were sending naval officers over to England for conference.

Friday, August 10, 1917

Cabinet. I brgt up proposition of Bethlehem Co. to build 750 submarines, some in 8 months & all in 18 months.

Gov. to pay $20,000,000 for plants & own plants after the war

---

[12] The Fore River Shipbuilding Corporation of Quincy, Massachusetts, a large Navy contractor.

[13] Rear Admiral Frederic R. Harris, chief of the Bureau of Yards and Docks.

Saturday, August 11, 1917

The President spoke to all the officers of the fleet on quarter deck of the Penna [14]

Hornets & the hornets nest

Plunkett [15] very angry about report of the Board of Selection.

At night went on Penna with the boys to moving picture show.

Sunday, August 12, 1917

On the River. Left Yorktown 9 a.m. Jonathan went over to the Texas. Capt Niblack [16] called & talked about his stay in Europe as naval attache & [blank]

Capt Downs [?] told N—— the English had never tried a smoke screen & when the Germans used it at Jutland some of the English ships thought they had destroyed the German fleet because they could not see it

Read ["]Germany after the Next War.["] Personal religion & national duty have no relation

Dropped Frank & Bennett at the Cranes

Monday, August 13, 1917

R——[oosevelt] said we would get nothing from the Naval officers who go to Europe. Needed a civilian on commission. Wanted to go himself No

Went to Fort Meyer [*sic*]. President there. Baker made fine speech

Tuesday, August 14, 1917

At Cabinet discussed building destroyers. Shall we build merchant ships or destroyers? McAdoo rather thought the first. W said much would depend upon how long the war would last. We are building 117 & the proposed 150 could not be secured until 1919 & later. Then it would be a top-heavy Navy whereas the merchant ships would get in trade & that was the chief need. Decided to confer with Taylor [17] & report

[14] Daniels had persuaded President Wilson to pay an unpublicized visit to the Atlantic Fleet and address the officers on the problems of the war. Wilson's informal remarks were noteworthy in their call for daring and imaginative methods to cope with the submarine menace. In the speech he used a favorite metaphor about the frustration of hunting hornets all over the farm while leaving the nest alone.

[15] Captain Charles P. Plunkett, director of gunnery exercises, who had not been selected for promotion to rear admiral.

[16] Captain Albert P. Niblack, commander of Division One of the battleship force of the Atlantic Fleet; subsequently promoted to rear admiral on August 31, 1917. Niblack had served as naval attaché in Berlin, 1911–1913.

[17] Rear Admiral David W. Taylor, chief of the Bureau of Construction and Repair.

Benson indignant at N[avy] L[eague] statement [18]

Went to see W about the charge of the Naval League & showed the statement and letter. Time for silence has ended—Speak out. He would, if necessary, demand investigation & examination

Wednesday, August 15, 1917

Philips [19] called about entertainment of Japanese mission.

Brittain [20] came to consult about becoming Private Secretary. Delighted to come

Roger Wells [*sic*] wished to commission men in the Intelligence service— men whose duties are purely civilian.

Pierce [?] called about his boat. Under English flag. Protested it had been undervalued.

Thursday, August 16, 1917

Took lunch with Saunders who told me of Edison's plan of using anthracite coal, cutting down smoke stacks & making a merchant ship so it cannot be seen until a sub-marine is very close to it. Wishes to bring it to the attention of the President. Will have engagement next week.

Called with Benson, Mayo and Jackson [21] to see the President. He spoke of absolute necessity of finding & ending the hornet's nest, & destroying the poison or removing the cork. He impressed upon them the need of an offensive and reiterated his view that we cannot win this war by merely hunting submarines when they have gotten into the great ocean. Mayo said he hoped the President would not expect too much. No, but he expected plans by which America could lead & be the senior partner in a successful naval campaign. He was ready to make great ventures for a chance to win but of course wished no policy that would mean suicide.

[18] In July a powder magazine had exploded mysteriously at the Mare Island Navy Yard. Daniels had immediately appointed a commission to investigate, but on this date the Navy League publicly charged that the Navy Department was blocking a full investigation under pressure from labor leaders. Daniels denounced the charge and demanded that it be retracted or the officers of the league resign from what he said had become an unpatriotic organization. Colonel Thompson, the league's head and longstanding Daniels critic, responded by suggesting that both he and Daniels resign their respective posts. Daniels in turn issued an order (see entry of August 17) that all officers and representatives of the league were henceforth excluded from Navy ships and stations.

[19] William Phillips, Assistant Secretary of State.

[20] Edward E. Britton, editor of the *News and Observer* since 1913.

[21] Captain Richard H. Jackson, newly appointed representative of the Navy Department with the French Navy in Paris. Jackson and Admiral Mayo, the commander-in-chief of the Atlantic Fleet, were en route to attend the Allied Naval Conference in London the following month.

Benson called & we went over his notes to Mayo & talked of the mission. Is Mayo hopeful enough?

Council of National Defense. Labor question

Friday, August 17, 1917

Sprague protested against action of Gen. Board turning down his 150 foot boats & baby torpedo idea. He revised it and we sent it to Mayo for consideration & discussion.

Letter came from Thompson. Issued orders that no connection be had between Navy League & Navy. Had many expressions of rejoicing that I uncovered the nest plotting against naval administration.

Cabinet. W W: Should all German newspapers be excluded? Should they be compelled to print in parallel column translation in English? Baker gave strong reasons against such course. W B W thought comparatively few saw the G—— papers & there was more danger from English papers. Burleson thought great danger from the new Peace organization that was calling convention in September to try to compel statement of peace terms. He thought there should be drastic action, but the President asked what? Better let them show their impotence than by suppression as long as they keep within the law.

Redfield indignant at action of Export Commission went to the President and threatened to resign [22]—

Saturday, August 18, 1917

Talked to Powell [23] of Fore River Co. & advised that in my opinion private ship building companies must pay same wages as navy yards.

Took lunch with Naval Consulting Board & told of visit to me by French scientists warning me not to rely upon discoveries by scientists.

Saw Chief of Secret Service who will undertake to help ferret out men who blew up magazine at Mare Island & try to find out who was giving out false stories from Mare Island in response to telegram from Commandant Mare Island Navy Yard.

Crawford Biggs here to see Attorney General who offered him position to succeed E. J. Justice in prosecution of billion dollar case in California. Wished my advice.

Josephus came home

Sims again wanted 4 coal burning dreadnaughts to take place of English ships. Lack of Personnel. No: not without a program

[22] Redfield had long been unhappy over the licensing policies of the Export Council.

[23] Joseph W. Powell, Annapolis graduate, president of the Fore River Shipbuilding Corporation.

Sunday, August 19, 1917

J D Jr home

Crawford Biggs for dinner. Offered position in California to succeed Justice.

Heard Dr Wood preach. The cry peace, peace where there is not peace. Will be no peace until the cause is removed. Havana suffered from yellow fever until doctors discovered it was imparted from bite of a certain mosquito. When that was learned & these mosquitoes exterminated, there was no more yellow fever

Napoleon III said "you can do anything with a bayonet except sit upon them." There are people now sitting on the sharp points of bayonets of denial of rights, equality, justice

May shut your eyes to evil & cry peace because one will not see

Jeremiah a statesman as well as a seer

Monday, August 20, 1917

J D Jr hospital for operation for hemorrhoids

Conference of all ship builders & manufacturers who make what goes into destroyers to see if facilities could be secured to build 150 more.

Went to White House with the President with Mr. Edison. He pointed out some of his experiments. Less visibility for merchant ships by using anthracite & cutting down masts & smoke stacks: method detecting sub-marines, & preventing torpedoes from sinking ships

Council of National Defense. Mr. Gompers spoke two hours against plan for Labor Committee. Said if 3 represented "the general public" they would be inclined to be against labor. Preferred one arbitrator. Spoke with great earnestness & feeling. Wanted basis made that of present trade agreements

Saw Stephen G. Porter.[24] Thompson [25] plead guilty to trying to corner cotton market & speculated for naval officers—a scandal

Perry Belmont [26] called—he had resigned fr[om] Navy League

Tuesday, August 21, 1917

Saw J D Jr suffered very much.

Arranged with Governor Cobb [27] & Mr Weatherly to speed up building of destroyers at Bath Iron Works

[24] Republican, U.S. Representative from Pennsylvania.

[25] Probably Colonel Robert M. Thompson, president of the Navy League, whose feud with Daniels was now at its peak.

[26] Democrat, former U.S. Representative from New York, and U.S. Minister to Spain, 1888–1889.

[27] William T. Cobb, Republican, governor of Maine, 1905–1909, head of a syndicate which had recently purchased the Bath Iron Works.

Orville Wright called. Told of first flying at Kitty Hawk. Invited all the people for ten miles around but only life savers came. One became tangled up in machine & was bruised & machine injured

News came that Germany had taken Riga & it was comparatively easy to go to Petrograd—F D R said "we ought to have sent T R over to Russia with 100,000 men. This would not have happened.["] Root did not speak their language. McKean said it was strange how many folks T R had fooled

Mrs. Stotesbury [28] phoned she had resigned from Navy League

Wednesday, August 22, 1917

Young Jew stood exam. Asst. P.M. [Paymaster] rejected because he did not look as if he would make a good Naval Officer. Was it racial prejudice? He looks OK.

Lord Northcliffe—vigorously criticized aeroplane co. in England for charging exorbitant prices and advised not to buy it. He criticized Lloyd George's speech and said submarine menace was greater than generally supposed. Is he interned by Lloyd George? [29]

Lehman, expert in cotton, wants commission. Vance McCormick called to see for him. Wants to wear brass buttons.

Japs. arrived today.[30]

Wife of Navy Dr. (Mrs. Curl) whose husband [31] [blank]

Man caught who impersonated my boy

Mr. Arthur Lambert [32] resigned as V. P. Navy League. Other letters repudiating organization

Saw Assistant Attorney General Knabel [33] [sic] just back from Cal. Wished

[28] Lucretia Roberts Cromwell Stotesbury (Mrs. Edward T.), wife of a prominent capitalist, the head of Drexel and Company, and a Morgan partner. Her resignation from the Navy League was a godsend to Daniels, for the league had charged that his exclusion order was depriving Navy enlisted men of the sweaters and socks being knitted by the thousands of women members of the league's Comforts Committee. To undercut this league criticism, Daniels arranged to have Mrs. Stotesbury head a new Naval Auxiliary of the Red Cross to take the place of the league's Comforts Committee in distributing knitted goods and other gifts to the sailors.

[29] Daniels apparently wondered whether Lloyd George had ulterior motives in keeping the outspoken Lord Northcliffe sidetracked away from home as head of the British war mission in the United States.

[30] The visiting Japanese war mission, headed by Viscount Kikujiro Ishii, who in 1918 became Japanese ambassador to the United States.

[31] Lieutenant Commander Holton C. Curl, a Navy surgeon, whose wife charged him with nonsupport.

[32] Albert B. Lambert, president of the Lambert Pharmacal Company.

[33] Francis J. Kearful, in charge of the Public Lands Division of the Justice Department. Daniels and the Navy Department were seeking to set aside certain allegedly fraudulent patents of California oil lands held by the Southern Pacific Railroad in order to expand the Naval Oil Reserve.

to swap some land with Southern Pacific—No. Condemn it all & work it & sell part & make reserve of other, & let money be divided as legal rights are adjusted

Thursday, August 23, 1917

Dr C—— [Curl] owed ½ his pay for 3 years to his wife. He looked like a ram-rod—Said not a word but did it.

Japs. called on me. I called on them. The Admiral Takeshita [34] had been attache here in 1903.

Palmer wanted to graduate men at Naval Academy in January—a little over 2 years. We all discussed it and I with Benson & Barnett opposed graduation in less than three years. Talked about getting destroyers. Hard to be sure they can be constructed.

Dinner at White House to Japs. Speaker Clark said he agreed about Thompson & the Navy League. Hiram Johnson said "We are not far apart," referring to levying taxes on wealth to carry on the war. Lodge & I talking to Mrs. Wilson. Uncle Joe [35] came up & said "Mrs. Wilson, do not believe a word Lodge says & not more than half the Secretary says." L—— said a Nebraska man went to Boston & was shown the finest house, & said "How did the man make his money?" He inherited it, & the Nebraska man said: "I am going to quit the stock-growing business & come to Boston and go into the inheritance business.["]

Friday, August 24, 1917

Cabinet. Is war popular? President said you usually obtained popular sentiment from his point of view. B said Kenyon [36] was quoted as saying ⅔ people did not favor war & President said he did believe K—— had said it. 100 years ago French people would not tolerate idea that Paris represented France. If N.Y. taken, Iowa would be glad. Race prejudice. Fight in Houston, Texas.[37] Negro in uniform wants the whole sidewalk.

Pres. Story of nicely dressed white lady, colored boy, poorly dressed, carried bag in car. She gave him some money, then turned and kissed him several times on lips, & as he shambled out she sat in seat and cried. Why? The observer wondered.

[34] Vice Admiral Takeshita of the visiting Japanese war mission.

[35] Joseph G. "Uncle Joe" Cannon, Republican, U.S. Representative from Illinois, and former Speaker of the House of Representatives.

[36] William S. Kenyon, Republican, U.S. Senator from Iowa.

[37] On August 23 there had been a bloody race riot in Houston, Texas, between white civilians and Negro troops of the 24th Infantry Regiment.

Col. Mott [38] felt that Russia would be OK even if Germany should take Petrograd.

Why is not Japan doing more? Is she demanding the price of control in the East?

Will LaFollette be expelled? [39] Talk of Stone & Reed.[40] Cannot understand Stone. R is a born prosecutor. Talked to Nick Ball who told Reed he had seen only one man in Mo. who approved his course & his neighbors said he was a d—— traitor.

Letter from Jonathan favoring promotion of men on ships.

Dinner to Japanese Vice Admiral

President signed paper for board to arrange to prevent strikes in private ship building plants, to settle differences & do justice. Capps wanted Bowles [41] —No

Saturday, August 25, 1917

Council of National Defense. Labor question up. Mr. Gompers spoke with great feeling detailing how certain employers were trying to destroy organized labor & how their acts gave encouragement & help to socialists & IWW's. He had been appealed to to call a general strike. "I'll see them in h—— before I will do it" but he plead that justice should be done to labor or he could not hold them in line, they will follow pacifists & socialists.

Matter of rooms. Dr. Franklin Martin [42] & others must move. Dr. M—— had protested when Baker told him he could carry on his work elsewhere better than War Industries Board, but Dr. M could not see it. We decided to rent room for Dr. M & others.

A. B. Lambert & Mrs. Stotesbury resigned from Navy League. Report of Mare Island Board fully vindicated my position and showed that League was guilty of falsehood.

J D Jr. better. Mrs. Woodrow Wilson sent him flowers.

About appointing Assistant Pay Masters by States as needed—took it up with Smith. Navigation wanted appoint. regardless of States [43]

[38] Colonel Thomas Bentley Mott, a member of the Root mission to Russia.

[39] A reference to the abortive movement to expel Senator La Follette from the Senate for his opposition to the war.

[40] Both Missouri senators, Democrats William J. Stone and James A. Reed, were critical of the administration's handling of the war, and Stone, chairman of the Senate Foreign Relations Committee, had opposed the war resolution.

[41] Francis T. Bowles, former chief constructor of the Navy, 1901–1903, subsequently president of the Fore River Shipbuilding Corporation, manager of construction division and later general manager of the Emergency Fleet Corporation of the U.S. Shipping Board, 1917–1919.

[42] Medical adviser on the Advisory Commission of the Council of National Defense.

[43] Since a regular naval commission was harder to obtain than one in the Pay Corps, there

Letter from J W Bailey stating that desperate blind tigers [44] in Raleigh had shipped trunk full of whiskey marked Mrs. J D.

Sunday, August 26, 1917

J D Jr. better.

Wrote little speech to make at Mt. Vernon. Perfect day. Japs very interesting. Ladies called Champ Clark "Senator" & Champ said there [were] 98 [96] Senators & only one Speaker.

Only person in the world to whom every nation could pay tribute was Washington. Received by Mrs. Rogers Vice Regent.

All Jap. Missions, Mr. Roland Morris [45] & many others on board. French Comm (Tardeau) [Tardieu] said no danger on Western front. Russia has munitions & men. 5 mil killed, but has 10 mil. more.

Mr. Gompers & daughter.

Japs showed sense of humor—more than other missions. Why? They had not been through the suffering others had been th[rough]

Dr. C. Alphonso Smith & wife. He outlines every Monday morning the course of instruction in English to the whole student body in English & to the teachers. It is an inspiration to teach them.

Judge Graham [46] had the original of letter from Perry [47] to his father who was then Se[c]y of Navy. It was not official, but personal & confidential. Said Japs were deceitful &c but had many fine quali[ties]. Thought show of steam ships, going without sail, which they had never seen, & guns, would impress Japan more than all Diplomacy

Monday, August 27, 1917

Interview with Judge Lovett.[48] We had commandeered tugs for Europe. Owners objected because needed to carry coal to New England. Which most important? He is getting figures and facts from experts and will see me Wednesday.

Talked to Mr. Davison [49] of Red Cross about a Navy Comforts Committee of the Red Cross. He thought it a good plan and will present a plan later.

---

existed a temptation, apparently resisted by Daniels, to grant Pay Corps commissions on a patronage basis.

[44] A slang expression for illegal saloons.

[45] Roland S. Morris, newly appointed U.S. Ambassador to Japan.

[46] Augustus W. Graham, former speaker of the North Carolina General Assembly, son of William A. Graham, Secretary of the Navy, 1850–1852.

[47] Commodore Matthew C. Perry, leader of the expedition to open the ports of Japan to western commerce in 1854.

[48] Robert S. Lovett, chairman of the executive committee of the Union Pacific Railroad, and commissioner of Priority in Transportation of the new War Industries Board.

[49] Henry P. Davison, Morgan partner and chairman of the war council of the American Red Cross.

Called on Gregory to help in trying to find criminal responsible for magazine explosion at Mare Island. Also gave him letters from J. W. Bailey about blind tigers who had dared to send shipment of whiskey to Raleigh in name of Mrs. J. D.

Young German [who] had been rejected for Pay Master called. Looked to me as if board failed him because he had a German name and talked German. Vouched for by Senator Husting.[50]

Tuesday, August 28, 1917

W. W. read his reply to Pope [51] at meeting of Cabinet. It leads all nations. Believed England wished us to lead off. L knew Italy did. France said nothing. It made peace talk impossible until the German Imperial Gove[rnme]nt had given place to government by the people.

Baker told good story. Went to Norfolk on Sylph. His flag was flying when he went ashore. English ship signalled "Who went ashore?" "Secretary of War." "Thanks awfully." "Don't mention it" said Martin in American slang. "We will be careful not to do so" said English ship. Good example of English ignorance of American slang.

New Orleans German wished to contribute to German Red Cross. No. England & France would not agree. Senator Hitchcock [52] wanted a German woman, whose father a German officer, sent home. England & France would not grant safe conduct. H wished this Govnt to compel. She lived with H in his summer home.

One Maryland man had 5 sons, 4 volunteered & 5th drafted. Last one needed to cultivate crop. One Mormon Elder had 11 out of 16 sons drafted.

Wilson's private secretary said "Mr. W cannot come because he is in Birmingham." Pres. amused: Man cannot in person take degree because he is in Europe.

B said Pres. ought to make a speech. People did not know what they were fighting for. Princeton man asked W W "How many times can you make the same speech varying the form.["] "I do not know—have not reached my limit yet.["]

Wednesday, August 29, 1917

Conference with Mr. Davison, Mr. Ryan [53] & others about the Red Cross directing comforts work for the Navy. Will have Auxiliary & have no further connection with the Navy League.

[50] Paul O. Husting, Democrat, U.S. Senator from Wisconsin.
[51] Pope Benedict XV on August 1 had written to the belligerents urging a negotiated peace.
[52] Gilbert M. Hitchcock, Democrat, U.S. Senator from Nebraska.
[53] John D. Ryan, president of the Anaconda Copper Mining Company and other western interests, a member of the war council of the American Red Cross.

Council of National Defense heard Gov. Stewart,[54] of Montana, & others, who said work was almost at stand-still in that State because of I.W.W. They had terrorized the workers & were really fighting the Government. Believed they were financed by foes. "To hell with the war"

Thursday, August 30, 1917

This ought to be Friday

Mrs. Frazer [55] called to talk about Navy League. She wished a Comforts Committee & she to be chairman & to have no connection with the Red Cross. Thought the Red Cross would not like her to serve

Had a call from Melville Stone about the telegram from America, A.P. correspondent who sent statement that the story of Gleaves was not true. America said he wrote "Private" & did not expect it to be printed but it sent for private information of Stone. S—— said he regretted it very much, for he esteemed me very highly, more so than any man in public life and he hoped I would believe he had called to express regret. He said that he believed Sims made the expression before he knew I had given out statement and that other officers were skeptical of any sinking of submarines

(Thursday we were at Charleston W Va at the breaking of ground for the new armor plate factory! Had good time. See paper & speech.)

Friday, August 31, 1917

Cabinet. President said a Georgia State Judge had issued an injunction against any employes striking or thinking about striking or almost looking at another man or quitting if another did. A DF——[Damned Fool] Judge W W said to a Georgia Congressman as his private opinion. Gregory said the Judge had issued a second order that it should remain in effect until passed on by a jury.

I brought up request of Gov. Stewart of Montana, requesting secret service men to go there to get evidence against I.W.W. 50 could do it. All copper mines closed & men who wish to work are terrified. If evidence could be had to put 25 in jail the others would subside. Gregory said: "Why do they not come to me? We have trails out—must have evide[nce].["]

I asked W W: Are you going to march in parade. With a twinkle in his eye he said: "I understand they wished good-looking men & so I agreed."

He spoke of the Peace League, who wished to hold meetings as "Eminent crooks and others who have sense in normal times"

---

[54] Samuel V. Stewart, Democrat, governor of Montana.

[55] Elizabeth Van Rensselaer Frazer (Mrs. James C.), chairman of the Comforts Committee of the Navy League, who was attempting to circumvent Daniels' ban against the league by heading an unofficial committee to accept knitted goods for the Navy.

Mrs. W—— named the ships we received from Germany. I was about to name them for all the Presidents.

Saturday, September 1, 1917

Wrote to Davison about Red Cross taking over the work of Navy League women. He had agreed. Mrs. Frazier did not come as she had said she would do.

Found I had to go to take Japanese mission to the fleet & Baker agreed to take my place and speak on Labor Day at Buckroe Beach near Newport News.

He brought over agreement of National Council of Defense to fix priority in A. B. & C class so we could get things needed for war first of all

Left at 11 pm. on special train for New York with Japanese mission to visit the fleet in Long Island sound near Port Jefferson

Sunday, September 2, 1917

Reached New York early & left at 9 o'clock on Destroyer Henley [1] for visit to the fleet. Mr & Mrs. Lansing & sisters (who are going to France) joined us in New York, went up in fog & saw sky-scrapers in impressionistic way. Reached ships at 12:45. Lunched on Penn. with Vice Admiral Coffman.[2] Officers eager to know if battle-ships would have chance to take part in the war. Sun came out and it was a beautiful sight to see the men lined up on every ship, with the "Star Spangled Banner" by every band. It was impressive.

Returned on Henley to New York and then came to Washington on special train reaching home about midnight. Took dinner on train with Sato [3] and Ishii, the resident and the special ambassador. Companionable. The first looks sad, said to be due to the fact that his son committed hari-kari last year. Viscount Ishii had an eye that twinkles, more like an American than an oriental. I asked him for his picture. He said "Will you exchange?"

Sato & Ishii

Monday, September 3, 1917

Left at 10 o'clock with Josephus, Addie, Belle and Ethel on the Sylph to

---

[1] One of the smaller yet modern destroyers of the Navy, built during the Taft administration.

[2] Vice Admiral De Witt Coffman, second-in-command of the Atlantic Fleet, commanding in the absence of Admiral Mayo.

[3] Aimaro Sato, Japanese Ambassador to the United States.

spend Labor Day on the Potomac. Had quiet & happy day of rest with plenty of sleep. Frank joined us, with the Crane boys, at Morgan's Landing, & after a sail we reached home, Monday morning.

Tuesday, September 4, 1917

Went direct from Sylph to Department. Mr. Britton arrived as private secretary. Talked to Mr. Westerfelt [4] (Naval constructor) just back from Europe, who went to study aviation. He confirmed the statement of Italian mission that Italy was building the largest air-craft in the world. He said the impression in England & America that Italy was not doing its best & doing well against fearful odds was all wrong, that nobody could understand the obstacles in their way unless he himself went to the front & saw how the Austrians held places on hills over-looking the Italian valleys. Praised Italy warmly.

Mrs. [Thomas F.] Bayard and Mrs. Frazier came to see me about Navy Comfort. Mrs. F—— urged a separate Comforts Committee. I said we will have a Navy Auxiliary of the Red Cross. Mrs. F—— does not wish to break away from the Navy League or fears to do so

Lunched at Shoreham with Roland Morris to meet Japanese mission.

Great parade in which President marched. Congress and all Departments in honor of the men who had been selected.

Wednesday, September 5, 1917

Mrs. Stotesbury and Mr. Gibson [5] came to see me She was enthusiastic & was pleased with letter to Red Cross. I had called to Mrs. Bayard, who favored an independent comforts committee. She spoke of the courage to issue wine mess order.

Had hearing with all builders of destroyers to see what could be done. Turned on ability to secure turbines. Looks very difficult. Decided to call Westinghouse and G.E. Co. to see what they could do.

Council of National Defense at my office. Willard wanted to say that Milwaukee ought not to require grade crossings during the war. We decided to urge all unnecessary work to be put off during the war, but declined to act in any local case.

Discussed labor question. Gifford said Gompers was opposed to plan of 3.3.1. the last to be an arbitrator.

Worth returned from Alaska.

[4] Lieutenant Commander George C. Westervelt.
[5] Harvey D. Gibson, banker and general manager of the American Red Cross.

Thursday, September 6, 1917

G.E. Co & Westinghouse Co came but gave little satisfaction as to speed in furnishing motive power for destroyers.

W. A. Erwin [6] of Durham—his son had been drafted & county board would not exempt because he was married & was needed in the business. He was greatly troubled because of the illness of his wife whose mental condition was such he feared the result

Letter from John N Cole

Council of Nat. Defense heard large committee of Manufacturers who wished labor to pledge it would not try to change conditions during the war. They seemed to think they spoke for all employers, & gave elegantly bound book to each member.

B M B [Baruch] talked about loan to GB & conditions abroad & prices. Pessimistic.

Friday, September 7, 1917

Lansing called & we talked about what Japan could do in the war. He said V. Adm'l was authorized to treat as to what J—— navy could do. Was willing to patrol on Pacific & release English & Am. ships. Would they send fleet to Europe or troops? L. thought they were not keen for taking part except in Pacific. Benson to see V. Admiral & also English attache.

Grif.[fin] Taylor & I had hearing before House Appro. Com. about 350 mil. for destroyers. Went fully into it. Sherley asked if the savings made by Department had delayed construction? That was the charge. It was inspired but had never been substantiated. On the contrary Fitz[gerald] went into it fully. Gillette [7] asked about factory for aircraft—we wished to know cost so as to keep up with it. I told Gillette of the reduction we had forced on Bliss Torpedo Company.

Cabinet. W. W. asked if he should give letter to lady who wished to do relief work in France. No said Baker—all should be done under the Red Cross. All agreed. RR brotherhood threatens to strike owing to trouble in Ga RR. Pres. had asked officers to reopen case. RR had acted arbitrarily.

Discussed strategy as to war in Europe. W W did not wish to ask Military Commission until more Americans were in Europe.

Could English Navy follow German ships & engage them in Battle in Baltic.

Dr. & Mrs. Cary Grayson called to talk about the Navy Auxiliary of the Red Cross.

[6] Prominent North Carolina cotton manufacturer.
[7] Frederick H. Gillett, Republican, U.S. Representative from Massachusetts.

Saturday, September 8, 1917

B. B. Thayer,[8] of Nav. Con. Brd. [Naval Consulting Board] called & said it was believed Chile hesitated to enter war because it had 40 mil. pesos on deposit in Germany and feared it would be confiscated. Saw splendid ships, forty in number, in Santiago harbor. He believed if we would guarantee Chile, we could obtain use of all the Cosmos line, load with nitrates, bring to America, and bring Chile in line

Long cablegram from Mayo and Sims telling of result of conference, with agreement to convoy, and suggestions of defensive not fully worked out. Italy complained it could not get supplies quick enough from America. More destroyers & convoys, even if battleships needed.

Thomas Mott Osborne talked long about prison reform. His confidential stenographer had been sent to prison for stealing & forgery. Doubted his guilt. Believed sentences should be long, & reduced & men sent back as soon as they made good.

Swiss Minister [9] called. Said his country was overrun with foreigners, some not very desirable. He thought the German people were tending toward demanding control of their government. That was hope[.] Switzerland suffers because it cannot get coal and material for its manufactures.

Miss Eula Morley [?] called & said brigs on ships were antiquated. Dark & men put in without sufficient cause at times.

Saunders wanted more money for naval consulting brd.

Sunday, September 9, 1917

James B. Morrow [10] in Star quoted Stanton [11] as in 1861 said "a ravenous crew pillage the Government & the soldiers on every side and used the Treasury of the nation as a fund to be divided among themselves." Stanton, writing of contracts to a clergyman, said that the bitter censure which burdened his life during the civil war was occasioned largely by "plunderers who had been driven from the Department, where they were gorging millions"

Went to hear Marine Corps band on El[l]ipse

At morning & night we went to hear Dr Wood preach. At night his subject was "The France our soldiers will see."

[8] Benjamin B. Thayer, mining engineer and member of the Naval Consulting Board.
[9] Hans Sulzer.
[10] A syndicated Washington columnist.
[11] Edwin M. Stanton, Secretary of War, 1862–1867, and 1868.

Monday, September 10, 1917

W. J. Bryan called. His daughter at hospital. What do you think of President's reply to Pope? It is like the saying of Luke "You cannot put new wine into old bottles." McCutcheon's [12] cartoon.

Took all boys to the theatre. Looked fine party.

Mrs. Story & her son. What to do with our boys

Ten per cent contract. Soldiering on the job.

Baker came over to say the threatened strike on Boston & Maine had been averted & I sent news to the President on the Mayflower

Saw Lansing about proposition to buy German ships in Chili

Tuesday, September 11, 1917

Cleveland, O, man with letter from Baker called to show plans to build ships out of concrete. His plans looked good & he took them up with Taylor. Why should we not build ships rapidly of concrete?

Clark, of Ala, & Bowdle of Ala who had roasted Thompson called & discussed Navy League and its wrong.

Went to photo. of Breck [?] & Addie & all boys had picture taken before Worth goes to University & Josephus returns to Philadelphia.

Long talk with Pulliam [?] and Fosdick [13] upon method of improving conditions at places where young men are in training. Must have detectives in naval uniforms to detect & secure punishment of violators of law.

Story of Midshipman who sent a negro in lowest negro section to find him a woman. Held him for hours in police station and gave him the scare of his life. Hope it will reform him

One submarine sunk. By mistake it was given out as six. Correction made, but it was a trouble. Balknap brought it in wrong. I gave to men to type write. Then he brought in paper with correction, but did not say it was a correction & Jenkins did not read

Wednesday, September 12, 1917

Long talk with Tumulty. He gave insight into making of cabinet. Once B's [Burleson?] name was erased from list. Some people advised P [14] I was not known & was editor of small paper. Jo talked of the President's appreciation

[12] John T. McCutcheon, popular political cartoonist for the *Chicago Tribune*.

[13] Raymond B. Fosdick, chairman of the joint Army-Navy Commission on Training Camp Activities.

[14] Daniels evidently meant Wilson, and the abbreviation might thus stand for "President," though this is not consistent with Daniels' general practice. The "P" might also be a Freudian slip and symbolize Walter Hines Page, of whose strong opposition to Daniels' being given a cabinet post the latter might now be aware.

of my friendship & regard. He did not know Mitchell Palmer [15] was a Quaker when he was asked to be Secretary of War, but P—— thought he did.

Lunched at New Willard with leaders of Civic Federation, Labor & Farm organizations. Lane, Houston & I spoke. Lane talked of A's provincialism & need of educating people ignorant of causes of war. Houston showed how little voice Germans had in their government from the lowest divisions to the highest & spoke of how farmers & laborers were working together.

I confessed that the printed page had less influence than I formerly thought & had come to see that the spoken word was most convincing & orators and leaders should go to the people.

Thursday, September 13, 1917

Vice Admiral Koltchalk [16] and staff called at Navy Department. He is reported to be an authority on mines and believes the mining in the Baltic sea will keep out German ships, certainly until next Spring. I returned his call at 5 pm at the Russian Embassy.

Met Mrs. Stotesbury who is to head Naval Auxiliary of Red Cross and talked with her about organizing the work to be done for the Navy. She told of her connection with the League and said it was a house of cards.

Went to capitol to lunch with Speaker Clark. He is writing recollections of Congress and Mrs. Clark said she was also writing her reminiscences. She told story of a relative, unreconstructed, who when McKinley was praised as a good man when he died, said "if McKinley had been a good man he would have returned the Presidency which he stole from him. He ought to have done this before facing his maker.["] That from Mrs. C—— when she had hated Mr. Bryan was interesting.

Dinner to Russian Vice Admiral at Army & Navy club. Toast "The oldest Republic in the new world welcomes the newest Republic in the old world.["] Big reception at home at night to all naval officers and their wives to meet Vice Admiral K—— Brilliant party. The Admiral believes whoever controls Asia Minor will win the war.

Friday, September 14, 1917

Rose early & went by auto—with Commander Belknap to Annapolis. Arrived 10:30. Over 700 new midshipmen drawn up. Went to Bancroft Hall where Eberle & I spoke to the 193 young Ensigns of the Naval Reserves who

[15] A. Mitchell Palmer, prominent Pennsylvania Democrat and former member of Congress, who was offered and declined the post of Secretary of War in 1913. Palmer served as Alien Property Custodian from October 22, 1917 to March 1, 1919, when he was named Attorney General.

[16] Vice Admiral Alexander V. Kolchak, head of a Russian naval mission to the United States, subsequently an anti-bolshevist leader in 1919.

had completed our intensive training of 10 weeks. I presented diplomas and then we all went to see progress on new building—the temporary barracks being erected there. McAdoo's boy led the class. Houston present & his boy among the number. Mrs. E—— told story of Jew who said "I have a boy at Fort Meyer and he will soon be an officer. Will he get a commission? No, he will get the full price." E wished men to graduate earlier than 3 years & if that could not be done, wished it announced they would be made junior lieutenants so the Reserve would not take rank above them.

Came back to office & signed mail. Baker called to know if I was willing for bill on Air Craft production board make contracts. He thought we could control it. I sent for Taylor. He thought power to make contracts ought to remain in Secretaries.

Roosevelt had report on wages. Will take it up to-morrow.

Saturday, September 15, 1917

Boston Transcript said W W & E M H were at outs because H had requested W W to get a new Secy. of Navy. I had letter from House saying he had denied it but "these things have to go a certain length after once begun. I regret it beyond measure because of my friendship & high regard for you" [17]

Sunday, September 16, 1917

Went to Mt. Vernon Meth Ch. Gen. Carr [18] came home to dinner—told of his trip to China. The first Chinese student in NC was educated by Gen C. She was the wife of the Prime Minister & their children were educated. Repaid him for his outlay to see the good he had done

Hubert Royster [19] came to dinner and we all went to the elipse to hear

---

[17] Whether or not Colonel House was intriguing against Daniels at this time, and there is no evidence that he was, he was definitely not the warm friend and supporter Daniels thought him to be. Daniels was unaware that after a conference with the quiet Colonel in 1915 House had noted in his diary: "I shall try and see more of Daniels in order to help him when and where I can. I think he needs it, although I do not consider him as inefficient as his critics claim." (Diary, August 26, 1915, Edward M. House Papers, Yale University.) The following year House recorded an even more significant entry: "The President had to go to another banquet, and Mrs. Wilson and I had a talk of an hour or more. We decided that the most helpful things that could be done for the President at this time, would be the elimination of good Josephus Daniels and Joseph Tumulty. She undertakes to eliminate Tumulty if I can manage the Daniels change. I do not know which is the more difficult feat, but I shall approach it with some enthusiasm and see what can be done." (Diary, April 6, 1916, House Papers.)

[18] Julian S. Carr, Confederate veteran and retired North Carolina manufacturer, serving as a volunteer aide to Food Administrator Herbert Hoover. General Carr had helped finance Daniels' early journalistic career in Raleigh.

[19] Dr. Hubert A. Royster, prominent Raleigh surgeon. Royster held a reserve commission as a lieutenant (junior grade) in the Navy Medical Reserve Corps.

Bishop Kinsolving [20] preach to soldiers and sailors—I introduced him. Later we went to National Theatre where "Damaged Goods" was played. Mr. Bennett [21] & I spoke. He told why he had written the play—daughter of neighbor given disease through no fault of her own. I quoted Osler [22] that 98,000 soldiers for England incapacitated from duty because of venereal diseases

Monday, September 17, 1917

Man from Dunn called [:] "Do you want to get the Kaiser?"—"What is there in it for me.["] Refused to tell how he would get him, but said he could do it.

Mr. Morgenthau called. Just returned from France where he went on special mission for the President. He reports French need many things & need America to give confidence. Like a woman in confinement she wants husband to hold her hand.

Mrs. Stotesbury & Dr. Grayson at dinner talked of comforts for the Navy through Red Cross.

Mrs. Dewey's letter & what to do about it.[23]

Tuesday, September 18, 1917

Saw Morgenthau who told of visiting the battle fields in France and of his conferences with Joffre. He was set aside from jealousy.

Lunched with Mrs. S[totesbury] & with Red Cross officers. She was depressed because it was to be only an auxiliary, but at night we talked it all over and her spirits rose.

Cabinet. The President back from his trip on the Mayflower.

Didn't you see how West voted? [24] At Princeton[.] Applied that to oppo[sition] of Hardwick & Vardaman who would raise a row if cotton seed oil were regulated.

He felt encouraged by news from France. Spoke highly of Ambassador

[20] Lucien L. Kinsolving, Protestant Episcopal missionary bishop of southern Brazil.

[21] Richard Bennett, actor and theatrical manager, who had prepared the French play *Damaged Goods* (*Les avariés*), by Eugène Brieux, for the American stage. The current movie version was intended to aid the Army-Navy campaign against venereal disease.

[22] Sir William Osler, Regius Professor of Medicine at Oxford.

[23] The Navy League had just announced that Admiral Dewey's widow had agreed to become honorary chairman of the league's Comforts Committee. This was an unexpected and embarrassing development for Daniels in his war against the League, since he was on good terms with Mrs. Dewey, but he promptly persuaded her to resign from the Comforts Committee and join the new Red Cross Naval Auxiliary.

[24] Either Wilson repeated the same story at the next cabinet meeting or Daniels wrote it down twice, for this refers to the same anecdote about the Wilson-West feud at Princeton that is recorded in fuller detail on September 21, 1917.

Sharp's [25] telegram. Before Kornelof [26] revolted, Sharp had quoted a man returned from Russia predicting it would happen & that he would win

Saw Mrs S——[totesbury] at night.

Wednesday, September 19, 1917

Capt. Bennett [27]—who was passed over twice—came to my house before breakfast. He felt that going to Pensacola was a come down. He asked that I make him a Temporary Admiral instead of leaving selection to Board of Admirals.

Took Mr. Young, War Editor N.Y. World, to lunch & talked of war conditions and preparation. He had predicted war bet Germany & Russia 3 months before it took place. During Russ-Jap war, Germany forced a treaty with R—— that gave Ger great commercial advantages. R—— refused to renew it & then Young said he knew G would go to war.

Admiral Winslow called and talked about reserves & particularly about what this Navy should do in the war. He wanted aggressive policy & did not wish us to play second to Grt Britain. He felt the English Navy should have done better during the earlier stages of the war & not to have let the submarines get such headway. He wanted to go to Europe when Mayo went.

Thursday, September 20, 1917

Spent morning before Appropriations Committee for additional appropriations for Navy, especially for destroyers & hospitals & training camps. Senator Martin: [28] "We are voting all this money for war and we do not know how it is being spent. Congress did not ask any questions at first, but now demands to be informed." I told him we were prepared for the closest scrutiny into every expenditure.

McGowan had seen Mrs. Dewey and thought she would be all right shortly. I saw her and urged her not to worry.

World [*New York World*] demanded publicity of naval operations on the other side. They had received a tip we were capturing very many submarines and were keeping back the news. A drive to secure Sims's reports.

Wish it were true.

---

[25] William G. Sharp, U.S. Ambassador to France.

[26] Lieutenant General Lavr G. Kornilov, commander-in-chief of the Russian armies who had just led a brief and unsuccessful revolt against the Kerensky government.

[27] Captain Frank M. Bennett, newly appointed commandant of the Pensacola Navy Yard.

[28] Thomas S. Martin, Democrat, U.S. Senator from Virginia, chairman of the Senate Appropriations Committee.

Friday, September 21, 1917

Naval Intelligence & Saunders had investigated Sperry's plant [29] & believe Germans know its secrets. We have very secret experiments being made there. Aircraft to carry tons of TNT that could be guided and dropped where it could create havoc. They recommended arrest of 96 German aliens employed & inspection of their homes to see if evidence against them and then to be interned. Detectives have been at work. Americans dismissed & Germans promoted & anti-American sentiment expressed by families of German employes. Urged me to arrest without letting Sperry know. I declined until I could consult the Attorney General on Monday.

Conference with Hurley,[30] Colby [31] & Thayer & Dr. Rowe [32] about way to secure German boats (60) in Chili. The Consul [33] at New York said his country believed America did not want Chili to enter the war. Lansing said great mistake. We wished them in war.

Cabinet. W W: It is a good idea to watch how some men vote & vote the other way. Told story of Dr West——"You fool didn't you see how West voted?" said a pro-Wilson member of faculty who had voted against W W's policies. "If you don't understand a question, never vote as West votes." Good rule in Congress.

Lansing's news about Bernstorff getting money caused us to call him old Sherlock Holmes.

Discussed ½ holiday for clerks in Departments. Lansing only advocate.

Saturday, September 22, 1917

Reached Raleigh 7 a.m. Discussed N&O business at office nearly all day. Gov. Bickett had prevented lynching of a negro by appearing at court house, & had organized & defied mob which tried to break into State Prison. He had instructed military and guard at prison to fire into mob & shoot to kill. If mob can break into penitentiary, said Governor, there is no responsible government.

Working on new subscribers and plan[n]ing how to get them—

Delightful how cordial was reception in R——

[29] The Sperry Gyroscope Company of Brooklyn, N.Y.

[30] Edward N. Hurley, former chairman of the Federal Trade Commission, since July 24 chairman of the U.S. Shipping Board and president of the Emergency Fleet Corporation.

[31] Bainbridge Colby, member of the U.S. Shipping Board and Emergency Fleet Corporation.

[32] Leo S. Rowe, Assistant Secretary of the Treasury and expert on Latin America.

[33] Carlos Castro Ruiz, Chilean consul general.

Dr. Haywood [34] & his boy & Ball [35] & McKimmon [36] said some of them had to sleep in same big room with colored men in Navy and to eat in same dining room. Had long talk with Dr H.

Worth came in afternoon from Chapel Hill, happy & we had good time together. He had joined DKE [37] & wore a pin.

Bailey talked of the bringing of liquor into State by freight & express & the difficulty of enforcing prohibition.

Sunday, September 23, 1917

Went to Sunday School & taught large A&E class. Subject—Daniel in the Lions Den. "Dare to be a Daniel"—Mr. Pearson's sermon.[38]

Went to Goldsboro with Worth to see mother. Several called to see about their sons who would probably be reached in the next draft. It is the most trying experience of all to talk to parents who wish to save their sons from the trenches.

Monday, September 24, 1917

Reached W[ashington] 9 am. Admiral Fletcher [39] met me at train with the price of steel fixed by War Industries Board and approved by President. F said as I had secured very low prices, he would not approve until I was consulted. Considerate as usual. The rate was $\frac{1}{4}$ cents higher on plates than I had secured but it gave same price to allies & to the public which was very important. Fletcher thought it best to approve and stimulate production. I agreed. Soon the President gave out statement of approval.

Went with Saunders & others to Dept. of Justice to talk to Davis [40] about alien enemies in Sperry's plant. Davis thought actions justified arrest, but agreed with me that Sperry ought first be informed, but not allowed to prevent it.

Polk had telegram from Page regretting our [41] any misunderstanding between Admiralty & our Navy. They had exaggerated ideas of misunderstand-

---

[34] Dr. Hubert Haywood, Daniels' personal physician in Raleigh.

[35] Probably Jesse G. Ball, prominent Raleigh wholesale grocer.

[36] Probably D. C. McKimmon, former North Carolina state legislator.

[37] Delta Kappa Epsilon, a social fraternity.

[38] A reference to the visit of the Rev. R. G. Pearson, an evangelist, to Raleigh in 1887, when Daniels was courting his future wife. See Daniels, *Tar Heel Editor* (Chapel Hill: University of North Carolina Press, 1939), p. 266.

[39] Since July, Rear Admiral Frank F. Fletcher had served as the Navy member of the War Industries Board.

[40] John W. Davis, Solicitor General of the United States.

[41] Daniels has crossed out what appears to be the word "notion," and probably meant to cross out the previous word "our" as well.

ing. We only wished to be informed & wished a policy of offensive to be agreed upon by admiralties of all countries fighting Germany

The Heflin [42] discussion in Congress

Tuesday, September 25, 1917

Senate Appro. Com. had put on amendment to authorize Sec. of Navy to receive comforts from Woman's Committee of League. I saw Overman, Hollis, & Swanson & it was knocked out.

Called on Garfield & warned him some coal operators would pretend they had contracts & refuse to deliver coal so as to try to compel increase of price.

Cabinet. Price of nitrates gone up very much, doubled—Houston said unwarranted. Navy had supply for 12 months.

Redfield told of bitter dispute between Dem & Rep, the latter being bitter against W. W. Finally he had to admit W W was right, but would not give him personal credit, but said: Wilson is making good only because he is inspired by the Almighty, by God!

Burleson said Man in small store in Nebraska had sign: "I have been drafted Serve your country by buying early from me Isaac Goldberg.["]

Benson 62 years old. I congratulated him that we had changed law making retirement 64, otherwise he would be retiring now

Went to see Mrs. Dewey & agreed that Womans Section of Navy League should be incorporated under name of Woman Navy Service, or something without the word League in it

President told of visit to Nantucket. Sea Captain became stage driver to Sconsett. On dark nights in a fog he would stop horses, drop the staff of his whip to the ground, draw it up, put it in his mouth. Why?—I know every foot of land and tell exactly where I am by tasting it.

Wednesday, September 26, 1917

Sperry came down in response to telegram. Told him we must arrest 96 German & Austrian aliens working in his factory, examine their homes, and intern those who were under suspicion. Intelligence and Naval Consulting Board believed in [it] dangerous to trust men in Sperry's works where most secret experiments are being carried on. 90% is for Navy—compasses, gyroscopes, new inventions, fire control &c are in the making there as well as the Flying Devil we are testing out. He believes they are loyal, or most of them, and was in distress. So was I, for while some are disloyal it is with deepest regret I cause internment of any who may not be disloyal. But under Presi-

[42] James Thomas Heflin, Democrat, U.S. Representative from Alabama, who had made sensational charges of pro-Germanism against some of his colleagues in the House.

dent's proclamation no alien can work on munitions & with so much smoke no other course. Sperry pledged to secrecy & accepted the inevitable with good grace

Telegraphed Norfolk strikers to come back to work without prejudice and appealed to their Americanism. Later they decided to come back tomorrow morning

Council of National Defense discussed labor questions & space for War Industries Board

Talked with Fletcher about relations as to purchase between War Industries Board & Bureau of Supplies & Accounts.

Met Julian Kennedy [43] at Baker's office & talked fuses till late at night

Thursday, September 27, 1917

Uncle of Ensign wished to marry divorced woman believed to be adventuress. Told him to go to see the young man.

McFarland "Carthage deleudo est." R——[oosevelt] If not loyal should not hesitate. Told Weeks N.D. [Navy Department] was not conducted properly & you should be certain. Hearst gave him control of editorial policy of papers.[44]

Talked to Sperry over the phone. He wished naval officer as Director of Works.

Ambassador Spring Rice called to present two English officers who had been wounded at the front. They thought Haig's gains yesterday important and said they knew every foot of land in that country.

Estimates—only those for conducting the Department, not for new ships.

Telegram from Page expressing regret that Am. Navy thought English were not frank and did not give all the facts to help us. I answered we had no such view and could not imagine how such an impression had been imparted.

Friday, September 28, 1917

Went to see members War Industries Board about reports that there was

---

[43] Consulting engineer and steel expert.

[44] This entry, virtually repeated on September 29, records a warning by Grenville S. MacFarland, editor of the *Boston American,* that Daniels' assistant, Franklin D. Roosevelt, was disloyal. Roosevelt was characteristically impatient with what he considered a lack of vigor and decision in the department, and had expressed his views freely to Winston Churchill in the hope that the latter's report would cause a shakeup. "The more I think over the talk with the President," Roosevelt wrote his wife an August 17, "the more I am encouraged to think that he has *begun* to catch on, but then it will take lots more of the Churchill type of attack." (*F. D. R.: His Personal Letters, 1905–1928,* Elliott Roosevelt, ed. [New York: Duell, Sloan and Pearce, 1948], pp. 356–357.) This entry suggests that Roosevelt had also carried his dissatisfaction to Republican Senator Weeks, a Naval Academy graduate. Whether Daniels was aware of the extent of Roosevelt's disloyalty is not clear, but in any event he was glad later that he had not on various occasions forced the issue to an open break. See entry of August 6, 1920.

friction between them and purchasing department of the Navy. Due to young egotists who wanted to control purchases. Urged that we permit no penny-a-liners to produce the friction they desired to bring about. McGowan to see Rosenwald and Scott.

Cabinet—short session. Mrs. McAdoo presided at Woman's meeting of Liberty Loan bonds. The President said she was very nervous, never having done such a thing before. He said to her "Why don't you follow the example of your father? When he does not know anything about what he must attempt, he makes a bluff at it."

Sir Stephenson Kent,[45] of Munitions Board of Great Brittain [*sic*], talked an hour before the Council of National Defense. Said early part of war there were colossal profits made by munition makers, and England soon saw it must make labor understand there should be no profiteering & lrg [large] profits allowed, & labor was to be fairly paid. That was essential. He is rich & big manufacturer & he showed his faith by his acts—

Norfolk strikers taken back. Regulations make them lose their leave. That reopened the trouble.

Saturday, September 29, 1917

McGowan made written report of meeting with Scott and Rosenwald & they agreed fully as to methods of purchases, leaving all matters to Navy Dept. & we to accept prices for fuel & food fixed by the constitu[t]ed authorities

McFarland, of Boston American, called & said he was now editor of all Hearst's papers. Said "Carthage deleuda [?] est"—F D R [46]

Josephus came at night from Phila & told us about his new home & how he liked Mrs. Brooke

Sunday, September 30, 1917

I was full of cold & remained in bed until 2 o'clock. Then went to see Mc-Adoo who was leaving that afternoon for his Western trip in the interest of Liberty Loan fund. He talked about his boys and wanted one to take the course at Annapolis. I told him it would be made all right. He had talked to the President.

Went to see Mrs. Dewey who showed me Chicago paper [47] showing how

---

[45] Sir Stephenson H. Kent, director general of the munitions labor supply of the British Ministry of Munitions.

[46] See entry and note of September 27, 1917.

[47] Possibly a reference to an article on "Woman's War Work" in the *Chicago Herald* of September 28. The article quoted W. H. Slayton, the executive secretary of the Navy League, as saying: "As a matter of fact, the sending of garments by the woman's section of the Navy League has gone right along at the rate of 11,000 a day. But instead of sending them in the name of the woman's section, they go forward in the name of Mrs. George Dewey."

Navy League was trying to use her. So she wrote Mrs. Frazier declining to serve as Chn of Comforts Committee

"Be calm: See how Damn Calm I am"—Brownson [48] went to Admiral Dewey in a rage because a Doctor had been put in charge of hospital ship. "Don't get excited" said D—— & counseled moderation & then, forgetting his counsel said: "By God, if I would get my hands on the men who abused my wife, I'd break his [sic] neck." [49]

Later went to hear Father Chidwick [50] preach on the elipse to soldiers and sailors. He was Chaplain on the Maine. [Franklin D.] Roosevelt introduced him.

At night at home with the boys and they were all very jolly

Picture taken at Friday [sic] White House with Naval Scouts from Balto

---

Monday, October 1, 1917

Visited Democratic Headquarters and saw the systematic way of keeping the people informed as to the acts of the administration. They feel that they do not get in close touch with the administration as they should.

Senator Swanson called about naval matters & wished a few appointments as Chief Yeoman

Ammunition carried into Mexico, reached Victoria, & Benson had telegram telling our Captain of Annapolis [1] not to permit ammunition to get to Car[r]anza forces in region of Tampico. The Mexican officer [2] in control of oil section of Tampico gets $35,000 a year from oil interests to protect oil wells. He is independent of Caranza and naturally wishes to get control of the oil wells & their revenue. Thought he wished ammunition for that purpose[.] I did not sign the telegram & waited to see Lansing.

[48] Rear Admiral (Ret.) Willard H. Brownson.

[49] Following his victory at Manila Bay in the Spanish-American War a group of admirers presented Admiral Dewey with a suitable house in Washington, D.C. Shortly afterward he married a wealthy Washington widow, Mrs. Mildred McLean Hazen, and gave her the house as a wedding present. Dewey never could understand nor forgive the flood of criticism resulting from his act.

[50] John P. S. Chidwick, Roman Catholic chaplain in the Navy, 1895–1903.

---

[1] A small gunboat stationed off Tampico to protect American lives and property.

[2] General Manuel Pelaez, a Mexican rebel chieftain in control of the oil fields around Tampico.

Coffin wanted F D R put on Aircraft Board & said he would have time to attend 2 or 3 meetings a week

Tuesday, October 2, 1917

Adams [3] had scheme to make merchant ships submerge & thus prevent injury by sub-marines. "I will see Taylor." He went up in the air & said Taylor had picked holes in it, & he was a beaurocrat [*sic*]. Most inventions have been made by outsiders

W W   What is G's chief trouble—men, money or munitions. Gregory said he had heard it was transportation—would give the submarines for engines. That reminded W W of the man who said he would like to swap a falsetto voice for a false set of teeth.

5 children girls. What are the other half?

Negro asked how he liked near beer: "It looks like beer, it tastes like beer, but when it gets inside of you it has no authority.["]

Discussion about exemptions in draft. Woman in Arizona who wanted her son exempted. He had 2 children & wife dependent upon him. W W said she was Pres. of a Wilson League & had been vigorous in his defense against the vile slanders upon him during campaign. His first reference in cabinet to it.

President thought it would do good if Mrs. Dewey would give out the suppressed chapters of Dewey's book on the German attitude.[4]

William & Mary. "I have come for your goods & all your goods"—Father of W W used that when Louisville offered money if Presbyterians would move seminary to that city.

Dined with Arthur Brisbane. Mrs. George J Gould [5] & Straus at the New Willard

Eberle said 1450 boys at Annapolis

Wednesday, October 3, 1917

Left at 12:30 with Mr. Davison, of Red Cross, for New York & spent night at his home at Peacocks Point. Young aviators there. His son, an aviator, had fallen in a flight, & sustained serious injury

[3] Commander Laurence S. Adams, a naval constructor.

[4] In his autobiography Admiral Dewey had deleted some material critical of Germany, including an account of a conversation with a German naval officer at Manila Bay in 1898 in which the latter predicted a German war for world conquest in fifteen years. Senator Lewis had recently created a stir by recounting this prediction in a Senate speech, and the President doubtless wanted to get maximum propaganda effect from the story by getting it in Dewey's own words. Mrs. Dewey demurred, however. See entry of October 15, 1917.

[5] Edith M. Kingdon Gould, wife of the prominent railroad capitalist.

Who is your favorite Jew? My husband

Saw young Davison & his friends. He had fallen from aeroplane & had been badly injured. Cheerful & fine

Thursday, October 4, 1917

Went to New York & reviewed Red Cross parade—Mayor Mitchell.[6]

Visited Navy Yard. Barracks in Brooklyn & Pelham Park.

Dinner & theatre with Mrs. Stotesbury

During parade, sent officer out to conduct my wife to reviewing stand. He did not know her & so I pointed out a lady about size & dress of my wife & she came somewhat demurring & I saw I did not know my own wife. Later when I sent for her, she would not come till she had marched by [?] several squares!

Friday, October 5, 1917

T. R. at large, writing and speaking in disparagement of America's preparation for war, is helping Germany more than the little fellows who are being arrested for giving aid and comfort to the enemy. Can Kansas City Star, containing his allusions to soldiers training with broom-sticks, be excluded from the mails along with other papers spreading what is construed as seditious? B—— said he was having paper read carefully and would not hesitate to act.

An Irish member of Parliament, who has four sons in the English army, here to try to get permission to enlist Irishmen to fight Germany who will not fight under the English flag. Baker gave a deaf ear. Wanted to begin here & then go to Ireland to recruit

Left Mayflower for Norfolk

Saturday, October 6, 1917

Reached Norfolk Navy Yard and went at once to Training Station where 4,500 young men drilled. Made them an address after they passed in review. Told of 1,600 men in ranks promoted since war was declared & counseled them to do all they could to win promotion.

Then visited Navy Yard and made thorough inspection. Dry Dock work going ahead rapidly. Navy needs to buy land opposite side of river for ingress and egress of big ships. Marine Barracks should be moved & space given to Navy Yard industrial work. Ways for building dreadnaughts & destroyers going ahead slowly.

Had officers of Navy Yard to lunch on Mayflower, then in auto went to

[6] John Purroy Mitchel, mayor of New York.

Hampton Roads. The Mayor promised to regard Norfolk as a branch or station of the Navy & do everything possible to safeguard young men. Would segregate the colored section of the town.

Sunday, October 7, 1917

Jonathan & friend Hoyle arrived on Washington boat & then we sailed for York river to visit the fleet, reached there at noon and all ships gave the honors, and Coffman and Grant came on Mayflower to lunch. We talked the war in Europe, the work of the fleet, how to improve what was being done. Coffman was doubtful of good work of YMCA. I told him Russia & Italy were asking us to send Y.M.C.A. workers there and we should be happy to have them make wholesome conditions.

Letter from Niblack giving his news on the European war.

Sailed for Washington at 4 p.m.

Berry leaving Mayflower.

Monday, October 8, 1917

Reached W[ashington] at 8 a.m. Went to meeting of Council of National Defense to hear report from Advisory Commission on housing men working in munition plants & ship-building yards. Many are poorly housed. Decided to appoint a special commission to make a study and report.

Talked to destroyer ship builders about contract for 150 destroyers & agreed upon terms.

Went to laying corner stone of new Southern Meth church.

At night dined at Willard with Gen Carr and Bishop Candler.[7]

Redfield wanted B & I to see Phila. Public Ledger man to discuss what we were doing as to getting men & supplies to France. Very pessimistic. Baker said we could not take time to talk to men who would not hear anything but their own theories

Tuesday, October 9, 1917

W W told of English sailors who entertained German sailors at banquet. After English petty officer proposed toast to 'is ighness the German H'emperor —he asked the G if he would not propose health of the English King. Asked twice. No answer. Then up comes your H-Emperor, putting his hand down his throat.

Burleson told of gentlemen just back from England who said all the country

[7] Warren A. Candler, bishop of the Methodist Episcopal Church, South.

was ringing with praise of what our destroyers were doing. "When will you be ready?" "I am ready now." [8]

Can wives of Army & Navy officers get passports to Europe? No, not even if member of Red Cross. Can wives of Cong. Yes—there is not executive jurisdiction over them. Redfield dissented & told of woman who had rented house to open it to American boys & Burleson said his old maid sister wished to go.

Talked to Atty Genl. about liquor to men in uniform.

Baruch called & we talked of War Industries Board. He had stood he said, alone for lower steel prices.

A Hun—Truth is a German lie

Wednesday, October 10, 1917

English Ambassador and Lord Reading [9] called. Spring Rice thanked me for giving prompt denial to rumors of differences between English and American naval authorities. Reading had presided when Roger Casement [10] was sentenced & was interested in telegram from Zimmerman [11] & other Germans who were trying to bring about sabotage & murder in America.

Roosevelt & Aircraft Production Board. He did not desire such responsibility. Letter from Winslow.

N.C. man who had the real invention for ending submarine menace—from the country & mountains, but was confident.

Mr. Edison came in & said he now felt quite sure he could put an end to Fritz and end submarine menace & had come here for advice and to gain information. I gave him Dewey's room & told him he could have anything except my job & he could have that if he made the discovery. He said he was happy. His ship [12] was up for 7 days repair.

Mrs. Dewey came to take me to Mason House and show what was being done for sailors. "I wish you to be my brother" she said

[8] The response given by Commander Joseph K. Taussig, commanding the first group of American destroyers sent to Europe after the United States entered the war, when asked by a British admiral how soon the Americans could begin patrol duty.

[9] Rufus Daniel Isaacs, Lord Reading, Lord Chief Justice of England, recently arrived on a special mission from Lloyd George to propose greater coordination of allied embargo policies and a high-level conference in London.

[10] Irish nationalist who in the early months of the war sought German aid for an Irish uprising. After landing from a German submarine to take part in the abortive Easter Rebellion of 1916, Casement was captured, convicted of treason, and hung.

[11] Arthur Zimmermann, German undersecretary for foreign affairs from 1911 to November, 1916; subsequently foreign secretary until August, 1917.

[12] Over the objections of some naval officers, Daniels gave Edison whatever facilities he desired for his naval experiments, including the use of small boats assigned to the New York Navy Yard.

Thursday, October 11, 1917

Col. House called. He said "You may see [say?] with a certain Governor of Texas 'I have made no mistakes[.']" My reply was I could not say that truthfully. He goes to Europe for the President for conference with the powers on our side. An army & navy officer will go with him. We talked of what Navy had done and the work of offensive ahead of it.

Conference between Baker, Hoover, Hurley[,] Gen Baker [13] & myself, at President's suggestion, to see how we could use ships to better advantage to carry food &c to France. At this time England has 5 months supply of flour. France only 1½ months. Coal is so high in France & Italy suffering must come to people. Hoover: "We should find out what ships allies have & see that all their shipping is used for the real needs. England should allocate a larger part of its shipping to France & Italy & stop 12 ships running from Australia to California. We must get Dutch, Norway & German Ships & put them in use. Further facts to be gathered.

Big meeting South end of War, State & Navy building. Speeches by Baker, Daniels and Phillips for Liberty Loan bonds.

Estimates finished—nearly a billion dollars.

Houston enthusiastic upon his visit to Providence and other places in Mecklinburg.

Friday, October 12, 1917

Satterlee [14] & Union [Navy] League—He hates to leave but wholly disapproves Thompson & Co.

Conference with builders of pumps, auxiliaries of destroyers. All wished advances and some wished too much profit.

Cabinet. Baker told of fact that most men drafted preferred infantry, small guns & artillery & few quartermaster duty & thus showed they wished to fight as much as the men who volunteered. The conscientious objectors are segregated, no harm done them, & one by one they come out and say they are ready to serve. Heads of churches opposed to fighting are writing urging that these men be put to work and not remain idle. More democratic feeling in the army.

W W talked of conditions abroad & spoke of suggestion that he appoint a commission on reconstruction. after the war. He said Jusserand went up in

[13] Brigadier General Chauncey B. Baker, chief of the War Department's embarkation service.
[14] Herbert L. Satterlee, son-in-law of J. Pierpont Morgan, Navy veteran of the Spanish-American War, and one of the founders of the Navy League.

the air when he read W's statement no selfish trade arrangements after the war. Some will wish to have league to prevent Germany trading with the world. This country will have the money & can compel the nations to measure up to our standard or not be given credit. We must impose these American views upon Europe for the good of all. To try to shut up Germany would be to plan to have another war & would be contrary to American views.

Lansing: England should put her Australian ships into carrying wheat for her & France.

Benson to go to France with House & Bliss [15]

Saturday, October 13, 1917

Luncheon with Saunders, Sperry, McGuire [16] & Earle discussing what to do with Sperry's work, to press the completion instruments & the flying torpedo and prevent spies getting information without keeping detectives in S's factory. McGuire had installed efficiency in Ford's factory & agreed to look in and help at Sperry's place.

At 11 o'clock went to Gun Factory to speak for Liberty Loan campaign. Great crowd. Band from Chicago Training station.

Saturday night had conference until midnight with Benson and Mayo. The latter told of his visit to England, of the conference with naval officers of all the allied powers, and his faith in the end, and told of the difficulties of an offensive. Germany may still control the air & until we can have aircraft to go over Heligoland [17] & photograph its guns and defenses a naval offensive might spell suicide. Told of a German aeroplane passing over Dunkirk & doing 1 mil pound damage while he was there. English suggestion of sinking old ships & shutting in submarines in Germany regarded as impossible. Mayo rather doubtful of any offensive. Benson aggressive for an offensive.

Sunday, October 14, 1917

Went to church with Frank. Communion at Dr. Wood's church. Soldiers and sailors here. Went there because Addie absent & it would make me feel nearer to her if I sat in her pew.

Josephus and the Brooke boys came to spend Sunday. We went driving in the afternoon

[15] General Tasker H. Bliss, recently appointed Army chief of staff.

[16] Possibly James C. McGuire, prominent New York engineer.

[17] A heavily fortified German island in the North Sea lying off the mouths of the Elbe and Weser Rivers.

Monday, October 15, 1917

Spoke at Keith's theatre at noon on Liberty bonds to good crowd. Praised Congress & spoke in optimistic vein & urged that dollars as well as men be mobilized &c.

Went to see Mrs. Dewey about her giving out for publication D's unpublished chapter telling of action of Germans at Manila & how Dewey read the riot act to officer who came on board the Olympia. W W thought it might be well to publish. She said the Admiral had decided not to print & if she gave it out now it might provoke controversy and she did not think it would please him.

Entertained at dinner Mayo, Benson, Fletcher, Badger, Winterhalter, Winslow, & Pratt [18] & discussed Mayo's visit to England & how to stop submarine menace. Hard nut to crack. Mayo favored barrage across North Sea, Benson to close straits of Dover & barrage around Heligoland. Talked till late but reached no plan.[19]

Tuesday, October 16, 1917

Spoke in Senate office room on Insurance for soldiers and sailors in bill passed by Congress and predicted that after the war the Government would continue the insurance feature and would enlarge it to reach all citizens so that saving would be encouraged and there would be end of high price charged for insurance.

Norman Mack [20] and New York city political campaign for Mayor. His son-in-law made Asst. Paymaster.

Cabinet. Houston brought up the fact that members of missions went about saying that if this or that were not done, the allies would be defeated,

[18] Captain William V. Pratt, assistant chief of Naval Operations. Daniels respected these officers and relied heavily upon their advice.

[19] Under discussion here was the proposal to plant a broad belt or barrage of mines in the path of German submarines, both to destroy the submarines and damage the morale of their crews. The scheme had early received the enthusiastic backing of Franklin Roosevelt and Secretary of Commerce Redfield and appealed to President Wilson's desire for aggressive action against the submarine menace. Many of the American admirals were skeptical of the plan, however, and the British Admiralty had at first rejected it as completely impractical. Daniels, too, had reservations about the mine barrage—a factor contributing to Roosevelt's impatience with his chief at this time. By the end of the month, though he had not been completely won over, Daniels had decided to proceed with the stupendous task of bottling up the submarines by laying some 70,000 mines across the North Sea and in the narrow neck of the English Channel. The barrage was not completed until late in the war and did not play a decisive part in the allied victory.

[20] Norman E. Mack, editor and publisher of the *Buffalo Times* and member of the Democratic National Committee.

& thought they ought to be told not to talk. President said Senator Hitchcock asked "is there anything hopeful?" having become blue by pessimistic talk. The President said he dissipated his pessimism to some extent. Trying to unload on us burdens they should bear, particularly the enmity of small neutral nations adjoining Germany. Wish us to press embargo without their help & shoulder all the odium.

Picture taken with Mayo & Benson.

At night went with Benson to see Edison. He had charts showing submarines [ships?] sunk in seven months, making an awful showing, worse than I thought. He insists sailing is not made with reference to location of submarines and that if ships would not sail when they could be seen the number would be greatly reduced. Less than 6% of sinkings at night. Edison full of subject & working hard [21]

Son of State Sup. Ct. Judge asked to resign from Annapolis because he had hereditary syphillis.

Wednesday, October 17, 1917

Folk Company wanted us to pay ⅔ for gears [22] new buildings &c. I offered ½, & we finally traded on ½, arbitrators to settle upon how much each should pay when war is over. Only people who can do the gear cutting and it was necessary to trade with them.

Admiral Winslow would like to take ships over to England if they are sent. He doubts suggestion of barrage in North Sea proposed by English and approved by Mayo.

Report that Cassin [23] had been torpedoed came from Sims. One man killed & 5 wounded. Ship taken into port to be repaired. At first news feared it had been sunk. Should it be given out? Benson said "Yes"; Belknap "No," but when later news that it had not been sunk all said No.

Egerton [24] had given one Parker placing of all bonds on destroyers. Joseph Wilson had wished them placed as usual and I had agreed. So had to turn Egerton down & tell me [him] I did not like having an intermediary.

[21] Edison was at this time working on an elaborate statistical analysis of submarine sinkings in order to determine the locations, hours of day, weather, and other conditions most favorable to submarine activity. Daniels and Wilson considered his lengthy report and recommendations for counteraction so valuable that it was at once dispatched to Sir Eric Geddes, the First Lord of the British Admiralty.

[22] Daniels has inserted the word "gears" here, evidently meaning to indicate that the discussion involved construction of a new gear factory to supply the Navy.

[23] A U.S. destroyer torpedoed while on patrol off the south coast of Ireland on October 15 with a loss of one killed and nine injured. Despite heavy damage the *Cassin* was brought safely to Queenstown.

[24] Graham Egerton, Solicitor of the Navy Department, whose bonding arrangements were successfully challenged by Joseph R. Wilson, brother of the President.

Conference on Sec 12 & 13.[25] Bawdy houses & saloons. Army had only ½ mile as to saloons in cities, 5 mi. for prostitution houses.

Thursday, October 18, 1917

Admiral Colchalk, Russian, leaving for home gave dinner in my honor at Shoreham. Russian and American naval officers present. He expressed thanks for American hospitality. I replied. Seas once thought created to divide nations. We have learned they were made to unite them. I proposed health of the President of the Republic of Russia. Is there such an officer? The Russian Admiral said "Yes, Kerensky is President.["] I rather think he is President of Council & not of Republic. But never mind. The Russian officers very much depressed and very blue over the victory of the Germans, and, as they are not good linguists, rather difficult to talk with them.

Signed order no house of prostitution within five miles of any navy yard or naval reservation.

Hinckley [?], from England, wants America to finance canal [tunnel?] from England to France. I referred him to English & French as we could not initiate it.

Saw Mrs. Stotesbury—very keen about comforts & work of Naval auxiliary.

Friday, October 19, 1917

Cabinet. Controller of RR wrote in Comptroller. When was P put in Controller. I don't know exactly, but think it was about the time the stock was watered.

Transport[26] submarined on return trip near French coast. Our first transport lost.

Went over with Mayo to see President. Mayo told him of message from the King. He told of what he had seen. The President said the English thought we were were [sic] Anglo-Saxons and like themselves. We are very different. He had said one of our troubles was we could understand the English & when they said things against us, we knew it while if F[rance] or G[ermany] did the same we knew nothing about it. He listened to M[ayo] & hoped some real offensive would come. He was disgusted with the idea of sinking 100 ships to shut up river beyond Heligoland when dynamite could clear the channel.

Dined at English Ambassador's to meet Lord and Lady Redding [sic]. I talked with a lady about the undefinable thing called charmed [charm].

[25] Sections 12 and 13 of the Selective Service Act of May 18, 1917, made applicable to the Navy by an act of October 6, authorized the prohibition of saloons and brothels in areas near military posts and establishments.

[26] The U.S. Army transport *Antilles*, sunk by a German submarine on October 17 while en route to the United States, with a loss of sixty-seven lives.

Who is the most charming person you ever met? asked lady. "I will not answer as to ladies, but make it men. You write down the two most charming & I will.["] I wrote Lloyd George & Balfour & she wrote Balfour & Lloyd George. When a boy Lord R—— said he had been a boy before the mast on a ship

He went to school in Germany & had many friends & yet 13 years ago he decided never to go there again. The people were offensive & made an Englishman feel they were a decadent nation (& in some ways we are) & I would not go again.

Morley: What you are, where you are; more than what you say

Saturday, October 20, 1917

Mayo spoke before the Naval Consulting Board. German trench & camp taken disclosed fact that mail written by German soldiers to their families had not been forwarded before captured. Examination of the mail showed that letters (not in knowledge of the soldiers) had been postmarked "London," "Paris" &c so that people at home would think soldiers had really taken London & Paris. One German prisoner, upon being asked what he wished most to see in Paris [*sic*], replied "The ruins of Westminster Abbey" really believing it had been destroyed. When he saw the Abbey untouched, he said: "We Germans are some liars."

Very busy trying to get away to Chicago and projecting myself ahead as much as possible.

Left on 6^{05} train for Chicago. Admiral Colchock, of Russia, & staff on train also Adlai Stevenson. His daughter had corresponded with German here who had later been caught in German propaganda & Navy had caused his arrest. I sent her word, in playfulness, that it might be necessary to publish her correspondence.

Sunday, October 21, 1917

Chicago

On Train

Tried to read up and get ready for Chicago addresses & read part of Gerard's book,[27] all the morning before getting to Chicago. At Chicago, 3 o'clock, met by Capt. Moffitt,[28] Braisted & others, & went in auto, to Great Lakes, where 15,000 men are in training, visited nearly all the houses, at least one of each kind, took dinner in the dining room of enlisted men with their menu. It was good & nourishing. Later visited hospital. Pleasant faced chap from Mississipii

[27] James W. Gerard, *My Four Years in Germany* (New York: Doran, 1917).
[28] Captain William A. Moffett, commandant of the Great Lakes Naval Training Station.

[*sic*] insisted upon my taking one [of] his oranges sent from home. Work is going on rapidly under difficulties of rain. Found men short in over coats and in thick underwear and telegraphed P.M. General [29] to at once rush orders as it was getting cold on the lakes and the men needed thicker clothes, & to get them even if he had to go to New York himself & take matter up.

At night spoke to large crowd at Y.M.C.A. & spoke of need of clean lives for clean thinking and steady nerves.

Monday, October 22, 1917
  Chicago
Arose early, had breakfast with Capt & Mrs. Moffitt and went to rifle range where men were making good record shooting. Visited other buildings & at 9 o'clock reviewed the 12 or 15 thousand men, led by John Philip Sousa's band, & made speech to them. Then left on train for Chicago, & hastened to Sherman house where I spoke at luncheon at Iroquois Club. It was a fine meeting & Bishop Fallows [30] made a militant invocation to the God of Battle. Jackson & wife, & Helen Towle [?] whose only son has gone to France. I made about the best speech I have made. Jefferson's "All Reps. All Federalists" Immediately after luncheon I went to Camp Grant and to the Municipal Pier where young men were under training for the Navy & spoke at both places. At 5 pm spoke to the Four Minute Men club.[31] At 6 pm dined with American Surgeon Clinical Asso's leaders, including English & French surgeons. Then I spoke & told doctors it was up to them to lessen the ravages of venereal diseases. Then I went to Hamilton Club and followed Ambassador Gerard in speaking on Causes of War & the Liberty Loan.

Tuesday, October 23, 1917
  Chicago
Had breakfast with Jacksons, talked to Rupert Blue [32] about Victor & the Texas, & left at 10 a.m. for Marion, Indiana.

Stopped with Mr. McCullough, President of Bank, visited Soldiers Home and factories, dined with Liberty Bond Committee where a lady sung [*sic*] delightfully. Then spoke to great crowd in hall. After speaking company went to Dr C's home and we spent hour in conversation. Good town and people very cordial

"Come to my bank and take anything you wish" said Doctor

[29] Rear Admiral Samuel McGowan, Navy Paymaster General.
[30] Bishop Samuel Fallows of the Reformed Episcopal Church, active member of the G.A.R. and other patriotic groups.
[31] Part of a nationwide network of volunteer speakers to promote the sale of Liberty bonds.
[32] Surgeon General of the U.S. Public Health Service and brother of Captain Victor Blue.

"The safe & deposit vaults are closed until tomorrow" said the Cashier. Good combination.

Canny Scotchman is the Doctor. Some of his associates wanted war contracts.

Lord Northcliffe came to train to see me and was deeply interested in Mayo's impressions in his visit to England and France

Wednesday, October 24, 1917

Left Marion at 9 o'clock on day train & reached Columbus, Ohio, ab[ou]t 3 o'clock. Met by Mayor Karb (5 times elected as Democrat) & Senator Pomerine.[33] Went to International Dairy Show and saw the finest cattle I ever dreamed of. Both Pomerine and I made short speeches.

After dinner, Pomerine and I spoke in large hall. Children sang patriotic songs. Pomerine was very severe on men with German sympathies. Said they ought to go to Germany unless they were in full sympathy with us in this war. Scored several in Canton who did not take bonds.

The Ohio State Journal came out for State Prohibition. Bryan had spoken the night before and made great impression. Looks better for prohibition, but big cities with large foreign vote will make victory difficult.

Thursday, October 25, 1917

Traveled all day, reaching New York at 3:30. Went to Plaza, met by Mr. Strong[34] and other members of committee, & after tea went to Central Park where German submarine had been set up. Mrs. Emerson[35] who had been rescued from the Lusitania, rechristened it "the U-Buy a Bond," & I spoke about the place in the Navy in this war, decried stiletto under sea stabs & hoped when peace conference came we would end forever submarine warfare. Went over submarine and then went to Brooklyn Navy Yard, dined with Admiral Usher & went with him to Patriotic Pageant at Metropolitan Opera House & then on night train to Washington.

Friday, October 26, 1917

Reached W[ashington] 9 am. My wife had left previous day for Atlanta for Y.W.C.A. meeting.

At Cabinet meeting the President spoke of good work I had been doing and of the other members. I took Admiral Browning, of the British Navy, &

[33] Atlee Pomerene, Democrat, U.S. Senator from Ohio.

[34] Benjamin Strong, governor of the New York Federal Reserve Bank and chairman of the New York Liberty Loan Committee.

[35] Margaret C. Smith Emerson, wife of New York banker Guy Emerson.

the President emphasized to him his earnest desire to do something audacious in the line of offense.

Pres. told of Aspinwall, Iowa, where Germans lived. They took no Liberty bonds. Delegations from near-by towns went over, shut up every store, arrested the owner of the town hall because he would not permit its use for a Liberty Loan meeting. W W: What right or authority? None[.] McAdoo thought obstructing the liberty bond campaign.

Burleson told of pro-German papers. When their editors were sent for he asked: Have you printed that Germans dropped bombs on Red Cross hospitals? Have you printed any atrocities practised by Germans? In every case such views had been deleted & they promised it would not occur again.

Worked late at night at Department trying to catch up.

Saturday, October 27, 1917

Finished contracts with auxiliary people for 150 destroyers—

Impressive Parade to Elipse in interest of Liberty Loan. All departments out & great crowd. McAdoo & John Davis spoke. Davis made classic. "Belgium replied to Germany: We are a country, not a road." Traced the time when Caessar fought the Huns on the roof of the world. McAdoo told of farmer who sent $1,000 for first Liberty bond & wrote to know to whom he should send the interest. He thought he had given the $1,000 & must also pay 3½ per cent interest on it during the continuance of the war.

Council of National Defense on improvement of water ways, specially up the Miss. Coal had been carried on War Dept barges from St. Louis at saving. Gen. Black,[36] Redfield, Parker [37] & others urged large improvts[.] President had ordered certain barges built[.] Willard did not approve. Feared it would hurt the rail roads.

Logic is: Transportation is a governmental function and Govt must own & control RR, water way & telegraph & telephone

Sunday, October 28, 1917

Went to Gun Factory to Memorial Service & to day of prayer according to the Proclamation of the President. I made brief tribute to the 28 sailors who had already lost their lives. Impressive service.

Dinner at Mrs. B[agley]'s—Ethel's birthday & then ride

In afternoon had a long talk with Admiral Benson about trip & the big question before us.

[36] Major General William M. Black, chief of engineers of the U.S. Army and chairman of the Inland Waterway Transportation Committee of the Council of National Defense.
[37] Edwin B. Parker, priorities commissioner of the War Industries Board.

"I have perfect faith that Providence orders our ways in our daily life" he said. It is beautiful to see a strong & able man with such child-like faith. He goes in that faith. I gave him W W's message & instructions—"All possible co-operation but we must be free.["]

B left [38]

Monday, October 29, 1917

Had talk with Lord Northcliffe who was evidently depressed & said he hoped we would build fire under English Navy. Jellico had but one thought and that was to preserve the great fleet. Not accustomed to fighting & had no real engagement since Nelson's day. Going to London to international conference, but feared there would be no commanding figure, with initiative. He saw me in Chicago and came back happy over the splendid spirit of the patriotic West.

McKean: After visiting Greece and seeing soldiers smoking and drinking in cafes & asking "Why don't the powers come and save us?" he no longer believed the story of Thermopylae—did not think such men could have begotten the men now inhabiting Greece. Felt about the same way about Italy.

Roosevelt after reading report of General Board for a bar[r]age across North Sea said "I told you so last May." Badger called and had long conference & said by process of elimination he had come to conclusion that the bar[r]age of mines, with closing of English Channel, in the North Sea was feasible and the only big thing the combined navies could do. All the General Board and Capt. Pratt held that view, and I authorized Pratt to put Capt. Belknap at work on the mining, it being regarded he was the most capable man on mining and for Admiral Hoogewerff's [39] division to take it in hand. A stupendous undertaking—perhaps not impossible but to my mind of doubtful practicability. North Sea too rough & will necessitate withdrawing all our ships from other work and then can we destroy the hornets nest or keep the hornets in?

Monday night. Edison spent whole evening, discussing a system of routing he thought would save many ships. He had maps showing all submarines since February

Tuesday, October 30, 1917

Went to capital to take part in departure over Bankhead good road through the South.

W W took up the General Board's & the Admiralty's plan of barrage across

---

[38] Admiral Benson accompanied Colonel House on the latter's mission to the Inter-Allied war conference in Europe. One of Benson's assignments was to arrange for the laying of the North Sea mine barrage.

[39] Rear Admiral John A. Hoogewerff, commander of the mine force of the Atlantic Fleet.

North Sea. I told W W it was very difficult, but was the only plan possible to shut off the submarines. It might cut off ½ & that would be important. Very costly & very difficult, but all things are possible.

Talk with Arther Pollen, who urged that I or some man in authority go to England and France and keep the Admiralty busy on plans to win the war. He seemed pessimistic.

Lord Reading, Chief Justice of England, called to say good-bye before his departure for home to be present at the conference & give his country benefit of all he had learned here. He was downcast over Italian news [40] & looked for a long war.

At night had long conference with Pratt and Belknap over the North Sea barrage. Will put Belknap in charge & told him to use all diligence & he would have the whole Dept. back of him.

Long talk with Baruch—not satisfied with progress of War Industries Board.

Wednesday, October 31, 1917

Got up at 6:30 and went to Quantico to the marine training camp, witnessed drill and maneovres [sic] & visited hospital and spoke to the men who will shortly go to France. Promised promotions to those who win them by fitness and urged them to keep their bodies and souls clean.

Will put Capt. Belknap in charge of the barrage in North Sea and of the mining division and transfer Admiral Hooggewerff [sic] to the fleet so that responsibility may be fully in hands of Belknap.

Went with Redfield to Bureau of Mines to see steel wings for air craft to take the place of wood. Steel as designed by Mr. Ropp [?], of Queens county, is lighter than ours [?], can be manufactured in quantities, and experts there seemed to think he had made a great hit. Wood is hard to get. If it is demonstrated as better, or as good, can manufacture thousands instead of hundreds. Dr. Stratton [41] told of young French Lieutent [sic] here, who is expert on radio, who was ten months in prison in France, and escaped as Red Cross employe. His tales of how Germans are kept in ignorance & of their brutality staggers belief, but who can doubt?

Lane's son [42] transferred from Army—wishes to go to France as Jr. Lieutenant. Too young. I knew nothing of it.

---

[40] The government of Italian Premier Paolo Boselli had fallen on October 26, following news of heavy Italian reverses on the Austrian front, losses that were continuing.

[41] Samuel W. Stratton, director of the National Bureau of Standards and secretary of the National Advisory Committee for Aeronautics.

[42] Ensign Franklin K. Lane, Jr., age nineteen, enrolled as a student pilot in the Naval Reserve Flying Corps.

Thursday, November 1, 1917

Council of National Defense met. Scott [1] had resigned and committee of Chamber of Commerce had presented an argument for such change as would co-ordinate all the purchases for war purposes. The Board of War Industries lacked power, War & Navy Departments bought without referring to the Board, & business men said they did not know where they "were at." Discussed matter and man for Chairmanship of the board & adjourned for further discussion

Navy Council talked about contracts—1 to [?] 10% & Harris [2] felt none other could be made and the work promptly done. Decided to build station in Ireland to repair torpedoes & keep our material in good shape. Could not get work done in England.

Council of Nat. Defense met in afternoon & heard Committee on Housing. In places where ships were being built & munitions on large scale the workers have no suitable places to live and this fact reduces production. Necessary for the Gov. to house mechanics or to furnish buildings & tools

Went to see Joseph Pannell's [3] pictures—many navy pictures

Friday, November 2, 1917

Sperry said he and another man had a plan by which ships in convoy could communicate with other ships without danger of detection. Very important now that wireless cannot be used by our ships going into danger zone and therefore can have no communication at night. This discovery would be of highest value.

Alfred Lucking [4] came about Eidsel [*sic*] Ford,[5] who had applied for exemption which had been denied by local board. I saw Baker who said it should be passed on on its merits by the board organized for that purpose. Mr. Ford says he is greatly needed to carry on big work of factory.

Cabinet. W W criticism is that this is rich man's war, & it was reported that sons of rich men were being given places in W[ashington] & others away

---

[1] Frank A. Scott, first head of the War Industries Board, had resigned for reasons of health on October 26, 1917, in the face of growing criticism that the board lacked both power and vigorous leadership.

[2] Rear Admiral Frederic R. Harris, chief of the Bureau of Yards and Docks, briefly general manager of the Emergency Fleet Corporation following Admiral Capps' resignation later in the month.

[3] Joseph Pennell, American artist whose lithographs of wartime scenes in the United States and England were on display at the National Gallery.

[4] Detroit attorney and former Democratic congressman from Michigan.

[5] Edsel B. Ford, the twenty-four-year-old son of automobile manufacturer Henry Ford. The Ford Motor Company did extensive work for the Navy during World War I, and Edsel Ford was given draft exemption on the ground that he was a key executive.

from firing line and this ought to be prevented. Mostly in new organizations. Lane said he thought this mistake & that rich men's sons were going quicker than others. Cannot be too careful said W. W.

Asked Baker to commandeer guns & hundred million rounds of ammunition belonging to Scandinavian country & then send to Italy. He said he could not approve Ordnance recomm. to let explosives go by express.

Council of National Defense. Too many organizations asking money to help soldiers. Some pay big salaries & there ought to be some way to prevent any except those approved to appeal &c

Saturday, November 3, 1917

Tumulty sent over several gentlemen who have sons in Naval Reserves who have sons in France [*sic*]. They complained that Commissions as Ensigns had been given to boys who had not gone to sea and denied to their sons who were in war zone. They wanted their sons sent to Annapolis to study for commissions. Palmer pointed out they could win commissions on ships by demonstrating ability & we could not bring men from actual service to give them opportunity to study. Trouble due to the way the first class was selected.

Lunched with Naval Consulting Board and made them a talk on the problems & difficulties. The French scientists who warned me not to depend as much on science as on guns and ships.

Revoked order that wives of officers should not go to places or in the vicinity of places where their husbands ships were.

Saw Henry Ford. Lucking was troubled because of order that pleasure autos be stopped but Henry Ford said he was ready to do whatever the govern[men]t said do in order to win the war. Is making trucks & parts for fly craft

Lane and his boy

Addie returned from Atlanta, Columbia and Raleigh at Y.W.C.A. Conventions.

Sunday, November 4, 1917

Went to church (Communion Sunday) at Mt. Vernon Place. Always greeted by friendly handshakes.

Upon return home Rev. Mr. Van Dyke [6] called on phone and said his father, Dr. Van Dyke,[7] could not come and it was desired that I take his place at Poli's theatre. I did so and took as my subject Van Dyke's "Keeping the Light"

[6] Tertius Van Dyke, Presbyterian clergyman and former secretary to his father during the latter's diplomatic service.

[7] Henry Van Dyke, prominent author, Presbyterian clergyman, professor of English literature, and former U.S. Minister to the Netherlands and Luxembourg, 1913–1917; subsequently commissioned a Navy chaplain.

and tried to tell the story of Natalie who kept the light and played the fife. Large crowd & friends were very cordial in compliment to impromptu address.

Went to hospital where Addie carried present to baby of Dr. Stryne.[8] His wife died when baby came

Mrs. John Hayes Hammond,[9] head of the Militia of Mercy, wishes to get wool for the Navy through her organization and wanted to call. No, I would call on her & so Addie & I went. She had no picture except of Kings & Queens, given her when her husband was in England at the Coronation. She spoke hinting of wrong on the part of a lady & as soon as possible I rose to go & wished no more of helping one who was interested more in her own exploits than in helping the Navy boys.

Monday, November 5, 1917

Council of National Defense. Dr. Monohan [10] (pronounced Munyan) and Dr. Triebe,[11] of Ohio, who had been in France, spoke to the Council with charts. Out of every 100,000 men who go into battle, hospital arrangements must be made for 20,000. Experience has shown this. Dr. M. urged need of hospitals and doctors & scientists. He said Germans were not as original or as scientific as allies. Two days after the first German gas, English physicians & scientists had gas masks that would save life, & when they reluctantly began the use of gas the quality was better than the Germans, ten times as effective.

Dr. M. said scientists had found a way to locate guns—not by air craft—& it was far superior to anything Germans had done. He urged higher rank for American doctors. He spoke well & as if from a large mind & large knowledge. The American doctor did not talk so well. Had not read so widely, but went direct to subject.

Strike at Fall River settled

Tuesday, November 6, 1917

Young man, who had been in Occoguan [workhouse] for drink, called & told me of half hour with President, in whose presence he had signed the pledge. The President had written below in his own hand "I will add this line to express my confidence that Morrison will keep this pledge now so solemnly taken. Woodrow Wilson." M—— had been pupil at Princeton

F D R wanted to name destroyers Indian names. No. Hold for heroes. We may lose many before this war ends.

Capps came and talked confidentially. He is not well & was annoyed by

---

[8] Lieutenant Commander Howard F. Strine, a Navy surgeon.

[9] Natalie Harris Hammond, wife of the wealthy mining engineer, John Hays Hammond.

[10] Colonel Sir Berkeley G. A. Moynihan, British Army surgeon.

[11] According to the Council minutes of this meeting, this was Major George W. Crile, prominent Cleveland surgeon currently serving in the U.S. Army.

publication of friction. He cannot possibly build the ships as rapidly as people expect and that troubles him. I told him not to worry about criticism for he had the President's confidence.

Gleaves talked of convoying & need of fast ships. Fletcher [12] let ships go out with slow speed & that invited destruction. F is recalled.

Ferguson [13] came & was at dinner with us. I told him he was offered Chm of War Industries Board. Big place & I felt it offered great opportunity. He was pleased and will see Baker to-morrow

Election of Hylan [14] as Mayor of New York

No Cabinet. President went to New Jersey to vote

Wednesday, November 7, 1917

Went with H. L. Ferguson to see Secy. Baker. B said "You cannot leave until you accept"

Saw Mr. Nesbit,[15] Insurance head in Treasury Department. Told me of his speech showing the very high cost of insurance management & talked to him about Alex J. Feild [*sic*] as assistant. Favorable.

A C Avery, of Morganton. I went with him to see Gen. Crowder [16] about commission in Judge Advocate General's office.

Telegram that House, Benson & Bliss had arrived safely in England. Telegraphed congratulations.

Decided to send Knight to pay visit to Vladivostock to pay visit of good will. No American ship had gone to Russia since it became a Republic.

News from Tampico (it comes often) of danger that oil wells might be endangered. 150 soldiers on the way and 300 expected. Saw Lansing who agreed that it would be well if marines were on the Gulf, with transport, so they be rushed to Tampico if necessary.

Thursday, November 8, 1917

Victor Blue at my request called and went over the report of investigation.[17] Thought Gleaves & Marbury Johnson [18] wished to pile up specifications so as to get him. He wished the court martial.

[12] Rear Admiral William B. Fletcher, commander of Squadron Three, Patrol Force, Atlantic Fleet.

[13] Homer L. Ferguson, president and general manager of the Newport News Shipbuilding and Drydock Company.

[14] John F. Hylan, Democrat.

[15] Charles F. Nesbit, recently appointed commissioner of military and naval insurance, War Risk Bureau, Treasury Department.

[16] Major General Enoch H. Crowder, Judge Advocate General of the Army.

[17] Through an error in navigation in September, Blue's battleship, the U.S.S. *Texas*, had been grounded off Block Island.

[18] Rear Admiral Marbury Johnston, commanding Divisions Three and Four, Cruiser Force, Atlantic Fleet. Rear Admiral Albert Gleaves was in overall command of the Cruiser Force.

Finland man came with idea about air ship that could go across the ocean in 60 hours. Wishes this government to build ships.

Council talked of building space and agreed the Navy to let War have all of building and to try to get building on Arlington site.

Judge Council and J. D. Elliott, of Catawba Co, called. Judge has son in the Navy & his wife said she sent her "God bless you" to me

Creel and O'Higgins [19] here to dinner. The latter to write an article about me and my service as Secretary of the Navy. Talked of the criticism and the policies I had tried to carry out.

J D Jr came home.

Friday, November 9, 1917

Shall retirement pay for clerks? W W favored. McAdoo thought some insurance measure would follow soldiers and sailors act. Lane said he dropped three old men and all three committed suicide. W W "That is the way out."

W W. Story of Vance trying to induce negro to join Pres. Ch. Said "I don't believe in this doctrine of election." V. said "I do & it is sound.["] Negro "I aint never heard you was a candidate."

Baker: Man loved to be in limelight. Wife wanted him to join Baptist ch. No. Didn't believe in immersion. Why not? Have to stay too long out of public eye

McAdoo: Shall we lend money to Russia? W W thought we could not yet presume R—— would fail. Must wait

W W pleased, on the whole, with election returns and must pay penalty by receiving Womans delegation today

McAdoo did not think Morgan interests trying to depress markets. Why stocks low? One thing people prefer governmt bonds.

Fosdick and I saw Baker about extending zone to 5 miles & making treating unlawful. He was doubtful—felt soldiers would resent it & good results would not follow

F D R. Lane & Lanes son. Mrs L—— felt troubled. He thought I had done right [20]

Blue was evidently aware that some of his colleagues resented his close relationship to Daniels. As subsequent entries indicate, Daniels spent many hours over whether to discipline his friend Blue.

[19] Harvey J. O'Higgins, writer working with Creel's Committee on Public Information, subsequently as associate chairman.

[20] This probably refers to Daniels' belief that Franklin K. Lane, Jr., was too young to be commissioned a lieutenant (junior grade) in the Navy and commissioned him instead as an ensign. (See entry of October 31, 1917.) Young Lane subsequently served in France as a naval aviator and was promoted to the higher rank.

Saturday, November 10, 1917

Telegram from Benson suggesting 4 dreadnaughts to be sent to English fleet. We approved and sent cable to Mayo to come to Washington to confer upon the ships to be sent.

Vanguard class [?] (E B Crow) sent meal to me and to the President. I sent to Mrs. Wilson and told her I thought the meal of the Presbyterian class was better than its theology though I would not dare to say so to my Presbyterian wife & she would bring down on her head the anathemas if she dared say so to her Presbyterian husband.

Mrs W answered as follows: "We had quite a laugh over your funny note when I read it to the President, and he says he is sure your Presbyterian wife did not see it as you were more considerate of her feelings than I of his. However he is [not?] above eating such sainted meal and we shall both enjoy it when we get back from Buffalo. We are starting in ten minutes, so pardon haste.

Faithfully

Edith Bolling Wilson["]

Jonathan had boy to supper—had engaged to go with a girl & told a social fib & we had quite a time. Jonath—— was troubled

Sunday, November 11, 1917

Slept late and did not go to church. Badger, Mayo, Pratt and Belknap came to dinner to discuss proposition for ships to go to England. They thought either T. S. Rogers [21] or Hugh Rodman should go and on the ground of seniority proposed Rogers, saying there was not much difference. Later I sent for Palmer and decided to send Rodman.

Meeting at Poli's theatre to celebrate Washington going dry. I presided. In presenting Bryan I quoted Brownings poem which fitly describes Bryan:

> "One who never turned his back but marched breast forward,
> Never doubted clouds would break,
> Never dreamed, though right were worsted wrong would triumph.
> Held we fall to rise, are baffled to fight better,
> Sleep to wake."

Jan. 9, 1912 Wilson said at Jackson banquet: "There have been times when some of us have differed. We differed, however, as to measures and methods but not as to principles. Through all the rise and fall, the ebb and flow of opinions and beliefs, we have all been following the one fixed goal—the goal

[21] Rear Admiral Thomas S. Rodgers, commander of Division Seven, Battleship Force, Atlantic Fleet.

pointed out by the principles and the preachings of William Jennings Bryan.["]

Monday, November 12, 1917

W. F. Fitzgerd [?] (Boston) said Morgan, Davison & Co. had sold out their stocks & behind the raid. Later he telegraphed "Ex-Gov. Foss [22] compelled to assign. Wrecking crew meeting with splendid success."

Call from Hurley about publication in Post of trouble in shipping board. He said it would be misfortune for Capps to retire. Able man but tries to do too much himself. Relies too much on Bowles in whom he [Hurley?] has no confidence. Bowles bitter partisan & did not wish to appoint a draftsman because John Sharp Williams recommended him. Schwab paid Bowles $200,000 to quit Fore River. Later Capps called. It seems that Hurley let Pezie,[23] Vice Chairman, to think he had power greater than he possessed & Capps had to show him. Evidently H—— who wishes things done quickly had confidence in P's making things move & did not define powers accurately. Capps not well and fear strain will tell on him. Hope trouble can be averted.

H L F[erguson] wrote could not accept Chairmanship of Board. Too busy building ships & feared Chm did not have powers to bring things to pass

Went to Navy Yard to see Berry's new destroyer, the Manly. Very proud of it and wants to go to Europe.

Tuesday, November 13, 1917

President returned from Buffalo where he spoke to Fed. of Labor. Hard trip but felt encouraged by reception.

Chief discussion about alien enemy. Gregory wanted to keep all out of DC & from docks and canals. Pres & Baker feared it would stop loading of transports as stevedores have strong organization & some are alien enemies.

What shall we do with aliens? Lansing said at request of War and Navy Departments a board would be created. Baker & I knew nothing about it & laugh at our over Lansing [*sic*] expense. Shall they be licensed? Why not take census of aliens? Burleson said P.O. Dept. could take it easily & cheaply, & we would know where every alien is. Have we right to arrest any who did not register? Gregory thought not. B—— said yes.

Talked to Lansing who will see Chilian Ambassador [24] and try to permit colliers to go to Chili and get nitrates.

[22] Eugene N. Foss, former Democratic congressman and governor of Massachusetts, whose financial empire had just collapsed.

[23] Charles A. Piez, vice-president of the Emergency Fleet Corporation.

[24] Santiago Aldunate.

C. Alphonso Smith came up & I read him parts of my report & he is helping on an introduction.

Wednesday, November 14, 1917

Admiral Capps came to see me & detailed trouble in the shipping board. H—— had told Chicago man [25] he was to be in charge and run things—in fact be over Capps who is President of corporation.[26] C—— will not permit and is greatly worried. I am to see Hurley.

Admiral Rodman came to be ready to go across in command of division of ships. He was very happy to have been selected for the duty and was plan[n]ing to get away four days before Mayo thought he could go.

Gen. Carr and Senator Swanson called. General troubled about his son who has been drafted for the army. He is expert in textiles and ought to be in that branch. Will try to help.

Judge Biggs, on way to California, here.[27]

Letter from Judge Brown said people would not stand for paying interned German officers The Hague treaty requires us to do it.

Thursday, November 15, 1917

Went to see the President. Took him telegram from Col. House proposing the Inter Ally body to conduct the war.

Discussed the shipping board situation as to Hurley and Capps, change by laws &c. He wished Capps to talk to him about it. I saw Hurley & told him I thought he ought to go to see the President and get his view before taking action.

Friday, November 16, 1917

Cabinet. Discussed the various secret-service agencies and the need for co-operation Also Gregory had the draft of proclamation on aliens.

Left at 4 p.m for New York with Capps & Morgenthau. M—— told us that Turks had only one round of ammunition when British withdrew and that even the German Ambassador was preparing to leave, so certain was everybody that the English and French would take Constantinople Stupidity he said

Spoke at Waldorf to Naval Architects & Marine Engineers. Big crowd & I had liberty & they received me warmly.

[25] Charles A. Piez.
[26] Actually Admiral Capps was serving as the general manager, not the president, of the Emergency Fleet Corporation.
[27] J. Crawford Biggs, now a special assistant to the Attorney General in charge of the oil litigation in California.

Labor & capital are better united   No response.

"Applaud that," I said. If you will not I will applaud it myself. Got the crowd

Saturday, November 17, 1917

Reached Newport 9 am & went at once to Training Station & reviewed the 5,000 boys. Talked to the leader of every corps & asked him why he enlisted in the Navy. Most of them "I wanted to serve my country" or "I wanted to go to France." I spoke to them.

Then went to torpedo works where they are turning out torpedoes. Many young women are employed there & seem of fine type   First women employed in Navy work of that character. They turn out more work than men.

Luncheon with R. Z. Johnson [28] & had pleasant time

Capt. Bryan [29] went with me to Fall River & talked of conditions at Newport. Authorities believe in a wide open town & do nothing to clean it up. I refer[re]d to their lack of proper hospitality.

Left at 3 pm for Portsmouth NH   Arrived at 9 pm

Sunday, November 18, 1917

Went to prison & talked to several hundred boys. Many had fine faces. Not criminal. Many were physically weak & others mentally. Delightful day and I spoke to them in the open from steps of Osborne's house. He is greatly interested and is trying to organize them to hold their own courts.

Lunch at Admiral Bousch's [30] & then spoke at Army & Navy Club built by Boatswain Hill. Good place. Spoke briefly.

Went up the river to see ship plant and then came to Boston on auto. Beautiful shore road drive

Did not stop in Boston   Powell said Endicott [31] could stop the strike, but if they thought they could appeal to me it would be deferred.

Hope he is right

Monday, November 19, 1917

Tillett [32] & son. Two boys already in. John wanted to go. Took him to see McCain.[33]

[28] Commander Rufus Z. Johnston, commander of the Newport Naval Training Station.
[29] Captain Henry F. Bryan, chief of staff, Second Naval District.
[30] Rear Admiral (Ret.) Clifford J. Boush.
[31] Henry B. Endicott, senior director of the Endicott-Johnson Company, shoe manufacturers; the official Massachusetts strike mediator during the war.
[32] Charles W. Tillett, a Charlotte, N.C., attorney and old friend.
[33] Major General Henry P. McCain, Adjutant General of the Army.

3 p.m. Went to White House with Air Production Board to see the President Had pictures & drawings to show the progress already made and all thought it satisfactory.

Council of National Defense. Sent Ray Stevens [34] to Buffalo to ask Federation of Labor to appoint committee to confer with us to try to get labor matters settled satisfactorily.

Capps came in. Health so bad he must quit.

Tuesday, November 20, 1917

Cabinet—What to do to help Italy. Ambassador had asked us for tank ships to carry oil, submarine chasers, mines & men to lay them, aeroplanes and men to fly them. Telegram from Italian Ambassador [35] saying reported [*sic*] Germans were sending diving submarines into Mediterranean to compel Italy to sue for peace. Page said he interpreted this to mean it was Italy's request for help. It came directly when Ambassador [36] from Italy called.

Discussed the matter of papers publishing false statements of treatment of troops on troop ships & in camps. Reports of inhumane treatment that were false. B—— said suppress them. W W asked for their authority instead of suppress.

Shall we have a Commissioner to control all boards or committees that help Army & Navy. One Bazaar took in $71,000 for Army & Navy, & gave $731 The balance was for expenses

Mr. & Mrs. Brooke [?] came over from Phila to see about son going on Gen. Footes [37] staff.

H L Ferg[us]on. Gen. Mgr. Shipping Board. Power had been taken from it. Doubt if he will accept.

W. W. Think of publish list of those whose feelings are hurt. Put personal pride above public service

Wednesday, November 21, 1917

Capt. Gaunt,[38] Naval Attache G.B. brought me letter from Benson. Said things were in bad condition, but was planning to do everything in our power to help. Capt G—— also brought me letter from Sir Eric Geddes [39] expressing

[34] Raymond B. Stevens, former Democratic congressman from New Hampshire, now vice-chairman of the U.S. Shipping Board.

[35] Thomas Nelson Page, U.S. Ambassador to Italy since 1913.

[36] Count Macchi di Cellere.

[37] Presumably Brigadier General Stephen M. Foote, commander of the 163rd Field Artillery Brigade, Camp Dodge, Iowa.

[38] Commodore Guy Gaunt, British naval liason officer.

[39] First Lord of the Admiralty.

sympathy for brave men who died in collision on the Chauncey,[40] & praise for those on Fanning [41] who had captured 40 Germans and sunk G submarine.

Had long talk with Mr Edison Not satisfied that navy officers give him all possible aid. Some seem self satisfied and do not quickly accept suggestions. Was severe   He thinks no merchant ship should sail in danger zone except at night. Only 7% of ships torpedoed have been destroyed in night. Edison has plan for routing which he is sending to Sir Eric Geddes. Out of 354 ships that go daily into French and English ports only 26 are American.

Mrs. George Vanderbilt [42] had heard women would be employed in ammunition factory in Navy Yard & she came to apply for position—wished no favors, only a chance to work. Very serious and very earnest & wished to do real war work. Is now in Red Cross work

While talking with Edison, Wiley Fort [?], of Pikeville of Confederate Navy, came in. He said he wished the Confederates had not invented the submarines.

Thursday, November 22, 1917

Council of National Defense. Edison advised to get all boats out of canals before they freeze over. A good idea. Can be used in South to transport freight of many kinds.

Gifford to make study of organizations made to help Army & Navy so as to keep unworthy organizations from getting money.

McAdoo and his boy. Wishes to go on submarine chaser with his brother.

Gentleman wanted to build concrete wall across English channel—to erect sky-scrapers & drop them in sea & that would shut in submarines. Would cost 500 mil. dollars he says. Pratt & Belknap did not think much of it.

Went to see Mrs. Wedderburn whose son [43] was lost on the Chauncey—collision with English transport

Friday, November 23, 1917

Talked to President about Capps and Hurley and he wrote letter to Capps while I was present expressing confidence and sympathy   Afterwards I talked to Capps who was greatly touched by Presidents confidence. Talked to Hurley

---

[40] The U.S.S. *Chauncey,* a small destroyer, sank after being rammed by the S.S. *Rose* early in the morning of November 19, 1917, with a loss of eighteen lives.

[41] The U.S. destroyer *Fanning,* aided by the U.S.S. *Nicholson,* had disabled and sunk a German submarine, the U-58, on November 17, capturing the crew of thirty-nine.

[42] Edith Stuyvesant Dresser Vanderbilt, widow of George W. Vanderbilt, the prominent capitalist.

[43] Lieutenant (junior grade) Charles F. Wedderburn.

who was glad W W had written to Capps. He wishes Navy man & President wishes one to succeed Capps. Gave out statement to papers with letters.

At meeting of cabinet, Baker told story of First Lieut. at camp who could not get supplies quick enough. His name was Baker. He sent telegram urgent. Signed "Baker" & they came by express. Now every man who wishes anything in a hurry gets Baker to send the order & it comes because they think Secretary of War is the man sending.

I brought up request of private companies to construct wireless in S. America & suggested we should unite with those countries and make them governmental. President agreed and Lansing will take it up.[44]

American sailors offered crosses and medals. Cannot accept them except by act of Congress.[45]

Bailey, Bank & Brodie [?]. Last named wanted a commission in Ordnance. When not given he felt aggrieved. He knew nothing of ordnance & I took it up with Earle whose subordinates had recommended it.

Saturday, November 24, 1917

Asked Harris to give sketch of himself for papers. He did so & it was full of praise. "His natural gait in getting things done is a gallop." We had great fun over it.

Baker agreed to Benson & Sims report that it was impossible to provide convoys all the way across the Atlantic They will go out part of the way and meet them in the danger zone.

Went to foot-ball game bet. Marine Corps team & Army team (Fort Lee) Marines won and the star & another marine took supper with Josephus.

Spoke at big war meeting gotten up by Masons at Convention Hall. Spoke on Compensations of War.

Sunday, November 25, 1917

Heard Mr. Prettyman at Mt. Vernon Place. Contrasted American with German ideals. Christ put *Man* before the institution. So does America. In Germany the individual is a cog in the wheel.

Went to see Mrs. Dewey. She wished me to present to the Red Cross $1,000.

[44] Daniels never lost an opportunity to urge government ownership and operation of radio facilities, preferably under the Navy.

[45] Both Daniels and Wilson were opposed to the awarding of foreign decorations to American military and naval personnel, believing that the practice might cause some officers to curry favor with foreign governments at the expense of their responsibilities to the United States. Eventually Daniels was obliged to modify his stand, as the War Department permitted its personnel to accept foreign decorations.

"I begrudge it but do as you say." She thought Mrs. Stotesbury fine because she was so devoted to men in the Navy

Mr. Moore [46] spent day and we talked about the paper. He wanted another deck on the press & we decided to put on two colored pages, though I had always opposed colored supplements

Addie arrived from St. Louis. Pale little girl who had come to work as stenographer. We took her in auto to boarding house in N.E. Washington.

Monday, November 26, 1917

Went to Red Cross—spoke to ladies of Naval Advisory Board. Mrs. Dewey present. I had gone to see her & she had given me check. I made a brief talk on the big thought in our work & the necessity of co-ordination through the Red Cross.

Went to see the President. I had 2 cablegrams from Benson   One recommended that our admiral in Europe accept position as honorary member of the British Admiralty. Very confidential & wished nothing said because if agreeable to us Geddes would see the King before it would be done   An emphatic *No.*[47]

Also Benson telegraphed plan of a Naval War Council. W W said the Military Council's plans would be changed to some extent and he suggested no action as to Naval Council be taken until changes were made known.

He said if Congress authorized acceptance by naval officers of honors &c from Great Britain he would veto the bill. It would cause them to be trying to secure foreign favor & would be unAmerican

Would Japs go to Russia? No, said Ishii   Too far, not enough ships.

Pres. looked weary—war-worn & said rather quizzically: "My mother did not raise her boy to be a War President—but it is a liberal education[."]

Tuesday, November 27, 1917

Picture taken as came out of house and went into office.

Council of National Defense with Hoover, Hurley, Garfield present and we decided to meet often as Co-ordinating body so as to prevent crossing wires and secure united action. Will make study of any overlapping.

Delegation called from Davenport, Iowa, to offer facilities for war work. I requested them to convert their machine & other shops engaged in war

[46] Victor C. Moore, business manager of the *News and Observer.*

[47] The British had offered to make Admiral Sims an honorary member of the British Admiralty and allow him to take full part in Admiralty deliberations. While appreciative of the unprecedented honor, both Daniels and Wilson felt that it would tie Sims, a strong Anglophile, too closely to the Admiralty point of view. Undoubtedly one factor in Sims' subsequent enmity and criticism of Daniels was this refusal to let him accept this honor.

work into shape so the war work can go into the West & not all be centered on Atlantic coast. This would prevent congestion of labor

Cabinet. The President read speech & message of Trotsky [48]—who said America entered war at behest of Wall Street and men whose prosperity came through making munitions. Lansing thought T—— misguided but honest. Once he worked at $12 a week on N.Y. Socialist paper & stopped writing for it because he thought paper was unfair to President. No answer now unless in message to Congress, for any answer would imply recognition. W W said action of Lenine [49] & Trotsky sounded like opera bouffe, talking of armistice with Germany when a child would know Germany would control & dominate & destroy any chance for the democracy they desire

Burleson & I advised President to take over all railroads.

W. W.   A man said he no longer admired W W style since reading Thanksgiving proclamation because he used word "stuff" & ended sentence with preposition.

Thursday, November 29, 1917

Turkeys from Col. J. P. Bass

Thanksgiving Dinner—14 young marines & sailors who are convalescent from the hospital. Fine young fellows. One had been in the gun crew on the Aztec which had been submarined (named Rucker). Told about the striking of torpedo just under the bridge. On one ship submarined, there were 7 men & 10 women. The men gave their food & coats to the women and all the men were dead & the women saved. Chivalry of the sea still lives. The boys sang. Mrs. Dewey was happy & cordial to them all.

Later went to the Mason House and saw the young sailors—11 to 15.

Went to the Navy Relief Ball. President and Mrs. Wilson there.

Morning went to church at Metropolitan Meth Ch   The President and Mrs. Wilson there. Bishop McDowell [50] preached splendid sermon on the war. It must drive men to drink, doubt or to God   Sir Philip Sidney. "If there be any good war I expect to attend."

Died from wound in Flanders & gave water offered him to a wounded fellow soldier

Emerson: It is not so much what we do as why we do it

Maine fisherman lost his life saving others. When anybody wanted anything he had he just gave it to them

---

[48] Leon D. Trotsky, Peoples Commissar for Foreign Affairs in the new Soviet government, brought to power by the November Revolution in Russia.

[49] Vladimir Ilyich Ulyanov (Nikolai Lenin), founder of Bolshevik communism and chairman of the new Soviet government in Russia.

[50] Bishop William F. McDowell of the Methodist Episcopal Church.

Friday, November 30, 1917

Cabinet. Russian situation discussed. Lane thought Trotsky government might maintain itself and should not be lightly dismissed. Others thought it would fail. W W said Cossacks & others in S. Russia would not follow T, had declared for continuance of war, & had asked help and recognition. Too chaotic to act yet.

Got your goat? Where did it come from. Lane said Kipling had a story of pious man in India who started to temple to sacrifice carrying a goat. 3 bad men conspired to get his goat. 1. Why do you carry a dirty dog. 2 & 3 also, & the third man got his goat

Dined with Dr. & Mrs. Boyd.

Wm. E. Chandler died. I telegraphed & sent Admiral Boush to represent Navy Dept

$$\begin{array}{r} 1865 \\ 1917 \\ \hline 8 \end{array}$$ [*sic*]

———

Saturday, December 1, 1917

Named new destroyers and to one gave the name of Maury.[1] Speaking to McKean about it he said M—— had left the service and joined the Confederacy and should not be honored. "But" I replied "they have Camp Lee and Camp Jackson. Why not honor Maury who did most for the Navy?" His answer was that these camps were temporary and did not signify so much while ships kept their names many years

Mr & Mrs. Edison dined with us. He ate toast, hot milk, & pumpkin pie. Full of fun & told jokes. We had onions & he said onions helped a deaf man —he could tell when one was coming who ate them. Refused whip cream on his pie, saying he did not like frills, & preferred the pie like his mother used to make

Jolly & full of joke. Told of foreman who was excellent as long as pay was small, but would go off on spree when pay was high. Had to reduce him & let him work up gradually & then reduce him. Could not stand prosperity

---

[1] Matthew Fontaine Maury, nineteenth-century naval officer who pioneered in establishing a uniform system of recording oceanographic data; served in England as an officer of the Confederate Navy during the Civil War.

Mr. Harrison,[2] author of Queed, also here to dinner.

Sunday, December 2, 1917
Went to church. Dr. Wood preached sermon of Life of Gen. Foster.[3]
Addie went in afternoon to YWCA
We called to see Mr. & Mrs. Lansing   Mrs. Scott there
J D Jr & I talked all afternoon
J D Jr returned, Mrs J D to Savannah & Worth to Chapel Hill
P M Wilson [4] & wife called   He thought there was a spirit of criticism among returning members of Congress

Monday, December 3, 1917
Co-ordinating Council met. Baker got in late from Florida. Mr. Willard said the need was to know whether we were to send 500,000 men or 1,500,000 men over to France in next 6 months. At present rail roads & all industry & shipping were brought into requisition to carry supplies to ocean. If it is not to be needed, private business, now stopped, could be cared for. Baker said the House commission was instructed to confer with allies & determine pooling of shipping so as to know whether ships could be used best for food & supplies, for men already under arms or whether for new soldiers. The ship is the neck of the bottle.

Garfield said he & Hoover were not quarreling, but that there had to be a fire built under somebody to get coal & food to the country & Detroit had been facing a coal famine.

Robison,[5] Taussig [6] & Johnson [7] came back from Europe. Johnson & Dave Bagley saved 487 men & women off of one ship that had been torpedoed. That was a work of which little is known. Not a person was killed on the boat & two destroyers saved all the people.

Robison warm in praise of Sims.

Mayo told me the court had ended Blue trial & he had been restored to duty. I have not seen the evidence or the finding.

[2] Henry S. Harrison, author of a number of novels, including *Queed* (Boston: Houghton Mifflin, 1911). On November 6, Harrison had been commissioned a lieutenant in the Naval Coast Defense Reserve.

[3] John W. Foster, Union veteran, lawyer, diplomat, and former Secretary of State, had died on November 15, 1917.

[4] Peter M. Wilson, a North Carolinian and chief clerk of the Senate.

[5] Captain John K. Robison, commanding the U.S.S. *Huntington* on convoy duty.

[6] Commander Joseph K. Taussig, commander of the first group of U.S. destroyers sent to European waters for convoy and patrol duty in April, 1917.

[7] Commander Alfred W. Johnson, in command of the U.S.S. *Conyngham,* one of the first destroyers sent to Europe.

Council of National Defense. Should we start counter propaganda in Spain &
S. America against Germany? Commission favored. Referred to the Presid[ent]

Roger Wells called & discussed Intelligence

Anderson [8] (Inter State) talked Gov. operation of RRs

Tuesday, December 4, 1917

Pres. spoke to Congress.[9] No tickets for wives of cabinet officers. Sinnot [10]
sent one to my wife & Ethel took her place. She was in Savannah speaking on
Y.W.C.A.

W W looked serious, confident, compelling. He had given much thought
to his message—read it deliberately & calmly, letting its logic and strength
make all the impression. It was received with marked approval & evoked
enthusiasm. After delivery we discussed it at cabinet meeting—all gave warm
commendation. W W seemed relieved & was plainly pleased at its reception.

Because of Roberts College [11] & such institutions he hoped we would not
have to declare war upon Turkey, but must be prepared for any eventualities.
He wished a plebiscite on Alsace & Lorrain. Suggested that many who had
owned & still owned land should be entitled to vote. Not certain all wish to
go to France. Children speak German. Wished to let the world know we stand
for no such treaties as would call for land or money beyond repairing Belgium
and Northern France.

More rooms needed by Departments.

Spent evening reading spotted record of E. D. Ryan [12] whom Vance Mc-
Cormick and Mitchell wished made Admiral I had almost promised to do
it, but could not after reading

Represt—— of Chili here to buy RR engines & cars. Can we trade & get
ships from Chili.

Wednesday, December 5, 1917

Gifford: Paper showing that if no ships are sunk we can transport 565,000
to France by June 1st & we have only half enough tonnage to carry necessary
supplies. This is carefully prepared & shows we need more ships very much.

Princess David, of Hawaii here & wished cruiser named Hawaii. Handsome
woman. Her son is going to school and hopes to be educated for the Navy.

---

[8] George W. Anderson, recently appointed to the Interstate Commerce Commission.

[9] Wilson's annual message to Congress. Among other things, he recommended a declaration of war against Germany's ally, Austria-Hungary, with whom relations had been broken
eight months earlier. Congress obliged three days later.

[10] Joseph J. Sinnott, doorkeeper of the House of Representatives.

[11] Robert College, an American supported school in Constantinople.

[12] Captain Eugene D. Ryan, supply officer of the Philadelphia Navy Yard.

Admiral W. B. Fletcher, who was relieved of his command in France because he was not efficient & Antilles was submarined near France owing to lack of convoys, called. He had prepared paper. Sims had declined court of inquiry and I had approved. He lacks initiative and resource—is a paper Admiral and should not have been promoted.

At night finished abstract of report [13] & it will go to printer.

Reports show steady sinkings of British ships, more yesterday and today than in some time. Menace still on us

Gov. Walsh & Matthew Hale,[14] of Boston. Wish me to go to Boston where I am not very popular. I told them I went there when I first came into office & perhaps they would have liked me better if I had not gone there

Thursday, December 6, 1917

Signed with Bethlehem Ship Co. biggest contract ever signed to build 80 destroyers.

Meeting of War Council. Discussed shipping at length and I sent by Knox [15] to England to Sims copy of secret data about shipping. Committee appointed to ascertain shipping of US, England and France, so that all ships will be fully loaded with the freight ready at seaboard. Now 1,800,000 tons on coast ready to go, but there are delays because all ships are not in the joint service. Shall we commandeer the Dutch and other ships in our waters? Discussed getting German ships laid up in South American countries France has obtained those in Brazil. Hurley & Redfield protested against Navy's taking trawlers and tugs. Cuts off fishing and reduces our food supply.

Senator Tillman attended meeting of Navy Council & we discussed many matters of interest & he took part. Increased pay for officers abroad. McGowan said pay $10,000 out of contingent fund. It was a new policy & I suggested we take it up with Congress.

Reception to W.C.T.U.

Friday, December 7, 1917

Cabinet

McAdoo said bankers were telling munition makers to depend on Federal treasury & it could not finance everything. "If banks refuse to transact the business for which they were created after awhile banks will wake up to find they have no business to transact." Said W. W.

[13] Daniels' annual report as Secretary of the Navy.
[14] Boston attorney and progressive leader.
[15] Commander Dudley W. Knox, subsequently a member of Admiral Sims' planning staff in London.

"What is law? Is it not to promote [and] secure justice? ["] asked W. W. "God forbid. It is to fix a system" said lawyer who had been steeped in learning and stupidity." W W: To quote my father: "You cannot reason out of a man what reason did not put into him"

Discussed what to do with Austrians & others in that Empire. The Bohemians are loyal,—so are others in that Empire. They are not to be troubled. Only the German-Austrians are to be interned. Suggested that legislation be obtained by which they can be made citizens. Many Bohemians volunteered in Canada. When captured by Germans they are invariably shot.

Council of National Defense met & we decided to ask people not to contribute to anything except such as authorized by State Councils of Defense.

Discussed stopping Com on Alcoholic Traffic & decided not to authorize any committee to give out anything except through the Council. First suggested a slap at Temperance Com. I opposed

News came that war had been declared with Austria & President signed it

Belknap telephoned that Rodman had arrived with ships across.

I telegraphed Benson that President approved Inter Allied Council. Cablegram that Jacob Jones [16] had been torpedoed.

Saturday, December 8, 1917

Last night at bedtime got news the Jacob Jones had been torpedoed & David's name not among those rescued. Early this morning W.H. [White House?] phone brought another telegram from Sims giving 27 rescued but David's name not among them. Had not told Addie at night hoping better news by morning. She was almost heartbroken. Then I went after Belle and Ethel. After we had told them, Mrs. B. was brought home & Dr. Dennis [17] summoned. She had feared it but was all broken up by news. Everybody sympathetic. 10 more reported saved but not David.

At 11:30 news came that David and five others picked up in motor boat. Woke everybody up. Great rejoicing, telephoned to friends & telegraphed & had regular thanksgiving.

President announced good news at Gridiron dinner & everybody stood up and applauded.

Josephus came. Worth got as far as Raleigh & got good news & went back to CH [Chapel Hill]

Dr. Wood came & had prayer

---

[16] The destroyer commanded by Daniels' brother-in-law, Lieutenant Commander David W. Bagley.

[17] Probably Commander John B. Dennis, a Navy surgeon assigned to the Naval Dispensary in Washington.

Sunday, December 9, 1917
Went to church & as we entered all were singing "Eternal father strong to save"
Much company and congratulations all day.

Monday, December 10, 1917
Mr. Gompers said oil producers in La & Texas would not even confer with employees   10,000 out & production of oil curtailed. Baker and I trying to straighten it out.
Council. Discussed food fixing price & all other commodities and recommended committee to frame laws. Hurley said shipping program depended on labor.
Andrew Joyner [18] and Cary Dowd

Tuesday, December 11, 1917
Cabinet
W. W.   Hate to do nothing about Russia but puzzled to know how to take hold. Lane   Perhaps Constituancy [*sic*] Assembly may point the way. No, neither party will have majority. Lansing: The Bolsheviki permits soldiers to vote wherever they are & charges them so they will have a majority for their party. Civil war possible. Everything now too chaotic to make any move.
Gregory presented proclamation as to Austrians, not along line of Germans, calling them denizens & not alien enemies   Sentiment not to regard Bohemians & others who came to this country to escape Austrian rule as alien enemies.
Burleson wanted us to call 5 million men at once. Baker & W W: Could not transport them & it would make it impossible to feed & equip our allies.
Redfield urged construction of concrete ships   Said Norway had built them. I thought still experimental. Hurley was watching experiment. Red: We are not using sailing ships. The President said he had talked it over with shipping board not once but several times
Decided to ask Congress to make $1,200 the lowest pay for stenographers.
Dined with Chinese minister.[19]
Reception of Woman Suffrage [20]
Train to New York.

[18] Former *News and Observer* correspondent in Greensboro, North Carolina.
[19] Vi Kyuin Wellington Koo.
[20] Daniels was an active supporter of women's suffrage.

Wednesday, December 12, 1917
New York
Navy Yard. Intelligence. Censorship   Pelham Park
Dinner of Southern Society. Baker made a great speech.

Thursday, December 13, 1917
Quantico.
Long conference with Hurley, Alfias [?],[21] Mc [*sic*] & other labor leaders
on how to prevent strikes & secure maximum of output.
Ask [?] Labor Department to have Employment Bureaus everywhere.

Friday, December 14, 1917
Mr. Crane said he had two experiences. Two new worlds. He found Russia
a new country. His previous knowledge of Russia was a hindrance rather
than a help. He left before war was declared, and returned to find a new,
united America. He left finding a divided, debating America.

Two kinds of Russians: 1. Red flag. 2 Black flag. One night the blacks
decided to attack American embassy. Francis [22] was informed while at dinner
party. All his guests hastened to their homes & invited & urged him to go.
He declined. The mob came and demanded admittance. It was refused. They
broke down the door & Francis drew his pistol, told them he stood upon
American soil, and that he would shoot down the first man that advanced.
They were not armed, they parleyed & departed. Nobody with Francis except
a colored servant. For five days he was the hero of Petrograd, he was serenaded
by men, women & school children.

Thomas Mott Osborne here & we talked prison reform. Will add temporary buildings at Portsmouth.

Boston street car company wanted to borrow coal we have in Boston. No.
But had to lend to Fore River Ship Building Company. Must keep work on
torpedoes going.

Gave out news of Inter-Allied Naval Council sent through Sims by Benson
Shall clerks pay be increased 25%

Saturday, December 15, 1917
Dr. Van Dyke [23] wished to know if there was not some service he could

[21] Probably N. P. Alifas, president of District 44, International Association of Machinists.
[22] David R. Francis, U.S. Ambassador to Russia since 1916.
[23] Henry Van Dyke was a vigorous sixty-five-year-old whose value to the Navy Daniels decided outweighed strict adherence to regulations.

render. Yes. Chaplain in Reserve Corps. Send for Frazier.[24] Are you less than 40? F "Looks like 38." "I was 38 once." Must examine you in theology. F & I both Methodists. Do you believe in Calvinism? I do not. "You have passed." Expect him to go to ships and camps and preach to sailors and marines. He is much interested and would like to go to sea.

Held session of Council to discuss action of Naval Affairs Committee to probe into naval affairs. Ready as soon as committee wishes information. Feeling of all that our situation is such that it is not open to just criticism.

Wrote President suggesting Governor Stuart[25] to control rail-roads.

Sunday, December 16, 1917

Sunday. Admiral Benson returned & gave me his report and we had conference. He found situation grave but was pleased with spirit of English and French navies.

Dr. Van Dyke at tea & a dozen sailors and marines

Monday, December 17, 1917

Commodore Wadhams[26] will represent Navy in Naval Auxiliary. Explained the differences.

Dr. Van Dyke came by & was examined to be chaplain.

Admiral Harris asked if position was vacant. He had fallen out with Hurley —tried to do too many things—appointed three publicity men at $5,000 a year—& rented building in Phila. He will retire. Had big head.

Council of National Defense. Redfield said he could get 200 sailing ships to go to S. America and Australia so as to release other ships for England. Hurley doubted if could do so, but wished them. R—— very positive and rather critical.

Benson, Bliss and McBryde[27] back from Europe and all report conditions are very serious.

Blue guilty of negligence & lose 20 numbers. Mayo reduce to 10. Guilty of only trusting his navigator. Ought that to tell against the captain? All recommended clemency.

Prohibition amend——t passed the House. Times (organ of brewers) threatened the South with suffrage of the negroes.

---

[24] Captain John B. Frazier, a Navy chaplain.

[25] Governor Henry C. Stuart of Virginia.

[26] Commodore (Ret.) Albion V. Wadhams, recalled to active duty to represent the Navy with the American Red Cross.

[27] Commander Lewis B. McBride, a naval constructor, formerly assistant naval attaché at the U.S. Embassy in London, later on Admiral Sims's staff.

Tuesday, December 18, 1917

W W   Many big men have been born in NC & left it

Cabinet. W. W. in reminiscent mood & story telling. Lady introduced herself & said you have heard of Bensons of Phila? I assented. Later my wife, who had more tender conscience, asked ["]Had you ever heard of Bensons?" I replied "Have you never heard of the Benson Porous Plaster?" This came up he said because he had lived in many places & people insisted that he ought to know their family tree. Once people made to do over a Mr. Biddle. What is it all about? A Biddle. Well, what is a Biddle? Andrew Jackson ought to know. W W had stick cut from the Hermitage. It is the Big Stick in the right hand said Burleson.

President read telegram from Francis. In Petrograd people broke into winter palace and took all wine & got drunk & went round shooting up the town, & spent night in building adjoining the Embassy. Chaos in Russia. Alexis [28] in palace with Lenine & Trotsky. Monarchists aiding the Boleskevis [*sic*]. Southern Russia the hope. W W wanted to help with money but saw no way with man power unless Roumanian troops could join the Russians who are fighting.

Investigate shipping board. Why do Democrats make such investigations? [29] Redfield said he could get sailing ships

I saw W W about Harris. Later saw Harris & told him how he had disappointed me. His letter might give news to Germany. Would change it. Said he had not precipitated trouble.

Wednesday, December 19, 1917

Went before Naval Affairs Committee and answered many questions and gave statement of what had been done before the war to strengthen the Navy and what had been done since. Britton [30] tried to show Dept. had not backed up Sims & I told him I had no time to answer petty gossip. (See my testimony in Official Gazette)

Shall we have a central organization to look after all questions relating to labor? Roosevelt went before Council of Natl Defense & said yes. Post [31] No—it was function of Labor Department.

[28] Probably a reference to a news report that the Grand Duke Paul Alexandrovitch was in Petrograd where the Bolshevists were treating him with respect.

[29] Following Admiral Harris' resignation as general manager of the Emergency Fleet Corporation, the Senate had voted to investigate Hurley's operation of the Shipping Board.

[30] Fred A. Britten, Republican, U.S. Representative from Illinois.

[31] Louis F. Post, Assistant Secretary of Labor.

Funston [?] wrote to B that Kaiser, in conference with von Hindenberg & the other generals offered to abdicate if it would bring peace to Germany. Von H—— dramatically said No & declared he would fight forever to preserve the House of Hohenzollern.

Baker promised to go to see Mrs. Dewey & see that she was given permission to erect the sort of monument she wished at Arlington.[32]

Thursday, December 20, 1917

Senators Swanson & Lodge came up and we went into Benson's office and he gave his impressions of conditions abroad. Serious. He spoke of the morale of the French Army & said the French on the Coast could do nothing. They lacked money & everything & whatever is done there we must do. Our ships are delayed in French ports because there is no place for landing & no facilities. One delayed 15 days. Army engineers are making provision at ports & Benson had arranged for better patrol of coast & detectives along coast. He thought German submarines might base on islands off France. He offered to furnish France material to repair its ships, but as to ships & repairing France is hopeless. England has promised to close up off [sic] English channel & work has already begun. Praised Geddes & said G spoke with pride of his stay in America and his work on the B&O. Fine man, resourceful & capable. English fleet well manned & kept in excellent condition.

Rep. Oliver [33] came in the evening, & we went over testimony before House Naval Affairs Committee & discussed naval affairs.

Woman Yeoman courtmartialled & reduced because she left when sick & Pratt did not like it. She was jerked up without time for advice. I overruled the action. Cannot deal with women as with men.

Decided to reappoint Griffin & he was to place resignation in hands at pleasure of the President.

Friday, December 21, 1917

W W read telegram that British censor had sent from N.Y. Tribune to Trotsky asking him for Christmas message. Why will an American paper be guilty of such stupidity or worse. B—— said it has been supporting the war

[32] After Admiral Dewey's body had been buried at Arlington Cemetery, Mrs. Dewey persuaded Daniels and Baker to permit her to erect a monument considerably larger and more elaborate than normally permitted. Following its completion and shortly before her own death, however, she changed her mind and moved the Admiral's body to the Washington Cathedral.

[33] William B. Oliver, Democrat, U.S. Representative from Alabama, member of the House Naval Affairs Committee.

policy. "Yes," said W W, "it was for war all the time, and cannot change, but it is not genuine in its real support." W W read telegram from Russian Commissionaire [*sic*] Minister of Foreign Affairs who proposed that consuls be given passports to America & other countries to propose the overturning of all governments not dominated by the working people. "The impudence of it" said W W. And the impotence. Should his message be printed. Lansing & Lane "Yes." Baker & I No. Baker said it would do no good & might encourage men of IWW type in America. W W said it was his reaction not to make it public. Why did American censors permit Tribune telegram to go out? I am to see.

By the way, W W said Crane's cook & housemaid said Trotsky owed them $10 & 20 each—money they had given to some sort of club he organized.

Admiral Winslow called & said a man of eminence believed he had discovered a principle that would enable one to detect presence of submarines 5 miles. Promised to experiment

White House dinner to Servian Mission. One officer told of leaving Salonica & of apprehension of danger from Austrian submarines. Austria confines submarines to the Adriatic.

Hoover said Russian revolution was spiritual—all revolutions are—& he expected to see movement after the war in this & other countries where people who labor will demand greater rights on property

Saturday, December 22, 1917

Went to luncheon Rotary Club. Garfield & I spoke briefly. Harry Lauder [34] was guest of honor. I sat beside him. Before he spoke he said "This has been a heart-breaking day. I have heard that the captain of my son's company has been killed. He was a teacher—a fine fellow—my son loved him. His death makes me live over again the anguish of my son's death." In his speech he
ow
said man in Balto. said "Is this Harry *Lau*-der," [*sic*] using the German pronunciation. "No; but I am Harry *Lau*-der." He spoke of Am. way of speaking about "the English fleet, the English Govt, the English Empire." There is no such thing. "Damn England" It is the Great Britain not Great England. Told of letter from a mother in Maine who had letter from her son, who while singing Lauder's song "Roaming in the Gloaming" ran upon grave. Union Jack twisted around it. He looked & saw it was son of Harry Lauder & he planted a rose bush upon the grave because he loved Harry Lauder's songs so. Made vigorous war speech. Wore kilts & had bare legs.

At night went with wife to Southern Society reception to soldiers & sailors

[34] Sir Harry Lauder, Scottish entertainer.

Dr. Stitt [35] & Dr. Barber [36] called
Boys home for Christmas

Sunday, December 23, 1917
Went to church. Dr. Hardin preached vigorous war sermon. No peace without removing menace. Peace with righteousness.
Went to community singing on steps of Treasury Building
Ridley McLean [37] talked about Victor Blue's case. Thought navigator was at fault.
Harrison author of Queed here

Monday, December 24, 1917
Chaplain T. P. Riddle [38] resigned as chaplain because he thought he could learn better to serve the Navy by becoming an enlisted man, without anybody in the Navy knowing he had been a chaplain. This is the real spirit & I commended him warmly.
Hurley & Baruch came over to talk about the work ahead. Hurley accepted Harris resignation before he presented it. Baruch thinks Govert should control & run RR's & many other facilities. Army will make powder. Overruled Ordnance that was ready to make contract with Duponts that would have given them 62 mil. profit.
Board of Selection reported. I sent to the President with my approval & he approved. Some heart-burnings & disappointments. But in a few years selection will have a better chance when the fetish of seniority has been fully eradicated.
Home at night. Addie went to Quantico & spoke to 2,500 marines

Tuesday, December 25, 1917
Jonathan Worth Jackson & wife here to dinner & all the boys.
At night talked to Dr Dodd [39] about newspaper experience.

Wednesday, December 26, 1917
Called with General Board to see Mrs. Dewey. It was anniversary of Admiral Dewey's birthday. George [40] was there. She was very happy and very sad—

[35] Rear Admiral Edward R. Stitt, recently appointed a medical director of the Navy.
[36] Rear Admiral George H. Barber, recently appointed a medical director of the Navy.
[37] Captain Ridley McLean, chief of staff of Battleship Force One.
[38] Lieutenant (junior grade) Truman P. Riddle, former chaplain on the U.S.S. *Pennsylvania*. In June, 1918, Riddle resumed his old rank and chaplain's duties.
[39] Probably William E. Dodd, North Carolina–born professor of history at the University of Chicago and an active supporter of the Wilson administration.
[40] George G. Dewey, Admiral Dewey's son by his first wife, Susan B. Goodwin Dewey, who died five days after giving birth.

talked about the Admiral with tears & told stories with laughter. Turned to Badger: "You were the midshipman with him, when, after the death of his little wife, he asked for far off sea duty. Badger woke Dewey up & said "The pilot says if we do not change our course the ship will certainly be lost." Dewey roused out of sleep & asked "Are we going on the course I marked out?" The answer was "Yes" "Then" Dewey said: ["]Keep on that course. Unless you do you will go to hell."

Plunkett and Roger Wells passed over. Plunkett attributed it to his incessant & vigorous hard work imposed in target practise. He had been offered a ship when war broke out but thought he could do better work by staying in target practise. He probably could explain it to his too much talking. Roger Wells not well—perhaps that was the cause.

Baroness ——— [*sic*] arrested in Louisville. Son in Annapolis. Husband in German army. She was under suspicion in Annapolis last year. Thought to be a spy.

President will take charge of all railroads. McAdoo Director

Talked to Ridley [41] about Blue

Pamphlet of speech at Surgeons Clinic[a]l Congress in Chicago

Thursday, December 27, 1917

Council (Secretaries) held long meeting and discussed proposition for Navy to take over manning of all merchant ships. Earlier I held conference with Hurley and Furoseth.[42] The latter vigorously opposed, saying it took 3 navy to 1 men [*sic*] to man ships taken over. He said the safest place in the war was in Navy & that is why so many men enlisted. He felt deeply it would be saying to sailors in merchant marine they could not be trusted. No decision.

Council of National Defense. Redfield & Lane said we had no program and were not moving rapidly enough. Baker detailed what he would say when he went before Con [?]

Sailing ships—Redfield.

Dinner at French Embassy to meet Admiral Grasse [43] of France.

The Ambassador [44] had predicted Tafts election & Wilsons to his government. He had said last election was too close for anybody to estimate. Now he predicts Prohibition will prevail and there will be a reaction to permit light wines

[41] Captain Ridley McLean.
[42] Andrew Furuseth, president of the International Seamen's Union and a longstanding champion of the rights of American sailors.
[43] Rear Admiral Grasset, commanding the visiting French battleship, *La Gloire*.
[44] Jules J. Jusserand.

Friday, December 28, 1917

Cabinet. Houston and ships for nitrates for farmers discussed. Must have them. He had been trying 4 weeks & had not been able to find anybody who could give rumor and farmers must know soon.

Talked to the Pres. about Admiral in the Pay Corps & recommend Peebles [45] who began work in Mare Island Navy Yard as a boy and worked his way up.

"I suppose he is a Republican" said W W "whereas Ryan is a Dem" I told him our Dem friends in Penn worked for Ryan but that Swanson, at request of Penrose, had asked for Rs appoint[men]t "When I heard Penrose was for him that was enough to settle him with me" said W. W.

Dinner at F. D. Roosevelt's. British captain present & Mrs. R—— mother. Left on Seaboard for Raleigh

After cabinet talked to President about Woman Suffrage amendment. Whether members of cabinet should handle [?] letters for submission of amendment to the States. He said each member should feel free to write his own views

Report from David of Jacob Jones

Saturday, December 29, 1917

Reached Raleigh. Coldest day I had felt. Spent most of day at N&O office talking with Moore & Haywood [46] and others. Went to Bank and ascertained how we stood. Had $57—in my wifes box. Went to see Aunt Sophie [47] who was full of messages & love to Addie & the boys.

Talked with C. J. Clark [48] about woman suffrage & the war. He looked old —never looked so before. He commended editorial in N&O I later found out from Haywood he had written most of it.

Told Alex Feild [?] place was ready for him & Shipping Board

Asked Hubert Royster how Jim [?] would like to come to Wash. & write the record of the Navy for the war.

Courtesy of the Griffins

Left at 8 pm for Goldsboro

[45] Rear Admiral Christian J. Peoples, assistant chief of the Bureau of Supplies and Accounts, currently holding a temporary rank of rear admiral which Daniels wished to make permanent.
[46] R. W. Haywood, currently editor of the *News and Observer*.
[47] Sophie Liggon, Negro nurse of the Daniels children for many years.
[48] Chief Justice Walter Clark of the North Carolina Supreme Court.

Sunday, December 30, 1917

Spent day with Mother. All Bordens called & some others who wished to ask me what to do with their boys in the draft age. That question follows me wherever I go and I can give no answer, for the Army has first claim on them.

. C C D Jr [49] came at 4 a.m. Couldnt wake anybody up & was bitterly cold. Left at 10 p.m. for Washington.

Monday, December 31, 1917

Attorney General of Great Britain [50] called. Very interesting man. Rodman well liked by English fleet. When he went on English Admirals ship, the Admiral said when they wished to confer, there would be no need for etiquette or writing. Rodman said "that suits me very well, for I am no pamphleteer myself."

Conference at McAdoo's office over freight situation, particularly as to coal. New England factories in great need of coal & must have water transportation.

Came home with Admiral Fletcher after talking of work of War Industries Board & adjusting the differences between Navy & Board over tin. It turned out Navy was right and we were commended.

[49] Daniels' nephew, Charles C. Daniels, Jr.
[50] Sir Frederick E. Smith, Attorney General of Great Britain since 1915.

1918

The Cabinet Diaries of Josephus Daniels, 1918

Tuesday, January 1, 1918

Spent all the morning at Attorney Generals. Senator Swanson present and we discussed how to conserve the Naval [Oil] Reserves and agreed on a bill giving the President power to take them all over, those in litigation as well as others, and operate them by Secy of the Navy, & pay over just & equitable sums to the owners and if they demanded more for them to be allowed to go into the courts. Land office & Int. Dept manned by Western men who think all lands & oil lands in the West ought to belong to the West and resent the idea that the Fed. Govert has any right to them. This tinges their point of view against the Govert.

Wednesday, January 2, 1918

Council of National Defense. Dean Gay [1] & Director Cary [2] gave figures of shipping, showing that the great need was ships & more ships. The sinkings by German U boats were large & the construction of new ships not large. Speeding up is *the* duty. Redfield brought up the sailing ships & need of using them.

Lane said we had not seriously taken up shipping in May, though it has been pressed by Shipping Board all the time, & resources have been employed to increase it.

Wrote President for a conference with Gregory[,] Swanson & I about oil.[3]

Lansing wrote over requesting the Brooklyn be sent Vladivostock to act with Japanese ships. It would have put the American Admiral in command and as we had no other ship there might prove unwise. Bolshekivi [*sic*] would say America was making war on Russia. Lansing thought it best for our ship to go. Otherwise Japan would go alone.

---

[1] Dean Edwin F. Gay of the Harvard School of Business Administration, currently a member of the Commercial Economy Board of the Council of National Defense and adviser on shipping priorities; subsequently a member of the War Trade Board.

[2] Edward F. Carry, director of operations, U.S. Shipping Board.

[3] Daniels was increasingly concerned lest the Navy lose its oil reserves in California, either through an adverse ruling by Secretary of the Interior Lane on the disputed claims or through congressional action to recognize the validity of the private claims and stimulate oil production in fuel-short California. While Lane, a Californian, was opposed to Daniels' view, the Navy had strong backing from Senator Claude A. Swanson and Attorney General Gregory, and ultimately from President Wilson.

We agreed to leave to President

He decided best not to send but order ship to pay a visit of courtesy to Japan and await instructions. That would put him near enough to V—— to go in

Thursday, January 3, 1918

Chadwick & Thompson [4] called to get us to break the ice up the river to get coal to Yonkers. Thompson had recently come from Russia & said only hope was in the Bolshekivi [*sic*] for if the classes won the German Emperor would practically dominate as the classes would wish to keep the people under. The English Ambassador [5] was not in sympathy with aspirations for a Republic & was with the owner class.

Council of Nat. Defense. Labor question up [?] Lane wanted Labor War Council of 3—Wilson (WB), one named by Gompers & one by Manufacturing organization. Baker wanted a Labor Director, one man, & thought that best. Decided to take the matter up with the President & obtain his views

Worth seemed to wish to go to Annapolis. I talked to Overman who would make him first alternate.

Went to see Otis Skinner [6] in Booth Tarkington's [7] play "Mister Antonia"

Friday, January 4, 1918

Talked again with Thompson. He put a million dollars of his own money in propaganda in Russia because he believed if they understood America they would stand against German propaganda. In English house, during Kerensky's [8] rule, a toast was drunk to the Czar. The E Ambassador & others so afraid of losing their perquisites & place they sympathize with autocracy. "I have been in Wall Street, but Russia gave me a new idea, & I have come home a better Democrat." Later L said he was a crank. W W said spending money in R for propaganda was like pouring water in a bottomless hole. Crane says no cement is left in Russia. We are with E[ngland] & F[rance] giving all aid possible to those in "Little Russia," where there is a fight against Germans & Anarchy. Summers,[9] consul at Moscow, says the only hope is in the men fighting in So. Russia. Baker said War College proposed, not recognition of

---

[4] William B. Thompson, New York banker, head of American Red Cross mission to Russia for four months in 1917.

[5] Sir George W. Buchanan, British Ambassador to Russia, 1910–1918.

[6] Prominent American actor.

[7] Newton Booth Tarkington, American novelist and playwright.

[8] Alexander F. Kerensky, prime minister of the Russian second provisional government until overthrown by the Bolshevists.

[9] Maddin Summers, U.S. consul general in Moscow.

the Bolsheviki but acceptance as the best way to keep Russia from coming under the dominion of Germany. One army report recommended giving $25 million dollars a month to a certain General with ample power to do any & all things in Germany. W W was astounded that any one would suggest such a thing.

Cooper Hewitt [10] said Germans have a bomb of gasses. When it falls on a place, nobody can live there for 2½ days. We are experimenting with it.

Presdt wrote Lane he would accept nothing further than the Swanson amendment—oil.[11]

Mrs. Catt [12] called to ask aid for woman suffrage amendment.

Labor War Board & Director of Shipping

Saturday, January 5, 1918

Saw Senator Swanson and talked with him about Blue and read him an opinion which would set aside sentence. He admires Blue & hoped it would be found well to set aside sentence but advised much consideration. See Benson

Also talked with him about oil lands & telephoned for appointment with the President to consider course to take.

Took lunch with Naval Consulting Board and made brief talk. No illusion. If there is glory for the Navy, it goes to Admiral or Captain. If blame it goes to the Secretary. Should be so   History shows that civil administrators rarely come out with approval. He must serve and expect his own consciousness of doing his best & approval of a few who know. Saunders read Montague poem "Josephus Is All Right." [13]

Council of National Defense sent statement to the President that if we put 1 mil men in France & supplied them, we must have 3¼ [million?] additional tons of shipping, & requested him to take up with Allied Powers what

[10] Peter Cooper Hewitt, wealthy scientist and inventor, member of the Naval Consulting Board since 1915.

[11] Swanson had successfully amended the leasing bill currently before the Senate so as to exclude the naval oil reserves from its operation, much to the dismay of the California oil interests which had hoped to validate their claims to the reserves.

[12] Carrie Chapman Catt, president of the National American Woman Suffrage Association.

[13] Daniels reproduced this poem, "Squaring Ourselves," by the popular columnist James J. Montague, in his *The Wilson Era: Years of Peace, 1910–1917* (Chapel Hill: University of North Carolina Press, 1944), pp. 402–403. After noting the early ridicule of Daniels' efforts to reform the Navy, Montague concludes:

> ". . . For his drinkless, curseless navy—every unit—thanks to him,
> From the dreadnaughts to the cutters, is in first-class fighting trim.
> Now at last the pitying jesters (we among them) see a light,
> For the fact has dawned upon us that Josephus is all right!"

to do. If they (England it means) will furnish ships, we can put the men over and feed the allies. If not, then our ability to help is limited by our tonnage. Cannot send many troops, & supplies for them & help allies for this year unless England helps in tonnage.

McAdoo desires Navy to furnish coal to Boston. Mc [?] has the coal

Earle thought Bliss must have 4 mil. advance or no torpedoes. I said $2. They came to it.

Talked to Benson about Blue. He opposed clemency

Sunday, January 6, 1918

Went to hear Billy Sunday preach & afterwards met him.

Lunched with Dr. Wood & young naval officer at Service club.

Monday, January 7, 1918

Council of National Defense. Gompers protest   Talked of his service

Billy Sunday called. Praised D & Baker.

Oil leasing bill passed

Telephoned Worth

Dined with Red Cross at Metropolitan Club

Tuesday, January 8, 1918

President delivered message to Congress on "War Aims." [14]

Cabinet. Discussion on President's message   What bait is there for Germany to go into Conference? Only freedom of the seas and partnership in the world's free commerce.

Talked with Mr. Davison & Mrs Stotesbury

Dined with Earle. The Bensons and Fletchers

Wednesday, January 9, 1918

Swanson, Gregory & I called to see W. W. about oil bill & he approved bill we had drawn for the Navy to take over all lands in oil reserve No 2 & to operate, paying to present claimants what is right, & if they decline compensation offered to offer them 75%, & if they decline permit them to go into the courts. We will oppose the jokers in the bill that passed the Senate. I am to see Ferris [15] & ask to have Swanson amendment incorporated in the bill.

Before discussing oil, Swanson congratulated the President upon his message

[14] Wilson's bold Fourteen Points address.

[15] Scott Ferris, Democrat, U.S. Representative from Oklahoma, chairman of the House Committee on Public Lands.

to Congress, & W W discussed various reasons that prompted him to state his war claims. "They never beat me to it if I see it first" quoting [?] Johnston Cornish [?]. I doubted his recommendation to let the Turks control Turkey in Europe. He said we could not undertake to dictate the form of government of any country or dismember. His autonomy in Austria-Hungary would permit the peoples to resolve their own governmt.

Talked to head of Servian mission.[16] He did not like what W. W. said about Turkey & Austria. Doubted if Greeks would fight. He believes America should send troops to Salonica & war can be won there & not on Western front

Dinner at British Embassy to meet Lord Devonshire,[17] Gov. Gen. of Canada Spring Rice greatly depressed.

Thursday, January 10, 1918

Decided to appoint the first Christian Scientist as Chaplain in Navy. The leader first assured me there would be no conflict with the surgeons.

Talked to Ferris about oil. He agreed to favor Swanson's bill to take over oil reserve.

My cabinet opposed creation of Minister of Munitions. Earle told how it would hamper ordnance

Council. Redfield vigorous in criticism that nothing was pressed & business men coming to W—— could get no information. Shipping Board, War Dept. & Shipping Board [*sic*] did not answer inquiries. He was too severe in his strictures.

Willard said his duties to B&O wo[ul]d require him to resign as Chm. of War Industries Board [18]

Friday, January 11, 1918

Cabinet. Discussed military minister. The President said he wished Americans could learn their country was not like Britain. Baker explained mistakes of Minister of Munitions in England. Baker detailed grilling to which he was subjected in the House. W W indignant at speech by Phelan, in presenting small bust of Emmett,[19] wishing the President to help Ireland secure its rights. At this time, with England fighting with us, such talk almost treasonable. President said he was so mad he could hardly restrain himself. Trots[k]y, it

[16] Dr. Milenko R. Vesnitch.

[17] Victor C. W. Cavendish, Lord Devonshire, former civil lord of the Admiralty, governor general of Canada since 1916.

[18] Daniel Willard had been appointed chairman of the War Industries Board on November 17.

[19] Robert Emmet, convicted of treason and hung after leading an unsuccessful Irish rebellion in 1803.

is said, will ask all allied nations to join in giving self-rule to Ireland, Egypt, India along with Belgium and Servia. That is playing into hands of Germans, but is shrewd move.

W W: Preacher in Orkney islands prayed for "the people of this land & the adjacent islands of England, Scotland and Ireland"

Why does Englishman wear monocle? So he cannot see more than he can understand.

Spring Rice & Capt. Harts: What is White House made of? Va sandstone. That is not white? No. It must be painted. Why? To cover up the burns &c after the fire. What caused the fire? The British.

Saw Dublin after catastrophe: "I did not know Ireland had home rule."

Talked with Pres. about Blue & 5 mile zone around Newport & Mare Island. What authority has he & how can he enforce it?

Talked to Mr. Davison and Mrs. Stotesbury

Saturday, January 12, 1918

Spent morning with Gregory and Lane on oil bill. We agreed to G's memorandum, ex. G's suggestion we add that innocent purchasers could get benefit of act. No! They would all swear they were innocent & open door to recognize the fraudulent claimants.

Blue spent evening with me. Said if record was approved it would be a record of guilt & would go to his children & nothing would hurt him more. Feels he had right to trust navigator & ought to be declared free from negligence

Sunday, January 13, 1918

Spoke on "Patriotism and Religion" at Church of the Covenant Bible class

Went to hear Billy Sunday at Tabernacle. He prayed for men on the seas & while denouncing hate & hard words lambasted the Kaiser in his prayer.

Bishop McDowell wished me to go to Baltimore Methodist Conference & speak on Patriotic might. Accepted

While at church, telephone from Earle & in afternoon went over statement showing that Navy in ordnance had done wonderfully well. Oliver to get up statement.

Vogelgesang [20] just returned from Japan & China. Thinks Japan could not fight us & little danger there.

Our trouble would be lack of a base

Pou's[21] son & bride here. War is hell. Too many boys marrying without knowledge of father & mother

[20] Captain Carl T. Vogelgesang, recently chief of staff of the U.S. Asiatic Fleet.
[21] Edward W. Pou, Democrat, U.S. Representative from North Carolina.

Monday, January 14, 1918

Council of National Defense discussed coal & voted it be their sense that coal and cars should not be given to breweries, piano mfs [manufacturers] & others not engaged strictly on war work. Hoover & Garfield to confer with McAdoo to bring about reduction & cessation in non-essential industries.

Dined with Mrs. J. W. Jackson

Mrs. J. Ham Lewis,[22] palmist, told my fortune from hand—

In youth was not ambitious, preferred friendship of those near to me to place or power. Hated to do or say what would offend, but followed convictions.

Olivers report giving Navy clean bill of health widely commended

Tuesday, January 15, 1918

W W

One woman had 2 stars, for her nephews & this caused Mrs W to tell her story of a Jew merchant who had 75 stars. Why It was not for his family in war but for the 75 customers he had lost because of the war.

W W. I saw a good adv. Sense—Common and Preferred

Lansing fearful introduction by Lewis of resolution endorsing W W's speech on war aims. W W not perturbed. Thought it a good thing if ⅔ should vote for it

W W asked Lansing to see Chamber of Commerce and ask them not to send out interrogatory as to whether American business men would refuse to trade with Germany unless it established a Democratic form of governt. We could not go so far & Pres. said such a referendum if in the affirmative would be embarassing [*sic*].

W W handed Baker petition from "Bible Students"—conscientious objectors. B said "They read the petition to me & also read the 17th & 18 Chap. of Revelations.["] W W said "They did not read to me, thinking I knew them by heart." B—— said they had no such presumptions as to him. "File it with your curious" said W W

McAdoo wished to know how much money each Dep. would draw from the treasury by July 1   Necessary to know how many bonds to sell

Discussed RR plan & Baker agreed to advance money for Russian engines

Wednesday, January 16, 1918

Long talk with Winterhalter about Blue.

Padgett and I discussed the naval bill & propositions for large permanent increase. He opposed that and doubted wisdom of increasing marine corps. Barnett strongly for.

Letter from Lane. He wished to say we approved relief to oil men. Wrote 1 could not do so.

Talked to Gregory about arrest of German spy in aviation camp near Norfolk. We must have co-operation.[23]

Baker & I went with Garfield to see President about coal. G wanted to cut down 4 days soon & then ex. Sat. & Monday. I suggested 1 week L[ayoff?] & the hope of no more. W W seemed doubtful Spoke of how it would affect men who needed daily wages to live & hoped employer would pay the wage

Decided to approve Garfield for 5 days

My phone rang all night with protests

Harris ordered to Norfolk, objected to going because he would have to serve under an officer of less rank. It was the limit of patience and I delivered myself.

Thursday, January 17, 1918

Padgett & P[almer] & I discussed personnel. Padgett & I agreed on only temporary & not permanent increase. It would make too many officers & we have now an abundance of Admirals.

Mr. Davison, of Red Cross & Naval Auxiliary. Saw Mrs. Stotesbury and committee resigned. The Army wished auxiliary & that would not be according to Red Cross rules

Storm over Garfield's order. I thought it was to cover only 5 days & not the 2 days a week he put into effect. Senate called on him to set it aside.

Dined with Frank Polk. The French Ambassador there & others. He does not believe in the capacity of the people for self government and fears a government of powers. Discussed RR owners

Story of W. B. Thompson who spent 1½ million dollars of his own money in Russia to try to make the people see the American point of view.

Gave all his coal & let his plant freeze to help the people.

Friday, January 18, 1918

"There is no expression of protest when a million men are called to jeopardize their lives, but the country is incensed to a pitch of indignation if money & profits must feel the pinch of war," said W W when cabinet met. Sometimes cannot refrain from "Damn" & recalled Luther Martins [24] defense of Judge Chase when impeached. Charged with profanity on the bench, it [?] was

---

[23] See entry of January 19, 1918.

[24] Luther Martin, member of the Continental Congress and Constitutional Convention, first Attorney General of Maryland, and defense attorney for Justice Samuel Chase at his impeachment trial in 1804.

shown he had used word "Damn" & Martin proved that was not profanity. 3 kinds of fools: Born fools, fools & Damn fools

A woman told her son he should not swear. Why   "Because it is wrong and worse because it is vulgar[."]

Reported the cabinet is divided. Is that true asked W W   Was it uncomfortable question? Not for any except —— [*sic*] [25]

Housing proposition. Should embrace all Depts.

All day telegrams asking exceptions for coal.

Conferred with Pres & Polk about Admiral Knight's cable. It had been agreed that England, Japan & US should not land or keep ships in Vladivostock. Japan had one ship. Another sailed for Korea but dropped in at V—— Consul at V—— wired that Knight should come. Knight said things were quiet at V & show of force might do harm

Is Japan trying to get a foothold in Russia? Shall we send ship to V or trust Japan alone? Delicate question. No solution reached.

Saturday, January 19, 1918

Long conference with Gregory & Lane, Ferris and Lenroot [26] on oil land legislation. Swanson amendment acceptable to all except Lenroot who wished to give Honolulu Co. [27] right to try case in court & if they lost there to apply for lease—"have their cake and eat it." Are to study Lenroots suggestion and report

Talked with Swanson about bill to create a Super War Cabinet & Minister of Munitions. We went to see Baker & agreed to see the President and fight the proposition. The President has his blood up & in a veto message would say some things. He has all the nerve any man needs.

Attorney General & I agreed on statement about Spoorman, [28] an ex-German officer, who was on military reservation. Stories had been printed that he was a No [1?] German spy   He is a plumber, pro-German, & an embezzler, but extravagant charges had been made & public had demanded he be shot. We decided to give out facts established by the evidence.

Conferred with Polk who sent suggested message to the President that Japan & England be asked each to send one ship alternately to Vladivostock & Japan to withdraw all but one now there so as to keep Russia from feeling

[25] Daniels probably meant Franklin K. Lane, the voluble Secretary of the Interior with whom he differed on a number of issues besides the naval oil reserves and who was increasingly critical of the administration's conduct of the war in his private correspondence.

[26] Irving L. Lenroot, Republican, U.S. Representative from Wisconsin, and member of the House Committee on Public Lands; subsequently elected to the Senate on April 2, 1918.

[27] The Honolulu Oil Company, one of the major claimants to lands within Naval Oil Reserve No. 2 in California.

[28] Walter Spoermann, a former German naval officer who had been apprehended near an army magazine at Newport News.

allies were disposed to make invasion. Will Japan agree? She takes it for granted she is to have full power in the Pacific

Sunday, January 20, 1918

David came early before I was out of bed. We talked of destruction of the Jacob Jones and his mother and the girls were here all day

Worth & I went to hear Billy Sunday

Mr. Herbert Swope[29] called. The NY World vicious toward Garfield & the administration on coal order. Swope approves and has been trying to get the World to look at the question in the right way

Monday, January 21, 1918

Letter from President enclosing one from Willard [30] criticizing Prof. Cusacks,[31] who has talked too much in Madrid—said America would obtain a naval base in Spain. Willard virtually said his resignation could be accepted if Cusacks was allowed to dip into very delicate diplomatic situation. Creel came over & said Willard was not well & was controlled, or influenced, by Wilson,[32] the counsellor of the legation. Wells said Cusacks was not discreet. He was recalled by wire.

Council of National Defense. Discussed the housing proposition in Washington. Decided to recommend building houses for 5,000 clerks who can now find no place to stay in Washington.

At night Billy Sunday tabernacle crowded. Patriotic program. I accepted paper signed by 9,000 employes in Washington Gun factory who pledged their best & every effort to win the war. It was presented to the Presd & Secretary of the Navy.

President gave out statement that Chamberlain [33] had made statement that was a perversion of truth

Tuesday, January 22, 1918

W W said he told Senators that War Council could not be established until he was dead. Republicans conspiring to make political capital by attacks on

[29] Herbert Bayward Swope, Pulitzer Prize journalist, now city editor of the *New York World*.

[30] Joseph E. Willard, U.S. Ambassador to Spain.

[31] Lieutenant Carlos V. Cusachs, a Navy professor of mathematics, or academic instructor, assigned to the U.S. Embassy in Madrid.

[32] Charles S. Wilson, counselor of the U.S. Embassy in Madrid.

[33] George E. Chamberlain, Democrat, U.S. Senator from Oregon, and chairman of the Senate Military Affairs Committee. Chamberlain had charged inefficiency in every government department and had announced his intention of introducing a bill to establish a powerful war cabinet, including a new Department of Munitions.

the conduct of the war. They want, said W W, a cabinet in which representatives of privilege will have seats & be in intimate touch. They do not think as we do because they wish to act for a class.

Carnora,[34] on day after Italian retreat, issued order naming as traitors the regiments that cowardly surrendered.

In cabinet discussed housing in D.C. & decided to ask legislation.

Ordered Cusacks to return from Spain because he was indiscreet.

Wednesday, January 23, 1918

Newton Baker came over to confer about a letter he had written to the President saying that he had but one purpose—to have the country united to win the war—and that in view of the criticism, he was ready to tender his resignation so the President could name a man as Secy. of War who would unite the country. I told him the President would not permit it, that the opposition would be satisfied with nobody except T R, Root or Wood, & the President would not name either & instead of composing & uniting, his resignation would have the opposite effect. Looks 5 years older. I told him that within a few months his critics would see how unjust they were.

Council of National Defense. Gifford had resolution for a committee on aliens looking to make all study in English. Deemed dangerous because all aliens would think they were not trusted.

Swanson read Blue's testimony & the argument & said I would make a mistake not to approve the report—that Blue ought to have quit coming & taken the fix of his ship

Thursday, January 24, 1918

Billy Sunday preached at home in the morning.

Council of National Defense met. Willard had resigned. Who should succeed him? Discussed Baruch as successor. Baker inclined. I favorable. Redfield rather opposed Houston decidedly opposed. I urged no man be appointed who was not devoted to success of Wilson administration. Chief trouble too many men in on war business who had no loyalty to Wilson.

Decided to take over wreckage companies to send over to Europe & do our own work in saving Navy & merchant ships aground or in trouble.

Called up W W to hope that heatless Mondays could end. No. He wished us not to add to no. of mfg plants exempted.

Chamberlain spoke in Senate [35]

---

[34] General Luigi Cadorna, former commander-in-chief of the Italian Army.

[35] Responding to President Wilson's charge that he had distorted the true picture of the American war effort, Senator Chamberlain declared that American soldiers had died of neglect in training camps.

T R came to town to set up rump gov. but failed.[36]

Friday, January 25, 1918

No cabinet. President sick.

Oliver talked to F.D.R. He said speed was not made, &c. T R had been in town two days.

Should D W B [David W. Bagley] & other Jacob Jones [survivors] go back at once or given leave. Latter.

Usher talked over New York, whether he would be in charge of district or Navy Yard.

Dined at 16¢ trench dinner at the Ebbitt House.[37] I spoke on making Democracy safe for the world [*sic*].

Dined with Mrs. Scott and the Vroomans

Saturday, January 26, 1918

Swope of N.Y. World came here to study & inclined to criticize. After investigation he found things going so well he had in honesty to praise. World got off on wrong foot on Garfield's coal program. He took other ground. He wanted Ralph Pulitzer released from naval reserve to guide the World. More important than commanding naval patrol ships

Talked to Benson about assignments. He told Fiske [38] if he discussed strategy again he would recommend that he be court-martialed.

Bryan in town. Had been speaking for ratification of prohibition amendment. 5 states ratified. He had no other business now but to advocate adoption of amendment. To Boston voters he said Miss. (Jefferson Davis's home) had ratified; S.C. (Calhouns); Va. Lee & Jackson. In other days Wendell Philips [*sic*] was the voice of conscience. Has Mass no voice now? Will it wait till Democratic States impose prohibition on the people?

Billy Sunday came after tabernacle to talk about some boys on the Harvard.

"Miss Mary Lee." My father said *"Never* is a long time, my child, & I rarely use it[."]

Sunday, January 27, 1918

Ralph Pulitzer called with Swope. Talked about the war and relationship of newspapers—how they could help by friendliness without bias, criticizing when necessary. Swope the ablest.

---

[36] Roosevelt had arrived in Washington on January 22 at the height of the congressional attacks against the administration's conduct of the war, with much press speculation that he had come to take command of the opposition forces.

[37] A meeting of the National Popular Government League, at which Daniels spoke.

[38] Rear Admiral (Ret.) Bradley A. Fiske was a frequent and outspoken critic of Daniels' and Benson's administration of the Navy.

Richard Hooker,[39] of Springfield Republican. He is quite able as to naval affairs, especially construction. He thinks more intimate news about what soldiers are doing for publication in home papers would make stronger sentiment for the war, shut off criticism, and nerve the people to make greater sacrifices. Thought more should be given out to the public. I told him of Ford's building 200 fast ships &c &c.

Monday, January 28, 1918

Ellis Island. Conference with Secy Wilson over letting Navy have it. War Dept. desires it. We must man 50 ships and there is no other place for us.

Col. House called. In all this talk and criticism, he said, the good condition of the Navy had saved the day. Nobody was so happy as W W

He said everybody abroad praised the alertness of the men of the Navy. Benson was easily the first man of the military men in the Council—towered over Jellico & told them what to do, & put them to doing it

Council of National Defense. Coal & food both short & shortage of both chiefly due to lack of cars & transportation Goods for abroad all rushed to NY Should go from Southern ports.

Need a Director of Shipping

Baker heard before Senate committee.

Tuesday, January 29, 1918

Lansing sent telegram from Petrograd and asked that 12 marines in civilian dress be sent to Petrograd to protect Ambassador Francis whose life seems in danger. Order sent to Sims but note sent to W W that such small force would tend to irritate and might jeopardize F's life rather than protect Embassy. Other embassies in Petrograd have guards but we have none

Garfield wanted marines sent to protect power plant on New River & Pocahontas coal fields. It would make a precedent. He is to furnish further information

Conference with Secy. of Labor about giving us Ellis Island during the war to have place for sailors to man ships for Europe

Orders for new Admirals. Naval districts changed for better organization.

Wednesday, January 30, 1918

Mrs. John D. Rockefeller [40] came to see about building houses for women employed in clothing factory at Charleston.

Attended conference at Wilson's office over housing proposition. Ship. Board

[39] President of the *Springfield Republican.*
[40] Abby G. Aldrich Rockefeller, wife of John D. Rockefeller, Jr.

had secured 50 mil appropriation from Senate. We wished all housing to be co-ordinated under Labor Dept. But Senator Fletcher [41] and Judge Alexander [42] thought it would delay & get into parliamentary tangle if change was made

Gov. McCorkle [43] of W Va. here & wanted detectives to arrest IWW who were fomenting strike & they were also German sympathizers.

Garfield called. The Boston Fuel Administrator had asked unreasonable things. G—— repudiated him

Baker going to Europe

Thursday, January 31, 1918

Page telegraphs that King wished to make Sims an honorary member of Admiralty—an honor never before given to an American. Lansing (through Polk) seemed to favor it. I opposed. President wrote me a note saying he thought it unwise and later I talked with him about it. Benson opposed and said it would do Sims harm. Officers were saying he was looking too much to English approval. W W: You see he would by such acceptance be tied up to English determination.[44]

Went before Com. of Naval Affairs & afterwards lunched with Butler.[45] We had great fun over time when Padgett put it over on Reps. when Calleway [46] & other little navy men voted for 5 cruisers & defeated Rep proposition

Went to Annapolis. Dined with Eberle & others.

Friday, February 1, 1918

Baker said stone-cutters were not employed & wondered what Gov. could do to give them employment. W W   Couldn't they get work on farms? W B W: The unskilled laborers might but the skilled ones, no. They worked with machine tools & could better work in munition factories   W W told of a stonemason at Princeton who had charge of building. His father & four generations

[41] Duncan U. Fletcher, Democrat, U.S. Senator from Florida, chairman of the Senate Commerce Committee.

[42] Joshua W. Alexander, Democrat, U.S. Representative from Missouri, chairman of the House Committee on Merchant Marine and Fisheries.

[43] William A. MacCorkle, Democrat, former governor of West Virginia, 1892–1897.

[44] See also entry of November 26, 1917.

[45] Thomas S. Butler, U.S. Representative from Pennsylvania, the ranking Republican member of the House Naval Affairs Committee.

[46] Oscar Callaway, Democrat, former U.S. Representative from Texas and member of the House Naval Affairs Committee.

had been the consulting mason of the cathedral of Canterbury. This man (Sutton) was a younger son, could not inherit the place, & so he came to America. He had a triangular piece of white marble. How did he get it? A door to the crypt of Thos. A Becket, moved from above, would not close. The Archbishop told the stone-cutter to cut off piece of marble so door could shut Two triangular pieces were cut off & Archbishop gave them to Sutton. The stone had been brought from Carthage & sent to England as gift from the Pope

Houston—Canada quietly trying to get American labor Lansing to see about it

Gregory Bill in Congress to except Austrians & others from laws against alien enemies. W W opposed it for it would free many enemies from espionage penalties

Talked to Pres. about Blue. He thought I should approve finding in case of Blue. Should take care of his ship.

Spoke at Annapolis & gave certificates to young Reserve officers

Saturday, February 2, 1918

Wrote State Dept. that thought it unwise to have Sims accept place as honorary member British Admiralty

Josephus came home

Sunday, February 3, 1918

Home all day

Monday, February 4, 1918

Mr. Gompers spoke feelingly about labor conditions. The Atty General had asked Supreme Court to postpone Harvester case [1] until after the war, but labor men were being haled before the Supreme Court. If one should go over, so should the other. Labor is in unrest he said

Mr. Rosenwald [2] showed that he had told army officers that 21 mil pair of shoes were enough for Army & yet they had insisted upon ordering 10 mil. more. His committee now had no duty.

Dr. Martin felt that Medical committee ought to have more power

Who for Chm. War Industries Board?

[1] On January 2, Attorney General Gregory had requested the Supreme Court to postpone arguments in the government's anti-trust suit against the International Harvester Company.

[2] Julius Rosenwald, philanthropist and president of Sears, Roebuck and Company, member of the Advisory Commission of the Council of National Defense and chairman of its committee on supplies.

Tuesday, February 5, 1918

Cabinet. Houston said last year we had 16 more million acres in cereals than in any previous year in spite of the complaint of lack of labor.

McAdoo: Roumania was to have 20 mil. ⅓ each from Great Britain, France & U.S. We have paid our part & now R asks for more. Lansing said R had 50 mil dollars on deposit at Moscow which the Bolsheviki Gov. had confiscated & we should help. Yes, but E & F must pay their part out of our loans to them.

McAdoo didn't like putting any set time for RR's to go back to private ownership or provision by committee to give Inter State Commerce Commission power to review Presidents fixing of rates. Not constitutional for any power to review or pass upon the Presidents action.

President approved building Pelham Park addition by direct work & not by 10% contract.

Dined with Phelan. Among others, Patton (Senatorial candidate) & Mr. Duvall [3] (cousin of Phelan) who helped defeat ship subsidy. Patton told of RR domination in Cal. He was Atty of So. Pacific & was told they expected him to oppose Foote, Dem. can. for RR Com. That was the policy & it produced a revolution.

John Sharp Williams on the Irish at Hughes's [4] funeral. Denounced them

Hitchcock had heard France wanted 600 sub-marine chasers & the Navy Dept. opposed

Wednesday, February 6, 1918

Depressing meeting of Council of National Defense. Hoover could not get food for our allies for lack of cars, Garfield could not get coal for lack of transportation, Hurley could not build ships because the cold weather, Houston troubled about wheat. Transportation fallen down. Weather made it worse. Hoover said he had urged McAdoo without result. Soft corn would be lost if not transported before March. Decided to name committee to see McAdoo

News came that Tuscania, a British Cunard steamer had been torpedoed. 2300 on board. 1,100 saved. Baker gave it out. Sims cabled report the ship was still afloat

Is God on the side of the Germans

Thursday, February 7, 1918

Loss of life less than at first reported on the Tuscania

Went to Baltimore to speak at the Press Club. News came while there that

---

[3] George S. Patton, California Democrat and unsuccessful candidate for U.S. senator in 1916, and George L. Duval of New York City.

[4] William Hughes, Democrat, former U.S. Representative and Senator from New Jersey.

Maryland had voted to ratify the Prohibition amendment. I spoke on the press as a quasi-governmental function & then on the war, replying particularly to the cry that labor is not patriotic

Spoke at Press Club   "Incomparably the greatest Navy"

Friday, February 8, 1918

Cabinet. Baker brought up that John Mitchell [5] and certain other miners had been cited to appear before Supreme Court for contempt. They had been adjudged guilty because they had tried to organize labor in a factory where the employes had been coerced into signing an agreement that they would not join the union. Mahlon Pitney had written the decision of the court in the face of the fact that the Clayton anti-trust act had exempted labor from its provisions. The act charged was committed prior to Clayton act. W. W. spoke contemptuously of Pitney & lawyers who had learned nothing & did not know the age they are living in. Wilson to see Gregory and see if same course—postponing till after war—could not be taken as in case against Harvester and other trusts.

Leonard Wood had sought to supplant Pershing [6] by telling French & English if he were in command he would divide Am. troops up in companies & have them lost or united with English & French divisions. Reading expected to request Wood to go to Europe. If he does, I will not reply in diplomatic language, said W W

Morally not straight & not truthful

Saturday, February 9, 1918

Saw Swager Sherley about new building for the Navy Department.

Delegation from Phila to ask to take over street cars so that Navy Yard workmen could get to work.

Navy night at Tabernacle. Billy Sunday preached to men of Navy

Sunday, February 10, 1918

Josephus & David at home

Wm. Wallace [7] called—seeking co-operation in enforcing the alien laws at New York

Robt W Bingham [8] & son here

[5] Chairman of the New York State Industrial Commission, former president of the United Mine Workers of America.

[6] General John J. Pershing, commander of the American Expeditionary Force in France and a strong advocate of a separate U.S. Army command in Europe.

[7] Probably William Wallace, Jr., former Assistant Attorney General, 1913–1917, now a New York attorney.

[8] An old friend and cousin of Mrs. Daniels', North Carolina–born and educated, now a Louisville attorney. In 1916, Bingham had married Mrs. Mary Lily Flagler, widow of Henry

Monday, February 11, 1918

At night went to White House to see Moving Pictures of the Navy by Dr. Dorsey.[9] Later went to University Club & spoke at banquet of Southern Commercial Congress given in honor of Senator Fletcher & Judge Bingham. I denounced pessimism & praised vision of Fletcher who advocated merchant marine bill. If that bill had been passed then we would not now be in such a sad plight for ships. Blunder of our decade.

Council of National Defense met. Hoover reported rail-road conditions better on RR for food. Garfield asked if Baker & I would join in requesting him to furnish oil to Carnegie. It developed Bethlehem had partly closed for lack of oil. Baker & I would not recommend Carnegie though it was doing most for us but thought it should be pro-rated between them

Baker had decided to go to Europe some weeks ago. Since the criticism, Justice Clark[10] had advised him to defer his visit. I agreed & thought it would be unwise to go now

Mrs Dewey called. She had letter from Thayer[11] asking her to let her [him?] print the chapter about the German admiral at Manila. She was opposed as the Admiral had decided to omit from book.

Tuesday, February 12, 1918

Lt. Comd. Babcock,[12] aide for Sims, talked about Sims who is very popular in Great Britain. Said he had heard much talk here that Sims was pro-English, but it was [not?] true. Sims believed in trusting our allies & was really more devoted to the French than the English. He had instructed all naval officers not to criticize what they did not approve in English or French navies. A Pay Master told him he suspected English holding back truth about oil. Sims said "Accept their statement; if they are lying it will come out to their discredit." Supposed French were not fully co-operating. Not a word from us. Strange the feeling between allied nations. One did not know what other was doing & a great Eng. general [?] had said "Before this war is over, we will be fighting among ourselves"

M. Flagler, the former Standard Oil partner. She died eight months later leaving Bingham an estate of $5,000,000. Bingham may have come to consult Daniels about the acquisition of the Louisville *Courier-Journal* and the Louisville *Times,* which he purchased in August, 1918.

[9] George A. Dorsey, anthropologist and lecturer.

[10] John H. Clarke, Associate Justice of the Supreme Court.

[11] Probably William Roscoe Thayer, author and popular historian who had recently published several anti-German books and articles.

[12] Commander John V. Babcock, Admiral Sims' personal aide since his assignment to London in April, 1917.

Lansing caused a laugh by reading a message from members of Russian Mission urging the Governmt not to recognize the Bolsheviki Government until Trotsky paid the ten dollars he borrowed from Mr. Crane's cook.

Wm. Bayard Hale [13] wrote asking whether he should print the interview he had with German Emperor in 1908. Emperor praised Roosevelt and denounced England for trying to make trade agreements that would bottle up Germany

Baker read telegram from Pershing. Encouraging

Burleson predicted 3 years war.

Wednesday, February 13, 1918

DuPont had plans to build explosive plant in Wisconsin—we to pay $3,675,000 in excess of regular price, enough to pay for plant & the company to own it & Government be responsible for all accidents. I declined and they went back to give us more facts.

Peebles [14] telephoned from Philadelphia that street car companies would deliver our men at Navy Yard promptly. I had signed papers if necessary to commandeer 30 cars & compel RR to give power. It had taken 2 hours to get to work & I had announced Saturday Peebles would go over to see that good service was given. "Don't shoot, I'll come down" worked.

Moore came up from Raleigh & brought reports for last year. I had drawn $12,000 from the paper & it had made $20[,]000.

Union at Raleigh had increased scale. We agreed. Then Union said—or some did—that if we discharged least efficient men, they would strike. I told Moore they regarded discharge now as spite for increasing scale & resented it for that reason. But in the long run we need keep only the men we regarded as efficient.

Thursday, February 14, 1918

Ralph Pulitzer.

Ellis Island. Labor to arbitrate

Baruch. Chicago Herald & Dupont.

Hayes,[15] Secy. International

Friday, February 15, 1918

McAdoo said chemists had experimented and found that nitroglycerine had been made from molasses & we will have interdepartmental board to study & make it commercially profitable.

---

[13] Author and editor, active in the Wilson campaign in 1912, subsequently special agent of President Wilson in Mexico, 1913–1914.

[14] Rear Admiral Christian J. Peoples.

[15] John W. Hays, secretary-treasurer of the International Typographical Union. See also the following entry.

Liberty bonds are selling at 96 [?]. Baker thought if McAdoo would offer to buy all at par very few would be offered. In Cleveland when Tom Johnson built street cars the stock of company went down to 65 & the city steadied & stopped run by agreeing to redeem at par   McAdoo said that would be impossible with 10 Billion dollars worth of bonds possible to be presented & the Treasury would not have the funds. Could not issue bonds in present condition of the country & might have to increase the interest rate on next bonds issued.

Went to capitol and picture taken of members of Naval Affairs Com. & Secretary's Council in front of the capitol. Went to see the ice in river   It endangers the bridges. Inspected site for new concrete navy building.

Went to see Secy. Wilson about Ellis Island.

Mr. Hays, of International Typographical Assoc. came to talk about wage conditions in Raleigh, but did not go to R.

Went to NY on midnight train to David's wedding.[16]

Saturday, February 16, 1918

Reached New York.

Saw Spencer Eddy [17] and Ralph Pulitzer about Intelligence work and its co-ordination with Justice and other secret service departments of Govt.

Went to call on bride & see David.

In afternoon went to matinee to see Ethel Barrymore.[18]

Wedding at Belmont 8:30 p.m. After beautiful wedding, 22 present, bride & groom got away with shower of rice.

Sunday, February 17, 1918

Heard Dr. Jowett [19] preach and he asked me about getting his sermons to England. He returns in April.

He preached on "Neither be silent no[r] rest until his righteousness is as the dawn or a torch."

Said it was better to have the emblem of doves than the bear, the lion or the eagle.

Ebenezer Elliott,[20] of Cornwall, in the Cornlaw [sic] agitation led for Cob-

[16] Mrs. Daniels' brother, Lieutenant Commander David W. Bagley, married Marie Louise Harrington of Colusa, California, the next day.

[17] Former U.S. diplomat, now a lieutenant commander in the Naval Coast Defense Reserve.

[18] Prominent American actress.

[19] John Henry Jowett, English-born Presbyterian clergyman, minister of Fifth Avenue Presbyterian Church in New York from 1911–1918, and subsequently of Westminster Chapel in London.

[20] Nineteenth-century English poet best known for his *Corn Law Rhymes*.

den.[21] Uneducated & had wonderful literary gift. Congregation sang Elliott's song: "Lord save thy people—Not kings & thrones."

Bunyan [22] & muck raking.

Left at 1 p.m. Reached home 7 p.m. Found letter from Gen. Barnett to Addie saying Josephus had been recommended and appointed Second Lieutenant in Marine Corps.

Monday, February 18, 1918

Delegation from New England to urge ships to carry coal to New England. Only two weeks supply. Will talk to McAdoo and Garfield.

Dr. Van Dyke wanted change in chaplains uniform. Likes his job.

Council of National Defense. Discussion on delay in transportation. Need of more cars in the West to bring wheat

Houston vigorous in criticizing Gore [23] for bill to increase price of wheat. Wilson said it would increase price of flour $5.00 a barrel and that would necessitate increase in wages and demand a new scale. Hoover criticized Mac.

Tuesday, February 19, 1918

Gov John A Dix [24] said his father taught a trade to all his sons—he was a mechanic. He wished to serve in some capacity as superintendent or on committee   No place for his service. He is clever man but failed as Governor of New York & was denied renomination.

Cabinet: Discussed taking over the Hamburg American line wharf. Owners would sell two large ships interned, one at Tampico & one in Columbia [*sic*] if they could have control of all other property. W W wished the ships, but wished to make no agreement that might embarass [*sic*] getting control of dock at Hoboken greatly needed. Decided to see Palmer.[25]

Wright-Martin Co. wish $2,000,000 for patent   I told them $1 mil enough as its value was chiefly due to Gov. war orders.

Went to Navy Yard to see model basin where they test model of Ford ships

Wednesday, February 20, 1918

Dupont would not agree for us to own plant after the war though we will advance the money. I saw Baker about commandeering the plant so we could make T.N.T. and T.N.Z. Am to see about it to-morrow.

[21] Richard Cobden, nineteenth-century English statesman and economist, leader of the Anti-Corn-Law League.

[22] John Bunyan, seventeenth-century religious dissenter and author of *Pilgrim's Progress*.

[23] Thomas P. Gore, Democrat, U.S. Senator from Oklahoma.

[24] Democrat, Governor of New York, 1910–1912.

[25] A. Mitchell Palmer, Alien Property Custodian.

I offered Wright-Martin people $750,000 for their basic pattern or a nominal sum for right of others to use in making planes

B——[aker] going to Europe. Wanted to know if in his absence I would give advice to Assistant Secretary [26] upon matters of policy.

Young Edmondson did not wish to wear yeoman's uniform. Telegraphed it would humiliate him to do so. I sent him word he would be honored and that was the only way to rise.

Dinner with Roger Wells

Barnett wanted to have same rank as Admiral.

J. D. Jr telephoned from Phila. He was the happiest person ever heard of now that he has won his commission

Thursday, February 21, 1918

Baker said the Germans would mass men on the Western front, take all of Russia and the Balkan states they could, and then after seeking to make the world think they were ready to strike would sue for peace, claiming that they were strong enough to win but would agree to peace.

Council of Nat. Defense. Hoover, Garfield & Hurley said everything depended upon transportation & there was no use of meeting unless McAdoo or his representative was present. He will be asked to come in future

Dinner at Barnett's. I told story of how we outgeneraled the Reps when Calloway voted for 5 battle cruisers

Josephus & his friends—2nd Lieuten[an]ts came home [27]

Yeager—Williams—Brooke

Friday, February 22, 1918

Reached New York. Worked on speech & reviewed N.Y. draft army in snow-storm at 2 p.m.

Spoke at Council of Labor and Democracy at Lexington Avenue theatre at night.

Saturday, February 23, 1918

Long talk with Dupont.[28] He wished us to put up 3½ mil. to add to factory in Wisconsin & at end of year belong to Dupont. I said "No." We will build & let board assess value at close of war. Told him Duponts made too much money & it was my intention not to put him to trouble of paying excess profits tax.

[26] Benedict Crowell.

[27] Listed in Mrs. Daniels' social diary as Lieutenants Charles H. Lovett and Allen G. Williams. The others were probably Joseph A. Yeager and William H. Brooke.

[28] Probably Pierre S. DuPont, president of E. I. DuPont de Nemours and Company, a major manufacturer of explosives.

Recommended Congress not to pay extra to flyers. Have been getting 50% more than others. Pershing says it is not more hazardous than trench service.

Also rec. end of plan to pay naval officers for carrying gold.

Ordered roster of heroes made & will name destroyers in their honor, whether sailors or officers

Theatre with J D Jr [?] & friends [?]

Sunday, February 24, 1918
Went to church with boys to hear Billy Sunday.

At 6 p.m. went to White House to see the President. Baker also present. He discussed the new regulations or chart for War Industry Board. He will make B M B [Bernard M. Baruch] the Chairman with large powers. W W wished to discuss now because Baker is going to Europe. With two or three suggested amendments we approved Presidents draft as wise & applicable. Judge Lovett wishes to get off. From racial or other reasons the Judge does not like Baruch & would not serve under him. He is a prima donna said W W. Necessary for McAdoo to find a good RR man to replace him. Lord R——[eading] was told by the Pres. that unless all allied countries agreed upon a Commander in chief we could not consent to our troops being under any but American command. Baker was told to say that to [Lloyd] George & Clemenceau.[29] George removed Robertson [30] & made Parliament believe it was as result of Allied War Conference & due to paper of Gen Bliss. Baker was instructed to see Bliss and ascertain what Bliss wrote. Believes George is playing politics & does not tell the truth. Petain [31] also criticized Pershing because he would not merge American soldiers with French commands. Will not stand for that. English Gen objected because orders agreed upon in Versailles council were sent direct by Gen Foche [32] & not through British Commander. W W expressed hatred of red tape.

Colored man told "Obey nobody but men with stripes on their shoulders[."]

Monday, February 25, 1918
Council of National Defense. Priorities to be settled by War Industries Board.

Roosevelt presented report of committee on rehabilitation and vocational education for wounded men after the war. Discussion as to who should be

[29] Georges Clemenceau, French premier and Minister for War since 1917.

[30] General Sir William R. Robertson, who had resigned as chief of the British imperial staff on February 16.

[31] General Henri Philippe B. O. J. Petain, commander-in-chief of French armies since May, 1917.

[32] General Ferdinand Foch, French chief of staff, subsequently made supreme commander of the Allied armies in France on April 14, 1918.

in control. Treasury wanted it under War Insurance Board. Will take it up with the President.

Shall April 6th be Win the War Day?

Dined at Miss Mabel Boardman's[33] Admiral Cowles[34]—joined church at 62 & joined Congregationalist because he thought his mother would like it. Liked Billy Sunday.

Tuesday, February 26, 1918

Cabinet. Discussed policy of rehabilitation of soldiers & decided to give the task to the Vocational Educational Board that had been studying the plan. McAdoo inclined to opinion that it ought to be under the War Insurance Board, but it was decided to prepare the bill & let all cabinet members give their opinion.

Baker left for France. Told me to tell Mrs. Dewey she could erect the kind of statue she desired at Arlington. He had sent some samples of what Art Commission had approved, but what she wanted he would order.

Will Bailey and Wake County politics. H Royster & Jos. G. Brown[35]

Mr. Davison wished to go to Europe for Red Cross. Wished advice as to best course

Dined with Vance McCormick.

Wednesday, February 27, 1918

Talked with Padgett about Navy bill. Decided to put all for Washington gun factory in deficiency & not in Naval bill

Flying machine patents. Ought to pay $1 million. They wanted royalties for $4 mil & then our patent. They offered to reduce royalty from $200 to $125.

Lady in Des Moines asked for the shirt-tail to make apron to be sold for the Red Cross. The President had like letter and said it was the limit[.] Certainly it is the tail end.

Swanson & Martin. The latter vigorous in criticism of Baker for going to Europe. Said of all times he was needed here now

Thursday, February 28, 1918

Talked with Tillman and Asst. Secy. of War on contract. War had selected contractor for big work on embarkation. Tillman wanted plans sent to local contractors to bid on. Crowell said this would delay & could not afford delay. Tillman used pitchfork

[33] Mabel T. Boardman, prominent Washington hostess, vice-chairman of the American Red Cross.
[34] Rear Admiral (Ret.) William S. Cowles, Theodore Roosevelt's brother-in-law.
[35] Banker and prominent Raleigh citizen.

Call from owners of air patents & wanted to know what I would do. Ready to come down.

Chas. A. Towne [36] wanted to sell Bliss Torpedo factory   No.

Friday, March 1, 1918

Peter Cooper Hewitt & his mistress supposed to be German   Asked to retire from Naval Consulting Board. Saunders and Thayer & Smith [1] had report of Naval Intelligence.

The President told us he was tired & when he was tired he first felt it by being unable to find language. Story of Rusty Pat he kicked out of recitation room. "That's me professor." Said when he lectured he poured everything of himself into the lecture & afterwards was so tired he could not recognize his best friend. Had no command of language. "I guess I had used up all language I had"

Why not join Japan & go into Russia? B & W said if Japan went in she would never come out & we ought to join. No said W W. "We have not ships to send soldiers and besides if we invade Russia will not Germany say we are doing exactly what she is doing. We will lose our moral position.["]

IWW. Should all alien IWW be interned. Wilson thought only those who were leaders. Lumber men in Wash. refused the 8 hours & to make better conditions for labor, & they enrich the soil on wh. [which] IWW propagates. W B W told to see them & War Dept. & tell them to accept 8 hr law before calling on Gov. to use strong arm.

Saturday, March 2, 1918

Went to lunch with Naval Consulting Board. English officer had drawings and talked on the system of camoflage [*sic*]. An English officer in court martial was acquitted because he proved he would not have made mistake in navigation but for successful camoflage. It made the ship appear to be going in one direction while it was in reality going in another. Is camoflage camoflage? I told Taylor I was inclined to think so.

Clark,[2] Com. on Public Buildings, thought by contract, we would erect new

---

[36] Democrat, former U.S. Representative and Senator from Minnesota, former U.S. Representative from New York, now an attorney in New York City.

---

[1] Rear Admiral William S. Smith, Navy representative to the Naval Consulting Board.
[2] Representative Frank Clark, chairman of the House Committee on Public Buildings and Grounds.

navy buildings better than on percentage contract which [?] F D R & Parks[3] recommended. Sent for Park [sic].

Martin & Swanson wanted us to build road to Quantico where we have marine barracks. Road badly cut up. Army agreed to build part it had cut up.

Hancock[4] saved $360,000 on contract for depth bombs. They ascertained the cost & company came down in figures

Sunday, March 3, 1918

Heard Billy Sunday. Rhodyheaver[5] said he wished all to sing "Brithen [sic] the corner right where you are" for Uncle Joe Cannon. He called on Cannon and Speaker Clark & Secy of Navy to come on platform. Said the friendship of Uncle Joe and Champ Clark would make the friendship of David and Jonathan look like thirty cents.

Young Thos. Gregory Jr.[6] wanted advice as to whether he should enter Marine Corps or the Navy. Sent him to see Palmer. Is chap who wishes to get in fighting line.

David & George here

Monday, March 4, 1918

Council of National Defense. Baker absent. I Acting Chmn. Telegram sent to Public Service Commission Minnesota urging taking back men who had struck at old positions. The St[reet] R[ailwa]y demanded the men take off Union Labor buttons. Men called meeting Monday night to decide upon course[.] When they went to work Monday morning they were told they could not take out cars unless they took off buttons. They struck. The[re] had been a strike before and Secy Wilson wanted telegram sent so that RR. would not send to other cities and employ men and let old employees walk the street. I sent urgent telegram in name of Council.

Telephoned Baruch congratulating him that President had named him Chr. of War Industries Board.[7]

Tuesday, March 5, 1918

Cabinet. W W. Reminiscent of Princeton told story of Prof of Chemistry.

---

[3] Rear Admiral Charles W. Parks, chief of the Bureau of Yards and Docks.

[4] Commander John M. Hancock of the Bureau of Supplies and Accounts.

[5] Homer A. Rodeheaver, musical director of Billy Sunday's evangelistic campaigns.

[6] Evidently young Gregory, the son of the Attorney General, decided in favor of the Navy, for he was commissioned an ensign in the Naval Reserve on October 2, 1918.

[7] President Wilson had just announced the appointment of Baruch as chairman of the War Industries Board, with greatly increased and centralized powers over industrial production and governmental purchasing.

"In my laboratory I am all mind; outside I am all soul." Given to big words: "Why did I have to take out that anaemic dessicated ——— female?" Like Disraeli said of Gladstone: "Inebriated by his own verbosity"

Gregory: What shall I do with whiskey taken by marshals? No authority to dispose of it. Much merriment. W W told of whiskey put in buckets at Army canteen and a mule got its head in the bucket and drank and drank and drank. Became so drunk it kicked over everything. ["]But did not kick the bucket." Burleson said it would be a sin to pour out good whiskey—it was getting too scarce & high. He suggested that it be given to hospitals

McAdoo: Hard to make people think Fed. Gov. should not pay everything. Secy. of Stock growers in Minn demanded more cars to carry stock to market. Cars were sent. Stock hurried in such quantities to market that price went down. They wrote McAdoo that the Gov. ought to pay loss of dif. in the price. W W thought this the limit. Everybody expecting the Fed. Gov. to do everything.

Dined with Mr & Mrs H. S. Rea [8] of Pittsburg

Gave $1000 & Sims suggested soda fountain. She was happy

Wednesday, March 6, 1918

Went to see Martin and Sherley about new building for Navy Department. Clark (Frank) had written it could be built for $1.50 sq. foot. concrete. We asked for $3.00. We had made tentative contract for 10% on 5 mil building not to exceed $250,000 fee. Telegraphed Clarks man asking him to come on if he could do it at suggestion of Swanson & Martin & Sherley. The latter said he would assume no responsibility. Wished to retire as soon as war is over. "You are surrounded by trained men who help you—I by selfish politicians who always want something."

Council met with Baruch, new chm. War Industries Board, Hoover, Garfield, Hurley. Baruch said England had only one months supply of nitrates. France and Italy none. Serious situation. Sent for Gen. March [9] just returned from France. He thought no lack of finished product. Inter Allied War Council feared could not hold line unless we send 90,000 men per month. He would telegraph Pershing & get fact about need of nitrates & whether 2 months waiting would seriously affect them.

Put Annapolis, Newport, Mare Island and other training stations under ɩ ry law

[8] Henry R. Rea, Pittsburgh manufacturer, a member of the Advisory Committee on Plants al d Munitions of the War Industries Board.

[9] Major General Peyton C. March, acting Army chief of staff.

Thursday, March 7, 1918

Council. Read the President's orders in his letter to Baruch as the chart by which we sail.

California man said I should be interested in developing water power so as to save the oil reserves in California. Otherwise need for oil for power would be so great the demand would compel use of oil set aside for Navy.

George went to Europe.

Dinner at Mrs. Marshall Fields.[10]

Friday, March 8, 1918

B—— was pessimistic—predicted Constantine [11] would be crowned King of Athens, Germany would defeat army at Salonica, & then go into Lombardy. Lane thought it would get help & provisions from Russia and other countries & could afford to wait before attacking on West front. "I am rather persuaded" said W W "that the friend who advised me to send members of cabinet out of Washington to learn what the country is thinking about is a good thing to do." Redfield thought Russia a liability instead of an assett [*sic*]. Lane disagreed. WW was grim, determined, & thought Japan should not go into Russia —it might throw Russia into protecting arms of Germany. He spoke of men in Wash. preaching pessimism—bitterly of dinner party gossip, and of others who lacked faith that history will repeat itself & that autocratic power must fall. It was glorious to hear his solemn & clear presentation of his faith & resolve—an antidote to selfish pessimism & it impressed all. McAdoo thought he ought to make a speech on April 6th. After discussing certain classes who were standing in way of victory &c., W W said "Now having proved that many of our fellow citizens are d—— fools let us come to business.["]

Houston and nitrates. Hurley had, without consultation, taken boats for nitrate & put them to carrying nitrates to France. Crops need them. W. W. did not like taking them without consultation. McAdoo talked of loan & queer proportion [?]. W W opposed class presentation whether of bankers or businessmen or labor men. W B W had said labor men had propaganda for labor man on Peace Commission

Henderson [12] thinking of coming here. W B W feared his preaching socialism might divide labor. W W said it would be worse [?] to make official protest.

[10] Delia Spencer Caton Field, widow of the Chicago merchant and a prominent figure in Washington society at this time.

[11] Constantine, King of the Hellenes, forced into exile by the Allies in June, 1917, because of his pro-German attitude.

[12] Arthur Henderson, prominent leader of the British Labour Party and former member of the Privy Council and War Cabinet.

Saturday, March 9, 1918

Gifford called to talk about War Industries Board. Baruch had offered him place as Secretary. He wanted to be member of the board. He asked if War Industries Board was under Council of National Defense or directly under the President. The Air-Craft Production Board wanted him to assist & he enquired what I thought. &c.

Act. Secy. of War [13] called with Coffin with a letter to the President proposing a board to investigate the Signal Service & work of Air Craft Board with Coffin as Chm. I said it would not do to have Coffin on a board to investigate himself & that he was needed now if ever to hasten production. They agreed. Coffin seemed rather to think he should be with the Board.

Sunday, March 10, 1918

Went to church with the boys.

Mrs. Dewey called with Mrs. Horatio Slater, who had invented or patented a blanket wrapper of 1½ blankets which would give greater comfort to soldiers & cover them twice over. Also a watch with a compass. Mrs. D gave me the watch. Jonathan kissed Mrs. Dewey goodbye.

Mrs Stotesbury & son called. She was full of the boy reserves she had seen in Florida & had helped them.

Baruch called. We talked at length about War Industries Board & fixing prices, &c &c. I wished a Navy man on board. He would not name another Jew because it was not good politics.

Monday, March 11, 1918

Council—at my office. *Baker reached France.* General talk about ships & need of RR's & cranes. We send more stuff to France than can be taken from ships and we are holding up ships until the way of getting things carried to the front is provided.

Hurley wanted us to officer and man Dutch ships we take over. Nav. [Bureau of Navigation] said we ought to have notice. Belknap & I said "We ought to meet the demand for men.["] It would be a miracle, he said, & we could do it. "All right" I said, "perform a miracle." It is our business to do the impossible.

Two young officers wrote in log of a patrol ship "The Commanding officer turned the ship & did not try to get submarine or protect ships convoyed." Niblack said it preposterous and insubordinate for them & he detached them from the ship & rebuked them. Was he right?

Secy Meyer died. Sent message & put flags at half mast.

---

[13] Benedict Crowell.

Griffin [14] Commd of Sailors Home, Phila, & Dr Braisted   "I will have no feelings, no question of precedence or anything like it during this war.["]

Tuesday, March 12, 1918

Cabinet. Discussed R.R. bill. McAdoo said States felt it would be OK now to impose heavier tax than when RRs were privately run and wished some check on it. Also some cities were withdrawing the police protection of RRs formerly given. Would see Secy. of War.

Redfield's man, clerk in Commerce, had lantern that revolved. Experimented at night when two secret service men demanded to be seen. Shows secret service men on their job.

Annapolis people auth[orities?] wanted more time on dry order. "Not a day" said W W "The city authorities had nothing to do with the order. They have therefore no responsibility." I so wrote Mayor.

United Fruit Co. wanted to get concessions in San Salvador & State Dept. wanted us to give $25,000 for Telefunken plant & aid United F Co. Polk & Benson recommended. W W said No, he would not be party to getting concessions for private companies, besides radio service was not a part of work of fruit Co

State Dept. wanted to allow Germans here to send messages to friends & relatives in Germany. "How is my father?["] &c Burleson said it would be a method of getting news into Germany by making such simple messages into a code. Polk & Intelligence think not. W W said he had three times decided no & would not permit it. Spain & Switzerland ministers had urged. "Spain is least neutral & Switzerland is the whispering gallery of Europe."

Wednesday, March 13, 1918

Gentleman claimed he had discovered a process by which he could bring down the power of a bolt of lightning, make it deal its death-giving blows where he chose & it would win the war. Is he crazy or a genius? Decided at his request to let him make experiment at Annapolis & if successful to give just compensation.

Decided not to ask reduction of aviators pay but only reduction of allowances unless army reduced. Should act together.

Our dreadnaughts in North Sea acting as convoys of merchant ships in North Sea. Two torpedoes fired at Florida but did not hit. Crew calm & cool. Should such ships do such duty? Wired Sims & offered to send second class ships if they would do.

[14] Commodore (Ret.) Thomas D. Griffin, governor of the Philadelphia Naval Home.

Thursday, March 14, 1918

Discussed at noon new building and securing expedition in work

H W Jackson   went with him to see Mitchell Palmer.

Conference with ship builders who contended that Gov. should pay income and excess profit tax on 10% contracts   No

Council of National Defense. Discussed importance of 100,000 tons of nitrates monthly from Chili. Am to see the President

Also talked of asking states to encourage trucks to hurry freight. States object because heavy trucks destroy costly roads.

My wife went to Raleigh   Aunt Sophie

Friday, March 15, 1918

Went to New York on midnight train

Saturday, March 16, 1918

Visited hospital ship Mercy at New York Navy Yard

Had Benson, Usher and Gleaves to lunch at Astor House

Spoke at Madison Square Garden at Military Meet to help France   Soldiers and sailors drilled

Spoke at banquet to Friendly Sons of St. Patrick on lessons in life of John Barry.[15]

Father Cavanaugh said: "I hate England"—then said hatred of England ought not to cause any American to fail to rally to the flag.

J Ham Lewis said after the war we might look for trouble because some of our allies oppose our Monroe Doctrine & do not agree on Asiatic exclusion

Sunday, March 17, 1918

Spoke at Grace Meth. Church on Paul's reaching appr. Tarsus [?] & thanking God & taking courage.

Dr Reisner.[16] 27 of 29 of his stewards were against Wilson. He was for him.

Spoke at night at Hippodrome to Knights of Columbus in launching campaign for fund to help in protecting young men.

Cardinal Farley.[17]

[15] Naval hero of the Revolutionary War and the quasi war with France, 1799–1800.

[16] Christian F. Reisner, minister of Grace Methodist Church in New York, pioneer of religious advertising in various media.

[17] John M. Farley, Roman Catholic cardinal and archbishop of New York.

Monday, March 18, 1918

Hoover urged fixing prices for salmon & packers products & whatever we lack enough of. Council approved & I was to see the President.

Took Governor Glynn [18] to lunch. He felt that Dems. did not receive enough consideration & that too many enemies of administration were recognized. Writing life of Martin Van Buren. He was glad I spoke to K of C. 1916? [19] Wanted me to go to Albany on Flag Day. Promised if possible.

Tuesday, March 19, 1918

Cabinet. Talked of ships & nitrates & need of priority. "There are not enough ships & I must decide how to employ them first["] said W W. "We must feed the world." Therefore the pledge to bring nitrates to farmers must be kept. McAdoo said coal must go to New England & President agreed we should commandeer no more ships from N.E. coal trade.

After Cabinet talked to W. W. He had had long talk with Lord Reading who urged encouraging Japan to go into Russia to fight Germany. What military advantage? It is 6,000 miles from Vladivostok to where Germans are fighting with a single rail and Japan does not propose at the most to go further than Ural mountains. He told Lord R to get what military men expected to accomplish. He did not trust their wisdom. Thought it most unwise.

Wednesday, March 20, 1918

The Manly collided with British ship & one officer and several men killed.[20]

Knight telegraphed about helping to set up government in Siberia. W W said telegraph him that Siberians must settle their own government & for K—— not to take any steps until directed by his Government. Also K—— cabled he & English would resist by force any attempt to move munitions from V—— [21] No. K—— had not conferred with Japs. Asked: Why not?

Many wires clamoring for Japs to go in. Lansing called. Said Japs were acting in best possible way and that they did not wish to go in unless it was agreed that it was best.

[18] Martin H. Glynn, Democrat, former governor of New York.

[19] Probably a reference to the fact that some Democrats had considered Daniels a political liability to the administration in 1916 because of his controversial reforms, especially his order abolishing the wine mess.

[20] The U.S. destroyer *Manley* suffered severe damage on March 19 when a depth charge exploded after the ship collided with a British naval vessel; 33 of the *Manley*'s crew were killed and 22 injured.

[21] The Allies were concerned about the future disposition of a large quantity of munitions and other supplies shipped to Vladivostock before the Bolshevik regime took Russia out of the war.

F D R wishes to go abroad

Mr Hall [?] (DKE) wants to go to France to look after fraternity men. Dined with us

I read Life of Maury [22] after dinner.

Thursday, March 21, 1918

Went to Anacostia to see flights in aerplanes [*sic*]—Taylor, Griffin & Earle. Two fine flights. The Liberty motor had brought machine up from Hampton Roads, 180 mi. in 2 hours—& it made a beautiful flight. Other machine also left water gracefully.

N.Y. Ship Co. wanted us to pay increase of wages since the war began on the Idaho. No—strong

Bought 6 Russian submarines $600,000 each. Wanted us to pay certain per cent

Friday, March 22, 1918

No cabinet—President had cold.

Saturday, March 23, 1918

Benson cabled Sims not to change policy until facts were sent here.

Roger Wells—Shall we take off a German engineer who is an American citizen going on transport.

Went to Raleigh.

Sunday, March 24, 1918

Taught SS. at Edenton Street. Lesson   The Miracle of the Loaves & the Fishes. I talked on Food Conservation and the Miracle. Many boys present. [?]

Raleigh. Spoke at Y.M.C.A. in A&M College. The glory of youth. Boy in France whose knees trembled. He prayed—& there came strength & a smile & he came back safe & said th[at] Christ was with him

Monday, March 25, 1918

Reached here 1 p.m.

Council of National Defense—Nitrates & Rehabilitation of wounded soldiers.

Gavin McNab. Air Craft. Praised Navy.

[22] Probably Diana F. Maury Corbin, *A Life of Matthew Fontaine Maury* (London: Low, Marston, Searle & Rivingston, 1888).

Tuesday, March 26, 1918

Cabinet—I brought up allocation of ships. Nitrates needed for agriculture and munitions & yet Shipping Board thinks of allocating ships to New England coal for next winter (& R.R. Director [23] urges) rather than leaving ships to Chili for nitrates. Baruch says we must have 100,000 tons of nitrate a month. France only has 1 mo supply, Italy less & our need is great. Only the President can allocate & facts given to him.

Lucy Burleson,[24] Yeoman, came in. Very pretty and proud of her uniform.

Yates Webb had banker who wanted to go in pay corps.

Tillman. Charleston dry dock. Small [25] objects to Naval Affairs Committee having anything to do with rivers and harbors. We must have 40 feet at Charleston in order to make dock most useful

Wednesday, March 27, 1918

The Presidents Council,[26] including McAdoo, Crowell & myself met at White House. Talked nitrates & decided to allocate ships to bring enough from Chili.

Shall all shipping of allies be pooled? England asked if we would give up 50-50 of Dutch & Norwegian ships? Will England give us 50 50 of all? Geddes said she had net loss of only 2½ mil. tons. Where is her 40 mil. tons left? McCormick thought we should pool. W W doubted until Stevens assured us that the suggestion of England was just.

Shall RR [Administration?] get usual low rates given to RRs? Or pay like others? McAdoo wants to furnish cars & get low rate. Garfield No. W W seemed to favor equal price to all even if RR's lost money

Thursday, March 28, 1918

Sent for Powell to hurry up destroyers

Griffin went to Phila. to see Cramps & NY Ship.[27] Very important to speed up.

Arranged to buy 6 submarines built for Russia. Shipping Board objected to fitting up in Skinner plant & that made a hitch

[23] William G. McAdoo.

[24] Daughter of Postmaster General Burleson, who had enlisted as a Navy Yeoman (F).

[25] Representative John H. Small, chairman of the House Committee on Rivers and Harbors.

[26] On Wednesday mornings President Wilson normally conferred with his war council, a small and changing group of his more trusted lieutenants. As this Diary makes amply clear, the Tuesday and Friday cabinet sessions had degenerated into a discussion of trivialities or mere storytelling, because Wilson had long since discovered that Secretary Lane was frequently indiscreet in revealing cabinet confidences.

[27] The New York Ship Building Company of Camden, New Jersey, a large Navy contractor, and William Cramp and Son, a large Philadelphia shipbuilding firm.

Friday, March 29, 1918

Cabinet. I presented telegram from Knight saying he might have to land at Vladivostok in view of presence of German officers & present and [prevent any?] shipment of munitions from that place to interior for fear it would fall into Japanese hands. Should Japan go into Russia? Lane & B thought it would be better than for Japanese to go in alone [*sic*]. W W & Lansing thought not. W W said: What military advantage. Japan has only 400,000 troops, regular & reserved—& is not keen to go in   Might drive resentful Russia into hands of Germany.

Spoke twice at Geographical Society

Saturday, March 30, 1918

Went to Belleview Magazine with Naval Consulting Board to see about location of laboratory.

Went with Barnett to see Assistant Secretary [of] War about sending marines to France. We can send 4,500 & equip and care for them. Question whether Army desires marines.[28]

Sunday, March 31, 1918

Heard Bishop James Atkins [29] at Mt Vernon Place Meth. Ch. He came to dinner with us.

At night heard the Archbishop of York [30] (named Lang)   When made Archbishop Andrew Lang [31] wrote and congratulated him & said "So far as I can learn you are the first man bearing the name who ever arrived at respectability."

Archbishop told of painting representing the Kaizer [*sic*] speaking to the King of Belgium.[32] Behind them were the chimneys, mute sentinels of devastation & ruin. "You see you have lost all" asked the Kaizer, "why do you longer resist?"

"No," said the King looking at the ruins, "I have not lost all. I have not lost my soul."

---

[28] By summer some 8,000 Marines were fighting in France, where they acquitted themselves well in the bitter fighting at Chateau Thierry, Belleau Wood, Soissons, and St. Mihiel. Ultimately nearly 31,000 Marines served in the A.E.F. in France, suffering more than 11,000 casualties.

[29] North Carolinian and bishop of the Methodist Episcopal Church (South).

[30] Cosmo Gordon Lang, in the United States on a speaking tour arranged by the war commission of the Protestant Episcopal Church.

[31] Scottish scholar and man of letters.

[32] Albert I, King of the Belgians.

Monday, April 1, 1918

Council of National Defense

Mr. Willard brought up matter of air-craft & was depressed at slow proceedure [*sic*]. When he learned what had been accomplished he & others were gratified and said a statement ought to be made that would reassure the people. I told him a special committee was making a study and would report shortly. We are behind & will not have full production expected in March until July.

Talked of delay in loading and unloading ships. Willard thought too slow.

Approved bill for Vocational Board to undertake rehabilitation of men from war.

Took lunch at British Embassy to meet Archbishop of York. He had spent three weeks with the Grand Fleet in the North Sea and was deeply interested in Navy. Was enthusiastic over Great Lake Training Station—the most wonderful sight he had seen in America

Tuesday, April 2, 1918

Cabinet discussed situation.

W W read letter from Ambassador Sharp of the destruction of church in Paris by 90 mi gun & 100 killed including Swiss Secy [?] of Legation. Wife of minister was violent in denunciation of conduct [?] of Germany.

Pres. decided to issue Proclamation requesting all parties to abide by action of Labor Adjustment Board.[1]

Spoke at night at Baltimore

Investigated vice conditions of Phila. Confer with Lt Col Hatch.[2] NY Times.

Wednesday, April 3, 1918

War Council met with President. First took up question of getting men to France. Hurley reported could send over 90,000 a month but this would require reduction of imports and in Japan and Brazilian trade. President said "Tell Great Britain how many we can send not taking out Japan & Brazil tonnage and then ask England and France to furnish ships for balance.["]

---

[1] The War Labor Conference Board had recently drawn up a set of principles to govern labor-management relations during the war and had recommended the creation of a War Labor Board to apply them.

[2] Lieutenant Colonel (Ret.) Charles B. Hatch, U.S.M.C., of the Philadelphia recruiting office. On March 31, Daniels had released a report by the Joint Commission on Training Camp Activities which sharply criticized vice conditions in Philadelphia as a threat to servicemen stationed in the area. Hatch subsequently supervised the reform of the Philadelphia police force.

John Skelton Williams [3] brought up buying coal for RR's at less figure than public pays—said operators were making unconscionable big profits, but were willing to continue practise of selling to RR cheaper if cars are furnished. Garfield opposed drop in price & said RR should pay same as public & Navy, & the practise of furnishing 100% cars to certain RR's [mines?] was indefensible. Williams said G's prop. made giving 40 mil dollars to operators & no benefit to anybody else. I asked why not commandeer. W W said the RR did not belong to the Governt & we could not commandeer.

W W—Not let cars go to certain mines but divide in zones, & require better prices for RR because coal to them is essential to keep all industries going.

Dinner at Gen McCauleys

Thursday, April 4, 1918
State Councils of National Defense met with Nat Council in office of Secretary of the Navy. I made brief address—how State & Fed. govs. had worked in harmony. Selective draft administered by local authorities as nearly perfect as possible. Must end treason but by law.

Lafe Pence & others wanted laws preventing teaching of German in our schools. It is the medium through which treason is preached. Going on now [?] not because it is better but to save teachers trouble of learning English & to give glamour to German Kultur. Wanted more vigorous laws to punish spies & men who were not true to their country. In Nebraska some German teachers refused to let children sing national air

Conference with McNab & others on air craft conditions.

Decided to furnish officers & men to put down pipe line across Scotland Theall [4] & Judge Advocate General

Friday, April 5, 1918
Went to Balti. Spoke to Meth Conference

Saturday, April 6, 1918
Spoke at Cleveland & told what Navy had done in the war [5]

Sunday, April 7, 1918
Reached Cin.
Spoke at Meth church 11 am briefly

[3] Comptroller of the Currency and director of the division of finance and purchases of the Railroad Administration.

[4] Colonel Elisha Theall, of the Marine Corps headquarters staff, formerly clerk of the House Naval Affairs Committee.

[5] Daniels was speaking in a number of Ohio cities on behalf of the current Liberty Loan drive.

Spoke at Luncheon at Country Club.

Spoke at 3 at Red Cross meeting to big audience

Monday, April 8, 1918

Reached Detroit early

Commodore Livingstone [6] told me of Henry Ford's beginning. F's partner did not like delay in producing & wished haste. Ford consulted Commodore L who advised saying you will buy or sell & ask him to name figure. He named low figure, knowing Ford had no money & thought he would get it cheap. But Ford took him up, Col. Livingstone lent the money, & Ford thereby became majority owner.

Spoke at Chamber of Commerce to Liberty Loan Committee—at Athletic Clubs & at the Theatre & visited Fords & other plants

Tuesday, April 9, 1918

Reached Buffalo early, breakfast at Mr. Walter Cooke's [7] with Norman Mack. Lunch & spoke to Liberty Loan Com. Went to factories & then spoke at Niagara Falls.

At night spoke at Buffalo

Wednesday, April 10, 1918

Reached Chicago—went to Training Station. Armour,[8] Swift, Sullivan [9] & others on Com.

Spoke at station (Great Lakes)

Received com. of ministers & others who urged asking City Council to quit giving license to Dance Halls to 3 p.m. & made brief talk.

Addressed National Chamber of Commerce

Thursday, April 11, 1918

On B&O train coming to Wash—Lane aboard. Clarence Howard [10] & wife of St Louis on train

Friday, April 12, 1918

Returned from western trip.

At Cabinet. W W said in [if] House cited George Creel for contempt he

---

[6] William Livingstone, Detroit banker and Great Lakes shipper.

[7] Walter P. Cooke, Buffalo attorney and chairman of the local Liberty Loan drive.

[8] J. Ogden Armour, Chicago meat packer and capitalist.

[9] Roger C. Sullivan, leader of the Cook County Democratic organization.

[10] Clarence H. Howard, president of the Commonwealth Steel Company.

would go up to the House as his attorney & say "It's me you are after. Here
I am. Be brave enough to go after me.["] [11]

Gregory: Said at Bridgeport the Judge sent for every German who would
not subscribe & after he talked to them awhile, they generally took bonds

Saturday, April 13, 1918

Went to New York & spoke before Democratic Club on Jefferson's birthday.
Also spoke in 69th Armory on Liberty Bonds

Sunday, April 14, 1918

Heard Dr. Jowett preach in New York farewell sermon "I will make him
the Morning Star." Quoted Tennyson on Arthur Hallom. Spoke of the Night
King & its blackness. The morning star harbinger & ambassador of light &
the end of bats & owls and fears & trembling.

Lunched with Samuel Untermeyer [12] at lovely Greystone (Tilden's home)
She is not a Jewess but spoke of the wonderful race and said prejudice was
so great she once wanted to live abroad and bring up her children there.

Dined with Ambassador Elkus

Monday, April 15, 1918

Mrs Baker was going to Cleveland and two men behind her were talking &
one expressed very vigorously the hope that the ship on which the Secretary
of War was returning would be sunk. She was so indignant she resented it &
told them who she was. His name was Wm. E. Lamb, a Chicago lawyer, and
bitter Republican partisan.

I went to see the President about it & he thought he ought to be punished
if seditious and other[wise?] should be brought here by the Attorney General
and given the 33rd degree and then the story of his comment given to the
public so he would be forever damned by the people.

Mayo came & urged that he go abroad with the fleet & Benson opposed.
We already have 5 & Mayo would supersede Sims. I saw the President & he
agreed not to send

"Fear I will come out of the war hating English"

Mrs. Dewey gave me the shaving cup (silver) which Admiral Dewey always
used—said she wished me to have it because he loved me and I loved him.
She said he had a little book—she never knew it until afterwards with Bible

---

[11] Creel, head of the Committee on Public Information, was under sharp attack in Congress as an alleged socialist with no respect for the legislative branch.

[12] Democrat and prominent New York attorney.

Texts he read every day. He had such faith and never talked of what he believed.

Tuesday, April 16, 1918

Cabinet. Navy had asked about taking Swan island [13]—little islands which nobody claims—so we could take over the radio controlled by fruit co. Not very far from Colon. He disliked the idea of claiming territory, or taking it. It would smack of doing what Austria had done but would be nothing like it, but would hate to put Americans on with radio without protecting them. Am to look into it.

National Research Council wished an Executive Proclamation setting forth what they should do. Houston objected that they wished to take over existing agencies of government and said it would not be wise.

Shall we favor Americans wearing French & English medals of honor & decorations? I had advised against—Senate had passed. House Mil. Chm [14] held up at our request. W W thought best to discuss with Baker and then see the Chn of House Naval [15] & Mil Com.

Went to Anacostia to see H 16 new air craft that had come up from Hampton Roads bringing up 5 men.

Saturday, April 20, 1918

At Squantum [16]—amazed to see workmen set up frame work for 5 destroyers in 50 minutes

Monday, April 22, 1918

Returned from New England

Attended funeral of Chilian Ambassador [17]

Saw Atty General about oil situation

Spoke at opening of the Service Club, young women in khaki learning how to cultivate farms during war.

Went to see Blanche Bates [18] in "All Together"

Tuesday, April 23, 1918

Cabinet. Talked with Baker about his trip abroad. Warm in commendation of naval transport service and of quality of marines. Talked incognito with

[13] A small but strategic island in the Caribbean off Honduras.
[14] S. Hubert Dent, Jr., Democrat, U.S. Representative from Alabama.
[15] Lemuel P. Padgett.
[16] A shipyard south of Boston.
[17] Santiago Aldunate.
[18] Actress wife of George Creel.

many soldiers. All are confident of ultimate victory. Foch believed to be ablest military genius but if Gen ———, very old & a royalist who helped save the day at the Marne, were younger, he would be the most resourceful.

Will bring indictment against profiteers   (NY Times)

Mr. Roys,[19] Naval Attache, under Sims came to see me

Wednesday, April 24, 1918

Went to N.Y.

Thursday, April 25, 1918

Spent day in New York—visited Publicity Department and saw color printing of war posters.

Went to dock at 23rd street & saw the St. Paul [20] which fell over, water going through ash hole, & it will be big job to get her out. She listed & probably bad navigation bringing her from basin into dry dock.

Had picture taken by Marceau.

Attended matinee.

Spoke at National Press Association at night at Waldorf banquet on The Press as Quasi Public Official. Governor Hughes [21] & Secy Baker also spoke. Baker was telling what he saw in France & he was interesting & inspiring.

Friday, April 26, 1918

No cabinet.

Half holiday. Liberty loan parade. I marched at head of Navy

At night Admiral H S Knapp called & we talked about our duty in San Domingo. He has large view—American view

Tuesday, April 30, 1918

Cabinet. Discussed pros & cons of declaring war on Bulgaria and Turkey. Sentiment against at this time and yet a suggestion that we would be forced to do so might help to keep them out of helping Germany. Bulgarians would like peace by keeping its territory.

Shall we give out addresses of men killed & wounded. Baker rather against because military men opposed fearing it would get to Germany. I favored. W W decided to give out

[19] Probably Lieutenant Commander John H. Roys.

[20] A large American Line passenger ship, which had heeled over and sunk at its pier when water accidentally shipped into an open ash door.

[21] Charles Evans Hughes, former governor of New York and former Associate Justice of the Supreme Court, Republican presidential nominee in 1916.

Saw Senator Tillman who wanted W W to give him a letter.[22] W. W. thought he ought not to run.

Discussed asking Japan to send cruisers. Swanson urged. W W doubted. Japs would not wish to send here to fight when England & US has [*sic*] greatly superior force to Germany

---

Sunday, May 5, 1918

V. C. Moore came to tell of Woolard[1] & the way he had collected money and wanted to know what to do   Could not bear to punish but ordered full audit of work

Went to Mt. Vernon with George Creel & party of French here with Commission

Monday, May 6, 1918

Spent morning with Naval Affairs Committee perfecting [appropriations] bill

Council of National Defense

Talked of getting ready plans for what should be done after war

Baker told of Am. boy in France, both legs shot off, who was happy because the Lt. who led the charge had been decorated

Tuesday, May 7, 1918

W W. Made a speech once at Princeton and said "no novelties are wanted here." The reporter printed "no new thoughts wanted here," the very thing that is desired   "Though they are not always welcome at colleges.["]

Hughes wrote wanting an Italian American day on May 24—the day Italy entered the war. Italy feels hurt that so little is said here about her participation & it was desired to have Italian flags waving everywhere to show our feeling.

Oil discussion

Talk with oil men. House agreed on a measure.

[22] Despite failing health and opposition from some leading South Carolina Democrats, Senator Tillman planned to run for another term. He died on July 3, however.

[1] C. S. Woolard, advertising manager of the *News and Observer*. Moore, the paper's business manager, was concerned about Woolard's lax accounting practices.

Talked with officers Clark & Robertson about sending Ensign to Portsmouth to report on Osborne [2]

Wednesday, May 8, 1918

Conference at Burleson's office with Josiah Quincy [3] & other Mass. Democrats to discuss getting together on a winning ticket in the Bay State. They favored Endicott [4] or Gaston [5] for Governor, & wanted the administration to say it would be pleased to have one. No. Administration cannot name candidate

Conference with Naval Affairs Subcommittee on bill. Selection for the staff.

Talked with Beckham [6] about woman suffrage. He opposes. I told him I was surprised that he was a reactionary.

Monday, May 13, 1918

Sent cable to Sims to give extra protection to ships carrying men to France

Tuesday, May 14, 1918

W W referred to new plan of Senate Military Com. to sit in recess and investigate & go to all places of war activity and virtually to try to take over the conduct of war. W. W. had told Martin he wished a record vote.

Should ministers be sent to England & English preachers come here? Pres. spoke of how most English preachers came here and regarded this as the mother country [sic] & that was not pleasing. Some were condescending. Might do more harm than good

Woman's War Council

Baker & Mrs. Anna Shaw spoke.

Wednesday, May 15, 1918

Went to Polo Grounds to see first airplane carry letters to New York. I wrote one to Josephus and received three. President, Mrs Wilson, Burleson & others down

Conference with Baker & Solicitor General Davis. Clerk in C&R [7] had

[2] There had been some criticism in and out of the Navy over Osborne's reforms at the Portsmouth Naval Prison, especially his relaxation of traditional discipline and his emphasis on rehabilitation rather than punishment.

[3] Former mayor of Boston and prominent Massachusetts Democrat.

[4] Probably Henry B. Endicott, industrialist and Massachusetts food administrator.

[5] William A. Gaston, Boston attorney and prominent Massachusetts Democrat.

[6] J. Crepps Wickliffe Beckham, Democrat, U.S. Senator from Kentucky.

[7] The Bureau of Construction and Repair, headed by Rear Admiral David W. Taylor.

written he had secured contract for certain parties at highest prices by using much bull on Asst. Secretary.[8] They had letter also written by clerk in War Dept. about same line. Lawyers & others get commissions on orders obtained. We will change form of contracts & prosecute men guilty.

Baker spoke at N.C. Society. I introduced him.

Thursday, May 16, 1918

Dinner at Hugh Wallace.[9] French General Vignol [10] said Germans would fail in drive & war would end this Summer.

Vignol said a good General was always kind & considerate

Pres. called me up & asked to see G. C. [George Creel] about his statement about Congress. Asked in a meeting in New York what he had to say about Congress, Creel answered "I haven't time to go slumming." Resolution in Congress. Creel will write a letter

Friday, May 17, 1918

Spoke at League to Enforce Peace [11] at Phila.

Urged no singing song of Hate & answering those who urged 5 mil. men for the Army pointed out that Congress in the Selective Draft provided 10 mil. as might be needed.

Something of reply to Taft & Alton B Parker [12]

Saturday, May 18, 1918

Red Cross Parade

Telegram that Mother was very ill & Addie & I went to Goldsboro. She had fallen [13]

Sunday, May 19, 1918

Reached Goldsboro early.

Mother was very weak, unconscious, and we thought she was passing. She

[8] It is not clear how seriously Daniels took this charge against his assistant, Franklin D. Roosevelt, or whether he advised Roosevelt of it. See also entry of June 26, 1918.

[9] Hugh C. Wallace, member of the Democratic National Committee from Washington State.

[10] General Paul Vignal, French military attaché.

[11] A nonpartisan group organized in 1915 to promote collective security through a league of nations concept.

[12] Both Taft and Parker, a New York attorney and former judge who had been the Democratic presidential nominee in 1904, had commented on mistakes and delays in mobilization in previous speeches to the League.

[13] Daniels has crossed out a similar entry on May 11, indicating an original error in dating this event.

rallied and by noon was herself and talked of getting crutches so she could soon be up and walking around.

Monday, May 20, 1918
Left Goldsboro at 11:30. Stopped at Wilson. Saw the Woodards & the Brutons [14]

Tuesday, May 21, 1918
Reached New York at 8. Had bath & breakfast & left on auto for New Brunswick, N.J. Heavy rain storm. Road part of way very bad & did not arrive until 12 o'clock. Rutgers College

Gave me degree of LL.D. I spoke at Alumni dinner. Told about my ancestor who lived in New Jersey and was named Van Pelt & thus put myself in touch with the Dutch who founded college—one of the oldest colleges and one of the best.

Spoke on war & the place college men had taken in it & how they had justified faith in them.

Thought of going to Raleigh, but mother was better & I did not go

Wednesday, May 22, 1918
Morgenthau called. Said I ought to go to France & he would like to go with me. Had second number of his article in World's Work

War Cabinet met with the President. Decided to have one board appraise ships. All law officers to bear same relation to Dept. of Justice that Solicitors of Depts. bear to him.

Talked to President about whether I should move out of present quarters? No

Barnett wrote to Penrose for promotions & I told him he was not acting properly without talking it over [15]

Dined with the Hamlins.

Thursday, May 23, 1918
Chicago News cor. who had been in Europe three years thinks war cannot last long, & believes it will end this summer. People out of food & clothes. Bacon one year ago in Berlin $6.00 a pound. Thinks Austrian Emperor is

[14] Probably John F. Bruton, Wilson, North Carolina, banker and attorney. It is not clear which of the several families named Woodard Daniels meant.

[15] Major General Barnett had quietly lobbied on behalf of an amendment to the Navy appropriation bill to authorize the President at his discretion to promote the Marine Corps commandant to a higher rank. Daniels disapproved and with the aid of the House Naval Affairs Committee the Senate amendment was dropped.

ambitious above all things to bring about peace & would go to almost any
length. English & French publications before America entered the war made
Germans believe Wilson not sincere in desiring peace. Says France sent to
Switzerland Wilson's letter to the Pope so mangled it made it appear he insulted the Pope. Thinks statesmen can do as much to end war as soldiers if
they will take the risk.

Went with Admiral Knapp to see McAdoo about this country advancing
money to take up [?] Haiti & Santo Domingo. Discussed our [blank]

Dined at Stetennius [16]

Friday, May 24, 1918

Saunders & Robbins [17] & [blank] talked of the position of Naval Consulting
Board. Robbins had been using propaganda to force building 250 Eagle boats [18]
and I told them such action was not in keeping with way board should act.

Taylor & Griffin & Benson opposed building more that class of boats
now.

Barnett felt aggrieved that Palmer had opposed promotions carried in Senate
bill for staff officers of Marine Corps—thought he had written a letter, but
Palmer said no

Dined at British Embassy to meet the Prince Arthur of Connaught [19]

Saturday, May 25, 1918

Lunched with naval consulting board. Sp[r]ague & others thought Navy
Department slow about building the ships needed for listening devices. Griffin
& Welles replied that Navy had more than one thing to do. Some feeling.

Lansing, Baker & I talked about rooms

Sent telegram to Allied Naval Body about two barrages in Medit.

Sunday, May 26, 1918

Goldsboro

George: [20] I am the guy that gave Lewis his first idea of machine guns.

Went out in hydroplane to hunt Zeps & Subs

[16] Edward R. Stettinius, banker active in war purchasing since 1915 when he organized
the Allied purchasing department at J. P. Morgan and Company; recently appointed second
Assistant Secretary of War.

[17] Thomas Robins, inventor and manufacturer, secretary of the Naval Consulting Board.

[18] Small fast boats favored by some members of the Naval Consulting Board as submarine
chasers because of their relatively silent operation. The Ford Motor Company was the chief
Navy contractor for the Eagle boats.

[19] Son of the Duke of Connaught and a cousin of King George V.

[20] Presumably George S. Daniels, Daniels' nephew, commenting about his exploits with
the Lewis machine gun.

Monday, May 27, 1918

Returned late from Goldsboro.

Went to capital to hear President Wilson. He urged a tax bill.

Talked to Kitchin who early in the year wished tax bill to reach profiteers but McAdoo thought best to wait. Now wished to postpone, but would accede to wishes of President. W W proposed to Kitchin, Simmons & others to postpone bill now if Reps. would agree to come back Nov. 10th & pass bill before Dec. 15 & put 40% of cost of war on excess profits, incomes and luxuries. Reps. refused & Pres. delivered message.

Council of National Defense. Woman's Council thinks agencies of housing & food & fuel should work with them. Some friction.[21]

Tuesday, May 28, 1918

W W told of preacher who prayed "O, Lord, you have doubtless seen from the morning papers[,"] &c. He said you have doubtless seen that Leonard Wood is here & I am to see him to-night. The papers will want to know why he is not sent to Europe. Then W W read paper he had prepared setting forth that Wood was an agitator and it was better that he agitate here than abroad— he could do less harm here for his agitation could be corrected in America. Most of cabinet opposed W W's saying anything. Baker said Pershing had not desired Wood & he had told Wood so & therefore he would not send him [22]

Gregory had caught 5 Irishmen busy with German spies & suggested giving out facts. The British wished it as backing up their statement. W W said No. G.B. had been stupid in its dealing with Ireland & we should not be stupid likewise. Let the traitors be arrested & indicted, & the news go from the courts & not from the Administration

W W said Carnegie once said there was no more reason to study Greek than Choctaw. "Not to a man who couldn't understand the difference & see

[21] Mrs. Anna Howard Shaw, chairman of the Woman's Committee of the Council of National Defense, had protested that her group was not being given anything substantial to do and had threatened to resign.

[22] Major General Leonard Wood's well-known desire for a prominent role in the war had long embarrassed the President, who resented Wood's previous criticism of Wilson's preparedness program. While on a visit to Europe early in 1918 to study Allied training methods, Wood had antagonized both Ambassador Page and General Pershing by his indiscreet criticism of the administration. Pershing, who commented to Secretary Baker that Wood was simply a political general, ordered him home, where he was assigned to command the 89th Division at Camp Funston, Kansas. In May the War Department belatedly discovered that the 89th Division was scheduled for imminent embarkation for France, and Baker, on the advice of Generals Pershing and March, hastily detached Wood from his command. Wood's Republican partisans in Congress and the press sought to use the episode to make a martyr of him, and Wood requested this interview with the President on May 28 to plead that he be allowed to join his troops. Wilson refused, despite the political cost.

that there was a literature in Greek & not in Choctaw" W W thought it silly to forbid teaching German and tearing down German statues. Baker said statue of Frederick the Great ought not to have been taken down at War College

Wednesday, May 29, 1918

Went to British Embassy to lunch to meet Prime Minister Hughes,[23] of Australia, and Secy of Marine Cook.[24] Went in Palm Beach suit & both the Ambassador & Lady Reading[25] admired my clothes. They looked so cool while the other guests were in hot clothes I felt comfortable. They wanted plates to finish ship building. Last Sept. the War Dept contracted for 50,000 tons of jam from Australia. Now they can get no tin cans & there is no shipping. The jam will be ruined and who is to pay—Australia or America. There is negotiation.

Met with War Cabinet with President. Discussed mainly coal & food. I told Garfield we ought to commandeer all the coal output to prevent the profiteering. Hoover agreed [?]

President told the story on watering stock when p was put into comptroller[26]

Left for Scranton 7 pm

Thursday, May 30, 1918

Reached Wilkes-Barre for breakfast. Spoke in park on Decoration Day and then addressed the Poles who were marching.

Small ship loaded with flowers launched on the Susquehanna & other craft following & bugler sounded taps.

Went to monument to men massacred in the Wyoming valley and to famous old church.

Big parade in Scranton and spoke at Park on Memorial Day

Friday, May 31, 1918

Returned from Scranton at 1 o'clock

The President Lincoln[27] torpedoed returning from France

---

[23] William M. Hughes, Labour Party leader and prime minister of Australia since 1915.

[24] Sir Joseph Cook, former prime minister of Australia, 1913–1914; Navy minister since 1917.

[25] After the retirement of Ambassador Spring Rice in January, 1918, Lord Reading had been designated to head the British Embassy in Washington under the title High Commissioner and Special Ambassador.

[26] See also entry of October 19, 1917.

[27] The U.S.S. *President Lincoln*, a large Navy transport, was torpedoed and sunk on May 31 with a loss of 26 lives out of the 715 persons aboard.

Saturday, June 1, 1918

Governor West,[1] of Oregon, wrote [?] to see if there could not be reconciliation between President and Chamberlain. He has been nominated for Senator & can win if administration is behind him. The West feels it has not been recognized because [sic] across the continent. He thought Reps. were having too much weight.

Sunday, June 2, 1918

Went to Annapolis. Last Sunday before graduation.

Chaplain Evans [2] preached appropriate sermon.

News came that submarine was seen off Barnegat Light [3] and S.O.S call had been seen heard [sic] from the Carolina.[4]

Sims had sent information that English Admiralty believed no danger of submarines on this coast. English felt they knew whereabouts of all but one. Is that the one?

Monday, June 3, 1918

Five ships torpedoed near Barnegat Light—one near mouth of the Delaware.[5]

Balloons, aeroplanes, Destroyers & Submarine chasers were sent out to locate

Met at Department at night.

[1] Former Governor Oswald West was understandably concerned lest the rift between President Wilson and Senator Chamberlain (see entries of January 21 and 24, 1918) hurt his chances in the forthcoming campaign against the Republican senatorial incumbent, Charles L. McNary.

[2] Commander Sydney K. Evans, chaplain at the Naval Academy, promoted to captain the following month.

[3] On the south New Jersey coast. The German submarine U-151 had arrived off the Virginia coast on May 21 where it remained for several days laying mines. On May 25 the U-151 sank three American schooners, the *Hattie Dunn*, the *Hauppauge,* and the *Edna,* taking their crews temporarily aboard the submarine. For the next week the U-151 cruised along the Atlantic coast, laying mines and cutting two cables. Then on June 2 the submarine struck again, sinking six vessels in the space of a few hours.

[4] A 5,000-ton New York—Puerto Rico liner, carrying 217 passengers and 113 crew members. Although the U-151 permitted the passengers and crew to leave the *Carolina* before sinking it, 13 lives were lost when one of the boats was subsequently swamped.

[5] In addition to the *Carolina,* the other vessels sunk by the U-151 on June 2, though with no lives lost, were: the small schooners *Edward H. Cole, Isabel B. Wiley,* and *Jacob M. Haskell,* the steamship *Winneconne,* and the small freighter *Texel.* The U-151 lingered in the area several days, dispatching other ships, and then proceeded home, leaving further destruction in its wake. During this voyage the U-151 successfully attacked 23 ships, totaling 58,028 gross tons, though three vessels with a gross tonnage of 7,143 were later salvaged. This first submarine activity in American waters caused widespread public concern and some newspaper and congressional criticism of the Navy.

Before Naval Affairs Committee today. Did not recommend the promotions in the Marine Corps.

Tuesday, June 4, 1918

Apropos of some topic (Gen Wood), W W said it recalled prayer by a Richmond preacher: "O Lord as Thou has doubtless seen in the morning paper." Wood had come to W to protest because he had not been allowed to go to France. W W prepared & read a statement as to why. He was an agitator & not amenable to discipline. We doubted wisdom & he acquiesced, but added "I wanted to get it off my chest.["]

Wednesday, June 5, 1918

Discussed coal & grain used in making beer & soft drinks. W W objected to Randall amendment [6] because there was no temperance in it. Felt like making a trade—cut out beer &c if Congress would give war-time prohibition. Told Baruch, Hoover, Garfield & McCormick to study & make recommendations.

Irish attitude.

Quoted Carnegie as saying no more reason to study Greek than Choctaw. Answer not [to] a man who did not know difference. Besides there was literature in one; none in the other.

At Department till late—on speech & correcting hearings.

Thursday, June 6, 1918

Annapolis. Made speech & presented diplomas to graduates

Lodge gave warm defense of the Navy Department.[7]

Tillman read letter in Senate (N.Y. Times) [8]

Talked to F. D. R. at Dept. on prison management & Osborne   He wishes to go abroad

Message to London: Road to France will be kept open

---

[6] An amendment to the Agriculture appropriation bill by Representative Charles H. Randall, Democrat of California, to prohibit the manufacture of beer and wine. The House had approved the amendment on May 21.

[7] Senator Lodge, a member of the Senate Naval Affairs Committee and not a particularly warm admirer of Daniels, nevertheless defended the Navy Department against criticism in a Senate speech on June 6, declaring that the Navy was taking every precaution to protect American shipping.

[8] Daniels is mistaken as to the date here, an indication that he wrote this entry sometime after the event. It was the following day, June 7, that Senator Tillman, chairman of the Naval Affairs Committee, read to the Senate a letter from Daniels declaring that the Navy was taking all possible steps to hunt down the marauding submarine.

Off[ere]d reward for information leading to discovery of U boat base off USA

(Ed. NY. Times) [9]

Friday, June 7, 1918

Gov. McCall [10] wanted Wood sent to France & thought it a mistake

Lodge & Weeks wants [*sic*] Gov. to take over the dry dock which Massachusetts has ⅓ built.

Saturday, June 8, 1918

Talked with Winslow & Benson about submarine capture. Suggested Winslow go to Norfolk Dist. as Commandant, but W thought he could do better as Inspector of all Districts than to be localized. Benson & I agreed, but could not let McLean [11] go it alone. Capt. Britton [12] was ordered there to be the active man.

Took lunch with Naval Consulting Board. Talked sending concrete ships, with nobody aboard, into Heligoland.

They thought I ought to go to Europe

Prof Fisher—wished $30,000 for certain work at Clark. Investigations Ballistics.

Sunday, June 9, 1918

Confed. Memorial Exercises. Mr. Padgett spoke.

Pres & Mrs. Wilson & Miss Mary Lee

Spoke at Georgetown University

Monday, June 10, 1918

Went to Charlott[e]sville

Tuesday, June 11, 1918

Spoke at Univ of Va.

[9] Presumably a reference to the *New York Times* editorial, "Mr. Lodge's Tribute to the Navy Department," on June 8, 1918.

[10] Samuel W. McCall, Republican, governor of Massachusetts.

[11] Rear Admiral Walter McLean, commandant of the Fifth Naval District and the Norfolk Navy Yard and Station.

[12] Captain Carlo B. Brittain, named to command the forces afloat of the Fifth Naval District, based at Norfolk, June–October, 1918. On June 3 the Navy had decided to convoy coastal shipping.

Wednesday, June 12, 1918

Went to see moving pictures of wheel of Theodore Edison.[13] It goes over trenches &c

War Council

Discussed at length plan of having Ministers, with executive powers, in Europe of Food, Fuel, Raw Material, Trade & Imports—with representative of President, all to make a Council & to allocate all things needed to win war.

Housing—in Wilsons hands

Friday, June 14, 1918

Albany

Saturday, June 15, 1918

Schen[ec]tedy

Syracuse

Sunday, June 16, 1918

Albany

Monday, June 17, 1918

Returned from Albany [14]

Roosevelt and France

Oil question. Mr. Kellogg.

Saw Hazleton's play "Pack Up Your Troubles [."] [15]

Tuesday, June 18, 1918

In Naval Allied Council the Italian Ad[miral] was not willing to act in concert. Sims wanted pressure. W W said tell L—— to talk to Italian Ambassador and tell him how embarrassing it was.

Clemenceau said might have to move valuable papers from Paris. W W not pleased.

W W said Empy's [16] play "Pack Up Your Troubles["] & talk would have America go into war with as much brutality as Germany.

[13] Undoubtedly Thomas A. Edison.

[14] Daniels had been a featured speaker at Flag Day celebrations in Albany and had addressed workers at the General Electric plant at Schenectady.

[15] A new war comedy at the National Theater by George C. Hazleton.

[16] Arthur Guy Empey, an American soldier of fortune who had served eighteen months with the British army in France before returning to write the best-selling *Over the Top* (1917); now playing the male lead in "Pack up Your Troubles."

Burleson: "If you induced Ford to enter race for Senate in Mich. it was a slick trick." [17]

Roosevelt to go to England.[18] W W said "He ought not to decline to run for Gov. of N.Y. if it is tendered to him.["]

I talked to F D R who was pleased at the President's view.

Should there be War Chest or separate drives. Red Cross does not favor War Chests.

WU Tel. Co. refuses to let its employes join union.

Wednesday, June 19, 1918
Council of War.
Dinner with Belgian Minister [19]

Thursday, June 20, 1918
Quantico
Baruch wanted us to take up with War Industries Board any plan to establish new industries in congested region. Hard to obtain power. Ford's plant at Newark would need it.[20]
Mrs. Barnett & Butler.[21] Criticism of General had made her ill

Friday, June 21, 1918
Mrs. Stotesbury & new organization. No solicition for the Navy.

Congressmen & Senators wanted their private secretaries made Chief Yeomen or given commissions. Hard to resist.

Ark. Congressman told of colored man who wanted to vote in primary because he wanted to vote for W W   1. Because he could make more time than Jesus. 2. Because he took the RR's away from all the rich men and gave them to his son-in-law

---

[17] Henry Ford had just announced that he would accept the Democratic nomination for U.S. Senator from Michigan, a race that administration leaders believed might be the decisive margin of control of the next Senate. Daniels, with a significant assist from the President himself, had been chiefly responsible for persuading the reluctant Ford to run as a patriotic duty to insure a satisfactory peace after the war.

[18] As previous entries indicate, Assistant Secretary Roosevelt had been badgering Daniels for weeks to go to Europe, either as a naval officer or on an official inspection tour. Daniels finally consented, and Roosevelt left on July 9, returning home ill with double pneumonia on September 19.

[19] Baron Emile de Cartier de Marchienne.

[20] Ford and the Navy wished to build an Eagle boat plant at Newark which Baruch opposed because of its drain on the critically short power facilities of the area.

[21] Representative Thomas S. Butler had led the fight against the Barnett promotion amendment to the Navy appropriation bill.

Saturday, June 22, 1918

Admiral Capps zealous and able. Worthington Pump Co. made to come to time & will save Gov. 1½ million dollars. Bethlehem Ship Building Co. mixes up accounts and does not show where money advanced goes. Must keep books in shape not to secure more money than they should

Dinner with Navy Consulting Board.

Dr. Webster [22] of Clark very sore because would not give large sum for ballistics at Clark. Ordnance did not approve

Marine Corps boys at home—Gravy Brooks, & Yaeger & H W Jackson

Commodore and Mrs. Wadhams.

Sunday, June 23, 1918

Dr. Winston to dinner. "A more equal distribution of hair & wealth."

Monday, June 24, 1918

C W Howard & A B Farquhar [23]—"Brother Charles and Brother Ned"—successful manufacturers—who said they loved me and would do anything for me they could.

Council of Nat. Defense. W W had referred suggestion that all health matters (ex. Army & Navy) be turned over to Public Health. Would they try to dictate to Army & Navy & say no contracts should go to any except where the health conditions they prescribed would be carried out? Meeting with Blue, Braisted & Gorgas tomorrow

Baker said Stet[t]inius was going to Europe to get business conditions & arrangements. When in France Baker heard the French were keeping books & putting down the things they would charge us. They were even going to charge us for the trenches we occupied. "Then" said Baker "we will evacuate at once"   If we were not in them the Germans would now be occupying them—

Austrian news cheers us [24]

Tuesday, June 25, 1918

Went before Agricultural Committee in favor of war-time prohibition bill. Burleson & shipping board had opposed bill.

Cabinet. Houston told how farmers said they could not plant full wheat

---

[22] Arthur G. Webster, professor of physics at Clark University and a member of the Naval Consulting Board.

[23] Arthur B. Farquhar, elderly York, Pennsylvania, manufacturer.

[24] Austria-Hungary was in the midst of a cabinet crisis following severe military losses on the Piave River front in Italy.

crop unless guaranteed $2⁵⁰ Have not only done that but raised biggest rye, barley &c & they now wished to be assured high prices for these.

Can President regulate street car fares? Baker thought not & that Congress could not either. Street car cos cannot, so they say, pay higher wages unless they raise fares. Secy Wilson will get Mr. Taft & Mr. Walsh of Labor Board [25] to file memorandum

Council Nat. Defense. Blue & then Surgeon Generals [26] discussed having all health functions under Public Health Service. We decided to recommend President to issue orders

8 pm   Spoke at Service Club to Army & Navy

Wednesday, June 26, 1918
Asso. Press printed one sided argument on hearings and I hauled them over the coals because they gave all that the liquor forces said & nothing that I said or other temperance men.

Clerk in C&R grilled to find out who was concerned with him in giving out information about bids. Sullivan [27] was arrested in Boston. He gave Sullivan tips so his concern could bid. Said he had to use a great deal of bull on F. D. R. to get him to give contract to his favorite—who was not lowest bidder.

Padgett & Butler both called about Marine Corps promotion. The Senate insisted on promotions of staff corps. Butler roasted Lodge—said he was the most selfish man in the world

Thursday, June 27, 1918
Italian sailors & officers on Bresto here. Dined at Navy Yard. Italian Ambassador there. Then we went to call on the President.

The Cronan case

Friday, June 28, 1918
Mrs Dewey & Miss Poe
Europe—wanted uniforms

Saturday, June 29, 1918
Navy bill all agreed upon
Picture taken in carriage with beautiful roan horses.

[25] In April, President Wilson had established the War Labor Board, under the joint chairmanship of former President Taft and Frank P. Walsh, to reconcile labor-management disputes affecting war production.

[26] Rear Admiral Braisted and Major General Gorgas.

[27] On June 17, Eugene Sullivan of Boston had been indicted in a crackdown on influence peddling. Sullivan had asked a fee from the Quaker City Raincoat Company and had promised in return a lucrative government contract for the firm.

Senator Tillman paralyzed. Did not wish it known. Law in S.C. permitted no entry after this date.

Went to Senator Phelans at night. Saw moving pictures showing danger of immoral diseases. Powerful.

Sunday, June 30, 1918
Went to Mt. Vernon Methodist Church
Senator Overman to dinner
Josephus returned with the Brookes

Monday, July 1, 1918
Harry Hawes & Mrs Adolph Busch. Searched in Havanna [*sic*]. At Key West, a rough neck doctor compelled Mrs. B—— to strip, examined her & did so in a way as to shock & disgust. He was indignant.[1]

W W signed pension bill.

Cou[nci]l of Nat Defense   Shall Board on Reconstruction be named? No —but shall study what Europe is doing and devise best plan for future consideration

Padgett & committee to go on Arkansas to Europe

Tuesday, July 2, 1918
Went with Baker & Burleson before House Committee in advocacy of bill to take over telegraph and telephone companies for the war. I advocated it for a permanent government policy.

Cabinet. I asked W W to see that S——[2] did not build two big plants—it would lead to scandal & we will have enough to build the ships we will need.

Discussed whether the President should tell Congress that he would veto certain bills if they embodied objectionable features. Burleson said no. Baker said if he wrote open message it would be O.K. Lansing thought a veto was more impressive.

Pres. objects to fixing higher price for wheat when the biggest crop in history is being harvested. Burleson fears Germany will recruit its man power from Russia and thinks President should act now.

[1] Lilly Anheuser Busch, wealthy widow of the St. Louis brewer, had been living in Germany since the outbreak of war in 1914, but had returned upon the advice of her attorney, Hawes, in the face of a government attempt to seize her holdings as alien property.

[2] Probably Charles M. Schwab, recently appointed director general of shipbuilding of the Emergency Fleet Corporation.

Talked to Baker about fact that names of marines killed & wounded were not wired.

Wednesday, July 3, 1918

War Councill [sic]—Discussed the question of power. There will be great shortages and Baruch wishes Navy to advance money to add to power in New Jersey; Baker for Pittsburg District; and Hurley for Phila Dist— I hated to put money in private plants Long discussion on coal & brewers. Decided to let brewers have coal to finish their mash and then no more. Some thought it best to reduce to 50%, but most thought the coal situation demanded above course & great reduction to all non-essentials

Thursday, July 4, 1918

Spent day in New York. Spoke at Tammany, Pelham Park, and Stadium at College Park.

Hearst entertained Congressional party Hyland [3] very courteous

Friday, July 5, 1918

Returned from New York

News that Covington [4] was torpedoed 6 navy men lost their lives. It was German ship

Had long talk with Capt. Foote,[5] of the President Lincoln torpedoed. Sunk in 18 minutes. No panic. After men were in boats submarine rose near them and one man on it was seen near the gun & one sailor called out "Now Fritzie is going to open the fire-works[."] [6]

Saturday, July 6, 1918

Conf. at WH on Russia   W W—Lansing, Baker, Daniels, Benson, Marsh.[7]
Chezk-Slovaks [sic] have taken Vladovostock—& wish to reach the Western

---

[3] Daniels undoubtedly meant Mayor John F. Hylan of New York.

[4] The U.S.S. Covington, a large Navy transport, formerly the Hamburg-American liner Cincinnati, was torpedoed on the night of July 1 while returning from France and sank the following day during unsuccessful salvage operations.

[5] Commander Percy W. Foote, ex-commander of the torpedoed transport President Lincoln and subsequently Daniels' personal aide.

[6] After the President Lincoln went down, the German submarine surfaced and searched among the survivors for Foote and the other senior U.S. officers. The U-boat crew managed to identify only one American officer, Lieutenant Edouard Victor M. Isaacs, who was taken aboard as a prisoner, though he later managed to escape from a German prison camp into Switzerland. While the search was going on, the Germans made menacing gestures with a deck gun, leading the President Lincoln survivors to fear the worst, but no one betrayed the officers the Germans were seeking.

[7] General Peyton C. March, Army chief of staff.

front. Pres. feels we must assist them, but does not believe in big Japanese army going in. Decided to send signal [?] force J&H [?] & to ask J. to furnish guns & ammunition for Chezk-Slovak forces so they can march to join their brethren 1,000 miles in the interior. Knight ordered to land marines to help C-S. hold Vladivostock. Baker fears Japs. W. W. thinks Germans can get little help from Russia in 18 months. Wishes to send a mission into Russia to help with provisions & clothes & give practical evidence of our sympathy

Dr Jacobi [8] came from Portsmouth to talk about man who brooded so he & Osborne thought only relief was to let him be discharged

Sunday, July 7, 1918
Went to church with Addie & Worth.

A family dinner.

Yeager & Charlie Brooks.

Went to station with Worth. We all cried and felt the going. A—— [Addie] could hardly bear it.[9]

Monday, July 8, 1918
Worth passed physical examination & came home to spend a few hours, for he yearned to see his mother and she was overjoyed to see him.

I went to New York to speak at Carnegie Hall at Y.M.C.A. 4,000 secretaries wanted to go to France.

Tuesday, July 9, 1918
W W. My father thought all sin came from Ego. Some men make themselves the centre of the universe instead of making God the centre & that [gave?] them a wrong outlook upon the world Everything was for self & that made sin

Speaking of War Councils advice on Russia, he said they proposed such impractical things to be done immediately that he often wondered whether he was crazy or whether they were. Once, after reading a page of examination paper & could make no sense he turned to Mrs W—— & asked her to read it. Is there any sense in it? He asked after she had read it & was overjoyed when she said "No" for he then was convinced that he was not crazy

Wednesday, July 10, 1918
War Council. Who shall take control of ships, their coaling and bunkering, at Hampton Roads, New York & other ports? Should be a single head. W. W.

---

[8] Lieutenant Arnold L. Jacoby, a Naval Reserve passed assistant surgeon stationed at the Portsmouth Navy Yard.

[9] Daniels' second son, nineteen-year-old Worth Bagley, was about to enter the Naval Academy as a midshipman.

suggested that all Departments concerned agree upon a plan and he would approve.

Discussed nitrates. Houston complained that private fertilizer manufacturers could get ships to bring up nitrates from Chili, but Dept. of Ag. could not get ships promised. Armour Fertilizer manager is Nitrate Executive? [10]

German interests won [?] in Chilian courts which compel American & other oil men to fill their contracts to supply oil & to take over any of their oil in Chili to make good the contract. Chili offers to sell us nitrates at advanced prices & we are forced to make big contract for nitrates or we can get nothing more

Thursday, July 11, 1918

Went to Atlantic City—reviewed parade and spoke. Mrs. Dewey was with me on reviewing stand

McGowan's story: The ancient and honorable society of "I will Arise and Go to My Father."

["]I am the Most Exalted King and Ruler.["]

"I take off my hat to you, for you are at the top[."]

["]No sir boss there are five above me[."]

Cong. Rodenburg [11] said now that Washington is dry, Congressmen love to come to Atlantic City as an oasis.

Friday, July 12, 1918

Bro. Frank returned to G[oldsboro]

Conference with Baker, Garfield & others about control of shipping. Benson insisted on full naval control.

Gave contract for 36 new submarine chasers

Spellacy,[12] candidate for Governor from Conn. Rep Governor [13] has controlled all war work through Republicans & hardly one Democrat on any board

Went to see plans for new building for Annapolis.

Padgett called. He goes to England on Ark. with Naval Affairs Committee.

Saturday, July 13, 1918

W W desired me to go to New York at meeting to celebrate France's great day & I left at midnight

[10] Charles H. MacDowell, director of both the nitrate section and chemicals division of the War Industries Board, was on leave from his position as president of the Armour Fertilizer Works.

[11] William A. Rodenberg, Republican, U.S. Representative from Illinois.

[12] Thomas J. Spellacy, a Hartford attorney and unsuccessful candidate for governor of Connecticut in 1918; subsequently appointed by Daniels as a legal adviser in Europe to assist in Navy demobilization after the war.

[13] Marcus H. Holcomb.

In afternoon with Commander Parsons,[14] Architect De Lebour [?], Mr. Olmsted [15] went to Annapolis to look over site for new seamanship and navigation building.

Saw Worth in his whites. He looked half a head taller and very handsome, somewhat self-conscious at being in Supt's home with officers His mother remained over until ten o'clock

Josephus came home. He has applied to go to France with Col Butler's [16] company.

Sunday, July 14, 1918

Reached New York. Spent nearly all Day reading Carlyle's "The French Revolution.["] What a masterpiece of insight and prophecy.

At night in Madison Square Garden at Bastile Celebration I read the President's message to the French people and later spoke, emphasizing close relationship between French and American Navies.

Hughes presided. During interruption in my speech, gentleman with carrying voice cried out: Who said Wilson did not [have a?] big man in his cabinet? D—— has more than made good. I exchanged glances with Hughes who began his campaign with attack upon me

Monday, July 15, 1918

Had call from Argentine Ambassador [17] & Admiral [18] who had come up with Rivadavia for overhaul.

Big drive on in France.[19] First news depressing. I could not shake it off. Seemed to see the brave American lads falling. The pity of it

This ought to be June 15 [20]

Heard T. P. O'Connor trace the story of England's treatment of Ireland. Said Kitchener said he only wanted 5,000 Irishmen & when 20,000 volunteered, though 90% were Nationalists 85% of the officers were Unionists.

Reception to Bishop McDowell

Went to depot to see Yaeger. How happy he was!

[14] Commander Archibald L. Parsons, assistant chief of the Bureau of Yards and Docks.

[15] Probably Frederick L. Olmsted, vice-chairman of the Commission of Fine Arts.

[16] Colonel Smedley D. Butler, subsequently promoted to brigadier general and appointed commander of Camp Pontanezen at Brest, France.

[17] Rómulo S. Naón.

[18] Captain Carlos Daireaux, commanding the Argentine battleship *Rivadavia*.

[19] The German attack around Reims, a prelude to the Allied victory in the Second Battle of the Marne.

[20] The following two paragraphs are written in heavier pencil and Daniels probably meant by this comment that he had written the entry on the wrong page (and obviously sometime after the event).

Tuesday, July 16, 1918

Conference between Redfield, Hurley, Wilson & J D on training men for merchant ships. We will train 20,000 officers and 200,000 men, & the coastwise & S. American ships will use merchant seamen   "Able bodied"

Cabinet. W. W. Should not all Depts. have a single Purchasing Agent? The Supply Dept. in part meets that need. It will be asked to make a study & report how it can be improved

W W: When young man he wore side-whiskers   One day in court, the Sheriff looked at him a long time & so hard he thought something must be the matter with him. Then the Sh[eri]ff took his long legs from table, & walked over and said: "Did you know that you had left one side of your whiskers longer than the other?"

Houston recommended advancing money to farmers in Montana & Kansas where wheat crops were failure so they could buy seed

Wednesday, July 17, 1918

War Council.

Coaling all ships & controlling all barges, tugs &c—so as to get maximum effic[ienc]y   I said Navy could do it.

W W: Each Dept. thinks there ought to be a single head, but that that Dept. ought to do it.

He read story of Ark. negro who thought W W great man for 2 reasons
1. He changed the time so we have Jesus's time & Woodrow Wilson's time.
2. He took all the RRs from the rich men and gave it [*sic*] to his son-in-law.

Conf. in Baker's office on power. Baruch wanted Baker to finance Pittsbg dist; Hurley Phila & Navy the NJ Dist. Where is the power

Thursday, July 18, 1918

Conference of builders of destroyers. Not more than ½ half [*sic*] up to estimated time. Benson had told allies we would furnish ships and companies had not lived up to their estimates. I was ashamed to go abroad until builders kept their pledges. Must speed up.

Shall we commandeer houses?

Josephus phoned he had been ordered to Quantico.

Mother here & Wilsons & Smalls

Friday, July 19, 1918

Wrote to Secy. of State that G.B. had tried to make arrangements by which it alone could build ships in Brazil. Said the U.S. was lending GB money &

if the people knew it was using money to protect its commerce against America after the war they would be indignant and it would disturb our friendly relations.

Heard of sinking of San Diego [21]

Saturday, July 20, 1918

Reached St. Helena & spoke to 5000 young men under training.

Met a com. of Real Estate men & others—some of whom had served notice that employees would be evicted & had put up rent. I told them the Navy Department would commandeer all such houses.

Spoke to all employees at Norfolk Navy Yard.

Went to Hampton Roads. Spoke to 9000 young men under training & then to class of young men studying to be Ensigns. Lunched with Admiral McLean.

Inspected land adjoining station and found owner wanted $1000 per acre. Taxed at 1$\frac{00}{}$ A [?]—

Inspected coaling piers at Newport News & returned to Mayflower

Sunday, July 21, 1918

Attended service (Catholic) on the flag ship. Admiral Grant's ship.

Walked over the land bought for oil storage on the York & picked out site for training station

Lunched with Admiral Grant

Inspected land (11,000 acres) Earle wishes for mines and high explosives.

Returned toward W—— Kites & aeroplanes following as they had preceded us.

Monday, July 22, 1918

Returned home.

Spoke at 11 o'clock to men who are working on new navy building. The Scotchman who worked in textile mills at Leeds. Negroes 100% loyal.

Lunched in his room with Justice Brandeis. Told of the hatred of a certain powerful man who had boosted in his three papers certain copper stock. He had been promised the stock & wrote "I have rented a new safe deposit box & wish that stock placed on the bottom and watch it grow"

Council of Natl Defense. The Woman's Com. dissatisfied because McAdoo,

---

[21] The armored cruiser *San Diego*, sunk by a mine off Fire Island on July 19 with a loss of six lives. The mine had been laid by the U-156, the second German submarine sent to raid off the U.S. Atlantic Coast. The *San Diego* was the first U.S. capital ship to be lost in the war and the most important victim of submarine activity in American waters.

Hoover, & Garfield turn over to other women the work that the Woman's Com. feel it was organized to do. Lane proposed to make new Advy Com ½ men, ½ women. No, we all said

Pond's Extract asked advice about advertising in Hearsts papers. We had taken no action on such matters

Tuesday, July 23, 1918
Cabinet

Gregory had been to Detroit & reported progress in building liberty motors. Also about submarine detectors.

W W told of a Scotch woman house keeper at White House. She was very suspicious of an unoffending German who made the fires in the White House and came in ominous tones and said "There is a German in the cellar."

W W: In order to disgust child who used slang very precise mother began to use it. Hearing an auto going by & making a noise, the daughter asked what it was & the mother said: "I think it is a tin lizzie panting for juice"

Making Liberty engines for $3,600 & England wanting them

Wednesday, July 24, 1918

War Council at White House discussed necessity of economizing in steel & making other things go as far as possible

Wrote Henry F[ord] not to make any statement until after Michigan primary

Thursday, July 25, 1918

Gen. Barnett came to talk about promotions in the Marine Corps   Went over the record of all Colonels

Friday, July 26, 1918

Talked to W L Saunders about the bird that will be managed without a pilot & carry TNT. It looks good. Will be tried out in Utah on a 75 mile plain.

Conf. with Fine Arts Commission with reference to new buildings at Annapolis.

Conf. about dredging in Hampton Roads. The delay has been great and we took action to expedite the work.

Twins in the Navy—one had slight defect in vision. I waived. They had never been separated.

Went before Senate Ag. Appro Com & advocated war time prohibiti[on]

Saturday, July 27, 1918
Luncheon with Navy Consulting Board
Saunders said "presidential timber." [22]
Josephus birthday

Sunday, July 28, 1918
J D Jr here
Mr Chappell [23] preached "Demos [?] forsook me, having [blank] for the world"

Merchant of Venice = Silver casket   Get
                 Gold   "   Get
                 Lead   "   Give

Arabian Nights. The nails & all the iron & steel fell out of the ship because it came to an island that was a magnet

Monday, July 29, 1918
P. A. Davison [24] wanted to send a mission to Siberia to help the Russians, but wanted to cross no wires with the plans of the President.
(W W: "It would be a Republican mission and I am preparing large plans which will include YMCA work[."])]
R. J. Reynolds [25] died

Tuesday, July 30, 1918
Cabinet. Gompers wanted to buy certain Mexican papers to help make favorable sentiment to Americans. W W No. Labor had helped Carranza and then C had turned on union labor. Instead of helping a subsidized paper, making propaganda, reacted. Witness German use of money to buy papers & writers.
   I brought up action of King of England in decorating Rodman and Strauss [26]

---

[22] It is doubtful that Daniels took seriously the occasional suggestions that he was a likely presidential prospect, but he was obviously flattered.

[23] Clovis G. Chappell, minister of Daniels' church, the Mount Vernon Place Church (Methodist Episcopal, South).

[24] Presumably Henry P. Davison, chairman of the War Council of the American Red Cross.

[25] North Carolina tobacco magnate, president of the firm of the same name.

[26] Rear Admiral Hugh Rodman, commanding the U.S. battle squadron with the British Grand Fleet, had been made a Knight Commander of the Order of the Bath. Rear Admiral Joseph Strauss, commanding the mine force of the Atlantic Fleet laying the North Sea barrage, had been made a Knight Commander of the Order of St. Michael and St. George. Daniels consistently opposed such decorations from foreign governments.

& advocated their non-acceptance   Sentiment was they could not be returned but that Secy. of State should inform European governments this Gov. did not desire such decorations to be given. I telegraphed Sims and approved his declination to accept tender from Italy

President discussed his letter to Slayden [27] saying he had not supported the administration & said Burleson had gotten him into that trouble.

"You wrote the telegram" said W W

B—— explained at request of Texas editor he had drafted telegram & sent to Tumulty for W W to sign if he thought fit, but said he did not think W W would sign. B's brother-in-law nominated.

Hardwick and Vardeman due such letters

How far should it go—

Wednesday, July 31, 1918

War Council—Discussed big profits steel men had made and Baruch talked of the meeting of Union Labor to try to compel steel men to admit unions into that industry. W. W. said grave problems after the war were such that he almost hoped the war would continue until his term of office expired. He said democratization of labor would not come through war between capital & union labor and collective bargaining but through partnership. If big industry does not invite labor to place on directorate and share in profits & responsibility, it will invite worse. Labor is entitled to this & when steel companies make big money labor should have better pay

I advocated Gov. fixing prices & if necessary commandeering coal & ore & preventing excess profits. Baker thought best way was to lay heavy excess profit tax—very difficult to fix varying prices and some concerns had to pay out more to produce coal &c

Talked to W W about Bethleh[em] having to pay 12% to NY bankers & McLean's protest. McLean did right [28]

---

[27] James L. Slayden, Democrat, U.S. Representative from Texas, had angrily withdrawn from the race for re-election several days earlier after Wilson had publicly accused him of failure to support the administration's war program. Wilson had not consulted the cabinet about this open interference in a Democratic primary, and some cabinet members and party leaders considered the action ill-advised. Slayden's withdrawal resulted in the nomination and election of Carlos Bee, Postmaster General Burleson's son-in-law.

[28] Angus W. McLean, a director of the War Finance Corporation.

Thursday, August 1, 1918

John R Mott & YMCA Campaign

Vance McCormick. New York politics. W W agreed that Osborne should come out and give Al Smith a free & open field [1]

Fine Arts Commission reported 2 buildings at Annapolis and against plan for auditorium that would obstruct view of the river.

Norfolk delegation wanted us to build place—men there rather than at Yorktown.

Friday, August 2, 1918

Meeting in Baker's office to organize commission to fight venereal disease & segregate women. Congress had appropriated 3 million for this work.

Council of National Defense   Discussed whether all agencies like Red Cross and Y.M.C.A. should have one campaign for contributions or have separate ones. Baker thought one. Fosdick spoke of difficulties of separate organization at first [?]. But Y.M.C.A. has world-wide places and must be considered differently.

Fosdick told of trip to France. What are the three greatest crimes? asked YMCA Secy   Cowardice   Selfishness   Big Itis [?].

French called for 2,000 men for special hazardous service. 2,000 Marines volunteered. They were sent to Paris to parade in Fourth [*sic*] of July celebration. They won the day at Chantilly—

When they saw a woman at Y.M.C.A. "Honest to goodness, there's a real American woman. Isn't she good to look at? ["] Helps them more than anything.

Saturday, August 3, 1918

J D Jr. came home

Sunday, August 4, 1918

Annapolis   Eberle wants to be V.A. [vice admiral]

McLean's wife [2] correspondence with German captain.

---

[1] William C. Osborn, a New York attorney and anti-Tammany Democrat, was seeking the Democratic nomination for governor against Alfred E. Smith, currently president of the Board of Aldermen of New York City. Despite suggestions that he withdraw in the interest of party harmony, Osborn remained in the race. Smith won both the nomination and the governorship, however.

[2] Emma Brown Jarvis McLean, wife of Rear Admiral Walter McLean. See also entry of August 9, 1918.

Monday, August 5, 1918

Davison, of Red Cross, wished to know if wise to provide clothing and over-coats for Checko Slovaks. Yes.

Council of National Defense. Baker absent. I presided.

Woman's Council. Felt they had no power. Wished their duties defined. Some wanted to resign. Others wished to amalgamate with com. of men and thus have one method of communication with State Councils

Tuesday, August 6, 1918

Overman and Kitchin called about Travis. They felt it was wrong to arrest & jail him upon charges & were disposed to be indignant. McDonald detailed how he began the work and the net woven in which three were bagged. First reported that Green was my nephew [3]

Cabinet. W W went to famed [?] doctor who pumped out his stomach & said: "This will be profoundly disagreeable but not intolerable." Princeton man went to Dr Delafield for prescription. Showed it to captain of foot-ball-team & he said: "There's strichnyne in it. Don't take it. Delafield is a Yale man." [4]

Gompers to go abroad. Shall Gov employ his assistants. No? [*sic*] But funds will be provided.

Agreed

Teleg fr Sims. King decorated him and he wrote that he did not feel like declining [5]

Wednesday, August 7, 1918

War Council   W. W. held meeting in basement room. He said it was too hot to bring up very serious questions.

Yale man read in Lit the prize oration & found it was the one he had de-livered 40 years before. He had not read a copy of Lit for 20 years, though taking it regularly except that issue. He exposed the young graduate.

[3] Navy Intelligence and secret service agent Richard F. McDonald had broken another case of influence peddling, this time in ship construction contracts. Involved were Edward L. Travis, prominent North Carolina Democrat and former law partner of Representative Kitchin, Selim B. Joseph, and Leon Green, who had posed as Daniels' nephew with great influence.

[4] This was evidently a favorite Wilson story, for Daniels recorded it earlier in his entry for August 3, 1917. Then the story referred to Dr. Theodore C. Janeway rather than Dr. Francis Delafield as here. Probably the confusion was Daniels' rather than Wilson's, al-though both Janeway and Delafield were Yale graduates and specialists in internal medicine.

[5] Sims had accepted the Grand Cross of the Order of St. Michael and St. George. In July, Congress had authorized the acceptance of foreign decorations by U.S. military and naval personnel, but Sims could hardly have been unaware that Daniels was still opposed to such awards.

Told of a man who, after graduation at Oxford, sealed his oration & hid it behind the oldest books in the library, thinking 100 years hence he would play a joke on posterity. He happened to be near Oxford at Exhibition half a century later, the first time since he graduated, & was astonished to hear the first honor man deliver his oration

We discussed [?] new 18 to 45 draft & how to protect men who ought to remain in their present position.

Thursday, August 8, 1918

Organized the new body authorized by Congress to fight venereal diseases. I was elected chairman.

W W called at my office with Baker & we decided not to allow any volunteer enlistments until Congress completed the present Army draft law.

President thought too many men, who wished to volunteer instead of being drafted, were rushing into the service who ought to remain at home, & a plan should be worked out by which such men should not have to ask exemption.

Wrote to Gen Carr about his boy who has been made Sergeant and will probably soon be made Lieut

Friday, August 9, 1918

Admiral McLean—forced to tell him he must retire. His wife had corresponded with a German officer and visited him at the place of internment in Georgia and the Secret Service had her letters and telegrams. She lacks sense, if she is not partly crazy. He had been drinking at Balto and had lost his power to act & initiative.

Jas. A. Garfield,[6] Judge Proctor [7] representing oil companies had conference with Polk, Baruch, & Garfield in Navy Department. They had been ordered to file their holdings by Mexican government. They said their lawyers advised them if they did so they would acknowledge the right of that Gov. to confiscate their property & would do it. We suggested it might be wise to file & protest. Lansing had already protested. Garfield & Requa [8] seemed to lean toward the oil men, Baruch & I [?] not. We went to see the President and he decided the oil men could not stampede us. I told oil men what they wanted amounted to a declaration of war

[6] James R. Garfield, Cleveland attorney and former Secretary of the Interior, brother of Harry A. Garfield, U.S. Fuel Administrator.
[7] Probably Frederick C. Proctor, Texas attorney representing the Mellon oil interests at this time.
[8] Mark L. Requa, general director of the oil division of the U.S. Fuel Administration.

Went to theatre and saw "Three Faces East" Told W W & Mrs. W. the story of Col. French,[9] his enrollment & how he was disenrolled.

Saturday, August 10, 1918

Mr. Gompers, who is going to Europe, called to say good-bye. He is deeply concerned and believes victory essential if labor is to receive what justly belongs to it. Above that, he is patriotic.

Mayo brought in report of Selection Board. He emphasized his opposition to it and said its bad results would outweigh many, or maybe most of the good work I had done as Secy of the Navy.

Benson felt that the order not permitting stars on any officers uniform unless he had qualified for sea duty was all wrong 34 Reserves had lost their lives in this war to 20 regulars and he thought there should only be one uniform for all in the line as there is for all in the staff corps. The Army has made that rule and he thought we should do likewise

Talked about commandeering Newport News Shipbuilding Yard. Norwegian capitalists wish to buy it.

Sunday, August 11, 1918

Heard Dr Chappell preach "The brook dried up"

Geo Matheson, becoming blind, wrote his sweetheart that he must live in the darkness and could not exact of her to marry him. She wrote accepting release. That sorrow drove him to God & made him seek divine consolation & to write the greatest of modern hymns "O Love that Will not Let Me Go"

Wife of Lt. Com. came to see me. Her husband was not selected for promotion and they were in deep distress and she was in tears. It is heartbreaking

J D Jr returning to Q. He thinks Headqts will not let Butler go unless I see to it

Monday, August 12, 1918

Lunched with Geo. Creel to meet delegation of Italian editors.

News of submarine gassing men at Smith's Island, north of Cape Fear, N.C.[10]

---

[9] Probably Leigh H. French, New York capitalist and former Rough Rider, who was briefly commissioned a lieutenant commander in the Naval Reserve as a naval attaché at the U.S. Embassy in Paris. Daniels strongly disapproved of the granting of reserve commissions to Americans who happened to be overseas and wished headquarters duty, considering this a rich man's dodge.

[10] This report seems to have been a false alarm. The only German submarine in the vicinity at this time was the U-140, which was fully occupied trying to elude pursuit and make repairs after being damaged by depth charges dropped by the U.S.S. *Stringham* on August 10.

Tuesday, August 13, 1918

Meeting of Board on Venereal Diseases. Will intern women

Cabinet. Shall men in military service run for office? Baker said they should be disenrolled when they accepted nomination. McAdoo agreed. Suppose Pershing should be candidate for President? asked McAdoo. I would bring him home at once said Baker   I: In Civil War Garfield [,] Hayes & others were elected to Congress. There are two sides to the question   President thought nothing should be done until after election & then they should vacate military position.

Discussed Labor questions & steadily mounting pay.

Should men at work have medals? Yes, if some arrangement free from abuse could be devised   Could it be?

Wednesday, August 14, 1918

Attended weekly meeting to review progress of the war at War Department. Admiral Benson explained in detail the barrage across the North Sea

War Cabinet. Discussed how to obtain water & power at Hampton Roads and elsewhere without giving too much money to private owners. Decided for Baruch to make study in conjunction with War & Navy

RR wished to use 180 engines belonging to Russia. They were paid for with money G.B. loaned Russia. Decided to use them & to replace them later & to assure Russia they would be ready when R—— had transportation and could use them.

W. W. Referred to C. Kitchin as that distinguished stubborn North Carolinian who when he made up his mind would never open it. Loves to argue. Reminded him of a certain Englishman who (Jeffers) [*sic*] loved to argue. One night he was ill. Some one out doors called out All is well & the sky clear with stars shining. He rose from his bed, saying "I doubt it" & pointed out a small cloud in the sky.

Friday, August 16, 1918

Saw Hubert Royster & talked about his taking position as Ex. Sec of National Commission on Vener[e]al Diseases. He is to let me know.

Barnett wanted to be made Major General. Can do it under the law but should I? Congress did not so intend.

Saturday, August 17, 1918

Officer in radio was rooming with representative of Federal Telegraph Co. He gave the order for wireless supplies. Other companies felt they had not fair chance as long as officer roomed with the Federal agent. I told Griffin to detach him & to let it be known why he was detached

Went to see Gen. March in interest of tank camp for Raleigh.

Conf. with Knapp, Barnett, Fosdick, & Ashe [?] about Y.M.C.A. undertaking work on large scale in Haitii [sic] & San Domingo. Natives drink rum but weaken it with water & rarely get drunk. Doubtful if prohibition by decree of military governor would be wise

Sunday, August 18, 1918

Josephus and Gravy spent the day and talked about the 13th regiment. They hope to go to France by Sept. 15th.

Went to church. Minister told about Bishop McMurray's [11] going to see Chinese Minister [12] (with letter from me) and when he complimented the Minister upon speaking English so well he replied that he was instructed in the Anglo-Chinese College founded by the Meth Church (South)

Monday, August 19, 1918

Radio officer who had charge of wireless contracts had an apartment with representative of Federal Telegraph Co. I had to send him to other duty, but sent for him and told him we did not doubt his integrity.

Roosevelt telegraphed from France that air craft materiel arrived with missing parts & there were only 8 machines in the air. Held conference and wired that all diligence would be used, but that 148 had been shipped & others would go forward.

Bailey here. Wanted to get tank camp in Raleigh

Went to theatre "Forever Afterward," by Alice Brady. Had box with boys & Moffitt

Council of National Defense. Discussed Woman's Committee.

Tuesday, August 20, 1918

W W returned from Mass

Cabinet discussed medals again. Liable to abuse & counterfeit. Failed in England.

Discussed revenue bill. McAdoo fretted at delay because he wished to begin Bond Drive on Sep. 28th, and he thought excess war profits should pay the main tax. He opposed drives for money except the Red Cross, YMCA & other recognized agencies.

---

[11] Bishop William F. McMurry of the Methodist Episcopal Church (South), who visited Methodist missions in Asia in 1918.

[12] V. K. Wellington Koo.

Gleaves asked me to make him a Vice Admiral.

Barnett here from Pensacola   Camoflaged! [*sic*]

Wednesday, August 21, 1918

Consultation at War Department where progress of Allies in France was shown on maps. The pressing need is cargo ships and Great Britain is to be asked to aid at least to the carrying of all supplies intended for her army.

She expects to ask 60[,]ooo £ [?] for her big ships if lost. You means [*sic*] dollars, don't you? No—pounds, & to charge $150 instead of 50 for every person taken over. Also desires us to agree to furnish ships equivalent to every day's work done on our ships & every day's docking. Worst of it is Sims approved

Went to N.Y. to banquet tendered to San Paulo [13] & Rividavio, Brazil and Argentine ships in our harbors. Argentine Ambassador (Naon) read his speech. His country is neutral; he is pro-ally and he must be diplomatic   Thinks Minister Brum's [14] visit (he is here from Uruguay) should take steps to unite Pan Americans in the war

De Gama [15] also spoke & Augustus Thomas [16]

Thursday, August 22, 1918

Had talk with the President. He thought France ought to be asked not to give decoration to Admiral Wilson,[17] even though Britain did give to Sims & I am to tell State Department.

I discussed titles & showed him an order I had drawn up, repeating old orders that staff officers could not be called Admiral, Captain, Commander &c but must be addressed as Pay Master &c. I told him Benson favored but the line opposed as a rule. He thought uniforms should be alike and men called by their rank. Tired of Annapolis caste.

Talked of our country making Hatii [*sic*] pay salary, as part of our officers there governing against their will

No

---

[13] The Brazilian battleship *Sao Paulo,* commanded by Captain Cesar Augusto de Mello.
[14] Dr. Baltazar Brum, head of a visiting Uruguayan mission.
[15] Domicio da Gama, the Brazilian Ambassador.
[16] Playwright and former journalist.
[17] Vice Admiral Henry B. Wilson, commander of U.S. naval forces in France since January.

Monday, September 2, 1918

Reached Indianapolis early. Mr. Bryan at the depot. He said his wife was at Hot Springs and he was anxious about her. Looked grave for they are real partners.

Took breakfast at home of ex-Gov. Ralston,[1] planted a tree, reviewed Labor parade, and spoke at Tomlinson [?] Hall to large crowd, & had liberty.

Lunched with labor committee who were worried because the war work had been committed to Governor of Indiana [2] who was using it for Republican politics. Most men called to Washington in war work were Republicans & Democrats were discouraged about it.

Said Labor Administrator was partisan Republican and would name in each of the 92 counties a Rep. who would try to use it to help the Reps. Will see W B W.

Tuesday, September 3, 1918

Returned from Indianapolis. Reached Cabinet meeting late.

W. W. said he was pained because W. J. B. [Bryan] represented Costa Rica, the President [3] who had assumed the presidency after revolution. The first act of the administration, said W W, in which W J B & I were in perfect accord, was we would not encourage revolutions in Central and South America. The present President, who came in by revolution, has had himself elected. Of course. He had the troops & the guns. If Mr. B—— knew the forces behind him, he would not have accepted to represent him. Hardly had he usurped the place before the United Fruit Company had telegraphed from Key West seeking recognition for him. The agencies behind him are as if Wall Street proposed a plot & Mr. B would not stand for it if he knew.

Burleson said he claimed his predecessor was pro-German and he had declared strongly against the Germans and ready to co-operate with us.

Lansing asked if F D R was authorized to tell Italy we favored the British plan of putting Jellico[e] in command of Mediterranean forces. I said no; on the contrary I had written him our [?] country [?] favored allied command but declined to say who should command. The French Ambassador was worried [?] at word [?] that in Rome F D R had said this country wanted English commander.

[1] Samuel M. Ralston, Democrat, governor of Indiana, 1913–1917.

[2] James P. Goodrich, Republican.

[3] Federico A. Tinoco, former Minister of War who in January, 1917, had overthrown the government of President Alfredo Gonzalez Flores and since had vainly sought U.S. recognition.

Wednesday, September 4, 1918

War Dept. Council—Better news from Europe & more cheer. Ships making better time & making turn-around trip quicker

Cong. Butler returned from France. Saw men as heroes who before the war were not dreamed worth $10 a week. He had bets that war would not end till 1920. Now he is ready to pay bets. It will end in 1919 he thinks or sooner. Confident our boys are too much for the Germans. Says his son is going next week—never expects to see him again, "but it is all right."

Cabinet discussed price fixing. Cotton seed men had agreed on price for cotton seed. Houston & Baruch authorized to call meetings of representative farmers to agree upon price for cotton. I said "Bad for NC [North Carolina]." We have big crop & Texas small & it will be unpopular with many, but it is right."

Ought to take over coal, oil & ore

Meeting of Board on Immoral Diseases [4] & disbursing officers elected

Thursday, September 5, 1918

Admiral Jones [5] to build barracks and enlist men to load ships & coal them at Hampton Roads. Army, Navy, Shipping Board & Fuel administration to pool all facilities under Jones.

Admiral Jayne [6] goes to San Francis[co]. Hurt because taken from the fleet. Mayo thought he did not show ability of that kind.

Saw Lansing. Ambassador J——[Jusserand] had heard Roosevelt had told Italians Gov. desired a British Admiral for Meditera——. We had urged allied command, but not of any particular country. Sims thought G. B & France agreed on Jellico & wanted us to say yes. I said Allied Council must name man.

Powell & destroyers. Delayed for forgings?

Conf. with Gen. Crowder & Palmer about naval recruiting & how to bring it about.

Friday, September 6, 1918

Quantico

[4] The Interdepartmental Social Hygiene Board, of which Daniels was chairman.

[5] Rear Admiral Hilary P. Jones, commanding the Newport News division of the cruiser and transport force.

[6] Rear Admiral Joseph L. Jayne, commanding Division Three of Battleship Force One, Atlantic Fleet, since February; now being assigned as commandant of the Twelfth Naval District.

Sunday, September 8, 1918
Annapolis

Tuesday, September 10, 1918
W W   Any persons, except on strict military service, going abroad, I wish to know their names & mission before they are designated. Often have a sidelight and too many men go over assuming to speak for the Government & W W did not wish this

W W had letter from Gregory explaining the wholesale rounding up of slackers in New York. Senators had severely criticized the action & Gregory had justified it by calling attention to the large number and the necessity of some measure outside the usual methods. It put the fear of God in others just before new draft

Council of National Defense   John R. Mott wished approval of drive for $17[,]000[,]000 for YMCA & the six other organizations working for soldiers & sailors

Agreed

Wednesday, September 11, 1918
War Council. Discussed fixing the price of cotton. Garfield & others said inasmuch as wheat & coal had been fixed, cotton this year

Baruch said notice was given to farmers about wheat. Should wait another year to fix price of cotton

Gov. can buy for itself & Allies & thus stableize [*sic*] price & compel use of other than the high grades. That is now the trouble

Thursday, September 12, 1918
Dry Dock at Boston. Senator Lodge and others.
Went to Quantico to spend the night with Josephus [7]
Dined with the Butlers
Slept with J D in Chaplain Niver's [8] room.
Presented commissions to men promoted in the Thirteenth Regiment

Friday, September 13, 1918
At 3 a.m. went to communion with Josephus and others of 13th Regiment. Sweet and impressive & holy.

[7] Josephus, Jr.'s Marine regiment was about to embark for service in France.
[8] Lieutenant Commander Edward B. Niver, Quantico chaplain.

Left at 6 a.m. Several wives down to see their husbands off—a dumb &
teary sort of good-bye

Congressman Butler at train in Wash. Red Cross furnished sandwiches &
coffee

At Phila. Red Cross ladies supplied lunch & ice cream

Father, you are now getting on very personal affairs—when I asked about
a certain girl.

Reached N.Y. Wife & Frank—Saw them off on ferry.

J D came to hotel at 10:30 & we had dinner

Saturday, September 14, 1918

J D Jr & mother & Frank went to the ship—Von Steuben. He bore up
bravely. I went down at ten. Saw Admiral Gleaves & inspected the overseas
transportation service   Then visited certain ships—the Agamemnon among
them. He had seen the torpedo strike the Mt. Vernon.[9]

I talked to the 13th Regt.

Had lunch with Cyrus Miller [10]

Sunday, September 15, 1918

Worked all day signing commissions

Tuesday, September 17, 1918

Cabinet. Discussed [blank]

Went to Annapolis

Wednesday, September 18, 1918

Spoke to 650 new Ensigns

War Council. Cotton discussed

Thursday, September 19, 1918

Met Prince Axtel,[11] of Denmark. Had him to dinner. He is Commander in
Navy and cousin of the King

McAdoo. Price of steel—putting it up—play into the hands of big interests.

Friday, September 20, 1918

Dined Lunched [*sic*] at White House with Prince Axtel [*sic*] W. W.
in fine spirit & full of anecdotes. Prince referred to the King of Bulgaria [12] as

---

[9] The transport *Agamemnon* had been in convoy with the transport *Mount Vernon* westbound off France on September 5 when the latter was hit by a torpedo with a loss of 36
lives. Through skillful seamanship the *Mount Vernon* was able to return to Brest.

[10] Commander Cyrus R. Miller, commanding the transport *Von Steuben*.

[11] Prince Axel, head of a visiting Danish naval mission.

[12] The pro-German King Ferdinand of Bulgaria, who was to abdicate in favor of his
son Boris three weeks later on October 4.

"a nasty King." W W told of playing golf with two secret service men (a maid called them silver service) near by. Two little boys came out of bushes and, pointing to W W & then to the secret service men one said to the other: "Them's his keepers."

Dined with Prince at Lansings.

Mrs. J D went to Raleigh in her Y.W.C.A. uniform

Saturday, September 21, 1918

Lunched with Minister from Denmark to meet Prince Axel

Dinner by Admiral Benson to Prince Naval attache from foreign countries present

Sunday, September 22, 1918

Took Prince and party to Mount Vernon on Mayflower

Spent evening with Jonathan who goes to Chapel Hill tomorrow

Monday, September 23, 1918

Jonathan went to see Secy of War & was greatly disappointed when he would not waive his age for the training school at Chapel Hill

Went to Eddystone, Pa. to speak at anniversary of first years success in making rifles—have made 1,000,000 in a year.

Mrs. J D went to Little Rock Jonathan to Chapel Hill

Tuesday, September 24, 1918

Appeared before Naval Affairs Committee in favor of buying dry dock from the Commonwealth of Massachusetts.

Talked with Padgett afterwards.

Cong. Hicks [13] gave me a [blank] he picked up on the field of Belleau Woods. Belonged to a Marine

Spoke twice at New York Ave. Presbyterian church before the Church Federation for War Work (Protestant) Church over-crowded & spoke also in SS room.

Council of National Defense. Approved organization of Field Board with Lane Chairman and Dr Shaw as Vice Chairman

No Cabinet meeting. President went to NJ to vote in primary

Wednesday, September 25, 1918

War Council What about ships to bring back Americans after the war? It will take 18 months unless ships are procured. Great Britain has ships.

[13] Frederick C. Hicks, Republican, U.S. Representative from New York, a member of the House Naval Affairs Committee.

Charges $50 to carry over soldiers & wants to increase to $150. France charges $50 and we furnish everything. McAdoo: We should use the power we have & make GB listen to reasonable arrangements after the war. If GB is asked now she will demand ships from us. That is already her desire. Decided to study situation & report.

Capt. Hasbrook.[14] Ship floated many hours after torpedoed. He did not go on board. Wilson and Gleaves said he should have done so. He says he thought tugs could get her to port & he could beach her

Monday, September 30, 1918

Went to capital with the President to draw in selective draft.

Went to Senate to hear President speak on Woman Suffrage amendment

Spoke before Athletic Club of New York   "How did the Americans get a-Cross[?"]

Tuesday, October 1, 1918

Spoke to military students at George Washington University

Lunch with Committee on Training Camp Activities at LaFayette hotel.

Cabinet. Change hours of beginning work at Depts on acct of influenza & to stop crowding of cars

Houston—House had asked for memorandum H had sent President on price of wheat. It is confidential.

Conf. with Marsh [March] and Hurley on how to get our soldiers back from Europe   Shall we ask Great Britain to help   Marsh "No." She wants to charge us more now to carry soldiers than the regular price charged for civilians.

McAdoo & Judge Lovett.[1] Price of Steel. War Industries Board thinks of putting price at $58. when it costs the Steel people $33 to make theirs   Should be varying price & a pool.

[14] Captain Raymond DeL. Hasbrouck, commanding the large transport *Covington* homebound from Brest when it was torpedoed on July 1, 1918, with a loss of 6 lives. Hasbrouck had abandoned ship, though prompt salvage action might have saved the vessel.

[1] Robert S. Lovett, currently director of the division of capital expenditures of the U.S. Railroad Administration.

Wednesday, October 2, 1918

Powell here—discussed delay in destroyers. He & Mc [blank] [2] (inspector) had a spat. The Admiral said they did not care about how much it cost.

Baker told that Plunkett [3] had U.S. Navy painted in big letters on cars carrying 14 inch guns & was not willing to take orders except from Pershing & not desiring to be under Chief of Artillery who was outranked by Plunkett. Told Benson to take it up and see that all rank nonsense be abolished.

War Meeting in War Department developed greatest need was horses & trucks & difficult to secure enough & sufficient tonnage. Truck builders put back by influenza.

Tuesday, October 8, 1918

W W came into cabinet room whistling. In response to inquiry said he whistled because he thought he had done right in answering Germans note.[4] Only one thing troubled him. How could he have correspondence with Germany under autocracy? Then we must go into G—— and set up a government ourselves, something unthinkable. Unless some sort of Gov. offers medium of communication, we might witness bolshevikism [*sic*] worse than in Russia. D [*sic*]

Wednesday, October 9, 1918

Discussed steel rails. Price fixing board wants to fix price of steel rails at $56. It costs Steel Trust $34 & Bethlehem about $60. A flat price would give Steel an ungodly profit. McAdoo & I urged pooling. Gov. to buy all at a reasonable profit & sell at fixed price. That would secure production & not give too high a price. Baruch thought varying price might well be applied on steel.

Saturday, October 12, 1918

Went to the train with Sir Eric Geddes [5]

[2] Rear Admiral George W. McElroy, an inspector for the Bureaus of Steam Engineering and Ordnance.

[3] As an answer to the German Big Bertha artillery, the Navy had organized a battery of 14-inch naval guns mounted on railroad cars under the command of Rear Admiral Charles P. Plunkett.

[4] Prince Max of Baden had become the German chancellor on October 4 and had promptly requested Wilson to initiate an armistice and a peace settlement based on Wilson's peace program. Wilson had responded by asking further assurances of Germany's true intentions.

[5] The First Lord of the British Admiralty had come to the United States to stress the urgency of the need for faster construction of destroyers to cope with the anticipated all-out German submarine campaign in the spring of 1919.

Sunday, October 13, 1918

Spent day in Raleigh. Influenza very bad in town and at camp. Germans note to President was all the topic. J H Pou [6] had an article "no let up until the Kaiser, Von Tirpitz [7] & Co were hung." Gov. Bickett thought it unconditional surrender by Germany. People ready for their boys to fight for Wilson principles, but if they are achieved, then to fight for vengeance is not American spirit. R W W [8] thought same, though Bishop Cheshire [9] & some ladies wanted Germany to feel what Belgium had felt

Jonathan and I had a chummy day. He had been sick but was better.

Went to see Mrs. J W Thompson whose son was killed in France. They had been able to get no particulars.

Attended Jo. Brown's meeting on Liberty Bonds   NC had so far raised only ½ quota for bonds. NC had never failed & must not now.

N&O boys & bonds. I agreed to pay the first 10% on bonds taken by employes on the paper & asked to have 100% subscribe. Told Moore if any failed to take them for me.

Returned to Washington

Monday, October 14, 1918

Returned from Raleigh at 10:10. Messenger met me with message to go at once to the White House. Found Col. House, [10] Lansing and Baker with the President discussing answer to German note. I read Gov. Bickett's letter wh[ich] the President thought fine. Agreed that until German submarines quit sinking passenger ships & killing non-combatants we could have no armistice & no peace with Germany until explicit acceptance of W Ws Fourth of July address—no autocratic government in Germany—was accepted & put into practise. I urged to express these views as already accepted, if G was honest, but not to close the door to peace

Read very happy letter from Josephus from ship, written just before he reached France

---

[6] James H. Pou, prominent Raleigh attorney and political leader.

[7] Grand Admiral Alfred von Tirpitz, German Minister of Marine, 1897–1916.

[8] Robert W. Winston, Raleigh attorney and close friend of Daniels'.

[9] Joseph B. Cheshire, Protestant Episcopal bishop of North Carolina.

[10] Presumably referring to this meeting, Colonel House noted in his diary: "The President soon formulated the points which appear in the Note, and we then decided to send for Lansing, Baker and Daniels to hear their reactions. The reason Daniels was sent for was because he wanted Baker, and the reason he wanted Baker was because he has just returned from the Western Front and we thought his knowledge would be of benefit." Diary, October 15, 1918, House MSS.

Long conference with General Board on program. They wish this country to have naval construction program authorized now that will make the US have the biggest Navy in the world by 1925.

Baker back & looked well. Enthusiastic about Navy men in France

Tuesday, October 15, 1918

Destroyer builders to speed up production.

British Educational Mission called at Council of National Defense.

Cabinet. W W thought not wise while discussing reduction of armament in case of peace to increase our program. Therefore did not favor Gen. Board's 7 years' program to give us navy as big as Great Britain's, but approved another three year program as adopted three years ago.

McAdoo urged economy & said if war went on 2 years longer it was hard to see how Treasury would finance it. We now finance not only our own cost of war but most of our allies.

Decided to dredge Buzzard's Bay entrance to Cape Cod Canal, but not to exercise right to buy it now.

Baker said the Division in which Marines fought so valiantly at Chateau Th[i]erry saved Paris. British and French were retreating. French soldiers sifting through Marines who went forward, sustained the brunt of battle & saved Paris. Archives were ready to be moved

What will happen in Germany.

A Princeton professor who did not believe in Democracy said the logic of a democracy would make a negro woman President of the US

Wednesday, October 16, 1918

W W said we must face such intolerant hatred of Germans I may have to become their advocate for justice & against American Prussianism. We must never do the things we condemn.

Baker said he heard many stories of cruelty & barbaric actions by Germans. Army traced them down & found only 2 of many cases true. Generally a man had heard that it happened in another regiment. Stories of cruelty & stories of our own cruelty were exaggerated. One Am soldier did shoot a German prisoner in the back but they found he was crazy.

W W: Men tell stories they say happened to them to make it more personal when it was only a rumor they adopted

Saw crazy man astride a trunk, saying "get up." Visitor said: "Is your horse hard to make go[?"] ["]This is no horse,["] said crazy man. ["]If it was a horse it would go. This is a hobby[."]

He told also of the story about his taking all the RRs & giving them to his Son-in-law & how many said they heard negro say it   Makes Mrs. McAdoo furious

Thursday, October 17, 1918

Discussed feeding Europe. Hoover thought we should begin now to send over food   W W said a preacher said the Lord's prayer began with "Give us this day our daily bread["] & said no man could worship God on an empty stomach Similarly hunger will bring on bolshevikism [*sic*] & anarchy. House had proposed in Allied Council that they arrange to prevent starvation. Why [not?] get Austrian ships interned in SA?

Discussing GB's selfish policy, W W said "I want to go into the Peace Conference armed with as many weapons as my pockets will hold so as to compel justice. England has agreed to trade conditions as I proposed. We must pool raw material & not permit it to be used for speculative purposes.["]

Fixing price of cotton. Baruch said committee reported it could not be done wisely. Texas man said South either wanted price fixed or not. The uncertainty had cause[d] loss of ten cents per pound.

Friday, October 18, 1918

Lansing here about increase in the Navy.

McAdoo resigned. I went to his house & told him of my deep regret. He said it had cost him 35,000 a year to live & he had practised as much economy as he knew how. He had spent all he had—was 55—had been ill twice this year—& must have rest and a chance to provide for his grand children.

Also saw Mrs. McAdoo. I think she is very sorry—but has such faith in Mc & such love for him she feels there was no other course. I think she is anxious about his health

Monday, October 21, 1918

German note came by radio.

Long conference at White House. W W[,] Lansing, Baker, J D & March. W W read it over and commented on it. General opinion that Germany had accepted W W's demands. Was she in good faith. Lansing thought first should put it up to military men as to armistice. Baker thought G—— had accepted. Why not ask allies for their views? March thought W. W. ought to act without conference with allies. W. W. felt it well to sleep over it. House on way to France. Benson with him. Wish they were there now so as to get view of Prime Minister there.

Public sentiment here wants blood or to put Kaiser on St. Helena. This was regarded as "ridiculous" said W. W.

W W told how Ashurst [11] rushed up to the White House and was afraid the Pres. would not [be] firm with the Germans. W W: "Why don't you Senators sometimes give me credit with not being a damned fool"

Ashurst was a cowboy: W W If you & I were in a fight & you held up your hands & asked for quits & would agree to all I said, and then I made you disarm, wouldn't that be all right? Ashurst thought it would ["]Had you rather have the Kaiser or the Bolsheviks"

Tuesday, October 22, 1918

Cabinet discussed German message.

McAdoo & Baker made strong statements. Baker left memorandum. McAdoo thought we could not go into Germany to set up government & with armistice arranged by military leaders we could accept Germany's statement it had or would comply with Presidents terms. Terrible responsibility to carry on war if it could be ended on our terms. Moreover there is a limit to our ability to finance this expensive war and our allies for two years more. Burleson wanted unconditional surrender, but the more discussed the more he felt this was getting what we were fighting for.

Wilson said labor was asking: What are we fighting for? They opposed war for what imperialistic England desired. McAdoo & Wilson wanted to confer with allies before answering Germany. Burleson & I felt he should answer Germany & I with an armistice safeguarded we should write to Germany & agree to propose peace on the 14 propositions & addresses. To-day America can have more influence in peace meeting than in future. In July all allies approved Wilson. If we continue to win their selfish aims will begin to be asserted.

Houston wanted to fix division of districts in Reichstag so the people could rule better than in present burgh system

Redfield & Lane felt could not trust Gers

But all finally came to side of unity to Solf [12]

Wednesday, October 23, 1918

War Council at White House. Long discussion of German note. McCormick rather wanted unconditional surrender. Hoover, Garfield, Hurley, Baruch, all, with McAdoo & myself favored such an armistice as our military would regard

[11] Henry F. Ashurst, Democrat, U.S. Senator from Arizona.
[12] Wilhelm Solf, the new German foreign secretary.

as safe. Hoover wanted note of encouragement to Germans who were trying to secure self government in Germany. Wanted to say the upper house should be changed & made popular in composition. W W said he had used a memo by Baker in the letter he thought of sending (wh. he read) but the last part he wrote himself. Like little girl whose mother said the devil put the temper & bad language & spitting in the face into her. Might as to the first two "but I thought of the spitting myself" What effect on politics? On election? W W could not avoid thinking of that & he might find popular opinion so much against him he might have to go into cyclone cellar for 48 hours. But after 48 hours, the people would quit being hysterical & become reasonable & prefer getting what they are fighting for now than to fight on to Berlin & keep up war. Baruch said it was right & we must go down if necessary for right.

At 12 o'clock the President sent for Lansing, March & I & read message to Solf. March said military opinion was to carry on war but the President could not fail to suggest armistice to the allies. Lansing thought paper OK. I suggested one verbal change. W W serious Public opinion he said was as much a fact as a mountain and must be considered.

Thursday, October 24, 1918

Presidents note well received by people & press.

Weekly Council. F. D. R. criticized our aviation department. We discussed plans to improve. Griffin, Taylor and Earle disagreed with him. Now we have machines to spare. Experience & ships have improved situation as R—— found it in Europe. Pratt, Earle & others approved 3 year program and hope we will not agree upon present type of battle cruiser until more study. They think battle of Jutland shows can sink too easily to invest 20 million dollars. Do not agree with the General Board.

Badger called to approve my programs and hoped no change will be made in battle cruisers. Thinks type already order[ed] should be continued. Telegraphed Benson to make study of all types so upon his return we could decide which to build.

Social Hygiene Board met and we took up with Dr. Chase [13] the way to make effective our fight against venereal diseases.

Friday, October 25, 1918

Calhoun wanted commission for his son. No!

Erie complained that Ordnance inspector was unfriendly and was too busy organizing company to do them justice

---

[13] J. Franklin Chase, Methodist minister and secretary of the New England Watch and Ward Society, New England executive of the Commission on Training Camp Activities.

Saturday, October 26, 1918

With Baruch, March & McKean talked with Baker about ship control. New York congested and not enough ships routed from other ports. After the war business responsible.

Lansing came around & thought of asking South American countries to give concessions to Marconi wireless. I told him Marconi belonged to Great Britain and we would be turning wireless over to them. Suggested he should ask S.A. countries to join with us in wireless as government agencies and have no private wireless. He seemed to agree

Ed. Graham [14] died at 8:10.

Sunday, November 3, 1918

Spent day at Annapolis. Frank drove me down. Admiral Coontz [1] & Capt. Pratt came down to bring some telegrams from Benson. I approved sending Bullard [2] with the Chester to the Adriatic. Benson had wired for definite instructions as to naval terms of an armistice to be proposed. The President had cabled that any ships taken over should be held in trust, but given no specific instructions. Upon return to Washington I went to the White House —had a talk with the President—and in accordance with his views sent this telegram:

"In advising Col. House with regard to the terms of armistice, you are authorized to use your judgment, but the President's judgment is clear that it ought to be distinctly understood that all armed vessels taken should be held in trust and that it is quite possible to goo [*sic*] too far in demanding excessive security"

Monday, November 4, 1918

Had long talk with Admiral Washington [3] about V. B. [4] He fears R—— [5] will not give him high marks and B—— is older and not happy & his ship

---

[14] Edward K. Graham, president of the University of North Carolina.

---

[1] Rear Admiral Robert E. Coontz, serving in Naval Operations; subsequently became chief of Naval Operations on October 26, 1919.

[2] Rear Admiral William H. G. Bullard, commanding U.S. naval forces in the eastern Mediterranean. The U.S.S. *Chester* was a third-class cruiser.

[3] Rear Admiral Thomas Washington, commander of the U.S.S. *Florida,* one of the battleships serving with the British Grand Fleet.

[4] Captain Victor Blue, commanding the battleship *Texas.* As in the past, Daniels resolved

is not quite up to the mark in R's judgment. What shall I do? is troubling me.

Had message to come to White House at 8:30. Lansing and Baker there. President had message from House. Supreme War Council agreed, but Great Britain raised question of freedom of the seas—did not understand exactly what is meant by it—and wished that left open for discussion. W W had cabled House if E[ngland] took course in opposition we would use our facilities to build the greatest navy. France accepted principle. Decided to accept inasmuch as G.B. agreed to all other 13 points & did not actually dissent from that in order to have unity. But he is resolved in later conference to win over the other countries to our point of view, and secure it from League of Nations. Great disappointment to me. Lansing & Baker thought it would work out all right. L—— does not believe in doctrine of blockade & thinks new conditions must make a change in it.

Baker told of Hughes, in War Drive speech, saying "unconditional surrender." Bourke Cochran: [6] "I approve of that doctrine first enunciated by W W who said there could be no compromise with autocracy[."]

Tuesday, November 5, 1918

Election day—very quiet.

Cabinet discussed German situation. W. W. said it would take months for people to get over passionate hate. Some wanted to get things—some special treaty—& even approved brutal treatment of Germans. I was a boy at Columbia & heard near relatives tell of outrageous deeds of Sherman's troops. The mob spirit of vengeance gets into some soldiers Baker said certain stock stories were current in Europe—awful cruelty but told of other regiments. Only two were substantiated. Most stories exaggerated.

Crazy man riding his trunk. Why cant you make your horse go. It is no horse it is a hobby

W. W. with some feeling "I have heard the story that infuriates Mrs McAdoo of the negro who liked me because I took all the rail roads away and gave it [*sic*] to my son-in-law" They make up tales

No Prussianism. Must not do the things we condemn.

Met in Cummings room at the Shoreham to hear election returns. First news was encouraging, but later left us in gloom.

---

his dilemma in favor of Blue, and reappointed him chief of the Bureau of Navigation with the rank of rear admiral on December 16.

[5] Rear Admiral Hugh Rodman, commanding the U.S. battleship force with the Grand Fleet.

[6] William Bourke Cockran, New York attorney, Democrat, and former U.S. Representative from New York.

Wednesday, November 6, 1918

War Council. Discussed getting food to Austria to feed starving people. Cannot use money for that purpose. Could we lend to Jugo-Slavs? Lansing to be asked to furnish statement as to whether we had power. If so, could be supplied to them and then we could send food-stuffs.

Hoover to go to Europe and Hurley too—Hoover on food and Hurley about ships. To try to get Austrian ships in S.A. ports & others tied up to transport food. Hoover thought as this country would have to furnish money direct or lend it to England & France we ought to undertake it and let it have our brand

Baruch said France wanted much steel, England wanted many things. "I wish no ships & nothing done till peace. I intend to carry as many weapons to the peace table as I can conceal on my person" I will be cold & firm. GB selfish. He looked for League of Nations to settle freedom of the seas

Thursday, November 7, 1918

Went to Phila. to Emergency Fleet Reception. Schwab. I told him I had forgiven him all his sins.

News that Germany had signed armistice printed by United Press and everybody wild and delirious with joy—paraded with bands &c.

Not true.

Could not sleep in Phila

Friday, November 8, 1918

Worked on report

Saturday, November 9, 1918

Wireless caught message from Max that Emperor would abdicate. Sent to Lansing.

Capps brought letter from Fore River. Men had stopped ¾ hours when I spoke & could not that time be charged to naval construction.

Republicans have raised question & is embar[r]assing.

Sunday, November 10, 1918

Spoke in Baltimore twice for United War Drive.

Telegram came from Solf, Minister of Foreign Affairs, who said "We are forced to accept armistice," but looked to President Wilson to prevent millions from starving. Objected to blockade provision because it would deny opportunity to secure food. Took it to Lansing who thought it ought not to be given out

Went to White House. W W said House had introduced resolution in Austrian matter that allies would co-operate to secure food for people of conquered country. W W is writing message & expects to appear before Congress to announce result when armistice is signed. Will touch upon food also. Must first of all support our soldiers.

Food must go to prevent bolshevikism [sic] & anarchy & help preserve the people. Danger of no government is call for our help

Monday, November 11, 1918

News of signing of armistice received at 2:45 a.m. Boys crying extra in the streets. Holiday ordered by the President in all public offices & navy yards.

Admiral Grant,[7] of British Navy, called to express thanks for all Navy had done.

At 1 o'clock the President addressed Congress giving details of armistice with Germany.

At 3:30 parade in interest of United War Work, reviewed by the President.

Banquet by Baruch to State Councils of National Defense. Baker, Hurley, Hoover, Redfield and I spoke.

Went to Italian ambassadors reception

Tuesday, November 12, 1918

Baker said he had cable that Am. soldiers held their watches & fought till 11 o'clock, the time of the armistice.

Discussed bringing troops home. How many will we need? Baker thought 600,000.

Burleson wished to abolish censorship—said it had never done any good. Lansing dissented & said War Trade Board needed it. France & GB continued theirs and we should do likewise until conditions were normal, say until Peace terms were agreed upon.

McAdoo thought could pass 6 billion dollar bill & no 8 bil dolls. He and Burleson urged economy W W said must not stop so hurriedly that labor will be idle.

Wheat discussion. Houston said Hoover never said same thing twice. Told him farmers ought to go slow increasing production & that he told others there would not be enough food. McAdoo thought price of wheat would go down & the Treasury would have to make up deficit to wheat growers, who all voted R ticket because price of wheat too low

[7] Vice Admiral Sir Lowther Grant.

W W will go to Peace Conference.
approved Sims & Gleaves [8]

Wednesday, November 13, 1918
War Council
Shall we annul contracts?
"   "   continue to fix prices?
W. W. Gradual. Do not disturb conditions   better make more shells than
we need
Shall Gov. own & run ships? Or let them go back   W W own them
McAdoo thought there must be some dislocation. Prices stimulated must
go down
Treasury cannot finance on present scale

Friday, November 15, 1918
Spoke at Phila to Society of Naval Architects and Marine Engineers

Saturday, November 16, 1918
Went to ball game at Brooklyn between Great Lakes & Rutgers. Navy won
Lunch at Chamber of Commerce with United War Workers—guest of Mr.
Bedford. Told story: "Next time send the $500 by K of C. The YMCA Secre-
taries took half of it.["]
Reviewed big parade.
Dined with John D. Rockefeller Jr
Spoke at Carnegie Hall   Portrait of President sold at auction. Police band
gave to my wife
Spoke at Astor ball by theatrical people.

Sunday, November 17, 1918
Worked all day with Wilbur Jenkins on my report

Monday, November 18, 1918
Funeral of Haitian Minister.[9]
Lunched at F. D. R.'s—good-bye to Capt Blannpre, French naval attache.
Council of National Defense discussed Reconstruction measures. Who shall
take them up?
Advisory Council—how to reduce expenses

[8] Promoted to admiral and vice admiral, respectively, on December 4.
[9] Solon Ménos.

Alf Scales [10] talked about his brother Arch [11]

W W to Burleson: "Ask their advice ——— a great English statesman, always made people whom he consulted think he was taking their advice[."]

Tuesday, November 19, 1918

Cabinet.

Uniform 8 hour law.

Talked to W W about man who came into the service & drew salary from concern that had big contract. Am to see Attorney General.

W W: State Council of Defense in states having Rep Governors had been made political agencies as had the Red Cross. Better dissolve slowly

To A. S .B.[12] Compact organized administration forces in House, elimination of C. C.[13] & C K.[14] Faithful men who will keep in touch. Same in Senate

League to Enforce Peace—now purged of Taftism should be encouraged along line of resolution passed.

Greg[ory]: Will you appoint C F Hughes No—there is no room big enough for Hughes & me to stay in

As to Chief of Navigation: No man not loyal. Baker imposed upon

Wednesday, November 20, 1918

Long confidential hearing before Naval Affairs Committee.

Butler opposed 3 yr. program which I urged because we need to strengthen our Navy & as a good instrument to use at the Peace Conference.

Brazil & GB's attempt to monopolize

War Cabinet. Baruch & McAdoo thought reconstruction would take care of itself. W W wanted to see that there was material for France & Belgium and not gobbled up by those who would boost prices to obtain it. McAdoo feared we were manufacturing munitions we did not need to keep labor employed. It is our business to reduce & protect finances. There is plenty for labor to do. But better to pay labor till adjusted than use it in what is not needed.

---

[10] Alfred M. Scales, Greensboro attorney and trustee of the University of North Carolina.

[11] Captain Archibald H. Scales, due for reassignment after commanding the U.S.S. *Delaware* with the British Grand Fleet. Scales subsequently served briefly as commandant of the Great Lakes Naval Training Station, and then in February, 1919, was appointed superintendent of the Naval Academy.

[12] Postmaster General Albert S. Burleson.

[13] Speaker Champ Clark, who would expect to be named (and was) minority leader in the Republican-controlled 66th Congress.

[14] Claude Kitchin, House majority leader in the 64th and 65th Congresses.

Thursday, November 21, 1918

Talked to Admiral Washington about Blue Record is very good.

Colby & I went to see the President about the purchase by G.B. of the 85 ships belonging to the International Mercantile Co. Very complicated. American money is in them but under English laws they are controlled by English directors and if owners attempt to control they are confiscated by England Colby to see Fletcher [15]

Tuesday, November 26, 1918

Cabinet. VP [16] to preside at future sessions.

Discussed what to do as to war activiti[es]

Wednesday, November 27, 1918

Went to Buffalo

Thursday, November 28, 1918

Spent day in Buffalo

Spoke on Thanksgiving to community service

Friday, November 29, 1918

Meeting of Council of National Defense Had picture taken of Council. We thought all war activities should cease & be taken over by regular departments as soon as possible.

Went to George Creel's banquet Friday night.

Saturday, November 30, 1918

Went at 5 to White House to see W W with Gregory to talk about oil reserves. I agreed to bill if all naval reserve agreements are left to the President to decide. He said he had lost interest in the bill and yet would agree on proposition but would not go one step further.

Wrote with his own hand nomination of Victor Blue, Chief of Navigation, & Taylor re-appointed Chief of C.&R.

Went to Annapolis

---

[15] Possibly Senator Duncan U. Fletcher, an outspoken advocate of a larger American merchant marine. Daniels and Colby wished to transfer the ships of the International Mercantile Company to the U.S. flag.

[16] Vice-President Thomas R. Marshall, designated to preside at cabinet meetings while President Wilson was in Europe attending the peace conference.

Sunday, December 1, 1918

Went to church at Chapel. Always impressive.

Dinner at Eberle's. He lobbied for Lanning.[1]

Called to see Dr. Smith

Talked to Worth. He thinks of resigning & seems to have his heart set upon study[ing] medicine. I told him he must settle it for himself. So did his mother

Went to Department. Benson cabled that Sims wished to man & send five German submarines to this country. England & France were taking them into ports. I cabled No—must remain in trust till Peace Conference determines their disposition. Benson thought best thing was to sink them both [?]

Monday, December 2, 1918

Told Lanning I would appoint Blue Chief of Navigation. He took it well.

F D R—

Went with Addie to capital to hear address of President to Congress. Republicans had said they would give him an ice bath and they were sullen and quiet, not even applauding his reference to brave soldiers and sailors. It was the most unhandsome performance—churlish. Later the President referred to it & said he was interested in remarks made to him by the special committee "Mann is a bitter partisan but he is a sport" he said[.] "He wished me a good voyage and success," ["]but Lodge put emphasis upon his wish for a good voyage—nothing else. When I get out of this office, I will tell them what I think of them.["]

Peter Gerry[2] came to see me & hoped some Reps. wd prevent Reps. organizing Senate and making Penrose Chairman of Finance Committee. "Why do you wish to help them when they desire to commit suicide?"

Council of Natl. Defense asked State Councils to continue in getting work for returned soldiers

Tuesday, December 3, 1918

Chas A Towne

Bliss Torpedo. They did not deliver on time & ask release. They charge high price for royalty on torpedoes made by us. They must treat us right on our royalties or pay for the delay, & Royalties come first.

Shipping Board agreed to continue Navy manning and officering of ships—

---

[1] Captain Harris Laning, formerly assistant chief and currently acting chief of the Bureau of Navigation, who was hopeful of being named chief in his own right.

[2] Peter G. Gerry, Democrat, U.S. Senator from Rhode Island.

50-50—*&* War Department requested us to man them. Will need larger personnel to man them.

Talked to Grayson as he was leaving

No Cabinet meeting

Mrs. Benson surprised the Admiral was not selected on Peace Commission

Wednesday, December 4, 1918

Went to Appropriations Committee. Sherley wants itemized account of all appropriations and what has been done *&* how much can be returned.

Went before Senate Finance Committee. It wished information Sherley desired *&* said it was needed as they had to raise the revenue.

Thursday, December 5, 1918

Went to Navy Yard *&* spoke to all employees who presented $12,000 and an ambulance to my wife for the Navy Department of the Red Cross. She declared she out ranked me because she was last on the program. The first man to die came out of the Navy Yard from the Dolphin *&* the last big gun fired was Plunketts 14 inch gun made in Washington Navy Yard.

Conference with Senator Knox[3] *&* Palmer about wireless. Should be owned, but owners of Fessenden[4] patent wanted ten million dollars for it. Navy owns Federal patent *&* Fessenden claims it is infringement

Photo from Sir Eric Geddes

Dined with Niblacks

Friday, December 6, 1918

Heard Maine *&* N.H. delegations ask Navy to help build bridge at Portsmouth, N.H.

Mayor Smith,[5] of Phila. wanted all Phila city employees returned from Navy to save the city which was paying their salary. Also wanted Phila embarkation point.

McFarland, of Boston, says Bolsheviki in Russia represent the people and it is the crime of the ages that US has sent troops into Russia to fight them.

Thinks Progressives are afraid Wilson will not stand against GB's wiles

Meets [?] at McAdoo's office.

[3] Philander C. Knox, Republican, former Attorney General and Secretary of State, currently U.S. Senator from Pennsylvania.

[4] Reginald A. Fessenden, Massachusetts inventor and electrical engineer, credited with the first American radio broadcast in 1906.

[5] Thomas B. Smith, Republican, mayor of Philadelphia.

Shall censorship be continued? Baker & I no. Others yes, in order to prevent trading with the Enemy through S.A. agencies

Sunday, December 8, 1918

Reached Springfield early—met by Richard Hooker. After breakfast went to his home. We went to Methodist Church. Went to breakfast at YMCA, & spoke to 150 boys.

Called to see Mrs. Samuel Bowles [6]—sister of Sherman Hoar [7]—who has a boy in the Marine Corps.

Spoke to Y.M.C.A. Quoted rebuke to Sims.[8]

Monday, December 9, 1918

Went from depot to Capitol before Appropriations Committee to go over statement showing sums appropriated for Navy during the war. Committee wished to know how much we could return. I told them we needed money for a deficit.

Lunched at Pan American buildg to meet his Royal Highness [9] & party who had been to Europe. Dined at home of Japanese Ambassador [10] at night

Tuesday, December 10, 1918

VP presided at Cabinet meeting. He was bright & full of jest. Gave out statement that his presiding was informal and unofficial & he wished this to go out to keep Reps. from saying the President doubted his right to go and therefore had asked him &c.

Burleson vigorous to take off all mail censorship.

Last meeting McAdoo present as member of Cabinet. "I hate to retire to private life, but there was no choice and I was compelled to take that action.["] All regretted his going.

Discussed wheat. V.P. said: "They voted against us because they said we put the price of wheat too low & next year they will vote against us because we wasted public money.["]

[6] Elizabeth Hoar Bowles, widow of the late editor of the *Springfield Republican*.

[7] Late Massachusetts Democrat and U.S. Representative, 1891–1893.

[8] Probably a reference to President Taft's formal reprimand of Sims, then a commander on a visit to England with the Atlantic Fleet, for his extemporaneous remarks at a Guildhall luncheon in London in 1910. Carried away by his faith in Anglo-Saxon destiny, the Canadian-born Sims had declared his belief that if the British Empire were ever seriously threatened England could count on all assistance from her kinsmen across the sea. The speech caused a sensation in the United States and drew an official rebuke from President Taft, who made clear that the Navy was an instrument of peace and that naval officers should say nothing to embarrass the government.

[9] Prince Higashi Fushimi of Japan, currently visiting the United States.

[10] Viscount Kikujiro Ishii.

Wednesday, December 11, 1918

Went to Baltimore & spoke at Southern Commercial Congress. Miss Grant & Col Lee danced to tune of Dixie. I told of Miss Mary Lee who was presented as "the daughter of the greatest American General" & called Miss Grant & she never corrected the person who so introduced her.

I spoke on America's contribution in gov. by consent of governed & Republic & contrasted Congress of Paris & Congress of Vienna "the meanest & unworthiest of assemblages of noted men."

Thursday, December 12, 1918

Went before Merchant Marine Committee in favor of government monopoly of wireless—must be in hands of one—government or one corporation. Interference makes anything else weaken or destroy value of wireless. Warned committee that a foreign owned or controlled corporation seeking concessions in South American Republics & thus gain control of high powered stations. The special interests present opposed any government ownership.

Friday, December 13, 1918

Architect who made plans for Squantum wished to appeal over Board of Compensation.

Went to dinner and theatre with Mrs. Edison.

Padgett had talked with Fletcher about B—— He respects Blue & says he has the kind of enemies all successful men have.

President & party reached Brest

Decided to have review when American dreadnaughts reached New York.

Saturday, December 14, 1918

Towne & Blue

Dinner at Admiral Fletcher

Sunday, December 15, 1918

Went to Corcoran Art Gallery to see war pictures.

Went to Senate to hear eulogies of Senator Tillman.

Gov Bickett & wife & Hoogewerff to dinner.

Addie to New York

Henry

Monday, December 16, 1918

Went to Quantico and spoke to 432 young men & gave them their commissions as Second Lieutenants

Tuesday, December 17, 1918

Cabinet. Marshall came in late.

Discussion turned on what to do as to wool, copper, sea island cotton, chrome & 20 other essentials whose production was stimulated for war purposes. Said that men incurred expense at request of government to get ready to produce—now in full production. If War Trade Board puts on embargo, or keeps it on, these infant industries can dispose of their product and be saved. If not, Congress may impose heavy tariff duties and compel their aid & make it entering wedge for high protective tariff. Marshall very uneasy for fear labor would be unemployed and said business men were anxious & something should be done. Redfield & Wilson said there was no real cause for alarm—that business men would go forward & no trouble now about labor.

Should we ask W W about embargo? Burleson said he would talk to Baker and get him to take it up with W W

Wednesday, December 18, 1918

Spoke to Methodist Temperance organization giving reasons for Wine Mess order. Bryan was there—said probably best he had not gone to Peace Conference—it looked like the allies would demand excessive indemnities of Germany.

Talked of my being candidate for Pres. if Reps put up military man two years hence   No.

Went to Annapolis on Mayflower to speak at Gov. Conf

Thursday, December 19, 1918

At Annapolis and spoke at Governors Conference.

Worth had written his resignation and was troubled but resolved to be a doctor. We talked heart to heart. I then talked to Eberle who was surprised & regretted it

"I was born to be a doctor"

Talked to boys on Miss [?]

Gov. & Mrs Bickett came back with us

Friday, December 20, 1918

Talked to Spellacy about trip

Talked to Padgett about Naval Committee going to New York to review. Could not pay their way

Edward Marshall.[11]

[11] Probably D. Edward Marshall, author and journalist, head of the Edward Marshall Newspaper Syndicate.

Worths resignation came in   Eberle & Standley [12] put on commendatory words

Worth came home. Fight.[13]

Jonathan came in middle of the night

Saturday, December 21, 1918

Burleson came to see about radio taking up work of overcrowded cables. Talked about W's going to Rome. Had letters from preachers protesting against W's going to R——. B—— suggested that he go to Piava [14] & ask King [15] to go with him and thus escape going to R—— &c.

Prof. Wilson said GB had staff of 100 men studying every phase of naval strength and sea power and would have 100 at Paris to try to press GBs point of view and would do it so adroitly there was danger something would be slipped in. Said if Baker went to take the President's place the Army would then be represented by two on the Mission & the Navy, which had the chief interest in freedom of seas, would have no representation.

Sunday, December 22, 1918

Boys at home.

Went to church   "There was no room for Him at the inn."

Phila. Council requested note to Captain of British Navy to exhibit naval paintings at Phila. I wrote. They first wanted Navy to take charge of it. Then Navy League asked. No. It must be a private exhibit. Govern't could not undertake it.

Went at night to Department. Met printer who wished help and Addie took it up with Red Cross

Monday, December 23, 1918

Uncle Joe Cannon wanted seven tickets to see Naval Review. Talked to him about Gideon Welles.[16] He said he had only talked to Wilson five minutes and wanted to know what kind of man he was in intimate association. I told

---

[12] Captain William H. Standley, on the staff of the Naval Academy.

[13] Before leaving the Naval Academy, Worth had challenged Midshipman Daniel V. Gallery, Jr., of the Third Class to a fistfight. Gallery had accused Worth of having entered the Academy only to escape the draft and then promptly resigning when the war was over. Gallery was evidently the victor, claiming a knockout. The accusation against young Daniels was understandable, but unfair nevertheless.

[14] The Piave River, scene of the Battle of Vittorio Veneto, the final defeat of the Austrian armies in northeastern Italy in October, 1918.

[15] Victor Emmanuel III, King of Italy.

[16] Secretary of the Navy, 1861–1869, the only other Navy Secretary to serve as long as Daniels.

him how he nearly always had a story before meeting of cabinet. "He is highly respected but walks alone"

Mrs. James R—— [17]   Gideon Welles & J. D.

No cabinet meeting.

C. A. Towne and the Bliss contract. We get the right to use patents & let them off on penalties.

Many officers came in to wish happy Christmas

Message to the fleet

Wednesday, December 25, 1918
Left for NY to attend Review
Gave out statement of how Sea Power had made victory possible

Thursday, December 26, 1918
Naval Review

Friday, December 27, 1918
Returned from New York

Saturday, December 28, 1918
Shallenberger: [18] "I wish you did not live in N.C. We would nominate you for President." The Germans had voted Republican practically solidly & without letting anybody know it. S—— was astounded at their move [?]

Talked with Mayo, Rodman, Blue. Mayo said it was suicide to send naval ships over to bring back troops. Benson had changed his mind and agreed with him. But I had promised the Army & could not change. Besides soldiers preferred some discomfort in order to get home in a hurry rather than wait for transports.

Sent out suggested law to every State asking laws against men & women with venereal disease.

Sunday, December 29, 1918
Heard Mr. Chappell preach. "Sleep on and take thine ease." No man can recall [?] tomorrow. "Rise let us go." Christ always calls men to fight their failures.

J. P. Dwyer, Phila Record, here to try to get Treasury Department order reversed which prevented bands on ships, blowing of sirens &c. This would

[17] Sara Delano Roosevelt, mother of Assistant Secretary Franklin D. Roosevelt.
[18] Ashton C. Shallenberger, Democrat, former governor and currently U.S. Representative from Nebraska.

prevent welcome to returning soldiers from Europe. We went to see Rowe who promised to make such change as is necessary to keep navigation safe

Monday, December 30, 1918

Went before House Naval Committee in advocacy of appropriation for 3 year programme

Dinner to McAdoos.

He said unless Congress keeps RR's in gov. hands for 5 years the President should turn them back at once. 5 years would give time to test. Less time would give RR's whip hand. If kept temporarily, Reps. will use issue to defeat Dems. by promising bigger wages & getting everybody dissatisfied.

A W McLean thought RR ought to be like Federal Reserve Board as to banks

Tuesday, December 31, 1918

Before Naval Affairs Committee.

Discussed personnel—how many should be put on each ship. Great Britain has 20% less than we have.

Lunched with Butler

Cabinet. Marshal[l] very witty [?]

Redfield said Home Market club had rebuked him for saying good bristles could be obtained from China & they had said he ought to be encouraging home trade instead of promoting trade in bristles from China. "Why don't those gents shave and furnish their own bristles?"

Baker said: What should he do with 350,000 men called in draft who did not report? Military men wanted them arrested & brought to camps, tried & punished. Would cost ten million dollars. Would public opinion uphold that. After discussion decided he should have letter sent to each one & then put up to Congress.

Gregory said he would prosecute every son of rich man who was sent out of the country to escape draft

Houston & G. Pinchot [19]

[19] Gifford Pinchot, prominent forester and conservationist.

1919

1919

The Cabinet Diaries of Josephus Daniels, 1919

Wednesday, January 1, 1919

Hearing before the Naval Affairs Committee continued.

Reception. Admirals and Captains and their wives at home for reception

Thursday, January 2, 1919

Went with Mrs. Dewey to District Court where she had suit. Dirty linen washed in public. Hoped to avert it. Ed. McLean told McGowan he would make it hot for me that we came with Mrs. Dewey.[1]

Before Naval Affairs Committee and finished hearing.

Electric drive.[2]

Went to moving pictures—showing Addie giving flowers to wounded marines in Brooklyn Naval Hospital. Also review of fleet coming into New York day after Christmas. Pratt, Blue and Mrs. Dewey went with us

Afterwards talked to Pratt & Blue about fleet and Atlantic & Pacific & new assignments for Admirals.

Friday, January 3, 1919

Rodman: When it got over, the Texas was rotten—just out of dry dock—but it came up splendidly and I gave him the best marks possible.

Towne and Earle. Shall we remit penalties?

Mrs. B[agley] & others hot about Post editorial[3] It was McLean's proof he "would make it hot"

Went to hear Isaacs tell of escape from German prison. A man sitting near Addie (not knowing her) said "There's D—— on the stage to introduce him Somebody ought to kick him off" "He will speak only two minutes and he will not trouble you long" And she got up and moved her seat

[1] Mrs. Dewey was suing her nephew, *Washington Post* publisher Edward B. McLean, over a financial transaction involving his father, the late John R. McLean. Daniels and McGowan had accompanied her to court as a gesture of moral support.

[2] During his advocacy of a new three-year building program before the House Naval Affairs Committee, Daniels announced that all future capital ships would be equipped with electrical drive instead of the previous turbine propulsion, an innovation Daniels had first authorized for the battleship *California* in 1914.

[3] McLean had carried out his threat of the day before in a long feature editorial entitled "The Secretary of the Navy"—a highly critical but generalized attack upon Daniels' Navy service.

Swanson: Wanted me to write President that he could not argue about a promise he had made   Must stand by 14 points

Vogelgesang [4]

Saturday, January 4, 1919

Plunkett back

Read the hearings

Sunday, January 5, 1919

Judge Lucking—Charles. Not to appear for Mr. Ford [5]

McLean. His 5 year old boy asked: Which is the biggest man

Uncle Sam

President Wilson

Mr. Daniels?

Jenkins and "Full Steam Ahead" [6]

Monday, January 6, 1919

Talked to Swanson about Ford boat & the Lodge resolution.[7] We will give facts to Senate committee.

Belknap back from laying mines—230 miles long & 10 miles wide & a great work was the barrage across the North Sea

Wells. Officer in IWW is secret service agent & gives view of labor. If wages continue good and there is plenty of work, no IWW. Otherwise[,] otherwise.

Venoble:[8] Shall we put into naval bill provision not to build ships if international agreement goes through? More logical not to do so.

Tuesday, January 7, 1919

Cabinet. Should V.P. go to funeral of T R? He said the papers had announced that it was a private funeral, with admission by card, and he would

---

[4] Captain Carl T. Vogelgesang, appointed to command the U.S.S. *Idaho* on January 7.

[5] Ford was currently facing two presumably related investigations, his own demand for a recount and probe of his recent senatorial election defeat by Truman H. Newberry, and a Republican charge of Ford profiteering in the Eagle boat contracts.

[6] John Wilber Jenkins, former *News and Observer* staff member now working in the Navy public relations department, was helping Daniels edit a book of his wartime speeches under the title *The Navy and the Nation* (New York: George H. Doran, 1919). The theme of Jenkins' introduction was "Full speed ahead."

[7] On January 3, Senator Lodge had called for an investigation of the Ford Eagle boat program.

[8] William W. Venable, Democrat, U.S. Representative from Mississippi and a member of the House Naval affairs Committee.

be butting in. Besides, Alice Longworth[9] did not speak to him or Mrs. M
& they might not like him to be present. We decided to telephone to Nicholas
Longworth & he answered it would be appreciated or something like that &
as the President had cabled asking him to go, he would go. Been married
24 years—never separated from his wife & she must go. Arranged private car
& we overpersuaded him

Burleson [to] V.P.: "You have been in office long enough & you may prepare to retire." Never out of official life since 21 yr old   Elected to Congress
from Dist Attorney & 2 months expired. His partner bought him a commission
as Deputy Sheriff & said: "I knew you could not survive out of office & I
procured [?] this for you to keep you alive till you get to Cong[ress."]

Jesse Williams—been shell-shocked & gone thr[ough] everything

Wednesday, January 8, 1919

Wrote to Mayor Smith, of Philadelphia, that if he did not clean up Philadelphia Baker and I would

Baker—as to Methodist University—said Tell the Bishop to keep setting
on the nest & he would be surprised at how many chickens he would hatch[10]

P S B Franklin [Philip A. S. Franklin] wanted captains of merchant ships,
who were Naval Reservists, advanced to Commanders. I recommended to
Padgett. They have been captains of transports during the war.

Oliver wanted me to reply to Post by statement in hearings

Thursday, January 9, 1919

Admiral Knight returned from Vladivostock. Said it would require half a
century for Russia to find herself. He seems to think America ought to have
sent 40,000 men into Russia 3 or 4 thousand miles to meet & encourage Checko-
Slovaks We should compel the Japs to co-operate. They are squatting on
the country, buying up public utilities &c. They would listen to us now. He
said Japanese Minister of Marine on day news came that America had voted
$600,000,000 for air craft. It immensely impressed him and other Japs. Also
they were greatly impressed when draft law passed. Before that many believed
Germany would win and were pro-German, especially any men trained in
Germany

W. C. Gonzales,[11] Minister to Cuba, here at dinner. Told of Anderson[12]

[9] Alice Lee Roosevelt Longworth, eldest daughter of Theodore Roosevelt; wife of Nicholas
Longworth, Republican, U.S. Representative from Ohio.
[10] Probably a reference to Daniels' interest in making the American University in Washington a more significant institution.
[11] William E. Gonzales, former editor-in-chief of the Columbia, S.C., *State*, U.S. Minister
to Cuba since 1913.

and Cuzachs.[13] Graft in flour in Cuba due to Morgan, of the War Trade Board. Morgan's clerk got commission sent to Cuba to relieve situation

Friday, January 10, 1919

Strike in N.Y. Baker called up from New York & will see RR administration to-night. W B Wilson cabled the President & requested him to ask Taft Board to act. Baker thought if we agreed to pay rate RR would agree upon it be wise. I agreed.

Dinner with Gonzales

Senator Johnson,[14] of SD wanted me to come out as candidate for President.

Saturday, January 11, 1919

Vilhjalmur Stefanson [15]   Lived 5 years in Arctic region

Went to see Steffinns, the explorer, at home of daughter of Commodore Wilkes [16]   I said it pleased him [me] to welcome him to our country.

["]What do you think is my country?" he asked to my rather discomfort.

"I am not sure. Are you not from Norway.[?"]

"I have lived in South Dakota since boyhood (born in Canada) and stumped the country for Bryan in 1900.["]

Went to Battleship Dinner at Y.M.C.A. hut & spoke. Edward Markham [17] read poem. "If my boy misbehaves, whip the boy that sits next to him. That will frighten Johnnie & he will behave.["]

Strike ended at New York harbor of marine workers after Wilson's telegram   Men agree to go to work, always ready to arbitrate. Tug owners would not

Cabled President whether he wanted German submarines sent here for exhibition to help in Liberty loan

Sunday, January 12, 1919

Heard Dr. Wood.

---

[12] Possibly P. Chauncey Anderson, a member of the Contraband Committee of the War Trade Board in 1918.

[13] Lieutenant Commander Carlos V. Cusachs, U.S. naval attaché in Havana.

[14] Edwin S. Johnson, Democrat, U.S. Senator from South Dakota, who in refreshing contrast to his less reticent colleagues described himself in the *Congressional Directory* simply as "born in Owen County, Ind., a long time ago; was always proud of his ancestors and family."

[15] Vilhjalmur Stefansson, arctic explorer. Daniels evidently added the first two lines of this entry after the rest.

[16] Jane Wilkes, daughter of Commodore Charles Wilkes, nineteenth-century naval officer and explorer, famed for his role in the *Trent* affair in 1861.

[17] Edwin Markham, poet and author.

Monday, January 13, 1919

George P. Hampton [18] told how the Farmers' organization had resolved to stand by Wilson and League for Peace. Will send a committee to Paris to join with labor in backing up the President.

J D regarded as p.t. [presidential timber?] When I became Secy of Navy, it was thought I had been shelved. Farmers are against the reactionaries & things look brighter for 1920.

Poindexter [19] & the Coast Guard boats to be built at Seattle

F D R telegraphed that J D Jr well but keen to get home & he saw no reason why not. I wired No.

Will be Captain in 6 mo

Tuesday, January 14, 1919

Went before Naval Affairs Committee on strength of the Marine Corps. Barnett wanted 70,000. I recommended 50,000—½ temporary. Kelly [20] wanted them all brought back from Europe now. "It is army duty. They have over a million men there. Let the marines get back to do only navy duty." I said marines had been ready to fight—equipped—had won glory in France & I could not feel it right to say to Baker "We wish our boys to come back & let army do it all." It helps to train our marines.

Cabinet: Mrs. T. R. wishes to go abroad in spite of rule that no mother of soldier can go to France Had been told the rule but insisted. It will make dissatisfaction among wives & mothers of others. Refusal would create a bomb. Let her go on the ground that she is the widow of a President—commander-in-chief of Army & Navy, & wishes to go to Italy. Makes no precedent. Baker did not feel that way but fell in with it.

Burleson wished us to go into Russia

Wednesday, January 15, 1919

War Council in Secretary of Treasury's office. Glass [21] urged Baker to release his colored butler. "I have two boys in the army, and I am asking nothing for them, but I need that darky."

---

[18] Farm leader, managing director of the Farmers National Council.

[19] Miles Poindexter, Republican, U.S. Senator from Washington and a member of the Senate Naval Affairs Committee.

[20] Patrick H. Kelley, Republican, U.S. Representative from Michigan and a member of the House Naval Affairs Committee.

[21] Representative Carter Glass of Virginia had been appointed Secretary of the Treasury upon McAdoo's resignation in December, 1918. Glass served in the cabinet until November, 1919, when he resigned to accept appointment to the Senate following the death of Senator Martin.

Discussed merchant marine, embargo on tin & taking off price on coal. Glass told Garfield the first letter he ever received from a public man was from his father. "I was a member of debating society." [']Does party spirit aid or injure national life?' & he wrote G's father, who answered writing a letter with his own hand. "My father was first of all an educator & I came naturally by it."

Luncheon at Training Camp Activities Commission. Mrs. Shepard [22] & others present.

Padgett said Com. thought $35 mil. to finish destroyers should be a deficiency and I am to make estimate to Sherley.

Burleson wanted to make change of certain functions— Architects office to PO Dept   Coast Guard to the Navy.

Thursday, January 16, 1919

Went to Senate & House Military Committee to urge change in Social Hygiene Law. Saw Dent and Chamberlain. The first was not in sympathy with Baker's policy of organizing army now, abolishing Assistant Secretaries, & putting power in the General Staff

Council discussed how to demobilize with the big problem & settlement ahead of us

Maj. Bastedo [23] & her corps of women autoists

Addie went to Raleigh.

Two boys here from Sixth Regiment to dinner. Both had been gassed & in hospitals. Fine & brave marines

Cullian [24] said we could keep house at same rent.

Nebraska was the 16th state to ratify [prohibition] amendment

Friday, January 17, 1919

Attended funeral of Italian Charge d Affairs.[25] A member of cavalry said "I wish he had died in their country. I had to get up this rainy morning at 6 o'clock & must now go to Arlington before I have anything to eat"

Conference of Social Hygiene.

[22] Helen Miller Gould Shepard, wealthy philanthropist and daughter of Jay Gould, member of the Navy's Commission on Training Camp Activities.

[23] Major Helen Bastedo, leader of the Woman's Motor Corps of America.

[24] Joseph S. Cullinan, Houston oil operator, had purchased Daniels' rented Washington house at 1851 Wyoming Avenue, N.W., but agreed to let the Danielses stay at the same rent while they were in Washington. If this was a bid for influence, there is no reason to suppose that it paid off in any way for Cullinan, for Daniels remained suspicious of American oil men as a group.

[25] Count F. Miniscalchi-Erizzo, counselor of the Italian Embassy and chargé d'affaires ad interim.

Swanson, Padgett & Taylor at home late discussing naval bill
General Board or Benson stat—— [?]

Saturday, January 18, 1919

Long talk with Taft about conditions at Bethlehem. In Oct. they agreed to confer with a committee of their men. After the armistice they declined.

Attended dinner given by Davies [26] to Hon Cramer,[27] new minister to [from] the Netherlands

Sunday, January 19, 1919

Spoke at opening of K of C at Fort Washington.

Cardinal Gibbons said I had been tried in the fire of hypercriticism and had come forth pure steel.

Monday, January 20, 1919

Funeral of Mrs. Willard.[28] Rodeheaver came to sing "Jesus remembers when the world forgets."

Saw Senator Martin who roasted Baker for using lump sum money for buying three camps after the armistice

Addie came back from Raleigh. Saw the boys. Jonathan told Judge W [29] that Bryan had offered his services and was as good a soldier as T. R.

M H Stacy,[30] Acting President of University, died of influenza

Tuesday, January 21, 1919

Ford boat investigation. Man who posed as expert & had said boats were not good had written the letter in office of King [31] who was the manager of Newberry's campaign.

Cabinet. W W had cabled for opinion of cabinet on whether his prohibition order should stand. It was based on necessity of conserving coal and food. There is now plenty of both. Burleson argued that under these circumstances the order should be annulled. Marshall thought should stand. So did Glass, Gregory, & I. Redfield thought should be removed as to non-alcoholic drinks.

---

[26] Joseph E. Davies, Washington attorney and former chairman of the Federal Trade Commission.

[27] Jacob T. Cremer, Netherlands Minister to the United States.

[28] Mae Stearns Willard, wife of Captain Arthur L. Willard, commandant of the Washington Navy Yard.

[29] Probably Robert W. Winston, a former superior court judge and good family friend in Raleigh.

[30] Marvin H. Stacy, professor of civil engineering and liberal arts dean, acting president of the University of North Carolina since October.

[31] Paul H. King, prominent Detroit attorney and Republican whom the Senate investigation now revealed to have been involved in the effort to discredit the Ford Eagle boats.

All agreed. So we advised the President to let order stand as to beer &c, but that it should be annulled as to non-alcoholic drinks

Dinner at Phelans—to meet V.P. & wife. Talked about oil & how Great Britain was controlling all over the world

Hurley & Thos. F Logan [32]

Wednesday, January 22, 1919

Senate Com. on Appropriations for money to write history of the Navy. War Cabinet in Glass's office. Discussed Merchant Marine.

Rosetti [33] had put rate at $24\underline{50}$ against $12 charged by Great Britain. Our minister to China said we could get contract for engines & RR material if we could secure lower rates. But Shipping Board said it must make money on investment. I said we ought to run our ships. Baker said it was the opposite of wisdom to tie our ships up at the docks because one could get no traffic at our high rates. Decided to telegraph Wilson we must meet Great Britains rates.

Discussed RR situation. Hines [34] said 5 year extension was needed. He will ask for 500 million dollars from Congress for the RR's

Thursday, January 23, 1919

Council. The way to resume is to resume.

Build battleships. Ferguson

Friday, January 24, 1919

Padgett came to house to talk about naval program. Sherley, Garner,[35] Oliver and others wished to ask if the President thought in view of the recent situation in Europe it was necessary to authorize the three year programme of construction.

If there is to be a League of Nations why build other ships?

I cabled the President

Saturday, January 25, 1919

Had talk with Senator Trammel [36] and urged him to change the tide and vote for submission of woman suffrage amendment

Went to New York

---

[32] Former journalist, vice-chairman of the welfare committee of the Council of National Defense in 1917, special U.S. shipping commissioner at Paris, 1918–1919.

[33] John H. Rosseter, director of the division of operations of the U.S. Shipping Board.

[34] Walker D. Hines, director general of the U.S. Railroad Administration.

[35] John N. Garner, Democrat, U.S. Representative from Texas and a member of the House Ways and Means Committee.

[36] Park Trammel, Democrat, U.S. Senator from Florida, whom Daniels was seeking to persuade to support the woman suffrage amendment which had been defeated in the Senate the previous October.

Sunday, January 26, 1919

Spoke at Italian victory meeting in New York at Metropolitan Opera House. La Guardia [37] defended the Treaty of London [38] and replied to criticism of Italy for making bargain for Adriatic ports before entering the war

Mr. Reihle,[39] Pres. Dem Club called. Doubted if Dems. could win in 1920. If so, he would favor J——

Monday, January 27, 1919

Talked to Baker about delay in hearing from marines & soldiers. Mothers at home are anxious. Will cable in any case.

Case of criticism of Army because returned wounded soldiers convalescent are forced to wash their own clothes at Walter Reed hospital. I told Braisted to see that clothes of marines & sailors in hospitals were washed at expense of the Navy.

Talked to Macy [40] about wages.

Took dinner at Mitchell Palmer's.

Tuesday, January 28, 1919

Went before Naval Committee in behalf of bridge from Portsmouth to Kittery.

Cabinet discussed Shipping Board and plan of Whipple [41] to have all shipping across ocean in one great corporation, the Government to guarantee dividend   Redfield said delays of Shipping Board had cost millions of dollars of business to be lost by this country   Decided to cable President

Cable from the President that it would be fatal not to build the three year programme.

Wednesday, January 29, 1919

At Carter Glass discussed in Weekly Conference ocean freight rates. Mr. Rossiter explained that we had all the freight our ships could carry at prices fixed. We had tried to work in agreement with Great Britain. They protested any reduction in rates and yet quietly booked orders at rates lower than quoted.

[37] Fiorello H. La Guardia, Republican, U.S. Representative from New York, former major, U.S. Flying Force on Italian front.

[38] By this treaty of April 26, 1915, the Allies induced Italy to enter the war in return for a promise of the south Tyrol, Istria, parts of Dalmatia and Albania, the Dodecanese Islands, and a share in Turkey and the German colonies.

[39] John M. Riehle, president of the National Democratic Club of New York.

[40] Valentine Everit Macy, chairman of the wartime shipbuilding wage adjustment committee and umpire for the War Labor Board.

[41] Sherman L. Whipple, general counsel of the U.S. Shipping Board.

We thought Rossiter should reduce to as near pre-war rates as possible so as to let us build up markets and get trade for our country. As to future policy on shipping, decided to lay facts before the President

Went to Balto. to speak at Eastern Shore Society

Dr. Finney: [42] Are you an American　No　I am a Marine

Banquet given to Mr. Bryan in recognition of his service in securing prohibition. They gave him a loving cup

Thursday, January 30, 1919

Went to Annapolis

Mrs. E[berle]—Husband perfect man

Mann said I ought to be impeached [43]

Appointed Scales to succeed Eberle

Friday, January 31, 1919

Spoke to class of 330 Reserve officers who graduated at Annapolis.

House Com. unanimously favored three year naval programme. It had been long and hard fight.

I sent cable to the President.

Dined at Miss Mabel Boardman's.

Sunday, February 2, 1919

Goldsboro

Monday, February 3, 1919

Raleigh.

Wednesday, February 5, 1919

Spoke before Rivers & Harbors Convention at the Willard Hotel

Dinner given by J. Hampton Moore [1] to John H. Small

[42] Brigadier General John M. T. Finney, professor of clinical surgery at Johns Hopkins, recently returned as chief consultant in surgery of the A.E.F. in France.

[43] The day before, Representative Mann had charged that Daniels ought to be impeached for using Navy uncommitted funds to begin purchase of the Marconi and Federal radio systems in the United States. In response the House deleted from a Navy deficiency appropriation bill the $4,300,000 Daniels had recommended for the purchase of these private radio systems. Daniels was eager to make radio transmission a government monopoly under the Navy before he left office.

---

[1] Joseph Hampton Moore, Republican, U.S. Representative from Pennsylvania.

"Let the Gold Dust twins do the work."
Com. on Appropriations on Social Hygiene Board
Dinner at Salisburys [2]

Thursday, February 6, 1919
I spoke before Woman's Congressional Club
Dinner to Naval Affairs Committee by Mr. Butler at Shoreham.
Roosevelt requested him to recommend Mr Dance, who had been friend of
R—— in the West. Dance did not go into P.O. but once in four years. Re-
appointed   "Tell him to go in and sleep at least one night in P.O." & "Remem-
ber this administration runs strictly on merit."
McKinley asked him to name a Southern woman P.M. Mrs. McK had
gone to school to the lady's mother. Butler agreed & McK said: "I will give
your man place as P.O. inspector.["]

Friday, February 7, 1919
Spoke at Congressional Club on The Navy & Woman in the War
Wrote to W W urging appoint[men]t of Mitchell Palmer [3]

Sunday, February 9, 1919
Heard Mr. Chappell
Lodge on Roosevelt at Capitol
Mrs. Lane told Addie J D was most talked about

Monday, February 10, 1919
Saw Spencer Wood [4] & talked about Boston conditions
Thomas Mott Osborne wanted a ship manned entirely by men from Ports-
mouth prison
Billy Sunday here to dinner
Bishop McDowell & others

Saturday, February 15, 1919
Went to New York
Spoke at St. Paul Meth ch. in New York
Also at banquet of Maritime Club on Merchant Marine.

Sunday, February 16, 1919
Spoke at the Cathedral of St John the Divine
Dined with Ambassador Gerard.

[2] Probably Willard Saulsbury, Democrat, U.S. Senator from Delaware.
[3] Palmer was appointed Attorney General on March 1.
[4] Rear Admiral Spencer S. Wood, commandant of the First Naval District, with headquarters at Boston.

Monday, February 17, 1919
Sitting with Mr. Baker for bust

Tuesday, February 18, 1919
Went to see Sen. Chamberlain about Hygiene bill
Went to give sitting for portrait
Cabinet discussed bond issue. Glass had asked Congress to pass bill without fixing rate of interest. To name rate two months in advance would cause depression & rush of sale of present bond issue.
Redfield said War & Navy were offering Coast & Geodetic men more pay than he could give & we ought to quit it.
Dined with Frank Polk. Mrs. Simon had been in Mexico—before that in Serbia—then Armenia. War in each country when she was there. Thought Mexicans bandits
Attended reception at Cong Club to Speaker and Mrs Clark

Wednesday, February 19, 1919
Talked with Garfield about importance of plan so that RR's & big corporations will not get coal at cost and make the people pay more
Conviction of Dr Benj. Davis [5] for selling approval of applicants to enter Naval Reserve & investigation of New York office.
Dined with William Philips
Dr. Draper [6] went to Great Lakes. Said Dr. Monk had right idea about carriers of meningitis & argued & convinced Dr. Flexner. Before idea was to isolate carrier. Dr M said "Give him direction of recruits for 6 weeks & there would be no danger[."]

Thursday, February 20, 1919
Conf. with Baker and Hurley. Last named had agreed no overtime work, but Board had permitted it instead of two shifts and now we are forced to grant it on transports to hasten return of soldiers to [*sic*] Europe.
Long talk with Whipple about what to do about ships & shipping board He favors selling all to a private corp, the Gov. to guarantee small dividend, & have power to fix salaries &c if it has to pay guarantee.
Dined with Minister from the Netherlands. V.P. criticized Burleson & Hitchcock for trying to line up men for League.

[5] Lieutenant Benjamin S. Davis, an assistant surgeon assigned to the New York receiving ship, had been convicted of accepting bribes to obtain soft Naval Reserve assignments for men facing the draft. Other arrests and convictions followed.
[6] Probably William K. Draper, professor of clinical medicine at the College of Physicians and Surgeons, New York.

Friday, February 21, 1919

Went with Aydlett [7] to ask Gregory to make address at NC Bar Asso

Talked to Swanson about Navy bill. Lodge & Penrose wish it to go over to next Congress. He hopes at the psychological moment to put it through, but odds are all against it. He favors returning RR's to the owners & not shouldering the loss.

Dinner with Egan [8] at the Shoreham to discuss turning work of Training Camp Activities over to the Navy, Navigation Department with a Morale officer at each station and on each ship.

Saturday, February 22, 1919

Called up President on the George Washington 800 miles at sea and gave him message that he would receive warm welcome here. Could not hear his voice, but New Mexico received it by telephone. Current not strong enough on George Washington

Dined with Vice President. Spanish Ambassador [9] the guest of honor.

Hugh Wallace and wife ready to go to France.

V.P. Rather talked against League of Peace. —said he had not made up his mind and that it ought to be discussed without attempt to line up Senators as Burleson was trying to do.

Sunday, February 23, 1919

Heard Mr. Chappell on "Thou Fool, This night shalt thy soul be required of thee." He quoted soldier in France who gave best definition of faith. "It is betting your life that God is true."

Jonathan Jackson & wife at dinner

DeWitt Lockman [10] also. He is painting portrait & went for sitting.

President arrived in Boston.

Monday, February 24, 1919

Senate Naval Affairs Committee seems inclined to debate every proposition. Are they resolved not to let the bill pass at this session?

Settled Bliss torpedo company & obtained right to manufacture by extending time of completion.

President reached Boston.

[7] Edwin F. Aydlett, prominent North Carolina Democrat and attorney.

[8] John J. Eagan, Atlanta capitalist, chairman of the Navy's Commission on Training Camp Activities during the war.

[9] Don Juan Riaño y Gayangos.

[10] New York artist specializing in portraits.

Tuesday, February 25, 1919

At Cabinet meeting W W detailed story of Peace Conference with many incidents. French resolved & British wish cost of war to be borne equally by all engaged. Would mean that this country would renounce all British, French & Italian debts & then some. He fenced to keep this direct proposition from coming to a head. He thought Venezolos [11] the biggest man he met. Smuts [12] he called "a brick" Lloyd George practical man but no idealist.

Told of gunner of Plunketts guns: "Kills everybody within 100 mi & hunts up his next of kin & kills them[."]

At first Press of Paris were told to do three things

1. Magnify Rep. opposition to Wilson
2. Make it appear conditions in Russia worse than they are
3. Cause it to appear that Germany is able to renew the war

Extra session talk. Reps. will not pass appro bills. Would he agree to call extra session within 30 days of his return from [Paris?]

Wednesday, February 26, 1919

Garfield at War Cabinet proposed councils of employes & employers
Dinner to National Dem. Com

Thursday, February 27, 1919

Wrote oil letter to Senator Swanson who put it in Congressional Record.[13]
Parade for soldiers from France
Senator Shafroth [14] on oil bill

Friday, February 28, 1919

Discussed medals of honor &c
Also uniforms
What shall we do with Merchant Marine?
 " about the ships Great B wishes to buy from American company?
Whipple

------

[11] Eleutherios Venizelos, premier of Greece.
[12] Jan Christiaan Smuts, South African statesman and supporter of the League of Nations.
[13] Daniels used this means to express his opposition to the conference committee's agreed version of the oil lands leasing bill, because he did not consider that it provided adequate protection for the naval oil reserves.
[14] John F. Shafroth, Democrat, U.S. Senator from Colorado, 1913–1919.

Saturday, March 1, 1919

Had talk with President about French decorations. Decided in view of their being given to Army men, to accept and confer them.

"I feel like swearing" said the President referring to the filibuster in Congress.

Weaver [1] unseated & Britt [2] seated

President said Great Britain would be very sore if we bought the stock in the Mercantile Marine Co & we would get so little advantage (we could not get ships since Maclay [3] says he would take them) would it be worthwhile?

Tuesday, March 11, 1919

Called to see Lord Reading at his request (he had gout or something in his foot). He wished to cable British Admiralty of my coming, party &c [4] "I never thought it work," he said "between 10 & 4 when in the court-room. I enjoyed it. My work was getting up early in the morning at 4 o'clock and preparing my briefs &c and in conference in the evening. If a man loves what he is doing it is not work.["] Said he was returning to GB to his duty as CJ. All right in war, but wished to go back on the bench before people asked. Said 6 weeks ago in Paris he favored sending food into Germany

Discussed League of Nations at Cabinet. Also need of Extra session wh. all members favored & I was to express their views to W W. Also discussed bond issue. Glass had not enough to give war insurance & allowance to soldiers. Ought to have extra session May 5 Reps. will investigate everything & Kitchin wanted strong Democrats named on all such committees.

Scales and Smith on status of civilian professors

Saunders & Naval Consulting Board

Gherardi [5] at home to-night. Talked of Germany & Bolshevism. Believed Russia would come to herself

Philips & decorations

[1] Zebulon Weaver, Democrat, U.S. Representative from North Carolina since 1917.

[2] James J. Britt, Republican, who had held Weaver's seat during the Sixty-fourth Congress (1915–1917), and who now successfully challenged Weaver's right to sit in the dying Sixty-fifth Congress and thus regained the seat for three days. Weaver resumed his seat in the new Sixty-sixth Congress after March 4, 1919, however.

[3] Sir Joseph P. Maclay, British Minister of Shipping and large shipowner.

[4] Daniels and his wife were about to depart on a two-month tour of Navy installations in Europe.

[5] Captain Walter R. Gherardi, just returned from service with the U.S. delegation at the Paris Peace Conference.

Friday, March 14, 1919
 Left for New York at 2 o'clock.
 Went to Ritz-Carlton, the guest of [blank]
 Spoke with Homer Cummings at New York Democratic Club.
 Hensley resolution [6] had committed us.

Saturday, March 15, 1919
 Went to Aeroplane Exhibition with Admirals
 Left [Hotel] Martinique 2 o'clock for Leviathan [7]   Welcomed with salutes

Sunday, March 16, 1919
 Spoke at 10 a.m.
 Spoke to sailors at 4 pm

Tuesday, March 18, 1919
 Conference with Y.M.C.A workers

Friday, March 21, 1919
 Spoke to Jewish Welfare workers

Sunday, March 23, 1919
 Reached Brest
 No
 Guest of Vice Admiral & Mrs Moreau [8]
 Dinner with Gen. Butler [9] & all officers
 Spoke to Sailors at Y.M.C.A. hut
 Dinner

Monday, March 24, 1919
 Spent most of day at Camp Pontanezon

[6] A reference to an amendment by Representative Walter L. Hensley, Democrat of Missouri, a member of the Naval Affairs Committee, to the naval appropriation act of August, 1916, which declared it to be U.S. policy to favor the peaceful settlement of disputes and authorized the President to call an international conference to achieve this end. Daniels argued that this was congressional approval of the League of Nations concept.

[7] The Daniels party sailed for France aboard the *Leviathan,* formerly the German transatlantic liner *Vaterland,* which had been interned in the United States upon the outbreak of the war and was subsequently taken over and operated by the Navy as a troop transport.

[8] The maritime prefect at Brest.

[9] Brigadier General Smedley D. Butler, commanding Camp Pontanezen, the U.S. embarkation center at Brest. Butler had shrewdly selected Josephus, Jr., as his aide, and assigned him to accompany his father on much of his trip around Europe.

Spoke to officers. Went all over camp
Lunch with officers at Navy Club given by Commodore Todd
Left at 5 30

Tuesday, March 25, 1919
Reached Paris 9:30
Saw M. E. Stone about using Naon station for wireless and took it up with
Benson and communication officer as [to] its practicability. Great complaint of
American correspondents that there are not enough facilities to send news to
America.
Long conference with Benson at rooms. Read long paper he prepared with
reference to disposition of German ships

Wednesday, March 26, 1919
Long talk with Benson & House. Lunched with the latter.
Called to see Minister of Marine. He asked the secret of success of Navy
administration & no criticism.
Visited sights.
House asked advice about [blank] [10]
Went to Opera—Henry VIII—with Admiral Long [11]
Capt Pomade [12] said State pensioned actors & actresses. They received very
little pay. Generally they are kept by some very rich man.

Thursday, March 27, 1919
Long talk with Grasty.[13] Shifty politician
Wilson is a Svengali & his tact & diplomacy have been wonderful & people
believe in him.
Went to see Peace Commission & arranged trip to Italy & gave dates for
Great Britain.
Lunched with the President & Mrs. W. He took us all over the house,
showing the wonderful bath-rooms. "Now come, let me show you the re-
frigerator where I sleep"—no heat at all in it. Also in Mrs. W's bath-room.
Painted cherry blossoms on the walls. "The only exercise I get is to my vo-
cabulary,["] W W said

[10] In his own diary Colonel House explained: "Secretary Daniels came in just before and
remained to lunch. I submitted to him the amendments we have in mind to made [*sic*]
to the Covenant in order to appease the recalcitrants in the Senate. He thought well of what
I had in mind." Diary, March 26, 1919, House MSS.
[11] Rear Admiral Andrew T. Long, assigned to the Supreme War Council in London and
naval attaché at the U.S. Embassy in Paris.
[12] Commander Lea Pamade, a French liaison officer assigned to the Daniels party.
[13] Charles H. Grasty, treasurer and staff correspondent of the *New York Times*.

Lloyd George wished me to see Mr. Long,[14] First Lord of the Admiralty, & Admiral Wemyss [15] about naval building program, & President hoped we could talk it over and reach some right understanding.[16]

Friday, March 28, 1919

Went to Chateau Therry [*sic*], Belleau Woods, Soissons and Rheims.

Gen Feelan [17] & Maj Chas M Busbee,[18] both of whom took part in the fight were with us

Saturday, March 29, 1919

Conference with Wemyss & Benson. Benson talked very straight to Wemyss who wanted us to agree to a larger Navy for G.B. than America should build. Not a minority stockholder

Lunched with Ambassador & Mrs. Jusserand

Sunday, March 30, 1919

Napoleon's Tomb.

Pasteurs tomb & monument.

Long talk with Col. House. He thought we could afford to have no programme of naval construction now if others would do likewise.[19]

[14] Walter H. Long, formerly Colonial Secretary, recently appointed First Lord of the Admiralty.

[15] Admiral of the Fleet Sir Rosslyn Erskine Wemyss, First Sea Lord, 1917–1918.

[16] Since the British had largely suspended the construction of capital ships during the war, they were much opposed to any continuation of American naval construction, such as the three-year program Daniels was advocating, that would threaten British naval supremacy. Daniels and Benson considered the three-year program necessary in and of itself; Wilson and certainly House looked upon it as a bargaining lever at the Peace Conference. House recorded in his Diary on this date: "Secretary Daniels was in for a moment this morning. Steed was about to interview him for the Northcliffe Press. I caught him in time to tell him what to say and what not to say. It was a dangerous interview because he does not know how thoroughly Lloyd George and the British dislike him, and how much they resent the foolish things he has been saying in the United States about our naval program." Diary, March 27, 1919, House MSS.

[17] Brigadier General Logan Feland, a much-decorated Marine Corps war hero.

[18] A prominent Raleigh attorney and old friend of Daniels'.

[19] House recorded this conversation as follows: "Secretary Daniels followed Balfour. He is having conferences with the British as to a naval program. The British are insisting, largely by direction of Lloyd George, that the American[s] agree that Great Britain shall always have a larger navy than the United States. Daniels wish[ed] advice. I told him it was utterly impossible to agree to such a condition. I thought he might consent to an agreement that both should stop building after our present building program was finished, so that the two navies would remain in relatively the same proportion as they then would be. I thought we should finish our two year program, which is now under way. This will put us fairly close to the British, perhaps, within 75% of them, but with a better class of ships." Diary, March 30, 1919, House MSS.

Long talk with Benson who thought we could not agree to any limitation on hulls. If any nation has preponderance of naval strength it will have an undue weight.

Monday, March 31, 1919

Had conference with Mr. Long (GB). He had been sent for by Lloyd George to come over after L G had asked W W to see if we could reach an agreement as to size of Navy. I explained that so far as programme already authorized, could do nothing but build those ships. The larger program (for 3 years) that passed the House was dependent upon League of Nations & would not be necessary if League was firmly established and all nations agreed to reduction of armament. He said L G could not support League of Nations if U.S. accompanied it by big building programs, for GB could not consent to any other nation having the supremacy of the sea. I pointed out that G.B. would still have more ships than America. Long said it would not be difficult for us to agree but public sentiment in Great Britain was very much alarmed by our building program. He said he was not fully informed as to Prime Ministers desire, but would see him and have later conference. Later I sent word to L. G. that I must go to Rome Tuesday & would like to see him (the President wished it) before going. He asked me to come to breakfast the next morning.

Saw Presidt at 6 pm.

Tuesday, April 1, 1919

Up early & breakfasted with Lloyd George and Long and discussed League of Nations. L. G said L[eague] of N[ations] would be worth nothing if we continued to build—he would ostentatiously throw into the sea & sink—all German ships awarded to GB, they had stopped work on their cruisers, & we ought to stop work if we really trusted the League Wilson wanted. I asked him if such an agreement was a condition precedent. Of course not, but L of N would be a mere piece of rhetoric if we continued to build—if America has no confidence in it, who could have. I told him I could not make such agreement or understanding, for anything done must be public & printed in all papers. He said he never meant any agreemt that could not be submitted to Parliamt & Congress. We parted to go to see President at 11. Saw him   L G rather insisted I should not go to Rome but go at some later date. I convinced President it would be unwise after all arrangements had been made to postpone but would cut my trip short & return Monday. Acquiesced. I called to see Long & told him.[1]

Wednesday, April 2, 1919

Met at Turin by Commander Sansonia who accompanied us to Rome. Senator [blank] called at Genoa.

Reached Rome at 9:30 met by Ambassador & Mrs Page, Admiral del Bono,[2] & others & taken to Hotel Grand. Out of window could see the Diocletian baths & glorious view of mountains.

Thursday, April 3, 1919

Went to call on Ambassador Page. Cordial. Told me incidents of interest, something of his troubles, & then we went sight-seeing, devoting the day also to calls on all the Ministers of State in the old palaces that had been converted into public buildings. Gave Page letters from Cardinal Gibbons & Archbishop Hayes,[3] but they could not be presented until I had first seen the King. Some captain, a Catholic, had called first on the Pope & then the King would not receive them until they had left Italy & had returned again. Brother of Mayor of Rome, who lives in the house his ancestors have occupied 1,000 years has two sons—one a secretary of the Pope; other in Foreign office. They live in the same house, but they cannot both call at Vatican or Foreign office so strict is the separation

Wonderful dinner of 50 or more at Ambassador Page's.

Friday, April 4, 1919

Went at 11 with Page to call on the King. He is dressed as high ranking officer, leggins [sic] & all. Rather short of stature. His wife is tall & an Italian told me with pride that the children are like their mother. King very frank, well informed, and courteous. Remained ¾ of an hour. He said 400,000 Italians killed & million wounded & died from sickness. He hoped Peace Commission would act soon. Uncertainty is injurious. He thinks little of Cheko-Slovaks [Yugoslavs?]. "I know them well. They will kill you— In 5 minutes they are very sorry—naturally very sorry, but you are dead.["] Not

---

[1] The ubiquitous Colonel House reported: "Secretary Daniels came to tell of the progress in the negotiations with the British regarding navy building. He is much worried over it, particularly of the insistence of Lloyd George that we should admit that Great Britain shall always have a larger navy than ours. Daniels says Benson takes the position that our Navy should be fully equal to that of Great Britain's. He said Benson was stubborn and asked me to talk with him." Diary, April 1, 1919, House MSS.

[2] Italian Minister of Marine.

[3] Patrick Joseph Hayes, Archbishop of New York.

capable of self control. Talked about Montenegro & its claims. Page talked of press propaganda & the King said it was like Achilles ——— it hurt when it cut but it healed before much harm was done. "But I must not detain you longer," he said after ¾ hour.

Went to St. Peters with Page & then to his house to lunch—just family lunch —& he said grace, the first time I had heard it since I left America. He has resigned and wishes time and leisure to write some books, the material for which he has been collecting. He has had a hard four years—most expensive too—is highly esteemed—& his wife needs the change which he seeks. She is fine & gave me card case made by Italian soldier

To Town [?], Coliseum, Catacombs &c

Admiral Del Bono gave beautiful dinner. He read a fine speech in Italian & I replied without notes in English.

Saturday, April 5, 1919

Went at 9 am to Methodist school in Rome in response to invitation of Miss Vickery. Over 200 bright faced children sang "The Star Spangled Banner" & Italian national air. Addie & I spoke. They could hardly let her leave. We were given Italian medals.

10 a.m. went with Senator [blank] (archeologist) to see statue of Juno just unearthed and brought to Rome & other ancient statues which had been discovered. He took us to St. Pauls, said the architecture might do for a dance hall or a theatre & was not fitting for church. Thomas Nelson Page with us.

Lunched at Hotel Excelsior with acting Prime Minister ———, who is acting in absence of Orlando.[4] Went to dinner with Countess ———, whose husband is in diplomatic service. She is a Cuban whose father became an American citizen. She had been ardent American & when A entered the war her friends in Rome asked: What can America do? It is 3,000 miles away— & she told them Americans can do the impossible and her faith was justified. Most of company could not speak English & I could not speak Italian.

Spoke at Y.M.C.A. to American soldiers & sailors.

Visited prison where Paul was incarcerated.

Left at 9:30 p.m. Ambassador Page, Del Bono & others at train. Addie and party remained behind.

Del Bono made us handsome presents.

Pope regretted owing to previous engagement with French priests & celebration in hon of Joan of Arc

---

[4] Vittorio E. Orlando, the Italian premier, in Paris as the head of the Italian peace delegation.

Sunday, April 6, 1919

Slept until after nine o'clock & dressed just before we reached Genoa. Went out to see the monument to Columbus erected there. After breakfast, we started again to Paris. The day bright and sunny and shortly we came in sight of the Alps covered with snow, rising directly from the plains, with the sun shining on the snow.

Supper 7:30 at Modane, France, filled with soldiers—Italians, French, Americans. Just before we left a train came in filled with British soldiers, most of them Australians, who had been away from home nearly four years—forty in a car—jolly, bright, and made the night merry with songs a la a college glee club. Some of them were cavalrymen. "The Egyptians made a bit of trouble" said one "and we had to postpone the armistice.["]

Two Am. chums (one from Brooklyn & one from Iowa) had been on leave in Italy. Fine fellows.

I felt bad to be riding in a special car & these brave fellows sleeping in box cars on the floor

Two years ago to-day the United States entered the war.

Monday, April 7, 1919

Reached Paris 10 a.m. Long talk with Benson who feels B——[ritain] is trying to dictate naval matters in order to control commerce. Suggested I do not talk with them unless he or someone else present as I might be misunderstood or misquoted to my great injury at home.[5] When Benson met me (½ hour late because train was ahead of time) he said Admiral Wemyss had been inquiring when I would arrive as he wished to meet me at the train. Benson thought it cheeky. I did not wish to see him or Long until I could communicate with the President. He said: ["]Please say you have seen the President and have found him deeply concerned about the whole method with which the whole peace program is being handled and that you have been instructed by the President to say that he cannot make any sort of agreement until he sees what the outcome is going to be." I made appt to see Long. Talked about my visit to G.B. and he thought it best to go to Scapa Flow and Rosyth &

[5] Admiral Benson was evidently afraid that Daniels might be persuaded to compromise on the U.S. big navy program, and preferred to handle the naval negotiations himself. After seeking to convince Benson that the new League of Nations ought not to be launched amidst a naval arms race, Colonel House noted: "He agrees to this, but insists there is a great principle involved. He wanted me to ask the President to keep Secretary Daniels away from Paris now that he has gone to Italy. The President flatly refused this when I put the matter to him." Diary, April 3, 1919, House MSS. Daniels, who had jumped Benson over five senior captains and twenty-six admirals to be the first Chief of Naval Operations in 1915 and who trusted him completely, would have been deeply hurt had he known of this disloyalty.

Scotland first and then come back to London when members of Parliament had returned from Easter holiday. He thought we might make agreements on principle to stop building and get together on details when I reached England. I then gave him the views of the President, & of course the matter was not pressed further. He will see L. G. Later I talked to the President & told him of conversation with Long. L. G. & W W will now take it up. W W's position greatly relieved me.

Dinner with B. Baruch. The more he saw of GB the more he felt US was only nation that approached unselfishness & our best hope to protect the peace of the world was a strong American Navy. Saw Vance McCormick. He and Baruch are doing very important work & will compromise anything except principle and justice. Others here have compromised and shifted so long think frank statement sensational. Met Belgian Minister to U.S. who invited us to come to Brussells. [sic]

Madame Jusserand called & brought letter to Addie about some lace for Mrs. Dewey. Had delightful talk with her. She told, with tears in her eyes, of French people returning to devastated homes. One party or family had returned & were getting ready. Had no water except from polluted wells & the question was who should first drink the water to see if were poisoned. The grandfather, 80 years old, said: "I will be the first. Most of my life is behind me and it is fittest for me to go if any are to be poisoned. You can say of me that I died trying to restore France[."]

Tuesday, April 8, 1919

Had call from E. J. Sadler,[6] of SO (Naval Academy graduate) who destroyed oil wells when Germany invaded Rumania. He said it too[k] G 9 months to get oil from wells, & now about a normal ¾ production was being secured. The British have purchased the Dutch Shell Company & Lord Cowdray's [7] interests in Mex. Two years ago Cowdray offered to sell to SO by [but?] GB would not permit, & GB was reaching out everywhere to obtain oil in order to strengthen its maritime commerce. It is believed it will be a mandatory for Mesopotamia & some provisions should be incorporated in treaty of peace that all mandatory countries should be open on equal terms to all allied countries. Otherwise GB will control oil in Mesipotamia [sic] and other countries where it is the mandatory power while enjoying equal or better advantages with U.S. in US & countries where U.S. has power. He will write memo. for the President.

[6] Everit J. Sadler, manager of Romano-Americano Oil Company of Bucharest, 1909–1916.
[7] Weetman D. Pearson, first Viscount Cowdray, who had developed extensive oil holdings in Mexico during the last years of the Díaz regime.

Calls from C M Busbee, John Hall Manning, Wright T. Dixon, Marvin W. Hardy, soldiers from North Carolina. Hardy said, when NC boys in 30th Div. were selected to lead in breaking Hindenburgs Line on Sep. 29th: "They are easy to kill but hard as hell to stop." I urged all these boys to write the history of that fight where N.C. troops did so well from his own standpoint while the memory of it was fresh in their minds and they promised they would do so and send home. N.C. boys in all wars have fought well, but delayed writing history of their deeds until others had in some cases pre-empted recognition belonging to them.

Benson detailed facts of how GB trying to get control of oil wells in countries.

He attended meeting of allied naval council who discussed action navies might have to take if Germany had no government to sign treaty of peace. There is fear Ebert [8] gov. may fall before peace is declared

Wednesday, April 9, 1919

Italian Ambassador [9] called and with much feeling spoke about the condition of his country—the need for two important ports on Dalmatian coast to protect Italy. He was most earnest and pleaded with me to see the President in behalf of his country which he feared would be sacrificed to help Cheko-Slovaks who had fought against Italy & predicted that if Servia, Checks & Slovaks were in one government there would be trouble as Croatians would not accept Servian King. They wanted a Republic. He feared if Italy did not get its claims the Gov. would be overthrown and Bolshevism would be enthroned. He spoke almost with tears in his eyes so deep was his feeling.

Thompson [10] (Asso. Press) called & he hoped President would exercise patience—that if he should leave Europe would go to pieces. Must make concessions. The order for the George Washington [11] had troubled the people & made them fear the President would lay down terms & leave if not accepted. Without League of Peace anything may happen here.

Benson brought up paper prepared by Scofield & McNamee [12] on naval needs & advocating America & England having equal navies to protect the peace of the world.

[8] Friedrich Ebert, German chancellor and socialist leader, subsequently the first provisional president of the German Republic.

[9] Count Macchi di Cellere.

[10] Charles T. Thompson, superintendent of foreign service of the Associated Press.

[11] Wilson's order that his ship, the *George Washington*, be made ready for his return to the United States if the Peace Conference remained deadlocked.

[12] Captain Frank H. Schofield and Captain Luke McNamee, members of the naval advisory staff of the U.S. delegation to the Peace Conference.

Lunched at Press Club with Mr. Solden [?] (N.Y. Times) Club Room is a palace built by wealthy merchant who tried to break into society. It did not succeed & French Gov. commandeered it for Press Club for all newspaper correspondents.

Went to Mrs. Wilson's reception. Met Mrs. Lamont [13] with her husband (She is sister in law to Gavitt [14] of N.Y. Evening Post). "I wished to meet you" she said & now my husband says we must go and I do not wish to go. Why do you go then? He has the car. Let him take the car and I will take you home.

Dinner with Vance McCormick & several army officers.

Thursday, April 10, 1919

Jap. Naval attache, Capt. Nomura,[15] called.

Lewis D. Cranshaw & Maj. Hugh O'Bear called to ask me to speak at 100th anniversary of founding Univ. of Va. Will place tablet of Jefferson on building occupied by Jefferson in Paris.

Call from Admiral Grou (Gront) [?] who represented French Navy in N.Y. during the war. He hopes to return.

Lunched with Lansings. Gen. Bliss there who said all the countries were planning to keep an army greater than they had before the war. American people curious. In peace they call soldiers murderers. In war they give no heed to man whose brain makes victory in the field possible and give glory only to those covered with the most gore of their own and their foes. Lansing told of writing in his diary his doubts about Russia when the Root Commission came back optimistic

Went to Senate where Senators spoke in praise of Sharp for his interest in aviation—said he was present when Wilbur Wright made first ascent at Fort Myers & to Alexandria. Americans conquered in flying first. France had done most to develop the conquest of the air, & he fully expected to see the U.S. Navy craft "which the great Sec. of Navy (applause) was making ready to send as he crossed the Atlantic the next week.["]

Called on Queen of Roumania [16] & discussed woman's place in the new world. She spoke with pride of the work she had done in the war—all kinds of work & of how proud it made her that the King & people fully trusted her

---

[13] Florence Haskell Corliss Lamont, wife of Thomas W. Lamont, J. P. Morgan partner and financial adviser to the U.S. delegation.

[14] John P. Gavit, former managing editor of the *New York Evening Post,* 1913–1918, currently a director of Harper and Brothers; brother-in-law of T. W. Lamont. Gavit had supported Daniels editorially in the past.

[15] Kichisaburo Nomura, Japanese naval attaché in Washington, 1915–1918.

[16] Marie, English-born Queen of Rumania, consort of King Ferdinand I.

and had sent her to try to help her country. When President Wilson called she asked how his League would touch other nations, & when he said it would help smaller nations she said she hoped, but looked with one eye behind her because she feared selfishness. The people must help Roumania, else who will wish to be virtuous? I complimented her on division of land so those who tilled it would become land owners. She said the King was very wise in that he took the step early before it was demanded. "But it isn't easy. Yesterday I could look over great stretches of corn [?] & say: It is mine. Now I can say it was mine.["]

Cary Grayson to dinner.

Friday, April 11, 1919

Went to find where John Paul Jones was buried. 43–45–47 Rue Grange Aux Belles. St. Louis hospital opposite & was formerly cemetery of St. Laurent but has been built over and no mark to show where Jones was buried.

Visited Tomb of LaFayette. Wilson, Pershing & Joffre had flowers. Is in Picpus [?] cemetery. Hard to find in yard of the Church of the Sacred heart. No longer used as a cemetery. Burial place of older families of France. 1300 bodies of people who lost their lives in French Revolution are buried there. Used dates they adopted at that time when they abandoned the year after Christ. Lafayette & wife buried in separate vaults & his son George Washington buried near.

"To the great Lafayette
From a fellow servant of liberty"   W. W.

Visited Y.W.C.A. headquarters in Place of Edward VII. Miss Harriet Taylor & Mrs. Cushman.

In afternoon attended session of Plenary Peace Council in Foreign office. Beautiful room crowded. Every delegate present. Clemenceau presided, Wilson & Lloyd George on either side. Mr. Barnes,[17] Labor M.P. prefaced resolutions by address depicting condition & menace of men of labor who had never had their rights, & said better conditions & steady employment must be provided. Others made addresses. Belgian delegate, M. Van de Heund [Emile Vandervelde] said choice was between the quick method of Russia or the slower method of Britain, and they had chosen the latter. W. W. invited first conference in Oct. to meet in Washington & expressed regret at enforced absence of Mr. Gompers, President of the Committee of Promotion of International

[17] George N. Barnes, Labor M.P. and former trade unionist, a member of the British delegation to the Peace Conference.

Regulations of Labor Conditions. Depends on Peace League and is fashioned on League of Nations lines. Afterwards talked to Lloyd George who spoke of presence & speeches of men from all parts of the world

Saturday, April 12, 1919
    Lunched with Col. House who "between us and the angels" told me of the steps taken at the two long sessions of the Council & how Cecil [18] had stood with us for M[onroe] D[octrine] and France had fought it for more than an hour. Clemenceau had promised H—— to do anything he could if Conference were held in Paris. Family rallied [?] Col—— on diplomacy and indirection. Talked about naval programme   "Nothing more important here than the questions you have touched." Discussed my trip to London & I outlined my speech which he thought good & said he would furnish extract from President's speech in London which might furnish a guide.[19]
    Went to see presentation of flags to first American aviators who served with France. Beautiful ceremony & good speeches. A French aviator hand[ed] flag to each American aviator, they saluted, then clasped hands. Lady dressed as Goddess of Liberty sang Star Spangled Banner and the curtain went down & an encore called for a second singing of Star Spangled Banner   an unheard of event, showing enthusiasm. Preceding presentation was a play "The Magic Cup," followed by ballet of women with such scant costumes as to be more than indecent. Benson and I agreed that such exhibitions to our young soldiers were disgraceful, but is America much better? Yes, decidedly in general if not in theatres.
    Attended exercises where overseas Alumni of Univ of Va. placed a tablet on Corner of rue de Berri and Avenue des Champs-Elysees on 100th anniversary of founding of University. It was on this spot Jefferson lived when he

[18] Lord Robert Cecil, one of the strong supporters of the League of Nations among the British delegates to the Peace Conference. Cecil, a close friend of Colonel House, was attempting with Lloyd George's blessing to settle the dispute over naval construction. Although Lloyd George and some members of the British delegation were disposed to tie the naval question with the United States–sponsored amendment specifying that the League Covenant did not affect the Monroe Doctrine, Cecil had backed the Americans against the French in the debate on April 10.
[19] Daniels was evidently irked by House's air of mystery and condescension—his frequent admonition "between us and the angels"—and his taking over the negotiations over the naval dispute. At the same time Daniels probably did not suspect the extent of the House-Cecil discussions. House reported after this meeting: "Secretary Daniels took lunch with us. I did not show him the letters and memoranda which has [*sic*] passed between Cecil and me regarding our naval building program, but I told him of our conversation. I outlined the character of speeches he should make in England and we went over these in much detail. If he does as we agreed, it will have a good effect and will clinch the work we have done here." Diary, April 12, 1919, House MSS. See also *ibid.*, April 8, 9, and 10, 1919.

was American Minister to France 1785–89. Addresses by Jefferson Randolph Kean,[20] lineal descendant of J, M. Chassaigne-Goyon, President of Council Municipal, Maj. Armistead Dobie,[21] Prof of Law Univ of Va, M. Lucian Poincaire, Rector University of Paris, Ambassador Sharp, Ambassador [blank] & J D.

Hundreds of alumni stood in damp rain, but it could not affect their enthusiasm, at its height when Dixie was played and cablegram read from President Alderman.

M. Ligge,[22] Minister of Marine, gave dinner at ministry. His daughter married Rockwell (a Rockhill?) [sic] of South Carolina. He is aviator & was injured. His brother from Asheville was decorated

Sunday, April 13, 1919

Damp & though ear was better did not risk it by going to cold church, though felt I ought to do so.

Hair cut & shampoo & wrote letters and started on a speech "The Return of the Mayflower"

Carter telephoned President of France [23] wished to confer distinguished honor on Admiral Benson if approved. I answered "Approved" per force though I think original position of opposition to all was the wise course. However, inasmuch as Army officers have received many decorations I could not say no without making naval officers feel I had withheld recognition which, so far as service is concerned, they richly deserve.

Long talk with Col. House. I outlined the speech I expect to make in Great Britain & he thought it was very good. Gave me copy of London Times containing interview with the President which shows his views.[24]

Talked over naval questions with Benson. 500 navy men busy building houses in France. Very good work, but gave directions to close up as that is not a Navy job.

Dined with Hoover. He thinks German efficiency will restore them to strong position (not military) in Germany. They work hard—he is sending food through Germany to Jugo Slavs & it moves like clock work. US. has put $350 mil dollars in relief work; England 12 mil   Italy $4 mil & France $1 mil-

[20] Brigadier general and deputy chief surgeon of the A.E.F.
[21] Chief of intelligence, publications section, General Headquarters, A.E.F.
[22] Georges Leygues, French Minister of Marine.
[23] Raymond Poincaré.
[24] Colonel House's version: "The Secretary of the Navy followed the Congressmen. I again went over the matter of his speeches in London. I even got him to phrase certain sentences which I thought it would be advisable to use. I hope he does this thing well for its importance is greater than appears on the surface." Diary, April 13, 1919, House MSS.

lion. Navy men at ports are doing great work. Army & Navy men carry food & help. GB, F, & I soldiers give orders & carry no help. They trust Americans

Mr. Taylor just returned from Roumania. Governing & wealthy class indifferent to condition of the poor. America is the only hope of the people

Monday, April 14, 1919

Left Paris for Chaumon [Chaumont], G.H.Q. upon invitation of Pershing. Lunch in Troyes. Woman who ran very good hotel said she had seen me in moving pictures the night before. Was told we were ahead of schedule & s[p]ent over hour at French lunch. Then it rained and we reached Chaumot $1\frac{1}{2}$ hrs. late and Gen. Liggett [25] had reviewed the troops because it was raining —very cold. They showed us map so we could see exactly how the German and allied armies were located on the day the armistice was signed, and what they showed proved the ability and grasp of American command. It became clear that cutting communications by American army was one of the decisive victories of the war.

Gen. Liggett had us to dinner. He is a big man—one of the ablest, broadest, & wisest military man [*sic*] I have ever talked to.

Went to Y.M.C.A. & met the press men in the army who were making a tour of camps. They had left the profession of journalism at outbreak of war.

Pershing sent message of regret. He was compelled to meet Secretary of War at Brest.

House built in twelfth century. Met Gen. Andrews,[26] Gen. Hines,[27] Col. Davis [28] & talked to Intelligence officer. Said Baker visited camp in Texas. "What is the best thing you saw?["] "The battery [?] of Col ———" who had piloted him through battlefields. We occupied same rooms occupied by King of Belgium, but we did not find it so cold because they found the King was found pinching the fires.

Col. [*sic*] Liggett said he knew I was the kind of man who would not wish men to stand in the rain. Otherwise I would not be worthy of giving a drill for.

Liggett had no hate—believed we should feed Germans. Our soldiers fought till 11 o'clock on Nov. 11 & then gave food to famished German soldiers on the front.

Maps of war

[25] Lieutenant General Hunter Liggett, commander of the U.S. First Army.
[26] Brigadier General Avery D. Andrews, assistant chief of staff, G-2 (Intelligence), at G.H.Q.
[27] Probably Major General John L. Hines, commander of the U.S. Third Corps.
[28] Probably Brigadier General Robert C. Davis, adjutant general at G.H.Q.

My wife & Admirals arrived first and were accompanied by Maj C. M. Busbee & we were met by Gen. Feland & Maj. Clendenin.[29]

Tuesday, April 15, 1919

Left at 8 a.m. Passed German prisoners at work with tall colored man directing the work.

What organization is this? Boy, this aint no organization. It is just 300 negroes working the road.

Stopped at Do[m]remy, Joan of Arc's home. Went into house where she was born. Long gave Addie breast-pin of Joan of Arc & she bought some rosaries. Went into church & saw the font in which she was baptized. Passed through Barleduc [Bar-le-Duc] (famous jelly town). Revigny (ruined) in charge of the French. Lunch at Mennehould [Ste. Menehould] Long poured water into wine & it was not very good. Thought it doctored & from chemicals and grapes. Went on to Argonne Forest & went into dug outs. One occupied by German royal family made of cement with marble mantle and bath & every convenience. Picked up shells which Addie has. Saw many graves. Saw Varennes (in ruins) Montfacon [Mont St. Martin?] (in ruins) Esnes [le Chesne?] (in ruins) and arrived in Verdun late in afternoon Passed Hill 304 and saw land all churned up. Had pointed out to us where Americans had fought. Germans had put up signs in all towns (big letters) to tell their troops distances. Passed through B[ou]illy & places occupied by Germans during the war. Raining & cold & roads bad & drove rapidly so as to reach Moraigne Farm before night. Had museum containing all kinds of armament Germans used. One German shell which carried message. If thrown in day, was white smoke. If at night made a white light. Big bow [?] used to send signal rockets. Saw the first 15 in[ch] brass cartridge case and many other things. Been used as German headquarters & had electricity. Mottoes on wall.

"Kein Trinken, Typhus-gefahr.["] "Drink no water, danger of typhoid"

On walls our room: Krankauhz—NJW.A. & JRKW. Fur—Tankfalle & Bestimmt Nicht adfahren Ortskomdts Durchgang—Verboten Waldhaus Gertrub Blink Station Bismarck Lagst

Jrnopr—Abt 569

Rained through wall in our room.

Woman, who owned house, came back. Everything gone except her picture. She was so infuriated she cut a hole in that.

Wednesday, April 16, 1919

Left Moraigne farm 9 am in rain. Went through Vitron [Virton] & town of Longuyon shelled by Navy's 14 in gun. Saw the RR station where Plunkett's

[29] Probably Marine Second Lieutenant Henry P. Glendinning.

guns worked well. German prisoner stated that a shell had detonated between troop trains at this station and killed many troops. At Longwy saw ruins. It had been shot all to pieces. Crossed Luxemburg border & saw big blast furnaces running [?] & stayed at L for lunch at Brasseur Hotel. We saw the garrison, house where Foch makes headquarters, & university. Met young man there [?] Maj. Denson, from High Point, N.C. who had been to Sunday School to my mother. I sent her a card and wrote her & sent her his regards. Boy Scout, who had learned to speak English from our soldiers, was our guide. Refused to accept money. True boy scout spirit. Queen [30] was away. At luncheon had discussion with Pomard who held that wine was necessary. I said doctors prescribed milk.

Met Dr. Coulcott's [?] daughter here. After lunch started for Treves under guidance of Army officer.

Just outside went to see mammoth big Zeppelin hangar & saw flights. En route people hard at work and at first came to the Moselle vineyards, high on the hills. Reached Treves before dinner. Put up at *Porta Nigra* Hotel opposite Porta Nigra arch, entrance of Roman walls around city. Built by Romans in the 3rd. Century. Visited Roman amphitheatre & baths & oldest church which we visited. Went into shops and bought some knives and trinkets as present. Gen. Hines had us to dinner.

After dinner went to K of C. & Y.M.C.A. & then went to wonderful theatre to see Mary's Ankle played by very good soldier troop, trained by a very bright lady. I spoke to the packed hall of soldiers. Took tea with Mrs. Walker [31] (Officers Y.M.C.A.) They called her "the waffle queen." She was from St. Albans School. Our first visit to German occupied city. Children looked anaemic. Our Army lived their own lives but had no dealings with German people who neither looked sullen nor friendly—seeming to act as if they were indifferent.

The General ———, after the entertainment, played on the organ for us— a deft touch. A charming gentleman and delightful host. Had delicious trout —must have caught them for not allowed to buy food

Negro: Biggest cemetery. Not tombstones, but Kilometer signs

Saw Miss Sylvia Sweet [?] at Treves

Thursday, April 17, 1919

Left Treves at 9:30. Saw German prisoners building roads. Logs distributed so newly built road would not be hurt by traffic   That made progress slower.

---

[30] Charlotte Adelgonde, Grand Duchess of Luxembourg.

[31] Mary A. Rogers Walker (Mrs. Barbour Walker), former principal of the National Cathedral School for Girls in Washington, on Red Cross and Y.M.C.A. duty in Europe since 1917.

Vineyards on the mountains   Looked like thatched roofs. Saw women working in vineyards. Reached Cochem. Looked at castle with U.S. flag flying over. Headquarters of Gen. Myers.[32] Very mountainous. Crossed the Moselle on a pontoon bridge. Rode down the Moselle until we reached Gen. Dickman's [33] headquarters. Received with honors & had fine lunch. Dickman's daughter had married Knauss, our navy friend. Wonderful windows looking out on the Rhine. Col. Williams [34] said bank clerks were about to strike & he sent word to strike leader that if banks were closed the leader would be jailed. No strike.

House occupied by Dickman belonged to Count von Oswald. They said Germans must have food by the 15th. Germans had had dried herrings or used them boiled. Quit buying because had no grease to cook them with. They were reduced to such extremity.

Lejeune [35] joined us & we left at 3:30 & went to Ehrenbr[e]itstein, where I inspected it. Col. McCable [36] took us through motor school & I rode on a tractor. American flag on ancient tower thrilled us.

Went with Lejeune to Nieu Weid [Neuwied]. Received by squadron of cavalry escorted us. Sent by Gen. Hines. Batalion [sic] of marines drawn up to receive us at Lejeunes. House belonged to Land Rat [sic] of town. Only thing he took out when Lejeune came was to remove from ball room two pictures of the Kaiser. He had first lived with Mayor [?] Von Runkle who lent him some silver to use while we were there. His aides Capt. Nelson [37] and Lt. Brown very courteous. Marine who was orderly at my door was asked by Addie how he received his decoration & he modestly answered "Only in the day's work," though it had been won by a courageous deed in hard fought battle.

Lejeune gave large dinner that night. He seemed very happy for us to be with him.

Friday, April 18, 1919

Clear and beautiful. Went by motor to Vallender [Vallendar] Field, overlooking Rhine where Kaiser had been wont to review picked troops. In sight of statue of Frederick & Ehrenb[re]its[t]ein. I pinned crosses upon soldiers and marines. Dickman commanded Third Army; Hines the Third Corps; Lejeune Second Div of 3rd Corps. 27,000 men passed in review, with ma-

[32] Probably Major General Charles H. Muir, commander of the U.S. Fourth Corps.

[33] Major General Joseph T. Dickman, commander of the U.S. Third Army.

[34] Colonel Richard H. Williams, assistant chief of staff, First Corps.

[35] Major General John A. Lejeune, commanding the Marine units in France during the war and the subsequent occupation of German territory; currently commander of the 2nd Division, A.E.F.

[36] Colonel E. Warner McCable, commander of Ehrenbreitstein fortress.

[37] Probably Captain Robert L. Nelson, U.S.M.C.

chine guns and tractors. Afterwards I spoke. French, American & Belgian crosses. Ground was slippery. Rode in tractors instead of motors to place where I spoke.

Lunched with Gen. Hines at his headquarters—the house of the Prince of Weid. Fine lunch. Several ladies there. Prince of Weid nephew of Carmine Sylva, formerly Queen of Roumania. Saw room in which she was born.

Motored to Honningen where Marines simulated trench warfare. First batallion [sic] of Sixth Regiment demonstrate[d] an attack on machine gun nest. They looked more like stories of Indian warfare than any other fighting. Saw men rise up from places who were not visible to the eye.

Rode by the old castle at Alten-wied, now disused, & visited our patrol at the bridge-head over the Weid river. Boys were cooking their supper. Addie went to Coblenz to see Y.W.C.A.

Dinner with Lejeune & he gave reception to all officers of the Third Army, & young women of Red Cross and Y.M.C.A. [sic]

Wife of Prince of Weid, rather young, smokes a pipe. They raise fine horses. Beautiful garden with wonderful pea-fowls. Army had ordered all arms surrendered & they had been taken down from the walls to comply with the order.

Saturday, April 19, 1919

Left at 8 a.m. up the Rhine in autos. Stopped at Bingen. Whenever we stopped, the children collected around Bob [38] who said he might charge admission. They were so anxious to see him. Then went to Mainz where Gen. Mangin [39] of the Tenth French Army Corps, who initiated the 1918 offensive at Soissons. The [?] house he was in was a castle in which Napoleon slept when he visited Mayance [sic]. Some of some furniture still there. German General had occupied Napoleon's room. When Mangin arrived he neither would occupy it himself or permit any one else. He said Germans did not wish people to have high wages to work or enough to give food because in future it would affect price of labor & make it impossible for German industry to sell to other countries. Said Germany had not suffered for food. Said people had not suffered.

Showed us picture of his children—seven. He had been married 11 years & 2 years were in Africa.

Went to Weisbaden [Wiesbaden]—garish furnishing. Then took steamer Preussen for trip over Rhine. Commanded by Marines. It flew Secretary of the Navy's flag & on way down the Rhine was saluted by the Tenth French Army

[38] Robert Gaines, Daniels' Negro servant.
[39] General Charles E. Mangin, commanding the X Army, which included the U.S. 2nd Division composed partly of Marines, at the Second Battle of the Marne in 1918.

Corps which was drawn up and had just been decorated by Gen. Mangin. Wherever there were French troops they saluted the flag & played Star Spangled banner. Our band played French national air. Passed wonderful castles on the Rhine.

Dined with Gen. Neville.[40] Full of jokes and jest. Va & N.C. jollied each other

His wife was ill & he had applied to go home, but withdrew his application to return when he found an Army & not Marine officer would succeed him.

Americans had let Germans have bacon & Madame Von Runkel had tears in her eyes when she told our Admirals about all people getting bacon. Had had none in 2 years.

Sunday, April 20, 1919

Cloudy

Went to Church at Honnengen [Hönningen]. Protestant & Catholic ministers officiated & Protestant preached. I then spoke. After church we went to luncheon with the 18th Co. of the 5th Regmt of Marines. The field kitchen, on which the dinner was cooked, had two wound stripes painted on it as it had been shot through twice. Clean & neat, men had planted flowers, & gave us cordial greetings. Capt. Jackson, who had been wounded in arm & eye, who had left company, was there. The Captain ―――― asked us to speak. Private Tucker, of Va. presented Addie with flowers & an insignia, colors of their shoulder piece, painted on satin. She created great enthusiasm by her speech saying she outranked me.

Went to Officers Y.M.C.A. Club (beautiful build.)& then to Y.M.C.A. used when men come from stations for 3 days leave. Big fire-places and comfortable place. Boys gathered around Addie & I asked YMCA girls to do me as well.

Photographed with a number of men and with one man who had been wounded 5 times.

Dinner at Gen. Lejeunes & after dinner I spoke in Theatre in Neuwied at night.

In morning visited castle of Col. Snyder's [41] headquarters

Stopped at Y.M.C.A. where ―――― very charming woman received us & we were photographed. Fine work everywhere.

Monday, April 21, 1919

Left Niu Weid [Neuwied] at 8:30 on the Rhine travelling on same steamer upon which we sailed down the Rhine from Weis-baden [Wiesbaden] on

---

[40] Brigadier General Wendell C. Neville, commanding the 4th Brigade Marines, A.E.F.
[41] Probably Lieutenant Colonel Harold C. Snyder, U.S.M.C.

Saturday. Rather cooler and spent portion of time in nice room below. Lejeune accompanied us as far as Cologne. At every place on the river where there are American troops, they were lined up on the river bank and saluted, the bands playing the Star Spangled Banner where there was a band. Passed points where English are in Control. They have headquarters at Cologne. Generals were changing commands & we saw no English officers officially. Visited the Cathedral. Much dif. in the military bearing there as well as where French were in control compared with American Army of Occupation. Gen. Biddle [42] did NOT meet us.

Passed through Aix la Chapelle & went into cathedral & went up and saw stone seat on which Charlemagne was crowned.

Fine country en route. Easter Monday & holiday. Passed place where Belgians were guarding frontier. Country had not been devastated & looked smiling.

Reached Leige [Liège] at 6:30. Stayed at Hotel du Suede big room. Consul Doutin [43] & Maj. Hoffman [44] (who came down from Brussels to meet us) met us & dined with us at other hotel. Germans had destroyed nearly everything in Hotel du Suede & they could not prepare food for us, but did give us coffee for breakfast.

Nothing had been destroyed at Liege—the Germans thinking they would own the town

Spent night at Liege

Tuesday, April 22, 1919

Governor & blind Burgomaster called. Took us to Visa [Visé], which had been burned. Family had been buried alive as warning to Leige. Met by Burgomaster who was made prisoner and taken to Germany. Visited Browning Plant, Fabrique Nationale d'Armes de Guerre. One building 4 acres. Plant 80 acres. Germans removed machinery & machine tools & no work can be done until new machinery can be had from America. Formerly they exported machinery & machine tools. Went to Fort Lovain [?] where Belgians held out so long & demolished Aug 15 1914. Saw the quarters & were told of fight by soldier who was in the Fort.

Passed Tronde [Tienen?] & reached Louvaine [Louvain] at 1.05. Had begun to be rebuilt. Saw City Hall & Library that had been demolished. Had lunch at Hotel de l'Industry.

[42] Probably Major General John Biddle, commander of U.S. forces in England at this time.
[43] J. Preston Doughton, U.S. consul at Liège.
[44] Major William W. Hoffman, military attaché at the U.S. Legation in Brussels.

Maj Commandate [sic] ——— joined us at Hotel Astoria & went to Waterloo. Pictures taken. 7 mi. extreme limit at Waterloo. Panorama. David [Bagley] joined us at Brussels. Dined with Minister Brand Whitlock [45] and wife   Only other guests Minister of Marine Braught [?] & wife and Armour [46] and wife

Wednesday, April 23, 1919

Called on Minister of War, Marine & Whitlock with Maj. Hoffman & City Hall & saw Petite ———.

Lunched with King Albert. Tall & spoke good English. Told my wife he was a teetotaler—did not touch wine. Silver on table had been kept in cistern during war, much of it presented by Queen Victoria when he was married. I had quite good talk after dinner. He said French were too imperialistic and spoke of the large spirit that must be shown to preserve the peace of the world. He hoped to visit America & told how much Belgium felt its indebtedness. Spoke of how lands had been destroyed. You can rebuild cities, but when land is destroyed & machinery removed it requires time for exporting country to get back into production. Many people in Belgium have no work. You cannot put mechanics to farming or mill men to building roads.

Went to Antwerp with Gen ——— & saw canals and big Army to work at that place. Better than Rotterdam for many things. Stopped at Ghent to see where 1814 treaty was signed. Then a hotel—afterwards first cotton factory which began that industry and now is a Catholic place for brothers. Went through some devastation. Spent night at Brugge at Hotel Flanders at that hotel Adml Schoeder [47] made headquarters during war.

Old time furniture but mattresses of straw. Germans had taken away all mattresses because Belgians make mattresses of wool. Delightful night & good supper

Thursday, April 24, 1919

Left Brugge 8 am. Reached Zebrugee [Zeebrugge] 8:30 & went out on the Mole & Belgian & British officers explained exploit.[48] Addie secured shell fired

---

[45] U.S. Minister to Belgium. Of this visit Whitlock noted in his journal: "Daniels and party, consisting of Mrs. Daniels, Josephus Jr., Mrs. Daniels' brother, Commander Bayley [sic], three admirals, a general of marines, and so on, thirteen in all, arrived today. We had them all to dinner tonight, with Renkin and his wife. The Daniels are not so bad; he a very intelligent and honest if narrow man, of good ideals, not lacking a certain distinction in appearance." *The Journal of Brand Whitlock*, Allan Nevins, ed. (New York: D. Appleton-Century, 1936), p. 558.

[46] Norman Armour, second secretary of the U.S. Legation.

[47] Rear Admiral Schroeder, commander of the German submarine base at Bruges during the war, noted for his harsh discipline of the Belgian population.

[48] The British naval attack on the night of April 22–23, 1918, which resulted in the blocking of the channel at Zeebrugge, one of the two entrances to the Bruges submarine base. The simultaneous attack on the other entrance at Ostend failed.

by Germans. Motored to Ostend & saw how it had been fired upon. Passed through ruined villages, saw pill boxes on front line. Rode through worst devastation because the flooded land had been destroyed & looked hopeless. Saw Nieuport which was destroyed & utter desolation. Saw German prisoners working on roads & otherwise. At Adinkerka [?] we crossed line into France and went to Dunkirke [Dunkerque]. There was the statue of Jean Bart, the pirate. By his statue stood a German shell fired from the big Bertha. Shell was 15 in taller than Josephus.

Reached Calais at 2 pm. had lunch at station. Met by Command[er] Barleon [49] of Wickes, French General & Navy & sailors drawn up. Saluted. Left at 3 pm. escorted by three British destroyers. Reached Dover 4:45. Met by Grant [50] & staff, Mayor of Dover & sister, Browning [51] & Knapp [52] Gen[er]al Commanding.[53] First salute fired since England went into the war in [?] 1914 was given. Mayor's sister gave flowers. Batallion [sic] of soldiers. Special train. Tea on way to London. Met at London by Davis [54] & Duff.[55] Went to Davis to dinner 36 Barclay Place. Talked about my speeches. He said British said they were reserved, paid few compliments & prided themselves on it, but they are avid for appreciation and compliments. "You cannot pile it on too thick—the thicker the better they like it.["] Left for Thurso 10:30 Ambassador Davis & Josephus went to train with us.

Friday, April 25, 1919
Cloudy and raw. McCune, RR man, pointed out objects of interest as we travelled.

Grampian Hills

Reached Thurso & went on Flying Kestral to Scapa Flow. Met by Admiral Pendergast.[56] Fine man. Expressed regret my wife had not come because his wife would have been delighted to welcome her. Went at once on the Lion. Sir Roger Keyes [57] received us on the Lyon [Lion]. "It seems so near and yet I thought of it as far away" when I told him that on previous day we were at

[49] Commander John S. Barleon, Jr., commanding the U.S. destroyer *Wickes*, which took the Daniels party to England.

[50] Vice Admiral Sir William Lowther Grant, whom Daniels had known previously as the commander-in-chief of British naval forces in North American waters, 1918–1919; assigned to the Daniels party in England.

[51] Vice Admiral Sir Montague Browning, Second Sea Lord of the British Admiralty.

[52] Rear Admiral Harry S. Knapp, who had succeeded Admiral Sims as commander of U.S. naval forces in Europe.

[53] Major General Sir Colin Campbell, commander of British Army forces at Dover.

[54] John W. Davis, U.S. Ambassador to Great Britain since November, 1918.

[55] Vice Admiral Sir Alexander Ludovic Duff, assistant chief of naval staff, whom Daniels had met in Washington as a member of the Geddes mission in October, 1918.

[56] Vice Admiral Robert J. Prendergast, commanding the Shetland and Orkney stations.

[57] Rear Admiral Sir Roger Keyes, who had commanded the attack on Zeebrugge and Ostend.

Zebrugee and saw the great achievement there. He was modestly proud of it and talked about it with reserve. He did not like Capt. Carpenter,[58] of the [blank], who had shown pictures and lectured about it in USA. He thought it too much like self exploitation

Saturday, April 26, 1919

Breakfast 8. My watch slow and was a little late. Each person helped himself on side table. Keyes in command of Atlantic squadron & hoped it would be sent to US during the year. Talked about efficiency in building German ships. Went on Flying Kestral and German fleet. Ad'l Von Reuter [59] had flag on Emden. Eleven battleships, including Baden & Bayern, five battle cruisers, 2 mine layers, six light cruisers, 50 destroyers & torpedo boats   Keyes had never been on either ship or talked to German Admiral. His chief of staff went on board every day & his chief business was to uphold German officers in executing punishment. One night on one ship crew raised red flag but pulled it down next morning. He laughed & pointed to 3 trawlers and said "These trawlers guard German fleet." Expressed undisguised admiration for German armor —better than British—on cruisers. Made for North Sea and not wide sailing radius. Pleased with Bob's statement: "I think, sir, these are some very fine ships but I think they are exactly where they ought to be."

Lunched with Admiral Pendergast. He spoke and so did I. He gave brass ash tray made out of rescued piece of last German submarine sunk during the war. One forced its way into protected Scapa Flow & if not discovered and sunk could have wrought great havoc. Keyes pointed out where it entered.

In afternoon visited Kirkwall in the Orkneys, visited St. Magnus Cathedral. He made a vow, did Reginald [?] that if he obtained dominion in Orkneys he would build a stone minister at Kirkwall, named for his kinsman, Earl Magnus, the Holy. In name of Magnus there were many cures, leprosy. Visited church and signed the register. House for King & Bishop. Visited site and ruins. Can be seen many miles.

There are firths [?] beyond Pentland and firths beyond Forth.

Went to Houton Air Station. Had tea at nice inn (all sorts of ancient weapons on wall) and visited quaint museum which recalled one at Nantucket. This was town of Stormness [Stromness]. Returned to Scapa and all dined on Lion with Keyes. He made briefest blessing I ever heard, but it was reverent. His wife had three brothers in British Army—all killed. He talked of Gal[l]ipoli & told me of his hearing before House of Commons. After they cross-examined him 2 days he made statement. He urged sinking or losing

---

[58] Captain Alfred F. B. Carpenter.
[59] Rear Admiral von Reuter, commander of the surrendered German fleet at Scapa Flow.

old ships with men to win Constantinople & still believes could have been done if Government had been willing to risk the loss. Would have saved life in the long run. He confirmed Morgenthau's statement [60] and criticized the Government.

Saluted as we passed British ship, Tiger, I think

Sunday, April 27, 1919

Fair but blowing hard. Heavy seas and swift current made rough trip to Sorabtrees [?] but cold and fine. At Thurso had tea with Capt. Meredith [Meredyth]. He, like Keyes, had passion for fishing which could be caught only by standing waist deep in water. Mrs. M—— looked like cold had taken strength from her. She did not like fishing or the country & was happy to entertain men from ships. Capt of old type—physically fit and loved the cold. She longed for balmy air. Reached Inverness at 5:20. Lord Provost [MacDonald] said he would like to have arranged public welcome but this was Sabbath. Straus, Bulmer, Fritman [61] met us & we inspected place where mines were received, put together and sent to North Sea for barrage. We got at least 10 subs. by mines and sent terror to Germans by barrage. We had taken over Old Glen Albyn distillery here and another one in Scotland. I told naval officers war ended too soon. My purpose was to make G.B. dry by taking over all distilleries for naval bases. Straus hoped 500 men held there would be sent home soon. There had been some trouble growing out of attention or worse to women in Inverness, and it was bad for sailors to be there in idleness. Explained method of taking up mines & difficulties. Strauss anxious to come home and boys anxious too. 4,000 barrels of whiskey stored away in distillery and owners wish us to leave so they can return to business. Mines were brought to West Coast & sent through canal to Inverness.

Heavy snow the previous night and we had to have snow plow for our train to come through mountains. Newspaper man at Thurso wanted to interview me & go on train to Edinboro [Edinburgh]. Permission granted. He wrote very good article.

Reached Edinboro at 10:30. Very cold and went to North British Hotel. Addie & Josephus had arrived Sunday morning, attended church at St. Giles, and dined with the Lord Provost, John Lorne McCloued [62] and his sister Mrs. Whigham—charmed with them.

[60] See entry of November 16, 1917.

[61] Rear Admiral Joseph Strauss, commanding the Mine Force; Captain Roscoe C. Bulmer, commanding the Mine Sweeping Detachment; and Lieutenant Martin Fritman, all working on the deactivation of the North Sea mine barrage.

[62] Sir John Lorne MacLeod, Lord Provost of Edinburgh.

Monday, April 28, 1919

Woke up to find it snowing and had to abandon program for that A.M. Left on train at noon for Rosyth, big naval base. Had lunch with Admiral Heath.[63] His daughter had been on duty in Egypt and had just returned. Lady ——— asked about Rodman and Blue and expressed warm friendship for them.

The Admiral in charge of construction took us over magnificent yard, big dry docks, cranes and pointed out big expansions contemplated before armistice. He feared yards established in So. England would not look with favor upon large expansion planned. Particularly interested in houses built for employees and plans for schools and parks by Government. Saw the Furious, the sea plane ship. Also Glorious and Courageous, each four 15 in. guns, 6″ triple mounts. Agincourt in dock. Blisters here & in Plymouth being put on all big ships. Queen Elizabeth, (Admiral Medden [64] [?]) in Forth.

Returned to Edinboro in time to dress for formal dinner in City Chambers. Beautiful banquet hall. Cold. Before going into dinner official with loud voice called out names & order of proceedure [*sic*] to banquet hall. Good dinner. Man behind Lord Provost began the "Hip" & crowd called out the hurrahs. Lord Provost made first address. Then I spoke. Then the Secretary for Scotland, Monroe [65] with some wit. Griffin said lady who sat next to him drank four glasses of champagne before toasts began, and had prost ready when he had to be excused to go to Glasgow. She was cold at first, but warmed up. Afterwards we went to the Museum and held reception and talk with Mr. Cowl, editor Scotsman, & offered to write some editorials for his paper if he would print them. He agreed if I would clearly set forth the future Navy policy of the U.S. Original letters of Burns, Carlyle, Robert Louis Stevenson & many interesting things explained by keeper of museum with enthusiasm and interest. Close of dinner sang songs concluding with Auld Lang Syne, everybody clasping hands.

Tuesday, April 29, 1919

Lord Provost, Chief Bailey Watson [66] called at hotel & Mrs. Whigham— & other officials. Went to the castle & Scotch Guard received us. Guide met us. Stood on high point & had fine view of country & saw the Dogs Cemetery where dogs of famous soldiers were buried. Went into chapel, the oldest build-

---

[63] Vice Admiral Sir Herbert L. Heath, commander-in-chief of the coast of Scotland.
[64] Probably Admiral Sir Charles E. Madden, second in command of the British Grand Fleet.
[65] Robert Munroe, Secretary of State for Scotland since 1916.
[66] Bailie Watson, senior magistrate of Edinburgh.

ing on the castle. Room in room [*sic*] where Mary Queen of Scots was living when her son was born. Saw window from which her son was let down to be baptized, thus eluding those who wished him baptized in the ——— faith in the hot contest between Catholics and Protestants. Went into banquet room filled with armor & armament of all kinds. Showed us little holes in wall where you could listen in and know what was being said. Saw there the first rifle where the first powder was put in pan to fire rifle. From this came the expression "flashed in the pan." Place where Crown Jewels of Scotland are placed. Had been in chest since Mary Queen of Scots. Sir Walter Scott had them taken out and now kept on exhibition.

Rode the Royal Mile—stopped at St. Giles. In old part John Knox preached. Tablet to Jean Geddes who threw her prayer at preacher because he started to read the prayer. He ran up into tower and no prayers read since. She won out. Went into Thistle Chapel where king bestowed royal orders. Went to Library. Only monmt [monument] to John Knox is simple memorial flat on ground. Then into old castle now courts [?] & saw originals of Burns & Stevenson. Then on Royal Mile and stopped at house where John Knox lived. To Hollyrood [Holyrood] saw [where] Mary Queen of Scots lived. Over mantel picture of Queen Elizabeth was [?]. Secret passage through which Reggio [?] was taken when he was discovered in Queen's apartments.

Lunched at hotel. Lord Provost & others.

Went to see the statue of Lincoln.

To University & especially Medical Dept. PM [67] had visited Naval Academy Alexander head of theory [?]

Then to Scotsman's office & all over it. Editor asked me to write leader.

Officers Y.M.C.A. Club. Edinboro loaned furniture. Col. Knight. I spoke. After dinner went to Y.M.C.A. Pinned Croix d[e] Guerre on boy from Indiana.[68] Very modest. I then spoke to the boys. Then took train for London. Lord Provost & sister with us. Consul [69] said no visit had done so much good.

Mrs. Hutchinson & daughter called. Her father bought for the Confederacy the ships that ran the blockade. She has the silver plate given him, Son in War Office. Friends of P. M. Wilson. He lived with them.

Wednesday, April 30, 1919

Reached London 7.30 & went to Carlton Hotel Saw reporters &c. At 11.45 left for Windsor Castle. Grant & Griffin scurried around to get swords to wear. Reached there just in time 1:30 luncheon. Met by Sir Derrick Kepple,[70] head

[67] Probably Principal Sir Alfred Ewing of the University of Edinburgh, Daniels' host.

[68] Corporal J. B. Tipton, decorated for bravery in a gas attack in October, 1918.

[69] Rufus Fleming, U.S. consul at Edinburgh.

[70] Sir Derek Keppel, Master of the King's Household and Extra Equerry.

of the King's household & ladies in waiting. Lady Bradford, Lady Cook & Miss Gye [?]

King & Queen came in. Prince of Wales, Princes Albert & George Princess Mary sick. Only 8 at lunch. As a course was served the attendants would retire & King would ring little silver bell when ready for next course. Here ate the first plovers eggs. King said white of egg rather indigestable. Soup, chicken, cold tongue & ham with salad. Hot egg pudding. Passed wines. Before K & fine cut glass bottles which I suppose had brandy & they would put water. None for George. All smoked including the Queen. King said "You live in only country that has an autocracy" Of Jutland, Admiralty delayed sending out news & when did send out only gave British losses, claimed no German losses & that left impression of German victory. Lunched leisurely & afterwards talked. Said Queen Victoria had the seat he occupied. Showed her picture, the best. From window he pointed out parts of castles & when built. I brought up housing question & they showed much interest & he pointed out how much more houses cost now. Discussed Jellico[e]'s book. Young men real boys. They talked to Addie and I to Queen & G to the King. Talked of friendly relations. Said Kaiser was good judge of men. He said Roosevelt & Cecil Rhodes two most remarkable men. I told of R's stat[emen]t to Kaiser "Those men can lick the world" & Kaiser believed it. Also proceedings of Naval Aff. Com. & House of Commons.

Shown about Castle—library by Fortescue.[71] Praised Geo III & said Chatham was crazy. He wrote book before the war & said Americans played not fair. Had tea with household & went to Chapel of St George—Dean Bailey.[72]

Bone [?] of behead[ed] Charles. King Edward buried [?] it in the chapel. Lowered box on casket of Charles. Tied hankerchifs [?]. King [?] on stomach. Quiet. Stalls where the Bath Knights sat. Foreign Knights & citizens [?] removed [?]

Dinner with Lord & Lady Mayor. Reception afterwards She is cynic & believes in old order

Mr. Wilde [?] called at 10:30 friend of Sims & Americans

Thursday, May 1, 1919

Called on First Lord of the Admiralty, Walter Long, & met Wemyss, Duff[,] Browning & others. Arranged for Griffin, Taylor & others to have conferences.

[71] John W. Fortescue, librarian at Windsor Castle.
[72] Albert V. Baillie, dean of Windsor.

Luncheon in hotel by Anglo American Society. Sir Robt Hadfield [1] presided. Duke of Connaught [2] there & he & Addie born on say [same] day of month— May 1—took her into luncheon & said in his speech: "We are birthday children." Later criticized for referring to German legend.[3]

Bryce spoke of his visit to Raleigh & he little thought then we would be here in London, partners in War. Very complimentary. Davis & all praised my speech.

At 3:30 went to House of Commons. Sir William Bull [4] took us all around and was interesting. He is friend of Walter Long. Met Lord Fisher [5] & others. Had tea. Heard Bottleny [6] & Whitaker [7] speak on the budget & demand changes in taxes. Also heard ———— in House of Lords. Commons well attended. Lords very slim. No interest.

Night. Long gave dinner in House of Commons. 98 men from it [?] present. Curson [8] proposed toast. Self made man—who when he made himself, made other men & other things. GB must open promotion to men below decks. Harvard students:

> "There was a farmer who had two sons.
> And these two sons were brothers,
> Josephus was the name of one
> Bo heepus was the other.["]

GB is Joheepus [?]. Spoke wonderfully well. I spoke fairly well. No reporters. Long praised Am Navy. Gen Haig said about time Pershing arrived Petain called & urged Haig to keep up fight, saying the French would not advance. Americans coming gave moral force even before present in great man power. After war Petain told him French demoralization worse than he had told him.

Private talk with Churchill. GB would build as big ships & guns as any. More in that than in size

[1] Sir Robert A. Hadfield, British industrialist and munitions manufacturer, to whom Daniels had awarded a three-million-dollar contract for 14- and 16-inch shells in January, 1917, when he believed that the Navy was being overcharged by American companies.

[2] Uncle of King George V.

[3] Daniels in his remarks at this luncheon referred gratefully to what he said was British naval support of Admiral Dewey against the German naval squadron at the time of the assault against Manila in 1898. The Duke evidently set him straight about this bit of American mythology.

[4] Conservative M.P. and parliamentary private secretary to Walter Long.

[5] Admiral of the Fleet John A. Fisher, 1st Baron of Kilverstone, former First Sea Lord.

[6] Horatio W. Bottomley, Independent M.P. and newspaper publisher.

[7] Sir Thomas P. Whittaker, Liberal M.P.

[8] George N. Curzon, 1st Earl Curzon of Kedleston, Lord President of the Council and leader of the House of Lords, subsequently foreign secretary.

Friday, May 2, 1919

Went out & bought wedding present for Addie. Saw Chester, of Times, & other newspaper men. Browning & Perks [9] & others called. Went sight-seeing & then luncheon with Sir Eric Geddes Hotel Grafton. He talked of his job of transportation & unifying water power and how difficult it was.

Visited Tower of London. Room & court of Sir Walter Raleigh & Crown Jewels. The Governor of Tower took us around.

To St. Paul's—"the gloomy dean." He was truly a gloomy Gus, but he showed us tombs of Nelson and Wellington & Roberts. Pigeons were fed there. Then to Westminster Abbey. Mr. Weller, the assistant, showed us through. Stopped at John & Charles Wesley,—Josephine [?] Gordon who introduced rhodendron [*sic*] into G.B. & lived to be 100 years old. Poets corner. Gladstone & Disraeli near together. G's back turned toward Dizzy

Hotel proprietor, Mr. Dreyfus had made wedding cake 1888–1919

Dinner given us by Ambassador Davis—anniversary of wedding day. They had just moved in new house. Endicotts daughter was widow of Joseph Chamberlain who was wife of Rector Carnegie.[10] Sloan (magistrate [?]) nephew of Mrs. Russell Sage,[11] returning to America with much money

Saturday, May 3, 1919

Went to the Embassy, met all officers & staff & employees 5 Ambassadors have been made Presidents. Visited Knapp & met all Navy personnel. Also had interview with correspondents of American newspapers. Lunched at 12:45 with Admiral Knapp—few ladies daughters of former naval officers. Claridges Hotel. After lunch went to Buckingham Palace to see review of Colonial troops. Fine looking men. King & queen & Queen Alexandria [12] & others reviewed. Air craft & good band. After review, Prince of Wales came to speak to us & said it had been pleasant at the castle. Later officer said King & Queen wished to see us—hoped we had had pleasant visit to London & the castle & had not been kept too long. Duke of Con[na]ught asked if we received his telegram of congratulations on Wedding Day. King spoke of Italy. 2 mistakes had been made   1. Orlando letting Italians know what was going on   2 The

---

[9] Sir Robert W. Perks, financier and public works contractor, prominent Methodist layman.

[10] William H. Carnegie, canon of Westminster, whose wife Mary was the widow of Joseph Chamberlain and daughter of William C. Endicott, Secretary of War in the first Cleveland administration, 1885–1889.

[11] Margaret Olivia Slocum Sage, prominent American philanthropist who had died the previous November.

[12] The Queen-Mother Alexandra.

Presidents Letter. He hoped & thought all would work out right and there would be found basis of compromise

Went to tea at Admiral Grants.

Early dinner & went to His Majesty's Theatre to see Cho Chin Chew [?].

Sunday, May 4, 1919

Left on train ten o'clock to Warrick [Warwick]. Passed through Oxford & Banbury Cross. Received at castle by Mrs. Henry [W.] Marsh & Lady Warrick & Adml Grant. Mr. Marsh rents the castle & has been active in war work. Lady Warrick poor. She is the famous Babbling Brook of King Edwards time. American & British flags flying from castle. Beautiful pictures. From the tower saw Queen Elizabeth's hunting Lodge. After lunch, drove to Stratford of [on] Avon, met by Mayor Flower [?] & his wife. Went to John Harvard house which Marie Corelli [13] had restored. Rector took us through church "Cursed be he who moves these bones." Visited school where Sha[k]espeare was taught. Sir [blank] had returned from Paris to welcome us. He & wife very courteous. Rector's wife cordial & daughters beautiful. Wreath furnished by American officers put on S's grave by me at their request. Tea at YMCA officers club & at Marie Corelli. Mayoress & Marie do not speak. She autographed her latest book.

Thence to Chequers, home of Lee of Fareham.[14] His wife was Miss Moore,[15] of NY (Schley & Moore)   Very courteous. Wonderful house wh. is to go to Prime Minister upon death of Lee & wife under certain conditions.

Many Cromwellian [?] portraits [?]. John Russell ward C's grandson [?] & it was preserved

Monday, May 5, 1919

Left Checkers [sic] & reached there in time for luncheon with American Luncheon club at Ritz. Large crowd & very cordial. Lord Fisher spoke. Davis presided and introduction was warm in commendation. President McFee [16] (once with Seaboard Air Line & knew Raleigh) spoke. I spoke. Fisher: "Damned fine hen that hatched the Amercian Eagle." King told him "I am your only friend."

Left at 3:45 by auto for Portsmouth. One puncture & one blow out. Passed through large army cantonments. Racing. Reached 6:45. Received with honors

---

[13] British novelist.

[14] Arthur Hamilton Lee, 1st Baron Lee of Fareham, former Conservative M.P. and personal military secretary to Lloyd George in 1916, whose country estate was deeded to the government as a summer home for the prime minister.

[15] Ruth Moore Lee, eldest daughter of John G. Moore, New York financier.

[16] John B. Macafee, chairman of the American Luncheon Club in London.

by Admiral Burney [17] & aid Kemble (who was Beattys flg lt) Burney commanded Marlbo[rou]gh at Jutland & had to abandon ship. Gave dinner at night. Toast to the President before the one to the King. Miss C [blank] fine girl. Admiral's son had invented the paravane and was said to have made much money by it. Storm had blown down trees behind commandants house and disclosed brewery & smoke, which was regretted. Why not transform brewery into some useful institution?

Tuesday, May 6, 1919

Portsmouth. Inspection of yard & ships with officers. Royal Sovereign K 10. Over dock yard. Big docks—bigger than we have.

Salute fired anniversary of the coronation of the King.

Went to Whale Island. Lunched with Capt. Bax.[18] Toasts. Given to the President first. Wrens had on table trophies & mementoes given by classes. Capt. Scotts [19] dog—Arctic or Esquimaux—stuffed and mounted and looked natural as life. Gunnery School. Went in turrets, saw night spot firing. No woman lives on island. War simulated & practise. But turrets were of old type of ships and Capt B—— wished modern ones put in. Island is made. Mine experimental depot. Saw Tank used in war

Received on board the Victory, saw spot where Nelson was killed, where he died. Saw signal flags. England had no signal for Duty & when Nelson gave order: "England Expects Every Man to do his Duty," the word Duty had to be spelled out.

They gave first salute fired by Victory since 1904. Saw Nelson's prayer and relics and writings. Officer in command told stories of Nelson and showed where his officers were placed &c.

Returned to Dock Yard & Commandants for tea. I told Lady B—— about Sir Eric Geddes opposition to hereditary title. "Wait and see" she said. She longed for sunshine

Left on train for London. Passed through Arundel & Essex—most conservative part of England.

Why don't they wake the people up? I asked. Duke of Norfolk's castle. He is the head of all Catholic efforts.

Reached London 7:15.

Telegraphed in station to drive with us Wednesday night.

Naval Architects dinner. About 30 present. Chief speech by Sir Ernest

---

[17] Admiral Sir Cecil Burney, commander-in-chief at Portsmouth.
[18] Probably Captain Robert N. Bax.
[19] Captain Robert F. Scott, who died with his companions while returning from the South Pole in 1912.

Shackleford [20] who told of his trip toward South Pole & hardships, & five attempts to rescue his associates before they could reach them.

Addie & J D Jr went to dinner and theatre with Sir Eric Geddes to see Russian ballet

"I, Hall & Lord George [*sic*] have broad [?] ideas to labor & believe can prevent trouble by just dealings.["]

Wednesday, May 7, 1919

Eagle Hut YMC[A]. Visited Eagle Hut & spoke to hundreds of soldiers of US and English

YMCA Officers Club. Mr. Britton,[21] M.P. & committee welcomed us.
———— had given the club during period of war for American officers club

Saw Hadfields big torpedo & visited his place in London.

Went to luncheon at Ritz with Sir Robert Perks. I spoke. Lord Fisher made very funny speech. Dr. Chadwick [22] spoke of his trips to America & asked about Dr. Broughton.[23] Sir Robert Perks & Rasmussen, of Government. Dr. Jowett [24] differentiates between American ways & British ways. Americans hung out silver stars when boys went to war. England no. A tearless England A national trait to repress feeling. Press button & fly away. "It is so good once again to worship in a real Meth. church" said an Australian who attended Westminster.

After lunch went to City Roads chapel, went in house where Wesley lived, saw his grave, & some memorials & relics. "Did you ever read Charles Wesley's poems [?] during the Revolution?" No. Then never do so. Perks father had been pastor at City Roads.

Opposite is cemetery where Non-Conformists were buried. Susannah Wesley, Daniel Defoe, John Bunyan & others.

Mrs. D. had luncheon with Mrs. Davis

Bessie Fulham [?] called & we went to see moving pictures of our visit to Warwick Castle & to Stratford-on-Avon. Very good—also of visit to Tower and St. Pauls

Our dinner at night to invited guests. I proposed toast to King & President

[20] Sir Ernest Shackleton, British antarctic explorer.

[21] Sir Harry E. Brittain, M.P., founder and chairman of American Officers Club in London, 1917–1919.

[22] Possibly Samuel Chadwick, Methodist minister, principal of Cliff College, and president of the Wesleyan Methodist Conference.

[23] Probably Leonard G. Broughton, North Carolina–born Baptist minister who established the Baptist Tabernacle in Atlanta as one of the largest churches in the South.

[24] John H. Jowett, minister of Westminster Chapel, formerly minister of the Fifth Avenue Presbyterian Church, New York.

& in a few words expressed the feeling of satisfaction of visit and common destiny of the English speaking people. Addie began new Guest Book

Left for Plymouth at midnight.

& Davenport [sic]

Adml B & others called.

Thursday, May 8, 1919

Reached Plymouth Thursday morning. Met by Admiral Thursby,[25] V. A. Freemarcete,[26] who had wished to have us to breakfast & show us sights. Beautiful place. Boarded Corsair across the quarter deck of the Resolution. Gangway was beflagged. Resolution was flying U.S. flag. Lt. Com. Porter,[27] commanding Corsair. Sailed at 8:45 escorted by USS Connor. As passing out of harbor passed the place from which the Mayflower sailed. Also passed several Eagle boats on their way to Archangel. Here received papers of terms of peace with Germany.

Sea was rolling, but we had fair and pleasant trip. Corsair J. Pierpont Morgans yacht & had good record and believed it had sunk a submarine. Morgan never sailed across in her. M. lived on it at nights in N.Y. & would sail out. Loved to play sol[i]taire. Kaiser had twice come on yacht twice. [sic]

Had man in engine room arrested—a German—who went regularly to the German Consul in N.Y. Believed to report who came to see Mr. Morgan, who was agent for G.B. in buying munitions. Man claimed he went to German consulate because as Naval Reservist he was compelled to do so. No evidence and he was discharged.

Mr. M—— wanted no radio outfit as he used yacht to get away from every-body, but consented, as he was always ready to accept suggestions.

Capt. Porter met Kaiser—put on cap as he should not have done. One morning when Kaiser called Mr Morgan had not shaved and was eating breakfast. Mr. Morgan came out as he was, made a brief visit & left Kaiser proposed M for a club & got in at once. After dinner left before the Kaiser

Reached Brest at 7:18. Halstead [28] & Butler came aboard to call & arrange for next day.

Friday, May 9, 1919

Admirals called 9:30: Moreau & Grant. Went ashore with Halstead and Butler and drove out to Camp Pontanazon. Butler wanted his wife to come

---

[25] Admiral Sir Cecil Fiennes Thursby, commander-in-chief at Plymouth.
[26] Probably Vice Admiral Sir Sydney Robert Fremantle, deputy chief of naval staff.
[27] Probably Lieutenant Commander William B. Porter.
[28] Rear Admiral Alexander S. Halstead, commanding U.S. Navy forces, French coast.

over. Saw big depot & noted great improvement in seven weeks. Went to see dam of water works put in by the army. Not enough water. Asked the French to secure additional supply. It would take years. Army men said: "We can put it in in 6 months." French did not believe it possible but said "Go ahead." Finished in 6 mo & 1 day & it made possible water for army and water for ships. Before that French would cut off supply. Sent word to Americans must have all the water for a time whereas Americans had furnished the pumps. Very well. We must have our pumps to get water elsewhere. Wrote they had looked more fully into it & found could be arranged to let Americans have water. Halstead told of dance given to British officers & difficulty in obtaining permission from French authorities. In one day made all arrangements to surprise of French.

Called on Admiral Moreau. He & Grant & wife, Gen. Helmic[29] & Gen. Butler[,] Commodore Todd dined with us on Corsair and Admirals dined at club with other officers. Then we went aboard the Imperator—met by Capt. J. K. Robison,[30] & I spoke to new crew. Then on the Mount Vernon—received by Capt. Dismukes.[31] Waited for Military Committee of the House & sailed at abt [?] 4:28. Good passage out behind the lights. It was a quick turn around. Arrived at 9 a.m.—6,931 men on board. Embarked 5,800 troops & officers, mainly 33rd Division, with Gen. Bell[32] in command. French ships, including submarine chasers purchased from us, fully dressed with band, escorted us to the entrance of the harbor. Commodore Todd & Torchy [?] were the last to leave.

Josephus left with Halsted & Butler & we strained our eyes to see him
Barnetts letter

Saturday, May 10, 1919

Fair & cooler till afternoon. Then strong gale.

Devoted most of day to reading and resting. Barries "The Little Bird" has the most perfect tribute to the real woman—like my wife.

4 p.m. at tea with the Captain & Congressional Committee. 6.30 p.m. Dined with the Captain and he told us graphically, with suppressed tears in his eyes at times, of the story of the torpedoing of the ship & heroism of all the men —collective heroism. Shortly before, on that voyage, doctor & engineer had represented that it was very hot in the firing room—temp. very high, & closing of doors made it terrible on men. Suggested doors be opened ten minutes

[29] Major General Eli A. Helmick, commanding the U.S. base at Brest.
[30] Captain John K. Robison, commanding the U.S.S. *Imperator,* a large former German passenger liner taken over by the Navy after the war for troop transport service.
[31] Captain Douglas E. Dismukes, commanding the transport U.S.S. *Mount Vernon.*
[32] Major General George Bell, Jr., commanding the 33rd Division.

when force was shifted. His heart wanted to do it. Place a death trap. Said he would sleep on it. Next day, at great regret, had shut his teeth & said No. If he had listened to his heart, the doors would have been been [*sic*] opened & ship would have sunk. Told particularly of wonderful courage of [O']Connor, Fitzgerald and miraculous escape of Hoke Smith. Also of great efficiency of Gutsufson [?], Chief Engineer, & anxiety & trouble of getting ship in dry dock.[33]

Sunday, May 11, 1919

I spoke to soldiers at 10:15 and to sailors at 10:30. To soldiers spoke of their cheerfulness & courage & how it had saved the world. To sailors (see speech taken down by May [34])

Sea heavy and had to slow down. 2,000 people did not turn up for meals, including Gen. Bell & Gen. Williams [35] & many soldiers. Our party all in good shape. Addie doctored her cold and stayed in her rooms. Most of the day reading.

Leviathan passed & sent us message

Monday, May 12, 1919

Stormy day. Read Life of Lord Nelson by [blank] Interesting volume & just. Excoriates Nelson for his infatuation for Lady Hamilton which caused him to linger at Naples and was the only blot on his career.

Capt. Dismukes told of Hines, big rotund colored mess attendant in officers galley.

Where were you when the torpedo hit? Right here boss

What happened?

The pans and pots & all went right up to the top of the Galley.

Well what happened then when they came down

Boss, I wasn't there then.

Toasts [?]. Admiral Taylor & the jolly

Dismukes put prisoners on bread & water in the brig—& let them out. Got to be a joke.

In Brest two boys committed themselves again. He told Master of Arms to take copper wire and they could unfasten it if anything happened.

Two hours after he sent for Master of Arms who said boys got out before he could get to them.

[33] The *Mount Vernon*, a large troop transport, had been torpedoed on September 5, 1918, while westbound about 250 miles off the French coast. Despite severe damage and the loss of thirty-six lives, however, the ship was able to return to Brest safely.

[34] John B. May, Jr., Daniels' confidential clerk.

[35] Probably Brigadier General Roger D. Williams.

Cabled Lejeune congratulations that second division had won in contest & Fifth Brigade led all.

Passed Va & RI & sent messages

"   G. Washington

Tuesday, May 13, 1919

Read Henry Watterson's [36] Recollections and wrote him correcting that President Johnson said "alleged to be my father."

Dr. Gilmer [37] came in and suggested I give him leave to try to secure vote of 3 Senators he named—J, H & C. He thought he could influence them through his brother in law & other agencies if he could have time to go. Quixotic.

Feeding of soldiers in 2 hours.

Gen. Bell called. Said 33rd Division was the only one that fought with all— the French & British. My wife said "I am a mother & are you sure you are impartial [?"]

Praised Marines and said they always looked neat & lack of this in soldiers due to Q.M. Department and he had got in bad by calling attention to it.

Australians said Americans are not soldiers. They are butchers. Said this because when American troops, capturing prisoners in early days, asked Australians: Where shall we carry these men to kill them? Albert Cox regiment had been with him.

Told story of Luke Lee [38] trying to capture the Kaiser. When threatened with Court Martial trial on charge of using automobile on private business. He & others tried to capture Kaiser and had authority to go to Holland. Kaiser asked if he was sent by his Gov. 200 Prussian Guards. Used auto by Gen. Custom & asked to summon 40 Generals to prove they had used it & told General "I will summon you, for you used one on personal trip to Nice,["] &c.

Wednesday, May 14, 1919

Went all over ship on tour of inspection & observed arrangements for carrying troops. When ship was first taken over it could carry less than 3,000 soldiers. Now carries over 5,300—every possible space utilized. No odor in toilets, but sleep five tiers deep. When weather is fair the men are OK because they spend all but 8 hours in the open. In rough weather, they have [to] stay under cover. Capt. D—— pointed out exactly where torpedo struck, the

[36] Recently retired editor of the Louisville *Courier-Journal*.

[37] Probably Lieutenant William P. Gilmer, an assistant surgeon from Virginia.

[38] Colonel Luke Lea, editor and publisher of the Nashville *Tennesseean*, former Democratic U.S. Senator from Tennessee, 1911–1917.

fire room where every man was killed, the rooms from which Fitzgerald, O'Connor & Hoke Smith escaped, and where the first two showed such wonderful bravery & presence of mind. I saw & shook hands with them and others and shoveled coal into furnaces as a photographer took pictures. Quite warm & when inspection finished was wet all over with perspiration. Men in engine force serve 4 hours on & 8 hours off & have only pants & undershirt. Capable & cheerful in important work.

Showed us how Germans had tampered with machinery and tried to ruin it without betraying their act. Made one engine make revolutions in one way & another in opposite directions.

Griffin predicted good day for Thursday

Pictures taken with men wounded in torpedoing with J D & Mrs J D & Captain

Thursday, May 15, 1919

Ran over trip & wrote up Diary.

After lunch called in Dent's room on Military Affairs Committee and talked about all kinds of problems. Green,[39] of Vermt, thought British Government superior to ours because of our rigid constitution. Most of them opposed any extension of governmental control & deplored extension to socialistic measures. Feared effect of too many men in Gov. service and their ability to throw their votes to carry their ends. I told them of my talks with Kings of Italy, Belgium & England. Green thought little of English King, who, he said, took his brothers promised wife along with the throne. Men who travelled with him across America thought little of him. But Green say[s] value in permanent chief ruler. Talked Prohibition & how foreigners could not understand it—nor Americans either.

Tea at Captains. He had invited ladies & officers of French army en route for Siberia. We told stories of colored men in war.

Beautiful sea & glorious sun set—passed the Minnesota and South Carolina and sent them message wishing good voyage

Captain dined with us. Griffin & the Jazz band

Went to show "Liberty Bell company." Very funny—particularly the shaving scene.

Friday, May 16, 1919

Passed full-rigged sailing ship. Beautiful.

Talked with Admirals about our visit and what we should report about new construction of big ships.

[39] Frank L. Greene, Republican, U.S. Representative from Vermont, member of the House Military Affairs Committee.

Fog, but it cleared after lunch.

Gen Bell & Gen. Williams & other army officers at tea at Capt. Dismukes

Saturday, May 17, 1919

Reached New York. 8. a.m.

Gave interview to the press. Gov. of Ill[40] & others to meet the Prairie Division.

Went to Martinique. Luke Lee came up and I asked him about capture of the Kaiser "General custom" permitted use of autos. Admiral Glennon[41] called. Charles. Misty [?].

Came on B&O & read N&O all the way to Washington

Met at depot by F D R, & others from the Navy Dept.

Navy boy drove auto in NY & told my wife "He is the nicest man I ever met"

Sunday, May 18, 1919

Birthday. Flowers. Went to church. Talked with Overman about the bomb sent to him. Saved because Post Office clerk suspected package. It was at the time of marriage of his daughters and presents were coming and it was remarkable that the clerk had the instinct to keep out deadly missile

Lane & wife & others called.

Mrs. Dewey & John Jenkins to dinner.

Went to see Admiral Blue. Better.

Many called.

Son of E B McLean killed by auto. Mrs. D[ewey] and Addie went out.

Ed Crow [?] & wife here to supper

Monday, May 19, 1919

Welcomed at Dept. by yeowomen & marinettes [?] & officers as I went into new building. Photo taken in front of building.

Council of National Defense to discuss its future. Clarkson[42] outlined plan and said Hayes[43] (Rep. Chn) opposed.

Went to see Secy Baker pin decorations on Anna Howard Shaw and others.

Went to Salvation Army ball.

Saw Padgett and talked about Navy program He thought we ought not to build new programme but trust the League of Nations Put it up to Congress to have faith in League

[40] Frank O. Lowden, Republican.

[41] Rear Admiral James H. Glennon, commandant of the Third Naval District at New York.

[42] Grosvenor B. Clarkson, formerly secretary now director of the Council of National Defense and its Advisory Commission.

[43] Will H. Hays, chairman of the Republican National Committee.

Tuesday, May 20, 1919

Went over the German U boat. Wonderful ship & no wonder von Tirpitz— Pinned decorations on marines in front of Navy building & made brief address. Marine Band

Congressman Butler called & discussed naval plans

Went to reception at Willard to the new Speaker [44]

Wednesday, May 21, 1919

Meeting of Social Hygiene Board.

Thursday, May 22, 1919

Council. Craven [45] discussed air craft   Also appropriations & how we could cut down expenses.

National Defense Council met at C of D office. Houston outlined plan Bullard [?], McKean & Bullard—plan of GE Co to have world-wide wireless & Navy to give them all its patents—& they not to let any other country have them without our consent

Benson's letter.

Friday, May 23, 1919

Conference with G.E. Co. about their organizing a wireless company—a monopoly in patents. They have important patents which Marconi company wish & would give that English company too much power in world communication. Wouldnt GE Co. with monopoly of patents, go in with cable companies & keep up high prices by wireless & cable?

Conference with the General Board upon result of visit to Europe

Talked with Capt. Leigh [46] about personnel

Niblack wrote letter wishing to be Chief of Operations

Sunday, June 1, 1919

Bryant [1] and Whedbee [2] here & discussed President of University. They

[44] Frederick H. Gillett.
[45] Captain Thomas T. Craven, director of naval aviation.
[46] Captain Richard H. Leigh, formerly chief of staff at Admiral Sims' headquarters.

---

[1] Victor S. Bryant, Durham attorney and trustee of the University of North Carolina.
[2] Probably Charles Whedbee of Hertford, N.C., who on November 25, 1918, had written Daniels suggesting that he sound out President Wilson to head the University of North Carolina upon the completion of his presidential term.

seemed to favor McVeagh [3] of Kentucky who is getting $9,000 salary. Connor [4] & Ivey Lewis.[5]

Monday, June 2, 1919

Spoke to graduating class at Georgetown on Joan of Arc and visions and voices. Ruskin's "Lilies: Queens Gardens." Cardinal Gibbons present and gave address. Afterwards lunched with the Cardinals and priests. Gibbons talked of Gaston, Catholic, who when denied right to hold office because of his faith, said he had [been] baptized in patriotism in the blood of his father—killed by the English.

Went to hearings before Naval Affairs Committee.

Telegram that Grayson en route would give me message from the President who seemed not to approve my not pressing for three year program.

Tuesday, June 3, 1919

Naval Affairs Com

Spoke at Anniversary of Chateau Thierry with Baker at Marine Barracks

Wednesday, June 4, 1919

Naval Affairs Com

Spoke at American University. Rev Mr. Tiplady [6] also spoke

Tree planted by Col. Bancroft

Reception by NC Society

Gen Carr.

Griffin, Taylor, Earle

Thursday, June 5, 1919

Naval Affairs Com

5:30   Went to Annapolis with Riordan.[7] Went to ball after dinner

Friday, June 6, 1919

Spoke to graduates at Annapolis

Attended Naval Affairs Com. till late at night

Saturday, June 7, 1919

Before Naval Affairs Com.   Navy League

Preacher—Rev. Mr. Howard—came to see me about better protection for

[3] Frank L. McVey, president of the University of Kentucky.
[4] Robert D. W. Connor, secretary of the board of trustees of the University of North Carolina and president of the alumni association.
[5] Ivey F. Lewis, Raleigh-born professor of biology (botany) at the University of Virginia.
[6] Thomas Tiplady, British army chaplain.
[7] Daniel J. Riordan, Democrat, U.S. Representative from New York, a member of the House Naval Affairs Committee and of the Board of Visitors to the Naval Academy.

air men   His boy had gone in from Yale, ordered to fly at Boston when the 26th Regt paraded, bad weather conditions. Should not have gone. Driven out to sea & boy drowned. He took off his coat & put his watch his father gave him & the Bible his dead mother had given him, and wrote a note to his father, which was picked up on the beach five or ten days later

Commandant at Chatham had married an Italian. Demanded to be called Lady E—— If anyone called her Mrs. he was socially blacklisted

Sunday, June 8, 1919

Frank's 15th birthday

Went to Arlington to hear Maj. Stedman [8] on Confederate Memorial Day Hearings

Sterling Ruffin came to talk about University of NC [9]

Monday, June 9, 1919

Talked to Joe Tumulty about League of Nations   He showed me letter he had written the President about the character of speeches he should make Springfield Rep. urged President to say he would not be a candidate for re-election—that was hurting the League. Joe said it would hurt if he announced it now, but should wait till he returns and then in a speech in the West he could do so by appealing to men to rise above selfish interests

McKean spent evening talking about the Admirals for the fleet. Wilson and Rodman.

Letters from Ralph Graves [10] and Judge Eichem [?] about being Pres. of the Univ of NC

Saw bust of me made by Baker.[11] Addie did not like it

Tuesday, June 10, 1919

Cabinet discussed deportation of aliens who advocated changing government by force. Palmer said very stringent alien & sedition laws were proposed and he thought would make it possible to reach radical socialists who did not resort to force and he thought them dangerous. Baker asked what we thought of his serving notice on Villa if he fired a shot over the American

[8] Charles M. Stedman, Democrat, U.S. Representative from North Carolina, and former major of the Confederate Army.

[9] Dr. Ruffin was evidently advising Daniels on whether he should openly seek the presidency of the University of North Carolina. A longstanding supporter and trustee of the University, Daniels was at least mildly interested in becoming its president. See entries of June 9, 14, and 16, 1919.

[10] Ralph H. Graves, Chapel Hill-born Sunday editor of the New York Times.

[11] Percy Bryant Baker, English-born sculptor, who had done a bust of Daniels and other cabinet members.

line our soldiers would go after him. Then we would be held as having been responsible for any trouble that followed. Carranza would wish us to drive Villa men back. He had plenty of men in his army but they had no stomach for fight. Redfield was for going over. Polk wanted to but feared we had not considered sufficiently the danger of bandits murdering Americans in Mexico.

Discussed action of Congress in asking every employe to give name of every relative in the public service and any compensation except government salary.

Saw Baker about storage space.

Mrs. Smedley Butler called

Thursday, June 12, 1919

Discussed Navy bill at Council and also uniforms. Signed order ending cocked hat and full dress suit. Long tailed coat *not* tabooed yet, but— [12]

Told Bureau Chiefs to write any recommendations to change bill they thought were absolutely necessary but nowhere else. Will write strong letter against cut in aviation.

Left 4:30 for Annapolis to speak at Post Graduate school. Dinner at Admiral Scales & talked about engineering & its importance. Came back in the moonlight Glorious night

Friday, June 13, 1919

President approved

   Gleaves   Asiatic

   Rodman   Pacific

   Wilson   Atlantic [13]

Addie went to NC

Mitchell Palmer wanted to talk to me & Lane about lands in the West. Lt. Wright says officers of both Depts have about agreed on program & it leaves out Naval Oil Reserve

Dined with Admiral & Mrs. Clark [14] Army officers who had been abroad and their wives.

Saturday, June 14, 1919

Worked till 2 p.m. & then went to Balto. to speak at the close of The University of Maryland in Lyric theatre. A number of North Carolina boys graduated. I spoke on the Flag—Ehrenburghstein-Rhine [*sic*] &c. Also on

[12] Daniels favored a simple and functional uniform and after much consultation and deliberation had decided to take a significant step toward that goal.

[13] Daniels' choices for the major fleet assignments.

[14] Rear Admiral George R. Clark, Judge Advocate General of the Navy.

League of Nations and danger of Junkers and Bolshevists. C. T. Williams [15] (Raleigh Call) brought me home. Judge Harlan [16] presented me for degree of LLD & it was conferred by President Fell.[17] Very courteous & complimentary references

Addie telegraphed that Worth & Jonathan agreed with Ruffin & Mac [18] (say nothing now but not decline presidency of the University)

Talked with Rodman about plans for Pacific fleet and told him the President had approved his promotion to be Admiral. He was pleased and will make the fleet popular in the Pacific. We are planning to send it around at the earliest possible day so as to reach there early in August. He is senior to Wilson and wishes to command when the fleets unite.

He thinks Panama Canal should be put under control of the Navy & wants Baker & J D to go down there & officially open the Canal

Sunday, June 15, 1919

Conferred with Wilson about Atlantic fleet. He wished to name supply officer independent of McGowan. No!

Heard Bishop Hendrix [19] preach and he came home to dinner

Monday, June 16, 1919

Conference with Senator Page about Navy hearings. Agreed to begin on Wednesday with bureau chiefs and let me go to Chapel Hill and be heard Thursday

Chase [20] elected Pres. Univ of NC

Law forbade election of any man who was a Trustee

Left for CH

Tuesday, June 17, 1919

Reached Raleigh 5. am & went to N&O office.

Reached Chapel Hill in time for alumni dinner   Spoke at Service Reunion of Univ men who went across the sea.

[15] Charles T. Williams, North Carolina–born Baltimore banker.

[16] Henry D. Harlan, former chief judge of the Supreme Court of Baltimore and dean of the University of Maryland law school.

[17] Thomas Fell, provost of the University of Maryland.

[18] Probably Angus W. McLean, a fellow trustee of the University of North Carolina.

[19] Eugene R. Hendrix, bishop of the Methodist Episcopal Church, South.

[20] Harry W. Chase, professor of psychology and chairman of the faculty at the University of North Carolina. Just how serious Daniels was about his own candidacy is not clear, but he may have permitted his name to be used in an unsuccessful effort to head off the front-running Chase who had strong faculty support but whose Massachusetts birth had aroused opposition.

Trustees decided to secure landscape architect and lay off 500 acres belonging to Univ. adjoining campus and to take over Battle Park, make roads, and get ready for a Woman's College. Also to take steps to buy all the frontage on Main street from [?] home of President to street, Columbus on Hospital [?] —& move all fraternity houses off campus.

To provide for Education of E K Graham Jr

Recpetion [sic] in Gymnasium

Wednesday, June 18, 1919
Lane & Bickett had puncture and arrived late from Raleigh. Lane spoke. I introduced him. Bickett spoke to graduates, a few women.

Dined with new President, Dr Chase.

Went in auto to Raleigh. Spent time in N&O office.

Banquet at night by Chamber of Commerce & Rotary Club

Thursday, June 19, 1919
Reached Washington

Hearing before Senate Naval Affairs Com. and urged increased appropriations for aviation &c

Saturday, June 21, 1919
Dinner with V.P. to meet the President-elect [Epitacio] Pessoa, of Brazil, at Pan American

Sunday, June 22, 1919
Bishop Candler preached first sermon in new Mt. Vernon Place Meth Ch.

Took Brazilian President and party to Mt. Vernon on Mayflower

Left for Carlisle Pa.

Monday, June 23, 1919
Spoke at Dickinson College, Carlysle [sic]. Dr. J. H. Morgan,[21] President. Received degree of LLD

Visited Gettysburg Battle field

Tuesday, June 24, 1919
Lunched at Willard with Redfield to meet President-elect of Brazil.

Cabinet discussed growing estrangement between executive and legislative. Glass & Redfield rather bitter. Both had been members of Congress and turned

[21] James H. Morgan, prominent Methodist layman and temperance leader, president of Dickinson College since 1915.

state's evidence. Baker thought only remedy for members of Cabinet to go to Congress and present their own measures

Glass protested against Coast Guard officers wishing to remain in the Navy through organization.

Dined with Frank Polk. Pres Brazil. Reception at Pan American

Wednesday, June 25, 1919

Went to depot to say good bye to Pres of Brazil

Sat for painting of portrait to Mr. Lockman

Talked with Wilson and Rodman about Atlantic & Pacific fleets

Leigh called about Navigation

Signed order restoring Blue's number

Thursday, June 26, 1919

Commander Wright & Mr. Kearful talked of oil litigation and legislation

Kearful's successor was appointed before he tendered resignation. Will he reverse policy [22]

Friday, June 27, 1919

Mother & Mary Cleaves came

Long talk with Butler and Swanson on naval bill. Asked Butler to take out the personnel (personal) legislation in Senate bill.

Saturday, June 28, 1919

Long talk with Gregory. P——[almer] is candidate for President & had said "D—— is unreasonable. Lane more reasonable." He will line up with the oil men.

Fears that naval reserve will be lost to those who have no valid claim & fears that K——[earful] will not argue the Honolulu case & nobody else can argue it. He has no doubt he will win it

Conference Committee agreed on Naval bill. Cut aviation to $25,000,000

Sunday, June 29, 1919

Took mother to Mt. Vernon Place, the first communion in new church

Spent afternoon with Mr. Lockman who is now painting my portrait standing.

[22] Assistant Attorney General Kearful had been outspokenly critical of Secretary Lane's oil leasing policies and his evident intention to uphold most of the Honolulu Oil Company's claims in the heart of the Navy's Oil Reserve No. 2 in California. Daniels was much afraid that the new Attorney General, Palmer, would side with Lane in the oil dispute, and that the Navy could no longer count on Justice Department support as in the days of Attorney General Gregory. See also entry of June 28, 1919.

The President sailed from Brest at 1 p.m. today

Talked to McAdoo about reception to the President & said we could send out ships if committee desired.

Mrs. Lit Alley [23] called to see mother—we talked of Wilson and Wilson people. Dr Lawrence [24] (Koskor) [?] & all the Wilson people who went to St Louis & got rich

Monday, June 30, 1919

Towers, Reed, Bellinger and all the others of the NC's which made the flight to Europe called.[25] I said a few words, and our photographs were taken together.

June 30th—last day of the fiscal year   Many requests for allottments [*sic*] of Aviation and Emergency funds to be used which would otherwise go into the Treasury. I had to say "No" very hard. A $700,000 warehouse wanted out of Aviation.

Talked to Baker about Joint Army & Navy Board on Aviation to prevent duplication.

———————

Saturday, July 5, 1919

Reached Columbus early 8 am & went to hotel. Reviewed parade of Minute Men & other Methodists. Went out to Exposition at 11—first calling to see Gov. Campbell,[1] the chairman of the Com.

Spoke to Minute Men—great audience.

"D for President" many cried

Sunday, July 6, 1919

Returned from Ohio & Indiana

[23] Mrs. R. L. ("Lit") Alley, wife of the foreman and job printer Daniels had worked with on the Wilson *Advance* in the 1870's.

[24] Dr. J. J. Lawrence, a Wilson physician in the days of Daniels' youth who later moved to St. Louis.

[25] On May 8, three Navy NC seaplanes, commanded by Commander John H. Towers, Lieutenant Commander Albert C. Read, and Lieutenant Commander Patrick N. L. Bellinger, left Rockaway, N.Y. on the first transatlantic flight. Only the NC-4 completed the flight to Plymouth, England, arriving there on May 31, after a flight of 4,513 miles in just under fifty-four hours flying time.

———————

[1] James E. Campbell, Democrat, former U.S. Representative and governor of Ohio.

Monday, July 7, 1919
Left to NY to meet the Presid[en]t

Tuesday, July 8, 1919
Went on Penn. at 8 am with V.P. & party. Sighted the G.W. [George Washington] at 11 o'clock & reached Hoboken about 3 o'clock. Thousands of children & great enthusiasm & crowd—

Pres. wirelessed   Why do we not go on in? Tide, like time, waits nor hurries for no man.

Pres. spoke in Carnegie Hall. Many cheered for D—— as we drove through N.Y.

C. Clark: Don't let McAdoo get ahead of you? He stands up and bows every time there is a single cheer.

Judge Gary asked to come on train.

Beautiful sight in Washington. Everything illuminated but the Capitol   To my wife who expressed regret he said: "It never is illuminated[."]

Wednesday, July 9, 1919
Mr Thomas (Labor Rep) of England here

L. G. has majority but any day he opposes Imperialism & Militarism he will lose his Tory maj[ority]

People getting weekly pay from Gov. will not work

Thursday, July 10, 1919
President spoke to the Senate—tense interest. Received with cheering but too serious for cheers

Bob Bingham & Davies came & we arranged to see Attorney General Palmer & urge Shepherd Bryan [2] for Judge

Friday, July 11, 1919
Had call from Mr. Thomas, Labor member of Parliament

The President came to see me

Saturday, July 12, 1919
Italy asked us to send coal & let them have a cable laying ship. This through Admiral Vantenlli.[3] Polk said Italy must be made to feel that she has no friends until she is ready to play with other nations and help toward world peace. We have no colliers with which we could send coal

[2] Shepard Bryan, North Carolina–born Atlanta attorney.
[3] Probably Rear Admiral Count Max Lovatelli, Italian naval attaché.

Gov. Folk came to see me about Jim Reed, Borah,[4] Hawes and others who talk about establishing a new party. Folk said if they did they would get more Republicans than Democrats and it would help our party

He advised me to have a friendly delegation from North Carolina at the next National Convention, that I had come out of war with warm friends everywhere and would make strong candidate—the Southern birth would not matter

Sunday, July 13, 1919
  Went to hear Dr. Chappell
  Sat for portrait

Monday, July 14, 1919
  Powell about dreadnaught at Fore River
  Armor plate men for conference. They wished 532 to 543 per ton. Made contract for 520.
  Went to F[rench] Embassy to see Legion of Honor to Barnett & others. Ambassador spoke & pointed to picture of Lafayette & Rochamb——[eau]
  Went to reception at French Embassy. Ambassador & President spoke. He said he & Mrs W—— came under irresistible compulsion though they had not been invited. Beautiful speeches. Speaking of seeing the flag on Ehren-burghst—[Ehrenbreitstein], he said to his wife: "I say, can you see? ["]
  Pres. "I did not intend to speak. I see Senators here. It is now time for them to speak[."]
  Talked by wireless telephone to Aero Dinner [?] in Cleveland, Ohio

Tuesday, July 15, 1919
  Attending meeting with reference to War Insurance Board. Former Justice Hughes, Baker, Glass, & others. Chomley Jones [5] explained situation. 30% of men released from service do not receive letters sent to them. How are they to be reached? Hughes said the Gov. must live up strictly to contract. I added "and do more for these youthful soldiers and sailors, who after the first year, will settle down, get married, and wish to renew their insurance.["]
  Cabinet. President discussed treaty. The B & French brought J into the war by promising big things—promised everything that was taken from Germany N of Equator. This included Shantung. He felt acquiescence a big price to pay to get J into League, but obtained J's renunciation of right Germany

---

[4] William E. Borah, Republican, U.S. Senator from Idaho, and one of the leaders of the anti-League of Nations "Irreconcilables" in the Senate.
[5] Richard G. Cholmeley-Jones, director of the Bureau of War Risk Insurance.

possessed of sovereignty, land[,] soldiers &c & to accept islands as mandatory under League of Nations instead of ownership as B & F promised Japan.

Dantsig [Danzig] as free port necessary to give Poland a port. Left future to plebiscite. Without League there will be trouble with G—— With treaty hope that G—— will acquiesce & Poland on [?] right to give equal treatment on rail roads.

Shall we continue Economic Board? or form new one.

He told Lloyd G that they wished G—— to pay & would not let her work to pay. L G had promised G—— should pay cost of war. Knew it was impossible, but framed up Reparation Com. to keep voters from knowing how much they will get

Shall we have civilian medals?

Benson, Sims, March, Pershing.

Wednesday, July 16, 1919

Talked with Swanson about conditions in Senate. He fears there must be some reservations to secure ratification of League. He hopes W will agree to such as will not destroy the effectiveness. If we can get 49 votes we can dictate the reservations.

Attended meeting of War Risk Insurance. Gov. Hughes said he did not come to white wash or approve legislation. He talked and talked & seemed to be trying to find something to criticize and then later to claim credit for reforming the bureau. Tiresome, very. Baker & I wanted action & to let the public know improvement & difficulties. 30% of men who had given allotments &c could not be found from the address they had given. That fact explains ⅓ of the complaints

YMCA of Boston criticized for circulating book to add to our friendship for G.B. I told them it was misuse of YMCA funds

Thursday, July 17, 1919

War Risk Insurance committee made report on improvement.

George Creel. "I am making money." Am looking to you as darkhorse.

Approved D.S. & NC [6] for British, French, Jap & other naval men.

Thomas Nelson Page here & with his brother took dinner with us. He is genuinely and earnestly pro-Italy & says France has financed Serbia which spent big sum of propaganda for Jugo-Slavs. We should flatter Italy, help it, and furnish coal & food. It may be made our best friend. If we do not, we lose its friendship and it will hurt the Democratic party.

[6] The Distinguished Service Medal and the Navy Cross.

Sunday, July 20, 1919
Stayed at home with mother
David & Mary Louise here to dinner.
Riot—race—following negro assaults on white women.
Long talk with mother and happy time. "Heaven sent her to you" she said talking of Addie who had such goodness of heart, executive ability, and charm.

Monday, July 21, 1919
Took up with Powell building dreadnaught No 54. He wished too much. "Race riots."
Marines ordered out to keep order. Carriage full of negroes drove by Naval Hospital and wantonly fired into party of convalescent sailors & marines
Mother went home

Tuesday, July 22, 1919
Powell came in to talk about building new battleship at Fore River. He wished Navy to let use tools & buildings built by Navy to construct destroyers & pay them for the slip. That would mean 18 mil dollars. Capps thought we ought first to take up the destroyer business and have that adjusted.
McFarland (Boston American) called and was hot against Shantung provision of the peace treaty. Said he feared it would put Russia under control of reactionists. France ought to help herself & we ought not to finance her if she insisted upon such provisions as Shantung treaty. France has not imposed any income tax.
Went before Naval Affairs Com. on bill to advance Benson and Sims to Admirals for life. Decided to give them Admiral salary for life, but not to keep them on active list expect [except] in the discretion of the President.
We took John [7] home on act [account] of race riots
Ordered naval guard & used marines to restore order. One marine killed

Wednesday, July 23, 1919
Went to see Baker. Com. on Pub. Information cannot wind up its affairs because it cannot spend any money on accountants & clerks. They have the money turned back or to be turned back to meet all expenses and wished to find a way to wind up. We asked him to file a statement and we would see what could be done.
Baker was reading report of Crowell Board on aviation.[8] He was warm

[7] John Pye, Daniels' Negro chauffeur.
[8] Assistant Secretary of War Benedict Crowell had just returned on July 20 from a visit

over Crowell's action in flying in the face of his orders and presenting a
report for an Air Ministry. At first he thought of sending for Crowell and
compelling action that would lead to resignation, but after reading report
found it so weak he decided to let it go to Congress with his statement that
it might be good for commercial aviation but would impose heavy burdens
on tax-payers and be of no military value. I had cancelled Mustin's [9] orders
issued by F D R but had decided, in view of passports &c, not to do so, upon
assurance that he did not favor air ministry. And yet he signed it! It is better
to stick to your hunch.

Marine wounded in race riot died

Thursday, July 24, 1919
   Belle & Geol. survey
   Peter Gerry. Must be some explanation, he feared, if Senate ratified the
League.

Friday, July 25, 1919
   Grayson called and talked about Wurtsbaugh.
   Saw Tumulty about President's going to California. He felt W W should
tell the country that resolutions expressing explanations would do no harm
and he would not oppose, but amendments and reservations would defeat
the League and ought not be engrafted   Impossible to re-assemble Peace Conference and therefore amendments would defeat League.
   Reps. (Standpat) will oppose anything and the President should not let
them mislead the man in the street by representing that the President opposes
any interpretation that would clarify the Covenant

Sunday, July 27, 1919
   Raleigh

Tuesday, July 29, 1919
   Cabinet. Discussed treaty. Pres. does not believe any reservation can secure
a majority in the Senate. Rumania wished a reservation of its sovereignty. The
League put other nationalities under it but must see that minorities & races
are treated right. If the US makes reservations other nations will do likewise
once it is opened up and where will it end—?

---

to Europe with a mission to investigate various aviation services. His report, which both
Daniels and Baker disapproved, recommended combining the Army and Navy aviation
services into a Department of Aviation of cabinet rank.
   [9] Captain Henry C. Mustin of the Bureau of Construction and Repair, a member of the
Crowell aviation mission.

Lane, Palmer & I discussed oil   W. W. felt that oil & coal ought to be saved for all the people. No agreement.

Talked about trip to California. The President cannot go now. Too hot and some Senators think he should stay—his going would be regarded as fight with the Senate

D. W. W.[10]

Washington [11] Chief of Navigation

Saturday, August 9, 1919

Left San Diego at 7 o'clock.[1] Reception Committee of Los Angeles went up with us on New Mexico to that city   Reached there at 2 o'clock. The Mayor [2] came on board and presented me with key to the city. Then we went up to Alexandria Hotel

Dinner at Jonathan Club.

Sunday, August 10, 1919

Went with Mayor to Meth Church in Hollywood. Sermon on Reciprocity. Man's ability & God's guidance. [?]

Spoke at Rodeo

Spoke at Auditorium (Treaty) & at Club for Enlisted Men.

Dined at night at University Club. They gave Addie wonderful basket of fruit. She made a speech & captivated all

Monday, August 11, 1919

Mrs. Foy [3] dined with us. She is Democratic representative of national committee. Told of her plans for organization—felt she should have funds to hold gatherings of women Dem. workers.

[10] Probably Captain Daniel W. Wurtsbaugh, whom Daniels may have considered as the new chief of the Bureau of Navigation. See also previous entry.

[11] Rear Admiral Thomas Washington, appointed chief of the Bureau of Navigation on August 5 to replace Victor Blue who had recently retired because of ill health.

---

[1] On August 1, Daniels, accompanied by Mrs. Daniels and their two youngest sons, Jonathan and Frank, had left Washington to meet the new Pacific Fleet at San Diego and tour naval installations on the West Coast prior to joining President Wilson for a great naval review at San Francisco on September 1.

[2] Meredith P. Snyder, Democrat.

[3] Mary E. Foy, associate member of the Democratic National Committee.

Had call from delegation on trying to prevent success of Americans who were going to Mexico to open saloons & slip it [liquor] over in autos to defy the American Pro.[hibition] law. They are to write me & I will take it up with Lansing

Call from Judge Bledsoe [4] who wanted me as the Dem. candidate for President. I told him I would not be candidate.

Went to Lasker's [5] studio. Met Mr De Mille [6] born in Washington.

Went out to Country Club to lunch

Then to Huntingtons [7]

Ball at night   Dinner at Dr Randolph Hills [8]

Tuesday, August 12, 1919

Went with Mayor and others to San Pedro and inspected site for proposed submarine base. Told the Mayor it would be necessary for us to have all the land to Army reservation and up to Pacific Avenue.

Went on board Texas. Mary Pickford [9] gave cup to crew who thanked her for help in Liberty Bond campaign. Had pictures taken.

Attended Business Men's Luncheon Club and spoke on the Navy & Profiteering, suggesting it was as great a crime to profiteer in peace as in war.

Spoke on the Peace Treaty at Pershing Square

Went with Addie to the Women's Club where she made a hit.

Had Mayor & Elliott [10] to dinner & we left on the New York & sailed at 9 pm

Wednesday, August 13, 1919

Quite a number of men sea sick. There was quite a roll and some rain. Most of the sailors are new men and this was their first experience of rough weather at sea.

The Mississippi had been good enough to lend us the band as it was better than the New York band.

Went to moving picture show

[4] Benjamin F. Bledsoe, U.S. district judge for southern California.

[5] Jesse L. Lasky, pioneer motion picture producer.

[6] Cecil B. De Mille, director general of the Jesse L. Lasky Feature Play Company.

[7] Henry E. Huntington, financier and railroad capitalist, a noted bibliophile.

[8] Randolph W. Hill, Los Angeles physician and Democrat, a leader of the Los Angeles Fleet Reception Committee.

[9] Popular motion picture actress.

[10] John B. Elliott, Collector of the Port of Los Angeles, in charge of harbor arrangements for the fleet visit.

Thursday, August 14, 1919

Received Secret Code message from Tumulty. Confidential. President tells me he will in all probability have to defer trip to Coast until later, but desires reception to fleet be held in San Francisco, Cal. Sept. 2nd just the same. ["]President does not wish this given out yet"

Gave tea in Admiral's quarters to one half of officers

Capt.[11] took dinner with us

Friday, August 15, 1919

Sent Radio messages to San Diego accepting offers for Hospital site, & storage warehouse.

Would you wish to live this life over again? Jonathan read an essay from "Pebbles From the Shore" and it said 5 elderly men discussed this question & 4 out of 5 said they would not

Gave tea to one half of officers

Saturday, August 16, 1919

Went with the Captain on tour of inspection of the ship

Dined with the Ward Room officers.

Moving Pictures

Sunday, August 17, 1919

Went to church at 10 a.m. The chaplain, Rev. Neff,[12] preached on "The Upper Room in our Lives"—a very good sermon   One of his hymns was by John Wesley and in his sermon he quoted from Bishop McDowell & I knew then that he was a Methodist. He lunched with us and Jonathan combatted his mother in a discussion on the doctrine of predestination.

In the afternoon took dinner with the Junior Officers. The young man who sat next to me came into the Navy as an electrician and had been promoted to commission rank. He was with the New York when it was in the North Sea and told of difference between B & A methods. They are very thorough and very conservative. There was friendship between A & B officers but none between sailors of the races

Monday, August 18, 1919

A sad and depressing day. Soon after breakfast news came that on Sunday night, as the turret was being moved, a young sailor was crushed to death.

[11] Captain William V. Pratt, commanding the U.S.S. *New York*.
[12] Lieutenant (Junior Grade) Josiah L. Neff.

It had to be stopped midway to fix some wires. He evidently thought it had stopped, crawled into what was a place of safety, and was killed immediately. It cast a gloom over the whole ship & depressed Addie all day.

Later in the day I went down to see Admiral McCormick,[13] who was not very well—ate nothing Sunday. He knew his symptoms and diagnosed them as appendicitis, and decided, in conference with the Ship's doctors, that an operation that day was necessary. He was cheerful and calm in the face of what he knew was the danger always incident to such operations. "My wife will be troubled and anxious" he said, and with a wistful smile that spoke of the love he bore her, said "for you know she is the only husband I have." [sic]

Did not feel in mood to go to moving pictures

Tuesday, August 19, 1919
Decided to have review in Frisco on Labor Day. That will give us a day less at Hila but more time in Frisco and have the review on a big holiday so the people of SF can see the fleet without losing a working day. Also sent radio we would go to the Yosemite from S.F.

Decided, after talk with Capt. Pratt, to radio that the young man accidentally killed when turret was moved, should not be buried at Honolulu as at first Pratt thought of doing, but taken to Mare Island and forwarded to Galesburg, Ill. if his parents desired. Otherwise would be buried in Mare Island

Wednesday, August 20, 1919
Reached Honolulu at 8 a.m. Admiral Fletcher,[14] Gov. McCarthy[15] & reception com. came on board. Before that submarines met us and escorted us in. Flying machines dropped lei on ship. Men out to meet ship & swimmers dived for money. Got in cars, went to hotel Monoa [Moana]. Daughters of warriors, wearing capes made of feathers of birds worn by warriors. Made of feathers of birds, the Oho, permitted only to royalty. Royal lei made of red carnations and tied with royal red ribbon placed on Addie's head & also on me.

Luncheon (Mrs. McGregor & son) gave me lei made of yellow ginger

Escorted by daughter of warrior to rooms, decorated in native flowers & fruits—Cape jasmine [?], white ginger. Also bread fruit, papai, & pine apples. Looked out on the sea.

[13] Rear Admiral Albert M. D. McCormick, medical director commanding the naval medical supply depot at Mare Island.
[14] Rear Admiral William B. Fletcher, commandant of the Fourteenth Naval District and the Naval Station at Hawaii.
[15] Charles J. McCarthy, governor of Hawaii.

I spoke at luncheon. Yellow lei (in paper in imitation of feather lei)   Gov. McCarthy, Judge Keen [16] (½ Chinese & ½ Hawaii   it makes good stock)[,] Judge Dole.[17] Hawaiian music & song. Spent afternoon at Pearl Harbor. Cottage on point built by Engineer in charge of coal plant.

Reception by Mrs. McCarthy in home of Queen Lil.[18] 60 year old woman [19] danced & Hawaiian band

Out to Country club at dinner with Fletcher. Very beautiful. Met most of ranking Army & Navy officers

Stopped to see hedge of night blooming *cereas* [*sic*].

Jap delegation gave two handsome vases in the morning. Other delegations called. Americans said Japs put one over on them by presentation.

Thursday, August 21, 1919

Centipede on floor in boys room. Foote stepped on it with his sandals & I killed it.

Left at 8:30 on Destroyer Dent (Capt. Shafroth) [20] to Pearl Harbor. Sailed all around Ford Island. Great crowd at opening of Dry Dock. Saw place where they would put dead horse to draw sharks in at high tide. Then when sharks came in they would be killed. Addie pressed button and water poured in. Fletcher & Hines [21] spoke. Then I spoke. Then reception & luncheon. Gave Addie pin. Built on place supposed to be home of shark god & natives predicted something terrible would happen if his home was invaded. When accident destroyed dock, they said it proved they were right. After present dock had been begun Dry Dock Smith [22] let Hawaiians get a Kalinin [?] woman, priestess, make sacrifice to Shark God. White chicken, black pig, bottle of gin & next day dead shark found in bottom of dock. At luncheon met native divers who helped build dock.

Visited Marine Barracks and heard delegation of workingmen

Dined with the Governor and later big reception at Palace. Japs, Chinese, Hawaiians   all colors & shades. No color line.

[16] Judge William H. Heen.

[17] Sanford B. Dole, former president of the Republic of Hawaii, 1894–1900, former governor and U.S. district judge of Hawaii.

[18] Former Queen Liliuokalani, overthrown by a revolt of American settlers in January, 1893, whose palace was now the governor's residence, Washington Place.

[19] Mrs. Manuel Reis, noted Hawaiian dancer.

[20] Lieutenant Commander John F. Shafroth, Jr.

[21] L. G. Hines, president of the San Francisco Bridge and Construction Company, main contractor for the Pearl Harbor drydock.

[22] Francis B. "Drydock" Smith, chief engineer of the San Francisco Bridge and Construction Company, in charge of the drydock construction.

Friday, August 22, 1919

Left early for trip around the island in autos. Went to Marconi radio station which is closed. Through pine apple groves, through the Pali, wonderful view. Stopped at Boys Ind. School, where Capt Berger,[23] who had trained bands & helped Queen Lil with her songs & music. At noon went to Luau, given by Mayor Fern,[24] a regular Hawaiian feast—raw fish, baked pig, poi, sweet potato poi with cocoanut milk. Speaking, I called on Addie to speak who made hit Gourd in middle of table. Chicken had been cooked with hot rocks. Pig cooked under ground & retained all its juices. Hot rocks inside and out. Addie selected her own piece of baked pig, with over skin. Stopped at Scofield barracks where saw games between Army & Navy, then to tea, then through the pine apple plantations to Honolulu.

Dinner by Commercial Club at Moana Hotel. Walter Dillingham[25] made speech & I followed

In afternoon visited [blank]

Saturday, August 23, 1919

Received officials at Moena.

Delegation of Democrats called and I spoke on Dem prospects and issues.

Addie visited YWCA, Agnes [?] Museum & had luncheon with wife of Gen. Morton[26]

Native Hawaii woman called. Presented me with cape like warriors way [*sic*]. Gave Addie a feathered cape & black eyed susan (red). Mrs. Atchley, whose husband is surgeon in British navy. Her daughter gave Jonathan a real feather lei.

Went to Mr. Garret Wilder's[27] & saw pink hybiscus to which he gave the name Adelaide. He had named others. His father was a trusted friend of the King.

Went to the luau at Mrs. [George] Beckleys, a regular Hawaiian feast. She is sister of Princess David. Beckley has royal blood. Hula-hula girls danced. More decent than the Spanish girl who danced or than many American women who look down on hula dancing girls.

Left at 8 o'clock. Great crowd to see us off & we felt we were leaving real

[23] Henri Berger, noted Hawaiian bandmaster.
[24] Joseph J. Fern, mayor of Honolulu.
[25] Walter F. Dillingham, president of the Honolulu Chamber of Commerce and president of the Hawaiian Dredging Company, the subcontractor for the drydock channel.
[26] Ida Hastings Morton, wife of Major General Charles G. Morton, commanding the Hawaiian Department.
[27] Gerrit P. Wilder of the Honolulu Chamber of Commerce.

friends. New York got under way, 9 o'clock. Everybody in Honolulu most hospitable & sugar & pine apples had made them prosperous

Sunday, August 24, 1919

Gov, Mr. Wilder & Maj. Doherty [28] went with us on New York. Reached Hilo about eleven. Maj. Scott [29] & Mr. Good [?] (Chamber of Commerce)[,] Mr. Hardy (editor) took us to club & there took us to Luau. Very good food. Made brief speech. Scotts very fine people. After Luau went in autos to Mt. KilAuea. Glorious drive. Sailors went up part of way on train & then by auto. Went through forest of fern trees. Ginger blossoming along the road.

Prof. Jagger [30] & wife gave us tea at his cottage called the Bird Cage in full view of volcanoes. Then went to volcano. Pela, is the goddess of volcano. Lava that looks like blown glass is called Pela's hair & it is found 300 miles at sea. Then went up on mountain. Saw extinct crater 780 feet deep. Walked over to volcano. In violent eruption. "Pela is behaving finely and giving us a fine exhibition" they said. Son of Greek proprietor Demosthenes Aristides showed sulphur bath and old building. Bright boy. Gave Addie lei of fuchias Very hot from burning lava which rushed violently against side of crater. Never dreamed of anything so terrible & grand. After staying into the night to see the moon rise, went to Volcano hotel, had dinner, and then drove to Hilo, all very sleepy & went to bed on the New York which got underway at once for San Francisco

Flowers for A D

Monday, August 25, 1919

Slept late.

Destroyer Philips returned to Honolulu with sick man.

The New York had 1,700 people aboard. They had enlisted about 300 in the four days at Honolulu, beside the band and brought back a number of soldiers whose enlistment had expired.

We enjoyed alligator pears given by Mr. Moir, of Island of Hawaii & the fruit by the Princess David & Mrs. A. F. Taylor [31] of Honolulu. Green cocoanuts, alligator pears, mangoes from Mr. Wilder.

Flowers for A D from Honolulu Chamber of Commerce

[28] Major James D. Dougherty, aide to Governor McCarthy.

[29] John A. Scott, chairman of the Hilo welcoming committee.

[30] Thomas A. Jaggar, Jr., geologist and volcanologist in charge of the Hawaiian Volcano Observatory of the U.S. Weather Bureau.

[31] Mrs. A. P. Taylor, a leader of the Daughters of Hawaiian Warriors and wife of a reporter on the *Pacific Commercial Advertiser.*

Tuesday, August 26, 1919

For lunch we had green mango pies and cocoanut cake sent by Mrs. Mc-Carthy, wife of the Governor

Dinner with the warrant officers. Had pictures of dinners given in that room on the North Sea. Also pictures of the King of England, Rodman and Sims. One officer had been with Dewey at the battle of Manila Bay. Another had been on Wyoming when we were on in April 1913 & recalled that Frank sat in his mothers lap in the happy hours on the Wyoming.

Music by Hawaiian band just enlisted while at Honolulu & the music recalled our delightful stay.

Flowers (carnations) from H. C of C [Honolulu Chamber of Commerce.]

Wednesday, August 27, 1919

Visited Admiral McCormick, who was improving. When we reached Honolulu he was very ill—bowels locked—and there was serious fear that he would not survive

Happy hour. Singing & boxing, with some vaudeville. Music was by new Hawaiian band.

Gladiolas for A D from H C of C

Thursday, August 28, 1919

At Sea

Friday, August 29, 1919

at sea

Saturday, August 30, 1919

Chauncey left early, 6 am. for San Francisco, carry mail & copies of four speeches I had written.

Reed Hayes, Asso. Press man, Tracy (United Press) took my speeches to send out in advance to the paper by mail.

Passed the only ship we saw en route

Sunday, August 31, 1919

Reached Monterey Sunday about ten o'clock Mayor & committee came on board. We went to Presbyterian church and heard very fine sermon by Rev. Dr. Freeman,[32] of Pasadena. (Rev. Barclay was pastor church). Then to din-

[32] Robert Freeman, minister of the Pasadena Presbyterian Church.

ner at Del Monte. Afterwards went to presidio where I spoke (Meth preacher I had met at Columbus, made prayer.[)] Had written speech on ship. Then went for a drive under direction of Mr. Green,[33] called Tin Can Green. He had been over all the world & brought trees of all kinds & plants & helped people to grow them in tin cans. Mayor of Pacific Grove Mr. Edward Berwick had glorious view over looking ocean. Town was original Methodist camp ground & many retired ministers lived there. Very strict old fashioned. Some original buildings taken over by U.S. Navy when Monterey was taken by the United States. Visited site they wished Navy to take over. Saw wonderful cypress tree over 4,00 [sic] years old. Cypress grove. Saw spot where the ship, of which Capt. Ward, of Raleigh, was captain, went down.

Left at 6 p.m. for San Francisco. Mayor [34] & Jayne [35] & Gen Liggett [36] & others met us & took us to Palace Hotel at 10:30 & then to bed.

Monday, September 1, 1919

Left at 10 a.m. for the Oregon. Governor, Mayor, & ship full of Committee-men & wives on board ship. A little fog. Passed Oregon exactly just as ships clock chimed seven bells—eleven o'clock—the time Rodman had agreed upon.

I went up on look-out station above the bridge to review fleet which came by in perfect order, all playing national air & saluting. All destroyers saluted with 19 guns. Ships came one by one out of fog, as if new born, & as last one passed Oregon the sun came out & made a beautiful scene. Hills all covered with people—literally black with them. After review, Rodman, Admirals & Captains came on board & luncheon was served for all. 2.30 went to Goat Island, inspected station, and spoke to new sailors from steps of administration station.

Tea with Mrs. Jayne & met officers, wives & others.

In evening Mayor gave dinner at Fairmont hotel & Y.W.C.A. gave reception to Mrs. D who pinned badges on 600 war nurses.

I made speech I had written on New York

Addie spoke to women & then went to enlisted mens ball at **Fairmont**

[33] Harry A. Greene, noted Monterey harbor booster.

[34] James Rolph, Jr., Republican, mayor of San Francisco.

[35] Rear Admiral Joseph L. Jayne, commandant of the Twelfth Naval District at San Francisco.

[36] Major General Hunter Liggett, commanding the Western Department with head-quarters at San Francisco.

Tuesday, September 2, 1919

Left early & made full inspection of new dry dock & suggested naval base at Hunters Point. Splendid dock.

Then to Union Iron Works where Addie launched the Chase, new destroyer. They are building 66. Diamond pin and flowers.

Luncheon by Commonwealth & Asso. Clubs. I spoke on the Oregon, the Panama canal ("Well I think it is worth it["]) & the Pacific fleet

Parade in honor of Women War Workers—soldiers, sailors, marines, & others, with women in carriages. Day fire works, air ships going over parade, Gov. Stephens held his grand-daughter, child of Capt. Zane [1] killed in France, up as Marines passed by. Recalled review in London where colonials passed before King at Buckingham Palace. Mrs. Stephens gave Addie a beautiful fan of California ostrich feathers.

5.30. Went to Letterman Hospital (army) where there are many men wounded in France. A woman, the only field secretary, in charge, beautiful. Dr. Boone,[2] decorated for service at Belle[a]u Woods, & wife there. I spoke. So did Addie.

Dined at Mrs. Eleanor Martins.[3]

Attended Grand Ball at Auditorium. Beautiful decorations.

Wednesday, September 3, 1919

Left early on the Versana [?] for Alameda. Met there by Mayor [4] & visited site suggested for naval base. Mayor gave me a silver key of the city. Spoke to hundreds of school children. Then to shipbuild—— plant where many merchant ships building I spoke & told my father was ship carpenter. Luncheon at Oakland hotel. Gov. Stephens, Chapin [5] & I spoke. Then to Berk[e]ley where I spoke at Greek Theatre on League of Nations to great crowd & presented medals to hundreds of Boy Scouts. Introduced by Acting President Goyler [6]

Went then to Richmond to see proposed naval site & they had large plans for a naval academy for the West. Then they kidnapped me & took me nearly to Mare Island, & I had to stop them. Got back too late for tea at

[1] Major Randolph T. Zane, who had died of wounds received while serving with the 6th Marine Regiment in France.

[2] Possibly Lieutenant Commander Joel T. Boone, a much-decorated Navy surgeon who had served with the Marine Brigade in France.

[3] Prominent San Francisco society hostess.

[4] Frank Otis, mayor of Alameda.

[5] W. W. Chapin, publisher of the San Francisco *Morning Call* and the Oakland *Enquirer*.

[6] Charles M. Gayley, professor of engineering and dean of faculties, acting president of the University of California.

Benj. Ide Wheeler,[7] but called later. Then hurried to Oakland where banquet was given. Rodman & I spoke. Editor Knowland [8] praised me very highly. He is Republican. Mayor Davie [9] interested in Wm. R Davie [10] of N.C. He is fine man—very interesting. Young Mr. Higgins,[11] Secy to Mayor, made excellent speech.

Reached Palace at 1 a.m.

Presented Addie with beautiful basket of flowers at Oakland.

Thursday, September 4, 1919

Left on Destroyer Ludlow (Capt Scott) for Mare Island. Beautiful day & beautiful trip. Reached there at 11 am. Honors. Inspected shops. Spoke to 6,000 men on excellent work done during war. Lunch at Commandments [12] [*sic*] & meet officers & wives. Visited place where magazine exploded wh. led Navy Leagues being barred out of Navy. Dedicated new Y.M.C.A. building and spoke.

Consulted with workingmen on wages, & left for S.F. at 4 p.m.

Dinner at Olympic club and spoke on the Navy as an athletic club.

Then to ball given to enlisted men.

Addie went to dinner of Daughters A.R. at the Fairmont. She made good speech. Then Mayor & I went after them to go to the ball.

Golden Gate truly golden.

Adml Field.[13]

Friday, September 5, 1919

Mr. and Mrs. Harrington [14] & Mrs. Justice [15] had lunch. Met oil men from Los Angeles & those in litigation.

Visited all war work organizations in city and met the ladies in charge.

Noon Luncheon at Commercial Club. Biggest meeting during stay and I had liberty & spoke at length on League of Nations. "It is the best speech I ever heard" said Admiral Twining.

[7] Benjamin Ide Wheeler, president-emeritus of the University of California.

[8] Joseph R. Knowland, Republican, former U.S. Representative from California, and publisher of the Oakland *Tribune*.

[9] John L. Davie, mayor of Oakland.

[10] William R. Davie, (1756–1820), Revolutionary War officer, governor of North Carolina, 1798, founder of the University of North Carolina.

[11] Preston Higgins, former secretary to Mayor Davie.

[12] Captain Edward L. Beach, commandant of the Mare Island Navy Yard.

[13] Rear Admiral Harry A. Field, commandant of the Puget Sound Navy Yard.

[14] Probably Mr. and Mrs. Tennent Harrington, parents of Mrs. David W. Bagley.

[15] Probably Louisa Cutlar Justice, widow of Edwin J. Justice, North Carolina attorney whom Daniels had persuaded to take charge of the Navy's fight to retain its California oil reserves.

Went to California Civic League (2,500 women) & spoke to them on woman's part in the new day.

Met appointments & talked to McNab and others. Judge Seawall.[16]

That night went to dinner with McNabs at Tates.[17] Gov & Mrs Stephens Addie went to lunch with Miss Phelan [18] & to tea at Tate's

Saturday, September 6, 1919

Left hotel at 10 am & boarded Arkansas for Astoria. Ad. & Mrs. Jayne, Mr & Mrs Harrington there to see us off. Left at 11 am. The Golden Gate beautiful & glorious day

Capt. Louis de Steiger [19]

Capt. [blank]

Found on board a deer sent by Mayor Rolph. Jonathan & Frank had gone to Mayor's ranch with his son trying to kill a deer, but had not obtained one. The Mayor supplied him and he was taken in charge by the butcher

Mrs. Monroe [?] & Mrs J had sent A D some flowers

Sunday, September 7, 1919

Went to church and heard sermon by Chaplain *Schrum* [20] ? [*sic*]. Afterwards the Chaplain came to luncheon. He and Jonathan engaged in some discussion on Predestination. He is Presbyterian

Monday, September 8, 1919

Reception committee came on board. Chm of Com. Mr. Stone. Also Mr Sanborn, Dr. Kinney, (picture taken 6 years ago) Col. Rafferty, of the Army, & the Mayor [21]

Upon landing went to luncheon with enlisted men—several hundred—and people surprised we would do this. Catholic priest made welcome address and I replied. Vermont, Oregon & N.C. in river. Inspector proposed Naval base at Tongue Point. Addie was guest of Mrs. Haradon [?] at her mother's Mrs. Elmores. Tea and reception. Miss Richardson, of Wales, sang there & also at dinner at hotel where two young ladies also sang

V. Ad. Williams [22] ranking officer here

[16] Emmet Seawell, judge of superior court, Sonoma County.

[17] Probably John Tait, a member of the Program and Special Events Committee for the fleet review.

[18] Mary Phelan, sister of Senator James D. Phelan.

[19] Captain Louis R. de Steiguer, commanding the U.S.S. *Arkansas*.

[20] Lieutenant (Junior Grade) Reuben W. Shrum, a Navy chaplain.

[21] George L. Baker, Republican, mayor of Portland, 1917–1929.

[22] Vice Admiral Clarence S. Williams, commanding Battleship Squadron One, Pacific Fleet.

Several speeches made. Mr. Jones stressed advantages of Astoria for naval base. Wanted Arkansas to come up to dock. No. Fog might hold it.

Spoke at theatre. Governor Olcott [23] introduced me as "a regular Westerner." 11 P.M. Left on special train for Portland with Gov, Mayor Baker & Com. A & J did not think my speech up to the standard.

Tuesday, September 9, 1919

Went to Multoonomah [Multnomah] hotel am after breakfast went on city [?] boat to inspect harbor.

1 pm. Luncheon at City Club. Packed house. Had very attentive & approving audience. "Best speech I ever heard" wrote Cliff [?] Shaw to A D   After luncheon met del. of Dems, who want scalp of Senator Chamberlain.

Drive on Columbia highway along Columbia river. Dinner at Crown Point Chalet—fine—good party. Piper,[24] of Oregonian, made speech of warm approval of my administration of the Navy. Jackson [25] and Irvine & the Mayor also spoke & I expressed thanks. Most wonderful highway & splendid memorial to early settlers, including Lane of N.C. After return to hotel had conference with number of prominent Democrats. Later saw Congressman Lea [26] of Calif, who is member of Cong. Invest. Com. investigating spruce pine War Department

Mr C S Jackson had in will $300[,]ooo Orthopedic hospital, & decided to give it now. His son Capt. Jackson, who had served in the war

Busy all day to prevent a strike.

A C Shaw sent flowers   Mrs. Rocky [A. E. Rockey] gave Addie luncheon

Wednesday, September 10, 1919

8 a.m. Left Portland on special car. Mr. Lilly, of RR, went with us. Mr. Lockey,[27] of Journal, went with us and interviewed us. Mr Stone & Mr. Sanders, Dr McKinney

Arrived Astoria at noon. Col. Rafferty & others met us. Col. R took us out to Ark. on his boat. Ladies of Astoria sent A box of famous Centenniel chocolates made in Astoria. First built on piles. Town spending millions to improve & put in permanent streets. Beautiful day but an hour after we left a fog came down.

Saw fishermen going out for first day of salmon fishing. Some Ark. officers

---

[23] Ben W. Olcott, Republican, governor of Oregon, 1919–1923.

[24] Edgar B. Piper, editor of the Portland *Morning Oregonian.*

[25] Charles S. Jackson, publisher of the *Oregon Journal.*

[26] Clarence F. Lea, Democrat.

[27] Fred Lockley, a reporter for the *Oregon Journal,* who was preparing a series of feature articles about Daniels.

had fished outside 3 mi limit. Rendezvous with New Mexico & other ships. Just as they came in sight, N.M. was reported disabled. It was trouble with wireless. Fog so thick we could not see N.M. and both ships blowed [*sic*] for fogs.

All officers at tea in afternoon and used Arkansas silver, the first time it had ever been used.

Ate deer and had Capt. de Steiger & Commander Kimmell [28] to dine with us

Thursday, September 11, 1919

10 a.m. Arrived at Port Angeles in the rain. Received by Mayor Pegram [?]. Addie rode with Ex-Mayor Walton. Abundance of flowers. I spoke in pouring rain to great concourse of people. Inspected hunter [?] spruce factory. Mayor & ex-Mayor took no stock in the Frear [29] investigation. Went over to inspect spit suggested for naval base—very courteous people.

At 12:30 got underway for Victoria.

At sunset went on deck where the Chaplain made prayer. The captain, many officers, and many men were present.

Reached Victoria 3 pm. Reception Com. headed by Grant, Gov. Gen. Nova Scotia [*sic*] & son (fears soldiers returning from war take little interest in church or religion) Mr. Cochrane, head Chamber of Commerce, Mr. Oliver, Premier of Victoria.

Friday, September 12, 1919

Discussed pay of officers with Butler

Council discussed economy.[30]

Sunday, September 28, 1919

Philips came early to house to bring dispatch from the President who approved what Polk had done, including action of Andrews at Trau. He thought naval force should be increased at Spelato. I sent for McKean and directed dispatch to be sent Knapp to concentrate all our ships in Adriatic & strengthen Andrews.[31]

[28] Commander Husband E. Kimmel of the U.S.S. *Arkansas*.

[29] James A. Frear, Republican, U.S. Representative from Wisconsin, a member of the Select Committee to Investigate Expenditures in the War Department which was currently looking into allegedly wasteful spruce purchases for airplane construction during the war.

[30] Daniels evidently wrote this entry on the wrong page when he resumed his diary after his return to Washington.

[31] Rear Admiral Philip Andrews, commanding U.S. naval forces in the eastern Mediterranean, had landed Marines at Trau, Dalmatia, in an effort to head off a clash between the Yugoslavs and Italians and prevent the Italians from seizing Yugoslav territory.

Later officer came from [*sic*] dispatch from Knapp saying he thought G.B.[,] France & US ought each to send 4 dreadnaughts into Adriatic & such display alone would have effect. Philips says GB & France have recognized Italy's right to Fiume & only W W stands against it. Cabled Knapp to let us know at once if GB & France agreed to send 4 battleships. We could not do so for some days.

Heard Mr Chappell preach fine sermon "And Demos forsook me loving the present world[."]   3 boys with us. Went to see Mrs. Dewey.

The President was sick, returned to Washington, and walked out unaided.

Monday, September 29, 1919

Conference with members of joint members [*sic*] Naval Affairs Committee on bill to increase pay. Most officers by reason of promotion, some temporary have had increase in pay.

Hampton Moore—to be new Mayor of Phila. About sending ships to Charleston in November to the Inland Water Ways Convention. Had you rather stay in Wash. & go to hell or go to Phila & go to heaven?

Talked to Com. of Machinists. New York machinists had quit work Saturday without agreement, taking the half holiday without authority. I told them that was not playing the game and they ought to go back and work the whole 8 hours, for many of their men would not wish to leave work as they needed the money

Went to depot to see Worth off—on his way to the University

Tuesday, September 30, 1919

Conference with labor men & Shipping Board over increased wages on Pacific coast

Spoke at Mothers of Soldiers at New Willard.

Jonathan (already nearly home-sick) went to University.

Addie to NY to War Council of YWCA

Wednesday, October 1, 1919

Buchanan [1] of Texas. Boy guilty of craps—not allowed to stand examination for Annapolis.

Roosevelt-Lansing. To meet King of Belgium. Telegram to Lansing. He

[1] James P. Buchanan, Democrat, U.S. Representative from Texas.

"went up in the air" R said it was "stupid." Philips said the President had selected the men to go and he could not add. I advised F D R to drop it & save embar[r]assment [2]

Received cable from Knapp giving facts about landing at Trau, Dalmatia. It knocks in the head Senators criticism.

Talked to Grayson. The President better.

Dr G T W [3]—finished Life of Tompkins & going to New York.

Banks trying to save soul of Tompkins

HGCB [?] telling him stories of Wash & Wash life

Thursday, October 2, 1919

Elkus on Americans

Council discussed pay of Navy. Annual Report

Badger on naval people   England and Japan.

Friday, October 3, 1919

The news of the serious illness of the President fell like a pall on all hearts. Could not work. Baker said he feared the worst. Joe Tumulty in tears. "We must all pray" he said.

Meeting of com on Inter Departmental Social Hygiene

Telegram from Dr Matthews [4] who fears Bolshevik trouble in Seattle. Saw Baker. Guns for Russia (shipped by Remington) on cars in Seattle. Should be under army control. Baker will wire Liggett

Saturday, October 4, 1919

Wrote to Mrs W W suggesting she ask every church to pray for the President.

Went to see Judge Payne [5] about turning over plant of shipping board to Marines at Quantico. Will let me know Tuesday.

Talked to Homer Cummings about candidate for President. All at sea as yet. Could a Pro.[hibitionist] be elected? He thinks might be if he is Rep. Could not if a Democrat.

President seemed better. No temperature said Grayson

But I'll show my temper if you keep me in this bed much longer

[2] Roosevelt was miffed because he had not been included in the official party to welcome visiting King Albert of Belgium.

[3] Probably George T. Winston, North Carolina–born educator and old friend.

[4] Mark A. Matthews, minister of First Presbyterian Church of Seattle.

[5] John Barton Payne, chairman of the U.S. Shipping Board, subsequently appointed Secretary of the Interior on March 1, 1920.

Sunday, October 5, 1919

Went to Pres. church. Frank was usher. Looked fine. V.P. & Mrs. Marshall. Said his mother was old fashioned Scotch Presbyterian—afraid to pray for her boy because of God's decrees. When she was old she said "Tommy, I have come to believe that hell is for other people's children." Said he defeated H C L by wearing old clothes.

Went to Ex. Office to see Tumulty. He was full of indignation because Post sent Fox [6] to report condition of President. ["]Ed McLean always said he was ready to do anything, but never did anything decent."

Grayson came in—he said W W had comfortable night, slept naturally, wished food this morning & wished stenographer so he could dictate a few letters. Grayson told him he ought not to work on Sunday. Feels better about W W but says we are not out of the woods.

Received reply from Mrs W W to my note. Hoped people would pray spontaneously for her "dear husband."

Willie Richardson—thought I would discharge him for not printing Raleigh Times in list of articles deposited in corner stone of Rex Hospital.

Monday, October 6, 1919

Attended Cabinet called by Lansing. He said important matters needed attention and if the President would not be able soon to attend to the public business we ought to consider what steps to take. Should the V.P. be called upon. He thought so. Referred to the Constitutional provision "in case of the inability of the President." What constitutes "inability" & who is to decide it. Garfield was shot early in July, said Houston & no "inability" was said to exist." L said "Wayne MacVeagh [7] ran the government." No decision & nothing but discussion.

Grayson came before Cabinet & said President was better but no business should come before him now. His condition encouraging but we are not out of the woods. President wanted to know why meeting of Cabinet was held—did not like it.

We talked estimates and Labor Conference [8] & gave that out as the business.

Attended Labor Conference. W B Wilson made excellent speech.

[6] Albert W. Fox, anti-administration feature writer for the *Washington Post*.

[7] Garfield's Attorney General in 1881.

[8] The Washington Industrial Conference, an administration-sponsored conference to deal with labor-management problems.

Long talk with Newberry [9] about Benson & Sims   Milk in cocoanut is that if B & S are made Admirals they will have to [make] March a General and this is not on the Rep. program. Playing small politics.

Went to see "Luck of the Navy"   Very good

Tuesday, October 7, 1919

Had telephone from Mrs W W that she was sending Mr Wagner with a message dictated by the President to her. It read:

["]Memorandum From the President to the Secretary of the Navy

If our Congress should ask questions concerning the employment of our Navy forces in the Adriatic or Mediterranean, please refer the questions to me at once, informing Congress that you have done so by my direction, and that the replies will be forthcoming in due course unless indeed the Executive should find it was not compatible with the public interest to convey to the Congress at this time the particular information desired"

I wrote what I had done & she replied. She said W W had not signed the note because Dr G did not wish any business brought to him. "Thank you for your personal word of rejoicing with us over the President's improvement."

Lady called—Mrs. Sellon of K City. Her boy had left ship without permission & she felt he was not responsible. Also added that boys great-grandfather had signed note for F D R's great grandfather. Result: Her father's utensils &c were sold to pay the debt of Roosevelt. She thought this ought to interest F D R. I told him I must help her out to protect his rascally ancestors. We had great fun.

Senate Com. put 3 vice admirals instead of 2 Admirals.

Wednesday, October 8, 1919

Baker had cablegr[am] from Gen Graves [10] indicating that Cossacks would attack American soldiers protecting R.R. in Siberia & J[apan] would aid them, covertly at first, actively if necessary. "Important if true." Lansing & Baker asked me to come over. W W had sent N D B to K City to give explicit instructions to G what he should do & what he should not do. Original purpose in sending our troops into Siberia was to protect RR & bring out Checko-Slovaks   We brought out a number, but balance are beyond the Ural

[9] Truman H. Newberry, Republican, U.S. Senator from Michigan, member of the Senate Naval Affairs Committee, former Secretary of the Navy, 1908–1909, and former lieutenant commander in the Navy Fleet Reserve during the war.

[10] Major General William S. Graves, commanding U.S. troops in Siberia, 1918–1919.

Mts the main backbone of Kolchak's [11] army. They cannot get to RR & K cannot consent for them to leave now. Lenin & Trotsky might give permission for them to return through Russia for then they would have K—— at their mercy. Many people must starve in Siberia. Many more will starve if we come out & the RRs are closed. Are J's playing game to get control of all Siberia bordering on the Pacific

Could the A Navy whip J—— navy? asked Baker. Yes, but we must have bases and supplies & they are wanting & we would require time. W W hesitates to withdraw leaving starving people to their fate.

Baker to see Grayson. Otherwise to hold another conference. "Government cannot stop functioning because President is sick" said Lansing.

Talked with Judge T—— [12] on Virgin Islands. Senate had passed bill for Com of 3 to go there & investigate Will be welcomed.

Thursday, October 9, 1919

J D Jr came up to talk about buying new press and adding to N&O building. Talked to representatives of three press dealers. All said 10 months before they could deliver and that prices would go higher. I am skeptical as to the last.

Took up estimates with Bureau Chiefs. All wish to keep the large force they now have, or at least 3 to 7 times as many clerks as they had before the war. What will Congress say?

Stevedores have struck in New York & tied up movement of ships. Acted contrary to advice of responsible labor leaders. Conference to see what Administration can do.

Friday, October 10, 1919

Baker & I approved statement of W B W that wage fixed by Compensation Board for Longshoreman was right and we would abide by it & Wilson made public telegram. Union of Longshoremen repudiated their agreement and would not listen to their officers who wished us to take the action taken.

As to Cossacks & Japs, matter was taken up with W W by Grayson. W W said "Tell Lansing to insist upon immediate answer to note." In meantime Baker had urged Lansing to see Earl Gray [13] and put him in possession of

[11] Alexander V. Kolchak, Russian admiral heading anti-Bolshevist forces in Siberia, subsequently captured and executed by the Bolshevists on February 7, 1920.

[12] Presumably Horace M. Towner, Republican and former Iowa judge, U.S. Representative from Iowa since 1911, chairman of the House Committee on Insular Affairs.

[13] Edward Grey, 1st Viscount Grey of Fallodon, former British foreign secretary, 1905–1916, recently arrived as special ambassador to discuss various problems not resolved at the Peace Conference. Among other things, Grey hoped to reassure Wilson that the British

facts that it was believed by Gen Graves that Japs. wished Cossacks to attack our troops & they would help & Cossacks would take Northeastern Siberia under Jap protection. Wished England & US to join in protest to Japan & believed that would settle matter for Japan would not antagonize position of both. Baker had advised against sending troops into China & was greatly troubled lest the small no. would be cut off & killed far from help. Wanted me to keep ship with powerful wireless at Vladivostock & be ready to send other ships. Agreed.

Senator Jones & Cato Sells talked woman suffrage & wanted us to work in Southern States so Reps could not say they held up woman suffrage

Saturday, October 11, 1919

Jusserand presented statue given by people of Grasse (in memory of Admiral de Grasse) to USS Seattle. That was the first naval ship to reach France after the US entered the war. It was Admiral Gleaves's flag ship & convoyed 14 transports   I replied. France & America are traditional friends.

Estimates. Marine Corps has blankets for 54 months & yet proposes to continue manufacture of blankets.

Sunday, October 12, 1919

Dr. Wood preached on "Come over into Macedonia & help us." Religion in France. Need for help.

Major died in Paris. What was the trouble? Paris—Full of temptresses.

Went to see Mrs. Dewey. Told her of nurse who baked my arm—locked in room.

Capt. McCauley [14] of the George Washington, called

J. D. Jr. returned from NY & we talked paper.

Addie returned from North Carolina & carried birds to the President

Monday, October 13, 1919

Had talk with Senator Page [15] on naval matters. He said sentiment was I had too many Southern Democrats around me. Said Coontz [16] was Mo. Democrat & that he was from So. Missouri. I pointed out that most of my ap-

---

government would not object if Wilson had to accept interpretive reservations to the League Covenant in order to get the Peace Treaty approved by the Senate. Wilson declined to see Grey, however, during his three months' stay in the United States.

[14] Captain Edward McCauley, Jr., commanding the U.S.S. *George Washington*.

[15] Now chairman of the Senate Naval Affairs Committee.

[16] Daniels had appointed Rear Admiral Robert E. Coontz to be chief of Naval Operations upon Admiral Benson's retirement on September 25. Coontz was confirmed by the Senate on October 26, 1919.

pointees were from other sections & he ought to tell them that. It is disheartening to see how even the best of Northern Reps seem to feel that no Southern man should have no [*sic*] recognition. Sims & Benson would have both been confirmed if both had been Northern Republicans.

Alumni of Univ. of NC met at our house & organized. I told of Graham's desiring to enter the army

Tuesday, October 14, 1919

Cabinet discussed sugar shortage & how to relieve it. Houston to discuss with Hoover and others and report to cabinet meeting on Friday.

Also labor question & steel strike. Labor has offered to arbitrate. I said Labor Conference should insist that Gary agree.

Lane thought that proclamation should be made that Gov. would send troops wherever there was disorder. I: This would be regarded as the Gov. advertising it would protect capital & be resented by labor

Lansing: If a man owns a plant the right of property gives him privilege to conduct it as he pleases.

Not so. The public has rights which he must consider. Public rights superior to employe or employer

Wednesday, October 15, 1919

Went to New York at 3 p.m. to Far [Near] East Relief & spoke at their banquet. Dr Barton [17] & Mr. Smith [18] & Elkus spoke. They had been in Armenia, the last two recently. Letter from Mr. Cleveland Dodge [19] who warmly praised Secy of Navy for the help given in getting supplies & help to those starving people. Cordial reception. McKinley: Our desire is concord; not conflict. Isolation is neither desirable nor possible.

A D [?] & the Presidency. No desire of [?] desire. Pro[hibitionism] & South stand in the way.

Thursday, October 16, 1919

Returned from New York 7 am

Went to foot of 7th Street, where N.C. 4 was lying, welcomed Reed and his crew, and made brief speech. Went to lunch with them—given by Chamber of Commerce.

Saw Lejeune

[17] James L. Barton, Congregationalist minister and director of the American Commission for Relief in the Near East.

[18] Walter George Smith, Philadelphia attorney.

[19] Cleveland H. Dodge, vice-president of Phelps Dodge Corporation, president of the board of trustees of Robert College in Constantinople, treasurer of the American Committee for Armenian and Syrian Relief.

Friday, October 17, 1919

Long Conf. at Atty Genl on high cost of living. Carter Glass said Government must set example of economy & reduce so labor would not be so high. "Cannot get a man to milk my cow because Navy & Ship[ping] Board pay so much.["]

Left for Raleigh

Saturday, October 18, 1919

Reached Raleigh. Saw architect about increasing our building. Talked press to Braddock at 4 am   He wants a Goss & says we must have it.

Looked up paper.

J W Bailey says Max Gardner [20] is not straight. Will Jones & Co are for Max—Bailey for Morrison.[21] Page [22] lacks organization. People are tired of war.

Reached Goldsboro & went to barbecue.

Marriage at night—beautiful

Mary Borden [23]—you next! Rice

Sunday, October 19, 1919

Spoke in Goldsboro Court House on Youth. Memorial for soldiers.

Reached Raleigh at 7 p.m.

Alford [24] tired & works too hard.

Signed Moores note for $4000

Monday, October 20, 1919

Conferred with Baker & Palmer about ways to decrease cost of living. What has the Navy it can sell? 9,000,000 pounds of sugar—would be a drop in the bucket.

Palmer said Cape Cod Canal would compromise on ten million. Baker said 8 mil was the very lowest & if the jury decided upon more he would advise Congress not to take it over at all. They wish the Gov. to pay for all their losses

[20] O. Max Gardner, lieutenant governor of North Carolina, 1916–1921, and a candidate for the Democratic nomination for governor in 1920.

[21] Cameron Morrison, governor of North Carolina, 1921–1925.

[22] Robert N. Page, Democrat, U.S. Representative from North Carolina, 1903–1917.

[23] An attendant at the marriage of Daniels' niece, Mary Cleaves Daniels, to Lieutenant Commander Henry M. Stenhouse.

[24] L. F. Alford, head of the linotype department of the *News and Observer*.

Talked to Baruch & Brookings [25] about Labor Conference. They were some-what discouraged because of Gary's attitude. The President has written a letter to be read only in case of adjournment without action

McKean saw McCormick [26] about the confirmation of Coontz. McK "I am Rep by tradition and Coontz is Dem by tradition[."] Said Coontz was better man for place than Sims or Wilson.

Tuesday, October 21, 1919

Cabinet—long meeting. Lansing brought up detention of Standard Oil tank-ers by England & Shipping Board's retention of ships leased from Germany to bring troops home. L. said we had agreed to return them after troops were brought & GB was very much excited because we had not done so. He said it was not keeping faith, & SB had no right to act on the question at all in any way. He was very indignant & most of the Cabinet seemed to agree. I said "Let us hear the SB's side before we act.["] Judge Payne came over & Lansing asked him if his action was not to benefit St Oil Co

"That is an impertinence" said Payne. Another question "That is an im-pertinence." Then Palmer saved the day by asking tactful questions. Payne said GB was trying to prevent an Amer merchant marine & he could not take any other course except by direction of the President. Briefs to go to him from L & Payne

Dupont wants order for 5,000 lb of powder per day so as to keep their chemists & skilled men

Morgenthau says if we take mandatory of Turkey we must jointly control Gibraltar with GB.

Wednesday, October 22, 1919

Powell & Beth Steel Co. Beth Steel Co. sold forgings to Beth Ship Co for 50¢ per lb. We obtained from Erie for 30½¢. Now Beth Steel offers to furnish for 30 cents. Nothing doing.

Spoke at Liberty Hut on League of Nations Oscar Straus [27] spoke. Frou-bert [?]: ["]Force and Right are the governors of the world. Force rules till Right is ready." Compared League Covenant with the tables Moses brought down from the mountains to find his people worshipping a golden calf. He

[25] Robert S. Brookings, former member of the War Industries Board, one of President Wilson's appointees to the Industrial Conference.

[26] Medill McCormick, Republican, U.S. Senator from Illinois, and a member of the Senate Naval Affairs Committee.

[27] Oscar S. Straus, brother of Nathan Straus, former Ambassador to Turkey, former Secretary of Commerce and Labor, 1906–1909, chairman of the Paris committee of the League to Enforce Peace, 1919.

threw the stones on the ground in indignation. Went again & the next time people adopted them. If any reservations they were not such as were referred back.

Thursday, October 23, 1919

Council. Discussed selling surplus food & clothing &c

Friday, October 24, 1919

Decided to sell sugar to naval employees & to furnish it to hospitals needing sugar

Went to funeral of Italian Ambassador de Cellare. V.P. sat on front pew, & glanced often at foreign ambassadors from Latin countries to get the cue to know when to rise. Sometimes they did not know themselves. Mrs. Wilson and Miss Benham there. The V.P. and Mrs. Marshal[1] came out before Mrs. Wilson. She looked troubled.

McKean & Barnett said it was frummery & could not understand how such men as Chf Justice could stand it.

Went to see Senator Page to urge him to support nomination of John Skeleton Williams.[28] He had been poisoned by Weeks. "Temperamentally" that was the trouble. Bankers had told him that & Reps. had held ex. session & decided to vote against confirmation.

Saturday, October 25, 1919

Cabinet met at 11 o'clock. Lansing sick. Glass presided. Called on Wilson to give result of negotiation on coal strike. He believed operators wanted a strike, feeling that coal men had presented demands greater than public sentiment would approve. Miners passed resolution to strike without vote of workers before negotiating unless they were given 5 day week & 6 hours per day & 60% increase in wages. Wilson thought miners did not expect to obtain all this. Crux of situation that miners had made contract for certain wages as long as the war lasted. They claimed the war was over & they were not bound. Operators claimed they were bound until peace treaty was signed even if war conditions were ended. Glass presented paper "that has been handed me" (Tumulty handed it to him) & suggestion of which W W should sign. Discussed generally and changes were made. Appointed Palmer Lane & Wilson to redraft & bring to Cabinet at meeting at 4 o'clock. Discussed & made a few verbal changes and then it was type-written (each member of Cabinet had copy) & when all had approved we sent for Dr Grayson who took it to the

---

[28] Williams' reappointment as Comptroller of the Currency was being opposed by a majority of the Senate Banking Committee.

President. He brought it back approved, but we suggested that he return & get the President to sign it. He did so & given to the press.

I left at 10:30 for Greensboro

Sunday, October 26, 1919

Met in Greensboro by the Mayor & went to Hotel O Henry.

Spoke to Chas. H. Ireland's [29] bible class at 10 am. Heard Bishop Darlington [30] preach at 11 am on Judas. Every day men who are trusted are doing exactly what Judas did. Powerful sermon.

Lunched in country with Albt [?] McAllister in country home. 3 p.m. Spoke to crowded theatre for Y.MCA. At 5 p.m. spoke at G.F.C.[31] to 300 young women [?].

At 8 pm spoke to Methodist Conference "The world is my parish.["]

Monday, October 27, 1919

Discussed estimates & used a sharp knife.

Talked with Padgett about pay of naval officers. He was inclined to favor the 30% increase. Thought no new building program should be proposed now.

Saw J P Tumulty about importance of big men to shape Industrial programme. He predicted a sweeping Democratic victory in NJ.

Late in afternoon Presidt vetoed Prohibition enforcement measure. Palmer, Glass, Redfield & I as soon as we heard of it felt big mistake & indefensible. On Saturday he had declared coal strike illegal, basing illegality on war measure that terminates at close of war. Now we virtually say war is over & no measure is needed to enforce the war prohibition act.

Tuesday, October 28, 1919

Called on King of Belgium at Long's. He recalled our visit to Brussels & spoke of courtesies of the Navy. Went to Capitol to see him received by Senate & House.

Cabinet meeting. Wilson to try to get Miners and Operators to hold meeting & secure postponement of strike

Lane, Baker, Wilson, Redfield & Daniels to see Mr. Gompers & urge his good offices. Burleson opposed. Sees red & thinks country is full of bolshevists.

Mitchell Palmer brought up case of packers. They wish to come in & agree

[29] Greensboro hardware merchant and prominent Methodist layman.
[30] Uban Valentine W. Darlington, bishop of the Methodist Episcopal Church, South.
[31] The Greensboro Female College, Methodist founded and the oldest women's college in North Carolina.

to give up wholesale & retail grocery business and &c, if not indicted   All agreed except Baker & D—— B raised question of what folks would say Daniels thought it would be dangerous

Dinner with King & Queen at Mrs Walsh's [32] given by the VP

Wednesday, October 29, 1919

To Mt. Vernon with King of Belgium and party.

Dined with King of B & party at Lansings. Duke of B[rabant] [33] had to leave the table sick. Later a bevy of girls invited to meet him afterwards disappointed that he had gone home sick.

Thursday, October 30, 1919

Left at 8 a.m. with the King of Belgium in auto for Annapolis in open car. Told him of story that when he visited U.S. as young man it was reported he assumed as name King Cummings & as such worked two weeks as reporter on Montana paper, his job having been secured for him by Jim Hill.[34] When I had finished he denied, saying "That is too fine [?] to be true."

Spoke of danger & fear under fire & said a man was always in fear & afraid also that he would prove a coward. "If any man tells you he did not have fear he is a liar."

Frank went with Prince Leopold & talked sports & automobiles

He decorated Scales & three other naval officers who had gone across.

Went to G.W. Univ. & saw King given degree

Dinner at Lansings—took Mrs Burleson in. "We have always lived on Albert's salary." [35]

Reception at Belgian Embassy & then on special train for Portsmouth

Friday, October 31, 1919

Reached Newport News at 9:30. Went over to P——[ortsmouth] on destroyer.

Brand Whitlock told sequel of his story of Carney the yegg [?] man. Showed his card as Chief Detective of NY Central only after he had delivered the King safely through Gary.

The Queen pressed button that flooded both docks at Portsmouth Navy Yard.

[32] Mrs. Thomas F. Walsh had allowed Vice-President Marshall to use her Massachusetts Avenue mansion to entertain the Belgian royalty.

[33] Leopold, Duke of Brabant, the Belgian crown prince.

[34] James J. Hill, late president and chairman of the Great Northern Railway system.

[35] This paragraph is crossed out, presumably to indicate that the entry belonged on the previous day.

Returned with King & Queen to Hampton Roads & went on board with them & said good-bye. Said would send photos

Then went to Mayflower & after lunch inspected naval base & station & made speech to boys just at sunset.

Dined with Admiral & Mrs. Felecter.[36]

Returned to Mayflower

Saturday, November 1, 1919

Left early for Yorktown on Mayflower with Lansings.

The [?] King said the President had full beard on face & it was white.

Visited oil base & mine station

Worked on my annual report

The quarters for men at the mine base far from river & next to the road— just opposite negro settlement.

Left for Wash

Sunday, November 2, 1919

Quiet day on Mayflower

Reached Wash. at 5 pm

Monday, November 3, 1919

O'Connell,[1] of Irish Committee, wrote letter criticizing Admiral Sims for his article in World's Work on Sein Fein [2]—said they were pro-German & had rows with our sailors in Cork because Irish girls liked our sailors & some married them. Denied permission to our sailors to go to Cork because of attacks. An American sailor killed an Irish tough. I replied that Admiral Sims had been given permission to write his story, I had not censored it, and he should write to him.

George Creel & statem[en]ts about loose methods.

Coontz came & I told him "No General Staff"

[36] Rear Admiral Augustus F. Fechteler, commandant of the Fifth Naval District at Norfolk.

---

[1] Daniel T. O'Connell, director of the Irish National Bureau, an American propaganda agency for the Irish republican movement.

[2] Sims had sharply criticized the Sinn Fein Irish republican party for alleged pro-German activities against U.S. naval forces stationed at Queenstown during the war. Despite sharp criticism from Irish-Americans, Daniels declined to reprimand Sims.

Bob[3]—has had baby—married only two weeks ago. Knew he had done wrong but loved her

Tuesday, November 4, 1919

Wrote to President that in naming Industrial Commission Brandeis[4] ought to head it—that in the list of names suggested by the Cabinet there was no Catholic & that would be taken as a discrimination & lose the force of any findings.

President sent me word to please see Brandeis. He expressed deep regret that Palmer had asked an injunction and thought in present situation no Commission should be appointed & he did not think he could do any public service. The miners had an excellent case, but it was so poorly handled that they placed themselves in the wrong & were not properly understood. Sympathy must go with justice

Americans are idealists and we are fundamentally good—the only country [?] that is

Wednesday, November 5, 1919

Went to see Director General Hines about special rates for midshipmen to game in NY, & talked coal strike &c. At first he said he thought it wise for Palmer to issue injunction against leaders of mine work[er]s, but at last cabinet meeting had advised against it. Enjoining mine leaders will dig no coal. He believed operators wanted strike & believed they could profiteer.

Justice Brandeis called and continued matter of strike and what should be done—Now nothing unless operators & miners both wanted to meet & reach agreement. There must be a total change Disease is deep-seated. Must go to the roots. As long as miners do not know how many days a month they will work, there will [be] demoralization. Some way must be found by which Gov. or RR's will buy regularly & miners be assured steady work. Otherwise bigger pay to miners will mean only higher price for coal & no settlement.

Conference with Wilson & Coontz & others. Papers had said fleet was tied up to the docks & going to pieces. Decided to have fleet go South as usual on 8th of January. Answer to charge.

Worked on report

Wrote to President the view of Brandeis

Report on Distinguished Service Crosses[5] Too many. Will cheapen them

[3] Presumably Robert Gaines, Daniels' Negro servant.

[4] Associate Justice Louis D. Brandeis, Daniels' choice to head a commission to try to settle the current coal strike.

[5] After Congress in February, 1919, had authorized various categories of medals and awards for wartime service, Daniels had appointed a board headed by Rear Admiral (Ret.)

Thursday, November 6, 1919
Pay of Navy. Butler called
Secured furlough fare for Annapolis boys to New York from RR administration
Council discussed economy.
Addie went to banquet of Labor women. Real folks trying to better conditions.
Mrs. Mary McArthur.[6] English delegate "The Presid[ent] was the only person that had an ideal. He was up against Clemenceau & Lloyd George who cared nothing for ideals. England Gov [?] sent Viscount Gray to make up to America for some of the men she sent over here during the war[."]

Friday, November 7, 1919
Meeting of cabinet. Discussed coal & coal strike. Palmer had make [*sic*] this proposition to Gompers to do these three things simultaneously
  1. Call off strike; 2 Do not ask injunction. 3. Operators & miners begin negotiations.
Palmer thought they would accept. Wilson doubted. All agreed to P's plan except Burleson. Houston sympathized with strikers. Lane thought we were losing labor sympathy because they thought we were against them.
Lansing suggested that Debs[7] be let out of prison. Burleson "No." All agreed that Pres. was right because he had agreed to do so with signing of treaty of peace.
Garfield & Wilson agreed as to figures on profits on coal. G—— thought Industrial Board figures wrong
Wilson said he had been out on strike 9 months without any strike benefit —miners did any odd job to live.

Austin M. Knight to review the recommendations by various Navy commanders for awards to their subordinates. In October, after receiving three reports from the Knight board, Daniels began his own review of the proposed awards. Both he and the Knight board revised the lists submitted by various commanders upward and downward, and Daniels added some names not previously recommended, rewarding enlisted men more generously than previously and generally emphasizing the importance of sea service over shore duty. Daniels' list of Navy awards was published in his annual report in December and promptly set off a bitter controversy with Admiral Sims.
  [6] Mary R. MacArthur, secretary of the Women's Trade Union League and National Federation of Women Workers, a British delegate to the International Labor Congress.
  [7] Eugene V. Debs, Socialist leader currently serving a ten-year prison sentence for violation of the wartime Espionage Act.

Saturday, November 8, 1919

Judge gave miners until Nov 11 to call off strike

Went to Mt. Vernon with Labor Congress.[8] Took them on the Mayflower. Very few hospitalities extended. The Checko-Slovaks carried down flowers and placed on W's tomb. It is the newest Republic. Very much impressed by taps & the ceremony. "I felt thrilled[,"] said Mary McArthur.

British delegates interested in prohibition. Will it last? They seemed skeptical. Labor leader Barnes was with Burns.

Ship builder Ross, on the Tyne, said wherever he went the Japs were all over everything and he had to go out and look at the flower garden. A rich American woman had told him that W W was not sick at all, only shamming, that his trip to the West was a bust [?] & he had taken to his bed

When Mrs. Ambassador Page christ—— launched [*sic*] the Eagle—destroyer —Named Eagle before known she would christen it. Was built for Chile & GB took it over. Boat went over into the stream it was taken in tow by two tugs, one named the President & the other the King George The first time an American woman christened a British ship.

A M.P. member from South Africa had been deported to England for propaganda. Now [?] had been seated to Parliament & sent here to represent his [?] govt

Saturday [9]

F. Hodoez, Czechoslovak delegate who put flowers on W's grave, clasped my hand & said "America helped us to win our freedom" & I replied: "We are proud to have been associated with you[."] Leon Jouhaux,[10] the French Gompers, quoted from Washington what he called "a prophetic phrase["]: "We have sown the seeds of liberty and union which will sprout little by little throughout the earth. One day on the model of the US of America will be formed the US of the world. The US will be the legislator of all nations." & Jouhaux added: "Our presence today at this place attests that this prophecy, profoundly human, taking the form of the Society of Nations, is in a fair way of being realized, for the great good of humanity.["]

Sunday, November 9, 1919

Dr. Wood: "Ferment in spirit." Communion.

---

[8] The first International Labor Congress, meeting in Washington. See entry of April 11, 1919.

[9] The rest of this entry was written on the following page for Sunday, November 9, but seems to be a continuation of the Saturday entry.

[10] Prominent French labor leader, secretary general of the French Confederation of Labor.

Monday, November 10, 1919

Went before Naval Affairs Com. on pay of Navy. Pointed out that Navy Dept and Congress had looked ahead and been just & liberal to the Navy. Out of 4400 officers 3800 had temporary commissions giving them larger pay & larger allowances & these go on until July next. Besides they get commutation and 10% at sea, something never given before. When I had reached this point, bells rang for members to vote on seating Berger [11] & Butler said "Lets all go and turn out that traitor"

Invited to dine Tuesday night with Mr. Barnes, Labor M.P. but had to decline because of acceptance to dine with V.P. to meet Prince of Wales.

Talked to Swanson about Navy pay

Charleston Dry Dock. $4,000,000. Kenyon introduced bill to withdraw appropriation for dredging to make channel & Calder introduced bill to repeal $4,000,000 appropriation for the dock. No dock South of Hatteras

Tuesday, November 11, 1919

Cabinet. A S B wanted Palmer to go into court and have Gompers and AFL. haled before the Judge because it had approved the strike & offered to support the miners. He said the reason we did not do it [was] because of cold feet. All of us disagreed & it was decided for Wilson to re-open the negotiations between operators and miners with a view to agreeing upon a scale. If they did not reach agreement shortly I said Section 55 ought to be invoked under which the President could take over and operate the mines. A S B "When we reach that point I want to be heard." Talk general on injunctions. I said it could be invoked only under Lever act & not otherwise. Palmer thought there could be cases. Dangerous.

Went to meet the Prince of Wales. Asked about Addie & said they never had a more jolly party

When Secy Wilson [left] the White House my wife said he was so engrossed he did not see his own car though he walked right by it. What was he thinking of? I told her.

Dined at Belmont's house as guest of V.P. to meet the Prince of Wales. He read a good speech

Coal strike ordered called off.

[11] Victor L. Berger, Milwaukee Socialist editor and former U.S. Representative from Wisconsin; elected to Congress from the Fifth Wisconsin District in November, 1918, while under indictment for wartime violation of the Espionage Act. Although subsequently convicted and sentenced to twenty years in prison, Berger attempted to take his seat in Congress while his case was on appeal. With only one dissenting vote the House on November 10 adopted a resolution refusing Berger his seat.

Wednesday, November 12, 1919

Went before Naval Affairs Committee on pay of the Navy and made recommendations for increase.

Senator Page wanted me to agree not to take any step on Charleston Dry Dock until Senate acted on Calder's bill not to build Charleston Dry Dock. Nay, nay Pauline. Sectional animosity & partisan littleness. Will be heard before action is taken.

Reception to the Prince of Wales at Library. Great throng

Went to Mrs. Deweys at 4:30. Tea. The Prince, Mrs Dewey, Admiral Halsey,[12] Admiral Niblock, Admiral McGowan, Foote. Ad. H had been at Manila when Dewey was there & Mrs. D was glad to meet him. She gave the Prince a flag whi[ch] England had taken from Spain & wh[ich] had been presented to the Admiral

McGowan was present when Fiske resigned in disgust

Thursday, November 13, 1919

Olney [13] & Mass delegation called about Squantum

In Council talked about reducing the personnel in naval districts.

Dined with British Ambassador & then reception to the Prince of Wales

Friday, November 14, 1919

Left at 10 am for Annapolis with Prince of Wales and party on special. Received with honors by Supt. He reviewed the regiments & parade & met faculty & ladies. Visited recitation rooms[,] laboratory & rooms. He thought quarters palatial & said when he was at naval school he lived in a trunk, & preferred that to fine quarters if he could get more leave. Made brief talk to boys & told of his experi—— at naval school. Lunch at Scales. Returned at 3 pm. He will send photo.

Addie went to NC

Saturday, November 15, 1919

Went before Senate Naval Affairs Committee on bill of Calder to withdraw appropriation and not build Charleston dry dock. I read long letter on chain of docks—Boston, N.Y., Phila., Norfolk and Charleston. All built but the last.

Went over list of men recommended for D.S.M and N.C.

Left on 8 o'clock train for Raleigh

[12] Rear Admiral Sir Lionel Halsey, Third Sea Lord.
[13] Richard Olney, Democrat, U.S. Representative from Massachusetts, who was concerned about the future of the great shipbuilding facilities built during the war at Squantum.

Sunday, November 16, 1919

Reached Raleigh 5 a.m.

Worked on a speech and went with Addie and three boys to church. Mr. Peele [14] preached & combatted the idea that discontent in itself was an evil.

Went out in country to see sites for a home when we go back to Raleigh.

Spoke for Tuberculosis Hospital at the Auditorium. Had fair liberty.

Went again in country.

Spent night at office with J D Jr who was greatly troubled because words [?] were lost & we were strained [?] in composing room

Biggs & Max Gardner bitter at Simmons's trying to dictate next Governor

Monday, November 17, 1919

Business at the office.

Lunched with insurance men. Mr Scofield, brother of the World correspondent who was driven out of Cuba by Shafter.[15] Scoville [*sic*] had roasted Shafter. Mr S said Shafter held on because of Michigan politics.

Crawford Biggs telephoned case vs. So. Pacific in oil reservation had been won in Supreme Court. Judge Biggs had argued case in Supreme Court. It affected Naval Reserve and was won on question of fraud by So Pacific officials

Long talk with Alford [16] [?]—deranged [?]

Had to raise pay of linotype operators

Returned at midnight to W

Tuesday, November 18, 1919

Reach office at 10 am. Saw delegation of colored people who wished me to speak at Hut in favor of proposition to erect a memorial to the colored men in the Army & Navy. Agreed.

Cabinet. Burleson wanted us to get into Mexico Conditions, he said, are very bad. Not so bad, I said, as at any time in 6½ years. Lane inclined to agree with B——

Wilson said when an American elected to go into a country like Mex & buy land & oil cheap because of conditions, he had no right to call upon the country he left to send in Army & Navy to make his property more valuable

Lansing, Palmer thought conditions did not justify going in. Baker thought if Mex wanted the kind of gov. they had now it was their country & we ought not to impose our will on them

[14] Rev. W. W. Peele, minister of Daniels' Edenton Street Methodist Church in Raleigh.
[15] Major General William R. Shafter, commanding the U.S. expeditionary force in Cuba in 1898.
[16] Probably L. F. Alford, in charge of the *News and Observer*'s linotype machines.

Garfield came in   talked coal. I protested that miners & operators should not be permitted to get together & put up prices on consumers.

Wednesday, November 19, 1919

Went over Distinguished service with Lee [17] & then said: "I am going to give myself a distinguished service medal. Any man who can stand the naval officer bunch seven years deserves a medal."

Dinner at F D R's. Lady Willett: [18] What do you think? I must be calm. "See how d—— calm I am."

Senate defeated the treaty. Lodge has one passion—hatred of Wilson.

A man who claimed to have had a message from T. R. went to see Mrs Derby (Ethel R) [19]   Must see her. Said T. R. made big noise and danced on his [?] table—told them he wanted the treaty ratified. Mrs D (Ethel R) said at least 150 people had thought they conected [?] with T R—some said he wanted ratification; some said no.

Thursday, November 20, 1919

Council discussed medals of honor—one like the ships & Columbus time. One of present destroyer—but bad representation of destroyer. Council decided upon ancient one

Discussed new cabinet choices with Tumulty. Why B—— C [Bainbridge Colby?] & not T

McAdoo—Joe T—— wrote to Mc

Doheny—Stronger hand with Mexico.

Left at 8 pm for Akron

Friday, November 21, 1919

Reached Akron early—8 am. Went to club. Then went through Goodrich Rubber Company. Lunched with the officers of the Chamber of Commerce

In afternoon went out to aviation site & hanger [*sic*] at Wingfall Lake where Navy had put up hangers and had place where 200 & more were taught to fly during the war. Went with Lt Langdowne who came over from England on R34.[20] Fine fellow and modest.

Spoke in Armory to big dinner on the Navy.

Goodyear Rubber Company has a Senate and House composed of their

---

[17] Possibly Senator Lee S. Overman of North Carolina.

[18] Florence Simpson Willert, wife of Sir Arthur Willert, longtime Washington correspondent of the London *Times*.

[19] Ethel Carow Roosevelt Derby, daughter of Theodore Roosevelt and wife of Richard Derby, a surgeon.

[20] A British dirigible, the prototype of a ship the Navy was considering purchasing.

employes where they discuss all matters of wages, hours, labor conditions &c. No labor union

Saturday, November 22, 1919

Reached Detroit 8 am. Mr. Tichar [?] Navy YMCA Secretary met me & we went out to hear John R. Mott, who made an excellent and inspiring speech, telling of world needs & American opportunity.

Lunched at Naval base with Commander Cook & wife & saw where Eagle boats were built. All had gotten out by hard work & would get through St. Lawrence before the river was frozen over.

Talked to Mr. & Mrs. Ford. He says people are leaving the farm. That with tractors and improved ag.[ricultural] machinery day will come when farmer will work half the year on the farm & half the year in factories. He thinks Jews & other money lenders wish to keep up differences between countries   It pays them to lend money.

Spoke at night to International YMCA Convention

Sunday, November 23, 1919

Reached Cleveland by lake steamer at 7 am. Tried to think out a speech. Went to Euclid Ave. Meth SS & spoke to the Sunday School

Spoke at 11 a.m. in the church. Dr Isaac Wood, minister & Dr. Price (?) [*sic*] very cordial. Touched on coal strike. They were at hotel to dinner & we had pleasant talk & discussed many problems, social and religious.

Left at 5 pm for New York.

Monday, November 24, 1919

Met at New York by Capt. Leigh & went to the Astor, & then on destroyer & steamed around the fifty 5 [*sic*] mine sweepers all just returned from the North Sea. Stand up lunch on Admiral Huse's [21] ship, the Columbia.

Crew & all lunched at the Astor, guests of KofC. "Shipmates.["] "Talk about Going Home." Significance of the Mine Barrage.

Spoke at Carnegie Hall at Jewish meeting to protest at murder of the Jews in Ukraine. Dr. Wise,[22] Mr. Cutler & others. Cheered & they were very enthusiastic.

Attended Hippodrome performance and left on midnight tr[ain]

Mrs. Caurristly [?]

"The Pres. wishes to go slow on this case[."]   W B W

[21] Rear Admiral Harry M. P. Huse, commanding the Atlantic Fleet Train.
[22] Stephen S. Wise, prominent New York rabbi and Zionist leader.

Tuesday, November 25, 1919

All day session of Cabinet over coal situation. Wilson, who had by request of cabinet, sought to conciliate & secure agreement, proposed increase of 30%. Garfield opposed & thought 14% as great an increase as ought to be made. Deadlock. Garfield said he could not agree to increase the price of coal to the public and believed operators could stand 15% increase, but miners ought not to get more. Hines was present and said if Wilsons increase were given to miners the RR men would demand it and up would go the freight rates & public could not stand that.

Adjourned & met again at 3:30   No agreement.

Dined at F D R's & Thomas Mott Osborne was there. We talked prison reform.

Wednesday, November 26, 1919

Cabinet met at 11 am. There was voiced criticism of McAdoo for "butting in" & showing that coal operators were making from 1 to 2,000 per cent. Glass gave figures from 15 to 800 per ct. Av. 150 to 300%. Getting very rich.

Garfield; Hines opposed Wilson's plan. W, L, H & I wanted to increase rate of pay. Others opposed.

I proposed asking the President to settle after making brief statement to him. Houston[,] Lane & I advocated   Others opposed. Wilson said Garfield had no voice in wage rates—or he so understood. Baker said law gave Garfield the right   Then Wilson would withdraw and let Garfield handle it. Gloomy outlook for digging coal.

Thursday, November 27, 1919

Mr. Chappell on not forgetting to give thanks—people forget. More trouble wrought by lack of thought than by lack of feeling. Two baskets—one for petitions, full to overflowing; one, thanks, empty

State Dept. officials wanted our advice based on request of Serbian Minister [23] on telegram to tell Italy we would resent landing at Spelato; & then if she landed we would sail away. We took ground the matter was not *now* local to Spelato & police duty in a given area [did?] not impose duty on us. Was a matter for joint protest & joint action of the allies, & not by us alone. Besides we have sailors on Austrian ships. We cannot sail away & leave them. Better no telegram. Things look better.

Col Theall run over or knocked down by auto. Went to Emergency Hospital where Dr Mitchell [24] operated on him. Just a chance

[23] Dr. Slavko Y. Grouitch.

[24] James F. Mitchell, chief surgeon at Emergency Hospital and clinical professor of surgery at George Washington University.

Addie to Navy Relief Ball

Friday, November 28, 1919
Talked to Lansing about the Jenkins [25] case. Had talked previously with B—— "Did you hear what L said at cabinet today[?"]—"If we go into Mexico it will settle our difficulties & unite us here"— B thought that sentiment at bottom of much talk of straightening out Mexico—& urged me, as he was going away, to try to prevent our doing what L seemed to favor. Said he was fanning the flames for war. I urged upon Lansing thorough investigation & pointed out that we had several times had [*sic*] been unable to grant demands of other govs. because they demanded Fed. Gov. to do what was in the province of national [local] governments.
Left with Frank & Addie for New York to see Army & Navy play.
Went to the Hippodrome

Saturday, November 29, 1919
Rainy & soggy.
George Creel was very bitter about the publication of charge that he had left things at sixes & sevens. Said G C [26] was no friend of ours—had men in possession of records who would like to disclose them to our hurt.
Game called at 2 pm in the rain. Before going to the ground I went down to speak to the team at their luncheon. Navy won 6 to 0. Baker & Pershing & March met Scales, F D R & myself in centre of field and Navy saluted Pershing.
Went to see Frank Bacon [27] in Lightenin & then to supper with Midshipmen

Sunday, November 30, 1919
Went to church—Grace Methodist—and heard Bishop Wilson.[28] Spoke on "The World Is My Parish."
Saw C. C. D. & Mary. He was strong vs P[almer?] & Mc[Adoo?]
Left at 3.30 & got home 9.[30]

---

[25] William O. Jenkins, U.S. consular agent at Puebla and owner of a large Mexican ranch, had allegedly been kidnaped and held for ransom by bandits. Following his release he was arrested by Puebla officials on a charge of complicity in a false kidnapping. Lansing favored a stern ultimatum to the Carranza government, possibly followed by military intervention if Jenkins was not released. Baker and Daniels and a majority of the cabinet were opposed to Lansing's militant course. The furor died down after Jenkins' bail was put up by a private American businessman in Mexico.
[26] Grosvenor B. Clarkson, director of the Council of National Defense, which had just issued a report to Congress criticizing the financial affairs of Creel's Committee on Public Information.
[27] Actor; author and star of the play *Lightnin*.
[28] Luther B. Wilson, bishop and president of the Board of Foreign Missions of the Methodist Episcopal Church.

Monday, December 1, 1919

Went over final list of Distinguished Service &c of Medals for officers & sailors. Straus gave his list

Lansing sent his note to Mexico

Granny & Navy ladies in pm.

Tuesday, December 2, 1919

Went up to capital to hear Presidents message read. "How is the President really & between us?" was the question asked of me by nearly every Congressman I saw. Kitchin wanted some way to prevent strikes—said he had always been with labor men but they now asked one side[d] arrangements and would not listen to reason. Talked to Overman who had given out statement about Creel & warned him that there were those who wished to embar[r]ass the President by trying to pry into Creel's management

Simmons is for Hitchcock for leader—too much South will give Reps. a chance to make a sectional campaign. Believed we must have reservations. Took lunch with Johnson, of South Dakota, who told of his sending resolution for renomination of Wilson & Marshall. He believed they deserved it—& then if not accept door open to others & not time to choose candidate yet.

Near East. Went to dinner at Shoreham with Mrs. Stevens [1] and then to DAR hall where Smith [2] & Morgenthau spoke.

Wednesday, December 3, 1919

Had invited Hoover to lunch with me & Coontz. I forgot and at 1:45 telephoned to Army and Navy Club & Hoover was waiting. I rushed over & told him the story of Hort Bower [?] who forgot his wife.

Col. Haskell [3] distributing food in Armenia & caught some of the men guilty of graft & rebuked the officers guilty & they resigned. This left nobody to function for the Republic recently organized. What shall I do? he wired in desperation to Hoover. "Don't accept their resignations" Hoover replied & they are still in office.

Dinner at La Fayette. Industrial Commission gave dinner to Governor John Franklin Fort [4]

---

[1] Mr. and Mrs. Cabot Stevens of the Committee on Near East Relief.

[2] Walter George Smith.

[3] Colonel William N. Haskell, Allied high commissioner to Armenia and director general of relief work in the Caucasus.

[4] President Wilson's predecessor as governor of New Jersey, recently retired member of the Federal Trade Commission.

Thursday, December 4, 1919

Long talk with Tumulty on coal & Mex. He told L that W W would not go to war with Mexico—& he ought not to make the issue vent [?]. If there is war, let the Reps do it.

Saw Lansing who said Mexican Embassy here was propaganda headquarters for red literature & Fall [5] was right. He told Com. he had not consulted Wilson about J——[enkins'] arrest & imprisonment. Fall & Hitchcock named to confer with the President about Mexican policy. Rec'd letter from Lansing enclosing letter from Justin McGrath [6] asking ships be sent to Mexico & telegraph from Wm. Randolph Hearst urging such course. Lansing requested ships be sent.

J D Jr up from Raleigh

Friday, December 5, 1919

Cabinet. Long session. Palmer said Judge Anderson [7] had taken case in his hands—had summoned the Grand Jury—and it looked like he was going to imprison many miners for contempt because they had not gone back to work. He was trying to prevent this as it was unjust to punish these small fellows & would react. As matter of fact there has been reaction because people were being thrown out of employment because they could not get coal to carry on industries. Public thinks Cabinet approves Garfields statement that 14% increase is right. Operators offered 20%. Decided to refer matter to the President, as I had urged at former meeting. Glass, Palmer & Houston to take matter up & get statement from Wilson, Garfield and Hines and then prepare suggestion to the President who would act. Tumulty had suggested a Committee of such men as Judge Gray, [8] Straus, & Endicott to try to get operators and miners together.

Chamberlain case. [9] Will dismiss him from the Navy.

Saturday, December 6, 1919

Houston presented our views to Mrs. Wilson [10]

[5] Albert B. Fall, Republican, U.S. Senator from New Mexico, currently heading a Senate subcommittee investigating affairs in Mexico.

[6] Washington editorial correspondent for the Hearst press.

[7] Albert B. Anderson, U.S. district judge in Indiana who in November had issued an injunction against the leaders of the striking United Mine Workers of America.

[8] George Gray, former U.S. Senator and U.S. circuit judge, chairman of the Anthracite Coal Strike Commission in 1902.

[9] Captain Edmund G. Chamberlain, Marine Corps aviator convicted of "falsehood" regarding his alleged wartime exploits in France.

[10] Daniels has drawn a line through this sentence, probably because it seems to refer to the entry of December 9.

Sunday, December 7, 1919

J D Jr. here from New York where he had to pay 7¼ cents a pound for paper in Canada. Five years ago we paid 2½ cents delivered in Raleigh.

Spent the morning at Department writing a speech, or speeches, to make in Ninth N.C. District [11]

Monday, December 8, 1919

Left in afternoon for Harrisburg, Pa, to speak at annual meeting of Chamber of Commerce and upon reception of organ & tablet presented to Grace Methodist church by Mr [blank]. Beautiful organ.

Spent the afternoon with Vance McCormick, his mother and sister quietly at their house in rainy afternoon.

Spoke on the glory of youth as seen in World War. "The world is my parish.["]

Had to leave 5:30 Tuesday morning for Washington.

Tuesday, December 9, 1919

Long cabinet meeting. Lansing had been told by Garfield that W W had approved G's stand as to coal situation which would defeat the idea of a commission to look into the whole matter already approved by the President & accepted by Lewis [12] and Greene.[13] At last session we had appointed Glass, Palmer and Houston to receive statements from Wilson, Garfield & Hines & present to the President & then to act for the cabinet. Garfield had, after learning of W W's approval, wh. [ich] was in a sense taking out of his hands sole power, sent a letter to the President which if approved would have favored nothing over 14% no matter what was established after study & investigation. Houston was appointed to go to see W W. He went over, saw Mrs. W—— & she brought back dictated letter to Garfield withdrawing his approval. We had dictated a joint note wh—— Houston took over.

Reported that W B W had decided to resign because the Cabinet, after authorizing him to negotiate had repudiated his action & sided with Garfield in coal matter. Every member expressed himself that it would be a calamity & asked me to see Wilson & assure him of our feeling. Wilson showed me

---

[11] For the special election to fill the seat of Representative Edwin Yates Webb who had resigned to accept a U.S. district judgeship for western North Carolina. Daniels was campaigning for Clyde R. Hoey, who won the election on December 16.

[12] John L. Lewis, acting president and subsequently president of the United Mine Workers of America.

[13] William Green, secretary-treasurer of the United Mine Workers of America.

letter he had drafted and I urged him that it was his duty to stick. He promised to take no action until I returned to city Friday

Wednesday, December 10, 1919

Reached Morganton on Southern at 10 o'clock Spoke to children at Deaf & Dumb School and spent morning with Prof. Goodwin.[14] First time I had spoken to the deaf, and had an interpreter.

Spoke in courthouse at Morganton in favor of election of Hoey to Congress to a crowded courthouse. Gen Carr stopped over.

Dinner at Goodwins. Visited Hospital for insane.

Reached Hickory at 7. Stopped with W. J. Shuford & spoke at night & was heckled—or he tried to—& the audience wanted to put him out, but got the best by calling for fair play Let him stay & hear the truth

Thursday, December 11, 1919

Reached Charlotte 1 p.m. Went to Manufacturers Club to lunch & spoke to Kanowa [?] Club on business men's devotion in war & scouted the danger of bolshevism overturning Americanism.

Drove over new part of city. Had callers all the evening & spoke in Auditorium at night.

Left at 11:30 for Washn

Cam Morrison brought in gubernatorial fight all the time but I was deaf. He was greatly overcome when he talked about the death of his wife

Friday, December 12, 1919

Late train from Charlotte and hurried to Cabinet meeting.

Hines was discussing what to do with rail-roads. W W had said he would turn them back on Jan 1 and now middle of December no legislation had been enacted—he feared that to turn them back without well-considered legislation might produce serious financial results and a panic was not impossible. Burleson favored fixing the responsibility—Reps had wasted seven months & done nothing. Majority favored turning them back Feb 1 or Mch 1 & Lansing was instructed to so report to the President.

I saw W B W. He said he had decided not to resign.

Gen. Harris [15] brought the record of the Roosevelt young men—all entered as officers with commissions.

[14] Edward McKee Goodwin, founder and president of the North Carolina School for the Deaf at Morganton since 1891.
[15] Major General Peter C. Harris, Adjutant General of the Army.

Had indignant letter from McAdoo smarting under reflection of yng Roosevelt [16]

Saturday, December 13, 1919

George Creel and the Public Information Bureau and the mixed up accounts. His Treasurer did not look after things as he should while George was in Europe—upon his return George discharged him, leaving the job in the hands of an incompetent. He was indignant because of statement by Accountant Ellsworth [17] & wanted to sue the Kansas City Star for libel. I advised against it & cited Ford's mistake when he obtained only a few cents. Dangerous

Gridiron Peace Dinner. Many hits, particularly McAdoo scrambling the eggs & Hines trying vainly to unscramble them. Peace Treaty Meeting good

Dinner not so enjoyable without liquor said one member. Quite as fine, said another You cannot prove it Yes, I can J D has attended banquets when there was plenty of wine & now when there is none, and he enjoys those where there is no wine just as much as where there is abundance.

Sunday, December 14, 1919

Went to hear Mr. Chappell. Stephen "and looking up he saw." Subject the upward looking man. The muck raker never saw the stars.

Read stories of negroes in wars—Crispus Attucks,[18] Peter Salmon,[19] Henry Johnson [20] & Brown [21] on the President Lincoln who refused to go in a boat that would have saved his life, saying "I must look after the old man," meaning the Captain.

Addie returned from NC at midnight

Monday, December 15, 1919

Fox in Post gave roast for crosses & medals—said I had overruled the Board —& put on David Bagley because he was kin to me [22]

[16] On December 10, McAdoo had written Daniels requesting information about the Navy war service of his three sons, in response to charges by Theodore Roosevelt, Jr., of favoritism for the sons of cabinet members. McAdoo had noted indignantly that the Roosevelt sons had all been commissioned promptly.

[17] E. K. Ellsworth, liquidation officer for the Council of National Defense.

[18] Negro victim at the Boston Massacre in 1770.

[19] Peter Salem, Negro hero of the Revolutionary War.

[20] Negro private cited by General Pershing for bravery in combat in France in 1918.

[21] Mess Attendant 1st Class Bernard Brown, killed when the U.S.S. *President Lincoln* was torpedoed and sunk on May 31, 1918.

[22] The highly critical *Washington Post* story by Albert W. Fox to which Daniels refers was given page one feature coverage under the headline: "Daniels Robs Naval Heroes of Honors Secretary's Friends Replace Those Named by Board." Fox suggested that Congress compare Daniels' list of awards with the original recommendations of the Knight board.

Foote & others indignant & wanted me to sue for libel. No. Gave facts

Martin H. Glynn and Victor S. Bryant and their wives here to supper. Then Glynn & I went to Liberty Hut and spoke at meeting in behalf of monument to negro soldiers. Baker also spoke. Justice Stafford [23] spoke & virtually apologized for being a white man.

Tuesday, December 16, 1919

Cabinet discussed Peace Treaty. Burleson said that the country understood the Presidents statement of yesterday made people feel that he would accept no reservation to the treaty and that was causing division among Senators. He thought Dem. Senators ought to be informed that this acceptance of Presidents statement was wrong & that he would accept interpretive reservations. Lansing agreed. Glass & Baker said that treaty was in better shape than ever and Reps. would accept no reservations that the President would approve and that it would be idle to make any move until public opinion compelled action by Republicans or go to the country

The Pres., said J P T[,] had sent over the statement that was printed & he would not be the one to take up any explanation with him.

Dined with Mr & Mrs. C. S. Hamlin,[24] Norman Davis,[25] who was at Paris. Told of Lloyd George in Peace Conference

Wednesday, December 17, 1919

Took lunch with W. J. Bryan. He had plan for meeting Mexican situation without intervention. In brief take Lower California as hostage that Mexico pay for loss of American citizens by reason of lack of protection by Mexican authorities. Then take strip 15 miles on border to police and guarantee protection against incursions over the border. I suggested they might destroy the oil wells. Then, he said, take over & operate the wells because of the necessity of the oil. Guarantee every American the money invested but not speculative profits. In course of time Mexico would be unable to pay and we could trade by taking Lower California & Magdelana [sic] Bay. Fine country for winter homes. Pay the owners the value for property. We should lend Mexico money for schools & improvements. We would then say to Mexico we do not make war upon you & if any fight ensued it would be a defensive one.

He feels that W W was glad he resigned. He said leave a door open. W W did so, changing the document substantially as he had suggested, but when

[23] Wendell Phillips Stafford, Associate Justice of the Supreme Court of the District of Columbia.
[24] Charles S. Hamlin, member of the Federal Reserve Board.
[25] Norman H. Davis, newly appointed Assistant Secretary of the Treasury, subsequently Under Secretary of State, June 15, 1920—March 7, 1921.

he asked him W W [?] said the changes were not such as would meet his objections & never said he hoped some way could be found by which objections could be met & he could stay. Felt he wished his retirement though at first he had said You must stay to help keep us out of war.

Saw Baker about Air Service

Dined with Adml & Mrs. Simpson.[26]

Thursday, December 18, 1919

Richard Hooker deplored Underwood's saying he wanted treaty as it is; would take Knox or Lodge. Reminded him of Grant's trade—Father told him to offer $20 for a colt & to go up dollar by dollar up to $25. Grant paid $25 because he told what his father had said. Wanted no Leonard Wood, who, speaking at Springfield, told about all the difficult & backward things at W & was interrupted by hard-headed Rep. business man who asked: Can't you tell of us [sic] one good thing? Wood was silenced & non-plussed.

Council discussed Squantum &c

Letter of Newberry complaining of publication connecting him with enrollment in Third district, published in Detroit News. Public record and surprise he had not been brought in before.

Massa. Senate resoluted [sic] why I was reducing work at Boston Navy Yard. Gave figures to show that in one year I had given more work at Boston yard than in a dozen years of Mass. secretaries

Dined with Admiral Earle. Mr Samuel Voclain [27] talked of war. Thought RR's ought to have been returned at once after armistice. Thessolonians "If a man will not work neither shall he eat[."]

Men who employ should go into factory am [?] & not late with golf sticks

Friday, December 19, 1919

Cabinet. Mostly a talk fest about politics & papers. Palmer told of his hearing before Committee investigating the settlement of the strike. The Reps seem sorry it was settled and wish to show that administration somewhere made a mistake.

Naval medals &c. Senator Pages letter.[28]

Minstrel show by Navy Yard employes.

[26] Rear Admiral Edward Simpson, Navy hydrographer, about to assume his new duties as commander of the Atlantic Fleet Train.

[27] Samuel M. Vauclain, president of the Baldwin Locomotive Works and during the war active in war production service under the Council of National Defense.

[28] On December 16, the day after publication of the Fox story in the *Post*, Senator Page, chairman of the Senate Naval Affairs Committee, had requested a copy of the list of awards recommended by the Knight board.

Bitterness in politics on league

Small boy to his mother: Aint that C L [29] a son of a b—— Stern rebuke by mother—Havent I often told you must not say aint?

Sims [30] & medals.

Saturday, December 20, 1919

Two American sailors jailed in Mazatlan [Mexico]. No news of it for 5 weeks. The boatswain said they did not come back from leave & were put in jail. He saw the consul, gave them food & bedding & sailed away. Papers make much of Mexican trouble. Sailor should have wired and stayed

Wrote letter to Speaker of House of difficulty in securing skilled men for the Navy & urged better pay.

Talked about medals & got up letter—or Foote did justifying my position. Will prepare it. Telephoned to Page & said after Christmas would do

Jonathan came home with the Tom [?] Baker's [31] Fine.

Dined at Gen. Barnetts

Sunday, December 21, 1919

Reed, going from New Orleans to Mobile, lost in a fog but he is fine and careful aviator & hope for the best

Worth came from Chapel Hill. We met him at the train after going to church.

C. T. Williams came to see me from Balto. Represented big company which thought Lane might accept important position.[32]

Mrs. Salene Jackson and Samuel S. Jackson arrived with body of Jonathan Worth Jackson, who died in Chicago.

Monday, December 22, 1919

Talked to Tumulty. Troubled about the President. Five important missions to be filled—& unless named soon nobody would regard it as desirable to accept, & Reps. might refuse to confirm. Also half a dozen other important

[29] Presumably Henry Cabot Lodge.

[30] On December 17, Admiral Sims, now president of the Naval War College, had written to Daniels declining his award of a Distinguished Service Medal on the ground that Daniels had not accepted all of Sims' recommendations for awards. Publication of the Sims letter aroused a storm of criticism and controversy.

[31] Probably Thomas S. Baker, director of the Jacob Tome Institute, Port Deposit, Maryland, 1909–1919, the private preparatory school attended by the younger Daniels boys during their father's service in Washington.

[32] Secretary Lane had let it be known to his intimates that he was eager to leave the cabinet for more lucrative employment.

places. Grayson came in. President improving slowly. T[:] if he had [blank] [33] when brought the treaty home it would have let him loom larger in history.

La Guardia & aviation in Italy. Called naval officer "a coward." Made no reply.

Sims &c

Tuesday, December 23, 1919

Cabinet   J P T had note from W W that the RR would go back to their owners Jan 1, as he had stated seven months ago. Hines thought time should be longer and some proposed that Presi[den]t be asked again to extend it. Not in face of his plain statement. Grayson said he refused to even talk RR. Proclamation to be sent over with date for turning over left blank. General opinion was that 30 days after signing proclamation should elapse before RR's go back to owners.

Sims letter—much abuse & criticism. I gave out my letter to Senator Page & let the papers have Sims letter

Wednesday, December 24, 1919

Sims protest made scramble for honors.

J D Jr came

Home quietly at night.

Thursday, December 25, 1919

At home all day except a brief visit to see Mrs. Dewey.

Capt. L. W. Mix, of Nogales, Arizona, called. He & party go to New York to present silver service to U.S.S. Arizona. He was member of Coleman's vigilantes in San Francisco. Told of time when a man, who had killed a man near Tombstone, Arizona, & compelled his wife to sleep with him, took her to town, & when he left her in wagon a moment she told of his crime. He was riddled & hanged on telephone pole & the jury brgt in verdict that his death was death was [*sic*] "justifiable homicide at the hands of parties unknown"

Many visitors

Turkey from Occoneechee [?]

Friday, December 26, 1919

Coontz, Taylor & Washington here

Decided to recall the Knight Board & gave out letter to the press

---

[33] Daniels evidently could not bring himself to write the word "died" in connection with his beloved chief.

Saturday, December 27, 1919
   Post said I had backed down
   Left on ACL for Goldsboro

Sunday, December 28, 1919
   Spent Sunday with mother
   O'Berry [34] called. Stopped taking N&O in 1894 when I had admitted Fusion victory. Said he had not been to bed, had no breakfast, and felt as Wayne had gone Democratic other counties must have done likewise.
   William said he saw Santa Claus. He asked me if I was a good boy   I said yes   Turned to his mother & said "I fooled him"

Monday, December 29, 1919
   Day in Raleigh.
   Dined with Bickett[,] G T & R W Winston [35]   R W said we ought to read the Education of Henry Adams [36] and he praised it as one of the greatest books ever written. "What did Henry Adams do? Who was he?["] Bob could not answer & G T W & I had fun by saying that if a man had done nothing worthwhile what was the value of our reading his unfolding of his life. Bob came back saying that the unfolding of a soul was worth more than the story of action, & that men of action rarely had time to write anything worth while.
   Cost 7.54 for every N&O printed & we get $7. Will talk (J D Jr will) with Chas H. [?] & E D Neil [?] to see if agreement on cash in advance will be made & subscription price increased.
   Talked about more State news. N&O should print every important piece of news in the State

Tuesday, December 30, 1919
   Cabinet   Sugar. Will Board [37] resign? They were miffed because President did not act on their advice in August. They wrote him twice & he did not answer. Now that Congress has given power to buy Cuban sugar crop, after the crop has been disposed of the Board does not feel anything can be done

[34] Captain Nathan O'Berry, chairman of the Wayne County Democratic organization in the hotly contested North Carolina election of 1894.

[35] George T., a retired university president, and Robert W. Winston, a prominent lawyer, were brothers.

[36] *The Education of Henry Adams,* an autobiographical account of the life of Adams, a distinguished author and observer of the Washington scene for many years, had just been published posthumously.

[37] The Sugar Equalization Board, established during the war to control the price and distribution of sugar.

to secure lower price & feel that the license can be invoked to prevent profiteering. They had threatened to resign and Houston went to Phila to urge them not to do so

Dined at Admiral Grants

Wednesday, December 31, 1919

Went to see Mr & Mrs. Padgett whose son had died. Distressing & P said how he would have gladly died in his stead

McG—— settled case of woman who was ready to bring suit against Mrs D—— because servants had roughly pushed her out of the house. She did not wish it done but McG & I agreed it was wise

Jonathan & I went to Foundry [Methodist] Church at 11:40 to watch night service

1920

The Cabinet Diaries of Josephus Daniels, 1920

Thursday, January 1, 1920

New York World carried my New Year expression.

New Year's Reception at home. Diplomats, naval attaches & others called. Marine Band. Mary Cleaves & husband.

Breakfast at Chas. Henry Butlers.[1] Saw many who approved my action in medals

Gen Brewster.[2] (we saw him at Cho^{au}mont) [sic] a fine officer

Friday, January 2, 1920

McCandless & State naval flags

Spent evening with Senator Page and discussed policy of medals and what steps should be taken. He approved recalling Knight Board and said I had acted wisely in having them to [sic] take up every case. We will not avoid such hearing as Republicans may wish to make. He thought that David's course OK & Sims's criticism was terrible. Let people get on to the feeling against Wilson and they will find the motive   Sims only 7 years of sea service

Saturday, January 3, 1920

Charles R. Crane came to see me to refute statement of Greek woman in this country that Admiral Bristol [3] was too favorable to Turks and thinking too much of Turkish society which was cultivating him. He said B was, of course, trying to do his duty as High Commissioner in Turkey and courteous to them, but was properly representing America & this Greek woman had been heard too much in Paris & here.

As to Russia he said it would be slow but the great peasant class would not follow Bolshevists who could hold on till their munitions gave out. They obtain great quantities that Germany had stored. Their brutality & cruelty was such that people would not now oppose them, but it would run its course. His faith was this: The people had driven out the Rasputin monks, reorganized their churches on democratic lines as they existed prior to Peter the Great

[1] Washington attorney.
[2] Major General André W. Brewster, Pershing's Inspector General.
[3] Rear Admiral Mark L. Bristol, U.S. High Commissioner to Turkey.

and observed the same freedom that was in vogue 260 years ago & had done so as if without interruption. Another reason why Russia would come back. All Russians speak same language, have same jokes & stories. Nothing like the culture & oneness of language elsewhere in so large a territory in the world.

Saw Baker about Creel

Sunday, January 4, 1920

Worked on Jackson Day speech

Dined at British Embassy to meet Lord Jellico at dinner given by Counsellor Lindsey.[4] Jellico said Admiral Bailey [5] was Naval Attache here twenty years ago and was recalled at our Gov's request & so when our destroyers were going over to Queenstown he sent for Bailey, who is a brusque man, and told him he must be very courteous to Americans. When Sims came in he was rude to him— d—— rude—so rude that he took him to Carson,[6] First Lord, & told him Bailey must be removed unless he improved his manners. B—— said he had not meant to be rude. Ten days later Sims wrote Jellico that Bailey was OK & all Americans liked him.

Had been to Honolulu. The Loop [?] by which through wires could detect presence of submarines was contributed by scientific men.

Believed in taking boys into Navy—catching them young—13½ to 14 years. They take to discipline better. Am. officers knew more than British officers, but B. of.[ficers] could manage their destroyers probably better

Monday, January 5, 1920

Admiral Jellicoe called and was interested in the John Paul Jones sword and I told him the history of how he became "Jones." Photographs taken and moving pictures. Went to lunch at Admiral Grant's [7] and saw a 16 inch gun lined. Impressed with magnitude of plant. "Our officers are not educated to this character of work" said Jellico, "our big guns are all made by contract."

Jellicoe at dinner with cabinet and certain naval officers. Agreeable & pleasant. Going to Havanna [*sic*] tomorrow. He said he supposed all our boats were tied up transporting liquor to Havanna. I asked if that was why he was leaving so soon and hastening to H——? He said he feared he could not prove an alibi.

Page and Butler had their heads together over the awards

---

[4] Ronald C. Lindsay, chancellor of the British Embassy.

[5] Admiral Sir Lewis Bayly, commanding the Anglo-American naval forces operating out of Queenstown, Ireland, during the war.

[6] Sir Edward Henry Carson, First Lord of the Admiralty in 1917.

[7] Rear Admiral Albert W. Grant, commandant of the Washington Navy Yard and superintendent of the Naval Gun Factory.

Tuesday, January 6, 1920

Went before Com. on Appropriations of the House (Wood [8] acting ch) for civilian employes in Navy Dept. & urged continuance of larger navy pay for the higher grade men whose pay was raised during the war.

Cabinet. Discussed probabilities of League of Nations. Most of members were not agreed to accept the Lodge reservations Thought better to let it fail than to back down on essentials. Burleson told of greatest insult offered to him. Life had printed a double page of modern paradise with St. William Bryan and St. Josephus & had confounded him with the Prohibitionists.

Alexander [9] read an extract from Everett Colby [10] who said Republicans had idiotic leadership and no foreign policy.

Senate Naval Affairs Committee decided to investigate award of naval medals. Walsh [11] spoke his mind. Lodge prevailed

Dinner to Vice President by Mrs. Walsh.[12] 80 people—gold plates. Went in with wife of the Polish minister [13]—agreeable & well posted Intended 2 dinners—V.P. & Secy of State—but [?] sent all invitations to the first dinner

Wednesday, January 7, 1920

House Naval Affairs Committee (Republican members) decided not to take any part in investigation of naval medals

Dined with the Chilian Ambassador minister [14] [*sic*]. Vice President Marshall there. Discussed newspapers & lands controlling press & the necessity of liberty of the press.

Thursday, January 8, 1920

Jackson Day dinner. So big had speaking at the Hotel Washington. Speakers at both places. The President opposed any except interpretive reservations. Bryan will take any he can get, believing, as he said, that it was so important to ratify that we ought to accept Section 10 as it was &c and then we could hope for change afterwards He was in a militant mood and when somebody called out: "Stand by Wilson" his eyes flashed fire and he said "If you can guarantee victory, then I will not speak" &c, or words to that effect. Most of

---

[8] William R. Wood, Republican, U.S. Representative from Indiana.

[9] Joshua W. Alexander, former Democratic U.S. Representative from Missouri, Secretary of Commerce since December 11, 1919.

[10] New Jersey attorney and Progressive Republican.

[11] Thomas J. Walsh, Democrat, U.S. Senator from Montana.

[12] Mrs. Thomas F. Walsh, prominent Washington hostess.

[13] Prince Casimir Lubomirski.

[14] Don Beltran Mathieu, Chilean Ambassador.

his speech was fine but he was deeply in earnest when he opposed delay in ratification and opposed making it an issue in the campaign. He got much applause and warmly praised Wilson about National Reserve Act & said no man since Andrew Jackson had so withstood the money power

Gov. Cornwall,[15] of West Va., preaching law & order, leaned so much, as it seemed against labor, that Mrs. Fairbanks,[16] of Chicago, said: "That's the kind of talk I have been hearing from Republicans all my life and I did not expect to hear it at a Democratic banquet. It was because of such talk I left the Republican party[."]

I talked on hyphenate politics

Got home at 3 a.m.

Friday, January 9, 1920

Slept late.

Cabinet talked of dinner and speeches. All were critical of the B——[ryan] especially G[lass] & H[ouston].

Lane & Alexander said it would be unwise to minimize Bryan's stren[g]th. Lane said he had 2 million followers. Palmer thought President ought to formulate the reservations he would accept. Then responsibility would be put up to Senate; otherwise Republicans would saddle rejection of treaty upon Democrats. Lane agreed. Baker opposed very strongly. Lane seemed to agree. I said if President made proposition they would say he weakened, refuse to accept, and would then make the issue on the two or three points instead upon their hostility & early opossition [*sic*] to the League. They had early wanted to pass peace treaty and reject League.

Called to see Bryan who strongly stood by his position & emphasized that we could not afford to go to the country on Section 10 as in the treaty. Referred to his advocacy of ratifying Philippine treaty which was his great mistake.

Lunch at Wilton McLeans [17] with National Committee

Call from Mayor of Vallejo about Mare Island Navy Yard.

Saturday, January 10, 1920

Addie went to Raleigh to see Judge Winston about buying his house

Talked to Lansing and Baker about fortifications of Guam and other Pacific military preparations and defense. Unless League is ratified we must spend hundreds of millions of dollars Decided to hold papers for the President.

[15] John J. Cornwell, Democrat.

[16] Probably Janet Ayer Fairbank, wife of Chicago attorney Kellogg Fairbank, and active in woman suffrage and Progressive and Democratic Party politics.

[17] Angus Wilton McLean, member of the Democratic National Committee from North Carolina.

I. L. Stone talked about Press. Advised postponement. Now is not time to buy. Should have tubuler press from him.

[House] Naval Affairs Committee, with only two dissenting votes, decided to have nothing to do with medal award matter, though invited by Senate Committee to join in investigation

Read up on speech before Holland Society & wrote part of it

Telegraphed Addie we were the guests of honor at dinner by the Russian Ambassador Tuesday night. She will come home to be present

Sunday, January 11, 1920

Went to St. Patricks to church and to reception to Cardinal Gibbon. Taken in the wrong way for usher thought I had been invited to lunch. Hurriedly escaped, after being told my name had been left off the seating arrangement by mistake and was on the other list. The preacher, I guess Mon[signor] Thomas, preached good sermon on need of parental obedience and national and personal obedience to God.

In afternoon went to see Senator Pittman[18] about Senate Committees investigation of awards and went over all the facts with him and left all letters written to Senator Page. He did not know what the policy would be. It was partisan. H C L [Lodge] had sneered at honors given to men who lost their ships. Explained unexpected attitude of Sims.

Miss Mary Graham[19] here to dinner. Over 250 students at Peace. She is fine

Read Dutch history.

Monday, January 12, 1920

Went before the Naval Affairs Committee for approval of appropriation to move marine railway from coaling station to concrete naval base at San Diego given Navy by Shipping Board. Governor Kelly[20] had been out there investigating shipping & thought Shipping Board contract too favorable to the private company—afraid if we put railway there company might get it under option & more afraid it would entail building new Navy Yard. Appointed Kelly & Oliver to look into it and present to the committee.

Saw Senator McCumber[21] about a doctor who was drunk in France & sentenced to two years. Excellent man and should be dismissed without prison

---

[18] Key Pittman, Democrat, U.S. Senator from Nevada, a member of the Naval Affairs subcommittee.

[19] Mary O. Graham, president of Peace Institute, a girls' junior college and preparatory school in Raleigh.

[20] Patrick H. Kelley, Republican, U.S. Representative from and former lieutenant governor of Michigan, member of the House Naval Affairs Committee.

[21] Porter J. McCumber, Republican, U.S. Senator from North Dakota.

sentence. Wife & child would starve. He was on leave & getting ready to come home & leave the service

Long talk with Grayson. President better some days & not others. L had written G—— long letter. W W "Damage done now." Glass wants Leffingwell [22] Secy of the Treasury. Baruch thinks it might hurt the party & advises that he be not considered. Shafroth wants to be Secy of the Interior. Grayson promised to send good letter for him

Tuesday, January 13, 1920

Cabinet meeting. Burleson blue about politics & said that as a matter of fact most of the people are dishonest and more that they are hypocrites.

Went to Annapolis to speak at the unveiling of the tablet to 800 first naval volunteers in the war & spoke. Scales & others spoke

Dinner at Ambassador Bakhmeteff of Russia to dinner—[sic] Serbian minister, Belgian minister & others present. Discussed many matters Serbian minister's wife very tactful—won her way in England despite the suspicion they had something to do with murder that brought on the world war

J D Jr here

Wednesday, January 14, 1920

Fox came out in Post with the statement that Sims had written letter criticizing Department. I had received letter in which Sims virtually indicted the whole Navy Department. I gave letter to Benson as it particularly roasted Operations [23]

Talked to Council about Naval bill. Hearings begin Friday

Swiss Ambassador [24] called to say goodbye

[22] Russell C. Leffingwell, Assistant Secretary of the Treasury since 1917. Carter Glass was resigning from the cabinet at the end of the month, having previously been appointed to the Senate on November 18, 1918, and subsequently elected to fill the seat vacated by the death of Thomas S. Martin.

[23] On January 7, a week before the Senate investigation of the Navy medal awards was to begin, Admiral Sims wrote Daniels a long critical letter entitled "Certain Naval Lessons of the Great War." A sweeping indictment of the administration and operation of the Navy during the war, Sims's letter was evidently intended to be the major gun in a new effort to reorganize the Navy along the lines of a professional general staff. Word of the sensational Sims charges leaked to the hostile *Washington Post,* which publicized them on January 14. Three days later at the Senate medal hearings Sims read his letter into the record, thus triggering a full-scale investigation of the operation of the Navy during the war. This second investigation, March 9—May 28, 1920, following the conclusion of the medal awards hearings, subjected Daniels' administration to searching scrutiny in which the original issues were soon lost in bitter partisanship and petty jealousy.

[24] Hans Sulzer.

Thursday, January 15, 1920
Finish my speech—
Went to New York to Holland Society Dinner and spoke on the Americanism— Judge Van Wyck [25] told why Raleigh went today [dry?]— He was in Raleigh & Gen. Hoke [26] told him Raleigh would go wet, but his young daughter Lily said "It will go dry because the people do not wish drunken negroes to push white ladies off of the sidewalks.["] It went dry
Went up with Clarkson, who will resign as Director of the Council of National Defense.

Friday, January 16, 1920
Sims before Naval Affairs Committee on awards of medals. Very cockey [*sic*] and sarcastic at first until Pittman pinned him down to fact that he had not recommended a single enlisted man for a medal & that certain service when a ship was lost might be distinguished. Pittman came to see me afterwards and said Sims was now on the defensive & he & not Daniels was on trial. But he will stop at nothing!
Lunched with Gavin McNab at Shoreham. He looked toward Hoover as our nominee but does not wish yet to commit. Present thought in California is to name Wilson & then delegates will be free. Plan to give great entertainment to delegates at S.F.
Long talk with Pittman & gave him data. Sims has been 16 years on shore & 7 at sea
Spoke at Lambs' Club—Masons from Navy Yard and at Congregational church on Watch Night Prohibition meeting. Bryan spoke at midnight
Cabinet spent 1 hr. discussing Bryan & Balto Convention—whether he wanted to nominate himself & how much he helped to name Wilson

Saturday, January 17, 1920
Sims read to the committee his statement "Lessons of the Great War."

Sunday, January 18, 1920
F D R came to see me and said he and Frank Polk thought I ought not to wait till called before the committee to say that the Department & I had made

[25] August Van Wyck, New York attorney and former Justice of the New York Supreme Court, president of the Holland Society.
[26] General Robert F. Hoke, railway official and North Carolina Confederate general. The reference is probably to the prohibition election of 1908 in Raleigh and North Carolina.

no such statement as Sims attributed to somebody in the Department.[27] So I sent for Coontz & Taylor and wrote letter to Senator Page. Showed it to F D R, who approved. So did Tumulty

It was sent to all the papers

Letter explains everything.

Monday, January 19, 1920

Sent the letter to Senator Page. Naval Committee ordered investigation of Sims's charges after they had finished hearings on medal awards. David Lawrence came to see me and wrote excellent article. N.Y. World printed good cartoon by Rol[l]in Kirby showing Sims trying to shoot holes in Navy record, and underneath these words: "Something The Enemy Never Did"

Gave interview with the newspaper men & told them situation, leaving strategy to be discussed by Benson. Distinct reaction in the mind of the public.

Saunders to dinner & talked Laboratory &c

Washington here. Talked of medals & of Sims' record

Tuesday, January 20, 1920

Cabinet meeting. I read Sims' letter to the cabinet about Wilson. Then talked to Grayson & Swope

Swope and David Lawrence at home & Swope went over whole matter of Sims & we took notes of some things that ought to be brought out.

Saw Mr. Bryan in the morning & he spoke of C G [Carter Glass] not inviting him to Pan American. Felt that it was unfriendly?

Wednesday, January 21, 1920

Preston home at dinner

Benson ordered on active duty & help to prepare his case.

Grant & Barnett before committee.

Thursday, January 22, 1920

Senate refused to vote money to employ attorney in investigation of Navy in the War.

Voted down Walsh's resolution to censure Sims by 2 majority

---

[27] Sims had declared that before he departed for England in March, 1917, he had received verbal instructions from an official of the Navy Department (later identified as Admiral Benson) as follows: "Don't let the British pull the wool over your eyes. It is none of our business pulling their chestnuts out of the fire. We would as soon fight the British as the Germans." In his letter to Senator Page, Daniels denied that he had said this or that it represented department policy.

Leigh & Foote at house on medal question
Addie went to Raleigh

Friday, January 23, 1920
Cabinet—Tumulty & Burleson jumped into Prohibition. Tumulty [28] said its harsh enforcement is going to injure prohibition & animadverted on the fact that a Southern man was in charge of enforcement in New York. This aroused Carter Glass's ire and he said the raid was made by New Yorkers & he would not stand for any reflection upon Southern men.

Burleson wanted no Hoover. Said Democrats had tried Greely [29] & it would be another case of leaving party principle for expediency & defeat. Palmer thought it would be to throw up our hands and say the Democratic party was a bankrupt

Congress does not have a program. Nick Longworth said "we cannot agree on anything." Hope to push everything aside until the election—appeal to people to turn the Democrats out & then they will reduce taxes

Newman [?] & others came to see me & said they were with me   J D

Saturday, January 24, 1920
Went over plans for Laboratory. Will Congress withdraw the money?

The House passed bill to increase pay of men & non-com officers in Navy but not for other officers. Will ask Senate to add officers. Would allow no amendment for fear Congressmen would propose a bonus for all soldiers.

Went over question of foreign decorations & prepared letters for my hearing

Telegram from Addie who said she had bought 11 lots for $8,500 on the hill beyond the Methodist Orphanage. We will build on the hill and be happy.

Sunday, January 25, 1920
Very bad day and did not leave the house. Prepared statement for the committee on D. W. B.[30] and the telegram to Sims. Sent for D. W. T.[31] who

[28] In the original entry this is written with ditto marks to the line above.

[29] Horace Greeley, unsuccessful Liberal Republican and Democratic candidate for president in 1872.

[30] One of Admiral Sims's major and perhaps most damaging criticisms of Daniels' medal awards was that he had given the Distinguished Service Medal to several officers, including his brother-in-law Commander David W. Bagley, who had lost their ships through enemy action during the war. Sims charged that such honors were destructive of morale and contrary to all naval tradition. Daniels argued that the stiletto nature of the submarine was a new element in naval warfare, and that a man might lose his ship by mine or torpedo through no fault of his own and so conduct himself with extraordinary heroism in the face of extreme danger as to merit reward. It should be noted that while Sims objected to such awards other flag officers had recommended them for subordinates who had acted

helped me to put it in shape and get it down into less space. Clear headed always

McGowan came around and brought article by Connelly [32] who roasted Sims and said he had O.K.'d telegram of July about ships coming over—when denial was made of Gleaves's telegram that they had been attacked by submarines.

Talked with Frank and Cora [33] about the house—Both glad of the hill and opportunity to build out there

Tuesday, January 27, 1920

Glass, Burleson & I talked politics at cabinet meeting. Nobody else came. Glass much disturbed because President had not appointed Leffingwell as Secretary of the Treasury. He had made sacrifices to stay during the war, had supported the President's policies, and knew all fiscal policies & would stand against speculators using money for speculative purposes &— But L is not Democrat.

Wednesday, January 28, 1920

Went to Phila. to speak at Pearce Business College   500 present   J Hampton Moore introduced me—said many bricks had recently been thrown at me but that none had hit me and that the people believed in the Secretary of the Navy & knew of the great work our Navy had done and criticism now could not dim it.

I can tell you who will be President—The man who embodies the best platform that secures to all men a fairer proportion of what their brain & toil have wrought

Met Governor McCall—who said that people in America were with me— that they took no stock in attack on me or Sims attempt to show we did nothing. Sentiment coming my way every day

Thursday, January 29, 1920

Gov. Glynn. Sec. Int. Any chance. Will see Tumulty.

Would a victory help us with H——[Hoover]   Would he help the D party or would it destroy the party and demoralize it? McAdoo seems our strongest man. Gov G said railroad men are for him.

---

heroically while losing their ships. While Sims expressed the highest regard for Bagley, he undoubtedly stressed this issue because Daniels was vulnerable to the charge of having rewarded a relative.

[31] Probably Rear Admiral David W. Taylor.

[32] James B. Connolly, writer on nautical subjects.

[33] Probably Frank B. and Rosa Daniels, Daniels' nephew and his wife.

Friday, January 30, 1920

Went over to the Industrial Conference [34] to invite them to dine next Friday night. Hoover presiding. And we joked about my Philadelphia speech and whether I meant Hoover or who? Three candidates thought I meant them

Talked with Joe & Cary about Secretary of the Interior and decided to write to W. W. in favor of Martin Glynn for Secy. of the Interior. Did so. Glynn came to see me

Dined at Lansings to meet the Secretary of State for Uraguay [35] [*sic*] & reception

Pittman & Benson

Saturday, January 31, 1920

Worked on material for hearing. Spent afternoon with architect and builder from Raleigh over plans for house.

Left on 10:30 train for New York

Sunday, February 1, 1920

Reached New York at 9 a.m.

McGowan came around & was optimistic as to result of Sims attack on the Navy

Lunched with Justice Elkus. Gentleman from Chamber of Commerce at Constantinople was there   Elkus thought Admiral Bristol, & particularly Mrs B was pro-Turk & gave too much social & other encouragement to Turks & was not sympathetic with the larger vision of our duty to end the rule of unspeakable Turks.

Went to Near East meeting at Hippodrome & spoke briefly. Elkus spoke strongly of what the Navy had done & commended Secy of the Navy and the people applauded & gave gracious reception

Spoke at Zion Dinner in Penna hotel on Religious liberty & freedom of the press. Mrs. Fels, [1] Mrs. Rabbi [blank] [,] Jacob Schiff [2] [,] sp[oke]

[34] After the collapse of the first Industrial Conference in October, 1919, over the issue of collective bargaining, President Wilson had appointed a second and smaller group of conferees to discuss labor-management problems. This second Industrial Conference began its deliberations in December.

[35] Juan A. Buero, Uruguayan foreign minister.

----

[1] Mary Fels, single tax and Zionist leader.
[2] Jacob H. Schiff, New York banker and member of Kuhn, Loeb & Company.

Gerard said "Daniels testimony [?] ought to put the soviet naval officers out of business[."]

Monday, February 2, 1920

Spent the morning with Senator Pittman going over my hearing & he approved, particularly the Wilson letter.[3] Spent all the morning at home

F D R had made speech in New York saying the President had not wanted preparation for war prior to our entrance. He had risked impeachment by spending $40 [million] for guns sixty days after we entered the war. I sent for Earle who said I had given orders in March for guns for merchant ships while F D R was in Haiti—& all orders had been made after conference by me—

Also we had no plans [4]

He wished News Bureau to send out explanation that did not explain and I told McIntyre [5] nothing went out without my approval

Talked house to [two illegible words] Rogers

Tuesday, February 3, 1920

Went before Sub-Committee of Naval Affairs and made statement about award of medals. Two hours and a half on stand. Afterwards Senator Ball [6]

[3] Daniels was planning to drop a bombshell of his own when he testified the next day as to why he had not always followed Sims's recommendations in making the medal awards. He intended to show that Sims had recommended a Distinguished Service Medal for every admiral who served abroad except Vice Admiral Henry B. Wilson, wartime commander of U.S. naval forces in France and currently commander-in-chief of the Atlantic Fleet. More damaging yet, Sims had written Daniels a long letter on January 12, 1919, protesting against the rumored appointment of Wilson to command the Atlantic Fleet, and complaining that Wilson had been a critical and disloyal subordinate whose promotion to a rank equal to Sims's without consulting the latter had damaged Navy morale. When Daniels read this letter into the record, along with Wilson's official fitness reports showing that Sims had unaccountably rated him much lower than had Admiral Mayo during the same period, Sims's charge that Daniels had acted with bias in the award of medals lost much of its force. See U.S. Congress, Senate, Subcommittee on Naval Affairs, Hearings, 66 Cong., 2 Sess., *Awarding of Medals in the Naval Service*, pp. 498–503 and *passim*.

[4] Roosevelt's ill-advised and extravagant remarks in Brooklyn on February 1 about the lack of naval preparation at the beginning of the war must have shocked and deeply wounded Daniels, coming as they did on top of the serious charges by Admiral Sims and various Republicans in Congress. Daniels would have been even unhappier had he known that Roosevelt had earlier congratulated Sims for his protest about the medal awards, though the Assistant Secretary understandably did not agree with Sims's subsequent more sweeping attack on the Navy Department. In later years Daniels chose to overlook the low points in his relationship with Roosevelt, but this was clearly one of their major crises, and for a time Daniels may have considered forcing an open break. See entries of February 9, 14, 16, 17, and 21, 1920.

[5] Marvin H. McIntyre, special assistant in Daniels' office in charge of Navy public relations.

[6] L. Heisler Ball, Republican, U.S. Senator from Delaware and a member of the parent Naval Affairs Committee.

told me he agreed with what I had said about rewarding the men in destroyers and like craft. Very few questions asked. Adjourned till Saturday.

Creech came from New York with letter from Van Sleich [7]—as to what line Benson should take.

Wednesday, February 4, 1920

Wrote to Senator Page in reply to inquiries Senator Hale [8] wished him to make that I had given orders to collect data—it would take some time and hoped to have it ready by the time Hale was ready to go ahead with the investigation. He only asks for it to try to help Sims get up data to try to make up his case

Man wanted to buy all submarine chasers at $5,000

Italian naval attache [9] called.

Council discussed getting tenders for destroyers.

House Naval Affairs Committee decided against ten million for repair of ships. Must discharge 13,000 men in Navy Yards.

Thursday, February 5, 1920

Went to New York to speak at dinner in honor of Homer Cummings who made a fine speech on the Democratic record and the hope of world peace through the League. Rung in Governor Edwards [10] who made a wet speech and criticized Bryan. He said he was going to S.F. to fight for an anti pro-[hibition?] platform

I spoke on Navy & the Merchant Marine. "Democracy and the Sea." John M. Riehle presided & roasted Sims who was hissed & hooted. R—— said Sims was the only Admiral who opposed laying the barrage across the North Sea while all other Navy leaders favored

Had many compliments & congratulations

Friday, February 6, 1920

Train from New York late

Cabinet talked about League and Prohibition and New York dinner & Finance. Houston said nothing could be done by this country to stabilize foreign exchange. Foreigners would buy less here and in the end prices of products in America would go down, but that would occur anyhow upon an-

---

[7] Possibly George Martin Van Slyke, Washington and Albany correspondent of the New York *Sun*.

[8] Frederick Hale, Republican, U.S. Senator from Maine, chairman of the Naval Affairs subcommittee investigating the Navy Department and a leading Sims partisan.

[9] Captain Pietro Civalleri, newly assigned to Washington.

[10] Edward I. Edwards, Democrat, new governor of New Jersey.

other harvest for England would buy from Australia & Argentina and thus employ shipping.

Meredith [11] trying to reduce the middle mans cost. Said the cost of lumber was the one thing that should be tackled—

Gave dinner to the Industrial Commission. Fine body of men. Hooker staid [sic] awhile. Gov. McCall said men would never forgive Sims betraying confidential instructions. Stewart [12] said he had seen nobody who approved

Saturday, February 7, 1920

Hearing before the Naval Affairs Committee (sub committee) on Awards. All day session. I felt that the cross examination left my position solid

Went to dinner with the Cuban Minister & Madame Cespedes [13]—in new Embassy Took Mme Jusserand in to dinner. Talked mostly with Senator Mrs. Sutherl[and?] [14] Mme J—— said it was to be regretted that Sims had violated confidence particularly where international matters were concerned.

Sunday, February 8, 1920

Stayed in bed until 11 & then saw a lady whose son had taken an auto & gone joy riding and was to have a summary court martial. She was in tears, said her boy had not stolen the car, but with other boys as a joke had taken it for a ride & had returned it. Her husband thought the boy was bad & she had no sympathy there. I comforted her

Wrote for N.Y. American sentiment on Lincoln's birth-day.

McGowan called. He had been thinking of best course to pursue as to S—— No inquiry, no board. Put him on w.o.[15] & not let any man stay at War College who had done certain things—enumerate them. He will get B[enson]'s opinion. He thought Reps. felt S—— was too heavy a load to carry, but he will go the limit.

Talked house building

Monday, February 9, 1920

F D R came in as usual. Osborne coming on Wednesday.

McGowan & Taylor thought no change should be made now at Newport.[16]

---

[11] Edwin T. Meredith, Secretary of Agriculture since February 2 to replace Houston, the new Secretary of the Treasury.

[12] Governor Henry C. Stuart of Virginia, a member of the Industrial Conference.

[13] Dr. Carlos Manuel de Céspedes.

[14] Presumably Effie Harris Sutherland, wife of Howard Sutherland, Republican, U.S. Senator from West Virginia.

[15] Waiting orders.

[16] Since mid-January the Navy Department had been under criticism for allegedly using enlisted men for entrapment in the investigation of vice in Newport, Rhode Island, during the war. The charges led to an investigation and further embarrassment for Daniels, though

Pittman wanted Foote to come to hearing to-morrow.

Dined with Gov. & Mrs. Martin H. Glynn at the Shoreham He told of Dr McDonald of Albany & how he would go to operate on washerwoman who could pay nothing instead of one who could pay big fees.

Negro stories.

Letter from Lansing "Personal & Confidential" There will be no more cabinet meetings except those called by the President.[17]

Will there be strike of RR men.

Straus showed resolution of committee on League of Nations & said he could not see any real difference between Hitchcock & Lodges reservations

Wrote Padgett recommending Padgett for [?] Inter State Commerce Commissioner

Tuesday, February 10, 1920

Sims appeared before the committee and denied he had said what Burns [Byrnes] and Whaley and Glass had said he told them overseas when they were there—said he told them the stories were circulated but not to believe them. All three testified to the contrary and Glass said it was unbelievable two Congressman [*sic*] would have traveled 150 miles to see the SOS forces if they had not been astounded and distressed at Sims's statement. Clear that Sims was untruthful or the three Congressmen were untruthful. They had no motive to make a story.[18] "Bottom has dropped out" said McGowan.

Who are the first thirteen naval officers, the men to be placed in the Arlington Memorial? President Lowell[19] & Alderman & other professors gave their choice of names. I asked Badger to look over & see what he thought was [*sic*] the first thirteen naval officers.

Went to dine with Admiral Thomas Washington—Earle, McVea[20] & Lewis— Pleasant evening.

---

he seems not to have known of the practice. Assistant Secretary Roosevelt was more closely involved.

[17] On February 7, Wilson had sharply reminded Lansing by letter that only the President had a right to call a meeting of the cabinet. Relations between Lansing and the White House had deteriorated badly and this rebuff, as Wilson had intended, led Lansing to resign.

[18] James F. Byrnes, Richard S. Whaley, and Carter Glass, at the time three Democratic congressmen investigating the war effort in Europe, had testified that Admiral Sims had told them in late October, 1918, that the Allies would have to grant Germany an armistice because the American supply lines had broken down. Upon further investigation they learned that this and other deprecatory statements by Sims were untrue and seemed based upon British propaganda designed to minimize the American contribution to the war. Sims's denial of the story was unconvincing and the episode strengthened Daniels' charge that Sims was overly susceptible to British influence during the war.

[19] A. Lawrence Lowell, president of Harvard University.

[20] Probably Captain Charles B. McVay, Jr., assigned to the Washington Navy Yard; appointed chief of the Bureau of Ordnance on June 19, 1920.

Wednesday, February 11, 1920

Meeting on Arlington Amphitheatre

G A R wanted to conduct dedication. Capt. Bealle not there but wrote a letter reaffirming what Judge Hiron [?] had said

Thought name of Confederate soldiers should go on memorial—

G A R No, only those who fought under US flag.

Spoke on Community Service at Navy Department

Letter from Taussig roasting Roosevelt—about prisoners going back [21]

Reception to Sponsors

Thursday, February 12, 1920

Council.

Spoke at Sponsor's luncheon

Friday, February 13, 1920

Letter from Taussig desiring a Court of Inquiry. F D R's letter which he said put him in bad light & said he had misrepresented conditions when he had not done so. Acknowledged letter.

Coontz & Washington strongly advise that Sims be detached & should be by order of the President

Appeared before House Appropriation Committee for Inter Department Social Hygiene Board.

Lansing resigned. Occasion unfortunate

Alameda presented site for Naval Base in San Francisco harbor

Saturday, February 14, 1920

Had long talk with Attorney General and Solicitor General [22] about appeal in case vs. Southern Pacific R.R. case which was won by RR & urged Palmer to appeal on account of Naval Reserve. He & King said they had no ground for appeal. Judge Bledsoe had held with them on the law and against them on the facts, & an appeal would not lie on facts. Gifford Pinchot has demanded appeal and matter is before Congress. Should appeal & urged it

Taussig case. F. D. R. decided to send for him and talk before any action taken in his request for a Court of Inquiry. I gave no advice and told him I doubted the wisdom of the action.

---

[21] Captain Joseph K. Taussig, recently in charge of the enlisted personnel division of the Bureau of Navigation, believed that the new rehabilitation policies in the naval prisons allowed too many undesirables to return to active duty.

[22] Alexander C. King.

Went to Senator Capper's [23] to reception given to Meredith. A Kansas sort of a time.

All the talk of L's resignation. P said the calling of the cabinet meetings not the reason—unfortunate that was the occasion. At Paris I found that W & L were not together— L opposing L of N—

Sunday, February 15, 1920

Went to Mt. Vernon Ch to hear Mr. Chappel on The Family Tree—the Methodist ancestry. Very good sermon. An old patriarch in Israel said: "We think of you often & pray for you"

Mrs. Dewey: Lansing had no imagination or initiative.

Oliver here & I read statement I thought of sending to Hale. He said "No, let Pittman have it & let it come out on cross examination." He thought with fair-minded men it would ruin Sims & show he was not truthful.

He was a little hazy about having seen the Sims telegrams but thought Benson had shown them to the Sub-committee

Mrs. Baker [24] (Woman Suffrage) called to get help in Woman Suffrage fight in Maryland

Monday, February 16, 1920

Decided not to go to Guantonimo [*sic*] just now.

Wrote letters to leaders at Annapolis in favor of woman suffrage, but it seems doomed to defeat.

Saw Mrs Dewey & McGowan & they were glad we were going to the F D Rs

Benson called at 7 o'clock and said he saw Mrs. Wilson who said the President wished to make him Chairman of the Shipping Board and to know how soon he could be ready. Grayson had spoken to me about it Saturday & I told him it would be a gratifying appointment & the best that could be made. B gratified

Went to theatre with Senator Overman, Mrs Gregory & the McLeans to see Elsie Ferguson [25] in Sacred and Profane Love. Very good

Tuesday, February 17, 1920

P M Wilson called

Polk called with Bishop Darlington

Long talk with Ambassador Sharp. Said he talked with Sims who thought

[23] Arthur Capper, Republican, U.S. Senator from Kansas.
[24] Mrs. Abby Scott Baker, leader of the Woman's Party.
[25] Prominent American actress.

no chance to end submarines except by surface craft & thought the menace was very slight until he reached England. Sent Sharp a pamphlet by some Englishmen to try to uphold Admiralty.

Jack Cohen: [26] Favors Hoover for President and wishes to talk with Hoover. Says Georgia will probably go for Hoover.

Dinner F D R To go or not to go? Mrs D & McGowa[n]

Maj. Glidge [?]: Here to oppose bonus for soldiers Said Convention at Detroit opposed bonus, but the Legion now asks $50 a month for those who served in the war. Would ruin the country's finances

Miller [27] thought England and France had plenty of American securities & should put them up for what is needed

Wednesday, February 18, 1920

Baker had seen Lansing correspondence with the President before it was made public and had advised L—— merely to submit resignation without the correspondence. Burleson had also seen it & both thought the reason assigned, calling the cabinet, not the one that should be assigned. But L—— said "No," he must give out the full correspondence.

Hoover has not answered telegram saying Jack Cohen wished to see him. I told Jack, that Hoover was afraid of entangling alliances with politicians

Saw Pittman to-night. Sims had written letter to Hale enclosing correspondence between Sims and Pershing, & saying in view of that correspondence Glass would wish to change his statement & retract. Pittman said Carter thought the correspondence added to proof of what he & Whaley and Byrnes had testified

Pittman said a Red Cross nurse had told him she heard Sims say in Paris that Pershing would have to be withdrawn because he had failed.

Thursday, February 19, 1920

Attended meeting of committee Asbury [28] committee [*sic*] on statue

Letter from Chairman Page who fears House will not increase pay of officers. Senate bill gives $3500 increase to Generals & Admirals and very little to machinists & others who need it most.

Council discussed action of Congress cutting down salary of high grade men.

Earle reported that first 16 inch projectile made at Charleston had stood the test & thus beaten private manufacturers.

[26] John S. Cohen, editor of the *Atlanta Journal*.
[27] Adolph C. Miller, member of the Federal Reserve Board.
[28] Francis Asbury, first Methodist bishop consecrated in America.

Dinner given by Naval Reserve officers at the Shoreham
In own handwriting the President wrote

Sorry. Cannot. W W

in reply to recommendation to name Rodman's nephew for Naval Academy.

Friday, February 20, 1920
Tumulty thinks President's letter to Allied Council is the best he ever wrote
and stands against the secret treaty known as the London Pact. Tumulty wishes
it printed and thinks people will see the talk of America yielding to foreign
countries is exactly the opposite.

Talked to A. Mitchell Palmer who is troubled as to whether to be a candidate for President in Pennsylvania. Otherwise liquor crowd might capture
delegation and be used against administration at San Francisco. But what
does the President want? Would he write "May I not suggest that you have
important enough duties without running for the presidency?" V. Mc-
C[ormick] lunched with Mrs. Wilson who, when he suggested that he ought
to say something about the candidate said it might be necessary for him to
run. This dazed.? [*sic*] McAdoo's action due to possibility of W W's running
& not because he wanted an open and free convention.

State Dept. wanted to know if we would take over tankers for the Navy
& then let Standard Oil operate for us

Roosevelt and Taussig fixed up their differences.

Dinner to Ambassador & Mrs. Sharp

Polk had story about cabinet meeting. Talking about gas masks I said I had
one on ½ hour & it was stifling. When? Burleson said when he wrote article
on Marines in France.

Saturday, February 21, 1920
Talked to Gregory about Leasing bill. Also Payne. I had asked him yesterday to read it carefully. He thought it all right. Gregory will give me his
views on Tuesday & I will write my letter then.

"I hate L" said E. Wanted T to tell L that Maj S must be sent back or would
not receive. T refused. Must put it on other grounds.[29]

F D R persona non grata with W. Better let speech pass.[30]

[29] Daniels had evidently learned from Tumulty of Edith Bolling Wilson's strong dislike
of Lansing. The Wilsons were also upset over a report that Major Charles Kennedy
Craufurd-Stuart, Lord Grey's secretary, had talked scandalously of Mrs. Wilson at a
Washington party. Wilson insisted that Craufurd-Stuart be recalled before he would meet
with Grey, who was equally firm in defending his subordinate.

[30] It is not clear whether Daniels believed Roosevelt had fallen into White House disfavor

Tried to get W W to put Lansing going on other grounds. Sent it over &
T did not know.

Council of National Defense accepted Clarkson's resignation. What of the
future?

Dunlap [31] wrote letter to the President cheering him up & pointing out that
national prosperity due to his vision and his wisdom.

John W Davis wrote that Beatty [32] would like to come over with his ships.
Cannot invite but glad to give welcome

Peary's [33] brother in law & son in law came to see about his funeral. I went
to War Dept & secured caisson & escort & air craft. Could not act as honorary
pall-bearer because had secured passage to go to Raleigh

Sunday, February 22, 1920

Reached Goldsboro 8 am. Mother looked well and was happy. Josephus and
Worth came down. Talked to Worth about what medical college he should
attend. He was undecided. I rather favored Johns Hopkins because it was
more scientific & because only graduates of universities are admitted and
because Drs. Welsh,[34] Finney [35] & Cullen [36] are among the faculty & because
it is nearer Raleigh & he may obtain a scholarship after the first year.

Went to Raleigh in afternoon & talked press & building with the boys.

Monday, February 23, 1920

Talked to Governor Bickett about revaluation. He printed sermon in N&O
on policy to which he has fully committed himself. From 1 billion NC's property will go up to 5 billion & we will have very low tax rate.

Nearly everybody thought W W had so many reasons for L's resignation
he ought to have obtained it upon some other reason than the one about
meetings of the cabinet.

---

because of his recent speech criticizing the administration's preparedness efforts (see entry
of February 2) or for some other reason such as his well-known friendships with members
of the British Embassy. In any event Daniels had decided that now was not the time for a
break with F. D. R. over his unfortunate Brooklyn speech. The resignation of Secretary
Lansing was evidence enough of trouble within the administration.

[31] John R. Dunlap, editor and publisher of engineering journals.

[32] Admiral of the Fleet Sir David Beatty, 1st Earl Beatty, commander of the British Grand
Fleet.

[33] Rear Admiral (Ret.) Robert E. Peary, the arctic explorer and discoverer of the North
Pole, had died on February 20.

[34] Probably William H. Welch, pathologist and director of the School of Hygiene and
Public Health of Johns Hopkins University.

[35] John M. T. Finney, professor of surgery.

[36] Thomas S. Cullen, surgeon and professor of gynecology.

Saw Tumulty about oil leasing bill. T thinks he should sign. So does Ferris & nearly all Westerners. Gregory gave me a memorandum showing that it would give too much relief to dummy entrymen or those who hold under title obtained by men who entered upon oil land after Taft's withdrawal order

Chas A Towne & buying Newport News Shipbuilding plant.

Col. Theall at home again. Called His restoration almost marvelous

Tuesday, February 24, 1920

Reached Raleigh [*sic*] at 10 am

Sent to Gregory for his memorandum on Oil Leasing bill. He gave reasons showing that it gave relief to those who claimed under dummy entries & otherwise gave leases to those guilty of fraud. But the bill safeguarded better than any former bill the naval reserves & I wrote to the President that I would not ask him to disapprove because of naval reserves. Tumulty thought he ought to sign the bill, but feared he would not do so because of Gregory's memo. I suggested that he get the written opinion of Judge Payne, the new Secretary of the Interior. He telephoned him.

Wednesday, February 25, 1920

Admiral Napier [37] called at War, State & Navy Bld

Bainbridge Colby appointed Secretary of State—a great surprise to everybody.

Saw moving picture of Social Hygiene Board showing life—to be shown only to women—life from the first to birth of baby. Wished me to say whether it should be exhibited. Also pictures of results of venereal diseases

Dinner to Vice Admiral Napier. Kelley saw Hale & asked him "Say Fred, can't you turn loose"

Thursday, February 26, 1920

Lunched with Lane. Other members of the Cabinet present at Interior Department. Talked of Prohibition. Burleson predicted that within 3 years the 18th. amendment would be as dead as the 15th. Wilson said Dem. Convention would not mention Prohibition—would not follow Bryan for or Edwards against.

Burleson said: "I will never attend another Cabinet meeting unless I get a written letter from the President asking me to come." Why not require him to send a White House car after you?

[37] Vice Admiral Sir Trevylyan D. W. Napier, in command of the British Light Cruiser Force during the war.

Burleson said W W said "Be neutral" & he had purchased Russian, German and French bonds before we entered the war & opposed, jokingly, Lenine because he would confiscate them.

Went before Naval Affairs Committee on School for Marines at Quantico. Lejeune made statement showing that 50% are taking the course. I also approved

Dined at British Embassy with Mr Lindsey Chg d'Aff. to meet Admiral Napier. Fine man. Had met him at Rosyth. Mr. Lindsey talked of Prohibition & of the superiority of British Parliament over American division of power

Friday, February 27, 1920

Repres Carlin [38] said he saw Sims in London who said to him: "America does not need a big Navy. We have always depended on England and can do so in the future" Said Sims charges had helped the Navy and helped the Democratic Party.

Interdepartmental Vener[ea]l Disease [Social Hygiene Board] decided to tell State and local institutions it could not help in their maintenance after July 1, but only where it was a military or national protection.

Britton & the sale of the Yale and the Harvard

Addie went to Raleigh

Jenkins here & we went over the Sims investigation getting up questions

Saturday, February 28, 1920

Talked to T. He is afraid W W will pocket treaty. He thinks it best to accept even Lodge reservations for if the League succeeds in spite of reservations it is Wilson's League. If it largely fails, it is because of delays & reservations. Art X was to prevent strong nations taking from small nations & to prevent imperialistic designs. It will be the spirit of League rather than any wording that will give it life

Talked in favor of Maxwell [39] for Inter State Commerce Commission. Saw Bob Wooley [40] who expects shortly to resign from Inter State Commerce Commission

Talked to Benson & Manning [41] about oil for the Navy & other ships. Am to see others Monday with a view to conference of oil producers to consider the oil situation. Great Britain taking over oil concessions & locking them

[38] Charles C. Carlin, Democrat, U.S. Representative from Virginia.

[39] A. J. Maxwell, North Carolina Commissioner of Corporations.

[40] Robert W. Woolley, Democrat and former journalist, member of the Interstate Commerce Commission since 1917.

[41] Vannoy H. Manning, director of the U.S. Bureau of Mines.

up & buying oil wells here. Would give her a great & controlling influence on trade and world commerce

Talked to Senator Pittman about Sims letter & investigation. Getting up data for him.

Admiral Chester [42] 74 years old. Went to his dinner. Commodore & Mrs Wadhams married 50 years

Sunday, February 29, 1920

Dr. Chappell preached fine sermon on the power of prayer

Lunched at Mrs. Bagleys

Vance McCormack came to see me. Interested in the Penn fight—and it will be a fight—for Penn delegation for Mitchell Palmer. Most of the I.C. [?] will be for Bonniwell [43] who obtained the nomination for Governor last year. At Paris [McCormick] said nothing except defeat of League would induce him to become a candidate again.

Lansing unbosomed himself to Vance in Paris—was specially bitter toward Col. House and Auchincloss [44] who did everything to make Col H *the* figure. Vance tried to prevent the feeling. Mrs. [Wilson] was bitter toward L at method of calling cabinet on idea that as President was ill some plan of carrying on government must be devised   That was the gravamen, added to the Bullitt [45] & the Jenkins [46] &c &c

McGowan called & stayed to tea. The Sims letter & Benson's reply will make it an Admiral's fight & he & Badger thought that should be the staging.

Commander Warren,[47] aid to Admiral Coontz, called. Fine fellow.

Jefferson M. Levy [48] called—wishes to be Inter State Com Com   Said party should not forget he had kept Monticello open

---

[42] Rear Admiral (Ret.) Colby M. Chester.

[43] Judge Eugene C. Bonniwell, a political foe of Attorney General Palmer within the Democratic Party in Pennsylvania.

[44] Gordon Auchincloss, Colonel House's son-in-law and private secretary during the Paris Peace Conference.

[45] William C. Bullitt, a disaffected former State Department staff member attached to the American delegation to the Peace Conference, had testified before the Senate Foreign Relations Committee in September that Lansing had declared privately at Paris that the League of Nations was useless.

[46] Wilson had disapproved of Lansing's highhanded actions in the Jenkins kidnapping case in Mexico. See entry of November 28, 1919.

[47] Lieutenant Commander Lee P. Warren.

[48] Democrat and attorney, former U.S. Representative from New York; owner of Monticello, former home of Thomas Jefferson.

Monday, March 1, 1920

C. W. Tillett here—oldest member of bar in Charlotte.

Conf. of Sec State, Commerce, Interior & others to discuss oil. Van Manning thought we ought to call members of Oil Institute here to discuss oil situation. Culinan [1] had proposed same thing & both thought we ought to write Rockefeller, Hoover & Requa—not the last. Always in war looked through oil men's glasses. Polk & I talked before the meeting & agreed it would not do to call them for they would talk nothing but Mexico. We are getting oil in Mexico now. G. B. is getting oil here & buying concessions everywhere & expects to control commerce & merchant marine through control of oil.

Went to hear Billy Sunday & introduced him as man who preached the old fashioned gospel in a new fashioned way & put his message hot from the bat over the plate & scored a home run. He roasted those trying to kill 18th Amendment. If Dems. do that, they will be put out & if Reps., they will lose. If both do, then Josephus & I will organize a temperance party and beat them both

Tuesday, March 2, 1920

At White House talked to T. He says W W will hear no argument for accepting Lodge reservations on Article X of Treaty. T had written an argument for holding original wording of X, saying imperialists wanted it &c— hoping W W would use it as basis for an article or letter.

You are looking well, Governor

"Yes, patiently waiting for disaster."

McAdoo thinks H's nom & election, if possible would wreck the Dem. party. Thinks H—— really wants to force Reps to nominate him & is not looking for Dems nomination. If nominated he thinks Dems. would not vote for Hoover. He says he will not enter in any primary—does not want nomination unless people want him enough to say so without contest.

Went to Shoreham to dinner with Gov. McCarthy & Hawaiian Commission. Jenkins found copies of Sims's letters to Benson & Bensons, & letters to Bailey [2] &c.

Wednesday, March 3, 1920

Jenkins found Sims correspondence with Admiral Bailey critical of America, opposed to League of Nations, &c &c. Is it confidential? Being in the public

---

[1] Joseph S. Cullinan, president of the American Republics Corporation, a large petroleum holding company, and incidentally Daniels' Washington landlord.

[2] Admiral Sir Lewis Bayly.

records & communications relating to operation of American ships by British Admiralty, can it be confidential?

Talked to Benson about his correspondence with Sims. It should be, or a part of it, given out in the hearings

Osborne came in from Portsmouth & said unless the restorations recommended by the Board could go through his usefulness at Portsmouth was ended. All who had not been guilty of crime were restored & sentences reduced. Clark would not recommend the others. Osborne felt this was a change of policy & men in prison felt it was not a square deal to deny them restoration when in former months men who had done the same things had been restored. Clark said he had not changed policy, but considered each case on merit.

Osborne wishes to be relieved since his policy is not wholly approved.

Thursday, March 4, 1920

Council advised to make building program in the alternative—to round out if League is ratified; Genl Board if not ratified by this Congress; 3 [year] program if we are definitely out.

F D R said when I gave Sims instructions he dropped in for a minute but did not hear any instructions given him & nobody there but Sims and myself. That confirmed by [my?] recollection & I was glad of assurance that Babcock was not there.

Hale wished Fletcher hearing postponed—Sims. I told him it could not be done but Sims [*sic*] would not be called until Sims [*sic*] had given his evidence.

Friday, March 5, 1920

Left at 9:50 for Quantico with Naval Affairs Committee to inspect the place, particularly the schools. Three fourths of the men have voluntarily undertaken some study and schools have been started to teach nearly everything any marine might wish to learn. There was a small class learning to read and write—two from New York, one from Washington, one from Tenn & one from Ky. One of them had served in the World War in Europe and had made a good soldier. Another had re-enlisted for the purpose of receiving an education. Upstanding, good-looking men they were, too. Pathetic to see how late in life they were thumbing their primers.

Committee was enthusiastic about the schools. A blizzard made it difficult to get aboard the Mayflower but once aboard we had delightful time coming back. Lejeune told of the battle of the Meuse-Argonne where his division, comprised of marines & army men, pushed through the German lines. A boy messenger was captured by Germans who told them [him?] (in sport) they would tear out his finger and toe nails, &c. They had him in tow when suddenly they found they were in American lines & prisoners & the boy said "Now we will cut out your toe nails and finger nails!"

Butler & others made speeches & were warm in commendation of J D.

Saturday, March 6, 1920

Went before Naval Affairs Committee on Appropriations bill & advocated program of only small ships to round out fleet now, but if we remain out of League of Nations favor large program. Our Rep. friends wish no League & no increase of the Navy. Also urged no reduction in Aviation estimate made by Capt. Craven.

Lt. Clifford [3] from Portsmouth with note from Thomas Mott Osborne who wishes to be relieved. He says Osborne is almost heart-broken—feels that his work is not permanent and has not had fair chance. It is depressing. Too many naval officers lack willingness to meet new measures & cling tenaciously to old rules which lack the human touch & comradeship.

Went with Frank—dear boy—to moving picture show

Sims' letters to Admiral Bayley show he lacked sense of loyalty & condemn him. Those letters came over from London office with official papers & if marked personal are truly official.

Sunday, March 7, 1920

Dr. Chappell preached on Thomas, who doubted after he had seen Christ buried, but whose faith gave him grace to die a martyr. Excellent sermon.

Sent for Commodore Wadhams and talked to him about going to Portsmouth to succeed Mr. Osborne who has resigned. Lt. Clifford said Osborne's heart is almost broken, but he wishes to go & there seems to be no other way.

Talked to Jenkins about the Sims letters & he went to see Senator Pittman to go over data which lets Sims answer Sims. Pittman sent me his report of the award & also Trammels. I had read the majority (all Republicans) who did not agree with Sims that no man whose ship was lost or disabled should receive D.S.M. In fact, so I have been informed, Senator Poindexter refused to sign the original Republican report which upheld Sims & threatened to write a separate report if it was not modified.

Monday, March 8, 1920

Hearing before Naval Affairs Committee on appropriations. Discussed Pacific Bases, Naval Reserve, and what to do with the buildings at training sta-

[3] Lieutenant Frederick Clifford, executive officer of the Portsmouth Naval Prison.

tions erected during the war. Shall we salvage them? Or keep them? They will deteriorate and cost money to guard &c.

Lunched with Chairman Butler.

Kelly hoped I would withdraw recommendation for any new ships "We get along so well together" &c &c

Taylor came up to talk Aviation &c. He does not think S[ims] is after me so much as B[enson]. It is S vs Operations and that will be the public view. Difference of opinion between Admirals. Should be kept that way because Operations ordered the ships & allocated them where it thought they were needed.

Josh McKean came to-night. He & Pratt agreed they had but few friends when they left Washington & would have none when they got through this hearing. We had 3,000 officers and needed 8,000 & of course nobody had enough. Broke up Operations several times to help Sims

Tuesday, March 9, 1920

Spent the day at final hearings before Naval Affairs Committee of the House. Executive discussion. Discussed naval bases on the Pacific and the necessity of being prepared if J[apan] should attack us. Coontz gave strategy as to Guam, Philippines and Hawaii.

Sims made his statement before the Sub-Committee of the Senate on his letter—said he was not responsible for its being given to the public, that it should have been studied only by naval officers. As a matter of fact some one from his force must have given it to the man Fox of the Washington Post which first published its substance

McGowan said, "Didn't I tell you so? Poor old Bill Sims"

Wednesday, March 10, 1920

Went to see Houston about continuing money on deposit in Commercial Nat Bk. Talked with him about Spellacy for Collector of Internal Revenue. R.C.[4] He asked me if he were good organizer. Cummings & Goltra[5] were there to urge Spellacy.

McFarland, of Boston, wanted me to release films taken by the Bolshevist government, given to our attache at Chinta [?][6] and "for such use as the Naval Intelligence might decide." He had paid $1.00, so papers said, for the

---

[4] Spellacy was a Roman Catholic.

[5] Probably Edward F. Goltra, St. Louis iron and steel manufacturer and member of the Democratic National Committee.

[6] Possibly Chita, a city on the Trans-Siberian Railroad in Central Asia near Mongolia and Manchuria.

films and they were his property. I talked to Baker and Palmer and felt unwilling to take anything from files of Intelligence now. McFarland greatly disappointed & said this Government had fought the only democratic government in Russia and now was practicing censorship.

Rodman, Wilson, McKean & Palmer here & talked to all three [*sic*].

Thursday, March 11, 1920

Talked to Hagner. Wanted to send telegram to B—— to resign at once & never put his foot on the shores of America again.

Deposition in case of buying Jamestown Exposition site. They agreed that $1,400,000 would be sufficient and are now suing for $1,200,000 more. Profiteers

Rodman, McKean, Twining & Palmer here at dinner. Thought Navy ought to control canal. Told about visit to Lord Hopes [7] at Hopeton. Lady named *Linothcomb* & he couldn't get her name. Called her Lady Linotype, Lady Lithograph, & Lady Linoleum. She said call me Mary.

Oliver called & said Naval Committee was so very friendly.

Friday, March 12, 1920

Letter from Geo. Creel about Senate Resolution to inquire into all expenditures by Committee on Public Information   Baker wrote George to come over and help prepare an answer. Money to Gompers & T. P. O'Connor.

Baldwin Locomotive Works presented models of 14 in. guns & mounts. Those used in France—Plunkett, Earle & some of the Captains were there Presentation speech & my reply

Conference with Benson on oil. S.O. & other companies plan to practise profiteering & we are trying to work in with the shipping board.

Brit[ton] & Jenkins here to go over Sims hearing.

Saturday, March 13, 1920

Went to Annapolis

Sunday, March 14, 1920

Annapolis

Monday, March 15, 1920

Talked to Geo Frick returning from Annapolis. He had been one of antisuffrage committee that went to W. Va. to defeat suffrage and got the cold

[7] John V. A. Hope, 2nd Marquess of Linlithgow, whose country home was Hopetoun House.

shoulder. He said John Walter Smith[8] would be nominated but would be defeated because he voted dry.

Talked with Pratt. Greatest piece of injustice he had ever known

Went to Homer Cumming[s'] banquet at the Shoreham. Speeches by members of Congress. Carter Glass said Lodge amendment meant nullification Owen[9] would vote for it. Baker made best speech of all

Tuesday, March 16, 1920

Bids opened for oil for ships. Only few received and prices very high

Spoke at Zion meeting in Baltimore

Wednesday, March 17, 1920

Hoover wanted second hand clothing for Poland. Cost $500,000. Appraised at $56,000.

Taylor & Oliver at home discussing cross-examination of Admiral Sims

Thursday, March 18, 1920

Council discussed House appropriation bill. Will ask the Senate to add S.F. base, new ships, naval reserve & certain items omitted

Discussed with F D R & Pratt & McKean and others the way to present evidence vs Sims & long conf. at night with Van Slyck, Jenkins & others.

Bryan did not call because he said facetiously he had quarantined himself so as to bring injury to none of his friends!

Saw Pittman & Trammell about hearing.

Hale insisted upon Fiske & Fullam[10]

Van Scheck[11]

Friday, March 19, 1920

Went to Capitol to see Pittman and Trammell about the hearing. They wished the cross examination of Sims to be confined to a few points that were not technical. They are so busy in treaty fight they could not go over the data until Sunday.

Pratt & McKean conferred about method of presenting the Department's side in the Senate investigating committee. They wish all called first & then Pratt & McKean to come, then Benson and then me. Pratt says he can answer all that Sims has said.

[8] Democrat, U.S. Senator from Maryland since 1908.

[9] Robert L. Owen, Democrat, U.S. Senator from Oklahoma since 1907.

[10] Daniels correctly suspected that Rear Admirals (Ret.) Fiske and Fullam would support Sims in his criticism of the Navy Department.

[11] Probably George M. Van Slyke.

Left at 4:30 p.m. on the Mayflower with Gov. of Maryland [12] and others for Newport News where the Maryland was to be launched

Saturday, March 20, 1920

Reached NPN early. Sun came out & was warm when Mrs. Brooke Lee [13] broke bottle of champagne on the Maryland. Some workmen had large paste-board box to collect any champagne that should spill. I told Gov. Ritchie, who opposes prohibition & favors a 3.5 bill for Maryland, that he could have 3.5% of all he could save from the smashing of the bottle and I would take 96.5 per cent.

Large delegation of Marylanders at lunch on the Mayflower which sailed to Hampton Roads. Speaking by Gov & J D   Then went over to operating base & to Navy Yard at Portsmouth where they are building the North Carolina. Tried to drive a rivet but it is hard work. Told the men that if anybody said they were getting too much pay I would not agree

The Sylph, carrying Maryland Congressmen got aground, and they arrived too late for the launching.

Started back to Washington on Mayflower.

Sunday, March 21, 1920

Reached W at 9 & home by 9:30 or a little later. Had cold and did not go to church.

Senators Pittman & Trammell here to discuss evidence in Sims charges against the Navy Department. Taylor also here.

Got telegram from Jonathan saying that he had gotten on well & completed 19 hours & by end of this school here [year?] he will have completed 23. Takes 36 hours to graduate, leaving 13 hours for next year & could by hard work graduate in 1920. Dr. Wilson [14] doubted the wisdom of it. I wired I was proud of him & hoped he would graduate in 1921 [1920?] so he could go to Columbia earlier.

Began work on my statement in reply to Sims.

Monday, March 22, 1920

Saw Dr. Chase, President of University, looking for commencement orator. Suggested Bainbridge Colby

Sims cross examined. Brought out that he was engaged in propaganda to prevent organization of an American army & wished that our Navy be a part

[12] Albert C. Ritchie, Democrat.
[13] Of the prominent Silver Spring, Maryland, family.
[14] Henry van P. Wilson, professor of zoology at the University of North Carolina.

of the B—— Navy. Also that he showed letter to H. P. Davison in New York though he had said nobody had seen the letter except his wife & his staff. He got excited when Pittman brought out memorandum and letter to Admiral Bailey.[15]

Dined with Senator Kendrick [16] to meet Gen. Pershing. His daughter talked of cow punching, circles [?] & was at home on a horse & loved riding & rounding up cattle

Tuesday, March 23, 1920

Baker sent letter in which Gen. Bliss denied the statement of Sims that he had recommended that American troops be breveted [brigaded?] with British. I forwarded it to Hale

Oliver came over and rode down with me and said that Pittman and Trammel had brilliantly conducted the cross examination of Sims & he was convicted of wanting American army incorporated with the British.

Went to see Trammell and gave him Lansing's letter in defense of the policy adopted by the Navy Department.

Wednesday, March 24, 1920

Saw Baker about what Bliss had said & at that time Sims had gone to see Bliss. Also talked to Baker about permission for Gen. Hines [17] to testify that nothing the Navy had failed to do had prevented taking troops to Europe. Baker was going to see Frank Polk about a Professor from Italy who was saying that the Italian defeat at Caprioni [?] would have been averted if Baker had kept his promise to send 60,000 American troops to Italy and they only sent 3,000 Baker had made no such promise.

I saw Bainbridge Colby who agreed to deliver address at University of North Carolina June 16th.

Harris Lanning testified that everything was wrong I delayed & delayed &c &c. Then Trammel presented letter written by Lanning to Sims declaring that everything was right and fully justifying the policy of the Department.

Rodman is cutting out   "Sims thought he was the whole show" &c &c

Admiral Capps said the tide had turned

[15] Sims had written to Admiral Bayly on January 24, 1918, indicating that he agreed with the British contention that U.S. troops should be brigaded with British and French units rather than put in a separate American Expeditionary Force as Pershing desired. Senator Pittman, Daniels' chief advocate on the subcommittee, was attempting to attack Sims's credibility by showing his pro-British leanings. See U.S. Congress, Senate, Subcommittee on Naval Affairs, Hearings, 66 Cong., 2 Sess., *Naval Investigation*, pp. 285–290.

[16] John B. Kendrick, Democrat, U.S. Senator from Wyoming.

[17] Brigadier General Frank T. Hines, chief of the Army Embarkation Service, 1918–1919.

Mr. W. J. Browning,[18] of N.J., member Naval Affairs died in barber shop chair this morning.

Thursday, March 25, 1920

Palmer on the stand—no written statement, but gave evidence that I had been dilatory & not pressed & delayed in enrolling reserve. Of all men he owed me most, but when Chief of Bureau I had to call him down often and he had not forgotten. But—Et Tu Brute [19]

Council discussed name of Steam Engineering Bureau. I had proposed to change to Engineering. Taylor, Parks and Earle objected.

Sale of aircraft to S. American countries to help.

Electric Boat Company wished to employ an English naval officer. We allow no American naval officers to serve in such companies & had to decline.

Col. Davidson [20] & Miss Carter called. The Col. is opposed to the treaty. Did not thing [think] much of Lincoln but the Gettysburg speech is a classic.

Friday, March 26, 1920

Made contract with armor plate crowd for armor for new cruisers—$525 a ton. They demanded 565 and we had quite an argument. My ultimatum was $520, but went up $5.00 & closed trade. Earle was well pleased—

Plunkett came in after his testimony & said he tried to do right. I told him I had a profound contempt for men who tried to throw mud on naval achievement in the war.

Mrs Dewey reads all the testimony & gets very hot & was particularly hot with Leigh Palmer.

Oil bids—only one—and very high

Spellacy said Palmer ought not to run in Geo. He might hurt because if defeated by Hoke Smith it would seem an administration repudiation

Saturday, March 27, 1920

Went to Senate to see Senator Warren [21] about adding three $4,000 places to Navy Department to keep efficient men.

[18] William J. Browning, Republican, U.S. Representative from New Jersey.

[19] Daniels had not expected criticism from Palmer, who as a lieutenant commander had been his first personal aide in 1913, and whom he had promoted to rear admiral and chief of the Bureau of Navigation from August, 1916, to November, 1918.

[20] Theodore F. Davidson, former Confederate colonel and prominent Asheville, N.C., attorney. The "Miss Carter" who accompanied him was probably his sister-in-law.

[21] Francis E. Warren, Republican, U.S. Senator from Wyoming, chairman of the Senate Appropriations Committee

Talked to Overman & Swanson about naval investigation. They thought there was no occasion to worry.

Sunday, March 28, 1920

Went to Mt. Vernon to hear Rev. Raymond Browning, evangelist from Hendersonville, N.C. Followers of Christ were first called Christians at Antioch

Admiral Rodman called and spoke of the statement he would give before the committee—free from bias & feeling—but to protect the good name of the Navy. Said he had been advised to tame down his original statement as it would have more effect than if he engaged in controversy

Went to Arlington & went over the new Arlington Amphitheatre. Beautiful—

Chas. came on his way to Franklin where young Charles is ill—not so well.

Monday, March 29, 1920

Admiral Grant appeared before Naval Committee today and wore his grouch. He said the submarines were no good & the battleships he commanded were not able to do much. For two years he had been in charge of the submarines and any fault was his own. But he had not been pleased with his honors & threw off on himself.

Had talk with Mayo. Said he wished to be fair. The British Admiralty had no faith in the barrage or in our ability to make the mines & sent officer over here to look us over before they would tentatively approve. Too judicial & had not recovered his difference with Benson.

Badger talked of Sims's charge of costing the lives of 500,000 men, & said it was not worthy of consideration. The blockade and the men in France won the war

Tuesday, March 30, 1920

Talked to J. P. Tumulty of letter written by the President to Sims & he thought it ought to be made public but the question is how—in my testimony, by questions, by cross examination.

Talked to Admiral F. F. Fletcher about Sims and his charges. He said he had warned me about Sims but agreed with me that Sims ought to go to London as observer, but not in command of forces.

Ralph Earle at home and we went over memorandum he had prepared on the barrage & got it in shape

Miss Legislature to vote on suffrage. Senate ratified amendment & I wired legislature urging House to ratify & make it OK

Wednesday, March 31, 1920
Star dinner—

Thursday, April 1, 1920
Executive session of Senate Naval Affairs Com—— considered recommendations for increased bases on Pacific Coast. Admiral Coontz was present and we discussed the Japanese situation. They have obtained control of the German islands in the Pacific & their building of new ships. Control of islands gives them chain where submarines could be used with great effect. They will control Hawaii within a few years.

Dinner with Commander Warren and Bellinger—Coontz & Craven & their wives present

Fullam testified that everything in the Navy O.K. but that the Secretary was not efficient &c.

Grayson saw the President about my using the speech of the President to the fleet and his telegram to Sims.[1] O.K.

Friday, April 2, 1920
Post carried article that I had told Senate Naval Affairs Committee that Japan menaced the United States and that we must build fortifications &c. against the menace. I wrote letter to Chairman Page & gave to the press that I had used no such terms & had gone to committee to urge San Francisco harbor & other developments on the West Coast. Also wrote Bainbridge Colby—so he could let Japan know.

Worked at office to-night

Mrs. Catt asked the President to appoint Addie to represent the U.S. government at the Woman Suffrage Conference to be held in Geneva in May. The Sufr. to pay her expenses.

Torn between going & staying at home

[1] In a telegram to Sims on July 4, 1917, and in his secret address to the officers of the Atlantic Fleet on August 11, 1917, Wilson had criticized the British for failing to adopt a more aggressive and imaginative anti-submarine campaign. Daniels planned to show that Sims's advice to the department had followed the British line. See Senate Subcommittee on Naval Affairs, *Naval Investigation*, pp. 2021–2024, 2080–2081, and *passim*.

Saturday, April 3, 1920

Talked to Admiral Benson about the necessity of being on the offensive in testimony & never let them put us on defensive. Also about going to Baltimore when Decoration from the Pope will be given him.

Wrote to Berryman [2] I could not come to Gridiron dinner as I had to go to Jefferson dinner in New York next Saturday night. Told Britton of data I wished for Jefferson speech

F D R recommended 3½ mil. dollars to go in with a concern to refine our oil we could buy in Mexico. Turned out that Homer [3] was in the company and would get $250[,]ooo if the contract went to that firm. Stewart [4] learned that R had some interest in it. Griffin warned against it.

McGowan: People are no longer interested in the Sims investigation.

Jonathan came & we had a rollicking time. He was reading poem of Rupert Brooke [5] who died in the war at 24 & had developed great power & talent.

"Blow bugles blow"

Sunday, April 4, 1920

Easter

Slept late and went to church to hear Dr Wood. Why should it be thought a thing incredible that one should rise from the dead? Inevitable also. Ship launched on inland sea—would run only half an hour. Would all its mighty power be placed in it for such short service? Man is a handful of matter glorified by inspiration—not made for this little life.

Young Cheatham brought Addie some flowers (Easter) His mother sick. She will give him clothes

A colored boy from Raleigh, just out of hospital, came here. Addie let him have money to go to Raleigh. Doubtful if she knew him. Jonathan and Frank voted to let him have the money.

Why have we no great preachers now? Discussed by John Wilber Jenkins & Jonathan.

Went to see Mrs Dewey. She said "It was a custom on Easter for the Czar

[2] Clifford K. Berryman, political cartoonist for the Washington *Evening Star.*

[3] Arthur P. Homer, Boston promoter and friend of Franklin Roosevelt, whose New England Oil Corporation proposed to build a refinery at Fall River, Massachusetts, with Navy funds to process Mexican oil for Navy use. Daniels believed the Navy was being overcharged by its current suppliers, but he was dubious about this scheme.

[4] Commander Harry A. Stuart, oil expert in the Bureau of Steam Engineering. There is no evidence that Roosevelt was financially involved in the New England Oil Corporation, though he did have other financial dealings with Homer.

[5] Gifted English poet who died at the age of twenty-seven in the first year of the war.

to kiss on the cheek the first person he met, newsboy or boot black or what not, to kiss on the cheek.["] With that she played the Czar. Beautiful act.

Went riding. Japanese Cherry trees in bloom Met Japs in rain taking walk to see the blossoms, reminding them of home

Worked on some reply to Sims Ambassador Page said Br. Ad. will furnish him with stuff.

Monday, April 5, 1920

Thos. Mott Osborne came in to see me this morning and handed me this extract from Gibbon's "Decline and Fall," Chapter XXX "The first moment of the public safety is devoted to gratitude and joy; but the second is diligently occupied by envy and calumny"

He said he brought it because when he read it he thought of me.

Senator Phelan came to see about San Francisco base.

Found telegram I had sent to Sims about barrage

Mrs Burleson [?] said to Addie: Did not feel like joining any of Wash. clubs—none of us knew how long we would be here Addie: Hard to know how the public will take that Mrs. B. I say it is not the public. It is just one husband and one man

Went to dinner at Hotel Washington of World Inter. Church movement. Rockefeller, Lansing, Mott, Milliken,[6] & Earle Taylor[7] spoke. Rodeheaver sang. I brought Bishop McDowell home Lansing received with applause. He asked me why I did not try [?] Sims

Tuesday, April 6, 1920

Went up to Naval Affairs Committee and spent three hours going over the bill, the Senate putting nearly everything in that we asked, particularly on the Pacific coast Lodge wanted more for Boston and I approved. No new construction of ships authorized.

Memorial to young men in Washington killed in the war unveiled at Municipal Building this afternoon by Miss Margaret Wilson.[8] Bainbridge Colby spoke and I tried but did not succeed well, but emphasized duty to soldiers and sailors who had returned.

Had long talk with Grasty. Sims had told him that the President ought not to butt in to naval matters, but let it alone. Grasty urged me to be very forgiving & act as the father and not to deal in crimination or recrimination. Sims was on pedestal but has ruined himself and best not to deal in persnly [personality?]

Be magnanimous & say all had made mistakes

[6] Carl E. Milliken, Republican, governor of Maine.
[7] Dr. S. Earl Taylor, general secretary of the Interchurch World Movement.
[8] Margaret Woodrow Wilson, eldest daughter of the President.

Wednesday, April 7, 1920

Rodman testified. Three kinds of liars—the lie, the d——d lie, statistics. Hale could not confuse him at any point, but he pointed out that he appeared to defend the Navy

Madame T [blank] called in Red Cross nurse uniform. Martens [9] (Bolshevik) came to her on the train & denounced her for wearing the Czar's decoration. She slapped his face. He turned the other cheek and said: Have you not read in the Scripture that if a pretty woman smites you on one cheek turn to her the other also.

Gov. McCorkle.: [10] Put pep in your statement.

Thursday, April 8, 1920

Wilson gave his testimony before the Senate Committee and gave testimony which showed that Sims was wrong.

Had conference with Mr. Crane who wished to be assured that Colby & Baker & I would give him assurance that all departments would cooperate and help. Since Europe has played hari-kari, he hoped to do something to save Asia. Told of Taft's ambition to carry out a Pacific policy & talked to him about it and wanted his cooperation & appointed him Minister to China, but Knox recalled him.

I spoke at conference of ME Church, ME Ch South & Protestant Meth Ch. on Francis Asbury

Worths birthday.

Friday, April 9, 1920

Washington went before committee & argued increase of pay—told the committee that the only thing the matter with the Navy was that men would not stay without better pay.

Admiral Fletcher testified & Hale in vain tried to get him to agree at least at one point with Sims but failed

Went to reception given by Col. Hines.[11] Judge Bingham here & went with us

Claude Kitchin had stroke after speech in the House. We went up. His wife was in North Carolina. Dr Battle [12] said he had had a slight stroke three months ago and he had urged him not to speak & be careful because of high blood pressure

[9] Ludwig C. A. K. Martens, who claimed to be the representative of the Soviet Commissariat of Foreign Affairs in the United States despite the State Department's refusal to recognize him.

[10] William A. MacCorkle, Democrat, former governor of West Virginia.

[11] Brigadier General Frank T. Hines.

[12] Dr. Lewis J. Battle, Kitchin's family physician.

Saturday, April 10, 1920

Discussed oil proposition with man who wished to put in plant to top oil & Navy to pay cost of 3½ mil dollars. Recm by F D R who said it would get us ⅓ of our oil cheaper than any other plan. Postponed to secure guarantees & look further into it

Admiral Fletcher went fully into questions raised by Sims in his testimony & answered effectively that our Atlantic coast should have been protected against possible German submarines in early days of the war. Made excellent witness. Said Sims statement about losing 500,000 men absurd.

Went to N.Y. to speak at Jefferson Day dinner by National Democratic Club. Train detained 2½ hrs by strike. Due at 6:35. Young man on who was to be married in church at 7:30. Could not arrive & could send no message. As he left the train at 9:30 I asked: "At what time will you be married?["]

["]At 7:30 sir"—I guess he moved back the clock.

Large crowd but not much enthusiasm when I arrived late and spoke on Free Press Jefferson & read what had been said of Jefferson[,] Lincoln & Wilson

Sunday, April 11, 1920

Left at 9 am for Balto—— Addie & Worth with me Reached Cathedral at 11. Bishop Russell [13] read letter from Secretary to the Pope making Admiral Benson a Knight of the Order of St. Gregory, the Great & preached on "Render Honor to whom honor—." Praised Benson Scored any naval officer who talks about "blood being thicker than water" and endangers peace. The duty of a naval officer to obey his commander in chief. Cardinal [14] commended Benson and said he had been recognized for his great work by the President and by the Secretary of the Navy who was present.

Luncheon with Cardinal who was gracious & courteous & full of anecdotes. Told stories of Vance [15]—Rum, Romanism & Rebellion Vance said: "I carry my law books in one side of my saddle bags[."] What do you carry in the other side [?] "None of your business[."] Remembered going to Greenville— Offered either the Court House or Methodist church to preach in—accepted the church Choir, janitor & everything Methodist except the preacher. I told him he preached so good a sermon the people thought he was a Methodist

Priests all spoke of his courtesy. One thing he will not stand & that is impugning motives.

[13] William T. Russell, Roman Catholic bishop of Charleston, formerly rector of St. Patrick's Church in Washington.

[14] James Cardinal Gibbons, archbishop of Baltimore.

[15] Zebulon B. Vance, former governor and U.S. Senator from North Carolina.

Monday, April 12, 1920

Went over to see Admiral Badger about inserting in his hearings certain reports of the General Board. He read me his statement which is fine and fully answers Sims in every important detail.

Talked to Coontz & Washington about personnel legislation on Appropriation bill. They went up to see Senators & found Kelly was urging them to put it on, though the House had said it would include no personnel legislation in the appropriation bill Swanson said they were seeming to hold out but would put it on

Admiral Scales. Changed Board on Selection Left off T [?] & put on Rogers.

Went to dine at Mrs. Cromwell Brooks. Talked to Mrs. Dimmock [16] who agreed with what Cardinal Gibbons told me yesterday—that Beveridge's [17] Life of Marshal[l] was a great book.

Tuesday, April 13, 1920

Henry Bagley came & went to Raleigh to confer with Josephus and advise about a press & building. He is doing very well in Texas.

Forster [18] telephoned to me that the President would have a cabinet meeting at ten o'clock in the White House proper, presumably to discuss the rail-road strike. No meeting held since he went West last Summer.

Cary Grayson's boy goes to see him every day. "Mr. Wilson I cannot hold your stick any longer. My hands are cold." He was riding with the President.

Dined with the Merediths. Fine dinner. He works every night until 1 o'clock.

Mrs. Hamlin said she cried when her husband told her she could not accept place on Dem. Com. because Fed. Reserve Board must not be in politics

Went to reception & dance by N.C. Society

Saw Mrs Helen Gardner [19] sworn in as Civil Service Commissioner

Wednesday, April 14, 1920

Cabinet in W Ws study at 10 o'clock. He was seated at his desk and did not rise when we entered as was his custom He looked fuller in the face, lips seemed thicker & face longer, but he was bright & cheerful.

[16] Mrs. Henry F. Dimock.

[17] Albert J. Beveridge, Republican Progressive, former U.S. Senator from Indiana, author whose final two volumes of a four-volume *Life of John Marshall* had recently been published.

[18] Rudolph Forster, White House executive secretary.

[19] Helen H. Gardener (Mrs. Selden A. Day), author and woman suffrage leader.

"I felt it well," he said "to put our heads together, not as the Chicago Aldermen who did so when they wished to make a solid pavement."

Palmer took up strike & attributed it to the Bolsheviks led by Martens and IWW who were the leaders of the strike. W B W thought they of course promoted it but economic conditions & the h.c.l. [high cost of living] had some part. Also men were against authority.

Palmer said Post, in absence of Wilson by sickness, had released alien anarchists who ought to be deported   W B W denied this—said all who committed overt acts or joined the Communist Labor party by signing had been deported, but those whose Com[munis]t party all went over in a body had not been deported because, while they wished to change government, they were not lawless & expected to compass change by legal ways

Palmer said if Post were removed from office it would end the strike. W B W thought it might aggravate it.

Mrs. Wilson & Dr. Grayson came in & Mrs W said "This is an experiment, you know" & ought not to stay long

Open season for critic[izin]g Burleson, he said with laugh. Told Palmer not to let the country see red

Thursday, April 15, 1920

Council discussed putting predreadnaughts out of commission for lack of skilled men. Must do it

Ferris & oil men talked about my bill to ask Congress to prevent any helium going out of country   His friends said they had gas that would produce great quantities but could not do so unless they could sell to foreign countries. The bill provided could sell if President agreed. Said foreign countries would furnish money; otherwise could not afford to operate because U.S. could use very little.

Said they had concessions in Mexico, but Carranza had provided if in any way any foreign gov had any interest they would forfeit concess

F D R & oil. Declined to advance money or oil payment to company wh. requests [?] us to furnish tankers to bring oil out of Mexico

Weeks—Karmany [?] & McLean—not honest

Mrs F A Woodard here.

Friday, April 16, 1920

Came home to lunch. Mrs. Dewey's birthday. McGowan & Col. Buckey, Mrs. Dewey & Mrs. Daniels the Big Four.

Wright [20] wanted all oil matters put in Operations. They have nothing to

---

[20] Probably Commander Nathaniel H. Wright of the Bureau of Steam Engineering.

do with oil & I told him that it could be handled by me—for Stewart to go into it fully & report by letter to Congress as to getting oil. Better ask money for opening reserves and wells in Osage reservation, from sections offered under lease to Navy.

Swanson thought Washington's bill gives too many Admirals & will see W—— Navigation always anxious to increase men because officers go up in proportion to number of men

Badger came in to tell me about his testimony & how for 3½ [hours] Hale asked him questions & then re-asked them to weariness. He gave solid arguments and reasons & would convince any who were open to reason

Saturday, April 17, 1920
Went out to the Cathedral to the marriage of Congressman Hicks[21] of Naval Affairs Committee, to Miss Stevens. Nearly all of the committee was there. Lunched at home. Twice in one week.

Gov. Folk said "Lightning may strike you at S.F.["]

Henry came back from Raleigh & said we greatly needed a press & new building. He and Josephus go to New York to-morrow. Henry has big idea of increasing N&O capital stock to $200,000 & borrowing $100,000 for new press and building. Also to inaugurate better business methods such as he did not have when in R—— &c &c &c

Ridley McLean said Sims had nothing personal against me. Rats. Mad because I did not let him belong to British Admiralty & get him full Admiral for life

Sunday, April 18, 1920
Went to Mt. Vernon church. Dr. Chappell preached on the scripture of the vine, and the branches.

Henry and his wife were here to dinner & the Bs.

Talked with Judge Smythe[22] about the Nebraska fight. He said most Democrats in Nebraska are wet and Bryan's only chance is with the votes of the women.

Went to train with J D Jr

Talked of adding to building and buying a larger and a faster press. Will cost $70,000, perhaps more. I hate to go in debt just as I am out of debt for the first time.

[21] Frederick C. Hicks, Republican, U.S. Representative from New York, who was married to Maria Christie Stevens.
[22] Constantine J. Smyth, former Democratic leader in Nebraska, now Chief Justice of the Court of Appeals of the District of Columbia.

Monday, April 19, 1920

Saw Colby about Mrs J D. Law Pres can appoint no Commission unless specially authorized by Congress, but Solicitor had held the President's right could not be infringed upon by Congress & he could appoint if it involved no expense to Government. At first State Dept. thought the President had no right, but Colby did not sign the letter & then Solicitors opinion was found.

Mr. Wallis,[23] of NY, wanted me to authorize ship loaned to New York to be called the John F. Hylan. I told him I could not do so, but if New York people choose to do so I would have nothing to say

Senator Ball telephoned me that Delaware would ratify suffrage on Wednesday.

Tuesday, April 20, 1920

Cabinet 10 o'clock.

The President (sitting) talked vigorously (if not viciously) about the men who had killed the treaty. "It is dead" he said, "and lies over there. Every morning I put flowers on its grave."

Burleson wanted W. W. to send treaty to Senate and say what reservations he would accept. Otherwise people thought it was his stubborn[n]ess that killed the treaty. If he sent it back & the Senate declined to accept what he proposed they would blame Senate. W W said many devils had taken him up the high mountain & he had tempted of them, but he had forced French & British stat[esmen] (I do not trust them) to sign an Americanized treaty. I am compelled to be sincere if they were not. I can stand defeat. I cannot stand to retreat from consci[en]tious duty. I may not talk as well but I can still use the English language and if the people do not see the issue clear I will put it so plain they must see it. Burleson said three issues would outweigh Treaty—Liquor, Taxes, Cost of Living. Meredith thought it would be good tactics. So did Palmer. W W said he would not play for position. No time for tactics, time to stand square. I said Borah would use an axe to cut the Treaty to pieces. Lodge uses poison gas & if W. W. sent it back the issue would be between which reservation instead of upon the principle of a peace treaty. Baker & Wilson opposed relea[sing?] it.

Wedding of Nancy Lane & Phil Kauffman.[24] Reception

C C D here. Nearly crazed about C C D Jr [25]

---

[23] Frederick A. Wallis, U.S. Commissioner of Immigration at Ellis Island, and active New York Democrat.

[24] Nancy Lane, the only daughter of the former Interior Secretary, was being married to Phillip C. Kauffman, a wartime Navy lieutenant.

[25] Daniels' nephew, Charles C. Daniels, Jr., had suffered a mental breakdown and died shortly thereafter.

Wednesday, April 21, 1920

Maj. Wench [26] of Dover, England presented £6,000 from citizens of Dover. They will erect a monument to memory of men in the Dover Patrol and will give this sum to us to erect a memorial in New York harbor. Speeches "hands across the sea." Pictures

Dr. Grayson called with eminent British surgeons en route to New Orleans to Medical Congress. Pictures.

At Guatamala [*sic*] the Minister [27] had placed naval force under control of military attache [28] who had no troops. I told Colby this was unprecedented and asked him to cable the Minister that naval forces ashore or afloat should be commanded by naval officers. He agreed.

F D R—said he told Hale if called he (Hale) would regret it. 2x3 history. Pratt finished his testimony. 90% good.

Thursday, April 22, 1920

Mrs J D received letter from the President designating her as delegate to represent the US at the Woman Suffrage World Convention at Geneva.

Butler said the Reps. were tired of the Sims business & if they knew how they would drop it. The House members are having fun with them

Admiral Carlo B. Brittain [29] killed himself at Guantonimo [*sic*]. Mr. Hanger of Ky had filed charges against him & I had transmitted them in letter deliv. by Coontz & directed him to answer. He had written obscene letter to Hangers wife, & H had told him he would kill him if he came back to the United States

Went to see Washington win in base-ball this afternoon with Frank, McGowan and Dr. Dennis. 8 to 5 but until 6th inning it looked like Boston would win.

McGowan thinks Sims ought to be removed from War College because he said our Navy did not enter whole-heartedly into the winning of the war.

Friday, April 23, 1920

Ships sent to West Coast of Mexico & papers exploited it as indicating Mexican trouble.

Pratt's letter to Sims like Lanings.

Addie went to Raleigh & has the idea of our living in a garage.

[26] John E. L. Wrench, chairman of the British Overseas Club.
[27] Benton McMillin, Democrat, former governor and U.S. Representative from Tennessee, U.S. Minister to Guatemala, 1919–1922.
[28] Captain Louis A. O'Donnell.
[29] Chief of staff of the Atlantic Fleet.

Martin H. Glynn. Said no Irish-Catholic [30] had been recognized by Cleveland or Wilson, both sons of Presbyterian preachers. Very well, when Mexican situation was acute, to ask me, an Irish Catholic, to make the speech at St. Louis and all over the country. I was urged to do it. But none of our people are deemed worthy to sit in the councils & it is about time to let the Dem. party leaders know what a great defeat means. If we are not good enough to hold positions of importance we ought to assert we will not vote the ticket. Frank Polk & Frank Roosevelt carry no votes & no strength & yet they are recognized

W W an ingrate.

Saturday, April 24, 1920
Engineers from Maine and New Hampshire here to talk about the bridge over the Piscatawa [Piscataqua] river to connect Portsmouth with the Navy Yard at Kittery. Swift current. We will ask War Department to grant the right.

Frank at Fairfax C.H.   auto broke down

Oliver came to see about having Naval officers who fought in the Confederate Navy to be regarded as having their resignations accepted instead of the present mark of discharged on their record

Sunday, April 25, 1920
Worked all day except time for a ride through the park on my statement for the Naval Affairs Committee— Jenkins came up to supper and we went over some of the most important things which we got ready for the typewriters. Read article in NY World by German Admiral which showed Germans did not think we could get the soldiers trained & get them to Germany.

Had lot of fun with Frank. In asking for passport for Addie to go to Geneva, we had to put down her occupation. I told Frank I must answer tomorrow & had postponed until I could consult him   He said "Just say Mother." No—not working at trade   Then say "None." That would disqualify her for nobody would wish a delegate who did nothing. Politician—General Boss—Globe Trotter. Frank resented the first.

McGowan prompt. Had protest from Boston from man who said he had been told he could get Kite only by buying [?] Monday. He asked for time. Telephoned McGowan who had everything in good shape & sent all telegms by dinner.

---

[30] In the margin here Daniels has written a question mark.

Monday, April 26, 1920

Butler said he would see B——

Kelly said Senate Reps would like to turn loose the last of the Sims investigation if they knew how

Wrote speech for Univ of NC & Press Club New York

Tuesday, April 27, 1920

Cabinet. W W told Colby to take [up] with British their selling ships to Chili. Also suggestion of Canada's sending a minister to their country who would be subordinate to British Ambassador. Favorable to Canada but thought a matter for Britain to decide rather than America.

Express Companies, now guaranteed 6%, have put an embargo upon carrying express and shifted burdens on P.O. Dept which lacks money to provide additional facilities.

Colonies wanted everything at Paris said W W.

GB financial experts at Paris had no heart and were trying to grab everything in sight.

Only reads the Balti. Sun in the morning & rarely sees other papers.

F D R had prospects to buy oil from certain company, advancing them money to begin July 1 & we would save money. "I hae me doots,["] but Griffin & all others agreed and I assented[,] voting against it, but saying I have only one vote. Ought to commandeer and compel the SO to come across

Left 7.50 for Raleigh to inauguration of President Chase.

Wednesday, April 28, 1920

Reached Raleigh 4:30 am. Went through the country with President and Mrs. Hibben,[31] of Princeton, with Mrs. John C. [?] Drewry to Chapel Hill to inauguration of Dr. Chase as President of University. Very impressive. I was toast master at banquet attended by representatives of other universities & colleges. (My speech in News & Observer) Introduced Dr. BASSett,[32] of Smith College, who when professor in Trinity wrote an article that Booker Washington was the greatest man who had been born in the South. As a result of my criticism I was burned in effigy at Trinity College. I praised his recent book on the war. I also introduced Senator Moses,[33] the celebrated key-hole

[31] John G. Hibben, Wilson's successor as president of Princeton University.

[32] John Spencer Bassett, former professor of history at Trinity College and since 1906 at Smith College. In attacking Bassett for praising Booker T. Washington, Daniels' *News and Observer* had always spelled his name bASSett.

[33] George H. Moses, newspaper publisher and Republican, U.S. Senator from New Hampshire.

diagnostician, who represented Dartmouth College. Reception that night after banquet and then Worth drove us through the country to Raleigh, arriving at 2 am. Thursday, Apr 28 [29]

Talked business & press & politics till 1.20 pm. when I went on SAL to Norfolk, Alford going with me as far as Norlina. Braddock had recommended buying the press which Henry & Josephus & Braddock had examined at Binghamton, N.Y.   Sextuple.

Reached Norfolk & dined with Admiral and Mrs. Burrage.[34]

Talked with W. W. Fuller [35] who thought Gov. was very poorly run.

Thursday, April 29, 1920

Politics busy in Raleigh between candidates for Governor

Judge Allen [36] thought Overman had hurt himself by coming to State Convention. His speech was not good and on woman suffrage he pleased nobody. He gave it out he was not going to oppose, then advocated referendum, and the publication that he had not stood for Simmons in the Kitchin-Simmons contest [37] hurt him.

Friday, April 30, 1920

Left Burrage's at 8 am. Went to base and left on the Goldsborough destroyer to Lynnhaven Bay where I went on board the flagship, the Pennsylvania. Well received. Beautiful day. Race in steaming by dreadnaughts, the North Dakota winning. Number of newspaper-men on board.

Nobody knew cause of Brittons [*sic*] shooting himself. He had been nervous of late. Nobody on ship had any idea of real cause except 2. After Coontz gave his letter from me, Britton sought no advice or counsel. For some time he had been practising with pistol & said he was going in for the contest by practising. He wrote letter to his son—to be good, care for his mother, and just such a letter as he would have written if only going on a journey. Also to his wife— nobody knows what he wrote her.

At 4 a.m. the shot was heard & he was dead

The tragedy of it

---

[34] Rear Admiral Guy H. Burrage, commandant of the Norfolk Navy Yard.

[35] Probably Williamson W. Fuller, North Carolina–born retired attorney, former general counsel of the American Tobacco Company.

[36] William R. Allen, Associate Justice of the Supreme Court of North Carolina.

[37] A reference to the heated 1912 senatorial primary contest between Senator Simmons and Governor William W. Kitchin, brother of Representative Claude Kitchin.

Saturday, May 1, 1920

Fleet reached New York a little after eleven o'clock. After lunch, liberty parties went ashore and I went with Coontz to Navy Yard and on inspection of Tennessee with Adml McDonald [1] & Capt Leigh. Great ship. Then went to inspect Bay Ridge station. Com of Bay Ridge Chamber of Commerce wished station moved as it was in the way of their view of the narrows &c &c.

Went to Press Club dinner & spoke & came to Wash on midnight train.

Sunday, May 2, 1920

Josephus here for the day.

Our Wedding anniversary and I had ordered flowers. A happy Sunday. Big boys here. Jenkins came after dinner & we went over my testimony & were getting into it pretty well when Adml Rodman called. He said sentiment was all one way on the Pacific and people condemned Sims.

Admiral Coontz called & said State Department wished Navy to send ships to Mexico & that Colby had seen me in N.Y. last night. He had but never mentioned Mexico & I wished request from State Department before any overt act, but told C to make ready & stand by so we could go in if necessary.

Went to ride & with Josephus to train.

Moon in eclips[e]

Monday, May 3, 1920

Admiral McKean called and said Pratt greatly appreciated my letter. He talked of his testimony & will be here to help out Benson with detail.

State Dept. asked us to send ships to Vera Cruz & other places in Mexico and Adee [2] wrote that he wished destroyers &c. I sent his letter to the President, told him I had sent destroyers to Hampton Roads & would be ready & yet I thought no announcement of sending ships to Mexico ought to be published. He wrote approving and said he wished me to send our best & wisest commander. Will be here to-morrow for consultation.

Addie got her passport.

Va. Power Company wants concessions at Charleston, W. Va. that would be injurious to Armor factory

Tuesday, May 4, 1920

Cabinet. W. W. in answer to statement by Colby that Dem. Senators wished

---

[1] Rear Admiral John D. McDonald, commandant of the New York Navy Yard.
[2] Alvey A. Adee, second Assistant Secretary of State since 1886.

his opinion about Knox resolution [3] said he would give his opinion in plain terms in a veto message. He could not trust E. & F. upon matters and did not believe we should open trade relations with Russia, for it would soon involve recognition of Soviet government. Alexander & Colby thought we might trade with her without recognition, and Alexander said American business interests believed England was controlling business while we were neglecting opportunities for foreign trade. Baker thought Soviet government weakening. Bakmeteff said Soviet controlled by saying outside govs. would not trade because they wished to force restoration of royalists.

W W opposed to sending the Peace Treaty back with suggestions of reservations he would accept

Meredith wanted to allow certain profits & then all above that would be paid to the Gov. Only way to prevent profiteering & return to normal conditions. Reducing excess profits would do no good as they would leave incentive to high prices

Jared Saunders [4] told me how La. converted 20,000 negro margin into a Dem margin in 1880.

Dinner at Franklin Roosevelts.

Wednesday, May 5, 1920

Ordnance experts from France here to visit our establishments and compare notes with our ordnance officers. They called and we were photographed.

Benson continued his cross-examination. Answered Hale's questions without preparation and did not get on well. Advocated making Chief of Operations virtually the Secretary of the Navy with seat in the cabinet when international questions were under discussion.

Saunders said La. would certainly ratify suffrage

Letter from Mrs T, wife of naval officer, retired, who was on duty during the war. Said she was on verge of suicide and must see me. Said she was French —her family had fought valorously. Was in France when war broke out—her husband told her to stay because of submarine danger. He accused her of being a spy—with her mother in Switzerland as helper. Accused her of all sorts of espionage & immorality. When she returned he would not see her. She obtained divorce with alimony. But she would go crazy unless her name was cleared of being a spy.

[3] A proposed congressional declaration to end the state of war with Germany without approving the Versailles Peace Treaty.

[4] Jared Y. Sanders, Democrat, U.S. Representative from Louisiana.

Thursday, May 6, 1920

Letters & calls because no Southern name is on the Arlington Memorial Amphitheatre. Left to a Board of College historians and presidents who assumed that only men who fought in the Federal army would be thus honored.

Went to House Committee to see pictures of Allison anchor & lunched with Chairman Butler.

Benson again on the stand. He said he warned Sims "not to let the British pull the wool over his eyes &c," but did not remember the actual words used, and he used them "in no such sense as has been represented["] &c. It has evidently given him great trouble and distress, for he said he had received high honors from Great Britain, had many friends there & the misrepresentation would make it impossible for him to go there again.

Naval militia. Commodore Forsham [?] vs. Admiral Washington.

Lejeune & Butler here with Addie from Quantico

Friday, May 7, 1920

Went to see Baker about letter protesting against leaving names of ex-Confederates off Arlington Memorial Amphitreatre. He read letter he had written to Mrs. Johnstock [?] explaining and saying if Congress would take action we would be glad to place names of Lee & Jackson on Amphitheatre but executives would not feel at liberty to do so. Senator Harris [5] called and urged that names be placed there of Confederate heroes

Dinner at Army and Navy Club to French ordnance officers here. The head of the mission spoke and I gave welcome address and Ambassador Jusserand spoke.

Then I went to Olympian dinner & spoke. Some one had said I had asked what an Olympian dinner was & I told story of Admiral Southerland & I said: "I never heard of you before[."] [6]

John Jenkins saw Benson & he was surprised that his testimony could be distorted as it had been

[5] William J. Harris, Democrat, former member and chairman of the Federal Trade Commission, U.S. Senator from Georgia since 1919.

[6] This was a favorite Daniels anecdote. When Daniels took office in 1913 the commander of the Pacific Fleet was Rear Admiral William H. H. Southerland. When later in the year Southerland returned to Washington he confessed to Daniels that the first time he had received an order signed "Daniels" he turned to his aide and said: "Who is this Daniels giving me orders? I never heard of him." Not to be outdone Daniels replied: "On the day it was decided to dispatch the order to the Admiral of the Pacific fleet, I turned to the Aide for Operations and asked, 'By the way, who is in command of that fleet?' He gave me your name, and I said: 'Strange isn't it, but I never heard of him.'" Daniels, *Wilson Era: Years of Peace,* p. 246.

Jusserand [?] said that an eminent French surgeon who had been here to attend Surgical Convention said he was convinced that Prohibition was a good thing, even excluding light wines. It had to be complete, even if later light wine was permitted [7]

Saturday, May 8, 1920

Senator Harris phoned about Arlington Amphitheatre. I urged him to urge our people to take part and I would see Newton [8] when he came on Saturday. I had not attended the meeting when Com of College Presidents was appointed.

Bernard Baruch said: "The world must decide between the constructive radicalism of Woodrow Wilson or the destructive radicalism of Lenine.["]

Two years ago he had bet $1,000 that Hi Johnson would be nominated   He thinks Reps. are doing all they can to let the Dems. win.

Dr. C. Alphonso Smith here at dinner. What caused the defeat of the Spanish armada? That was the question asked of midshipmen at Annapolis. One boy —a genius—replied   They lost by the lack of three ships: Seaman-Ship—
Marksman-Ship
Leader-Ship

Finished my statement for the hearings at the Department.

Sunday, May 9, 1920

Went to hear Dr. Wood.

Telegram from Capt. [of the] Sacramento [9] at Tampico. Rebels in charge and hostile to Americans. Told Coontz to order Oklahoma & three more destroyers to Mexico. He came to see me. He was to call up Wilson & arrange for ships & get marines at Phila. ready for the Henderson to leave Phila Monday night.

Called at night. Rebels had taken Tuxpam.

McGowan gave the following to Mrs. Dewey.

In re Secretary Daniels:
"I would go down to the gates of hell[,"]
Said one "for a friend, through
thick and thin"

[7] This paragraph is written in the margin and may have been added later.

[8] Charles W. Newton, a member of the Arlington Memorial Amphitheatre Commission representing the United Spanish War Veterans.

[9] Commander Otto C. Dowling, commanding the gunboat U.S.S. *Sacramento* on Mexican patrol duty.

The other smiled as he
bit off a Concha's end
"I would go in."
                S McG

8 May 20 [*sic*]

Mrs. Dewey took me aside to tell me to go after them.

"Give them hell." That is the message George Dewey would give you if he were here.

"Post editorial [10] clear proof that in the classic language of ——— "their goat has been got."

"Go with staunchest friends with you"

Henry & his wife here

Monday, May 10, 1920

Went before Sub-Committee of Naval Affairs and began my reply to Admiral Sims' charges of naval conduct of the war. The newspaper boys & others seemed to think I scored and the afternoon papers had good accounts, the Star giving it three columns.

Ordered ships to Key West & tried to get news from Mexico City. Car[r]anza reported to have left but no news comes through.

Tuesday, May 11, 1920

Hearing before Senate Naval Affairs Committee. Read speech of President to the fleet in Aug. 1917. Also followed with barrage story. Papers gave good play to it.

Osborne here & will make recommendations for reforms in prison & on ships when guilty of offenses.

Cabinet meeting. President looked better than last Tuesday, but talks very slowly. Baker brought up bill of Merchant Marine to turn over all docks &c to Shipping Board, & President to let Army & Navy have them when needed and so long as needed. Baker objected vigorously. President had not heard of it. Payne said that Hoboken dock should belong to shipping board & certain other docks also. We are to see Benson

Burleson said "When this is over, you should jack up Sims."

Telegrams from KofC societies congratulating me on my testimony in re

[10] The feature editorial in the *Washington Post* on May 9, entitled "Condition of the Navy," reviewed the testimony given in the Sims investigation thus far with a strongly anti-Daniels bias. Since Daniels was scheduled to begin his reply to Sims on Monday, the purpose behind the editorial was transparent.

Sims The Irish are all with me. Operator of telephone said "We are with you. Keep your eyes on Weeks"

"I am heart and soul with you" said Bishop Bratton [11]

Wednesday, May 12, 1920

Benson, Baker & I had talk. Benson said for advancing the American merchant marine the Shipping Board should have control of docks & piers, & the Army should not continue its transport service. Baker dissented from the last. Navy or sea service should control everything afloat. Baker to write memo. to the President & submit to us.

At hearing today read the President's cable to Sims in 1917 & other replies to criticisms.

Conference with labor men who urge increase of wages in ship yards.

Rodman & Senator Stanley [12] came to talk about young officer guilty of crimes (sod[om]y.) in Norfolk. He was the vilest of the vile.

Taylor said Operations was going too far

Thursday, May 13, 1920

When I finished my hearings today Pittman asked me if I was writing a history of the Navy. I told him I was in part.

Took up Troop transportation, showed Sims placed emphasis on cargoes & things rather than soldiers.

Conference with Benson and Labor leaders & agreed each to name a man who should make careful study of conditions & then we would take up request for increase of wages.

Hale asked how long I would be & I told him I was like John Paul Jones: "I had just begun to fight"

Talked to Dr. Vann [13] & Livingston Johnson [14] who are attending the Baptist Convention

Friday, May 14, 1920

Herald said President would rebuke me for printing his speech to the fleet. Later the President gave out statement that he knew & approved making speech and letter to Sims public. Gave orders to print a large number of the speeches for distribution.

---

[11] Theodore D. Bratton, Protestant Episcopal bishop of Mississippi.

[12] Augustus O. Stanley, Democrat, former U.S. Representative, governor, and now U.S. Senator from Kentucky.

[13] Richard T. Vann, Baptist minister and retired president of the Baptist University for Women in Raleigh.

[14] Baptist minister and editor of the *Biblical Recorder*, published in Raleigh.

I wrote Baker that, while I believed the Navy ought to be only navigating department, but [*sic*] wished to make no request now.

Hearing from 10 am to 12 m *&* others again in the afternoon.

Found speech made by Penrose in Aug. 1918, in which he said my procrastination delayed 3 months *&* cost 15 billion dollars. Did he send mental telegram to Sims or Sims to Penrose?

Mexican situation more quiet

Blue wrote letter answering Adml McKean

Saturday, May 15, 1920

Hearing continued before Naval Affairs Committee

The Arlington Memorial Amphitheatre dedicated. Baker *&* I, among others spoke. Large crowd. All the diplomats and distinguished company. I had read so much at the hearings *&* had taken cold so that I could not be heard well. And of all the days I wished to have my voice!

Later I spoke at Baptist meeting in interest of great memorial Baptist church for this city. RI *&* NC refused to ratify the Constitution without freedom of religion. Due largely to Baptist belief

Capt Newton of Spanish War Veterans, member of Commission at home, to dinner. I hoped he would favor Lee's name *&* Jackson's being placed on Arlington Amphitheatre. He doubted the right.

Sunday, May 16, 1920

Slept until 12 o'clock.

Went to Navy Department and with Jenkins went over matter for my hearing.

Admiral Caperton [15] called. Senator Fall had sent for him to give testimony of Mexican conditions. Fullam had told Fall that Caperton said must [not?] do anything in Mexico because of elections. No such instructions had ever been given to any officer.

Monday, May 17, 1920

Hearing again. Prussianizing the Navy.

Went before House Naval Affairs Committee and urged bill to establish a Bureau for Aviation

Gen Mitchell [16] had secured the incorporation into the Army bill of a pro-

[15] Rear Admiral (Ret.) William B. Caperton, served at Veracruz and in charge of the pacification of Haiti and Santo Domingo in 1915–1916, commander-in-chief of the Pacific Fleet from July, 1916 to June, 1919.

[16] Brigadier General William Mitchell, the Army's leading exponent of air power.

vision putting all aviation shore stations under the Army. This would take 5 naval stations & transfer them to the Army. I went to see Senator Lodge who agreed it was a vicious principle. Will try to get it out

Went to hearing again & put in Benson's speech, the Wine Mess order &c &c

Dinner at Mrs. Bagley's—birthday. Addie left for New York. She hated to go now that she is ready & it is hard on all of us.

Tuesday, May 18, 1920

Gave testimony to Committee—gave Penrose's speech and Sims's charges and showed how alike they were. Also printed Sims's letter complaining that he was not permitted to accept position on British Admiralty.

Went before House Com. & favored Air Bureau

Cabinet discussed helping people in Europe. Burleson and I favored $100 million dollars. Houston opposed. President agreed with Houston who spoke of condition of the treasury & the need of revenues for regular appropriations. I brought up whether we should ask permission of Congress to sell ships to So Am countries. The President thought not, even though England was doing so. Directed Colby to ascertain—thought it a gross infringement on the Monroe doctrine

Left at 4 pm for New York. Worked all the way on my conclusion to Sims & Foote brought it back that night

Addie well & writing letters to her loved ones

Wednesday, May 19, 1920

Rose early and wrote my speech which I delivered at 2 pm in memorial meeting of honor of youths brought back from France. Their mothers and loved ones were there.

We left hotel shortly after eleven. Commander Parker [17] with us & went to the Royal George where Addie was received by Mrs. Catt and other woman suffragists on the way to Geneva.

Addie yearned so for her bairns but was brave & cheerful, & we had a short sweet time together before I had to leave to go to Memorial

Lunched with Mrs. Capt Bastedo who wished her Womans Corps made permanent. Did great service in war & should be continued.

Returned home, reaching here 10:30

All well

---

[17] Probably Commander Edward C. S. Parker, assigned to the Third Naval District at New York.

Thursday, May 20, 1920
Naval Affairs Committee, morning and afternoon.
Worked tonight at Department.

Friday, May 21, 1920
Naval Affairs Committee met and all day was taken up with cross-examination by Hale, most of it having to do with plans, seeking to show we entered the war without any plans. Quoted Pratt, Palmer and Lanning, & I confounded him with Pratt's statement about plans and with Badger's statement.
Talked with Niblack about the Newport case.
He is ambitious to be V.A. & comes next on the list.
Talked with Coontz and with Washington about next assignment for Sims. What?

Saturday, May 22, 1920
Colby said Porter [18] of Foreign Relations Committee wanted him to go before Com. Bill is pending to receive Minister from Irish Republic. Irish are pressing for action. Reps. are catering to Irish vote & trying to pass the buck by getting Colby to advise against passage of the bill. He declined to walk into their trap. They must act or expose pretense of being friendly to those Irish who wish Irish Republic recognized.
Appeared before Newport Board in connection with charge of ministers that Navy Department authorized enlisted men to be guilty of immoral acts in order to obtain testimony against Rev. Kent [19] Bishop Perry [20] demanded apology. Naval officers who have investigated case believe Kent guilty Court said he was innocent.
Attended meeting of Jacob Jones post of Yeoman (f) Camp, named the Jacob Jones & spoke & then went to their club house.

Sunday, May 23, 1920
Went to hear Mr. Chappell on "The Man Who Encouraged Himself"—David "who encouraged himself and trusted in the Lord"—in substance the words.
Took dinner at Mrs. Bagleys.

[18] Stephen G. Porter, chairman of the House Foreign Affairs Committee.
[19] The Navy had charged that Rev. Samuel N. Kent, head of a Newport sailors' welfare organization, had engaged in homosexual activities. Kent had been acquitted by a local court, however, and his superior, Bishop Perry, had in turn accused the Navy of using immoral methods to obtain evidence.
[20] James De Wolf Perry, Jr., Protestant Episcopal bishop of Rhode Island.

Went to hear Bishop [blank] preach baccalaureate sermon at Cathedral with Mrs B & the girls. Frank's school.

All religions come from the East because they ask Why?

All inventions come from Western civilization because they ask How.

The lad had the loaves & fishes & men who use what they have somewhere find it is multiplied

Foote brought me the plans & the introduction I had dictated

Jenkins came up to-night with important data on destroyers across & on this side

Monday, May 24, 1920

Before committee all day. "Answer yes or no" said Hale. I told him I would make my own answers. "Have you stopped whipping your wife.["]

Morning devoted to plans. Afternoon to use of destroyers in the war.

Spoke at Christian Endeavor tonight & dined there. Calvary Baptist church.

Tuesday, May 25, 1920

Hearing continued. Took up Fiske & Knight's letters. I had forgotten Knights. The 1914 action in the light of 1917 seems very small & my position is not so strong [21]

Cabinet discussed at great length the resolution declaring peace. Would we still be at war with Germany? &c

Hearing again at 3 30

Wednesday, May 26, 1920

Hearing all day ended.

Capt Hutchison [22] had sent up figures that gave Hale a false idea & he said certain ships were not ready to fight which needed only a few repairs or a few men

Very tired & went to bed at 9

Thursday, May 27, 1920

Sims on stand today—took out certain extracts from testimony of officers which seemed to bolster up his case. Nothing new. The burden of his statement was that the Navy Department was slow & lacked initiative until the President's speech and the Presidents letter.

Went to tea at lovely home given by Gen. Pershing. Saw Thomas Nelson

[21] See Senate Subcommittee on Naval Affairs, *Naval Investigation*, pp. 3025–3046.

[22] Captain Benjamin F. Hutchison, assistant to the chief of Naval Operations.

Page. Also Mrs Hugh Scott who said Hugh could settle the Mexican trouble —he could fix both Obregon and Villa.

Conference with Taylor and others about Sims testimony. Decided to do nothing about it & let things take their course.

Friday, May 28, 1920

Went before House Committee to advocate turning the Coast Guard over to the Navy. Also all other government ships.

Sims finished and Fiske and Fullam had additional statements. All advocated naval organization on Prussian lines.

Meredith said Payne had given settlers forests wh. ought to be reserved for national forests.

Saturday, May 29, 1920

Took Mrs. Dewey & Mrs. Bagley, McGowan and Dr Rowe to Annapolis to the game between Annapolis and West Point. The Navy won 11 to 1. But the Army is still ahead in the series. Lunched with Scales. Perfect day. Hale, Ball and Keyes [23] & other Senators telegraphed they wished to come down and I had to give them seats in my box. Wasn't that heaping coals of fire on their heads, but Hale hasn't anything inside his skull that isn't poured in by somebody else.

At night went to French Ambassador's to dinner to meet British Ambassador and wife, Aukland Geddes.[24] Quite a company. Promised to take Geddes & wife down some day to Annapolis. Talked to him. He says British are not increasing their Navy. J—— talked of French help in Am. Independence, not anti British but pro-Independence. Geddes said British people were fighting parliamentary battles for their liberty against tyranical [sic] King.

Talked to Porter about his controversy with Colby about passing the buck. Very sore with Colby.

Mrs Baker told of book written saying Newton is not named Baker but Becker & is a Jew & she is a Jew, & that Newton favors Bolsheviks She is hot all over. The female of the species

Sunday, May 30, 1920

Worked on my Annapolis speech. Saw a Mrs. Ring who is greatly interested in two lads who are a fraction short in examination & she is deeply interested. Talked to Coontz & Washington. They had written letters to Hale & will

[23] Henry W. Keyes, Republican, U.S. Senator from New Hampshire. Hale, Ball, and Keyes were the Republican members of the subcommittee investigating the Navy.
[24] Sir Auckland Campbell Geddes, the new British Ambassador.

furnish them. I tried my hand on two or three & talked to C & W about what to do with S—— Is it waiting orders or is it Honolulu or what?

Cablegram from Addie that party arrived safe and well. Very happy

Jusserand & Geddes agreed that majorities never rule—that minorities know what they want, are compact, well organized, have the experience and can compel acceptance of what they want against desire of majorities & they said it was so everywhere. Are they right? Is it always to be so? What is the remedy? They thought there was none

Jusserand fears Germany will fight again & France is the frontier. Geddes says they will not fight in this generation, though Junkers have not changed a whit

Monday, May 31, 1920

Worked on my Annapolis speech.

Had call from Mr. Henry, editor Jackson (Miss) Clarion-Ledger, who wished a new census taken of Jackson as they had proof of mistakes. Will see Rogers.[25]

Went to ball game between Army and Marines.

Talked to Washington about his letter to Naval Sub-Committee. We had enough men to man all fighting ships.

Tuesday, June 1, 1920

Civil Service Commission called. They had opposed my order that no aliens be employed in Navy Yards if citizens wished place. The President wrote them that he approved my position & they came over to discuss a rule to carry out my idea. It was the first official call Mrs Helen Gardner had made.

Cabinet. Houston & Burleson opposed certain provisions in the Shipping bill. Alexander and I favored larger [?] merchant marine. President said he favored freedom of the seas but wished the American flag to float there & was strong for merchant shipping

["]To-day is the day for killing the Armenian mandate" said one cabinet officer. "I did not know what particular day had been selected for the assassination.["]

Speaking of British shipping & oil the President said "Daniels and I know the feeling of the British & their selfishness. We were up against that in Paris.["]

[25] Samuel L. Rogers, director of the Bureau of the Census.

Dined at Bainbridge Colby's & then went to the Department & finished last letter to Hale

Wednesday, June 2, 1920

Went to meeting of trustees of American University Proposition to join forces with the George Washington University presented & com. headed by Bishop McDowell appointed to confer. Bryan present He had an idea that we should offer to surrender bonds held for money loaned abroad to help the world & stop armament. I tried to dissuade him. Our people will compel payment for Britain is using money to buy oil lands when we are having trouble to get oil Some oil men say they are using the money we loaned her to get oil reserves for later period & buy oil from America for present needs

Went to Annapolis after finishing letter to Hale & my Annapolis speech. Garden party—lante[r]ns &c for graduates & their fathers & mothers Capt Blake [1] of British Navy present at dinner.

Ambassador Geddes & wife said they would accept my invitation to go to Annapolis some time on Thursday. Could not arrange it.

Thursday, June 3, 1920

Spoke to the graduating class on Tradition & Loyalty & gave some facts about naval participation in the war

Scales spoke & presented diplomas. Lunch Went to see Farragut window unveiled

Busby & his boy—failed in 2 studies.

Dined at British Ambassador's on Birthday of the King.

Friday, June 4, 1920

President sent over naval passed [bill] that passed Congress & I recommended that he sign it. He did so

Heard Admiral Winterhalter was ill & went to the hospital & saw his wife who felt that his death was a question of but a few hours

Worked late correcting my cross examination before Senate Committee

Saturday, June 5, 1920

Admiral Winterhalter died at 5 am. An able, loyal and true man. We had worked together with loyal friendship.

Roosevelt wrote letter to Hale opposing military organization.

Left at 9 pm for Goldsboro

[1] Captain Geoffrey Blake, British naval attaché.

Sunday, June 6, 1920

Found mother looking well but feeble & with her old kidney trouble. She is rarely free from pain, but is so cheerful, brave, & a blessing to all about her. Brother Frank is uneasy about her.

Josephus came down to Goldsboro & we returned to Raleigh & had a pleasant evening together.

Primary for Governor was very close between Morrison & Gardner   neck & neck. It looks like M—— in the second primary, for labor is against Gardner & most of Page's vote will go to M——

Monday, June 7, 1920

Reached office at 11 am

Swanson said on the whole he would not advise me to go to S.F. Sure to be a dif. between W & B and as I was not a delegate I had no compelling reason & need not go.   might be embar[r]assing

Went to Admiral Winterhalter's funeral at Arlington.

20 grad. class of Methodist Orphanage here & I took them to see the Mayflower & invited them to dinner   It was the best of parties

Tuesday, June 8, 1920

Conference on oil—to exchange certain land in California owned by Navy, in litigation, for others so as to have a solid reserve.

F D R urged me to go to Convention—said I might be of great service in helping along with harmony. Tammany sullen but friendly to me as was also Bryan.

Cabinet. W W full of anecdote. Discussed sending ships to Armenia. Urged by Colby. I said we could not land unless we had real force behind us. Am to prepare statement for W W.

Colby said Geddes had called & was very anxious about conditions abroad. England regarded Germany as a bankrupt; France as a conquered province. Believed America & England had the right view & could work together. Wished us to have representation at Spa & confer on finance. Houston doubted England's good faith seeing it had broken off conversation about paying its debt.

Colby proposed that 2 members Tariff Commission go abroad to study oil situation. Payne said we already knew much & Van Manning was going abroad for Oil Industry.

Talked to Grayson ab[out] Sims

What is Congress? A person from Congo

Wednesday, June 9, 1920

Lunched with George Creel. He said the Com. on Pub. Inf cost us $3,900,000 whereas England spent 5 mil. a year alone in tolls. Wishes all papers sent to the President who will make a statement wh. Creel deserves in view of unjust criticism.

Civil Service Commission came over & complained that Naval Constructor Gleason[2] employed mechanics on clerical work to the cost of the government & would not cooperate with Civil Service Commission to stop it. Wanted him removed. Nix.

Talked to Jameison:[3] Most people who come to headquarters favor McAdoo though organization men do not generally wish him named. He wanted dry plank.

Thursday, June 10, 1920

Long talk with Pittman. He thinks Sims should be sent to Hawaii at once. Wishes us to prepare full brief, quoting exactly what witnesses said so he and Trammell may each have copies so they can prepare their reports to be given simultaneously with Hale's to the public. He thinks it looks like Sproul[4] at Chicago

Council discussed exercise and the kind that officers should take. The F. D. R. plan of ½ a day each month in work-hours was not approved by any. Decided on plan of at least ½ hour each day & physical examination.

To go to SF or not to go—that is the question!

W W said he would see me Saturday morning. I am to be in Jersey City. He said not to break the engagement & he would see me next week about Sims &c

Barnett returned from the Pacific. It is a rather troublesome problem on my hands[5]

[2] Captain Henry M. Gleason, naval constructor at the Mare Island Navy Yard.

[3] William D. Jamieson, editor and former U.S. Representative from Iowa, director of finance of the Democratic National Committee since 1919.

[4] William C. Sproul, Republican, governor of Pennsylvania, a dark horse for the Republican presidential nomination.

[5] Daniels had decided to replace General Barnett, who had been Major General Commandant of the Marine Corps since 1914, with General Lejeune. Daniels believed that Barnett had held the post long enough, and that Lejeune's distinguished war service in France merited the reward of the Corps' highest honor. The problem was that Barnett refused to resign, contending that his appointment was for a second four-year term. Daniels was consequently obliged to remove him from office, after which Barnett's Republican friends in the Senate delayed confirmation of Lejeune's appointment. Thanks to the intervention of Representative Butler and the House Naval Affairs Committee, however, Lejeune was reappointed and confirmed under the Harding administration. Daniels, *Wilson Era: Years of War and After*, pp. 155–156.

Friday, June 11, 1920

Wrote some extracts for Flag Day speech at Jersey City.

Left at night with Frank for Jersey City

Very hot—too hot to sleep well on the Pullman

Saturday, June 12, 1920

Reached NY. Frank was my aide & we went to Hotel Penna & after bath & breakfast Dr. Pollock and Mr. McKee, of Jersey City Elks, with escort of policemen came over to take me to Jersey City. Frank elected to stay in New York and take Evelyn to the theatre.

Elks gave cordial reception & dinner. 5,000 children in red, white & blue on hill side made an American flag. Beautiful I spoke on duty to the men who died under the flag to see to it that this was a War against War.

Dined with George Creel & saw Blanche Bates in "The Notorious Mrs Fair"

Returned on midnight.

News of Harding's [6] nomination. Is he weak or strong? Not big, reactionary & Penrose choice

Sunday, June 13, 1920

John Jenkins came up and I went over with him summary of the hearings on Sims charges. We decided to make them rather full with the material evidence condensed. McIntyre came up & we went over Navy chapter for Text Book. Penrose & Sims—partners in partisan charges.

The Smalls here to dinner. He was defeated in primary for Congress to the surprise of everybody including his opponent. Takes it philosophically. I think his wife not so much so but we did not talk about it but about national politics.

Letter from Addie

Monday, June 14, 1920

Spoke at el[l]ipse as 150 soldiers left with autos on Bankhead highway for Los Angeles, California. Baker & Alexander & others spoke.

Spoke at night at East Front of Capital at beautiful Flag Day celebration.

Tuesday, June 15, 1920

After cabinet talked to Presidt about Sims. He has ruined himself. Why not let him stay in the hole he has dug for himself?

[6] Senator Warren G. Harding, dark-horse Republican nominee for President.

Barnett—approved naming Lejeune
Also MacVea.[7]
Colby couldn't go to CH [8] because he must write a speech for SF Convention
Roland Morris went down with me.

Wednesday, June 16, 1920

Arrived at the Governors 4:30 in Raleigh   Went to sleep.
Left at 9 am for Chapel Hill
Morris made an excellent speech.
Dined with Gov. Bickett. In answer to questions, Ambassador Morris discussed in most illuminating way the Russian & Japanese situations

Thursday, June 17, 1920

Reached here at 1 pm. Sat up in station in Raleigh fr[om] 12:30 this morning until 4:15
Lejeune relieved my mind. Maj. Gen. Com Marine Corps "four years or until relieved.["]
McLean spent the evening talking politics
Apprehensive of course anti-Wilson men & wet men will take at SF

Friday, June 18, 1920

Lejeune. Letter to Barnett. Wanted to see President.
McAdoo would not accept.
Bryan for Prohibition; Wilson still wants his fourteen points

Saturday, June 19, 1920

Reached Gettysburg just before night with [blank] [9]

Tuesday, August 3, 1920

Cabinet. Payne & I told of our trip to Alaska.[1]

[7] Captain Charles B. McVay, Jr., whom Daniels wished to appoint chief of the Bureau of Ordnance.

[8] Colby had earlier promised Daniels to go to Chapel Hill to make a commencement address at the University of North Carolina. See entry of March 24, 1920.

[9] Daniels was en route to the Democratic National Convention at San Francisco, but unfortunately seems to have been too busy to continue his diary for the next month-and-a-half.

---

[1] After attending the Democratic National Convention in San Francisco in early July, Daniels had inspected Navy coal lands in Alaska with Secretary Payne. Daniels evidently kept no diary record during this period.

Palmer wanted his Fair Price Com. to fix a price for coal and prosecute all who charged more. They were all int.[erested?] as buyers or producers. W. W. told Palmer that the Fed. Trade Com. was authorized to investigate & he would be wise to get that Board to make report instead of depending on voluntary & interests [?] committees.

Palmer spoke of the growth of the Communist & Bolshevik sentiment & wanted to take action against it.

Colby brought up the suggestion that the President or Dept of State make known the dangers of Bolshevist propaganda from Russia as obtained by State Dept. Suggested that John Spargo,[2] who had written on autocratic bolshevism, get out the facts. The President thought Duncan [3] (Labor Delegate to Russia) might be able to reach many. Colby to see Wilson.

After cabinet I talked of F D R's resignation [4] & asked if President had any man in view for vacancy. No.

"I resent & deeply resent["] &c he said.[5]

Senator King,[6] who is going to Newport on Com of Newport affair, & F. D. R. at home to talk about conditions at Newport. A political investigation

Brew from berries in Alaska said Payne

Did Daniels drink it

"Then there was no kick in it"

Wednesday, August 4, 1920

Mrs. Mark St. Clair Ellis,[7] who had married him for 3rd husband, called to see about his retirement. Another woman claimed he had been her husband & sued for bills.

Brave little widow from Dayton, Ohio, whose boy had passed examination at Annapolis, was almost heart-broken because he had been rejected on account of eyes. Braisted told her that if he started with weak eyes, it would be progressive.

Woman from La. with home in N.C. was willing to give $50,000 to help woman suffrage in N.C.

F D R & wife here to dinner. They leave for Columbus and then to Hyde

---

[2] Prominent Socialist writer and anti-Bolshevist.

[3] James Duncan, president of the Granite Cutters' International Association and A.F.L. leader, a member of the Root mission to Russia in 1917.

[4] Roosevelt was resigning from the Navy Department to accept the Democratic vice-presidential nomination.

[5] This cryptic comment suggests that Roosevelt was still *persona non grata* with Wilson. See entry of February 21, 1920.

[6] William H. King, Democrat, U.S. Senator from Utah and a member of the Senate Naval Affairs Committee.

[7] Commander Ellis was due to retire in two days.

Park, & he resigns on Monday. He is full of campaign & goes West at once. McGowan here & told of Barnetts complaint that bureau chiefs had been tipped not to come to his party.

Western Union had sent ship from Hampton Roads to lay cable off Miami. The President had refused license & I had sent destroyers by force if necessary to prevent laying of cable. Decker [8] wired that he had conferred with W.U. people. I wired him to carry out his orders and have no conferences. Admiral Anderson [9] was sent to take charge & carry out orders.

Worth went to Balto & got room for time he enters Med College

Thursday, August 5, 1920

Council met & had picture taken—the last one that F D R will attend.

Powell and Ferguson talked about the inquiry of the special board studying the wage question & said any increase in wages would increase the costs of building ships, & that we could not compete with England. Moreover our naval scale is already higher than the rate recently given to the rail-road men.

Powell said he could not get the plates for the Mars & had urged expedition. I wrote Grace that Powell was delayed & told him he must get busy. We placed Navy Order with Bethlehem & Powell & Grace are both Bethlehem. They wish to make us to compel Carnegie to furnish steel for Beth ships & that is the rub.

Anderson arrived at Miami & took charge. Telegraph him not to let cable be laid at Key West as we learned British Co. hoped to do.

Badger said Regulations were being drawn to put General Board under Operations and he had written his views in a memo. to Coontz stating his opposition. He would like to stay on General Board until March & I hoped he would.

Friday, August 6, 1920

A Loving Cup presented to F. D. R. upon his departure previous to his retirement as Asst. Scy on Monday when he accepts the [vice] presidential nomination. I was requested by Mr. Morning Star, Chief Electrician of the Washington Navy Yard, to make the presentation for the men in the service & spoke of only two compensations for men in public office—consciousness of giving ones best to the public weal & appreciation & friendship of co-workers. F D R had both. He left in afternoon, but before leaving wrote me a letter

[8] Rear Admiral Benton C. Decker, commandant of the Seventh Naval District at Key West.

[9] Rear Admiral Edwin A. Anderson, commandant of the Charleston Navy Yard.

most friendly & almost loving wh. made me glad I had never acted upon my impulse when he seemed to take sides with my critics.

Sam McGowan wants to retire in December. F D R suggested no Asst. Secy be appointed now. He would like Howe for a short time & said Howe had bona offer of $20,000. He believes it but I have a great big swallow but cannot swallow that

Wrote to the ship-builders that they must make more progress on Dreadnaughts they are building.

George Creel here & he hopes to get Pres W to write and let him publish & sell to all countries. He said he could make Wilson a rich man.

Saturday, August 7, 1920

Left Wash. at 1:30 in auto with Addie and Frank for Gettysbg—a perfect day through beautiful hills & valleys & mountains.

Dr. Dennis new anti- [?] disease

Wrote Ethel & sent copy of my letter to F D R & my speech.

Reached Gettysburg just before night—went to Eagle Hotel. Met by Martin F. Olsen C.B.M. & J. W Cranston, Chf Storekeeper

The CBM had written to John Shaybaugh [?], a guide engaged "You are not to approach the Secretary or any of his party until ordered to do so by the Chief Petty Officer." There's naval directness for you.

After dinner went over the first day's fight where the Confederates had the best of the fighting

Sunday, August 8, 1920

Started out early to see the battle field with petty officers & guide. Drove over the 2nd & 3rd days fight. Guide said [illegible name] company lost more men than any other. I had always supposed Pettigrew.[10] Must be enquired into.

It was depressing to see how Confederates were ordered across open space to Little Round Top where death was certain. The Federals had the ridge & must have won under the conditions.

Went to Antietam. Saw place where L O'B. Branch [11] was killed. Near by, where Federal officers were killed, there stands a statue. We ought to have a statue of Branch on the spot where he was killed. There is a Branch avenue and the guide said before the fighting Branch notified the people of Sharpsburg that the fight was to take place and his name is still remembered pleasantly.

[10] James Johnston Pettigrew, Confederate general and North Carolina brigade commander, killed at the Battle of Gettysburg in 1863.

[11] Lawrence O'Bryan Branch, U.S. Representative from North Carolina, 1855–1861, subsequently a major general, C.S.A., killed at the Battle of Antietam, September 17, 1862.

Sent telegrams & wrote letter to Cox.[12] Left for Hyde Park to R's notification

Monday, August 9, 1920

Reached N.Y. early & left on 8:45 for Poughkeepsie. Went up with lady Democrats on train. Mrs F D R met me at Depot & we drove to Hyde Park. Met most of Com. on Notification. Both Mrs. R's spoke of my letter to Franklin & were pleased by it. Cummings took me off and said the President was considering him for cabinet portfolio & no Conn. man should be named for other place—reference to Crosby.[13]

I was with Mrs. James Roosevelt [14] at exercises. Cummings & F D R both made good speeches. Geo White [15] said "It is the business of the Chairman to work, not to talk." He was disconcerted when some one cried out "Right you are," & it had reference to Whites saying folks in Ohio did not take much interest in the League.

Came back with McAdoo's & we had jolly time. McAdoo was disappointed that F. D. R made no reference to W. W. They had kept tab on all states & delegates at S.F. & while happy to be out of politics they remembered those who had not been for Mc. He thinks danger is that national ticket will be sacrificed for State ticket. Wilson got the largest up-State vote any Dem. had ever received & T had not supported him in New York.

Mother came home with me

Tuesday, August 10, 1920

Cabinet. I brought up Haiti & San Domingo & the propaganda to try to make people believe conditions were bad & the government was killing people & having a despotic government. Colby said the Uruguay minister had called to see him about it. Baker said the governor of Porto Rico had wanted to send surplus population to Santo Domingo. I suggested as answer to the criticisms that we ask Cong. Com on Insular Affairs to continue the study.[16]

Shall Debs & the others who have served 15 months sentence be pardoned. Palmer, Payne & I advocated it & Baker also. Burleson opposed & Colby

[12] James M. Cox, governor of Ohio and the Democratic nominee for president.
[13] Probably John F. Crosby, Connecticut Democratic leader, who may have desired to succeed Roosevelt as Assistant Navy Secretary.
[14] Roosevelt's mother, Sara Delano Roosevelt.
[15] U.S. Representative from Ohio who had succeeded Cummings as chairman of the Democratic National Committee.
[16] There had been reports, at least partly substantiated, of brutality by U.S. Marines stationed in Haiti. As Daniels seems to have feared, Senator Harding and the Republicans later used the issue in an effort to discredit the Wilson administration and win Negro votes. To undercut the criticism Daniels launched several official investigations of the situation in Haiti which played down the discreditable side of the Marine occupation since 1915.

doubted. "In N.J.,["] said the Presidt ["]the Governor is a member of the Board of Pardons. He cannot pardon by himself, but his vote is necessary to secure pardon.["] He said that with finality & that ended hope for Debs and the others

Burleson says Cox is sure to win.

Houston said GB had broken off negotiations with Treas officials about 5 mil pounds Engl owes us in open debt [?] & said Lloyd George would take it up with Wilson. "I have had no com.[munication] with the [sic] Lloyd George on any subject" W W.

Addie went to Annapolis & spoke to all enlisted men who had passed exam & could not get in.

Wednesday, August 11, 1920

Talked to Baker about George Creel and the report of the com. to examine into his report. George thought report should say that Congress put the Com. out of business and that he & others had served without pay, and that there was no suggestion that anything was lacking in honesty &c I agreed & Baker will see Director Shenton.[17]

"I've no interest in Debs" said Baker. "He made all the trouble he could. What do you think the President meant yesterday?["] he asked. "He meant" I said that Debs had no chance to obtain liberty.

Story that a Cuban came to Wash & visited British Embassy in great dudgeon. He had heard that Margaret Wilson was to marry the Prince of Wales & W. W had promised to give Cuba as a dowry. He said Cuba would not stand for it & he had come to Washington to say that to the British Government.

Coontz & Foote at home and we went over the revised list of medal awards. What a task & how hopeless to differentiate.

Simmons will give out interview tomorrow for suffrage. He believes women will vote before he runs again. His position may save the day, though he comes very late

Thursday, August 12, 1920

Italian naval attache [18] called to request us to furnish crew and deliver the Austrian ships in an Italian port for fear if Italians went into Spalato there would be trouble. I am to see Colby tomorrow.

J D Jr came here—very much in the dumps. We must borrow $20,000.

---

[17] Herbert N. Shenton, director of the Council of National Defense and its Advisory Commission.
[18] Captain Pietro Civalleri.

Friday, August 13, 1920

Long talk with Wilton McLean about NC and suffrage. He had given up hope, said he had done all he could, and said he could not go to North Carolina.

Left at 8 p.m. with Josephus for Raleigh. He came up to talk about business conditions. We are paying 13c for most of our paper and it has stuck [?] us so hard we have to borrow $20,000. He was depressed but I cheered him up.

Saturday, August 14, 1920

Reached Raleigh 7:30.

Talked to Governor and legislators. The Round Robin signed by members of the House (a majority) was regarded as settling adversely the question in the General Assembly.[19] Lt. Gov. Gardner thinks it will pass the Senate but the vote is close and I tried to talk to some Senators but those anti just say their people are against it and they must represent their people.

The Governor's speech on previous day had not helped. It came too late, and besides he spoke against it the first ten minutes and then for it on grounds of expediency the last ten minutes. "It is the longest straddle for a short-legged man I ever saw" said a lady who heard it. He is chiefly interested in taxing question. I talked with Bailey who says it discriminates against landowners in favor of railroads & corporations & to Maxwell[20] who has worked very hard on it. He is trying to work out a better plan. It looks like they can raise revenue from other sources and exempt all land from taxation

Sunday, August 15, 1920

Had talk with Judge Clark. He says Bickett is going to Winston when his term expires at $25,000 a year and he has helped Reynolds[21] to escape tax. Bailey said same thing last night. He says Reynolds & like interests control North Carolina & I should hurry back.

Went to church. Rev Peele read list of all of our church who served in the war to be placed on bronze tablet in the church. Josephus & Worth among others. To be unveiled in November. I will make address.

Conference with Mrs. Jerman[22] & Com. of 5 on Suffrage on plans of reaching members. The opposition has much better organization. Many members afraid people at home will repudiate. Deep seated hostility to permitting any woman to vote.

[19] Ratification of the woman suffrage amendment.
[20] A. J. Maxwell, North Carolina Commissioner of Corporations.
[21] The R. J. Reynolds Tobacco Company of Winston-Salem.
[22] Cornelia Petty Jerman (Mrs. Thomas P.), Raleigh woman suffrage leader.

Long talk with Doughton [23] & Frank Ray.[24] Hopeless on suffrage

My interview reply, to Will Williamson [25] who said Wilson, Cox & I had sought to perpetrat[e] a crime created much interest & talk.

Monday, August 16, 1920

Returned home.

Funeral of General Gorgas. Great tribute to great & good man.

Baker, Meredith & I went to Arlington. Baker said no newspaper went to his house—he read NY Times and told his people at dinner if there was anything in it worthwhile & said papers ought to be required to pay letter postage on all advertisements

Went to see Judge Payne about offer of Standard Oil Co. to exchange lands in the Naval Reserve for their worth [?] I have a hunch it will be not wise for Dept. but am to see Payne tomorrow.

Our Atty, Mr. May seemed to favor

Tuesday, August 17, 1920

Cabinet. Colby stated that the French Charge d'Affairs [26] had sent to his gov. as its official position a story in the Wash. Post by that "skunk Fox" (as W W called him) and the French foreign office had given it out as America's action. W W told Colby to let the French gov. know that the French chg de Affairs was persona non grata & should be sent home.

Colby had intercepted telgm that England was in sympathy with Japan's position. It had been talking otherwise. W W said "Take it up & let us know if such hypocrisy is going on." England sympathizes with any nation that follows its example—grabs everything it can. It hated Germany because that nation got into the grab game but got in too late.

Poland minister [27] had been told he must not make appeal to the people here & start propaganda. An Ambassador was sent home for doing so, though we had sympathy for Poland and its plight.

W W read Oliver Herford's [28] poem on "The Marionette" in N.Y. World of the 16th. with zest & appreciation

[23] Robert L. Doughton, Democrat, U.S. Representative from North Carolina since 1911.
[24] J. Frank Ray, veteran Macon County legislator.
[25] William H. Williamson, Raleigh cotton manufacturer, in a public telegram to Tennessee legislative leaders, had accused Daniels and others of attempting to perpetrate a crime by pushing through woman suffrage. The incident gave Daniels a chance to restate his support of the Nineteenth Amendment.
[26] Prince de Béarn et de Chalais, counselor of the French Embassy and chargé d'affaires in the absence of Ambassador Jusserand.
[27] Prince Casimir Lubomirski.
[28] Author of light prose and verse.

Senator Dahl,[29] of SC said money was so scarce farmers could not get money & Houston ought to restore Finance Board

Meredith agreed.

Wednesday, August 18, 1920

Went with Meredith [30] to see Federal Trade Commission. Colvin? [31] [*sic*] pointed out that Gregory, when he had paper magnates at his mercy, consented to a consent decree that permitted publishers to waive their rights under decree and make contracts. Under that by duress all big publishers waived & got paper at contract rates while other pubs. have to go into open market and pay two or three prices for $\frac{1}{3}$ of their paper. That was a joker. All concerns have moved to Toronto & are now out of jurisdiction of the court. Cannot begin a new suit. We are to see Palmer, but Gregory by not seeing the joker enabled Canada & print papers to practise extortion & favoritism

New England Company wishes to make exchange in certain oil lands in reserve for oil lands outside reserve. Am to see Judge Payne.

Three Master Mechanics from Norfolk yard, 67 & 68 years old, wish to be retained. Swanson with them. I agreed. All wanted retirement pay. None want to be retired.

Tennessee ratified woman suffrage. NC postponed. Addie telegraph that as good news came from Tenn the prospects improved for North Carolina

Thursday, August 19, 1920

Council talked about Regulations. O——[perations] is thinking of more power. Vetoed.

Eugene Reed came here with Gordon Woodbury,[32] of NH, who wishes to be Asst. Secy. Grandfather was Secretary. Impressed me favorably.

Talked with State Department about situation in Haitii. [*sic*] City Nat. Bk.[33] has purchased old French Bank which has the sole right to issue money. Canadians tried to buy it. Report is that Canadians have stirred up trouble. State Department has authorized Americans in Haiti to pay no salary to President [34] or Cabinet unless they stand by bank regulations as approved by State Dept. I protested that we should withdraw that directive which

[29] Nathaniel B. Dial, Democrat, U.S. Senator from South Carolina.

[30] Like Daniels, Secretary Meredith, a magazine publisher in private life, was concerned about the high price of paper.

[31] William B. Colver, former journalist, member of the Federal Trade Commission.

[32] Former editor of the *Manchester* (N.H.) *Union,* who replaced Roosevelt as Assistant Secretary for the remainder of the Wilson administration.

[33] The National City Bank of New York.

[34] Sudre Dartiguenave, president of Haiti since 1915 through the support of the U.S. occupation authorities.

has been extended 30 days & assume the issue of money by Gov. & not permit it by City National Bank

P. M. Wilson & family here to dinner

Capt. Helweg,[35] who brought over German ships, told of their sabotage & stealing & how they almost made it impossible to bring them over. The sailors stole the electric bulbs &c

Friday, August 20, 1920

Baker & I conferred on aviation co-operation & use of North Island for great naval hangar. Army officers denied permission.

Capt. [blank],[36] long naval attache at Rio here. He had outwitted British & secured for us job to repair two of Brazil's greatest ships in our Navy Yards.

Relatives of Admiral Harris [37] protested that we gave too much honor to Gorgas & not enough to Harris. I told McGowan to investigate & he reported: "The deceased Paymaster General got all that was coming to him, I assure you."

Decided to install new fire control in Maryland & Colorado.

Broth[er] Frank at home. Woman suffrage

Saturday, August 21, 1920

Long talk with Norman Davis about Haitii. The Minister [38] & Financial Adviser [39] told President and Cabinet their salaries would not be paid unless they agreed to changes in concessions to National City Bank which purchased French bank with large concessions. The changes are favorable to Haitians, but they oppose. State Dept. directed minister not to deny salaries & give 30 days to Pres. to carry out provisions of treaty

Davis told of interview with Geddes who said letter of Earl Gray [40] was worse than stupid; that Lloyd George was hampered by imperialistic cabinet; & that Wilson was a greater man to-day than ever & would grow in history

Telegraphed Evans [41] to see Boucher.[42] I think we have done injustice to

[35] Captain Julius F. Hellweg.

[36] Captain Frank K. Hill.

[37] Rear Admiral Henry T. B. Harris, Paymaster General of the Navy, 1903–1905, had died on July 12, 1920.

[38] Arthur Bailly-Blanchard, U.S. Minister to Haiti since 1914.

[39] John A. McIlhenny. Under terms of a 1915 treaty, Haiti agreed to accept a U.S.-designated financial adviser in the Haitian Ministry of Finance.

[40] After his return to England from his unsuccessful mission to the United States, Lord Grey had written a letter to the London *Times* suggesting that the Lodge reservations to the Peace Treaty would probably prove harmless in practice and ought not to stand in the way of American ratification. The letter was given wide publicity and antagonized the Wilsons.

[41] Captain Waldo Evans, heading a Navy court of inquiry at Samoa; subsequently commandant of the naval station at Tutuila, Samoa, and governor of American Samoa.

[42] Lieutenant Commander Creed H. Boucher, who had preferred charges against Commander Terhune.

Terhune [43] & should not have removed him as Govnr of Guam [Samoa]. May order him to remain

Dinner at Army and Navy Club. Gen. Crowder talked of Selective Draft. W W called on Secy. Baker & said he wished an act drawn by 10 next day to call every young man into military service. The War College had worked out a plan for Registration by P.O. Dept. mail carriers. In Civil War there had been a system which required months to [44]

Sunday, August 22, 1920

get into action. Crowder said he did not think either would serve the purpose and was trying to devise a plan when a member of Congress called. He told him at some length of the problem, and as the Congressman was leaving he said to Gen C "If we can arrange for every man to vote on one day why can't it be managed for every man to register in one day" Having said this in passing, without thinking he had contributed to what later developed in the act, the Congressman went out. With that as the germ Gen C——— says he presented the draft of the act to Baker next morning, it was approved & passed with little change, & Baker assigned him to carry it out. Gen C——— is now engaged in a plan for like draft in war for men to register for all kinds of labor. Thinks it should include all men and women under 65

Spent day reading Cox & newspapers, trying to get in campaign spirit, ready when the call comes to make campaign speech. I feel like the man from Maine who said "I am going down to Boston to get drunk and, O Lord, how I hate it.["]

Monday, August 23, 1920

Craven, Pye [45] & Aviation officer went to conference with Baker & Menoher [46] & aviation Army officers over North Island San Diego.[47] The Joint Aer[o]nautic Board had agreed we should build large hangar 1000 feet long for dirigible, Menoher agreeing. Later he opposed in letter to Secy of War. As member of Board, I favored; as Army officer I opposed. We referred question back to Aer[o]nautic Board. Hard for Army and Navy to agree

Delegation from Wilmington wanted Shipping Board to agree that 2 ships (tankers), $\frac{1}{10}$ completed, might be sold to Great Britain. Benson had declined. We went to see him. In view of fact that material &c had been purchased

---

[43] Commander Warren J. Terhune, former commandant and governor of Samoa, who committed suicide on November 3 shortly before his exoneration by the court of inquiry.

[44] At this point the entry is continued onto the following page.

[45] Commander William S. Pye, serving in Naval Operations, and a member of the Joint Army and Navy Planning Committee.

[46] Major General Charles T. Menoher, director of the Army's Air Service.

[47] The words "San Diego" are enclosed in a box.

from shipping board & so little done, Benson was willing to make exception. Law permits no ships to be sold to foreign country ex. by permission of Shipping Board.

Gov. West said Portland was up in arms because put in Seattle District. Wanted change or a Portland man named as Member of Shipping Board

Tuesday, August 24, 1920

Cabinet. The Jones Shipping bill undertakes to denounce certain parts of 28 treaties giving equal rights in shipping with our own people, "the favored nation" clause. It would enable InterState Com. to give lower rates to goods brought in American ships & give other privileges amounting to a subsidy. The other nations protest that a treaty is not a scrap of paper & cannot be abrogated except by mutual consent & Congress undertakes to exercise executive functions when it impairs terms of treaty. Under act notice must be given in 30 days   Colby must act or defy Congress. W W was for declaring Congress could not change a treaty, but Alexander & W B W said he had signed the bill and therefore approved it. Best thought seemed that Colby should notify countries of the law & ask them to consent. If they refused then to take matter up with Congress which would shortly thereafter be in session. But troublesome question.

Decided upon Gordon W[oodbury] as Asst Secy & telegraphed him. Hope it is wise

Tribune roasted F D R for saying he had had Haitii & San Domingo and I now had them & therefore we had as many votes as Great Britain

Read over extracts for armor plate fight.

Wednesday, August 25, 1920

Long talk with Colby and Norman Davis on Haitii & San Domingo. Decided to rescind order about right of military government to imprison for articles in papers, and substitute for same rule as to papers and speech as prevail in our own country. Colby ordered Solicitor [48] to draw up such orders. I suggested that we send Admiral Knapp to Haitii to make study—a new man might succeed where mistake of manner by Minister and Financial Adviser had put us in an impasse with Haitian President and Congress. Approved.

Suggested to Colby to have signing of 19th amendment made a function & invite Cabinet &c & have pictures taken—it will make history

Mrs. Helen Gardner phoned that she had asked Colby not to have any of the Picketting crowd of women present. "The female of the Species—"

Young man Graham, just from Rio, took an hour to explain organized

[48] Presumably Fred K. Nielsen, the State Department Solicitor.

German-Mexican-Japanese propaganda   Anti-American all over South America? [*sic*]   Not very convincing.

Thursday, August 26, 1920
  Admiral Knapp and Haitii
  Mr. Gordon Woodbury arrived
  Woman Suffrage celebration. Colbys speech a classic

Friday, August 27, 1920
  Long talk with Colby and Knapp about Haitii. Nat. City Bank has purchased Bank of H—— formerly belonging to the French   State Dept. insisted upon Haitii standing by the changes. They refused & their salaries were cut off by the Minister and the Financial Adviser
  Can Knapp compose differences and prevent military rule? Colby thinks he can. Knapp dubitante [?]. Will go down on battleship & spy out the land.

Saturday, August 28, 1920
  Lejeune showed me letter from Col. Haines,[49] Adjutant General, that after I had ordered full investigation in Haittii [*sic*], he had told Barnett that he (Haines) did not think there was anything much in the charges and to avoid publicity he wrote a confidential letter to Gen. Russell[50] in Haitti [*sic*] not to continue & Barnett approved. This stunned me. Russell was cabled for report and Barnett ordered here on Tuesday.
  Knapp feels he should have large powers if he is to compose differences in Haitii & Secy. Colby agreed. He will sail next week. We must clean house and if anybody has been unwise or has done wrong, we must punish the wrong-doers and show they were exceptional and in violation of orders.
  Talked to Mr. Wheeler, Y.M.C.A. worker & Eng [?] leader, who said trouble is we do not mingle socially with Haitians & that until this done Americans cannot reach them. No Haitian has been invited to American Club & they have invited no Americans to either of their two clubs. This is a barrier. D'Artinav,[51] the President, could not live a day without military protection. He is nice old fellow who gets $25,000 for doing nothing. The Occupation is the govt.
  Marines often immoral.

Sunday, August 29, 1920
  Charleston

---

[49] Colonel Henry C. Haines, Assistant Adjutant General of the Marine Corps.
[50] Colonel John H. Russell, commander of the Marine brigade in Haiti.
[51] Sudre Dartiguenave.

Monday, August 30, 1920
Charleston

Tuesday, August 31, 1920
Gen Barnett said he had written letter to Gen. Russell scoring any lack of consideration and urging full investigation and fixing of responsibility. He is to see me on Friday.

Larson,[52] who owns patents for aluminum aircraft, came. Reported he had paid $6,000 for machines and charged us $27,500. He said "I am no profiteer["] & had spent all he had assembling, testing and getting ready to make more aeroplanes which he thinks will revolutionize flying. Very light, takes less gasoline.

W W at cabinet meeting asked if I had ordered ship to Dantzig, as the papers printed. Yes, at the request of the State Department for the protection of American citizens

"Rats" he said. That is the excuse always given for sending ships that ought not to go. French & British wish them to help us [*sic*] & we have no right there & State Dept ought not to have asked ship.

Taylor & I went over Pittman's suggested state[ment]

Prince of Roumania [?]: When will prohibition go into effect in US

Wednesday, September 1, 1920
Colby showed me letter from the President saying he was surprised to see in the papers that a ship had been ordered to Danzig. I had ordered it at C's request. C—— wrote President the reasons, he had information that American refugees had been coming into D—— & thought it wise for their protection, & had not thought neces[sar]y to confer with Predt & he regretted it, & said I hoped to detain Huse[1] before he reached D——. W W wants to be consulted & keep in touch with all things growing out of treaty. Colby told me that he had since had information that an Am. ship going into D—— might be misunderstood.

W. W. had objected to Knapp's going as his personal representative, as

---

[52] John M. Larsen, whose aluminum airplane, the J.L. 6, had just completed a round-trip transcontinental flight.

---

[1] Rear Admiral Harry McL. P. Huse, commanding U.S. naval forces in European waters.

suggested by Colby at K's request. I told him I agreed with W W & thought all Knapp needed was a letter from him & his mission was to compose differences and that I would regard a military govt as a tragedy.

Lejeune & Butler left for Haitii to study conditions and to make reports as to marine occupation. They do not like possibility of Knapp's being in charge of marines on the island.

Sam McGowan to dinner—his 50th birthday

Lejeune & Butler went to Haitii to study the situation and make report

Thursday, September 2, 1920

Report of Board on Wages for civil employes, recommending increase of wages amounting to six million dollars or more, with recommendation for ½ holiday on Saturday without pay.

Discussed fact that could not keep up with accounting without more money and I assigned 1½ mil. dollars to Supply and Accounts for clerical & accounting assistance.

Gave orders to Bethlehem and Midville for 6 each 16 inch guns, the last for the 3 year program, most of which will be built in the Washington Gun factory—cost $265,000 each.

Dined with Spanish Ambassador to meet officers of Alphonso XIII.[2] Colby was to propose health of the King of Spain. He made elegant speech, but forgot to propose health & then asked me [to] propose it which I did

Colby enthusiastic over trip on Destroyer to Provincetown

Friday, September 3, 1920

Officers of Alphonso XIII called and we had picture taken on portico.

Talked to Gen. Barnett and Gen. Haines about conditions in H—— Haines had written letter that he thought there was not sufficient evidence to convict men charged with killing Haiitians [*sic*]—that Barnett knew he had written but did not see the letter & H said he had not advised calling off the investigation. Russell said he had forwarded report and recommendations March 20th —never received.

Grayson said President was better and in fine spirits

S5 [3] 42 hours under water at Cape Henlopen. Brought in by the Governor Goethals—everybody saved. Ordered destroyers out to assistance

Gov. Stephens, of California, out to dinner.

[2] A Spanish naval training ship, the first Spanish warship to visit the United States since the Spanish American War.

[3] The crew of the U.S. submarine S-5 had been saved by the S.S. *General Goethals*, which had pumped air into the stricken submarine until its release could be effected.

Jeunett [?] & daughter here.

Saturday, September 4, 1920

Officer Gatewood [4] from Raleigh said he made a mistake—thought it was his own berth on the Pullman. Wrote to Raleigh to see if lady was willing to prefer charges.

Talked to Barnett about Haitii & he is to write full account of American Marines in Haitii to answer Harding's statement.

Roosevelt denied what Harding said "I wrote the Constitution of Haitii.["] [5]

Zeb Vance Weaver here. Reps. in Asheville offered Registrar $5,000 in gold if he would change the mail votes from Dem. to Rep. Wishes a detective

Sunday, September 5, 1920

Judge Samuel J. Graham [6] came around to talk about the campaign and the matter of getting a capable man to go to Asheville. He feels that we have the right with us in the campaign.

Houston Thompson [7] called. The Anti Saloon League had endorsed Watson [8] for Senator in Indiana. Watson had sought to destroy the Trade Commission & that body had replied that Watson was a lobbyist who was paid $500 a week by the Mfr Assn. He wanted the League not to endorse so unworthy a man as Watson. I will see Wheeler [9] and Bryan

Thompson said that Baruch, Cleve Dodge, Chadbourn [10] & others, including Taggert,[11] had signed a telegram urging Cox to say that he would veto any bill that sought to change the Volstead act.[12] Cox had declined. T——

---

[4] Lieutenant Commander Robert Gatewood, of the Navy recruiting station at Raleigh, had been accused by a young Raleigh woman of attempting to enter her Pullman berth. Gatewood claimed it was simply a misunderstanding, but Daniels promptly transferred him to the Asiatic Fleet.

[5] In a campaign speech at Butte, Montana, on August 18, Roosevelt had boasted of writing the constitution of Haiti and of the Navy's control of the votes of Haiti and Santo Domingo in any League of Nations. Although Roosevelt claimed he had been misquoted, the Republicans tried to make political capital of the indiscretion.

[6] Assistant Attorney General, 1913–1919, now judge of U.S. Court of Claims.

[7] Huston Thompson, Assistant Attorney General, 1913–1918, subsequently a member of the Federal Trade Commission.

[8] James E. Watson, Republican, U.S. Senator from Indiana.

[9] Wayne B. Wheeler, temperance leader and general counsel of the Anti-Saloon League of America.

[10] Thomas L. Chadbourne, Jr., prominent New York corporation attorney and chairman of the State Finance Committee of the Democratic National Committee in 1916.

[11] Probably Thomas Taggart, unsuccessful Democratic candidate for U.S. senator from Indiana in 1920.

[12] The Volstead Act, passed over Wilson's veto on October 18, 1919, attempted to enforce

said Tumulty & others had been greatly exercised when they heard such a telegram had been sent & had advised Cox the opposite.

Sunday, September 12, 1920

Reached New York coming from Maine with the McAdoos. He said he had urged Cox to declare he was opposed to the repeal of the Volstead act— wine and beer, for authorizing the sale of wine and beer would restore the saloon. That was Cox's mistake, he thought.

Saw George White and Pat Harrison [13] at Democratic headquarters. White thought Irish were offish and Harrison said he could not get them out to speak. They do not feel hopeful about New York, but trust the good reports from the West. Very little money coming in and organization lags. I promised to give dates when I could speak.

Reached home at 4.50

Monday, September 13, 1920

Howe told me that McIntyre came out of N.Y. headquarters one day two weeks ago, & said "Cox will come out for Prohibition." He got in touch with labor leaders who got message to Cox that such a declaration would cut heavily into the labor vote. Cox did not do what White predicted.

Talked to Colby about Haitii. Had letter from Lejeune who finds marine force in that island all right. He goes to San Domingo.

Republican com. asks questions which will be answ[ered?]

Labor men came to talk about wage. Object to uniform 8 hour day, say they have enjoy[ed] 7 or 7½ hour day for a long time and it ought not to be taken away even if mechanics work 8 hours in some navy yards. Shall we increase 5% or give up 8 hr day. They want both.

Tuesday, September 14, 1920

Gompers said reducing the hours for any (draftsmen & clerks) would be a step backward and earnestly hoped it would not be done. Board had recommended all in Navy Yards be put on 8 hour rule

Cabinet. Colby suggested that a committee of publishers be asked to take up with Canadian authorities question of pulp. Said it was serious and the publishers felt it would result in good. W. W. said he had refused to approve the Underwood bill for like purpose & it would not be consistent. Burleson said it was contrary to law to appoint such a Board. Colby said he would not

the prohibition decreed by the Eighteenth Amendment. The controversial law was named for its author, Representative Andrew J. Volstead, Republican, of Minnesota.
[13] Pat (Byron Patton) Harrison, Democrat, U.S. Senator from Mississippi.

make official appointment but make it informal. He had talked to Ambassador Geddes, who said it would be welcomed by Canada. W W said he sympathized with Canada in trying to conserve its trees & that newspapers had too much paper now, & hit the papers very hard. I put in that Canada was not trying to conserve but was robbing publishers; that Burleson had almost sent us to the poor house & that paper mfs. had gone further, & some good might come from taking this step. He was adamant

At night reviewed parade of veterans of all wars and spoke

Wednesday, September 15, 1920

Settled question of wages & let hours remain as now.

Mr. Cortes, of Mf [?] Paper Co., talked paper & the conditions that faced us—with small supply & high cost.

Worth operated on for tonsils.

Dinner at Pan American given by Colby to Dr. Parros,[14] the newly elected President of Panama. Both spoke. Argentine Ambassador [15] talked of our big navy. Cuban Ambassador said Cuba had made 4 mil. tons of sugar this year. The most ever raised under Spanish rule was 1 million.

Thursday, September 16, 1920

Took lunch at A&N Club. Asst. Secy. of War [16] gave lunch to Dr Porras, President-elect of Panama.

In afternoon I took party to Mount Vernon on Mayflower.

Addie went to Chevy Chase Md. to make her first speech on politics "Put the key under the mat for ma"

Sent $4,000 of bonds to C C D

Friday, September 17, 1920

Naval officer at Raleigh in night in Pullman entered berth of young lady and said "Let's talk awhile." I detached him and ordered him to Washington.

Ordered Barnett to prepare detailed report of Marine occupation in Haitii.

Long talk with Minister from Haiti,[17] who said he had forfeited confidence of his country by his welcome of American occupancy, & now by reason of lack of consideration of Haitians the people had lost faith in America and had recalled him. He had written letter to Secy of State in Apr 1919 detailing wrongs committed by Americans, but got no hearing or redress. Said a Haitian,

[14] Dr. Belesario Porras.
[15] Tomas A. Le Breton.
[16] William R. Williams, Assistant Secretary of War since July 29.
[17] Charles Moravia.

caught stealing was captured by Marines and then killed though he was in the custody of the Marines.

I felt sorry for the Minister, who goes home discredited & feels we have not acted toward his countrymen as we did in Cuba.

Monday, September 20, 1920

N.Y. American said delegation was here from Haitii saying Nat. City Bank was in control of island

Tuesday, September 21, 1920

Spoke at International Congress against alcohol. Article 22 of League

Cabinet. W. W. told stories & there was little discussion of public topics.

Cabinet thought League of Nations ought to be the only issue & Cox was making a mistake by discussing other topics

Creel. Chadburn [?] & others put up to Cox that he and R[oosevelt] ought to themselves put up $50,000 each & then they would help.

Reception at Pan American

Wednesday, September 22, 1920

Left for Bluefields [18]

Thursday, September 23, 1920

Reached Bluefields.

In afternoon drove to Princeton and spoke

At night spoke to great crowd at Bluefields   Louis Davis (col) met me

Supper by the North Carolina Society

Friday, September 24, 1920

Arrived 1 hr. late at Welch

Spoke at North Fork and spent night with Col. Lawrence Tierny.

Saturday, September 25, 1920

Went to Williamson where the miners are on a strike.

Some have been evicted and are living in tents—evicted by detectives by orders of operators who have been indicted

Spoke to ousted & striking miners at Matewan

"The first time I was ever ashamed of being a Democrat. You made me ashamed by your speaking to those murderers[."]

[18] Daniels was on a short campaign tour through West Virginia.

Sunday, September 26, 1920

Left Williamson 7:30; Lunch at Bluefields; travelled with Mr. Tiernan, coal operator; went to hear Billy Sunday at Roanoke and told them I had been preaching the gospel in W Va.

Monday, September 27, 1920

Reached Washington

Tuesday, September 28, 1920

Cabinet. Houston spoke at length against the misunderstanding in the South about the Federal Reserve Board & said they wanted money to hold cotton. "The people of the South ought to depend on themselves" said W W   Much politics talked

Left on 7 pm for Asheville

Wednesday, September 29, 1920

Reached Asheville at 11:40. Spoke at Reunion of 30th. Division.
In afternoon spoke at Bingham School.
At night spoke at Court House. Gov Craig introduced me
Dr Shorty [?] Battle [19] said "Since Democracy has destroyed S/R [States Rights?] & free gov.["]   No

Thursday, September 30, 1920

Left Asheville at 7 a.m. for Rutherfordton via Chimney Rock
Shelby
Gastonia
Col. Armstrong—governors [?] spirit.
Left at 12.40 for Greensboro

Friday, October 1, 1920

Left at 1 p.m. for Reidsville & spoke in warehouse. 2,000 people
Spoke at Normal & Ind. College 6 pm
At night in C[hapel] H[ill]

[19] Probably Dr. S. Westray Battle, prominent Asheville physician and civic leader.

Saturday, October 2, 1920
Took Tercentenary party to Mt Vernon on Mayflower

Sunday, October 3, 1920
Both boys at home   Worth & Frank
Went over estimates at Department
Completed medal list at home with Foote & McGowan

Monday, October 4, 1920
Gen. Lejeune report on Haiti.
Swanson & Labor. Increased pay of Master Mechanics & Supervising force
Social Hygiene Board's estimates.

Tuesday, October 5, 1920
Cabinet. "You cannot reason out of a man what reason did not put [in] him" said W W speaking of ———
Left for Illinois to enter campaign.

Wednesday, October 6, 1920
Reached Chicago at 3:30. Publicity man met me at train with some reporters. Left for Joliet to speak. Reached there and nobody expected me. Judge Hooper very courteous & took me to club for supper and then a company of Democrats called. They had not even heard that I was expected to speak there. The Nat. Speakers Bureau had notified State Com. I would be assigned to Joliett [*sic*]. OK they said but every hall in Joliet had been engaged & no place to speak could be obtained, but no notice to that effect was given to National Headquarters which failed to telephone to Joliet & so I reached there on a wild goose chase, & went back to Chicago. Joliet Democrats much chagrined & I upon return to Chicago felt like expressing myself, but McClintock was so upset I hadn't the heart to say a word & slept the sleep of the just—on a bed in the Congress Hotel that cost 10\underline{^{00}}$—such robbery. A few years ago I paid 4\underline{^{00}}$ for a like room.

Thursday, October 7, 1920
Spent the morning at Headquarters. Walsh troubled about Beckham [1] and hoped Bryan could go into that State and give a helping hand. He telegraphed Beckham and wanted me to co-operate if I could as I came on back. Mark Sullivan [2] said Dems. had no organization in most Western states & that Pro-

[1] Senator Beckham of Kentucky was engaged in a hard (and unsuccessful) re-election fight.
[2] Author and prominent political columnist, former editor of *Collier's Weekly*.

gressives had all gone back. Progressive sentiment was dormant and Wilson had lost out. He said it was incongruous for Cox to talk like a preacher for the League & wear loud checked overcoat & sporting hat, & Reps. were circulating a cartoon showing the incongruity of it.

Reps depend on Irish, Italians, Germans & Negroes & had them all docketed.

Reached Rockford at 6 pm & met by Mr. Howells (ex-Navy man) & others & spoke in Shriner Hall to a great crowd.

Friday, October 8, 1920

Left Rockford & went out to Camp Grant where Gen. Bell is carrying on schools for the enlisted men. He married daughter of Gen. Bob Ransom.[3]

By auto went to Rochelle along Black Hawk trail. Spoke at Rochelle and went to Clinton, Iowa, on train. Met there by several autos, Chairman Pender & Editor Potter & drove up Miss Riv to Rock Island. Beautiful trip. Dinner at Rock Island. Spoke at Swedish College [4] hall. Fine auditorium & introduced by Presidt of College who said: "I am a Bull Moose." Is hot Republican. I told him I was glad for they had been telling me the Bull Moose was an extinct animal. Reps. had said the Bull Moose was swall[ow]ed. If so they have more brains in their belly than they have in their head.

Judge Wade [5] there & thinks Iowa will elect a Democratic Senator

Saturday, October 9, 1920

Left Rock Island early. Stopped at Peoria & took lunch with Pindell.[6] He runs the papers, all there are in Peoria, one Rep & one Dem. Says he has everything his own way. He is Democrat. How long can he keep the monopoly?

Reached Alton 6 p.m. Spoke at night to large crowd—& left in auto for St Louis at stated hour at 11.50.

Sunday, October 10, 1920

On train Sunday.

Met Senator Harris, just from Japan, who discussed Gengro [Negro?] policy

Monday, October 11, 1920

Had meeting of Council on Estimates. Over $700 million dollars with no new construction. Worked hard & cut down 25 million dollars.

Held meeting of Social Hygiene Board and sent up estimates for next year

[3] Confederate major general from North Carolina. The Danielses had met General Bell returning from Europe in May, 1919.

[4] Presumably Augustana College.

[5] Martin J. Wade, former U.S. Representative from Iowa and member of the Democratic National Committee, U.S. district judge since 1915.

[6] Henry M. Pindell, Democrat, publisher of the Peoria *Transcript* and *Evening Journal*.

Worked at Departmt at night

Heard mother was better

Tuesday, October 12, 1920

Cabinet. The Presdt thinks Cox will win.

Palmer brought up the consent decree of the packers. Preice [?] wants to buy up & have a monopoly of all packing houses, with trustees appointed by the court to choose directors. Payne, Meredith & I opposed. Payne said all dissolutions of trusts resulted in failure & this would only strengthen monopoly. President told Palmer to take matter up with the Industrial Com. & he felt like following their unanimous opinion.

W W said if he were candidate he would say he did not wish the vote of any hyphenates.

Should Davis speak at Cooper Union? The Irish might break up the meeting. Colby suggested Davis might be ill. Would that do? No, said the President. Let him go & he is brave & staunch [?] man. If they break up the meeting, they will not break up another

Left at 9 pm for Dunn—

Tuesday, November 9, 1920

Cabinet. Burleson said the Republicans had plenty of trouble. "But what I am thinking about" said W. W., "is the trouble that will come to the poor country."

What about Treaty? Should the President send it back to the Senate when it meets in December? B—— said he should say in his message that he would send it in later, & then hold till 4 or 5 days before session & then send so it would be before the Senate when that body convened March 4th. W W said that would look like a trick & if he sent it in at all it should be in good faith. Long discussion as to whether he should send. Payne & I opposed or rather expressed our feeling that no good could come. Reps would either do nothing or would send it back with such amendments the President could not ratify & people would say he was stubborn. Baker thought he could not accept without Section 10. Colby thought much reason for sending. Has any President ever returned treaty to Senate when it has been returned to him without assent? Colby was asked to investigate & inform Senate [*sic*]

Took lunch at Army & Navy club to meet Gen. Neville.[1]

[1] General Robert Georges Nivelle, official French representative at the Pilgrims Tercentenary celebration.

Baruch thought enough attention had not been paid to & not enough credit given to War Industries Board. He talked about campaign & is planning to organize a Trust Co. to finance cotton crop. Must have warehouse certificate plan.

Neville said when he went to a certain place where Germans had dominated for two years, many women with babes in their arms. Germans had forced them to become mothers.

Wednesday, November 10, 1920

Conference with Gov. Milliken [2] & Gov. Bartlett [3] on building bridge across Piscataqua river. Decided to give contract to construct sub-structure and advertise for bids for superstructure.

McAdoo called about Aztec—thought Burrage, [4] the owner who had leased at $1 $\underline{^{00}}$ a year had not been treated well.

He thinks Democrats can win if they are wise, for there is sure to be a revulsion in feeling when Harding begins to act

Dined with Gen. Neveille at New Willard. He is the only Protestant General in France. He was the French General at Verdun & he lost 600,000 men while Germans lost 500,000 Later he was forced to make the offensive by British & French politicians. It was against his judgment. He lost 80,000 men & he did not gain a foot of ground. The Germans withdrew 30 miles & all his supplies had to be carried up. The people had to have some one to punish & he was sent to Africa. He is fine man—looks like Gen. Wood, only he is of kind spirit & simple. He was delighted with visit to Annapolis

Friday, November 12, 1920

Dinner at Pan American building as guest of Uruguay Minister [5] who gave it to Secretary Colby upon eve of his trip to Uruguay & other South Am. countries

"I am not a stranger in land of free peoples"

Saturday, November 13, 1920 [6]

F D R. told of a German who was gardener for his mother for 20 years. He said he voted for Harding. Why? Because of letter from Germany telling

---

[2] Carl E. Milliken, Republican, governor of Maine.

[3] John H. Bartlett, Republican, governor of New Hampshire.

[4] Albert C. Burrage, wealthy Boston attorney and yachtsman, had given his yacht, the *Aztec*, to the Navy during the war at a nominal rental but was seeking to have the Navy live up to its agreement to pay for its reconversion to its original state.

[5] Dr. Jacobo Varela, Uruguayan minister.

[6] Daniels mistakenly wrote this entry on the page for October 13, but corrected the date.

him of lack of food and of clothes & it was because Wilson entered the war. Are you not an Am. citizen. Yes, but if America joins with England & France against Germany I am a German.

Thos. B. Love [7] active & thinks we can win two years hence   He thought my idea of a weekly paper a great one

Decorations awards

Tuesday, November 16, 1920

Cabinet. Palmer said proposition to Alien Prop. Cust. by Americans to organize a 10 mil. co. & be given control of $170 mil. of money belonging to Germans—debentures to be issued. Germans in Germany to give their consent —& money to be used to open trade with Germany   He said Sec. 9, conferred the power. Would help cotton. "Damn cotton" said W. W. Scheme a gigantic one for the favored company   The President sat down on it hard as he did on Palmer's suggestion that the 500,000 cash belonging to the German Government be used to pay the holders of German bonds who live in the U.S. "Most of the holders of these bonds were German sympathizers" I said "and should wait until all other claims are met"

Ralph D. Paine [8] came to see about writing history of the Navy in the war.

Arranged with Powell of Fore River Co. to pay fixed profit of $2 million on battle cruiser instead of 10%. Will save $500,000 by this arrangement.

Went to theatre to see "The Little Visitors" by young girl—Austin.[9] "We will go on our wedding journey for six weeks & expect to return with a son and heir.["]

W. W.: Quoted Thackery [*sic*] saying to Mrs. King: "I hear you are very fast"   Don't believe all you hear. I heard you were a gentleman

W W   Disgusted because Taggert & Senator Harrison said no party responsibility [?] now [?]

Wednesday, November 17, 1920

Powell came up about contract for cruisers—agreed to a fixed fee of 2 million dollars instead of 10% which would be nearer 3 million.

Admiral Scales came up to go over story of the hazing at Annapolis. The first class had drawn up a set of regulations under which their hazing, without personal injury but most humiliating, would be approved by the Superintendent. If he would accept them and thereby abdicate in favor of gov. by

[7] Thomas B. Love, Texas attorney and Democrat, former Assistant Secretary of the Treasury, 1917–1918.
[8] Journalist and author specializing in nautical subjects.
[9] A stage adaptation of Daisy Ashford's book of the same name.

First Class they agreed not to engage in brutal hazing. He hoped he would
not have to see newspaper men. I advised him to see them & talk frankly, for
unless he gave them his side they would think things were worse than they
are and would publish all the gossip possible

Thursday, November 18, 1920
Finished proof of report.
J. D. Jr came here on way to New York about paper contract

Friday, November 19, 1920
John H. Fahey [?] said he had returned from Europe and had found that
America had lost all it had gained in the war. He felt that the permitting the
high rates of interest had made a present of 450 million dollars to the bankers;
that the War Finance Corporation should have continued functioning; &
predicted that if something was not done soon we were in for a panic next
Spring.
Roosevelt—Woodbury—oil.[10]
Reception at British Embassy

Saturday, November 20, 1920
Talked to Colby about our preventing W.U. Tel Co laying cable at Miami.
The War Department has given permission & they intended to lay cable
on 24th of November—have moving pictures and newspaper men present and
lay claims for damages if we prevent. I told Colby that Baker ought to withdraw permission and there ought to be nothing so unseemly as the Navy Department preventing laying of cable for which the War Department had granted
permission.
Rogers told me at French dinner to-night that one reason the President was
so hot against laying cable was because McAdoo had written W W urging him
to give permission. Dinner by French representatives. The new blue sky law—
wireless [?] men charting the heavens.
Burleson will advocate further increase in postage rate. I told him that killed
us in the campaign & Reps wd be too smart to do it. He said it cost the Gov
[for the] Sat Ev Post 4 mil. dollars dollars [*sic*] more to carry it than it paid
in postage & he intended that papers should pay all that it cost.

---

[10] Roosevelt was evidently still supporting the oil refinery scheme referred to in the entry
for April 3, 1920, and subsequently. He may have run up against additional objections from
his successor, Gordon Woodbury, for a week later Roosevelt wrote his wife: "Yesterday was
very busy—many conferences in New York and Washington, and I really think that Woodbury person is either crooked or pin-headed!" [November 27, 1920] *F. D. R.: His Personal
Letters, 1905–1928*, p. 511.

He agreed with me that new gov. in Mexico ought to be recognized.[11]

Sunday, November 21, 1920

Went to hear Dr. Chappell

Jason's voyage with the Argonauts. The song of the syrens carried the bow of the ship to the rocks—sailors put wool in their ears. But Jason got Orpheus to make music. You must drive out evil or discord with good or harmony.

In afternoon went to Quantico to speak in new Methodist church. Rev. Mr. Johnson [12] earns $125 a month as teacher & his wife $90. He gives $75 a month & his wife $50 to pay off the debt of the church. Such devotion made me feel very humble.

Spoke at Auditorium to 3,000 marines and presented the colors to the new Fifth Division which has the name of the regiment which played such a glorious part in France

Got lost on Manassas road & did not get home till nearly two o'clock

Monday, November 22, 1920

Commodore Wadhams here. He is 74 & is doing a young man's work at the Portsmouth prison.

Went to theatre—"Honors are even" with C S. Hamlin & R W Woolley & their wives

Tuesday, November 23, 1920

Cabinet. Shall we permit the WU to lay cable at Miami? They have contract by which the British would control the cable to South America. The President denied them permission to land some weeks ago & Navy had given directions not to permit it. It turned out that the Secy. of War had years ago given the permission to put cable over causeway. We have information that they will lay cable & connect it with cable to S.A. & thus defeat the President's determination that cable cannot be permitted to land in America. Pres. directed Baker to annul permit & let matters take their case in the courts.

Dined at British Embassy to meet Vice Admiral Packingham [13] Lady Geddes [14] talked of her being new at the business of politics & diplomacy.

---

[11] Alvaro Obregón, a former supporter and general of Carranza, had been inaugurated president of Mexico on December 1, and was hopeful of obtaining U.S. recognition.

[12] Rev. Wade Johnson.

[13] Vice Admiral Sir William C. Pakenham, commander of the British Battle Cruiser Fleet, 1917–1919.

[14] Isabella Gamble Ross Geddes, New York–born wife of the British Ambassador, Sir Auckland Geddes.

She had never met Mr. Balfour. She said people often mistook her for Lady Astor,[15] & she thought their coloring the same. She has charm.

Wednesday, November 24, 1920

Pakenham went to Annapolis.

Pakenham at home at dinner. He is such a stickler for form & uniform that his sailors said during his service in the North Sea he slept in a stiff shirt so as to be able to be properly attired to receive the surrender of the German ships. An upstanding & frank man—a total abstainer

Thursday, November 25, 1920

Reached New York & met by Commander Parker. He is working on apparatus to make colored moving pictures and thinks he has found the principle.

Went to Mineola to Pulitzer flying contest. Pershing there. He said he had not seen me since the election. I told him that N.C. was the only State that increased its Democratic majority in 1920, & that I was there on election day—had provided myself with a cyclone cellar.

Went to theatre with Josephus

Friday, November 26, 1920

Spent the entire day going with Josephus to see the paper companies, taking lunch with Mr. Dodge[16] & Mr. Lyman[17] of International   They would as a favor see we had supply of paper at 7½ c at the mills to April 1st by which time Booth would probably be able to supply us. The Mfr Paper Co. could give no guarantee.

All of them wish to get all they can. The Great Northern is selling paper to its old customers at 5c while the others are charging 6½ cents. After the price is stableized, [sic] the Great Northern will be the favorite because of its square dealing

I felt like Josephus & I were two lambs going about to be shorn.

Went to see the Bat by Mary Rhinhart Roberts[18] with Addie & others after dinner with A. W. McNeill[19] of Bridgeport, Conn.

[15] Nancy W. Langhorne Astor, Virginia-born wife of Waldorf Astor, 2nd Viscount Astor. In 1919 she was elected to her husband's former seat in the House of Commons as a Unionist, becoming the first woman M.P.

[16] Philip T. Dodge, president of the International Paper Company and the Mergenthaler Linotype Company.

[17] Chester W. Lyman, vice-president and director of sales of the International Paper Company.

[18] Mary Roberts Rinehart, author of the current play "The Bat."

[19] Archibald McNeil, Bridgeport newspaper publisher and prominent Connecticut Democrat.

Saturday, November 27, 1920

Went again on paper hunt & Seaman [20] arranged for enough to last us till April at 6½ cents

Went to ball game & Navy won by 7 to o "The moral[e] of the Navy is *not* shot all to pieces." [21] Glad because it vindicated Scales' policy at Annapolis.

Told Pershing he would need a cyclone cellar before the game was over.

Saunders, Swope, Creel, McNeills & the boys with us.

Met Baker, Neville, Pershing among the field

Hippodrome at night

Pershing told me he was writing a history of A.E.F before recollection of it fades

Sunday, November 28, 1920

Heard Dr Kellar [?] preach on the Plymouth colony. Extremely pro-British.

Went to Hippodrome to Marine Band concert

Jonathan and his doubts [?]

Monday, November 29, 1920

Boy less than 17, son of Greek, with mother & father & all who had run away, came to get him out of the Navy. Distressed. I arranged it. Addie said "do all you can"

Crawford [22] came to see me & said Mr. Ochs [23] wanted him to sound me to see if I would consider newspaper proposition.

Norman Davis said that Navy men did not support policy. He had requested Decker to be ordered here. Decker had, as usual, talked against our policy.

I made affidavit giving the real facts about refusing to permit British Corporation to lay cable at Miami. It gave monopoly to England of cable to South America.

Dinner at Rauschers [24] by Italian delegation to Communication Conference [25]

[20] George M. Seaman, president of several Chicago paper companies.

[21] A charge made by Admiral Sims before the Senate Naval Affairs subcommittee the previous spring.

[22] Probably William H. Crawford, political feature writer for the *New York Times.*

[23] Adolph S. Ochs, publisher and principal owner of the *New York Times,* who was interested in having Daniels do a series of articles for the *Times* after his retirement from office.

[24] A popular Washington restaurant.

[25] The International Communications Conference, sponsored by the League of Nations to decide the disposition and use of the former German cable facilities.

Burleson said he had changed his mind & now thought the Presdt ought not to send the Peace treaty to the Senate

Tuesday, November 30, 1920

Cabinet. Discussed low prices for farmers and the demand for legislation to assist them. Houston said we were exporting larger volume of agricultural products than ever, more he believed than Europe could pay for. He said that Eugene Myers,[26] formerly member of War Finance Corporation, resigned and went to help Harding, was urging it, but was more interested in getting money for his copper mines than for farmers. He deplored the sudden drop in farm prices but saw nothing the Treasury could do. He feared panic if the Treasury went in for inflation. He criticized John Skelton Williams for saying banks were sending money to New York to lend to speculators at high rate of interest & said very little went and that New York & New England banks were lending money to the South & West. He said merchants & manufacturers needed money as much as farmers did—indeed that the trouble with price of farmers products was that other people lacked money to buy farm products.

President seemed better & said he had not yet written his message & would like suggestions

Again declined to sell destroyers to Peru

He disapproved sending troops to West Va & Baker is to withdraw them. The Gov. of W Va wants him to declare martial law instead of the State taking care of conditions as it should do.[27]

At home with Taylor, McGowan & Theall on Regulations

Wednesday, December 1, 1920

Went to St. John's Church to the funeral of Mr. Ekengnen [1][,] Minister from Sweden.

Wells [2] from State Department came over to talk about Santo Domingo. I had

[26] Eugene Meyer, Jr., banker, former member and managing director of the War Finance Corporation until his resignation the previous May.

[27] U.S. troops had been sent into West Virginia to quell violence arising from the bitterly contested coal strike.

---

[1] Wilhelm A. F. Ekengren, who had died November 26.

[2] Sumner Welles, recently appointed chief of the Division of Latin American Affairs of the State Department.

written letter to Colby, Snowden,[3] Knapp with reference to turning government over to the people of the Republic

C C D here & distressed about his boy

J. D. Jr came from New York

McFadden [4] wanted coal & gave to him when requested by Venezuela minister.[5]

Went to Naval Moving Picture at Interior Dept.

Thursday, December 2, 1920

Coontz returned from trip to Pacific coast. He favors big naval base at Alameda.

Council: How many officers on duty in Washington? 390 & most bureau chiefs say they cannot now reduce the number. I stated that there were too many and the number should be reduced.

Telegram from Haitii saying Mayo Board [6] had left without inquiring into all the cases charged against the Marines. I telegraphed them to present any proof they had to Admiral Knapp.

Friday, December 3, 1920

Lunched with Dr. Rowe [7] at Pan American building to meet the President of Panama. Chester Rowell,[8] a California editor was present & Baker and others had their say. Rowell told of a Roman publisher who sent part of a copy of his paper to Cicero, who wrote him that the paper contained matter that no one would dare talk to him about. See Rowell [9]

Samuel McGowan came up to the house & will retire.

Saturday, December 4, 1920

Shall the compulsory salute when off duty be abolished? That is to be decided in the next regulations. I asked Gen. Butler and he said a salute was only like saying "good morning."

Went to Baltimore to see game between Marines at Quantico and sailors at Great Lakes   Score 7 to 7.

[3] Rear Admiral Thomas Snowden, military governor of Santo Domingo.

[4] Probably Preston McGoodwin, U.S. Minister to Venezuela.

[5] Dr. Don Santos A. Dominici.

[6] On October 16, Daniels had appointed a court of inquiry, headed by Rear Admiral Henry T. Mayo, to investigate the charges of Marine brutality in Haiti.

[7] Leo S. Rowe, director general of the Pan American Union since September.

[8] Chester H. Rowell, California Republican, editor and publisher of the *Fresno Republican*, currently serving briefly as a member of the U.S. Shipping Board.

[9] Daniels has circled these two words.

Talked to Butler, Chm of Naval Affairs Com., who said the Appropriations Committee will control naval appr, but Kelly will go on Naval Committee & that will help. He thinks Rep. maj. is too great and there will be divisions.

Sunday, December 5, 1920

Heard Dr. Chappell on the Passover & communion.

Worth over from Balto. J D Jr returned to Raleigh

Taylor & McGowan came over and we went over the Regulations. I had cut out compulsory saluting off duty, put discipline under J.A.G.[10] & changed other harsh regulations, but decided not to do so inasmuch as I am going out of office so soon.

Monday, December 6, 1920

Went to Bellevue Magazine & threw the first dirt in new Laboratory Building.

The Bliss Torpedo Co. claimed more money and appealed from Ord[n]ance over McVea [McVay], Earle & Block.[11] I decided against the torpedo [company] & told them they ought to be thankful the Navy had enabled them to make so much money.

Took Gov & Mrs Bickett to the theatre

Tuesday, December 7, 1920

Solicitor of State Department brought over agreement between the lawyers in Miami cable case by which suit would be withdrawn to enjoin me, the WU Tel Co would agree not to connect with cable to Barbadoes unless Congress, the executive or the courts should grant permission. In it I promised to secure revocation of order from the President. I said I could not sign but would put it up to the President. At Cabinet meeting the President declined to compromise, saying the paper by implication surrendered the right of the executive to deny permission to land cable in this country. Baker, Burleson & Davis thought W W was wrong but he would not compromise.

Went to Capitol to hear President's Message. It was well read, but it was a great contrast to the days when he delivered it in person. It was unlike any other

W W said he could not understand how Lodge could have the effrontory to come to the White House, said he stood all the while and did not shake hands with any because he would not shake hands with Lodge.

Houston very bitter on Eugene Myers   was liar

---

[10] The Judge Advocate General.
[11] Captain Claude C. Bloch, assistant chief of the Bureau of Ordnance.

McLean [12] said Leffenwell & NY bankers behind action of Treasury. The NY bankers got themselves in good fix & brought on present conditions just as Morgan brought on 1907 panic because refused to increase the interest charge.

Wednesday, December 8, 1920

McGowan retired & resigned to take effect Dec. 31st. "They will not pick my bones"

Dr. S. H. Lyle, of Frankin here. Refreshing to see so fine & stout a partisan. Told Jenkins he had never seen a really honest Republican.

Saw Redpath's [13] man about a lecture tour. He thought Out But Not Down a good subject.

Settled matter of building cruisers for fixed fee with Bethlehem Shipbuilding Corporation

Went to Meredith's ball

Thursday, December 9, 1920

Went before Naval Affairs Com

Friday, December 10, 1920

Mr. Ward, of Los Angeles, proposed if lease given on Honolulu oil reserve be given to the company and they would surrender all claims on the property. No. He said if new administration should reverse Payne I would lose all for Navy. I told him I must act on the assumption that Reps. would protect the naval oil reserve. But I would have a newspaper & would keep in touch & if the Ho[no]lulu oil co. were before Interior Department I would make that fact known to the public.

F D R here. He said that in 1854 a man named Butler killed a man named Smith for calling his wife a negro. Later Gov. of Ohio at request of Harding's grandfather pardoned the murderer

Saturday, December 11, 1920

Oil matter   F. D. R. here. Woodbury handled it.

B. M. Baruch came to see me. Only way for better conditions is to fix German reparation. Until that is fixed neither Germany nor France can obtain credit. Germany will have credit to buy raw material and will not work until

[12] Angus W. McLean, managing director of the War Finance Corporation.

[13] Redpath's Lyceum Bureau, which Daniels was considering as a booking agent for lecture tours after he left office.

it knows how much it is to pay. Other things are palliatives. Talked to him about my affairs.

Cam Morrison here. Says rich men in N.C. think only of making money & few can be depended on for any constructive policy. He discussed desire to advance State. But what will he propose? I suggested warehousing for cotton.

Went to Gridiron dinner & spoke on how editors in America served in World War without censorship. "When are you Democrats going to vote[?"]
Camoflage [sic]
Some mine, some yours, some ours & some mistake [?]
Lodge asked for patience & resented the World's editorial, showing that its remark that Senate leadership was morally bankrupt had stung

Sunday, December 12, 1920

H W J [14] here & we went to church. Then to Lincoln Memorial. What a beautiful memorial to a simple American! It is a statue worthy—his eyes have meaning & love in them. The only sitting statue I ever saw that was impressive.

Went out to Arlington. How noble a monument are the pillars of Lee's house. Strange that he has a monument here, not of national making, so close to Lincoln's. Noblest figures of their day

Addie went to Raleigh to-night to see about renting the house for the Legislature. What a brave girl she is and how blessed I am in her love & strength.

Monday, December 13, 1920

Regulations & McGowan & Taylor.
Judge Towner [15] & Virgin Islands

Tuesday, December 14, 1920

Cabinet. Wilson (W B) read long opinion in case of Martens closing with opinion that he should be deported. Suggested that his opinion wasn't conclusive though his finding was just, the President said he had learned that no gathering or company could frame a paper—that Secy of Labor knew the thought and he could make such change as might be necessary.

Davis reported that cable convention had reached agreement to agree as to disposition of ex German cables by March. France, Japan & England now have all the cables & seem to wish to keep them

I dont see I grow any better said the President when after cabinet I asked how he felt

[14] Herbert Worth Jackson.
[15] Horace M. Towner, Republican, U.S. Representative from Iowa, and chairman of the House Committee on Insular Affairs.

Appeared before Naval Affairs Committee & discussed building program. Should we enter agreement with England & Japan to stop. England has 800,-000 tons to our 400,000, & Japan has 200,000 & they have an alliance

Wednesday, December 15, 1920
Raleigh

Thursday, December 16, 1920
Before Naval Affairs Committee. Urged conference of all nations looking to reduction of armament as opposed to suggestion of a US[,] Jap & British agreement.
Advocated law to do away with bread and water.
Discussed submarines and told story of what had been done and the difficulties.
Kelly & reduction of the Navy to 100,000
Taylor & McGowan   Settled Regulations

Friday, December 17, 1920
Powell on Destroyer contracts.
      ?
Spear & Crose [*sic*] on Submarines made by the Electric Boat Co.

Saturday, December 18, 1920
Went to Shipping Board to discuss serious need of oil.
Marshall [?] & others wanted $25,000,000 to hold oil for U.S.   Great Britain would put up twice as much
California oil men wanted Shipping Board to get oil elsewhere while a number of Japanese tankers were taking oil from Calif to Japan
Dinner by Naval Architects
Oil & coal should be nationalized

Sunday, December 19, 1920
Went to Richmond and read Taylor's Life of Mahan.[16] He was a deeply religious man & the writer shows the secret of his greatness.
Talked to Herbert [17] of business. He is a joy and a comfort and strength & gave me good advice.

---

[16] A newly published biography of the American naval philosopher. Charles C. Taylor, *The Life of Admiral Mahan* (New York: Doran, 1920).
[17] Herbert W. Jackson.

Monday, December 20, 1920

Naval Affairs Committee—decided to postpone meeting until full membership has returned from New England. We talked about tariff & War Finance Corporation &c &c

Saw Electric Boat Co.

Tuesday, December 21, 1920

Went to Treasury Dept. Houston sick. Talked to Harding [18] and McLean about War Finance Corporation.

Harding said nothing could be done—that farmers should sell their crops —& that the interest rate had been delayed—should have been adopted sooner —like a cold fish. I asked him what he thought of McAdoo's suggestion. He said he interpreted it to be an announcement of his candidacy for the Presidency. I could hardly retain my indignation, seeing McAdoo had put him in office & trusted him. But since the election he has shown that he is a weather vane. He has since McAdoo left taken advice from the big interests.

Lunched at Shoreham with McLean and Cameron Morrison. Afterwards Morrison came over and had a long talk

Son of Secy Alexander killed at Bolling Field.[19]

Osborne on prison reform—he could not write because he would say things that he did not wish to say now

Wednesday, December 22, 1920

Ambassador Sharp called—said before we entered the war Clemenceau sent wire to the President asking to see that France had ships engaged in Pacific trade to take gasoline over to France. "Unless we get gasoline for the 101 purposes for which we need it" said Clemenceau "France cannot carry on the war more than a few weeks." Sharp approved the appeal.

He also told story that Schwab told him. He had contract to build submarines for Great Britain—to build them here—but Bryan ruled it was not neutral to build war ships here & so they were built in Canada. Schwab said England fixed the price for a short period & said he must pay penalty for every day over time. Agreed. Then Schwab said he ought to have a bonus for every day he saved in building & it should be twice the penalty. He made bonus of 4 million dollars.

Sharp said these statistics [?] showed that in war nations had to agree to pay any price for speed.

[18] William P. G. Harding, governor of the Federal Reserve Board.

[19] Army Reserve Lieutenant Walter R. Alexander, son of the Secretary of Commerce, killed when he accidentally walked into the propeller of his plane.

Sumner Wells on Santo Domingo.

Thursday, December 23, 1920

Went to see Mr. Merrimon [?] at Corcoron Gallery about painting portrait & went to see one he had painted of Mr. Alfred Douglas—a strong face & good portrait.

Council discussed reduction of appropriations to $400,000.

Argentine officer wanted to go to Portsmouth, N.H. to see work on submarines. McVea [McVay], who always opposed letting foreigners see anything, said "I am in favor of the permission because they are already there and have seen everything already."

Addie went over & brought Worth from Baltimore.

Shall we prosecute men accused of wrong doings in Haitii now that the Mayo board has reported that conditions are good? McGowan said "A Court of Inquiry is like a grand jury. It did not find a true bill and they cannot be tried."

Meeting of the Interdepartmental Board. Dr Pierce [20] wanted all matters to go through Public Health Service. Dr Story [21] wishes no change. Better wait to see if Congress appropriates any money

Friday, December 24, 1920

Telegram from Snowden who said he had issued the proclamation looking to self government in Santo Domingo. Saw Secy of State who made announcement of purpose because Marines had brought about peace and security.

Ordered certain of men put in prison for talking & writing against Occupation released

Dr. Grayson told about M & the quacks who talked against G & R [22] & the others. Greatly irritated W W.

Decided to get Mr. Merrimon [?] to paint my portrait.

Talked to Kelley who wishes Navy reduced to 100,000 men & cut off building of the big ships, or rather to build more slowly

Saturday, December 25, 1920

Boys all here & girls came to breakfast. McGowan and Hilton,[23] Mrs. George Dewey & George, Admiral & Mrs. Eberle called.

---

[20] Claude C. Pierce, Assistant Surgeon General of the U.S. Public Health Service, a member and chairman of the executive committee of the U.S. Interdepartmental Social Hygiene Board, of which Daniels was chairman.

[21] Thomas A. Storey, executive secretary of the Social Hygiene Board.

[22] Presumably Grayson and Dr. Sterling Ruffin, another of Wilson's physicians.

[23] Commander James C. Hilton of the Bureau of Supplies and Accounts.

Coontz called. W.U. had coil of wire for laying cable near Key West. Davis said to keep outlook and not permit landing & connection with cable to Barbadoes. I gave orders not to permit landing.

Telegrams from various friends.

J D & I talked business.

Addie told of story of the President that when he returned from Paris she said "I regret the capitol is not illuminated[."] "The more important thing is that there are some people under the capitol who are more in need of illumination[."] [24]

Sunday, December 26, 1920

Addie and I and boys went to church   Dr. Chappell. Little boy so fidgetty he could not keep still—therefore could not learn

Man had a grove—owls & hawks & like animals who made hideous noises. He had them all killed & "then one nightingale sang & then others until it became known as nightingale grove.["]

"No place for him at the inn." These busy days there is no time for Christ —no welcome—no room.

J D Jr & I went to Dept. & met Mayo and signed some papers. He left for Raleigh on night train

I talked to Herbert on the phone & decided not to increase stock & call it J D Pub Co

Went to see Mrs. Dewey. Said the best sermon she ever heard was in Italy. Priest came down—crossed himself, & said "Little children, love one another. God is love." In the name of the father, son & Holy Ghost.

Jonathan & I spent evening

Rode by Capitol.

Monday, December 27, 1920

Council & General Board met to go to call on Mrs. Dewey on anniversary of the Admiral's birth—an annual custom. Picture taken. She was very happy to receive us & had luncheon for all. Badger told of having Brownson on ship when Usher & Winslow were having a battle. Brownson nervous & thought Winslow did not understand. Suddenly a new move was taken & Badger said it showed the Navy would go on after the old Admirals retired. "I hope for the best and fear the worst" I said

Gave contract for super structure bridge across the Piscatqua at Portsmouth NH

[24] Cf. entry of July 8, 1919.

New York World began crusade to end navy building. Walker & others joined forces.

Talked to Joyce about paper. He could give us no contract.

Coontz wanted me to approve $55 mil. dollars for Guam. No

Tuesday, December 28, 1920

Went to Mr. Merrimon at Corcoron Art Gallery for first sitting for portrait.

Cabinet. Bristol had telegraphed from Constantinople that Greek King was going to Athens & should he salute him? Is he King? asked the President. If King, salute. France and England will not salute. Bristol telegraphed to avoid Greek fleet & let recognition be extended in some other way.

President's birthday. In answer to congratulations he said rather sadly that he did not know whether he deserved to be congratulated.

Wilson br[ough]t up immigration bill   W W said he wished to send back those who were not Americans—he wished he had an X ray to determine where ones heart was—in this country or some other.

Worth & his experience under arrest in Richmond.

Senator Pat Harrison talked about his speech on peanut protectionists in the Senate, & hoped President would sign War Finance Corporation bill. It would hurt very much if he did not do so. H—— had almost ruined the Dem party

Houston talked of foreign debt & our plan to permit its refunding—to require no int. for 3 years after 1919. Congress interested

Thursday, December 30, 1920

Reached Raleigh at 7:30 a.m. & went to room of Josephus and woke him up.

Meeting of the Board of Trustees. President Chase proposed plan for six years, involving 5½ million dollars for new buildings and for increased facilities approved by Board of Trustees.

Lunched with Alf. Scales. Said cotton & tobacco low prices ought not to be permitted to interfere with progress of schools.

Talked business & reduction with boys at the Dept

Slept at night at new home on New Bern Avenue.

Friday, December 31, 1920

Saw Jones & Bailey and arranged about mortgage

1921

The Cabinet Diaries of Josephus Daniels, 1921

Saturday, January 1, 1921

New Year's Reception

Gen Crowder gone to Cuba to look into elections—sent on the N.H. to tell Presidt of Cuba that the US must do its duty & see legally elected President is inaugurated.[1]

Mondell[2] says Harding favors big Navy

Monday, January 3, 1921

Jan 3. Gov. McCorkle, of West Va. says Gov Sproul told him armor plant at Charleston would be dismantled—that it showed the actual cost of production—and what it cost would keep many steel mills going—& they would close it up

Bob. Doughton served with notice of contest—alleged that negroes were not allowed to vote.[3] Conf. with Overman and Doughton

Tuesday, January 4, 1921

Jan. 4. W. W. said he did not wish to make position of Sec or Asst Sec a a stepping stone to a place on a commission (Woodbury exit)

Shall Eugene Meyers be appointed? Burleson & others seemed to think "yes" & Houston said he would not like to work with a liar. Burleson said "offer place to Senators who were active in putting it over the veto." W W No. He said Dems, had better traditions than Republicans but did not live up to them. H—— evidently not keen to make loans & doubtful if Corporation[4] functions with spirit to make it meet the needs.

Davis talked about Cuba. Is Gomez part negro? W G H[5] Sent Gen.

---

[1] A dispute over the recent Cuban presidential election seemed likely to explode into violence which might lead to U.S. intervention. The election of Alfredo Zayas y Alfonso, backed by incumbent President Mario G. Menocal, was being challenged by General José M. Gómez, a former president (1909–1913). Ultimately Gómez withdrew and Zayas served the presidential term, 1921–1925.

[2] Frank W. Mondell, U.S. Representative from Wyoming, Republican floor leader in the 66th Congress.

[3] Doughton's re-election was being unsuccessfully contested by his Republican opponent, James I. Campbell.

[4] The War Finance Corporation.

[5] Probably a reference to the rumored Negro blood of President-elect Warren G. Harding, a whisper-charge in the recent campaign. See also entry of December 10, 1920.

Crowder down on ship to confer with Menocal to secure settlement of presidential election. Moritorium ordered, ships in harbor unloaded, & conditions bad. I said Marines had 4 yrs ago helped keep Menocal in when he was not elected.

Should Morgan's [6] offer of house in London for Am. Embassy be accepted? He said he would hold it open only till March. W W said yes

Coontz went before Com. & said Japan & England were working together & Japan was building ships in GB. Japs here troubled when they learned we knew it—said they were not war ships

Wednesday, January 5, 1921

Jan 5. Admiral McCully,[7] who had brought home seven children from Russia, came to see me. The children had been detained at Ellis island. Secy. Wilson said they would be paroled in his care until all the papers arrived and the question could be passed upon.

Overman, Simmons & Doughton came over to talk about the contest for Doughton's seat. It is an attempt to compel registration and vote of negroes and illiterates in N.C. & is fraught with danger to politics of our State.

Gov. of Santo Domingo, Admiral Snowden, had issued proclamation that was very drastic about criticism of American Government & officers. I ordered it annulled after talking with the State Department

Champ Clark came up about young man who was denied com. at Annapolis because he had tuberculosis—given his diploma, but denied commission & his mother was in distress

Begin to see light on Sat Eve Post article [8]

Sam McG & Mrs Dewey   Twenty [?] sent to Herbert

Thursday, January 6, 1921

Jan 6. Went before Naval Affairs Committee—proposed monument to Dewey & other legislation.

Calder called to praise Navy's action in commandeering coal.

Dined with A. Mitchell Palmer to meet Supreme Court Justices   Took Mrs. Sproul [9] in to dinner. Her father, John Roach, built the Dolphin & he swore he would never again build for the Navy because Whitney [10] would not as fit accept [*sic*]

[6] J. Pierpont Morgan, New York banker.

[7] Rear Admiral Newton A. McCully, formerly in command of U.S. naval forces in Russian waters.

[8] Daniels had agreed to do a series of articles on the Navy for the *Saturday Evening Post,* published in April and May, 1921.

[9] Emeline W. Roach Sproul, wife of Governor William C. Sproul of Pennsylvania.

[10] William C. Whitney, Secretary of the Navy in the first Cleveland administration, 1885–1889.

Friday, January 7, 1921

Jan 7. Spanish Ambassador called to introduce the new Naval Attache.[11] All youths in America should learn Spanish. Spain has left its indelible impress upon this continent because all speak Spanish.

Approved policy to fortify Guam.

Dinner with the Woodbury's at the Willard   He made very gracious speech of friendship for himself & the Council.

Saturday, January 8, 1921

Jan 8. Took Commander Mayo [12] over to see Under Secretary Davis about bond issue to complete roads & schools in Santo Domingo. Davis did not agree to pay 8% just as we were getting ready to try to give them self government. Bankers would not lend money. Harding intimated that we would come out of Haiti as soon as he came in office. I cabled Snowden to call on Commission and show them that unless they approved loan work would have to stop. Cocoa [?] is so low it does not pay to gather it, & conditions, financial, are bad. Mayo thought they would not approve. Davis thought Snowden's proclamation had ended his usefulness. Why not send Knapp?

Cuban Presidt Menocal [13] first said he would not see Crowder—unless he was consulted & knew his mission. Davis telegraphed that our relations to Cuba justified our going without asking & Menocal saw Crowder. Truth is we put Menocal in 4 yrs ago when he had not been elected & he thought he could bluff it through again. Voted in Nov. & nobody knows who is elected. Menocal hopes to keep matter in the courts until May & then hold over

Sunday, January 9, 1921

Sunday Jan 9. Gray day. Addie not well and felt gray

Dr. Sterling Ruffin brought me a goose. Tom Ruffin called. Returned from N.C. said Charlotte seemed more prosperous and had more faith than other places he visited.

Mr. Oliver came over and I read him what I would say to the Naval Affairs Committee Tuesday. Will advise Harding to call a conference under Act of Aug. 1916.

He talked of big Army waste.

Weeks said Harding would call off inauguration ceremonies & he would ride to capitol on a mule. I offered the Dem. donkey & guaranteed he would not throw him off

[11] Lieutenant Commander Gabriel Ferrer.
[12] Probably Commander Chester G. Mayo of the Bureau of Supplies and Accounts.
[13] Word encircled.

Monday, January 10, 1921
Jan 10 Chatauqua people called—said the business had gone to pieces. Instead of $250 per lecture they offered $100 & ½ of all other receipts. I went to see V.P. & he advised a fixed sum rather than ½ over $100.

Dined with the V.P. Talked to Sterling Ruffin

Saw Admiral Knight about history of War College. Sims had written that Knight was taking some credit to himself which belonged to Rogers.[14] I asked Rogers to read Knight's report for Admiral K—— wished to change it if any such statement appeared in it

Tuesday, January 11, 1921
Jan 11. Went before Naval Affairs Committee and read statement. Davis also there. Said no overtures had been made to secure reduction of armaments.

Cabinet. Davis read letter from Crowder that outlook of securing result in Cuba [*sic*]. Houston said there had been no applications under War Finance Board.

Dined at Merediths

Wednesday, January 12, 1921
Before Naval Affairs Committee. Gen. Bliss urged a conference between the 5 big powers and repeated arguments he had made in Boston & elsewhere.

I gave the relative standing of all great navies of the world
                              (See Testimony)
Took Reynolds & Chatham to Army and Navy Club to lunch.

They wanted [blank]

Dr [blank]

Thursday, January 13, 1921
Telegram from Gleaves about killing of Lt Langford [15] at Vladivostok by a Jap. sentry. L—— was going to the Albany, asked if an American, said yes & was fired upon in the back. Died after making that statement. Saw Davis & Morris. Latter said Japs. assumed to police everybody & subordinates were heady. They will file serious representations to Japanese government which expresses deep regret. A Col. John F. Stevens [16] sent for. He has been building

[14] Rear Admiral William L. Rodgers, Knight's predecessor as president of the Naval War College, 1911–1913; currently a member of the General Board.

[15] Lieutenant Warren H. Langdon, serving on the U.S.S. *Albany* at Vladivostok. The killing of Langdon brought a minor diplomatic crisis with Japan for the next two months.

[16] Civil engineer and railroad expert, head of the American Railway Mission to Russia in 1917.

RRs in Siberia. Says the Russian city gov. at V is on paper. Japs. police & control & told of incident where a Red Cross man was beaten over head by Jap because he was passing through place which had been public until day before Japs had stretched wire over it. Young officer killed had gone up from the ranks and had exemplary character.

Afterwards wrote to State Dept. asking them to take steps to protect Americans & secure proper action in case of young officer.

A lady journalist from London came to see me. She will write about this country. Said she wanted to be President of something like de Valera so America would support her. Discussed Irish question.

Received from Ambassador Davis clippings about my report & policy of continuing naval construction. First Lord explained why estimates were high & why deficiencies necessary

Friday, January 14, 1921

London Globe showed naval deficit of 92 million pounds for Navy without new construction. Sent to Butler & Kelly

San Diego gives 25 acres for flying field. Shall we lease 300 acres more at 8\underline{^{00}}$ an acre? Bill Ketner [17] called & said San Diego could never forget what I had done &c &c

Dined at McVeas [McVay]

Worth came home from Baltimore. Had letters from Richmond about his awful experience & suggestions from Parsons that they bring suit.

Saturday, January 15, 1921

Worth came to office and told me all about the Richmond affair and was deeply troubled.

Talked to Woodbury and Peebles [18] about deficiency estimates.

Wrote to Aviation Board of Inquiry to hold it in public, permit press to be present, have each aviator tell the full story of the trip so as to have a real official report, they have sent only a brief cryptic message.[19]

Sunday, January 16, 1921

Sat for my portrait till one o'clock

Admiral McGowan and Dr. Sterling Ruffin here to dinner.

[17] William Kettner, Democrat, U.S. Representative from California.

[18] Rear Admiral Christian J. Peoples, acting chief of the Bureau of Supplies and Accounts.

[19] A reference to the crash and rescue of a group of U.S. Navy balloonists in Canada. Daniels had ordered an investigation and had forbidden the aviators to sell their story to the press until the inquiry was completed.

Took Worth to the train

At night spoke at the Gorgas Memorial   While Marine Band was playing "Nearer My God to Thee" the Minister from Ecudor [20] [*sic*] asked me if they were playing "Carry me back to Old Virginia[."]

Fourth anniversary of Admiral Dewey's death—wrote to Mrs. Dewey and sent flowers

Monday, January 17, 1921

Went before the Appropriation Com. on Bulletin of Shipping.

Rosseau [21] had sent report on contract which he had never read asking construction of Comptroller in advance. Declined to do so   Contract was expected to be for $390,000. Cost $1,800,000. & they wanted ten per cent on the larger sum. No.

Dined with Mr. Hubbard [22] at Wardman Park Inn. Regular Maryland dinner—oysters, terrepin [*sic*], duck.

J. Ham Lewis, speaking to the Supreme Court   C.J. said, "Mr. Lewis I do not follow you—["]

"You are lost Judge"

When decision is given it will be Lewis who will be lost

British Embassy to meet ———. Music & pleasant time

Tuesday, January 18, 1921

Cabinet. W of M [?] suggests ——— for War Finance Corporation. Said Houston. "Nothing doing. Never anything else to do with him.["]

Will you ride with Harding asked Baker. ["]I hope you will not go if it is a cold & sleety day." "O that will not matter. I will wear a gas mask anyhow.["]

Davis talked of how Lloyd George asked him to talk to British rep. & ask him to agree with Am on G. reparation. Davis said he had done so & if L. G. could not influence him D could not. L G said he had a letter from the former President of Bk of England saying G. ought to pay 25 billion. "Give him that letter & you may influence him. But L G would not give up letter.

W W did not want Army reduced—said France would yet involve Europe in another war—that Foch and his party were determined to take the Rhine territory.

W W gave two limericks. Houston said his daughter had found new book of Limericks. W. W. said let me know the name of the publisher.

[20] Dr. Don Rafael H. Elizalde.
[21] Probably Rear Admiral Harry H. Rousseau, a Navy civil engineer assigned to the Commission on Navy Yards and Naval Stations.
[22] Wilbur W. Hubbard, a prominent Eastern Shore Marylander.

Woodbury went up about deficiencies—looks for trouble.

Telephoned J D Jr to come here and go to New York to get facts straight about the press—so we will know where we are at

Saw Mrs. Dewey & she said she had put my letter inside the Admiral's tomb.

Wednesday, January 19, 1921

Peebles & Woodbury & all Bureau Chiefs before both the Naval and Appropriations Committee discussed deficiencies. Peebles feels hopeful of adopting legislation which will avoid large appropriation for so-called deficiencies.

Josephus here from Raleigh & went to New York to see if we can get released from press contract. A hard mission which he does not relish & which is doubtful.

Knapp saw State Department. Coontz thinks & so does Knapp that their San Domingo plan just now is a mistake and ought not to have been undertaken. Knapp says only hope of those negroes is wise white guidance & he is a Connecticutt [sic] Yankee

Peters [23] and Venable came to see about Stanley Mitchell.

Hineman.[24] Judge Advocate in case of Newport here for stenographic [?] help—said he could not complete until 2 or 3 months. I told him I desired to pass upon question before my term expired. Clark will expedite.

Thursday, January 20, 1921

Woodbury and Peebles told of appearing before committees on naval deficiencies. W had blood in his eye when Good [25] suggested I had played politics in making estimates too low. I did not make them high enough

Talked to Sumner Wells about San Domingo. He feels that Snowden made mistake in notifying 5 named on Com. & talking with them before announcing all 9. Thinks that gave the 5 chance to object to the two and that made things difficult. Knapp backed Snowden. I told Davis & Wells I would keep Snowden there, for if not always tactful he was honest & had done a man's job in a hard place. Would not sign letter for we must co-operate rather than correspond.

Talked to Davis. Lodge had said that Davis knew his job   Why not ask him to stay?

[23] John A. Peters, Republican, U.S. Representative from Maine, like Venable a member of the House Naval Affairs Committee.

[24] Ensign Henry I. Hyneman, the judge advocate conducting the naval court of inquiry into the Newport vice charges. Since the inquiry might be used politically against Franklin D. Roosevelt, Daniels wished to complete it before leaving office.

[25] James W. Good, Republican, U.S. Representative from Iowa, chairman of the House Appropriations Committee.

Scales came about man who had confessed to killing woman nurse at Annapolis. Told him to deliver him to civilian courts.

Talked to Josephus about press. There will be delay of 6 months

Taylor said: I have had to stand 2 Roosevelts   I cannot try another [26]

Delegation called to protest against cutting down Great Lakes Trng Stat.

Friday, January 21, 1921

Read Knapp's report on Haitii & talked with him. He says if whites were withdrawn from the South negroes would lapse. He believes Occupation is the only hope of $\frac{9}{10}$ of Haitians. The agitators wish to graft on the others.

Worth came home

Almost finished article for Sat. Ev Post. Lacks convincing quality & spontaneity.

Council discussed appropriations

Padgett came to see me. As he was leaving I thanked him for his help & friendly counsel, & he said "It is because I love you"

Saturday, January 22, 1921

Dinner of North Carolina delegation at A. W. McLeans. Discussed how failure of European credit affected price of cotton and tobacco. McLean praised Houston's ability.

J. D. Jr. came from New York where he went to see about the press.

George Creel here—talked about his visit to Mexico at request of Wilson & how the plans written out came to naught because Davis insisted on treaty, thus leaving matter in hands of Republican Senate when Wilson might have settled it now. Of course now Obregon thinks it is better to come to terms with Harding. He says Doheny wishes intervention & speaks of adding 28 stars to our flag by adding Mexico. McAdoo represents Doheny, who is in with or has close relations with S. O. Co.

Colby wanted ship to bring his party back from Hampton Roads

Denman said Franklin was working for Great Britain when he thought he was working for Shipping Board.

Sunday, January 23, 1921

Went to hear Dr Chappell with Addie[,] J D Jr & Worth. "Teach us how to pray." Teach me how to paint, how to play (country boy on fiddle[)].

Saw Geo. Creel & took him to Lincoln Memorial & he went to White House to lunch.

[26] Theodore Roosevelt, Jr., was reported to be in line for a high Navy Department position in the incoming Harding administration.

After dinner Addie[,] J D Jr & I went to Balto. with Worth

J D Jr went to Raleigh after talks about press &c. He had found out that matter need not be taken up for five or six months. This gives us breathing time.

Admiral Taylor & J W J [27] here. Taylor liked article. Said he quit reading as article & read on because he was interested

Monday, January 24, 1921

Hollis Godfrey (Drexel Institute) called and said I was the only one of the associates who drew forth affection. Said since 1624 every generation in his family had held a commission under the King or under this government.

Talked to Knapp about Santo Domingo & Haitii He said it would be fatal to turn the gov. over to the negroes, as fatal or worse than to turn the South over to the negroes after the war

Went to dinner at Willard. With officers of the Reserve Corps who have met here to confer about best thing for Reserve

One reserve officer told in report that one of his officers was too bow legged to be a Jr. Lt but not too bow legged to have military qualities for an Ensign

Tuesday, January 25, 1921

Cabinet. Palmer told of German doctor in Wash. [?] whose property was taken over by the Alien property custodian. His wife was American & under recent act of Congress she is entitled to her property if not obtained through German sources. It was all returned, but when he examined he complained it lacked a priceless possession—the appendix of Alice Roosevelt Longworth in alcohol.

Houston said British evidently intended not to deal with the administration on debt due this country. Twice they had made date for Lord Chalmers [28] & twice postponed. He wished to give Congress Lloyd George's letter & the Presidents. Davis objected because it contained some things bearing on French affairs and W. W. said that part should be omitted. Decided to give facts & show this administration had left no stone unturned.

Harding will send Root abroad to have Powers define what is international law.

Went before Naval Affairs Committee (Appropriations rather) on estimates. They will reduce appropriation to 100,000 men & cut down all along the line.

[27] Probably John Wilber Jenkins.
[28] Robert Chalmers, 1st Baron Chalmers, designated by the British government to confer with U.S. Treasury experts about refunding the British war debt to the United States.

Dined at Merediths to meet Cox and wife. He said the best editorial in any American newspaper on Cleveland's death apprd in N&O

People wrote him of the election & tried to cheer him up by saying that the vote was not personal. Reminded him of note somebody wrote Lord Kimberly [29] they intended to kill him. And they sent word they had no personal feeling against him

W W. New house.[30] Among other things, "I can look down on Phelan[."]

Wednesday, January 26, 1921

Went to have portrait finished.

Went to see Theall—very sick

Mr. Filene, of Boston, said my policy as to disarmament absolutely sound—must have international agreement or keep on building. Progressive Democrats must go forward & be ready to receive the support of the people who will not stand for Harding's reaction

Said he bought a N&O—did not know whose paper it was—but told fellow traveller that every State needed such a paper.

Dined at Lejeune's. Senator Ransdell told of German agent who wants US to lend Germany 1 billion dollars & says it will all be used to buy raw material here—& allies will let Germany pay that before it pays anything else.

Neville said it reminded him of the man who would get rich selling skins of cats for fur. How would you feed them? On rats. How will you feed the rats. On cats after they have been skinned. Senator thought it was a flippant way of dealing with a serious question. R—— spoke dejectedly of the outlook for the South

Thursday, January 27, 1921

Saw head of Worthington Pump Co. We made contract on a price which he said would give him profit of 20% From his own figures he made over 60%. We decline to permit profiteering.

Council. Discussed how to reduce telephone and telegraph expense.

Lunched at Mitchell Palmer to meet Gov & Mrs Cox

Gov. Cox said that when Cleveland died my editorial was the best one that appeared in any of the papers.

[29] John Wodehouse, 1st Earl of Kimberley, nineteenth-century British statesman, Lord Lieutenant of Ireland, 1864–1866, where he repressed the Fenian Revolt, subsequently colonial secretary.

[30] Wilson had purchased a house at 2340 S Street, N.W. for his retirement upon leaving the White House.

Friday, January 28, 1921

Woodbury came over about a letter Howe had written with reference to labor. Federation of Labor said some Navy Yard commandants proposed to reduce pay of men instead of making discharges. Reduced appropriations compels [*sic*] reduction. Shall 1st class machinists be made second class? Or discharge   A.F.L. wants discharge; Woodbury think[s] probably other way. W does not trust Howe.

In afternoon AFL called for conference. I will not reduce pay. It would be contrary to all my policy.

W. T. Ellis [31] came to see me. Hopes Bristol will not be removed from Constantinople—believes W W will come back into popular favor, or rather his policies. Cannot understand the bitter hatred people feel toward him.

Saw Baker—says he is wearied *&* waiting for March 4th.

Saturday, January 29, 1921

Gen Mitchell, advocating single air service, said all future wars would be in the air *&* that battle ships were as out of date as armor when fire arms came in vogue. Craven[,] Lay [32] *&* Coontz got up answers for the Admiral *&* then I decided only to give out Lay's statement as to the Indiana

Went to Annapolis through the country   Admiral *&* Mrs Scales had commanders and their wives to dinner.

Sunday, January 30, 1921

Went to church in Chapel at Annapolis   "Eternal father strong to save" Callers.

I spoke at YMCA at Annapolis to midshipmen

Scales doubted whether wise for me to send him to sea now in important command and he wished no other. He would have to be preferred over others *&* it might hurt him with incoming administration

Monday, January 31, 1921

Funeral of Col. Theall at St. Matthews church *&* went to Arlington. The priest said "You lost a good friend."

[31] William T. Ellis, journalist and author, correspondent of the *New York Herald* in Turkey and the Balkans in 1919.
[32] Captain William D. Leahy, director of the Gunnery Exercises and Engineering Division, who denied that the bombing test against the U.S.S. *Indiana* supported General Mitchell's faith in the superiority of air power.

Mr. Ayers [33] called. He wishes to make speech on the Navy when the bill comes up in House and wishes some facts and figures.

Foss [34] said when Great Lakes station was open[ed?] Philip Andrews, who did Myers [35] dirty work came to him and said Myers wished to compliment me and hoped I would stand by him in all his policies. Foss replied he did not care for and [?] did not need Myers praise

Foss said he was the fi[rs]t American to greet Dewey on return from Manila —met him at Trieste. Hearst through Creelman [36] offered $5,000 for anything he would say. Dewey declined to say anything.

Foss said he had built Naval Hospital & Marine Barracks and was proud of it.

Went to dinner with Capt Dayton [37]

Reception at Congressional Club to V.P

Tuesday, February 1, 1921

Cabinet. Burleson urged President to protest against allies compelling Germany in addition to 54 bil dollars to pay 12% on all exports. This makes impossible our trading with Germany & injuriously affects all countries not receiving indemnity. Houston said W W had offered the way and Senate had rejected it. W W said nations would laugh at our protest & it would have no effect. W. B. W. said we should protest. Otherwise when Harding comes in & plan injurious to us has been settled we will be charged with not having done our duty. W. W. told State & Treasury to study proposed settlement & let him have the facts.

Colby said S.A. feels we are not helping & not cordial.

Should Cabinet officers resign? W W said he would not accept any of our resignations if we did

> There was a young man of St Louis
> Who married a beautiful Jewess

[33] William A. Ayers, Democrat, U.S. Representative from Kansas, a member of the House Naval Affairs Committee.

[34] George E. Foss, Republican, former U.S. Representative from Illinois, chairman of the House Naval Affairs Committee, 1899–1911.

[35] Presumably George von L. Meyer, Secretary of the Navy in the Taft administration, 1909–1913.

[36] James Creelman, journalist and editor, at the time a correspondent for Hearst's *New York Journal.*

[37] Captain John H. Dayton, commandant of the Washington Navy Yard.

Her talk was so bold
And her stories so old
He called [her] his Chauncey Depewess.[1]

There was a monk in Siberia
His lot was dreary and drearier,
So he broke from his cell
With a [blank] hell
And eloped with the mother superior

France will ask us to accept or float German bonds. If England & F cannot
pay us
Naval Consulting Board here. I made talk to them. Passed resolutions

Wednesday, February 2, 1921
Addie's reception. The last one before we return to North Carolina. I came
home & many called—expressed regrets we were leaving Washington.
Left on train for Raleigh with Addie

Thursday, February 3, 1921
Reached Raleigh 7:30 & went to new home on New Bern Avenue.
Went to see the Governor[2] & at 11:30 received note from Powell that Senate
had passed resolution asking me to deliver address at noon.
"Mr. Jedg, you don't mean June of this year do you?"—
With 15 min notice I spoke.

Friday, February 4, 1921
Lindsay Warren,[3] ex-Senator from Beaufort came to see me having telegraphed from Washington & wished me not to say that I would not be candidate for office

Sunday, February 6, 1921
Spoke at Vanguard class of Second Presbyterian church. When the country
went Democratic & Presbyterian.
Heard Bishop Lambuth[4] at Centenary Methodist church. The Chinese

---

[1] A reference to Chauncey M. Depew, Republican, former U.S. Senator from New York,
and a prominent after-dinner speaker.

[2] Cameron Morrison.

[3] Lindsay C. Warren, president *pro tem.* of the North Carolina senate in 1919 and prominent Beaufort County politician.

[4] Walter R. Lambuth, bishop of the Methodist Episcopal Church, South, with long missionary service in China and Japan.

ferment & our duty to help the world. He intended no collection, but the Chm of the Board was so moved he asked Dr. Smoot [5] to take up a collection. "Not a prophet or son of a prophet"

Spoke on Christian Education at John Marshall auditorium in afternoon & returned to Washington at night.

Monday, February 7, 1921

Dr. Story and the Social Hygiene Board. The Treasury and Public Health wish Board to fade away and be absorbed by Public Health. I went to see Houston who was deeply interested in work & thought we ought to work together. Will see Baker.

Jo Tumulty came over to see me about an aviator who had been drinking too much. I let him have another trial. He will stay here. Would not let Dave Walsh pass upon him and therefore would not accept the Judgeship. Said he would stay here to see the the [sic] resurrection, if one comes. Did not wish to go back to Jersey & take fees for practising before Judges W had appointed.

Dined at Mrs Dimmocks to meet V.P. Gen. Pershing told Mrs Marshall he respected her all the more because she stuck to her principles when she declined to help him receive on Sunday reception

Spellacy wanted me to agree to lease on naval oil reserve. No.

Southern Relief Ball

Public Health Service wishes to oust the Social Hygiene Board. I saw Houston

Tuesday, February 8, 1921

Each cabinet officer should send his resignation to the President on March 4th.

W. W. said a newspaperman said he had been much with Harding—he had good intentions & good character—all he lacked was "mentality" W W said he hated the word "mentality."

Dawes [6] & his profanity. When Judge [Samuel Chase] was under impeachment, the charge against him that he said "Damn" & his attorney contended that "damn" was in no sense profane—only a word of emphasis.

Payne & Baker said Dawes had talked that way all along & Burleson thought Dawes talked as he did because it was sour grapes because he did not get

---

[5] Thomas A. Smoot, minister of the Centenary Methodist Church in Richmond.

[6] Charles G. Dawes, Illinois financier hopeful of a position in the incoming Harding administration.

assurance [of?] office   W W said he had heard Dawes had written to Harding
he did not want his G——d office.

After cabinet meeting, Burleson & Payne & I talked to Tumulty—all deplored calling meeting of Dem Nat Com by Love & Woolley. T told of the
statements of W W at Paris on Art 10 which if published would have changed
opinion but W W would not let him print them

St Marys dinner
Press Post of Am. Legion

Wednesday, February 9, 1921

Mr. Eggleston—is he a dreamer?—from the South has been busy on aviation
since 1917. Thinks he has something that will revolutionize warfare. Experts
in Dept. fight shy of him. In 1918 he had fight with man in McAlpin who
had criticized me. The next week the man called on Mr E & apologized &
said "D is all right."

Mr. Hall [7] wants me to write article every Sunday on some current topic.
Am to see him again.

McGowan: "I would go down to the gates of hell" said one

> ["]For a friend,
>   Through thick and thin[."]
> Then the other smiled
>   as he bit off [a] conchas end
>   ["]I would go in.["]

Worked at office on Aviation
167 new subscribers of N.&O.

Thursday, February 10, 1921

Our naval rep. in Berlin wrote that Krupp wished a naval representative
to meet their agent at Havanna [*sic*] to make arrangements to secure manufacture of munitions by private company in U.S. No negotiations or meeting
with Krupp. I told McVea [McVay] to so telegraph them.

Niblack cabled advising an ordnance expert be sent to Berlin to confer
about patents on optical instruments   Deemed very important. McVea had
doubted necessity, but when Niblack & naval attache continued to urge it felt

[7] Blakely Hall, head of the Twenty First Century Press, a newspaper syndicate for which
Daniels agreed to do a series of weekly articles after leaving office.

it was best for us to send expert. He had only 3. I do not believe they have anything superior, but they say have & decided to send expert

Commerce refused to license sub chasers & Taylor, Preston [8] and I went over for conference with Commerce

Geneld [?] & Beckley of Hawaii here

Justice Clark gave dinner to the Bakers.

Friday, February 11, 1921

Wrote letter to Senate Naval Affairs Com. protesting against repealing authority for Charleston dry dock.

Wrote to Senate that all wireless ought to be gov. monopoly.

Went to see Hoke Smith—never felt so well in my life & anxious to work. Had plenty of money. Houston had been unwise in Federal Reserve Board.

Eggleston had air craft idea & model and wanted money to develop.

Barker [?] of NY asked if I knew W W Fuller Told him story of [?] R. W. Winston who wished me to quit calling Am. Tob. Co. the trust—should call it Co. "Didn't Will Fuller ever speak to you about this." No; he had too much respect for me

President didnt like Woolley's letter to White [9] said he had no upper story, was built like a bungalow

Baker: W W sent insulting messages to Lansing— Mrs W & J P T softened them & W W thought L got them like he sent them

Like Admiral Kirkland and Aaron Ward [10]

Dr. Pierce & Dr. [blank]— Int—— Dept Board

Saturday, February 12, 1921

Went to Garl [?] Brown to have photo taken for bust.

Peebles talked about the House not giving rule to pass bill for Supply Account & wished me to sign letter & telegrams that unless it became a law Navy Yards must be closed and [sic] &c &c. I declined & he is drafting another letter Woodbury said he had presented it to Congress & I had done everything possible & that if they did act with the knowledge they had he would advise us to do nothing. Peebles is to see McGowan tonight

P.M. Wilson wanted me to see Glass—proposition to knock out his place

Col Newman came to see me about Dr. ——— who had been convicted of

[8] Probably Captain Charles F. Preston of Naval Operations.

[9] Woolley had urged a full meeting of the Democratic National Committee, presumably to try to oust George White as national chairman.

[10] Probably the late Rear Admiral Aaron Ward (1851–1918), a naval hero of the Spanish American War who had risen to the position of second in command of the Atlantic Fleet before retiring in 1913.

sodomy & escaped the day he knew sentence had been pronounced. His friends said the Doctor was very ill and could bring doctors certificate. I said "We have hospitals for sick people." I told him that the only thing the doctor could do would be to surrender and go to prison. I could promise nothing until he surrendered. Remember the case of C. W. Morse.[11]

Saw Baker about officer for Bingham School. The officer now is a hell-roaring sort.

Sunday, February 13, 1921
Spoke at Baptist Sunday School—16th & O. "I ought to be a Baptist.["]
Heard Dr. Chappell & saw Lanny [?] Webb,[12] former U.S. Senator from Tenn. "I am standing by you and Woodrow Wilson.["] "Greatest teacher the South has produced" said Dr. Chappell.
Went to Church of the Covenant. Shook hands with several [?] as they came out & the V.P. said "Are you the pastor of this church?"
Sam McGowan here for dinner & talked to him about letter to Senate Appropriations Committee.
Read "A Perfect Tribute" & several speeches on Lincoln
Mrs. Dewey called & wanted us to stay with her after we left our house
Supper at Mrs Bs
Spoke at Knights of Columbus

Monday, February 14, 1921
Dinner at Willard by House Naval Affairs Committee.

Tuesday, February 15, 1921
Lawyer: But that is the law
Pitney: I don't care a damn about the law; you are trying to cheat this man and you shant do it
Photo taken
W W wished his letter printed to Lloyd George refusing to agree to remit debt due by allied nations.

Wednesday, February 16, 1921
Admiral Bailey [Bayly] & Miss Vosney [13] here at dinner. Told my wife

[11] Charles W. Morse, a speculator currently in financial and legal difficulties because of illegal wartime operations.
[12] William R. Webb, North Carolina–born educator, Democrat, U.S. Senator from Tennessee briefly in 1913.
[13] Violet Volney, Admiral Bayly's niece.

she did not pronounce a word correctly & Addie said he ought to learn the American way

Bailey & the Trippe [?]

"   [sic] was to have gone to sea but machinery was out of order, & signalled if she would take the Admiral & when would be ready. Been out 7 days. Can we stop to get food

Historic flag

Woodbury's party

Thursday, February 17, 1921

Sat with Boush [?] Brown for bas-relief.

F D R here.

Wrote to Badger regretting retirement from General Board

Hale asked Peebles why I did not send in the estimates for '20 and '21 earlier. P said we had money in General Account [?] of Advances & felt it well to transfer from those where there was a surplus. Tried to get basis for criticism

P said his amendment was a bill

Dined with Admiral Clark

Friday, February 18, 1921

Meeting of Council to discuss asking Senate for increased estimates & all went before Naval Affairs Committee.

I wrote to Com. urging larger appropriations for aviation & aircraft carriers. Coontz urged 120,000 to Senate Committee.

Dinner at Colby's. French Ambassador referred to visit of Virick[14] & Thompson[15] to Harding: "Looks like a separate peace with Germany." Regrets to see friends to go.

Sedgwick,[16] Ed. Atlantic Monthly thinks serious question about journalism. Chic. Tribune thinks of nothing but money.

Saturday, February 19, 1921

Peebles telephoned that Senate had passed deficiency bill with provision to transfer from one navy account to another to prevent a deficiency. Good navigator!

Edward DeValue [?] Co. had made shells—claimed to have lost 1 mil.

---

[14] George Sylvester Viereck, German-American journalist and pro-German publicist before U.S. entry into the war.

[15] William Hale Thompson, anti-British mayor of Chicago, Republican.

[16] Ellery Sedgwick, editor of the *Atlantic Monthly* since 1909.

dollars. War Dept. was making cost $+$ contracts & they ought to have cost. Ordnance said no.

Lufkin [17] want[s] man who entered as pharmacists mate & has been practising dentistry 13 years examined on his record. Dental Society demanded exam. from Dental College. Stitt agreed

Dr. Tullidge—escaped. Miss Margaret Wilson called & said that he was sick & she believed it was a frame up. Night before she had spoken against a special woman's party.

Went over my diary & was sorry I had not kept fuller notes.

Fullam went before Naval Affairs Com & advocated scrapping dreadnaughts & using money to build subs & aircraft   Made no impression. Taylor corrected him

Sunday, February 20, 1921

Spoke at Foundry Meth. SS. in morning on need of same spirit of old fashioned religion as the founders of Foundry had. Snow & cold but good crowd.

Mr. & Mrs. Padgett at home for dinner. Said R—— had so many Secretaries [?] they knew nothing or little about naval affairs. Nobody could take from W W glory of League of Nations

Jenkins here at night & we finished the fifth article for Saturday Evening Post & discussed series of 30 articles I am to write for papers. It is a big job & I am fearful of ability to succeed

Monday, February 21, 1921

McCully came & talked about Kolchak & will write his impressions for me.

Meeting of Council of National Defense elected Ellsworth, now acting as Director.

Talked over some tribute to the President. Baker thought a letter signed by all. Wilson agreed. Meredith a separate letter but to be bound.

Colby thought something in silver.

Why not his chair?

I suggested that all members of cabinet meet & talk it over—for Colby to ask them.

"One Secy of State was bounced for calling a cabinet meeting.["] Did I wish to get rid of him?

Dr Story showed letter by Pierce saying I had sought to perpetuate Board without authority. Very indignant

---

[17] Willfred W. Lufkin, Republican, U.S. Representative from Massachusetts and a member of the House Naval Affairs Committee.

Badger said he prized and would hand down my letter

Tuesday, February 22, 1921

Went to Army & Navy Club to attend reception given to Gen. Pershing. Great crowd there of Army & Navy men men [*sic*] "Why did you leave Press Club before I spoke?["] he asked. I had said the Army helped us to win this war &c.

Jack Cohen here. He wishes my articles for Journal. Hard times in Ga. You go out most honored of all &c.

S. R. [?] Fuller came to see me. Said Sims was speaking privately to clubs. He wished he could be soaked.

Worked at office all day trying to get a start on articles to run 30 days. I find it hard.

Dinner at Japanese Embassy. "Fisk tires."[18] Panama canal. Descendant of Drake.

Colby: At Washington's birthday in Paris.

Sorry head of mission could not come but has sent a substitute. First time I ever knew Silence had to have a spokesman.

Admiral Le Bon said after he had called Joffre "the immortal" (cheers) & Viviani "the incomparable." "You have saved my life. I did not think after what you had said of Joffre there was anything else that could be said about Viviani that would be suitable. O you have saved me & the day.["]

Wednesday, February 23, 1921

Worthington Pump Co. accepts & we save $3 million dollars and also a law suit.

That [?] New England Oil Co., wants us to take bonds on second mortgage and release our first mortgage.

Dined with the Taylors—real folks—& we hate to leave them. He is the ablest man here.

Wadhams here & recommended leniency in cases. Granted. But not in case of those who had taken money for enlisting men in soft jobs.

Announced that Denby[19] is to be Secretary of the Navy.

Thursday, February 24, 1921

W. J. [blank] President of Carnegie Trust Co. who was sent to N.J. penitentiary when trust co. failed, called to urge that Dye [?] be turned out—

---

[18] Daniels liked to use the slogan of the Fisk Tire Company in describing his feelings toward his former Aid for Operations, Rear Admiral Bradley A. Fiske.

[19] Edwin Denby, Republican, former U.S. Representative from Michigan, 1905–1911.

his brother is tutor for rich man. Guilty of sodomy at Newport. Did not believe he was guilty. Wadhams said he did not deserve clemency. The man who asked clemency was author of Golden Rule Club. He cried as he told his experiences in prison & how he obtained better treatment of men in prison.

Alford operated on.

Everett, of Durham, here. I told him to advocate 6% on incomes over $25,000 & make RRs pay franchise tax

Dined with Admiral Stitt at Washington Hotel

Friday, February 25, 1921

New England Oil Company. Lodge, Weeks, & House Committee favored proposition to aid that company.

Texas Oil Company presented me with pair of binoculars, wh. I had used going to & from Europe.

Invited by Gen. Board & Bureau Chiefs to go to luncheon A&N Club on Thursday of next week

Went to Quantico

Saturday, February 26, 1921

Telegram from Denby thanking me for cordial expression and saying he would come to Washington soon. Young Theodore Roosevelt to be Assistant Secretary—carry the news to F. D. R.

Mechanics object to reducing men in Navy Yards from first to second class—a plan they believe is to [be] a "regular smash" in wages. I ordered yards not to follow that course.

Henry Van Dyke came to see me "You are my Secretary & the world appreciates the great work you have done[."]

Dinner at Chevy Chase Club with Foote

Sunday, February 27, 1921

Went to St Elizabeths in the morning to talk to the shell shocked & those afflicted in mind. My experience in the hospital. Forgot the pain & remember only kindnesses

Buddies

Went to hear Dr. Chappell. In China, got gold & silver & made bell. King frowned—not normal [?]. Tried again. Failed. Would kill the man if he failed the third time

Daughter went to wise man; said sweet tone only if some sacrifice, must be bought with blood Threw herself into the caldron & perfect tone & men could hear the songs of angels.

Dr Wood: This is your last Sunday
Addie   till [?] we return
McGowan & Hilton
Wash. paper said I would run for Senate.

Monday, February 28, 1921
Monday—Pershing luncheon for Baker
N.C. Society Reception

Tuesday, March 1, 1921
Dined at British Embassy

Wednesday, March 2, 1921
Denby called
Barnett. Lejeune.[1]
Favored in a speech cancelling all war debts
Dr Boyd

Thursday, March 3, 1921
Attended meeting of Ericson Committee
Went to Marine Barracks   "Dixie"—
General Board & Council luncheon.
Reception
Resolutions
Marked off numbers lost.
Dinner at Mrs Deweys

[1] Republican supporters of General Barnett had thus far been successful in blocking Senate confirmation of General Lejeune as Barnett's successor as Major General Commandant of the Marine Corps. Daniels was consequently fearful that Lejeune might lose the post under the Harding administration. Fortunately for Lejeune the House Naval Affairs Committee was solidly behind him and after consulting Daniels the committee requested the incoming Secretary Denby to retain him. Daniels subsequently recalled: "Later Denby called to see me, told me of the earnest request, almost a demand, that Lejeune be reappointed. He asked, 'If you were coming into office with such an insistent request from the Naval Affairs Committee, what would you do?' I replied that whatever of success I had been able to achieve was due to the help and coöperation of that committee, members of the two parties, and added, 'I'd hate to start in by turning down a request for the retention of an able officer they were unanimously urging.'" Denby saw the point and Lejeune was promptly reappointed and confirmed. Daniels noted, however, "But for the insistence of Butler and the House Naval Affairs Committee, he might have been sacrificed." Daniels, *Wilson Era: Years of War and After,* p. 156.

INDEX

Index

NOTE.—to conserve space the following abbreviations have been used throughout the Index:

A.E.F.:   American Expeditionary Force   F. D. R.:   Franklin D. Roosevelt
J. D.:   Josephus Daniels   T. R.:   Theodore Roosevelt
I.W.W.:   Industrial Workers of the World   W. W.:   Woodrow Wilson

Abbott, Ernest Hamlin, 12–13
Abbott, Wilbur C., 149
Accidents: aviation, 417–18, 587; defective shells, 124, 132, 134, 155, 156, 157, 160, 163, 164; Mare Island explosion, 191, 192, 196, 198; maritime, 301, 555
Adams, Henry, 475
Adams, Laurence S., 113, 215
Adamson Eight Hour Act, 115 n., 117
Addicks, Lawrence, 148, 149
Adee, Alvey A., 525
Agamemnon, U.S.S., 336
Agriculture: conservation, 165; and nitrates shortage, 257, 319; politics, 367; prices, 281, 334, 335, 338, 560, 570, 576, 590; production, 276, 314–15; and prohibition, 310 n., 323; relief, 321; mentioned, 165, 549. *See also* Hoover, Herbert C.; Houston, David F.
Aguilar, Cándido, 111
Aircraft. *See* Aviation
Aircraft Production Board: investigation of, 289; and F. D. R., 215, 218; mentioned, 239
Air mail: start of, 303
Alaska: coal, 48; J. D. visits, 541
Albert I, King of Belgium: entertains J. D., 398; visits U.S., 443–44, 453, 454; mentioned, 295, 391, 414
Albert, Prince of England, 404
Albertson, Robert B., 77
Alderman, Edwin A.: and Naval Academy, 140 n., 164; mentioned, 39, 128, 389
Aldunate, Santiago, 236, 300
Alexander, Joshua W.: and housing, 274; and oil, 502; on politics, 481, 482; on Russia, 526; and shipping, 536, 552; son's death, 576; speech of, 540

Alexander, Walter R., 576
Alexandria, Queen of England, 406
Alexandrovitch, Paul, Grand Duke of Russia, 252 n.
Alford, L. F., 450, 461, 524, 603
Alien Property Custodian, 565, 591
Aliens: deportation of, 178, 418, 574, 579; employment in navy yards, 536; registration of, 236, 237, 275; and wartime restrictions, 271, 277
Alifas, N. P., 250
Allen, Ethen, 78
Allen, William R., 524
Alley, Mrs. R. L., 423
Alphonso XIII (Spanish warship), 555
Alsace-Lorraine, 159, 246
Alte, Viscount ―― de, 134
America, Mr. ―― (war correspondent), 199
American Commission for Relief in the Near East, 449
American Expeditionary Force: delayed news from, 371; naval protection of, 303; Pershing on, 277 n., 569; return of, 348, 358; as separate force, 283; and shipping, 263–64, 296; Sims on, 509 n.
American Federation of Labor, 593
American Iron and Steel Institute, 185
American Legion, 496
American Tobacco Co., 524 n., 598
American University, 365, 417, 537
Ammons, Elias M., 82
Anaconda Copper Mining Co., 198 n.
Anderson, Dr. Albert, 91, 95
Anderson, Albert B., 467
Anderson, Edwin A., 543
Anderson, George W., 246
Anderson, P. Chauncey, 365

607